A THEMATIC COMMENTARY ON THE QUR'AN

Shaykh Muhammad al-Ghazālī

Translated from the Arabic by
ASHUR A. SHAMIS

Revised by
ZAYNAB ALAWIYE

INTERNATIONAL INSTITUTE OF ISLAMIC THOUGHT

© THE INTERNATIONAL INSTITUTE OF ISLAMIC THOUGHT

FIRST PUBLISHED 1421AH/2000CE

THIS EDITION 3RD REPRINT 1445AH/2024CE

WASHINGTON OFFICE

P.O. BOX 669, HERNDON, VA 20172, USA

www.iiit.org

LONDON OFFICE

P.O. BOX 126, RICHMOND, SURREY TW9 2UD, UK

www.iiituk.com

TITLE: A THEMATIC COMMENTARY ON THE QUR'AN

AUTHOR: SHAYKH MUHAMMAD AL-GHAZALI

ISBN: 978-1-56564-260-7 Paperback

ISBN: 978-1-56564-261-4 Hardback

ISBN: 978-1-56564-502-8 eBook

Layout and Design by Sohail Nakhooda

Printed in the USA

CONTENTS

                                                                page

Foreword   vii

Author's Introduction   x

SURAH 1   *Al-Fātiḥah* (The Opening Chapter)   1

SURAH 2   *Al-Baqarah* (The Cow)   6

SURAH 3   *Āl ʿImrān* (House of ʿImrān)   30

SURAH 4   *Al-Nisā'* (Women)   55

SURAH 5   *Al-Mā'idah* (The Table)   88

SURAH 6   *Al-Anʿām* (The Cattle)   115

SURAH 7   *Al-Aʿrāf* (The Heights)   138

SURAH 8   *Al-Anfāl* (The Spoils of War)   160

SURAH 9   *Al-Tawbah* (Repentance)   177

SURAH 10   *Yūnus* (Jonah)   197

SURAH 11   *Hūd* (Hūd)   216

SURAH 12   *Yūsuf* (Joseph)   234

SURAH 13   *Al-Raʿd* (Thunder)   250

SURAH 14   *Ibrāhīm* (Abraham)   258

SURAH 15   *Al-Ḥijr*   266

SURAH 16   *Al-Naḥl* (Bees)   274

SURAH 17   *Al-Isrā'* (The Night Journey)   292

SURAH 18   *Al-Kahf* (The Cave)   308

SURAH 19   *Maryam* (Mary)   323

SURAH 20   *Ṭā Hā*   333

SURAH 21   *Al-Anbiyā'* (The Prophets)   343

SURAH 22   *Al-Ḥajj* (The Pilgrimage)   352

SURAH 23   *Al-Mu'minūn* (The Believers)   366

SURAH 24   *Al-Nūr* (Light)   375

Contents

SURAH 25   *Al-Furqān* (The Criterion)   385

SURAH 26   *Al-Shuʿarā'* (The Poets)   394

SURAH 27   *Al-Naml* (The Ants)   403

SURAH 28   *Al-Qaṣaṣ* (The Story)   413

SURAH 29   *Al-ʿAnkabūt* (The Spider)   425

SURAH 30   *Al-Rūm* (The Romans)   433

SURAH 31   *Luqmān*   442

SURAH 32   *Al-Sajdah* (The Prostration)   447

SURAH 33   *Al-Aḥzāb* (The Confederate Tribes)   452

SURAH 34   *Saba'* (Sheba)   463

SURAH 35   *Fāṭir* (The Creator)   471

SURAH 36   *Yā Sīn*   478

SURAH 37   *Al-Ṣāffāt* (The Ranks)   486

SURAH 38   *Ṣād*   494

SURAH 39   *Al-Zumar* (The Crowds)   502

SURAH 40   *Ghāfir* (The Forgiver)   513

SURAH 41   *Fuṣṣilat* (Revelation Well-Expounded)   522

SURAH 42   *Al-Shūrā* (Counsel)   530

SURAH 43   *Al-Zukhruf* (Ornaments)   538

SURAH 44   *Al-Dukhān* (Smoke)   546

SURAH 45   *Al-Jāthiyah* (The Kneeling One)   551

SURAH 46   *Al-Aḥqāf* (Sand Dunes)   556

SURAH 47   *Muḥammad*   564

SURAH 48   *Al-Fatḥ* (Victory)   569

SURAH 49   *Al-Ḥujurāt* (The Chambers)   577

SURAH 50   *Qāf*   581

SURAH 51   *Al-Dhāriyāt* (The Dust-Scattering Winds)   585

SURAH 52   *Al-Ṭūr* (The Mount)   589

SURAH 53   *Al-Najm* (The Star)   594

SURAH 54   *Al-Qamar* (The Moon)   599

SURAH 55   *Al-Raḥmān* (The Merciful)   603

SURAH 56   *Al-Wāqiʿah* (The Inevitable Event)   607

SURAH 57   *Al-Ḥadīd* (Iron)   626

Contents

SURAH 58   *Al-Mujādilah* (She Who Pleaded)   633

SURAH 59   *Al-Ḥashr* (The Gathering)   637

SURAH 60   *Al-Mumtaḥanah* (The Tested Woman)   641

SURAH 61   *Al-Ṣaff* (The Ranks)   645

SURAH 62   *Al-Jumuʿah* (Friday)   649

SURAH 63   *Al-Munāfiqūn* (The Hypocrites)   652

SURAH 64   *Al-Taghābun* (Loss and Gain)   654

SURAH 65   *Al-Ṭalāq* (Divorce)   658

SURAH 66   *Al-Taḥrīm* (The Prohibition)   661

SURAH 67   *Al-Mulk* (Dominion)   665

SURAH 68   *Al-Qalam* (The Pen)   669

SURAH 69   *Al-Ḥāqqah* (The Reality)   671

SURAH 70   *Al-Maʿārij* (The Ways of Ascent)   674

SURAH 71   *Nūḥ* (Noah)   676

SURAH 72   *Al-Jinn* (The Jinn)   678

SURAH 73   *Al-Muzzammil* (The Mantled One)   682

SURAH 74   *Al-Muddaththir* (The Cloaked One)   684

SURAH 75   *Al-Qiyāmah* (The Resurrection)   687

SURAH 76   *Al-Insān* (Man)   689

SURAH 77   *Al-Mursalāt* (Those Sent Forth)   691

SURAH 78   *Al-Nabaʾ* (The Great News)   694

SURAH 79   *Al-Nāziʿāt* (The Setting Stars)   696

SURAH 80   *ʿAbasa* (He Frowned)   699

SURAH 81   *Al-Takwīr* (The Folding Up)   702

SURAH 82   *Al-Infiṭār* (The Cataclysm)   705

SURAH 83   *Al-Muṭaffifīn* (The Stinters)   707

SURAH 84   *Al-Inshiqāq* (The Rending)   710

SURAH 85   *Al-Burūj* (The Constellations)   712

SURAH 86   *Al-Ṭāriq* (The Night-Visitor)   713

SURAH 87   *Al-Aʿlā* (The Most High)   715

SURAH 88   *Al-Ghāshiyah* (The Overwhelming Event)   717

SURAH 89   *Al-Fajr* (The Dawn)   719

SURAH 90   *Al-Balad* (The City)   723

Contents

SURAH 91 *Al-Shams* (The Sun)   725

SURAH 92 *Al-Layl* (The Night)   727

SURAH 93 *Al-Ḍuḥā* (Daylight)   729

SURAH 94 *Al-Sharḥ* (The Consolation)   732

SURAH 95 *Al-Tīn* (The Fig)   734

SURAH 96 *Al-ʿAlaq* (The Blood Clot)   736

SURAH 97 *Al-Qadr* (Power)   739

SURAH 98 *Al-Bayyinah* (The Proof)   741

SURAH 99 *Al-Zalzalah* (The Earthquake)   744

SURAH 100 *Al-ʿĀdiyāt* (The War Steeds)   746

SURAH 101 *Al-Qāriʿah* (The Calamity)   748

SURAH 102 *Al-Takāthur* (Wordly Gain)   749

SURAH 103 *Al-ʿAṣr* (The Flight of Time)   751

SURAH 104 *Al-Humazah* (The Slanderer)   753

SURAH 105 *Al-Fīl* (The Elephant)   754

SURAH 106 *Quraysh*   756

SURAH 107 *Al-Maʿūn* (Charity)   757

SURAH 108 *Al-Kawthar* (Good in Abundance)   758

SURAH 109 *Al-Kāfirūn* (The Unbelievers)   760

SURAH 110 *Al-Naṣr* (Victory)   762

SURAH 111 *Al-Masad* (The Fiber)   764

SURAH 112 *Al-Ikhlāṣ* (Purity of Faith)   766

SURAH 113 *Al-Falaq* (Daybreak)   768

SURAH 114 *Al-Nās* (Mankind)   769

Index of Qur'anic Quotations   771

General Index   775

FOREWORD

MUSLIMS ARE ENJOINED, along with the rest of humanity, to "read" the two great books of Revelation and Creation, i.e. the Qur'an and the natural world. Reading one without the other will result in an imbalance detrimental to the existence (and prosperity) of humankind on earth, indeed to the divine purpose in the cosmos. Fatalism, world-rejection and stultification of the intellect and the imagination are some of the results of a "reading" that excludes the real-existential. Arrogance and a rampant lust for power at whatever cost are among the by-products of an absorption with the material world at the expense of the spiritual and moral. In both cases, people walk away from their role as *khulafā'* (stewards) on earth and from all the responsibilities of compassion, mercy, fraternity, moderation, and other duties which that role implies in relation to God, fellow human beings, and the environment.

A Thematic Commentary by the late Shaykh al-Ghazālī is a signifi-cant contribution to the first reading, i.e., that of the Qur'an—the repository of divine truth and enlightenment. Already of course there is a wealth, indeed an abundance, of exegetical work on the Qur'an. But while the ancient scholars have endeavored to elucidate many linguistic, historical, and miraculous aspects of the sacred, ever-won-drous and challenging text, al-Ghazālī's contribution is somewhat unique (and contemporary) in the sense that it focuses on the organic unity of each surah (chapter) highlighting the logic or inherent rea-soning that courses through the surah and unifies its various com-ponents and images.

Indeed, to the uninitiated, the Qur'an can seem quite daunting, even bewildering. The titles of the surahs do not appear to reflect their subject matter; the ordering of the verses and the surahs does not seem to fall into a set pattern; the structuring of the topics within the individual surahs, especially the longer ones, does not appear systematic; there is often a blend of narrative, polemics, anecdotes, and straightforward instruction. The diction resorts to a variety of linguistic and stylistic devices.

There is no dispute among Muslims over the authenticity or integrity of the Qur'anic text; even secular students of Islam no longer seem to argue very much over this issue. Differences have always existed, though, over the precise interpretation and application of Qur'anic statements and injunctions. As issues proliferate and life becomes more complex, the need to throw a new light on the meaning of the Qur'anic text grows.

Shaykh al-Ghazālī's cogent method of interpretation takes account of the fact (or premise) that each surah has its unique coherent and integral character. This character is defined by a main subject, or a theme of interrelated topics which together form the body of the surah's subject matter. Once the central subject or theme is identified, the jigsaw pieces come together, enunciating how the rest of the surah falls into line with, or can be related to, that theme.

This is where Shaykh al-Ghazālī's greatest contribution lies. By adopting this method, he is able to make the Qur'an more easily accessible, and the task of unlocking its secrets less daunting, more rewarding. In addition to appreciating the beauty of the Qur'an, the reader is now able to have a clearer understanding of its meaning and flow. The surahs come alive, each one assuming distinct features and characteristics that make it stand out and claim its unique position within the whole design and sweep.

Another feature of Shaykh al-Ghazālī's work is that he places the Qur'anic subjects within their proper historic and cultural context. This has the effect of relating the Qur'anic subject matter not only to the life and career of Prophet Muhammad, but also to today's world, thereby transforming it into a source of practical guidance and a ready reference for dealing with contemporary issues.

No exegesis is by itself sufficient for a full understanding of the Qur'an. But this work is an indispensable companion in the quest for a better comprehension of, and a closer affinity with, the sacred text.

Al-Tafsīr al-Mawḍūʿī was originally published in Arabic in three volumes. The IIIT translated and published the first two volumes separately in 1997 and 1999. The current volume incorporates all three volumes into one edition.

The translation of the meaning of the Qur'an used in this book is mainly ʿAbdullah Yūsuf ʿAlī's *The Meaning of the Holy Qur'an* (Amana Publications, 1996) and *The Message of the Qur'an* by Muhammad Asad (Dar al-Andalus Limited, 1980). However, we used several other translations and made changes whenever we deemed it necessary for the sake of elucidation and precision of meaning. Footnotes have been added by the editorial team for further clarification or explanation of terms. Following the IIIT house style, Arabic words appearing in English dictionaries have not been italicized.

We would like to express our thanks and gratitude to the translator, Ashur Shamis; the editorial and production team at the London Office and those who were directly or indirectly involved in the completion of this book: Zaynab Alawiye, Sohail Nakhooda, Shiraz Khan, Ataiya Pathan, Amanda Adams and Alexandra Grayson.

Jumada (II) 1421   IIIT LONDON OFFICE
September 2000

AUTHOR'S INTRODUCTION

THIS WORK PRESENTS a new approach to the study of the Qur'an which I had adopted in some of my earlier writings. Ever since I embarked on the task of producing this work, I have been daunted by a feeling of inadequacy, a fear of being unable to do the Qur'an the justice it deserves. My decision to go ahead with it nevertheless has been as much for my own sake as for that of the readers.

The Qur'an is a vast and rich world, with widely varying themes and subjects and endless possibilities for interpretation and analysis. This work is but a small contribution to the noble objective of understanding the Qur'an, and it is being undertaken in the hope that I might tap certain areas or open certain doors not tapped nor opened before. According to this approach, each surah of the Qur'an is treated as one whole unit. A thematic explanation, or overview, of each surah is then presented, identifying its main theme, or themes, and the subtle threads of meaning and ideas that link its subject matter. I have taken meticulous care in dealing with the main theme of each surah, regardless of the number of different issues it raises or addresses. In this, I have emulated the excellent pioneering work of the late Shaykh Muhammad ʿAbd Allah Darrāz in his study of *al-Baqarah*, the longest chapter in the Qur'an.

I began learning the Qur'an during my early childhood, and committed it all to memory by the age of ten. Ever since I started to study it seriously, I have been convinced that there is a need for this type of commentary. But, as I read the Qur'an today, going through my eighties, I still find that I have grasped only a fraction of its meaning. I feel a pressing need to go deeper into it and to try and link the themes, passages, and sections found in each surah, in order to identify its character and its overall purpose.

The method I have adopted consists of highlighting only those verses and passages that represent or enhance the features and the character of the main theme of the surah. This implicitly assumes that readers have to fill in the gaps and fit the rest of the surah into the overall picture themselves. Needless to say, this method of studying the Qur'an in no way undervalues or replaces the traditional methods and approaches adopted by other students and scholars of the Qur'an. It merely complements their great works and facilitates an easier and more accessible way of understanding the text.

Another aspect of thematic commentary on the Qur'an which I have not attempted to adopt here, is to identify the major themes of the Qur'an as a whole and discuss the issues and subjects it covers in the light of those themes. I had made use of this feature in other writings of mine, published in Arabic, such as: *Al-Maḥāwir al-Khamsah li al-Qur'an al-Karīm* (Five Central Themes of the Qur'an) and *Naẓarāt fī al-Qur'an* (Glimpses into the Qur'an). Surely, the study and understanding of the Qur'an can benefit from both approaches and from all efforts that will make its meaning, wisdom, and beauty easier to grasp and appreciate. The Qur'an shall remain an eternal fountain of knowledge, a guidance for all humanity, and a living proof of the Power and Glory of God Almighty.

Ṣafar 1413   MUHAMMAD AL-GHAZĀLĪ
August 1992

Al-Fātiḥah
(The Opening Chapter)

"IN THE NAME OF GOD the Merciful, the Compassionate" (1). This surah, like all other surahs in the Qur'an with the exception of *al-Tawbah*, opens in the name of God, Allah (SWT),[1] the most exalted and holiest of names which, when invoked, provides protection from all harm and evil. As an expression of praise and gratitude to God the surah represents the very heart and soul of the Qur'an and, although it is one of the shorter surahs, it is often considered to be the most illustrious of them all. *Al-Fātiḥah* conveys the quintessential ideal of Islam giving expression and definition to the covenant made between human beings and God upon which the mission and task of humankind in this world has been founded. It is, moreover, an earnest prayer to God, a heartfelt plea to show humans the right way, give them guidance and make them deserving of His pleasure and benevolence.

Let us take a close look at the verse: "Praise be to God, Lord of all creation" (2). This verse articulates three concepts:

1. praise and glorification of the grandeur, magnificence, and perfection of God Almighty;
2. praise to God, the Creator and Provider, for the grace, generosity, and kindness He has shown towards His creation; and

---

[1] SWT—*Subḥānahu wa Taʿālā*: May He be praised and may His transcendence be affirmed. Said when referring to Allah.

I

3. gratitude and thankfulness to the Creator and Provider, for all the favors and the grace He has bestowed upon His creation.

Every time one utters these words or expresses these feelings, one not only glorifies God, but praises and thanks Him at the same time. "Lord of all creation" (2) is an assertion that God is Master of all, from the mightiest to the humblest of creatures, wherever they may be on earth and in the universe. He is the Master of humans, animals, plants, angels, planets, stars, systems, the seen and the unseen. Everything that has existed or shall ever exist in this world is subordinate to God, subservient to Him, bound to His power, and totally dependent upon His grace, blessings, and compassion. God says elsewhere in the Qur'an:

To God is praise, Lord of the heavens and of the earth, Lord of all creation. Glory to Him in the heavens and on earth. He is Mighty and Wise. (al-Jāthiyah: 36–37)

"The Merciful, the Compassionate" (3). Human beings, and all other creation, live by the grace of God's mercy, which is abundant beyond all estimation. Were it not for His mercy, our existence would have been eroded by both our sins and ingratitude as well as by our arrogance and high-handed tendencies.

"Master of the Day of Judgment" (4). This refers to the day of reckoning, which heralds the beginning of a new life that will be in total contrast to our present transient one. The concept of a "Day of Judgment" has been all but obliterated and forgotten in today's materialistic society. It has become a subject for satire and ridicule. In areas of education, law, national and international politics, it has been deliberately omitted or swept aside. Nevertheless, it represents a most basic and fundamental fact of human existence and should be cherished and reckoned with.

"You alone we worship, and to You alone we turn for help" (5). Everyone and everything is in need of God and His favors. Prophet Muhammad (ṢAAS)[2] was known to appeal to God: "Help me to be mindful of You and thank You and worship You, the best I can." He was reported to have advised: "When you have a specific need, ask God to provide it, and when you are short of help seek it from God."[3]

"Guide us to the straight path, the path of those whom You have favored" (6-7). A straight line is the shortest distance between two points and is therefore unique. Whoever leads a straight and righteous life will be on the right path to God, for that is the one and only sure and direct way that leads to Him. God's religion is one religion, preached by all prophets and messengers at all stages of human history. It is founded on the oneness of God who deserves total allegiance and full praise and on whom everyone and everything depend.

This concept seems to be a matter for considerable confusion and debate among followers of some contemporary religions. But Muslims believe with certainty that everything in existence, human or otherwise, is totally subservient to and dependent on God in every aspect of its existence, now and in the life to come. And there are no exceptions to this rule; neither among human beings nor other creatures. Those who deny or overlook this fact are doomed to ruin and humiliation.

On the other hand, whoever submits willingly to God and obeys Him and His Messenger, Muhammad, will find the right and straight path and would follow it. God says elsewhere in the Qur'an:

whoever obeys God and the Messenger [Muhammad] will be in the company of those whom God has favored: the prophets, the

---

2 ṢAAS—*Ṣalla Allāhu ʿAlayhi wa Sallam*: May the peace and blessings of Allah be upon him; said whenever the name of Prophet Muhammad is mentioned or whenever he is referred to as the Prophet of Allah.

3 Narrated by Abū Dāwūd and al-Nasāʾī in their Sunan.

believers, the martyrs and the pious; and what good company they will be! (*al-Nisā'*: 69)

As for those who take other gods, or deities, besides God or flout His commands, their plight will be hopeless and they will be wasted, wallowing under the combined effect of a total loss of direction and the wrath of God. People should strive to be clear and correct in their thinking and sincere in their vision and perception. Once shown the truth, people should uphold it, show humility towards God, and kindness and benevolence towards other beings.

God prescribed the recitation of this surah as part of all Muslim prayers, including the obligatory five daily ones. It is a refreshing, regenerative, and intimate communication between people and their Lord. It is a manifesto of fundamental truths and ideals, and an overture of humility from a modest apologetic servant to the All-Powerful Lord and Master. Prophet Muhammad is reported to have quoted God as saying:

[the fruits] of prayer are shared equally between Me and My servant, and My servant will be granted what he had asked for. As he recites: "Praise be to God," God would say: "My servant has praised Me." As he recites: "The Merciful, the Compassionate," God would say: "My servant has thanked Me." As he recites: "Master of the Day of Judgment," God would say: "My servant has glorified Me and surrendered to Me." As he says: "You alone we worship, and You alone we turn to for help," God would say: "This is between Me and My servant, and My servant will receive what he has asked for." And, as he says: "Guide us to the straight path, the path of those whom You have favored, not those who have incurred Your wrath, nor those who have gone astray," God would say: "This is for My servant, and he will be granted his wish."[4]

---

4 Narrated by Muslim in his *Ṣaḥīḥ*.

We recite these blessed words of supplication and praise for the benefit of our own souls, just as washing regularly is necessary for the health of our bodies. The benefits we reap justify the regularity and repetition of the recitation. A body would not remain clean by washing it only now and then; it needs to be washed regularly all through one's life. Likewise, human temperament and behavior are never put right by a short prayer, casually repeated but soon forgotten. One has to stand before God as frequently as possible, because human recklessness and imprudence, as well as Satan's insinuations, never cease nor know any bounds. Prayer, supplication, and submission to God have to be observed and performed as a matter of habit. God says elsewhere in the Qur'an: "Prayer has been enjoined on the believers at set times" (*al-Nisā'*: 103).

In a few short lines, therefore, we have a true expression and a full definition of the natural and proper relationship between people and their Lord. The essence of this relationship is people's acknowledgement of God, their unqualified praise of Him, their eagerness to reach closer to Him, their commitment to worship Him, and their continual active and sincere efforts to beg for His favor, mercy, and grace. All this in order that God may help people to exist and live as He wishes them to do.

SURAH 2

Al-Baqarah
(The Cow)

FOLLOWING THE MUSLIMS' emigration from Makkah and their settlement in Madinah around 622 AC, all attention was focused on building the first Muslim autonomous community there. By embracing the new religion, members of that community had, each in his/her own right, succeeded in breaking away from idolatry, polytheism, and other forms of pagan traditions and practices of Arabia. They had now found security and safety in their new sanctuary where they could group together and set up a state of their own.

Nevertheless, they were to face fresh hostilities from a rather unexpected source. The Jewish rabbis had always believed that religion was the prerogative of their own people and a monopoly of their 'Chosen Race.' Predictably, they were somewhat ruffled and unhappy at the arrival in Madinah of Prophet Muhammad and his followers preaching Islam. They quickly embarked on preparations for how to react to that threat and for the best way to deal with it. Scheming, overt as well as covert, began.

The Hebrew tribes who had settled in Madinah, or Yathrib as it was known then, in the fertile northwestern part of the Hijaz, had gone there as refugees to escape the oppression and persecution of Byzantine, the Eastern Roman Empire whose capital was Constantinople. Although welcome to live among the illiterate Arab tribes, they rather looked down upon them. The Jews made no effort to combat idol worship, which was widespread in the area; nor did they feel the need to pass on the teachings of their religion to their native hosts. They recognized no obligation to propagate

6

God's message or establish His order to replace the existing man-made one. Their view of the Arabs was wholly sanctimonious, adopting the proverbial condescending 'holier-than-thou' attitude, holding jealously onto their religious heritage, and totally beholden to the erroneous belief that religion was their privilege and theirs alone.

What, then, was their (or, more specifically, their elders') reaction to Islam? They rejected it. They began to distort, conceal and otherwise obliterate religious and historical facts in order to pre-empt the spread of the new religion.

In contrast, Prophet Muhammad, the last of God's prophets and the benefactor of the new religion, spared no effort in appealing to them and soliciting their understanding and cooperation. However, their malaise was deep and irrepressible, and increasingly their hostile intentions began to be reflected in their behavior. In view of this the Muslims found themselves, in their new sanctuary, building their community on the one hand and defending it on the other. They were laying the foundations of their nascent state, under the guidance and direction of the divine Revelation being received by Muhammad, while at the same time having to ward off the impending threat posed by enemies living in their midst, who were intent on undermining their existence and everything they were building.

It was in this atmosphere that *al-Baqarah*, the longest and most wide-ranging chapter in the Qur'an, was received. The surah obliquely cited the fallacy of Jewish claims of exclusivity by describing the Qur'an as "the Book over which there is no doubt, a guidance to those who fear God" (2), thereby highlighting the view that other 'Books' or scriptures were less viable as sources of guidance and law, and less authoritative as references for or expressions of the divine will.

In over thirty different places, the surah elaborates extensively on the features and merits of the God-fearing category of human beings. This aspect is unique to the surah. Fear (alternatively,

7

awareness) of God is a quality required of human beings by all religions. God says in the Qur'an: "To God belongs all that is in the heavens and on the earth; and We have recommended to those who had received the Book before you, as We have recommended to you, that you should all fear God" (*al-Nisā'*: 131).

The surah is also remarkable for referring to all the five principles of the religion of Islam in the following verses:

Tawḥīd: "People; worship your Lord who had created you and those before you" (21);

Salah: "Observe salah, especially the middle one, and submit to God" (238);

Zakah: "Believers; spend of what We have given you before a day comes when there will be no trade and no friendship and no intercession" (254);

Sawm: "Believers, sawm has been prescribed for you as it had been for your predecessors" (183); and

Hajj: "Complete the Hajj and the ʿumrah for God's sake"(196).

The revelation of the surah was completed over a period, with the Prophet adding verses and passages that related to its subject matter when he was directed to do so through revelation.

According to established sources, the last Qur'anic verse revealed to Muhammad was number 281 of this surah, which says, "Fear the day when you shall return to God; when each soul shall be requited according to its deserts and none shall be wronged." The Prophet instructed the scribes to include it with the verses dealing with usury, which appear towards the end of the surah.

Reading through the early part of the surah, we find that it describes God-fearing people in three verses, the unbelievers in two, and the hypocrites in thirteen, an indication of the last's wickedness and the threat they pose to the whole Muslim community. Following a general call for belief in God and the Day of Judgment, and a brief

account of the miraculous aspects of the Qur'an itself, the veracity of
Muhammad, its proponent, and the ill-fate awaiting his opponents,
the surah returns to the description of the various human groups: the
believers, the rejectionists, and the renegades, and how each reacted
to God's message. The surah then inquires whether God deserves to
be understood and addressed in such an improper and ungrateful
manner by the unbelievers and the skeptics who fail to acknowledge
His grace and benevolence. It asks them pointedly:

> How can you deny God when He gave you life, after you were
> dead, and He will cause you again to die and then restore you to life
> so that you eventually return unto Him? (28)

Having dealt with that subject, it would follow naturally to
address the issue of creation and how humans came to be charged
with their role in this world, and the perennial confrontation
between Adam, father of the human race, and Satan, humankind's
archetypal enemy, along with his supporters. This confrontation
was reenacted in a bitter conflict between Muhammad, the last of
God's prophets to humankind, and some descendants of Israel who
in that instance chose to take Satan's side in a crucial battle between
truth and falsehood.

Being the first surah revealed in Madinah, it was imperative that
it should deal with the issue of the Jews; their elders' negative attitude towards the message of Islam, and their history, both ancient
and recent. This begins in the surah with:

> Children of Israel, remember the favors I have bestowed upon you,
> keep your covenant and I shall keep Mine and fear Me. Believe in
> what I have revealed, confirming that which you had received [the
> scriptures], and do not be the first to deny it. (40–41)

The confirmation in the Qur'an of the scriptures of which the

9

Jews had possession was a confirmation in general terms and not in all details. The People of the Book, Jews and Christians, were seen as different from other religious groups because they believed in the One and only God. Unlike the idolaters and the pagans, they did not deny the existence of God and divine Revelation. The Qur'an endorsed the claims of the Jews with regard to their belief in the One God, revelation, and the responsibility and accountability of human-kind. But it did not endorse, among other things, the allegation in their scriptures that God regretted bringing about the Great Flood or His needing to be reminded not to do it again. Likewise, the Qur'an does not endorse the Old Testament tale of God walking on earth, leaning towards Abraham, and eating with him. Nor does it accept the story of God's wrestling with Jacob one long night, and not being released until He promised Jacob the name 'Israel.' The Qur'an's endorsement of the Jewish scriptural legacy was general and not specific nor total. Furthermore, the Qur'an cites those parts of Jewish scriptures it endorses mainly to hold their elders accountable for their faithfulness to and respect for those scriptures and their teachings. All in all, this surah cites sixteen different issues concerning Jewish dissent all through the people's long and checkered history as docu-mented in the Torah. In all these cases, the dissenters prove disap-pointing even to their own prophets, and wanting in their obser-vance of God's commands and their gratitude to and reverence for Him.

The account begins with the verse: "Remember how We deli-vered you from Pharaoh's people, who had inflicted upon you the worst type of torture" (49). Did the rebellious among the Jews appreciate that favor? Although God went on to drown their enemy before their eyes, did they recognize God's justice or acknowledge His grace as He destroyed their oppressors? These issues are debated over several passages, always inquiring whether the Jewish con-science had been aroused or the Jewish faith in God rekindled. Would the Jews of Arabia, after such a detailed interrogation and analysis of their ancestors' record, persist with their obduracy and rejection of Prophet Muhammad, to whom the Qur'an was being revealed? The outcome of this discussion of the long history of the Jews is an assertion of the veracity and efficacy of the concept of religious unity as expounded in the Qur'an.

In the face of narrow-minded religious fanaticism, Islam emerged to promote a tolerant religious unity, addressed to and embracing all of humankind, built on pristine human nature and sound common sense. The Jewish and the Christian establishments had grown accustomed to seeing truth as their own monopoly, and salvation as theirs alone. Islam questioned that judgment and the attitudes underlying it. We read in the surah:

> They [the Jewish and the Christian elders] declared, "Only Jews and Christians shall enter Paradise!" Such are their wishful fancies. Say, "Bring forth your proof, if you were really truthful." (111)

There are other people in the world who have come to know God truly, and who have submitted themselves to Him and dedicated their lives and energies to His service, and whose efforts should not be allowed to go to waste. The surah thus affirms:

> Indeed, those who surrender themselves to God and do good works shall be rewarded by their Lord; they shall have nothing to fear or to regret. (112)

It was on this basis that the Qur'an called upon the People of the Book to believe in God and *all* His messengers, and to cast aside their religio-centricity which led each group to claim a monopoly on truth. The surah cites their spokesmen's allegations:

They said, "Accept the faith of the Jews or the Christians and you shall be rightly guided." Say, "By no means! We shall accept the religion of Abraham, the pious one, who was never an idolater." (135)

It also advised them to believe in all the prophets sent by God to guide humanity, since there would be no meaning in excluding any one of them. The surah says:

Say, "We believe in God and in that which is revealed to us, and that which was revealed to Abraham, Ishmael, Isaac, Jacob, and the Tribes, and in what Moses, Jesus, and the prophets received from their Lord. We make no distinction among any of them, and to God we have surrendered ourselves." (136)

These are the basic principles of the unity of religion as expounded in this surah and presented to the Jews and the Christians, for them to adopt and share with the Muslims. At the beginning of this exposition, the Qur'an makes it clear that Islam, as such, is not a new religion but the same religion preached by all preceding messengers.

Jews have always taken pride in the fact that they are the sons of Jacob, known also as Israel, after whom the modern Jewish state is named. But who was Jacob? He was a pious man who acknowledged God and surrendered to Him, and who taught his children to do likewise. Before he passed away, he made sure that his legacy continued intact in his descendants. The surah relates:

Were you present when death came to Jacob, and he said to his children: "What will you worship after I die?" They said: "We shall worship your God and the God of your forefathers Abraham, Ishmael, and Isaac; the One God to whom we all surrender." (133)

Surrender to God or, to use the Arabic term, *Islām*, is the only natural and logical position creation can assume in relation to the Creator, the definitive bond between humankind and God. It is only natural for creation to surrender to its Creator and yearn for His mercy and pleasure. This is the essence of true religion rather than rebellion against God; it is neither transgression nor adherence to manmade religions.

Muhammad restored for religion its true and proper place in the world and chartered a unique and sure way towards God, as the surah states:

> So if they accept what you have believed in, they shall be rightly guided; but if they reject it, they shall be in schism. God will defend you against them; He hears all and knows all. (137)

The verse advances two morals, the first being to offer the Jews of Madinah the choice of accepting the new faith, and the second being neither to condemn nor scold them for their rejection of it. They were merely left to their own devices, and if they were to initiate hostilities, God would help and protect the Muslims against them.

Thus was the overall framework of religious unity as presented in this surah. However, one possible misunderstanding remains to be clarified: this concerns the statement that all messengers were Muslims, although we know that Islam was the message that Muhammad, the last Prophet and Messenger, had established. The answer lies in the fact that religion has always been one. It entails faith in God and a righteous life of good deeds, which are the very essence of the religion of Islam. For faith to be complete, mere or abstract knowledge is not sufficient. A believer has to attest to his or her belief and indicate to God that he or she has received the message and is ready and willing to obey Him; or as the Qur'an puts it: "We hear and we obey, grant us Your forgiveness, Lord; to You we shall all return" (285). Satan's knowledge of the fact that one God was the

Creator of all things did not spare him, because knowledge has to be supported by submission to God's commands and followed by exertions to please Him. Having refused to do so, Satan was ostracized and banished from God's grace.

All messengers have declared their knowledge of the true God and demonstrated their obedience to Him. This was the case with Noah, Abraham, Moses, Jesus, and Muhammad. To list the Qur'anic verses that confirm this would take much space, but suffice it to say that they were all advocates of surrender to the will and power of God, despite the minor variations in what they had taught and preached at various periods of human history.

When people are born, they are given names which remain with them right through to their old age, although their personalities and spheres of activity widen quite extensively. Likewise, it would be naive to think that the scope and sphere of religion today can be compared to those during Noah's time, for example. The focal point and the central theme may remain the same in both cases, but the outer limits can expand according to the needs and level of development of the period. In today's technological terms, the national power grid in certain small towns can extend to only a few square kilometers, whereas in big cities it has to cover hundreds or perhaps thousands of times that area; however, the electric current flowing through both grid systems remains the same and performs the same function.

Muhammad was preceded by the tumultuous experiences of Moses and Jesus, and it would not be unusual that his commission should introduce certain amendments and corrections, or make alterations and additions that had become necessary by the passage of time. It would also have been quite normal for him to throw a new light on, or reveal fresh aspects of, religion that may not have been dealt with by his predecessors. Thus his coming was a matter of urgency to correct the direction of human history and to alert the People of the Book to the malaise and confusion they had brought upon themselves and humankind as a whole.

As far as Christians were concerned, it was necessary to reemphasize the concept of *tawḥīd*, to reinstate the identity of Jesus as a human being, and to point out that he and his disciples were ordinary mortal advocates of the true religion of Islam. In the case of the Arabian Jews, there was a need to reprimand them for their arrogance, to weaken their encroachment on authentic divine revelation, and to reaffirm the fact that God had no biased affinity towards any particular ethnic group of the human race. The surah stresses the fact that sincere and honest followers of Moses and Jesus are one with those of Muhammad in the beliefs they hold and the fate they are to receive:

> The believers, the Jews, the Christians, and the Sabaeans; whoever believes in God and the Last Day and does good deeds, shall be rewarded by their Lord; they have nothing to fear or to regret. (62)

But those of the People of the Book who discarded revelation, neglected their obligations towards the Lord, and chose to pursue their capricious worldly desires, vying with idolaters, would have no claim to godliness. Their plight would be made worse by their envy and hostility towards the believers. The surah inquires:

> Who is more wicked than those who seek to destroy the mosques of God and forbid His name to be invoked in them? These perpetrators can only enter mosques in fear. They shall be held up to shame in this world and shall receive stern punishment in the hereafter. (114)

Having been revealed immediately after the Prophet's emigration from Makkah to Madinah, during the formative days of the new Muslim community, the surah lays down the fundamentals upon which relations among followers of various religions ought to be conducted. At the same time it calls for the unity of religion by advocating a return to the common basic teachings of all messengers.

When Islam first emerged, the elders of the Jewish community in Arabia received it with cynicism, denial, and disdain, since they believed in their God-given monopoly over religion, and in the notion that after their race, religion would never be revealed to another human group. When the Muslims emigrated from Makkah to Madinah, Islam became too close for comfort for some Jews who were already settled there. They resolved to fight it by all available means and to scheme against its followers. Prophet Muhammad offered them a charter as a code of conduct for their relationship with the Muslims and other inhabitants of the area. The agreement was based on peace and mutual cooperation. It seems that the local Jews accepted that agreement with reluctance, for they continued to deride the new religion, to lobby against it in a hostile manner, and to undermine its veracity and stability.

Meanwhile, the Qur'anic revelations also continued with their relentless scolding and rebuke of certain Jewish attitudes in the past. However, this had little effect in subduing the more recent arrogance or softening hardened hearts. The detractors persisted in their belief in the exclusivity of their religion and in the assertion that God could not and should not have chosen prophets from outside their race. The Qur'an rejects all their claims, querying their denial of the new religion which endorsed, supported, and blessed what had been revealed to their forefathers. We read in the surah:

> And when it is said to them, "Believe in what God had revealed," they reply, "We [only] believe in what was revealed to us," but they deny what had since been revealed, although it is the truth, corroborating what they had already received. Say, "Why did you then kill the prophets of God, if you were true believers?" (91)

The surah lists over ten different reminders of this kind, in the hope that the Jews of Madinah would heed God's advice and come to their senses. While those reminders might not have dissuaded Jewish zealots from pursuing their policy, they were extremely instructive for the Muslims themselves and served as a warning to them. God had said to the Jews, "Keep My covenant and I shall keep yours" (40), and He advised the Muslims saying, "Remember Me and then I shall remember you; be thankful to Me and do not deny Me. Believers, seek help in patience and prayer" (152–53). It is saying to the Muslims that whereas other groups had clung to the outward form of their religion but ignored its essence and true spirit, and drained it of its authentic universal meaning, they, the Muslims, should look into the heart and the essence of their religion and live it with sincerity and true faith. The surah puts it thus: "Righteousness does not come about by turning your faces towards the East or the West. It is belief in God and the Last Day" (177).

The surah then gets down to the task of laying the solid ground on which the new community was to emerge and grow. It outlines the five basic foundations or pillars of Islam and turns to dealing with Muslim family affairs, giving many of the principles on which they should be established, strengthened, and preserved.

From time to time references to narrow-minded or rebellious attitudes by previous groups and nations serve as a timely, if oblique, warning to the Muslims themselves: "To whoever tampers with God's boon after it has been bestowed on him God would mete out a severe chastisement" (211). The surah also deals with the question of protecting the larger community by means of sacrifice and hard work (Arabic: jihad) as well as protecting the smaller one, the family unit, with a number of rules and provisions that ensure its health, safety, and welfare—two counts on which we, the Muslims, have unfortunately been so negligent. Let us for the time being leave the family issue aside and deal briefly with the subject of war and the manner in which the Qur'an has presented it, contending, in the process, with some persistent misconceptions about jihad.

We Muslims abhor war, and dislike the destruction and loss of life it causes. Our natural disposition and tendency favor peace, harmony, and stability among relatives, neighbors, and friends. However, while condoning and encouraging these tendencies, the Qur'an also says:

> Much as you dislike it, fighting has been prescribed for you. But you may despise something that is good for you, and you may love something that is bad for you. God knows, but you do not. (216)

Peace is to be welcomed when rights are protected and beliefs are respected; but if peace means abject surrender and subjugation, it cannot be easily defended on moral or realistic grounds. This delicate balance is well presented in the verse: "They ask you whether fighting is permitted during the sacred month. Say, 'fighting in it is a grave matter'" (217), meaning it is not permitted. However, what should be done if aggression is perpetrated, terrorizing peaceful communities and jeopardizing their rights of worship and belief? Should not aggression be repelled, in order to protect one's rights? The verse continues:

> ...but to deny God and debar people from His path and prevent them from worshiping in the Holy Mosque, and to drive its inhabitants away, is far more grave in the sight of God... (217)

In short "sedition [Arabic: *fitnah*] is a greater threat than killing" (217), and fighting or armed resistance should be permitted in defense of one's integrity and beliefs. However, in circumstances in which we are faced with enemies who will not be satisfied until we forsake our religion and way of life and adopt theirs, defensive action becomes obligatory and the blame for instigating the conflict will not fall on us but on those who were the cause of it.

These introductory remarks enable us to appreciate fully the meaning of the following verse; "fight for the cause of God those who fight against you, but do not commit aggression because God does not love the aggressors" (190). This is an eternal principle, and everything else the Qur'an has to say on this subject agrees with it. Some commentators have been erroneously misled into believing that surah *al-Tawbah* contains injunctions that contradict this principle. The command given in that surah to undertake to fight back does not, however, prescribe fighting against fair-minded, neutral, or reasonable people. It condones it against groups who have grudges against the Muslims and are actively undermining their peace and security and inflicting harm upon them. That is the reason for the Qur'an's condemnation that: "Evil is what they [the unbelievers] have done; they respect no pacts or agreements with the believers and they are the aggressors" (*al-Tawbah*: 9–10). Furthermore, the Qur'an emphasizes the need to confront those aggressors in a just and clean fight, by asking:

> Would you not fight against those who have broken their oaths and conspired to drive the Messenger out, and attacked you first? Do you fear them? Surely you should fear God instead, if you are true believers. (*al-Tawbah*: 13)

It is difficult to see how this can be seen as prescribing waging war against those who do not commit aggression, or that it overrides the principle given in *al-Baqarah* which states clearly that fighting is undertaken only in response to aggression. This—when propounded by some Muslims—is at best a misunderstanding, and at worst an objectionable undermining of eternal Islamic principles, inviting noxious charges against Islam, for which we have only ourselves to blame. Here it is worth stressing that the Qur'an prescribes legitimate defensive war on condition that it is undertaken for the cause of God and not for personal glory nor to gain a special advantage; nor should wars be prescribed for the sake of vainglorious and bigoted nationalist interests to prove that a particular country is supreme and master of all! Wars conducted in recent times have been organized to usurp the wealth and the resources of weaker nations, and to colonize and control their lands and destinies for the benefit of strong and mighty ones. Far from being "just wars," fought in the name of God, they are true works of evil. Wars are said to be conducted for God's cause when they are fought to uphold God's supremacy and drive out godless powers. True believers have always undertaken such proper fighting in order to keep alive the belief in and worship of the One God. The surah asks: "Who is more wicked than those who forbid God's name being invoked in His mosques and seek to destroy them?" (114). The Qur'an observes:

> And if God had not enabled people to defend themselves against one another, corruption would surely overwhelm the earth: but God is limitless in His bounty unto all the worlds. (251)

Indeed, right can only triumph and become firmly established when those who defend it are selfless, brave, and totally devoted to uphold and preserve it.

※※

Al-Baqarah contains a long and detailed discussion of family affairs. Since it appears at the beginning of the Qur'an, some may be misled into thinking that what it has to say about this subject is the first to be presented in the Qur'an. However, about two thirds of the Qur'an had been revealed before this surah, and the subject was dealt with extensively. In studying what the surah says about family affairs, one has to refer to what has already been said elsewhere in the Qur'an.

One of the topics under the family heading is equality between the sexes, expressed in *al-Nahl* in these words: "Those who do good, be they male or female, and are true believers, We shall certainly grant them a good life and give them their rewards according to their best deeds" (*al-Naḥl*: 97). The same principle was advocated by a believer from Moses' generation who defied Egypt's Pharaoh and his henchmen, and is quoted elsewhere in the Qur'an to have said:

> Those who do evil shall be rewarded with like evil, but whoever do good, be they males or females, and are true believers, shall enter Paradise, and therein receive limitless blessings. (*Ghāfir*: 40)

In another surah, we read: "One of His signs is that He created for you spouses from among yourselves, that you may find peace and harmony with them, and induce among you love and kindness" (*al-Rūm*: 21). This was stressed again in surah *al-Naḥl*, when listing God's favors upon people, which included giving them "spouses from among yourselves, and through them He gave you children and grandchildren" (*al-Naḥl*: 72).

Since the status of women and the position of the family in society have already been dealt with in other parts of the Qur'an, it will not come as a surprise that *al-Baqarah* should deal with details relating to family disputes or other aspects of family life that may arise for which God's rulings and guidance have to be sought. Hence, we find the surah dealing with oaths, divorce, childbearing, breast-feeding, and so on. However, family legislation cannot endure and be effective without a firm basis of morality, faith, and piety. The surah points out that divorcees, men and women, might have second thoughts and choose not to sever the relationship altogether. They should use reason and common sense, on which the surah gives eight successive guidelines, for it says:

> If you divorce women and they have reached [the end of] their waiting period,
> a) retain them with honor, or
> b) let them go with dignity.
> c) You shall not detain them to harm them or to do them wrong.

d) Whoever does this will wrong his own soul.

e) Do not take God's revelations in vain;

f) remember God's favors upon you and what He had revealed to you of the Book and wisdom in order to enlighten you.

g) Fear God and

h) remember that He is aware of all things. (231)

What more can any religious system offer for a more amicable and courteous separation, and a more equitable and responsible way of protecting the rights and the future of all concerned in the family? Nevertheless, divorce in some Muslim communities has become rife, and one still comes across some ludicrous situations that have led to tragic family breakups, with the blame being put on Islam as being unfair to women!

I have referred on other occasions to the Qur'anic expression "the bounds [or terms] set by God," which appears six times in verses 229 and 230 of this surah, dealing with the subject of divorce. Very few Muslims have a clear understanding of this expression or the emphasis placed on it in the Qur'an and the context in which it is used. Women have been badly treated in many societies, but the odd thing is that this maltreatment is often blamed on the teachings of Islam, which have shown utmost respect and justice towards women. God says in the Qur'an: "Wives shall with justice have rights equal to those exercised against them, although men have precedence [in terms of financial responsibilities] over them" (228), which is quite clear in setting out the mutual rights and liabilities of husbands and wives. Nevertheless one notices, in certain backward communities, that women tend to give more than what they have a right to receive, or that they are treated with undue harshness and disdain. It is difficult to believe that such an attitude can have anything to do with any religion, let alone the religion of Islam.

Of course, the wife herself may sometimes instigate the quarrel, and such disputes cannot always be settled at the hands of the law.

There has to be an environment of trust in, and respect for "the terms [bounds] set by God" on the part of both sides. Enlightenment, generosity, moral integrity, as well as a sense of equity and fairness, and a God-fearing community are all essential requirements for strong, happy, and well-protected families.

The treatment of women in certain Muslim societies has been a soft target for the enemies of Islam, and has proved a dangerous breach through which they have relentlessly attacked its teachings and laws. This issue has been the Trojan horse for those who want to undermine Islam and Muslim societies by calling for the "liberation of Muslim women from the injustice and cruelty of Islam!" This has led to a bandwagon of opinion among sections of the intelligentsia in some Muslim countries, especially amongst women, who have taken up this issue with great enthusiasm. But certainly, some of those who claim to speak for Islam and grossly misrepresent it or are ignorant of the spirit of its legislation, are partly to blame.

I once described the wife's right to divorce from her husband in return for a monetary compensation she pays to the husband (the *khulaʿah*) as being equivalent to the husband's right to divorce her. Accordingly, I argued, when a woman can no longer bear to live with a man for whatever reasons that she may reveal or keep to herself, and she offers to pay him back the dowry he has advanced to her, the legal authorities concerned should have no reason not to grant her wish. Someone in the audience commented that a judge could grant a wife divorce if she were threatened with real harm. I replied that even if she were not, but nevertheless were not able to live with her husband for some reason and were willing to compensate him for what he had spent on her, there should be no reason why she should be forced to stay with him. My opponent insisted it would not be permissible as long as the husband was not agreeable to the divorce. I replied that it would be permissible and it would be up to the judge either to bring about reconciliation between them or rule that the husband accept compensation in return for a divorce.

Some religious zealots tend to deny a woman her individual entity, while in the Qur'an we read that the wives of Noah and Pharaoh, for example, were independent of their husbands and were under no obligation to share in their actions or liabilities. When it comes to having children and setting up a family, husbands and wives share responsibilities and advantages equally, as the Qur'an says:

> None should be charged with more than they can bear. A mother should not be allowed to suffer on account of her child, nor should a father...But if, after consultation, they decide by mutual consent to wean the child [or separate it from its mother], they shall incur no guilt. (233)

One important aspect of divorce which has been neglected in our societies is that of providing maintenance for divorced women. Divorce normally follows a period of much disagreement, acrimony, and bitter emotional tussles that could destroy hearts and wipe out the best goodwill in the world. However, once divorce is agreed upon, the emotional animosity it leaves behind has to be watered down with some gracious gestures. This is clearly stated in the verse that says:

> Divorced women, too, have a right to maintenance that is duly incumbent on God-fearing men. Thus God makes clear His requisitions that you may comprehend. (241–42).

I earnestly call upon Muslims today to refer to the Qur'an and the example of the Messenger Muhammad and to learn properly the rules and principles governing family life in Islam, and the most honorable ways of promoting happiness and efficiency in Muslim homes. We must look around, examine and understand what is happening in the world today. It is incredible that we should ban women from driving cars, when other societies allow them to lead nations.

✹✹

In Madinah, and following their emigration from Makkah, the Muslims continued to receive Qur'anic revelation as they had done previously over a period of thirteen years. The environment and the circumstances, however, had changed. For, whereas episodes from Jewish history had hitherto been cited and related for information and education, the talk about Jews now took a much more relevant, topical, and contemporary significance, affecting the present as well as the future.

At Makkah, Muslims used to perform prayers individually, but now the mosque became the focus of the community and they flocked to it to pray collectively. Only the hypocrites or the weak and infirm stayed behind in their houses during prayer times. The essential characteristics of the new state began to emerge slowly and a new society was gradually taking shape. Narrow-minded individualism was slowly but surely giving way to collective consolidated allegiance to God's laws, in defense of which the Muslims sought strength in unity and collective vigilance.

The unitarian belief in the one God had its roots firmly established by Makkan revelation, and to expound it further in Madinah was necessary for a clearer and more enlightened understanding of its significance. The Qur'an, after all, is a self-explanatory and self-sustaining book; it resorts to a great deal of repetition and paraphrasing of ideas and concepts. This can be seen in the many verses in this surah that talk of the unity of God, such as verse 163 which says: "Your God is one God; there is no god but Him, the Compassionate, the Merciful," and verse 164 which says:

In the creation of the heavens and the earth, the alternation of night and day, the ships that sail the ocean carrying goods that are useful to humanity…there are signs for people who understand.

These are followed by verses explaining the common bases that underlie people's emotions, feelings, and behavior. Believers who love their God more than anything else reflect the fruits of this love in their actions and expressions.

God is deserving of this adoration, because He is the ultimate manifestation of all glory, and greatness belongs to Him alone. This is beautifully articulated in the most magnificent verse of the Qur'an, also known as the verse of the Throne, which begins with the words: "God: there is no god but Him, the Living, the Eternal. Neither slumber nor sleep overtakes Him. His is what the heavens and the earth contain" (255). Yet, in order to establish the faith, it may be necessary to debate and argue on its behalf with those who deny or suppress it. The surah cites the confrontation of the prophet Abraham with a king of his time. It says: "Have you not heard of him who argued with Abraham about his Lord, because He had granted him power and sovereignty?" (258). Abraham, with God's guidance and support, using sincere and simple arguments, was able to confound the arrogant tyrant.

Thus we find in this surah, which was revealed early on in Madinah, another Qur'anic approach in dealing with major issues of faith and belief, without deviation from the main objectives of divine revelation. The Qur'an is a Book, as the surah states, "about which there is no doubt" (2). Muhammad and his followers excelled in their response to the teachings and commands of this surah and the revelation that followed it. As the Qur'an was being revealed, they were acting on its instructions and advice, eagerly and willingly. The Qur'an was setting out the characteristics, the framework, and the principles, showing the Muslims the way forward for them as individuals, and as members of society and citizens of a state.

They were building and implementing, turning the ideas and concepts into living realities. With the diligence and devotion of those early pioneers, Madinah was well on its way to becoming the great new capital of one of the most formidable and enduring religions the world has ever known; a citadel for what verse 143 describes as the "middle nation," and the most righteous. It is a nation raised by divine revelation, and teachings containing guidance, sent by God to His Messenger, who in turn passed it on to his followers. The verse says: "Thus We have made you a middle nation, so that you may bear witness over all humanity, and the Messenger [Muhammad] shall in turn bear witness over you" (143).

In the last two verses of this surah, God Almighty states that Prophet Muhammad and his followers were true to their faith and diligent in their understanding and implementation of the commands and exhortations contained in this surah and in others after it, and had acted upon them faithfully and with enthusiasm, to the best of their abilities. For this reason, God had given them His support and His blessings. They excelled their predecessors who had received divine revelation but did not respect or act according to it.

The Arabs were an illiterate people who, prior to receiving the Qur'anic revelations, had little influence on the course of human civilization. Since then, however, their reputation and standing in the world began to rise and spread until they became the leading nation of the world. For centuries they were world pioneers in all fields of religion, science, law, and social affairs. The contribution they made to human civilization, when untainted by worldly or divisive concerns, was free of racial ethnocentricity and materialistic aggrandizement. Their civilization was in essence devoted to God and looked on this world as a prelude to a more meaningful and fulfilled life hereafter. The penultimate verse says:

The Messenger believes in what has been revealed to him by his Lord, and so do the believers. They all believe in God and His

27

angels, His books, and His messengers, making no distinction among any of His messengers. They say: "We have heard and we obey; grant us Your forgiveness, our Lord; to You we shall all return." (285)

Muslims have no race to be biased towards, nor a homeland to identify with, because their allegiance is to the universal God, the Creator and Lord of all. They have no advantage over other nations or human groups except by what they pass on to them of the religion of Islam, and they are distinguished by their piety and sincere faith. The special reputation and place gained by the city of Madinah in the history of Islam are directly linked to the fact that it was the cradle of revelation and first city of the great Islamic nation that has since emerged. In it were created the first Muslim families, marketplaces, government cadres, centers of learning, trade enterprises, farms, and legislative councils; all under the guidance of divine revelation and the enlightened leadership of the exponent of that revelation, Muhammad. History tells us that the Prophet had once selected a very young man for a leadership post because he had memorized and learnt this surah well, indicating its distinguished and prestigious status in the Qur'an.

Finally, as we look at the last verse in the surah, our attention is drawn to the historic phenomenon that nations which attain ascendancy and supremacy usually display arrogance and conceit, and look down upon other weaker nations. Today's domineering vainglorious civilization, which has encompassed both east and west, is a vivid living example—a culture of decadence and gross injustice thriving on the great achievements and glory of a genius elite who have split the atom and made inroads into outer space. When the Muslims were a leading nation, however, and at the height of their achievement, they were overwhelmed by a sense of submission to God and a need for His support and guidance. They have always sought God's forgiveness and looked up to His grace, praying:

> Our Lord, do not take us to task if we forget or make mistakes,
> Our Lord, do not lay upon us a burden such as You had laid
>   upon those before us,
> Our Lord, do not burden us with more than what we can bear.
> Pardon us, forgive us our sins, and have mercy upon us.
> You are our Lord,
> Grant us victory over the unbelievers. (286)

Āl ʿImrān
(House of ʿImrān)

IT IS EASY TO IDENTIFY immediately the subject matter of this surah. It revolves around two major issues: the debate with the People of the Book, the Jews and the Christians, of whom the Jews were Madinah natives incited to oppose Islam; and a review and assessment of the humiliating and tragic defeat suffered by the Muslims at the battle of Uḥud in 625 AC. The two issues are treated separately to begin with, but halfway through the surah they are brought together and from then on are discussed as almost one subject. The outcome of the whole discussion seems to focus on the fact that perseverance and steadfastness are required to face both issues: the scheming of the Jewish establishment inside Madinah and the attacks by the infidels from outside it.

Islam is a religion addressed to all human societies without coercion or discrimination. Whoever responds positively is taken into the fold, while those who turn away are left in peace. However—as mentioned earlier—those who commit aggression against Islam and the Muslims are boldly confronted. This is clear from the verse:

> If they argue with you, say: "I have surrendered myself to God and so have those who followed me." As for those who had received the scriptures and the illiterates [pagan Arabs with no revealed scriptures], ask them: "Have you surrendered yourselves to God?" If they have they shall be rightly guided; but if they turn away, then your only duty is to deliver the message to them. God is watching His servants. (20)

The surah begins by stressing that Islam is a universal guidance, and the Qur'an a confirmation of all previous revelation. God's revelation is one, in the sense that it sets the truth apart from falsehood in a sharp and unequivocal manner. The surah highlights the fact that Moses, Jesus and Muhammad have trodden the same path, and that the scope of Islam encompasses all other revealed religions regardless of their time and place. The Torah and the Gospel are both referred to here as "God's revelation [or messages]." This phrase occurs ten times in the surah, as in verse 4 which says: "Those who deny God's revelations [messages], grievous suffering awaits them; for God is Mighty and capable of retribution," and verse 199, towards the end of the surah:

There are among the People of the Book [Jews and Christians] those who believe in God and what has been revealed to you and to them. They humble themselves before God and do not exchange God's revelations [messages] for a trifling price.

There could be no contradiction nor differences in the basic tenets and principles of divine faith, nor in what was revealed to Muhammad and his earlier brothers in the line of prophets, Moses and Jesus. Contradictions can exist only between God's revelation and the false notions and philosophies that people put forward. Belief, as presented in the Qur'an, applies to what has been revealed to the Muslims and to those before them. Those who deviate from it ought to repent and return to the straight path. The "People of the Book" is a term that refers to Jews and Christians. Unlike the debate with the Jews, that with the Christians in Madinah was calm and unhurried. The Jews had their own settlements inside Madinah itself and in other parts of northern Hijaz. Their elders resisted Islam, gainsaid God's revelations and berated His Messenger. Moreover, they collaborated with the pagan Arabs in their insidious efforts and fights against Islam and the Muslims. They were encouraged by their wealth and economic power and the strong foothold they had secured in Madinah. This was repeatedly condemned in the surah (10, 21, 116, 196, 197), for excessive wealth and affluence would lead individuals as well as nations to ignore God and overreach themselves in pursuit of power and influence.

Although the Jewish settlements in Hijaz were much more developed and economically prosperous than other cities and towns in Arabia, they had never used any of their wealth or expertise for the development and welfare of the region as a whole. With its well-established traditions of self-dignity, honesty, and hospitality, the pagan Arab society could, in fact, be said to have been more liberal and charitable than other communities in their midst. When Prophet Muhammad began to spread his teachings, he proved to be more persuasive and endearing, and less condescending, than the Jewish spokesmen who had been exposed as arrogant and self-centered. Their attitudes and conduct had in the end led to their defeat and the end of their influence and existence in the area.

The Jews had enjoyed the honor and privilege of custodianship of God's revelation for several successive generations. They had been entrusted with it for so long that they had come to nurture the false belief that God's revelation belonged to them and to them alone—a nation that would have the eternal indisputable right to hold and interpret God's revelations and reap their benefit for ever. They were hopelessly mistaken. Honor, privilege, status, and leadership in the world have to be earned through devotion and hard work.

By the time Prophet Muhammad had emerged, the Jews' capacity to carry God's revelation forward had reached its nadir. Their rabbis' hearts had turned hard, morals had deteriorated, and selfishness had gained the upper hand; greed for material and worldly possessions and privileges had become their sole preoccupation. Worse than that, they had also displayed signs of insolence and insubordination towards and rejection of God and the mission with which He had entrusted their race. And so it was necessary to transfer the responsibility and the trust to another human group, which was better qualified and which would give it the effort and devotion it deserved. The surah expresses this in the following verse:

> Say, "Lord, Sovereign of all creation, You bestow sovereignty on whom You will and take away from whom You will. You raise whomever You will and abase whomever You will. All Goodness lies in Your hands. You have power over all things." (26)

This fundamental assertion is preceded by elaborate reasons and considerations such as:

> Have you not taken note of those who received portions of the Book [revelation]? When they are called upon to accept the judgment of God's Book, some of them turn away and take no heed. It is because they said, "We shall suffer the fire for a few days only." (23–24)

They were so overcome by that false sense of security that they turned to open rebellion, squandering the divine injunctions and reneging on their commitment to them.

God's response to that was to confirm divine justice towards all people and to dispel the erroneous idea that God was biased towards any particular ethnic or racial group, saying: "What will they do when We gather them all together upon a day that is sure to come, when every soul will be given what it earned with no injustice whatsoever?" (25). In God's eyes, people are all equal; each shall reap his or her just rewards according to their behavior and conduct. When humankind is brought before God for judgment, each human being shall face the Creator alone. The one thing that would redeem any of them shall be their piety, and the depth and sincerity of their belief in God.

It is important to keep in mind that although those words are addressed to Jews in Arabia, they also serve as a subtle reminder to other human groups. God was not going to chastise the Jews for their deviation, and overlook the misdemeanor of the Arabs if they were to follow their example. Similar actions and activities would earn similar reactions and responses. The pitfall in which errant Jews were caught was their misconception that the Torah had been graced by them rather than the other way around, and this had led to their fateful fall from God's grace and favor. Today, there are Arabs who refuse to be associated with Islam and try to separate it from Arab culture and history. Their fate could not be any different from that of the misguided Jews of Madinah before them. God does not make any undue or unmerited preferences among humans.

The debate with the People of the Book is covered over a large part of this surah, and apart from a fleeting allusion in verse 6 to the birth of Jesus, was mainly directed at the Jews of Arabia whose animosity towards the early Muslims was much more pronounced. In saying: "It is He who creates you as He pleases inside the mothers' wombs; there is no god but Him, the Mighty, the Wise," the surah outlines God's stupendous power to create human beings and shape their form, soul, and body, and in the same breath alludes to the fact that Jesus' miraculous birth was but one of a multitude of feats and incredible acts of God. He has shown humankind veritable signs of superiority and ingenuity in His creation, endowing some people with higher qualities and aptitudes than others. Jesus' fatherless conception and birth were but two of these extraordinary and exceptional acts. This is a subject which we shall come to discuss later.

As to the hostility exhibited towards the Muslims by the Jewish establishment in Madinah, its main underlying reason was the transfer of prophethood from their patriarchs to Muhammad. That prophethood had given them such a special and unique status over all the rest of humankind, and seeing it being taken away from them and entrusted to the Arabs enraged them and fired up their fury and hatred towards them. Their reaction was severely and immediately condemned in the Qur'an: "People of the Book! Why do you deny God's revelations when you are witnesses to their veracity? Why do you confound the true with the false and hide the truth knowingly?" (70–71). It is clear from the tone of this reprimand that the Jewish priests and elders were aware that Muhammad was genuine in his claim of relaying God's words and being His spokesman. It is also implicit in the address that they were guilty of transgression against God, that they rejected a reconciliation with Him, that they persisted with their refusal to acknowledge Muhammad's prophethood, and went on to oppose and resist it with arms, seditious scheming, and active collaboration with his other enemies, the pagan Arabs. The reproach is repeated several times in the surah: "How would God guide people who rejected the faith after believing in it and having borne witness that the Messenger is true and after receiving veritable signs!" (86). Elsewhere God's Messenger is directed to ask them, saying:

> "People of the Book, why do you deny God's revelations, when God is witness to what you do?" Say, "People of the Book, why do you drive believers away from God's path, seeking to mislead and confuse, when you yourselves are witnesses? God is not unaware of what you do." (98–99)

To countermand this criticism, some Jews came up with the brilliant stratagem of feigning their acceptance of Islam in order to conceal their antagonism and prove their tolerance and fair-mindedness towards the new religion. The logic of their argument would lead them to say that their rejection of, and opposition to Islam had come as a result of direct firsthand experience of it. The surah says: "Some of the People of the Book said [to one another], 'Believe in that which is revealed to the faithful in the morning and abandon it in the evening, so that they may themselves go back on their faith'" (72). The surah also exposes this group's determined rejection of the new revelation and their dogged resentment of the transfer of divine trust away from the Hebrews, by reporting their statement: "Believe in none except those who follow your own religion" (73). The inference here is that they firmly believed in the superiority of their religion over all others.

So it was clear that the rabbis were not happy with God's decision to give preference to the Arabs and choose them this time round to be the custodians of His revelation. If they only could, they would force God to go back on that choice and change the course of history by restoring the leadership of humankind to them. God's response was clear and decisive: "Grace is in the hand of God; He bestows it on whom He will. God is Munificent and All-Knowing. He favors with His mercy whom He will. His grace is immense" (73–74). However, the group had acquired several vices, not least their self-importance, hard-headedness, and conceit, that could at times of weakness turn into deep-seated hatred and, at times of prosperity and triumph, into open hostility and belligerence. These characteristics seem to have colored much rabbinical writing, driving the Jewish people into isolation and making them tragically vulnerable to persecution by other societies and groups. The surah offers the explanation that "they [the Jewish elders] say, 'We are not bound to keep faith with the unlettered [the Gentiles].' They knowingly tell lies about God" (75). The Arabic term *ummiyīn* used in this verse literally means "unlettered," but could also mean "non-Jews" or Gentiles (Hebrew: *Goyim*). In the one case it would be a reference to the Arabs, while in the other it would be a reference to non-Jewish communities in general. Jewish religious scriptures, especially the Torah and the Talmud, as well as parts of their literature, do advocate the idea of the superiority of the Jewish nation over other nations, and propound the concept of Jews as the 'chosen people of God.' The Qur'an explains very clearly that the relationship between God and humans cannot be based on false claims, but rather on sound ethical grounds, and on faith and trust. In it we read: "Indeed, for those who keep their covenant and fear God, God loves the righteous" (76).

At this point in the surah we may inquire why the subject of the pilgrimage is suddenly brought up for discussion halfway through it, having covered the debates with the People of the Book and their behavior. Indeed, we may even ask why the subject of permitted and forbidden foods is raised here also. After a great deal of reflection, and with reference to Shaykh Muhammad Rashīd Riḍā's commentary in *al-Manār*, I was able to find the answer. As Islam was being introduced to the Jews, they questioned the idea of adopting a religion which allowed them to eat certain foods that their own religion had forbidden them. The answer they were given was that the embargo imposed on them regarding the consumption of certain foods had been temporary, and had come about as punishment for earlier intransigence and insubordination to God's commands. This is covered more fully in surah *al-Anʿām* where it is stated:

> Such is the penalty We imposed on them for their misdeeds. What We declare is true. If they do not believe you say, "Your Lord's mercy is vast, but His punishment cannot be averted by the transgressors." (*al-Anʿām*: 146–47)

Jesus, as we know, sought to relieve the Jews of some of the burdens placed upon them. This is given in verse 50 of this surah, which quotes Jesus as saying to the Jews: "'I come to confirm the Torah already revealed and to make lawful to you some of what was forbidden you.'" The Qur'an restored the divine law to its original form, forbidding only certain types of carrion meat, swine flesh, spilt

37

blood, and the meat of animals slaughtered without invoking God's name—all other types of food would be permissible. Verse 93 of the surah says: "All food was lawful to the Israelites except what Israel [Jacob] forbade himself before the Torah was revealed."

The same argument applies in the case of the *qiblah*, or the direction faced by Muslims during salah. As verse 96 affirms, the Ka'bah at Makkah was the first and only *qiblah* for all humankind. And although Jerusalem, for certain temporary reasons, had been chosen as the *qibla* for worshipers of God, those reasons no longer applied and the Ka'bah was reinstated as the legitimate *qiblah* for all believers.

Putting differences between various religions and human ideologies aside, the fact remains that sound moral and ethical discipline and education have proved to be the basis for human progress at all phases of human history. We find reference to this very early in the surah where God says:

> Men are tempted by the allure of women and offspring, of hoarded treasures of gold and silver, of splendid horses, cattle and vast plantations. These are the comforts of this life, but to God is the best return. (14)

True, for human life to continue, the satisfaction and pursuance of these desires is necessary. Without the sexual relationship between men and women, human existence would have ceased long ago. The same can be said of all other human desires. The crucial point here is that they should be pursued in moderation, with discipline, and within a framework of reason and common sense. Islam has permitted all that is good and useful to people, and forbidden what is harmful. Islamic laws and teachings are built on the foundation of faith in God and positive action, and they have provided for a great deal that would nurture people's relationship with God and maintain their awareness of the hereafter.

We are used nowadays to hearing national leaders warning their citizens against the AIDS virus and advising them to take certain precautions during illicit sexual acts. They no longer call for proper lawful sexual relationships between people because they no longer believe that these are possible. This is only true in a society that has lost its faith and trust in God. Followers of formal religion shall continue to suffer from their uncontrollable desires, unless they heed the words of God, especially when He says:

> Say, "Shall I tell of better things than these? For the righteous their Lord has gardens beneath which rivers flow, where they shall dwell forever, spouses of high purity and God's grace." God is aware of His servants, those who say: "Our Lord, we believed in You, so forgive us our sins and save us the torment of the hellfire," those who are steadfast, sincere, devout, charitable and who pray for forgiveness during the small hours of the night. (15–17)

So we find the surah opening with a statement addressed to the People of the Book that salvation could come only with a faith based on the belief in "God, there is no god but Him, the Living, the Ever-Existing one" (2), and in a way of life that acknowledges human nature within a discipline of decency and virtue that discourages all forms of excessive deprivation or overindulgence; a discipline that renders enlightened life in this world a natural and meaningful prelude to the life that is to come.

Mary was a virgin throughout her pregnancy, having miraculously conceived Jesus. When some people began saying that Jesus was the son of God, it was clear that a groundless myth, a fallacy, was being created, pointing towards the existence of a special and intimate relationship between God and Mary, the outcome of which was Jesus. This outrageous notion reflects a deep-seated ignorance of the nature and status of God and the exaltation and glorification that humans owe Him. Surely, God could not be conceived of as an agent of reproduction in such a crude and salacious manner, for as God says in the Qur'an: "Were God to have offspring, He would have chosen the best of His creatures at will; Glorified is God, the One, the Almighty" (*al-Zumar:* 4). It is true that Jesus' conception and birth were abnormal and extraordinary events. Such was the will and wisdom of God in order to show humankind that God is not bound by the natural laws of causality, but rather He overrides and controls these laws. The story of Jesus and his mother is related following that of Zachariah and his wife, which had also entailed certain miraculous aspects.

Mary's own conception and birth were unexpected by her mother. As soon as she knew that she was pregnant, she dedicated her baby to serving the temple in Jerusalem, and to worshiping and being devoted to the service of other worshipers. The Qur'an quotes her as saying: "'Lord, I completely dedicate to Your service that which is in my womb. Accept it from me; You are All-Hearing, All-Knowing'" (35). However, contrary to her expectation, the baby turned out to be a girl and would not, therefore, be of much use in fulfilling that task which required men of strength and endurance. In the circumstances, the son she was hoping to have would have given more happiness than a daughter who would herself probably need care and looking after. Naturally, the mother was not to know that her newly born daughter was destined to be the mother of a highly regarded and noble human being and would have the privilege of nursing him in his infancy, just as Moses and Muhammad were nursed by their respective mothers. It is interesting to note in passing that these three great senior prophets had been respectively reared by mothers of humble means and status who had to seek and depend on God's help alone. History is witness here as elsewhere that women too can reach great heights in society with their nobility, magnanimity, and strong belief. Mary's mother prayed to her Lord saying:

"Lord, I have given birth to a daughter"—and God knows well of what she was delivered, and that a male is not like a female,—"and I have named her Mary. I seek Your protection for her and her offspring against Satan, the accursed one." Her Lord graciously accepted her and made her grow up a goodly child. (36–37)

Mary was brought up by Zachariah, an old and frail man, and his as yet childless wife. Zachariah was himself melancholy and heartbroken for not having children of his own to inherit the leadership of the Israelites in whom he had little faith, but for whose future he was concerned. Despite his frailty, though, Zachariah struggled and persevered in bringing up the new addition to his family. However, Zachariah began to notice some unusually fortunate developments taking place within his household and certain provisions coming to the possession of the new girl, and so he asked her: "Mary, how did you come by this food?" She replied, "It is from God, who gives to whom He wills without stint" (37).

This inflamed Zachariah's heart with love for, and devotion to, God. He began to look up to God for more extraordinary acts and for such favors to be bestowed on him personally. He knew that God could make a hitherto infertile female conceive and have children and give an elderly man the virility to produce offspring, and so he prayed to God, saying:

"Lord, grant me goodly offspring, You hear all prayers." The angels called out to him while he was praying in the shrine, "God bids you rejoice in the birth of John, who shall confirm the word of God."
(38-39)

Life had returned to the despairing old couple; the barren wife would be made to conceive by her elderly and infertile husband. This only goes to show that when God wills, all the laws of nature succumb to His will. He can create and cause things to happen completely at will.

Mary grew up in that—by then—happy, pious, and blessed household, where God's angels would be no strangers. They called on Mary with more good news:

> The angels said to Mary, "God gives you glad tidings of a word from Him, whose name is the Messiah, Jesus the son of Mary. He shall be noble in this world and in the hereafter, and shall be favored by God. He shall talk to people in his cradle and in his adulthood, and shall lead a righteous life." She said, "Lord, how can I have a child when no man has touched me?" He replied, "Such is the will of God who creates whom He will. Once He decides on a matter, He says, 'Be' and it is." (45–47)

Thus Mary found herself on the threshold of a new and overwhelming experience, which a virgin girl would naturally undergo with extreme apprehension and trepidation. At one point she wished she were dead. Nevertheless, the will of God was declared and Jesus was born in that astounding and extraordinary way. Jesus was then charged with the mission to address the Israelites with the message of God in order to reform their state of affairs, break the arrogance of their chiefs, and commit them to a humble attitude towards God and their fellow humans.

Mary's family was highly respected and venerated by people, and her son was held in high esteem by those who recognized the blessings that accompanied his coming. However, there were Israelites who took a different stand towards him. The Pharisees and skeptics rejected the miracles Jesus performed and refused to recognize him as an apostle of God. Furthermore, they claimed that his birth was no act of God, but the outcome of an illicit relationship between Mary and a suitor of hers named Joseph the carpenter. Thus they compounded their disbelief with slander. Jesus sought the support and the backing of reasonable and fair-minded people, some of whom rallied around him and offered their backing, saying: "Lord, we have believed in what You have sent down and have followed the messenger, so please enlist us among the witnesses [to the truth]" (53). The Pharisees, however, went on with their intrigues against Jesus and his followers even after, having delivered his Lord's message, Jesus had passed away and was saved from their treachery and vicious scheming.

Although a large number of scholars believe that Jesus was raised to heaven alive, I find myself more in agreement with those scholars who say that he died a natural normal death. This would not discount the idea, as the scholar Ibn Ḥazm says, that he could have been brought back to normal life again to pursue his mission of spreading the creed of monotheism. Jesus' story could, in this context, be compared to that of the man who passed by a town which had been destroyed, and inquired: "'How can God bring life back to this town, now that it is dead?' Thereupon, God caused him to die, and after one hundred years brought him back to life" (*al-Baqarah*: 259). It also can be compared to the story of the People of the Cave, who remained dead for a few hundred years and then were brought back to life. The matter is very simple and the dispute is fickle. Jesus must be perceived as an ordinary human being, not as a god or a son of God.

The surah recalls the visit to Madinah by a Christian delegation who went to debate with Prophet Muhammad aspects of the new religion he was advocating. They argued that Jesus was human in form, only asking, of course, that if he were human, who was his father? The Prophet replied that the absence of a human father did not necessarily mean Jesus was the son of God. Based on their reasoning, Adam, who had neither father nor mother, would have been more eligible to divine parentage. We read in the surah that: "Jesus is like Adam in the sight of God. He created him of dust and then said to him, 'Be' and he was. Truth comes from your Lord; do not ever doubt it" (59–60). Nevertheless, the quibblers insisted on their viewpoint and defended it with vehemence. The Prophet

43

then proposed that the two camps, Christians and Muslims, should unite in prayer to God to curse the liars of either side. The surah continues:

> Whoever disputes with you concerning Jesus after all the knowledge you have received, say to them, "Come, let us call out our sons and your sons, our women and your women, ourselves and yourselves, and then let us all jointly and earnestly pray that God's curse should fall upon the liars." This is the true version [of events]. There is no god but God; He is Mighty and Wise. (61–62)

The Christian delegation refused to take part in that joint prayer to establish the truth regarding the nature and status of Jesus, and up to this day the two religions have continued to exist apart from one another. It seems that the matter shall be settled only by Jesus himself on his second coming to earth. He might be the one who will point out the liars and confirm that the world knows only one overpowering and almighty Master.

Before closing the chapter on the People of the Book, the surah gives a critical account of the battle of Uḥud, at which the Muslims of Madinah sustained a humiliating defeat at the hands of the pagan Arabs in 625 AC. These were the original enemies of the early Muslims, who had no alternative but to face them and, as has been the case ever since, fight on two fronts simultaneously. The story begins with verse 121 referring to the Prophet's preparation for battle, and then it suddenly breaks into a discussion of usury, spending, and the urgent need for repentance. Having covered these topics, the surah picks up the account of the battle of Uḥud again, which takes us right to the end of the surah.

This leads us to look for a reason for this brief, but intriguing, digression. The explanation seems to lie in the need for a cleansing, a review, of the Muslim internal condition; to purge it of all signs of weakness and corruption in order to qualify the Muslims for victory in the battlefield. fights such as the ones the Muslims were engaged in were not personal or nationalistic wars, but wars for values and principles. This is made very clear in the surah when it says: "It is of no concern of yours [Muhammad] when He [God] should forgive or punish them. They are transgressors" (128). Reconciliation or antipathy should be perpetrated for the sake of God only; for today's enemies could very well be the allies of tomorrow, if they reconcile their situation with God and submit to His will and teachings. Under Islam, there is no room for private grudges or personal animosity.

The defeat at Uḥud contained a sharp lesson for the Muslims. Their earlier triumph at Badr in 624 AC had opened the door for opportunists and those with special interests to join the growing Muslim community which showed clear promise of dominating the region. One such prominent personality, ʿAbd Allah ibn Ubayy, saw it coming and recognized the victory at Badr as setting an irreversible trend that would result in the dominance of Islam. He decided to convert and take all his followers with him. The surah comments on this by saying: "God would not leave the believers in their current plight, without separating the bad from the good; nor was God to let you in on the unknown" (179). The scene was then set for a setback, a test, that would distinguish those who were sincerely upholding Islam and supporting the Prophet and the Muslims through thick and thin from those who were in it merely for personal gain or prestige.

Under such circumstances, one can normally distinguish two main groups of people: those who are sincere and dedicated to the common cause, no matter what happens; and those whose main concern is their own safety and self-interest, who hold little faith in God or their fellow human beings. The surah describes these by

45

saying: "And a group who were only concerned about themselves, doubting God in their ignorant ways. They ask, 'Do we stand to gain anything?'" (154). The latter group are always disgruntled and restless, because their views are rarely given credence and they are seldom, if ever, accorded respect or prominence. Any society, and far more an army, would be wiser to be rid of such people.

Contrary to the opinion of some, the Muslims' defeat at Uḥud did not come as a result of bad planning or faulty tactics. It was the result of insubordination, for some Muslim fighters, at a very critical point during the battle, neglected their duties by abandoning their battle positions in pursuit of the loot. Had those fighters adhered to their orders as given by the Prophet, the outcome would have been totally different. The surah recalls:

> God fulfilled His pledge to you when, by His leave, you trounced them [the unbelievers at Uḥud], until the moment when you lost heart, started squabbling among yourselves and disobeyed the Messenger just as you were close to victory. Some of you chose the gains of this world, but others chose the rewards of the life to come. (152)

The Muslims' attitude in the battlefield had changed and therefore the outcome had also to change. "He [God] prevented you from defeating them in order to test you. But now He has forgiven you, for He is gracious to the believers" (152).

The defeat came as a shock to the Muslims and they were shaken by it. They questioned how and why it could have happened at all, and God's answer was:

> Now that a disaster has befallen you, after you yourselves have inflicted [on your enemies] losses twice as heavy, you come to ask, "How could this have come about?" Say to them, "You have brought it upon yourselves." God has power over all things. (165)

True, the defeat sustained by the Muslims at Uḥud was only half as
heavy as that sustained a couple of years earlier by the Arabs and their
allies at Badr, giving the Muslims a slightly higher advantage.
Nevertheless, they were defeated and had to face up to the consequences, especially that their defeat could have been avoided if they
had not become greedy and ignored their leader's battle orders.
However, the surah eloquently offers a most encouraging consolation for that tragic episode by saying to the Muslims:

> This often happened to others before you. Look all over the world
> and see what was the fate of the unbelievers. This is a proclamation
> to all mankind; it is also a guide and an admonition to the God-
> fearing. Do not, therefore, lose heart or grieve, for you shall reign
> supreme as long as you uphold your belief. (137–39)

In the Qur'an, God has given the Muslims accounts of previous
nations and civilizations which collapsed or were destroyed as a consequence of their stubborn rejection of God's messages and their
refusal to believe. The triumph of the non-Muslim Arabs at Uḥud
would be short-lived. Things would change, allowing Islam to prevail. However, for the Muslims to achieve supremacy and triumph,
two things, not mutually exclusive, would be required: sincerity of
intent and a proper execution of duty. Muslims are always in need of
emphasizing the second condition, for some tend to imagine that
good intentions and sincerity alone are sufficient to achieve success.
When the Muslims' performance is assessed, their shortcomings or
lack of fighting skills are not likely to be glossed over or overlooked.
They have to give their utmost, no matter how little it may be, to
the cause for which they are fighting and then God will give them
aid and support.

We have seen wars between equally equipped sides that go on for
years or decades, and others that are brought to an end in a matter of
days or weeks. The worst defeat is that which comes from within, as

a result of internal faults and weaknesses, rather than due to an enemy's strength or superiority. And so it is with Muslims all through their history. Their reversals have most often been self-inflicted, being a result of disunity and internal squabbling rather than the power of their enemies. Once they overcome those weaknesses, they regain the initiative and move ahead. The surah stresses this point very strongly when it says:

> Do not, therefore, lose heart or grieve, for you shall reign supreme as long as you uphold your belief. If you have sustained casualties and loss, so has the other side, and that is how We alternate [victory and defeat] among people so that God may distinguish the true believers and choose martyrs from among you; for God does not love the transgressors. (139–40)

Human history is a continual struggle between the forces of good and evil, beauty and repugnance, meanness and nobility. God says in the Qur'an: "They will remain at odds [with one another], except for those to whom your Lord has shown mercy, and that is what He created them for" (*Hūd*: 118–19), and "We made some of you as means to test others, to see if you would endure, and your Lord is ever aware of all" (*al-Furqān*: 20). God is no doubt capable of destroying false beliefs and their adherents, but that would negate the role of the believers and undermine their efforts and the favors they would receive from God, who says: "Had God willed, He could Himself have dispersed them, but He so ordained it that He might test some of you by means of others" (*Muhammad*: 4). And so it has been with all the previous prophets and messengers and their followers. Every achievement made on earth on behalf of God has come about as a result of human effort and endeavor. God asserts:

> For, if God had not enabled people to defend themselves against one another, [all] monasteries and churches and synagogues and

mosques—in [all of] which God's name is abundantly extolled—would surely have been destroyed [ere now]. (*al-Ḥajj*: 40)

So God most wisely recalled these facts in the present surah to Muhammad's followers when He was consoling them over their ordeal at Uḥud. He said:

Many a prophet went into battle supported by multitudes of devotees, but they were never daunted by what befell them for the sake of God. They neither weakened nor let up abjectly; God loves the steadfast. Their only words were, "Our Lord, forgive us our sins and our excesses, give us strength and victory over the unbelievers." (146–47)

The surah then continues to dress the Muslims' wounds and raise their morale and prompt them to regain their unity and self-confidence. It is important to recall here that the defeat at Uḥud had uncovered some high-caliber individuals who had displayed extreme courage and self-denial, and cared nothing for worldly gains. There were men who held to their positions even as things looked very desperate. Women too entered the battlefield with a tenacity and valor like that of the men. The battle claimed a number of martyrs, men and women, who sacrificed their own lives for the cause of God and His Messenger. The battle of Uḥud was to remain engraved in the memory of Muslims, generation after generation. Muhammad himself was to remember Uḥud constantly for the rest of his life, saying, "Uḥud is a mountain that loves us as we love it."

Martyrdom commands a place of very high regard in Islam. Martyrs are chosen by God Himself, as the surah confirms, saying: "And [God] chooses martyrs from among you" (140). Those chosen are usually the believers who give God's cause precedence in their actions over all else and who devote their whole life to the promotion, reinforcement, and defense of their faith and the Islamic way of

49

life. We have some exceptional examples among the martyrs of Uḥud. Take Muṣʿab ibn ʿUmayr, for instance, who was one of the most handsome and well-to-do youths of Makkah. He adopted Islam, left all his wealth behind, and spent the rest of his days in poverty; instead of silk, he was reduced to wearing clothes made of sheepskin. He emigrated to Madinah very early and was charged with teaching the new religion to its inhabitants. He spared no effort to carry out that task. But there he was dying in Uḥud, unable to afford his own burial cloth. And look at ʿAbd Allah ibn Ḥaram, father of a son and six daughters, who asked his son to stay and look after his sisters because he did not want to remain behind when the Messenger went to battle. He joined the fighters and was killed.

Martyrs were extolled in the surah as God says:

Never think that those who were slain in the cause of God are dead. They are alive and well provided for by their Lord. They are pleased with God's gifts and rejoicing for those they left behind that they should have nothing to fear or to regret. (169–70)

God has thereby reassured those who were martyred that their fellow Muslims will continue to uphold the true faith and support the cause of God and His Messenger, and that they will eventually join them in Paradise.

During the battle of Uḥud, the Muslim camp became extremely dangerously exposed when the archers abandoned their positions. In a desperate struggle, seventy of their number were killed and rumor had spread that the Prophet himself was among them. Despite the Muslims' defeat, the Arab tribes were not able to proceed to enter Madinah and were forced to return to Makkah. It is important, moreover, to remember here what the Muslims did after their defeat at Uḥud. They regrouped, tried to rise above their wounds, and made their way towards Makkah, chasing their Arab enemies who were still contemplating a return to Madinah to complete their attack on it. When they realized that they were being followed by the Muslims, the Arabs hastened their pace and made for Makkah. This was noted in the surah which says: "As for those who after sustaining defeat responded to the call of God and the Messenger, those of them who do what is right and fear God shall be richly rewarded" (172).

At this point the surah, for a while, turns back to recount the behavior of the local Jews, and we note that the discussion alternates between them and the pagan Arabs. This is not surprising, since the Muslim community was facing both camps at the same time, as the surah itself indicates:

You shall be tested in your possessions and your persons, and you shall hear much that is hurtful from among those to whom the Book was given before you and from the pagans. However, if you persevere and remain God-conscious, then that will indeed be a commendable act. (186)

The Jews of Madinah had by then overreached themselves. In the Qur'an, God calls on the Muslims to spend of their wealth for the cause of God, whether to support the war effort or to provide welfare and help for their needy and poor people. This appeal is made in another surah with such eloquence and with a powerful incentive. It says: "Who will grant God a generous loan? He will repay him many times over. God retains and He gives abundantly and to Him you shall all return" (al-Baqarah: 245). Some Jews in Madinah, nonetheless, were saying something different. They were claiming that God was in need of people's aid, and that He was resorting to usury while condemning it. Surah *Āl ʿImrān* quotes them as saying: "'God is poor, but we are rich.' We [God] shall record what they have said" (181). Such statements were more suited to people who had neither faith in God nor consciousness of Him, and were symptomatic of a group who lived on corruption and traded spite and envy in contravention of the teachings of the wise and pious among them. Earlier prophets could only exhort their people to lead other nations in piety, teach them God's word, and show kindness towards them, but never look down upon them or manipulate and exploit them. The surah observes:

> God made a covenant with those to whom the Book was given that they should proclaim it to all humanity and never suppress it. But they cast it behind their backs and sold it for a paltry sum. What an evil bargain they had made! Never think that those who congratulate themselves and love to be praised for what they had not done, will escape the scourge. A woeful chastening awaits them. (187–88)

Then the surah takes us into a different atmosphere, far removed from the past and its bittersweet reminiscences.

As ordinary honest human beings living in this world, experiencing and observing its complexities, intricacies, and marvels, are we not sometimes tempted to conclude that there is a God behind it all? Does it not then lead us to thank that God and praise Him? Let us leave religion and interreligious strife aside for a while. Let us simply use our minds and our logic and think of where we shall all end after we depart from this world in which we live. Why should people deny the existence of God and turn away from Him? Would it not be more sensible and more conducive to acknowledge and accommodate Him in our hearts and our lives? All through human history, voices have called forth and exhorted humanity to believe in God and be close to Him. Is it not time that people stopped to think and give heed to these calls, as the surah says:

> Our Lord, we have heard someone calling to the true faith saying, "Believe in your Lord," and we believed. Our Lord, forgive us our sins and absolve us of our misdeeds and make us die righteous. (193)

God replies that He will overlook none of the good actions and deeds of people, whether men or women, black or white. Race and rank do not come into this at all and only good deeds count.

What is it, we may ask, that some people find so difficult in believing a person who calls them to lead a righteous life based on surrender to God and the pleasure of His grace? What is it that drives some of us to oppose such individuals, stand in their way, and persecute them? Such was the way in which the pagan Arabs and the bigots among the People of the Book greeted the mission of Prophet Muhammad and behaved towards him and his followers. They repressed and persecuted them, and drove them out of their homes and homelands. The Muslims withstood all that persecution, faced up to all kinds of hardship, and eventually had to emigrate from Makkah and seek refuge in Madinah. Their sole concern was the preservation of their faith and the defense and protection of their new religion and their community. Accordingly, the surah reassured them:

> Their Lord answered them, saying: "I shall not deny any of you, man or woman, the reward of their labor... Those who emigrated, were driven out of their homes, suffered persecution for My sake and fought and were slain, I shall forgive them their sins and admit them to gardens with rivers running thereunder." (195)

Following this extensive coverage of the surah's two main subjects, it closes with two verses. The first one talks about the People of the Book and the stance expected of them towards Prophet Muhammad. It says:

> There are some from among the People of the Book who truly believe in God, and in what was revealed to you and what had been revealed to them. They humble themselves before God and do not sell God's revelations for a trifling price. These shall be rewarded by their Lord. (199)

The verse, as we can see, extends to the Jews and the Christians an open invitation that is there for posterity, to heed the call of the Prophet of Islam and accept the message he delivered on behalf of God to all humankind.

The second verse, and the closing one in the surah, is addressed to the Muslims. "Believers, persevere in patience and constancy; vie in such perseverance; strengthen each other; and fear God; that you may prosper" (200). This is a directive addressed to those who believed in Muhammad and followed him to hold fast to the message he delivered and with which God had honored them. They are expected to show a much higher degree of steadfastness than their predecessors in upholding it, and to vigorously defend it, its followers, and their lands at all times. They are not to give any leeway to their enemies to overwhelm or dominate them, as witnessed over the last century or so when European colonialism swept over Muslim lands and controlled the lives and destinies of hundreds of millions of Muslims for decades. It is a call addressed to Muslims everywhere and of every generation, and it is up to every one of us to respond to it.

Al-Nisā'
(Women)

ABOUT A THIRD OF THIS SURAH deals with the nucleus of
human society, the family, and issues related to it. The rest is a discussion of wider issues pertaining to the larger human community,
or to use the Arabic term, the Ummah. The subject of the surah
overall then is human social relations and how they are to be conducted and regulated. This is made quite clear right at the outset, for
the surah opens with the words: "People, fear your Lord who created you from a single soul, and from it He created its spouse, and
from them both He brought forward multitudes of men and
women" (1). Although we human beings may look and seem different, we are in fact all related, sharing the same origins and the same
common ancestry. It is indeed important for everyone to remember
this fact and strive to maintain good and constructive contact with
other fellow humans, no matter how near or far. This is one of
Islam's major principles. The sense of belonging and togetherness
should be extended beyond blood relations in order to encompass
all human groups, races, and colors, and bring about cooperation
and cohesion between people.

In order to drive this home, the opening verse instructs
humankind to fear God, and emphasizes His omnipotence and total
control over the destiny of man. That notwithstanding, we can also
find in the surah passages that encourage optimism and raise hope in
God's grace and mercy. Verse 31 says: "If you avoid the greater sins
you are forbidden, We shall pardon your misdeeds;" while verse 110

says: "Whoever commits evil deeds or does his own self an injustice and then seeks God's forgiveness, shall find God Forgiving and Merciful." Verse 48 states: "God will not forgive the act of taking other gods besides Him, but He will forgive whom He will for other sins;" and verse 17 says: "God forgives those who commit evil in ignorance and then quickly regret it and repent;" while verses 26 to 28 read:

> God wishes to make matters clear to you and guide you along the paths of those who have gone before you, and to turn to you with forgiveness. God is All-Knowing and Wise. God wishes to forgive you, but those who follow their own base desires wish you to go completely astray. God wishes to lighten your burden, for man was created weak.

God has no desire to overburden His servants with obligations and rituals that are beyond their human ability and scope. The efforts they are required to exert are those which are necessary but bearable and within their capabilities in order for them to gain knowledge, understanding, and experience, and achieve progress in life. A believer's life is controlled by his or her fear of God and the promise of His mercy and compassion. These are the two strong forces guiding believers in this world and preparing them to account before their Lord sooner or later in the hereafter.

The part of the surah dealing with family affairs begins with defining the rights of orphans in a Muslim society. Being a dynamic, expanding, and struggling society, it is not surprising that the Muslim community will always have an appreciable number of orphans living in it. Orphans, even today, are always easy prey for influence, domination, and exploitation by various individuals as well as groups with ideological or political interests—hence the concern in Islam for their position in society, their rights, and well-being.

At this point, the Qur'an refers in passing to marriage, pointing out that men are allowed to marry up to four wives. There is nothing abnormal or abhorrent about this, as Islam did not deviate from the laws of other religions preceding it, none of which has prohibited polygamy. In fact, when we look at societies of contemporary Europe and America, we find that they are in many cases grossly unfair and demeaning in their treatment of women. In these societies, polygamy is rife but under different guises, and promiscuous relationships between the sexes are considered normal and practised openly. What Islam permits is clearly defined and tightly regulated. Single men who cannot afford to marry and raise a family are encouraged to abstain from sexual contact until they are able to get married. Those who wish to take a second wife are not considered eligible unless they can show that they can afford to keep and be equally fair to both wives. Furthermore, marriage in Islam is never allowed without the consent of both parties, and any woman who does not wish to enter into a polygamous marriage has the right to refuse. Islamic law goes even further than that and grants the wife the right to incorporate her refusal of polygamy in the marriage contract. According to the renowned jurist Aḥmad ibn Ḥanbal, the husband is obliged to abide by that condition or the wife can demand a divorce and be granted it.[5]

The surah then turns to the rules governing inheritance of wealth and how it is to be dispensed and distributed among surviving family members and relatives. Women, hitherto completely deprived of inheritance, are specifically mentioned as having the right to inherit and their share is clearly defined. The poor and the needy are also entitled to a proportion of any wealth left behind. A man has the discretion to bequeath one third of his wealth to whatever public or

---

5 The fact that women in 'Muslim' societies are sometimes coerced into marriage or do not opt to practise their rights is mainly due to ignorance and should not belie the remarkable achievements of Muslim law. (Ed.)

private causes he may choose, a ruling subsequently reinforced by Prophet Muhammad. It is also established that, in the majority of cases, Islam entitles a man to twice the share of a woman; the reason being that men undertake more financial responsibilities, such as dowries, and bear the greater burden in supporting their wives and children. A woman is not obliged to work or earn an income and her male relative or relatives, if she has any, should support her financially; otherwise she is the responsibility of the state which should provide adequately for her. This is prescribed by Islamic law in order to preserve the dignity and honor of the female members of society, and save them the degradation, misery, and humiliation they have to endure in order to earn their living. One has only to look at the situation in today's Western societies, the so-called bastions of women's rights, to appreciate the wisdom and justice of Islam, when correctly and humanely applied.

In saying this, we are not trying to be apologetic for an unrepresentative minority of inconsiderate and irresponsible Muslims who maltreat their women, whether wives, sisters, or daughters, and deprive them of their right to education and freedom. ʿĀʾishah (RAA),[6] the Prophet's wife, is reported to have related that the Prophet said: "Believers with the most excellent faith are those with the best manners and those who are kindest to their wives." Ibn ʿAbbās, a Companion of the Prophet, is also reported to have quoted the Prophet as saying: "The best among you are those who are kindest towards their wives, and I am the kindest among you towards mine."[7] It is indeed regrettable that some zealous Muslims today make the mistake of believing that the maltreatment of women and the undermining of their rights is a prerequisite of religious purity and righteousness. This has given Islam a negative image and caused

---

[6] RAA—*Raḍiya Allāhu ʿAnha/ʿAnhu* (May Allah be with her/him). Said whenever a Companion of the prophet is mentioned by name.

[7] Narrated by al-Tirmidhī.

women the world over to detest Islam and fear the promotion and spread of its teachings and beliefs.

Prior to the advent of Islam, women had no rights to speak of. When a woman's husband died, any of his male relatives would simply appropriate her, as if she was an animal or a commodity. The norm in pagan Arab societies was similar to that of the ancient Hebrews in the sense that when a man died childless, his brother was obliged to marry his widow in order for her to have children to be called after their deceased father. What was this if not forced marriage and contrived lineage? Most certainly this practise was not based on revealed Jewish scriptures but one which some Jews had devised. God says in the Qur'an:

> Believers, it is unlawful for you to inherit the women of your
> deceased kinsmen against their will, or make life difficult for them
> in order that you may take back some of what you have given them,
> unless they are guilty of a proven shameful act. (19)

The idea here is that a woman must not be under any pressure to leave her family home or pay a ransom for her freedom and dignity. The verses direct men to: "treat them with kindness; for even if you dislike them, it may well be that you dislike something which God has invested with abundant goodness" (19).

In cases of impending separation or divorce, Islamic law forbids a husband from bargaining with his wife over the dowry he has paid her, no matter how high it is. A woman's dowry is her indisputable right and cannot be taken away from her. Accordingly, if a man is not satisfied with his first wife and wishes to take a second one, he must meet all the expenses and cannot retrieve any money he has paid the first one. The following verses make this very clear:

> If you wish to replace a wife with another, do not take from her any
> of the dowry you have given her, even if it were a talent of gold.

Would you take it illegally and improperly? How can you take it back when you have been so intimate with each other and have entered into a firm contract with them? (20–21)

We note the above before going on to talk about the need to set up happy and loving marital relations. The passage refers to two abhorrent social diseases: sodomy and lesbianism. This reference is not superfluous, since the fight against both these loathsome practices is an essential protection for family life and the healthy environment it represents in society. About lesbianism, God says:

And those women who commit unlawful sexual acts, call in four witnesses from among yourselves, and if they testify against them confine them to their homes until they either die or God provides another way out for them. (15)

As for those guilty of committing homosexual acts, God says: "If any two of your men commit indecency, punish them both" (16). The West, having completely turned away from God and all but abandoned religious guidance, has come to take these social crimes very lightly, as it has done with others, resulting in the tragic breakup of family life and the epidemic spread of deadly conditions such as AIDS and other sexually transmitted diseases. The foundations of Western civilization are, in fact, being eroded very fast. Its dominance can be guaranteed to continue only for so long as an alternative sane civilization, by which I mean a genuine Islamic one, remains absent.

For family life to flourish and be productive, family members have to be disciplined and well behaved. Selfishness has to be firmly suppressed, while mutual kindness and cooperation have to be encouraged between all of them. A married woman once came to me complaining about her husband, and I could see from the way she was talking that she was badly affected and wished to leave him, were it not for some other compelling reasons. I advised her to

follow the example of the Pharaoh's wife and put up with his insolence for a little longer. Reluctantly, she agreed.

A pertinent question arises here: what is to be done when it is the
woman who persecutes the husband or treats him with insolence?
The family home is certain to turn into hell. Under these exceptional
circumstances, Islam prescribes a gradual solution that allows, as a
first step, for simple advice and gentle persuasion, followed by a temporary cessation of sexual contact, and then, and only then, permits
resort to physical measures. The main condition attached to this last
method is that physical punishment must be moderate and should
not in any way touch the face or harm it. Looking closely into the
sunnah of the Prophet, however, I cannot find a justification for this
last measure except when the wife refuses her husband's bed, or
brings male outsiders into their home, both of which represent, as we
can see, very serious problems indeed.

Prior to presenting these directives concerning family life, the
surah strongly emphasizes the unlawfulness of the appropriation of
other people's wealth or property. It also encourages acceptance of
one's lot in this life, and refraining from eyeing the fortunes of others.
The passage then turns to address all humankind, saying: "Worship
God and associate no one else with Him. Show kindness to parents
and kindred, to orphans and to the helpless" (36). Though giving
priority to the family, this directive applies also to society as a whole.
The surah then turns to deal with spending, which should always be
done in moderation, identifying two distinct types of people: the
grudging miserly ones, and the overspending pretentious ones. It
singles out one particular type of people who are uncharitable in
certain ways, encouraging others also to be stingy and grudging, but
who, in other ways, are pretentious and ostentatious with their
wealth. Were they to use their wealth according to God's teachings,
they would reap a higher reward. "What harm could befall them if
they believed in God and the Last Day, and spent charitably of what
God had bestowed on them? God is aware of all their affairs" (39).

The surah continues for a while longer to touch upon the current and future state of the Muslim community, before turning to a different theme. This other theme relates to the various religious communities existing within Arabian society at the time, and how the Muslims should deal with them. The striking similarity between those groups and the ones the Muslims are facing today is quite uncanny.

Muslims of the Prophet's generation were very keen to befriend the Jews. Recognizing their seniority as the first recipients of God's revelations, they expected them to stand on their side if the Muslims were to enter into any conflicts with the unbelieving Arabs. However, as noted in earlier chapters, the Jews in Arabia proved largely disappointing. Their elders had no respect for any treaties or neighborly relations, and they were to offend badly against Islam and cause it the worst damage. God addresses the Prophet, saying: "Look at how those who have received some revelation court error, and wish for you to go astray. But God best knows your enemies" (44–45). The verses state clearly that those people had lost most of the revelation sent to their ancestors. This had come about as a result of their failure to maintain the continuity of their faith and preserve the texts of their scriptures intact. Furthermore, they had failed to implement properly those parts that were still in their possession. Corrupted religious laws and practices could indeed cause more harm to society than no religion at all, and those who adulterate and misuse religion should expect a worse fate than those who have had no religion at all to follow.

In this surah, Muslims are given a pledge that God will be on their side in this confrontation and will favor them with victory. It states: "sufficient is God as an ally and sufficient is God to bring victory" (45). However, this divine intervention and support are not granted to those who sit and wait, nor are they ever won by those who neglect the duty of preparing their own defenses and making the plans necessary to achieve victory. We read in Shaykh Rashīd Riḍā's commentary on the Qur'an, *al-Manār*:

> God Almighty does not alter the established laws of social change in favor of Muslims, Jews or Christians. These laws apply equally even to those select few, the prophets. At the battle of Uḥud, Muhammad himself suffered physical injuries to the head, had a tooth broken and fell into a ditch, owing to negligence by his troops and shortcomings in preparing for war. How long, then, could Muslims continue arrogantly claiming identification with Islam, while discarding its teachings and refusing to abide by its laws or heed its warnings? Can Muslims not see how the tables have been turned against them? As other nations have armed themselves with science and hard work, and taken note of the dynamic forces of social change, they have come to sweep over most of the Muslim lands and dominate their people...Muslims are in need of turning back to the teachings of the Book of God, the Qur'an, and fully appreciating the laws of civilization and social change which He has laid down. They must cast aside all calls to abandon Islam or do away with the guidance that God has placed in their hands. They must break away from all superstitions and wake up to God's eternal justice, and realize that their glory and dignity have been undermined only as a result of their own negligence and deviation.

Although today new and far more threatening social and moral diseases have infiltrated the fabric and body of the Muslim Ummah, the Shaykh's diagnosis remains basically valid.

The surah then goes on to explain what the rabbis had done with their own religion so that the Muslims could avoid it. Verse 46 begins by saying: "Some Jews take words out of their context." Priests and scribes did this by seeking esoteric or ulterior, rather than the obvious, meanings to what was said to them, in order to satisfy their own prejudices, serve certain interests, or justify stances or claims of their own. They had clear indications in their scriptures of, for example, the forthcoming Messenger of God, but they twisted those words and interpreted them in such a way so as not to commit them to accepting Muhammad or recognizing him as that promised messenger. Tampering with their scriptures also included adding words or phrases to the text. Shaykh Raḥmat Allah of India, in a monumental and most authoritative work on the subject entitled *Izhār al-Ḥaqq*, available in Arabic, lists a hundred such instances of deliberate and obvious adulterations that can be found in the Old Testament. Even so, the rabbis continued to claim, "'This is from God,' whereas it is not; and they ascribe falsehood to God, knowingly" (*Āl ʿImrān*: 78). Their stubborn and disrespectful behavior also led them to say to Muhammad: "'We hear, but disobey; may you [Muhammad] be bereft of hearing!' and they say, 'foolhardy!', twisting words with their tongues and reviling the religion" (*al-Nisā'*: 46). Although God warned them of severe punishment if they were to persist in their stubbornness, still they did not desist. However, glory and domination will be the reward of those who show greater sincerity in and make higher sacrifices for upholding God's message and promoting His laws and teachings.

The surah then turns to another topic, saying: "God shall not forgive those who take other gods besides Him; but He will forgive whom He will for other sins" (48). The concept of associating other gods with God is known in Arabic as *shirk*, and it is of two types. The first one is when one believes that in this world there are two or more creators, providers, or controllers. The second is when one turns to someone else other than God for legislation or guidance relating to what is lawful and what is unlawful, or to seek help and support from them without recognizing God's role in providing that assistance. Both types of *shirk* are grave crimes against God and the rest of humanity, and their perpetrators must be exposed.

There is yet another type of *shirk*, which has found a wider following in modern times, and that is the complete denial of God's existence, and His role and influence or control over the world. Thus, Muslims these days find themselves confronted with an unprecedented multitude of forms of *shirk*, which in turn makes their responsibility to explain, inform, and persuade that much greater. They must endeavor to avoid the "Chosen People of God" trap, into which others have fallen. To such arrogant people, religion does not mean justice or benevolence or fear of God; it is a mere tool to enhance their racial aims and satisfy their selfish nationalistic pride. Indeed such pretenders "have no share in [God's] Kingdom; otherwise they would not give others so much as a speck of it" (53). A nation that is in charge of dispensing God's favors must not be mean to other nations or groups.

The surah continues: "Or do they envy other people what God has given them of His bounty? We gave Abraham's descendants the scriptures and wisdom, and a glorious kingdom" (54). This is a subtle reference to some Jewish elders from Madinah who accorded the pagan Arabs in Makkah a higher status over the Muslims and gave them pledges of moral and material support. However, the surah has a more general application. People of faith are always obliged to give an honest and fair testimony, as the surah confirms:

> God commands you to hand back what you had been entrusted with to its rightful owners, and, when you sit in judgment among people, to judge with fairness. Noble is that which God exhorts you. (58)

Trust, here, is both material and metaphorical, and refers to the preservation and protection of all kinds of commitments and obligations towards God as well as towards fellow human beings. Those who do not fulfill their duty with regard to trusts cannot claim to possess true belief, and the religious faith of those who do not keep their word or fulfill their promises must always be in question.

Having related part of the past history and attitudes which impinged on contemporary events, God in this surah turns to the characteristics and behavior of a noxious group of human beings, the double-faced hypocrites who had posed a great threat to Islam and Muslims. These were the people who in public declared their belief and acceptance of Islam and the Prophet, but in private they rejected them and harbored deep-seated hatred and spite towards the Prophet and the Muslims. However, as their actions betrayed them, their sinister schemes were foiled. The surah continues:

> Have you seen those who profess to believe in what has been revealed to you and had been revealed before you? They seek judgment of someone else other than God, although they were commanded not to do that; and Satan would wish to lead them far astray. (60)

The verse clearly affirms that they were lying. To believe truly in God, it is necessary and essential to abandon other deities or powers. God says elsewhere in the Qur'an:

> God is the Patron of the believers. He leads them out of darkness and into the light. As for the infidels, their patrons are false deities who lead them out of the light into darkness. (*al-Baqarah*: 257)

In this surah, He says: "The believers fight for the cause of God, but the infidels fight for the cause of false deities" (76).

False deities are bound to lead people away from God's true path and turn them against Him and the way of life He ordained for humankind. Although the hypocrites pretend to listen to the exhortations of the Muslims, they go ahead with whatever they think serves their interests. The more they do this, the more arrogant and

66

proud they grow, and the more difficult it becomes for them to acknowledge their mistakes and reverse their actions. People with these characters can be very close to the believers physically, but their hearts and minds are far removed from them, and they can hardly appreciate or understand the guidance being offered to them. As the surah points out: "When it is said to them, 'Come to what God has revealed and to the Messenger,' you shall see the hypocrites turn away from you" (61). In another surah they are identified as those who, "when it is said to them, 'Come, God's Messenger will ask forgiveness for you,' they turn their heads and you see them walk arrogantly away" (*al-Munāfiqūn*: 5). Of course every unbeliever or hypocrite has his or her own point of view to uphold and argue. Many of these believe that they are right, but sooner or later they will realize the error of their stance. Many of them will then seek to apologize and justify their positions. The surah asks:

> But how would it be if some disaster befell them on account of what their hands committed, and then they came to you swearing by God that they desired nothing but amity and conciliation? (62)

Many people are today prepared to defend man-made laws and systems, believing them to be the best and most beneficial to humankind. However, when societies begin disintegrating and crime starts to eat into the fabric of society at all levels, they retreat from their positions and start to think again. Concerning these, the surah says: "God knows what is in their hearts. Ignore them, and admonish them, and speak to them about themselves with eloquence and force" (63).

Two reactions can reveal a person's hypocrisy: revulsion towards God's revelation and refusal to defend the truth and fight for the cause of God. Hypocrites also feel ill at ease when it comes to performing religious obligations, such as prayers and alms-giving. Although they might be able to disguise their reluctance to perform the latter, one would find them totally exposed when it comes to the former. Apostles, on the other hand, deliver God's messages as comprehensive guidance for a better life on earth. Their followers believe, listen, and obey without deviation. God says in the surah:

> By your Lord, they shall not be true believers until they resort to your judgment in what they disagree upon among themselves. They will not find any difficulty in accepting your judgment, and they will submit totally. (65)

Indeed, there is nothing in religious teachings that is unfair or difficult for people to carry out. It is only those with weak hearts and lack of will that flinch from them and cower at performing their religious duties, be they fighting for the cause of God or the observance of daily prayers.

The surah then elaborates on the characteristics of the hypocrites, touching briefly on another social group that needs attention, those of weak faith. If not attended to, these are always in real danger of losing their faith altogether. This weakness of faith manifests itself in several forms. One of them is referred to in the surah as follows:

> There is among you he who is sure to lag behind, so that if a disaster befell you, he would say, "God has been gracious to me that I was not present with them." But if God's grace came your way, he would say, as though there was no amity between you and him, "Would that I had been with them, I might have gained immensely." (72–73)

This is a person motivated by sheer self-interest, and cares nothing for the faith or its future. He is dithering, wavering between satisfying his own ego and the honest fulfillment of his duty towards others. Another type is the person who observes religious obligations, such as prayers and fasting, but when it comes to fighting for the cause of God, shudders and wavers and asks for time to think. The surah continues:

> Have you not seen those to whom it has been said, "lay down your arms and observe your prayers and give alms," but when they were ordered to fight, some of them were as fearful of other people as they were of God, if not more so. (77)

The surah offers considerable guidance and counsel to those of weak faith, and confirms that God is so gracious as not to leave them to their own fate or to drift away completely from their religion. To the first group, God advises that in deciding what direction to take, they should not be led by their personal narrow interests only. It is shameful, indeed despicable, that those who do not take part in fighting should lament their reluctance to participate in battle after victory has been achieved, or feel self-satisfaction and happiness when the outcome is defeat. They are told to devote their energies to God and be forthright in responding to the call to defend His religion:

> Let those who are ready to exchange life in this world for life in the hereafter, fight for the cause of God. Whoever fights for the cause of God, and is then killed or achieves victory, We shall richly reward him. (74)

As for the second group, they are told that a person's term of life and his or her moment of death are determined by God beforehand. This is confirmed in *Āl ʿImrān*: "No soul will die without God's permission, after a certain fixed term" (145). Indeed, some people come out alive from the most horrific accidents, such as airplane crashes, while others die for no apparent reason while relaxing in their own living rooms.

The world is full of those who oscillate between hypocrisy and weak faith, and the surah has mentioned some of them. God says:

When they are blessed with good fortune, they say, "This is from God," but when misfortune befalls them, they say, "This is from you [Muhammad]." Say to them, "It is all from God." (78)

This reminds us of the Pharaoh's stance towards Moses, which is described in another surah as follows: "When good fortune came to them, they said, 'This is our due,' but when a misfortune befell them, they blamed Moses and his followers" (*al-A'rāf*: 131). This cynicism, which might have characterized the attitude of the People of the Book or some of the new converts to Islam at the time towards God's revelations and messages, is a sign of a serious flaw and a lack of faith in God.

As Muslims, we believe that God is the source of good fortune and He is the only power that can cause real harm. He is the creator of all, in whose hands lies the destiny of the whole world and everything that is in it. Despite their active free will, human beings can neither create things nor cause them to happen. However, within the context of this universe, about which we still know very little, a person's will and power to do things is limited and constrained. This is the significance of the words: "Say, 'It is all from God.'" The verses that follow elaborate on this theme further and place it in a proper perspective. They explain that most of the evil that befalls people can be attributed to their negligence or to certain undesirable actions or behavior on their part. Addressing the Prophet as well as every human being, the surah goes on to say: "Whatever good you [Muhammad] encounter is from God, and whatever misfortune befalls you is due to yourself" (79). God is the creator and the origin of everything, while people commit acts and acquire results, and they are the cause of most of what they suffer. Another type of people the surah mentions are those who:

when they hear any news, whether good or bad, they broadcast it; whereas if they had [first] referred it to the Messenger and to those in positions of responsibility, they would have verified it properly. (83)

Indeed, one of the most unfortunate phenomena in society is when ignorant incompetents take charge of its affairs and begin to pontificate, give advice and direction to others, and control their lives and destinies. It is still possible today to find ignorant people who issue religious edicts, or *fatāwā* (sing. fatwa), relating to fundamental issues of Islamic law, or pronounce on the most important matters of war and peace. There are people who spend all their energy trying to change the world, whereas they are not capable of influencing their own closest family members or friends. It is imperative that we should spare our energies by leaving things to those properly qualified and competent to deal with them or carry them out. Ignorant people should not be spokespersons for God or Islam, and specialists in all fields ought to be accorded the highest respect and allowed to serve society in the best possible manner, without being denigrated or undermined. It is far healthier for people to make their contribution in areas that they know best, and allow others to contribute similarly. Prophet Muhammad is reported to have said: "He is not one of us who is not kind to our children, or does not respect our elders, or denies our learned people the esteem they deserve."[8]

God commanded the Prophet not to be disconcerted by those who were weak of heart or cowardly, and to stand up to the troublemakers and the aggressors until they relented and would no longer pose a threat to the Muslim community. The surah expresses that as follows:

---

8 Narrated by Abū Dāwūd and al-Tirmidhī.

fight you, then, in God's cause—since you are but responsible for your own self—and inspire the believers to overcome all fear of death. God may well curb the might of those who are bent on denying the truth: for God is stronger in might, and stronger in ability to deter. (84)

It was up to individual people to decide whether they would join the Prophet and the Muslims and support them, or not. The surah continues:

Whoever lends support for a good cause shall be a beneficiary of its goodness, but whoever gives support for a bad cause shall suffer part of its consequences. God controls and assigns all things. (85)

God also commanded the Muslims to observe and assess the attitudes and stances of others towards them, and to reciprocate with them accordingly. The surah says: "When you are greeted, reply with a similar or better greeting..." (86). This would apply to normal everyday greetings exchanged between people. The Muslims in Madinah used to extend greetings to Muslims and non-Muslims alike until some People of the Book resorted to distorting the word *al-salāmu*, meaning peace, to *al-sāmu*, meaning death; that is, in return for the greeting *al-salāmu ʿalaykum* (peace be upon you) used by the Muslims, they would reply *al-sāmu ʿalaykum* (death be upon you). In this situation the Muslims were instructed to counter with the single word, *wa ʿalaykum*, that is, "upon you also"! This, it seems to me, was a specific instance. However, the general meaning of the verse is that it becomes Muslims to undertake social interaction with others, Muslims and non-Muslims, as that would be more conducive to creating amity, peace, and trust among all. Ibn Jarīr quotes Ibn ʿAbbās as saying: "Greet in return everyone who greets you, even if they are Magians, because God says, 'When you are greeted, reply with a similar or better greeting.'" Al-Shaʿbī once greeted a

Christian person, saying: "Peace and God's mercy be upon you." When someone criticized him for doing that, he replied: "Does not he too live by the mercy of God?"9

The surah then turns to talk about the hypocrites and how to deal with them. In this context, the hypocrites are not a particular group of Madinan residents, such as ʿAbd Allah ibn Ubayy and his coterie, but other tribes and communities, or in modern terminology, foreign nations, who express support and solidarity with Muslims and Muslim causes in public, while behind the scenes they resort to scheming and intrigue against them. Some Muslims at the time were taken in by such people until the revelations from God alerted them to the facts, saying:

> Why should you split into two camps concerning the hypocrites, when God had thwarted them on account of their misdeeds? Would you guide those whom God had confounded? Those whom God confounds you can never guide. (88)

Then the surah continues to provide more details on the nature and type of those enemy groups. Some of them wish hardship for the Muslims, connive against them, and are eager to see them abandon Islam. However, the surah warns: "Do not take some of them as allies until they leave their homes for the cause of God and join you" (89). Those who are neutral should be offered peace. "If they leave you alone, do not fight you, and offer you peace, then God gives you no authority over them" (90).

Nevertheless, the opportunists should be given firm and sharp treatment. The offer of peace extended to the genuine neutrals must not include them. Still, fighting these people would not be for the purpose of forcing them to convert to Islam, but to persuade

---

9 Narrated by al-Bukhārī and Muslim.

them to remain neutral in any war forced upon Muslims. However, if in fact it became clear that they reneged or showed hostility towards the Muslims, then there would be no justification in letting them off.

The classification of these enemies given in the surah is extremely equitable. Muslims neither force others to convert to their religion, nor object to them taking a neutral stand in any conflict that develops between Muslims and non-Muslims, as long as that neutrality remains true and effective. What Muslims object to and would resist is naked and open aggression.

The surah then gives the Islamic ruling with respect to premeditated murder and unintentional killing or manslaughter. This came about in the wake of an incident, during one of the battles, when the Muslims captured people from the enemy side. As they were closing in on them, a man came forward to announce his conversion to Islam. Some Muslims immediately thought that he was only doing that to save his neck and could only be bluffing or trying to deceive them. He was killed by Usāmah ibn Zayd.

When the news reached the Prophet, he was deeply affected, and reprimanding Usāmah, he said: "What have you to say to the fact that he had proclaimed the faith?" Usāmah replied: "He only did so out of fear." To which the Prophet responded, "How do you know? Had you cut open his heart and made certain whether he did so in fear or not?" After that, Usāmah said, "The Messenger of God would continue to reproach me over that incident so that I wished I had not been a Muslim before that day."[10] On that occasion the following verse was revealed:

Believers, show discernment when you go out to fight for the cause of God, and do not say to him who surrenders to you that he is not a

---

[10] Narrated by Imam Aḥmad and al-Bayhaqī.

believer, seeking worldly gain. God has abundant rewards. You had been in similar situations previously, but God was gracious towards you. Therefore, show discernment as God is cognizant of all you do. (94)

As a matter of fact, it was inappropriate at that time for Muslims to continue to live among the infidels. There was a need for converts to emigrate and join their fellow Muslims in Madinah, in order to partake in setting up the new Muslim state and share in the effort of building the future of Islam. Hiding their belief made new converts to Islam open to persecution when discovered. The Qur'an was quite critical of such a stand when it said:

Those who die sinning shall be asked by the angels, "What were you doing?" They would reply, "We were oppressed in the land." The angels would say, "Was not God's earth wide enough for you to emigrate?" (97)

Emigration for the sake of preserving one's own beliefs is one way of securing peace and security. There is nothing more degrading than having to live under suppression, humiliation, and duress when God has promised those who seek refuge for the sake of their religious belief a better and far more prosperous and happy life, now and in the hereafter. Indeed, human societies all over the world have always migrated and moved around, building and contributing, materially as well as spiritually, to human culture and civilization. As believers in God and custodians of the message of Islam, Muslims should be at the forefront of this vital human activity to dispense their duty of spreading God's message.

With travelling comes the concession of shortening some of the obligatory daily Muslim prayers, as indicated in the following verse: "When you travel, you incur no offense in shortening the prayers, if you fear that the unbelievers might cause you harm" (101). It seems that this verse and the one following it apply to prayers when one is under the threat of enemy attack, but the ruling on prayers during normal travel are expounded elsewhere in the Qur'an. Further details on this subject can be found in numerous books on jurisprudence.

The next verse addresses Prophet Muhammad as the religious as well as military leader of the Muslims:

> When you [Muhammad] are with them [Muslims] and it is time to conduct the prayer, let a group of them rise up [to pray] with you, carrying their weapons. When these finish praying, let them stay behind you [to your back] and let another group who had not performed the prayer join you, and let them be on their guard and carry their weapons. (102)

Most scholars tend to be of the view that this ruling applied when the Prophet was leading the prayer and groups of Muslims took turns in praying behind him. My personal interpretation of this statement is that it applies only in the case of the Prophet, as it would be inconceivable that someone else would lead the prayer in his presence. But today, prayers could be held in the battlefield by several groups, behind different *a'immah* (sing. imam), or leaders, and at various times, without fear of being taken unawares by the enemy. It would not be practical or necessary otherwise to tie up a whole army of several thousand people to a single imam or demand that they all pray together in one congregation at the same time.

The surah continues with further description of people whose faith is weak and whose hearts are feeble or sick. It comments on one of the most intriguing incidents dealt with in the Qur'an, which concerned one of those Muslims whose perception and understanding of Islam was, to say the least, lacking. A Muslim called Ṭuʿmah committed a theft, and to conceal the evidence, he entrusted the stolen goods to a Jew to keep them for him. Investigations focused suspicion on him and the Jew, and eventually the stolen goods were retrieved from the Jew's house. The Jew said, quite rightly, that Ṭuʿmah had placed them in his custody. Ṭuʿmah, however, denied the offense and pointed to the Jew as the culprit. Ṭuʿmah's clan also entered the fray, defending their man and accusing the Jew, a soft target as a result of Jewish animosity towards Islam, of committing the crime.

Prophet Muhammad showed a certain inclination to believe Ṭuʿmah and his people, giving them, as Muslims, the benefit of the doubt. But God intervened to put the matter right. The surah goes on:

> We have revealed to you [Muhammad] the Book containing the truth, so that you may judge between people by that which God has shown you. You shall not plead for those who are perfidious. Implore God's forgiveness; He is ever Forgiving and Merciful. (105–6)

God, therefore, had forbidden the Prophet to defend deceitful and untrustworthy Muslims, and directed him not to believe their claims. God says to the Prophet:

> But for God's grace and mercy you would have been led astray by some of them. They would only mislead themselves, and could do you no harm. God has revealed to you the Book and the Wisdom and taught you what you did not know before. (113)

Commenting on the Ṭuʿmah case, the surah says: "Whoever commits a misdemeanor or an offense and accuses an innocent person of it, shall bear the guilt of calumny and gross injustice" (112). As for the offender, the surah invites him to repent, saying: "Whoever pursues evil or wrongs his own soul and then seeks God's forgiveness, will find God Forgiving and Merciful" (110). As for the collusion of the guilty man's clan and their efforts to pervert the course of justice, the surah asserts:

> There is no virtue in much of their counsel, except for those who call for charity, kindness, or reconciliation among people. Whoever does this seeking the pleasure of God, We shall grant them a great reward. But he who disobeys the Messenger after the guidance is made clear to him and pursues a path other than that of the believers, We will leave him to his choice, but will assign him to hell; a dismal abode. (114–15)

Thus, once again, Islam's fairness is made manifest! These arguments were put forward for the sake of establishing the rule of law, to grant justice to a person whose community were in the main antagonistic towards Islam, and to prove his innocence in a crime for which he was clearly being victimized.

Having closed that chapter, the surah turns to another diminishing but significant community that was still to be found in Madinah, the idol-worshipping Arabs. The surah hits at them very hard:

> God will not forgive taking other gods besides Him, although He will forgive whom He will all other misdemeanors. He who takes other gods besides God has indeed strayed far away. (116)

Certainly polytheism, or the belief in and worship of several gods, is a mental and spiritual aberration which totally negates human nature and values. True believers in God can neither submit their will to, nor place their trust in, nor seek guidance from anyone else but the one and only God, the Creator and Sustainer of all creation. This belief generates in the believer's heart total reassurance and peace of mind, so that he or she will not submit to anyone else, nor seek their support or reward. On the other hand, the recognition of several gods divides one's loyalties, and causes one to be guided and motivated by several contradictory, delusive, and fallacious principles and ends. One's life turns into a long, continuous delusion that ends in a mirage.

> Those who take Satan rather than God for an ally shall indeed suffer total and evident loss. He [Satan] promises them and raises false hopes for them, but he only does that to deceive them. (119–20)

Boasting about one's religion or beliefs is a hopeless pursuit. Sincere actions and sensible behavior shall be the final criterion. Today we meet people who are so eager to express their pride in Islam, bragging about its superiority, integrity, and justice. However, when these same individuals are asked what contributions or sacrifices they have made for Islam, or what distinguishes them from followers of other religions in the world, they become dumbfounded. In response to these people, God says:

> It is not by your own wishful thinking, nor by the wishful thinking of the People of the Book. Whoever does evil shall be requited for it, and shall find none, other than God, to protect and support him. (123)

Nowadays, although while we find Christian and Jewish leaders openly and proudly identifying with the ideals and traditions of their religions, we rarely find political leaders of Muslim countries observing or respecting even the simple daily prayers.

The surah returns to the discussion of family relationships dealt with earlier. At the outset, it sets out the general principles of equity and reconciliation upon which these relationships must rest:

> They consult you [Muhammad] concerning women. Say, "God provides you with answers about them, and so do those parts of the Book concerning orphan girls, whose rights you deny but whom you wish to marry, and concerning helpless children. God has also instructed you to treat orphans fairly." (127)

We have already seen how at the beginning the surah dealt extensively with the subject of orphans; here it concentrates on disputes and disagreements that might arise between married couples. In this context, the Qur'an strongly recommends the resort to reconciliation, mutual kindness, and fairness, and urges resistance to securing selfish gains as much as it is humanly possible. Still, if that option fails and the relationship breaks down, each party is advised to seek redress, first and foremost, with God Himself; "But if they separate, God will compensate both out of His own abundance; God is Munificent and Wise" (130). Indeed, God's grace and generosity are boundless. With deep and sincere faith in and obedience to God, one should not despair or become pessimistic:

> To God belongs all that the heavens and the earth contain. We have exhorted those who had received the Book before you, as well as yourselves, to fear God. For, if you deny Him, know well that to God belongs all that the heavens and earth contain. God is Self-Sufficient and Worthy of praise. (131)

This last phrase is repeated in this part of the surah three times to stop people despairing and give both spouses encouragement and hope in a better future if they have to divorce and lead separate lives.

The surah then goes on to emphasize that married life is based on fairness, and that society as a whole can in fact grow and survive only on foundations of equity and justice among its members. "Believers, uphold justice and bear true witness before God, even if you have to attest against yourselves, your parents, or your kinsfolk" (135). Upholding justice has been the tradition and the motto of all the prophets who had received from God the guidance and the law, and were assigned to ensure its proper and fair implementation. This is what the next verse seems to affirm, when it says: "Believers, believe in God, His Messenger, the Book He revealed to His Messenger, and the Book He had revealed previously" (136). Oppression and the absence of justice within a family home are a threat to both spouses and to all their children. Broken homes and dislocated families spread unhappiness through the rest of society and threaten its cohesion and the safety and quality of life within it.

So far, we have seen how the surah has discussed the various groups of people in society and their respective roles, and has not limited the discussion to family affairs alone. We have also been given a taste of the Qur'an's approach in dealing with the hypocrites or fifth columnists in society against whom it gives stern warnings. Before the surah is brought to a close, however, we are taken back to this subject to see the surah highlighting one very important aspect of this matter.

True believers respect and revere God's words. They take them seriously and never allow them to be ridiculed, reviled, distorted, or taken in vain. It is for this reason that outrage is always provoked in Muslims by others who take God's words in vain. Nevertheless, there are always the weak-minded, dim-witted Muslims who are so lax in this regard and who are hardly ever moved by slanders or attacks against their religion or their holy Book. It is these who are addressed in the next verse:

Inform the hypocrites that a stern chastisement awaits them; those who choose to take the infidels rather than the believers as allies. Are they seeking glory at their hands? Surely, all glory belongs to God. (138–39)

The point here is that no matter how powerful their enemy, Muslims should never appease or succumb to him at the expense of their religion and their honor. It is a characteristic of the hypocrites alone that they do not care about truth or principle, but sincere believers are told:

> He [God] has instructed you in the Book that whenever you hear God's revelations being denied or ridiculed you must not remain in that company until they move on to another subject of conversation; or else you would be like them. (140)

All through Islamic history, Islam and Muslims have repeatedly suffered as a result of scheming and intrigues at the hands of such hypocrites, and it is no wonder that the Qur'an refers to the subject over and over again to stress its various aspects.

Towards the end, the surah returns to the subject of the People of the Book, Jews and Christians, shedding some new but vital light on aspects of their history and official conduct. The Jewish elders reject both Jesus and Muhammad. They accuse Jesus of being an impostor and of being born out of wedlock by an adulterous mother, while Muhammad was a bedouin with a false claim to prophethood. To the Church, Muhammad was simply a charlatan and a pretender. The surah replies to all these allegations as follows:

> Those who deny God and His messengers, and wish to draw a line between God and His messengers, saying, "We believe in some, but deny others," and seek to find a way to justify this, are the real infidels, and for the infidels We have prepared a humiliating punishment. But those who believe in God and His messengers

and discriminate against none of them, God shall give them their reward; and God is Forgiving and Merciful. (150–52)

Following a short debate with the People of the Book, God addresses Prophet Muhammad:

We have sent you revelation as We sent it to Noah and to the prophets who came after him. We also sent revelation to Abraham, Ishmael, Isaac, Jacob, and the [Hebrew] Tribes, and to Jesus, Job, Jonah, Aaron, Solomon and David, to whom We gave the Psalms. (163)

The source of the revelation and guidance received by all of these messengers and that received by Muhammad is one. They are all envoys of God to humanity, assigned the same basic mission which they delivered with equal honesty, care, and diligence. Muhammad's only merit over his fellow messengers was that the revelation he had received was more detailed, more profound and comprehensive in communicating with people's basic nature and instincts as well as higher aspirations. His legacy is bound to endure and the mission of enlightenment, guidance, and service to God which he launched is set to continue and persist as long as humans are due to live in this world. God has endorsed Muhammad's mission by saying: "God bears witness to what He sent down to you [Muhammad], and He sent it down with His knowledge; and so do the angels, and God is a sufficient witness" (166). Indeed, any detached and fair examination of the Qur'an would in fact show that it is unique among all the divinely revealed Books of all the other prophets and messengers. A similar examination of Muhammad's own character, life, and work would establish that he was ideally and uniquely suited for the mission he was chosen to undertake.

As for the Qur'an's debate with the People of the Book, the surah tells us:

> The People of the Book ask you [Muhammad] to bring down for
> them a book from heaven. They demanded something greater than
> that from Moses, saying, "Show us God face to face." (153)

This could not be the attitude of a group seeking truth for its own
sake. This demand could only be made by individuals with an arrogant overreaching mentality, and so when it came from members of
Moses' party, who should have known better, they were reprimanded and punished severely. The surah portrays the group as
people who had accepted God's covenant only out of fear, and went
on to renege on it and break it, to which God responded:

> That was a consequence of their breaking their covenant, their
> denial of God's revelation, their killing of the prophets unjustly and
> their saying, "Our hearts are sealed." It is God who sealed their
> hearts, on account of their denial, and only a few of them would
> truly believe. It was also a consequence of their denial and their
> utterance of monstrous falsehoods against Mary. (155–56)

When Jesus became the target of slander and murderous intents,
God saved him and confounded his enemies.

> They had neither killed him, nor crucified him, but it was made to
> seem to them that they did. Those who disagree about that are con-
> fused; they have no knowledge thereof, going by pure conjecture,
> since they had certainly not killed him. God lifted him up to Him;
> God is Mighty and Wise. (157–58)

Nevertheless, for historical and other reasons, many people have
come to believe in the crucifixion and salvation myths that have
become a central part of Christian dogma and doctrine. This is due
to ignorance, narrow-mindedness, and lack of enlightenment. God,
affirming the escape and eventual ascent of Jesus and his submission

to Him, maintains in these verses that were the people more enlightened, they would have taken a more sensible attitude:

> But those of them who are deeply rooted in knowledge and
> the believers do believe in what has been sent down to you
> [Muhammad] and what was sent before you; and so do those who
> observe the prayer and give alms, and so do believers in God and the
> Last Day. We shall give all of these a great reward. (162)

Here we come to the closing verses of this surah which give decisive judgment on all the human social and religious groups mentioned earlier. The infidels and the hypocrites fare the worst, because
they are bigoted and base their beliefs on myth and ignorance, and
they try to mislead and confuse others. They in fact stand as obstacles
to other people's endeavor to know God and avail themselves of His
guidance. "Those who disbelieved and debarred others from the
path of God have gone far astray. God does not forgive those who
disbelieve and act unjustly, nor will He guide them" (167–68).
Looking at the history of modern colonialism and imperialism, one
can see clearly that it quite distinctly bears these two features: disbelief in God and the oppression of humankind.

Then, in such an intriguing manner, the verses address the
Jews thus:

> O people, the Messenger has come to you with the truth from your
> Lord, and so believe for your own good. If, however, you disbe-
> lieve, know that to God belongs all that the heavens and the earth
> contain. God is All-Knowing and Wise. (170)

This is followed by a statement directed at the Christians, who are
seen as being overwhelmed by confusion and lack of direction,
which have led to their highly outlandish, self-contradictory, and
paradoxical doctrines and beliefs. With respect to that, God says:

People of the Book [Christians], do not exceed the proper bounds of your religion, and say nothing but the truth about God. The Messiah, Jesus, son of Mary, is no more than the messenger of God and His word which He had bestowed on Mary, and a soul from Him. So believe in God and His messengers and do not say [God is] three. Desist for your own good. God is but One God; He is far too glorified to have a son of His own. To Him belongs all that the heavens and the earth contain. God is a sufficient Protector. (171)

The truth is that honest inquiry into and the study of the mysteries of the universe and natural phenomena will only confirm the fact that there could only be one God. If other gods exist, then where are they? What have they created? What is their contribution to the world and what role do they play in its destiny? Where is this corporate godhead that is running our world and deciding our future? No! There are not, nor could there be, more than one God; obedience and total submission are due to Him alone, and all are obliged to thank and worship Him and nobody else. God says:

The Messiah would never feel too proud to be a servant of God, nor would the angels who are close [to God]. He [God] shall bring before Him all those who are arrogant and look down on those worshiping Him. (172)

The surah ends with a verse setting out the rules for inheritance with respect to deceased childless couples and orphans. This takes us full circle to the subject of family affairs with which the surah had opened. Thus we can see that the subject matter of this surah revolves around the theme of social life and social relations in general and the various groups that make up society and its cultural and religious structure. The family unit is a miniature model for society as a whole, while society is a larger model of the family, and God's grace and guidance encompass them all. To those lacking in perception, however, the surah may appear to be made up of a collection of disjointed passages, which is a serious misunderstanding.

I simply refuse to judge Qur'anic surahs by their titles, which are quite different from their subject matter. The titles are no more than restrictive tags or labels, while the content is often complex, elaborate, and intertwined. We may take *al-Baqarah* as an example; it extends over forty pages of normal size, out of which the story of the cow, which gives the surah its title, comprises no more than half a page. The rest of the surah extends into a vast ocean of subjects dealing with history, law, theology, morals, ethics, and other themes. The same applies to this surah. A few short passages of it are devoted to matters relating to women, such as the family and family affairs, but the rest deals with wider social and religious issues that are of interest and relevance to human groups throughout the world.

Al-Mā'idah
(The Table)

THIS SURAH IS KNOWN by two titles: *al-Mā'idah,* meaning "the table;" and *al-ʿUqūd,* meaning "the covenants." The second title reflects the surah's wide-ranging subject matter much more accurately. The first title comes from the request made by the Christian disciples to the prophet Jesus to ask God to send them a meal from heaven for them to enjoy and celebrate, as evidence for his truthfulness. However, the story of this meal receives only a very brief mention towards the end of the surah, whereas the subject of covenants and obligations occupies almost the rest of it.

The main feature of this surah is the frequent use of declamatory, direct, and emphatic speech. Sixteen such statements are addressed specifically to Muslim believers:

Believers, be true to your obligations...(1)

Believers, do not violate the rites of God, or the sacred month...(2)

Believers, when you rise to pray, wash your faces and your hands as far as the elbows (6)

Believers, fulfill your duties to God and bear true witness over others...(8)

Believers, remember the favor which God bestowed upon you... (11)

Believers, have fear of God and seek the right path to Him...(35)

Believers, take neither Jews nor Christians as protectors...(51)

Believers, whoever of you recants of his Faith, God will bring forth others who love Him and are loved by Him...(54)

Believers, do not take as mentors the infidels and those who were given the Book before you, who have mocked your religion and taken it in vain...(57)

Believers, do not forbid the wholesome things which God has made lawful to you (87)

Believers, wine and games of chance, idols and divining arrows, are abominations devised by Satan (90)

Believers, God will put you to the test...(94)

Believers, kill no game while you are in the state of *iḥrām*... (95)

Believers, do not ask questions about matters which, if made known to you, would only cause you harm...(101)

Believers, you are accountable for none but yourselves...(105)

Believers, when death approaches you, let two just men from among you be witnesses as you make your testament...(106)

In two instances, the orders are addressed to Prophet Muhammad himself:

Messenger, do not grieve over those who plunge into unbelief... (41)

Messenger, proclaim what is revealed to you from your Lord...(67)

On five other occasions, the exhortations are addressed to the People of the Book:

People of the Book, Our Messenger has come to reveal to you much of what you have concealed of the Scriptures... (15)

People of the Book, Our Messenger has come to you with revelations after an interval... (19)

Say, "People of the Book, would you hate us only because we believe in God..." (59)

Say, "People of the Book, you can claim no faith until you observe the Torah and the Gospel..." (68)

Say, "People of the Book, do not transgress the bounds of truth in your religion..." (77)

Throughout, the tone is stern and solemn, fully conveying the seriousness and weight of the issues being discussed, while the declarations and statements are usually followed by explanations, elaborations, instructions, or specific factual information, which are necessary to inspire Muslims to build and organize their community life in accordance with the laws and teachings of Islam. All the time it is quite clear that this set of rules and proclamations is being presented by God in the form of binding obligations that must be fulfilled by Muslims. Among these, we find the call to wash in a certain manner before performing the prayers, as well as rules pertaining to prayer which is itself the first clause in God's covenant with the Israelites.

Having outlined a number of rules, duties, and responsibilities required for the establishment of a Muslim society, God says:

And remember God's favor to you [the believers], and the covenant with which He bound you when you said, "We hear and we obey." Fear God, for God knows what is in people's hearts. (7)

Doubtless, the relationship between God and humankind is a serious and solemn one which calls for sincerity, tenacity, and diligence. An essential corollary of true faith in God is to take one's obligations towards Him seriously and hold them in high regard, and discharge them fully to the best possible standard. God has taken an undertaking from the Muslims that they will believe in His oneness, submit to and serve Him alone. Having become Muslim, they have pledged to promote and spread His religion, to be a good and faithful example to others, and to teach and dispense virtue and goodness to all.

Muslims are not the first group of humans to undertake such far-reaching and binding obligations towards God, for they had been preceded by others. The surah explains:

> God had made a covenant with the Israelites and raised among them twelve chieftains, and God said to them, "I shall be with you. If you observe prayer, and give alms, and believe in My apostles and support them, and if you offer God a generous advance, I shall forgive you your sins and admit you to gardens with rivers running thereunder. But any of you who thereafter renege shall stray from the right path." (12)

The Israelites' responses to that covenant are well known, having been documented—along with God's own reactions to them—in various sources, Jewish ones included. Elsewhere, there are people (nominal Muslims) who, no matter how much piety and sincerity they try to convey, or no matter how religious they might claim to be, are always betrayed by their attitudes and actions. Their contrived devotion to Islam leads some of them to censure and condemn more severely Muslim believers who commit minor misdemeanors than they would unbelievers. In the minds of such people, the very concept of right and wrong is confused and turned upside down. They would show more tolerance towards the infidel enemies of Islam than they would towards some Muslims. The well-known sect of the Khawārij, who emerged around 659 AC, some twenty-seven years after the death of Prophet Muhammad, and who were vehemently opposed to the Prophet's cousin and fourth Caliph, ʿAlī ibn Abī Ṭālib, whose blood they demanded, are the progenitors of this school of misguided religious behavior. The Khawārij allowed the killing of Muslims whom they judged to be sinners or lacking in faith, but refused to fight unbelievers on the pretext that these were asylum seekers. In a way, one could understand the reaction of the eighth century AC Muslim scholar, Wāṣil ibn ʿAṭā', founder of the Muʿtazilah school of Islamic thought, and his followers who, when confronted by followers of the Khawārij, feigned unbelief, because otherwise they would have been killed. They based their view on the literal interpretation of the Qur'anic verse: "If an idolater seeks asylum with you [Muhammad], give him protection so that he may come to know the words of God, and then deliver him to his place of safety" (al-Tawbah: 6).

Such ruthlessness and insensitivity are totally alien to Islam. Jewish elders in Arabia displayed a strong sense of insincerity and artificial religious piety towards Islam and its followers, as the surah affirms: "You [Muhammad] will ever find them deceitful" (13). Nevertheless, the same verse ends with the directive to the Prophet to: "Pardon them and excuse their deeds, for God loves those who are benevolent" (13).

As God had made a covenant with the Jews, so He made a similar one with the Christians. The way this is expressed in the surah merits reflection for it distinguishes between the later Christian generations and the one contemporary to Jesus and his disciples who were true representatives of his teachings. Accordingly, the surah says:

And with those who claimed to be Christian We made a covenant, but they forgot much of what We had impressed on them. Therefore We allowed them to be drawn by their enmity and hatred, which shall endure till the Day of Resurrection, when God shall inform them of all that they had done. (14)

A cursory look at the history of Christianity would bear this out completely. Relations between the various Christian churches are replete with dissension, bloody feuding and schisms. Europe can never forget the interreligious wars that plagued it during the Middle Ages. Although they have abated somewhat in recent decades, they have left deep-rooted divisions and suspicion, temporarily overshadowed by the need to face up to the challenge of modern anti-religious secularism that is threatening the very existence of all the Christian sects and churches. This standoff can be only temporary, for as long as the underlying causes of those divisions and schisms continue to exist, those ugly and bloody feuds are bound to rear their heads again, as the verse makes quite clear.

Genuine peace, conciliation, and understanding among people can truly come about only under Islam. Bloodshed and conflict between various national, religious, ethnic, and other human groups can be avoided only when the hearts of people are filled with the love of the one and true God. Only God's incontrovertible and unambiguous guidance can bring people to live in peace and harmony with one another. This is what the surah affirms:

A light has come to you from God and a perspicuous Book, with which God will guide to the paths of peace those who seek to please Him. He will lead them by His will out of darkness and into the light and onto the straight path. (15–16)

The greatest and most irrevocable covenant humankind has made with God is to uphold His absolute oneness. Those who insist on the belief in the existence of other gods besides the one God are drifting rudderless in high seas, with no hope of rescue or redemption. All followers of divinely revealed religions are assumed to affirm belief in monotheism. The Christian view of Jesus Christ, however, is shrouded in mystery and confusion. Since Christians also claim to believe in and worship the one God, there immediately arises the question of what is the true and proper status and position of Jesus Christ in Christianity. Under proper and calm scrutiny it is possible to see how contrived, disingenuous and unconvincing present Christian doctrines are. My own study of the subject has led me to take seriously the claim made by Dr. Muhammad Maʿrūf al-Dawālībī—though to my knowledge uncorroborated by other sources—that he is in possession of a Vatican document confirming the total humanity and non-divinity of Jesus. The document is the result of extensive studies carried out by competent authoritative scholars over a forty-year period. It is said to contain specific and unequivocal instructions to Christians that Jesus should never be referred to as divine. More interestingly, the document categorically accuses the Church of numerous injustices against Islam and Muslims, and recommends wider contact and more reconciliation with Islam in the future. The document also apologizes for the role of the Church in the twelfth to fifteenth centuries AC, when the Crusaders waged war against the world of Islam in the Middle Ages, and its implication in the European colonization of the Muslim world during the nineteenth and twentieth centuries. It reportedly regrets the plunder of Arab rights in Palestine and calls for direct dialog with Arab and Muslim peoples to remedy the past and heal old wounds. The Vatican, according to Dr. al-Dawālībī, later succumbed to various pressures and had this document "suppressed and eventually withdrawn."

Be that as it may, the Christian view of Jesus Christ is extremely ambiguous and self-contradictory, as pointed out in the Qur'an:

They had neither killed him, nor crucified him, but it was made to seem to them that they did. Those who disagree about that are

94

confused; they have no knowledge thereof, going by pure conjecture, since they had certainly not killed him. God lifted him up to Him; God is Mighty and Wise. (*al-Nisā'*: 157-158)

The real and true God is but the one God, and that is the reason for this angry retort that:

Those who held that God was the Messiah, the son of Mary, are infidels. Say, "Who could then ever prevent God if He wanted to annihilate the Messiah, the son of Mary, and his mother and everyone else on earth?" (17)

Rabbinical teachings, on the other hand, though spurning the Trinity doctrine, are nonetheless guilty of insolence and of showing a lack of proper respect towards God Almighty. They are known to be less than forthright in their expression of devotion to or fear of God, whom they depict as the Jews' own benefactor to the exclusion of almost all other beneficiaries.

Both Jews and Christians, therefore, claim a special relationship with God and assume for themselves a privileged and unique status in the world order. But, in fact, God's favor and grace may be earned only through sincere, unadulterated, and unshakable faith and real tangible actions to back up that faith. Nothing else can, in the sight of God, give people, whether individuals or groups, any particular advantage over others. This applies just as much to Muslims, who have to show the same required degree of humility and submission to God, and show the courage and fortitude necessary to uphold His laws and teachings and face up to His enemies and detractors. Mere verbal identification with Islam or the teachings of Prophet Muhammad is no substitute for real action and tangible endeavor. To illustrate this point, the surah relates two examples; one concerns some Israelites, and the other the two sons of Adam: Cain and Abel.

In the first example, we are told about the group who refused to

carry out the order by Moses to enter the Promised Land and fight
those who were in control of it at the time. Moses tried all manner of
inducement to persuade them to do so:

> My people, remember God's favor which He has bestowed upon
> you. He has appointed some of you as prophets, made you kings,
> and given you that which He has given no other nation. (20)

For generations the Israelites had borne the great and honorable task
of carrying God's message. Compared with other human groups
such as the Arabs, the Israelites received scores of prophets and messengers. They enjoyed dominance and prosperity and were made
secure in their own land. However, many failed to appreciate that
privileged status, and as time went by they developed a strong sense
of complacency and arrogance. They took God's grace for granted
and believed that God was more in need of them than they were of
Him. At that point they were put to the test, with Moses telling
them: "'My people, enter the Holy Land which God has assigned
for you and do not turn back, or you shall be the losers'" (21). They
flinched and disobeyed, unashamedly telling Moses: "'Go, you and
your Lord, and fight, we shall be waiting here'" (24). As punishment, God caused them to spend forty long years lost in the
wilderness of the Sinai desert, where, except for a few sincere
believers, most of them perished.

The second example is the episode concerning Adam's two sons:
Cain and Abel. Out of jealousy and spite, Cain murdered his brother, Abel, in cold blood. Having killed him, the story goes, he was
at a loss as to what to do with his body. The surah picks up the story:

> Then God sent a crow which started digging into the earth to show
> him how to inter his brother's body. "Alas!" he cried, "Am I not
> as able as this crow that I can not inter my brother's body?" He
> became full of remorse. (31)

Cain's attitude proved to be symptomatic of human behavior. Killers are always under the illusion that they somehow benefit from the murder of their victims. However, the cold-blooded destruction of one soul can in no way be an enhancement for another. To build, promote, and reform human life is a positive deliberate act of virtue that is likely to invoke God's pleasure and favor. God, in the verses that follow, deems the cold-blooded murder of one human being to be a crime against the whole of humanity:

> Whoever kills a human being, other than as punishment for murder or for the spreading of corruption on earth, it shall be considered as though he had killed the whole of mankind; and whoever spares a human life shall be deemed as though he has spared the whole of humankind. (32)

These stories are related in the Qur'an for the benefit of the Muslims, to enable them to learn from the experience of earlier generations. They also contain specific rulings that are designed to guide the Muslims and protect their society from falling into the traps that caught their predecessors. In this instance, verses 33 and 34 specify the penalties for highway robbery, while verse 38 specifies that for theft, stressing with respect to both penalties the need to be fearful and conscious of God; "Believers, have fear of God and seek what brings you closer to Him, and strive for His cause, so that you may be successful" (35). The means that take us closer to God and help us achieve success in life, are good deeds and positive action, which in turn require strength of will and selfless dedication.

Divine revelation is a unique source of legislation for religious matters as well as issues relating to the inheritance of wealth and penal codes. Once God has ruled on a certain issue, there is no longer room for human speculation or sophistry. This is a legacy that has been passed on by believers from one generation to another, although some have deviated from these traditions and neglected God's laws and guidance. Crimes affecting life, property, or personal honor are vile, with far-reaching social consequences. It was God's own decision not to leave legislation in these areas to the prejudices, whims, and vulnerability of ordinary mortals, for human legislation is bound to be biased and influenced by countless factors that would be prejudicial and impair judgment in one way or another. The whole process of justice would be in jeopardy. This is exactly what happened with earlier Jewish and Christian generations. Prophet Muhammad said:

> Those before you were condemned because when a nobleman committed theft they let him go, but when a hapless citizen did the same they punished him. By God! If Fāṭimah, the daughter of Muhammad, herself were to be convicted of theft, I would have her hand cut off.[11]

Indeed, as those people became more lax, they dropped the punishment of cutting off a thief's hand and replaced it with varying terms of imprisonment which encouraged more larceny and crime. How could this be considered more just than divine justice? The same happened with respect to other crimes and penalties.

Having looked very closely at crime in various societies, it is clear to me how deeply serious and hugely costly this problem has become. In several modern cities today, personal safety and security are almost nonexistent. As frightening statistics have shown, women, children, and old people are raped, abused, and attacked every minute of the day and night, with the criminals enjoying immunity

---

[11] Narrated by al-Bukhārī.

from real and effective punishment. This only goes to prove the wisdom of the Prophet's comment: "The administration of God's punishment in one case is better for humanity than thirty days of continuous rain."[12] He was also reported to have said, "Apply God's punishment to near and far alike, and do not allow yourselves to be swayed in the way of justice by kinship or criticism."[13] The Islamic penal system, as defined by the Qur'an, continued to be in use all over the Muslim world until the thirteenth-century AC Mongol invasion, when some parts were replaced with legislation laid down by the rulers themselves.

The Mongols ruled Iraq and Syria for almost a century (1256–1336 AC), and their precedent was later to be emulated and taken even further forward by European colonialism, which ruled Muslim lands from the seventeenth century AC. This brought about radical transformations by replacing Islamic law with European laws and legislation, some of which permitted extramarital sex, prostitution, and homosexuality. In some Muslim countries, the Islamic penal code was pushed aside or completely condemned and rejected as brutal, inhumane, and retrogressive.

When the Prophet arrived in Madinah, two Jews accused of adultery were brought to him for judgment. He asked them what was the punishment for their crime according to their own religion. They said it was flogging and blackening of the face, to which he replied that it was in fact stoning to death. They insisted that he was wrong, until reference was made to the Torah and the Prophet's view was shown to be the correct one. To this effect the following verse was revealed:

Messenger, do not be unduly worried by those who plunge headlong into disbelief, who say, "We believe," only with their lips but

---

12 Narrated by al-Nasā'ī, Ibn Mājah and Imam Aḥmad.
13 Narrated by Ibn Mājah and al-Nasā'ī.

have no faith within their hearts, and those from among the Jews. They listen to lies and to other people who never come to you. They tamper with [God's] words and take them out of their context and say [to one another], "If you are given such-and-such [judgment], take it, otherwise beware." (41)

The only course of action left for those exposed by God's Messenger was to hurl abuse at God Almighty and the prophets. However, the Prophet refused to give in to them, and was supported by the words of God which said:

> You [Muhammad] can do nothing to help someone whom God wishes to confound. Those whose hearts God does not wish to cleanse shall be disgraced in this life, and an awesome torment awaits them in the hereafter. (41)

This is a statement for all time concerning falsifiers and hypocrites and is an affirmation of the fact that whoever chooses to get on the evil bandwagon should expect only to be doomed and condemned. This is in tune with the words in the following verse: "Those who persist in the error of their own ways, the Merciful shall leave [them] to their own devices" (*Maryam*: 75).

The law in any country applies to all who live under its jurisdiction, no matter what their religious beliefs are. The Jews in Madinah led an autonomous existence which had been guaranteed and protected by the treaties concluded with the Prophet on his arrival to settle in Madinah. Accordingly, the Prophet did not force them to apply his judgment, but was rather instructed by the Qur'an thus:

> If they [the Jews] come to you, you can either give them your judgment or turn away from them. If you do turn away from them they can do you no harm, but if you judge between them, do so with justice. (42)

More generally, Muslims are required to respect and apply the statutes and ordinances of Islamic law in their own countries, and cannot be expected to do so everywhere else in the world. Followers of other religions living in Muslim countries are, with few exceptions, free to conduct their own religious ceremonies and rituals, and pursue their religious beliefs in peace and security, but in all other matters they are subject to the law of the land like everyone else.

The Prophet's judgment should not have surprised the Jews, since the "Book of Deuteronomy" in the Old Testament explicitly recommends stoning (22:20–21) as the punishment for the unmarried woman who commits illicit sex. It says: "If a man is found lying with the wife of another man, both of them shall die" (22:22). It further states,

> If there is a betrothed virgin, and a man meets her in the city and lies with her, then you shall bring them both out to the gate of that city, and you shall stone them to death with stones, the young woman because she did not cry for help though she was in the city, and the man because he violated his neighbor's wife; so you shall purge the evil from the midst of you. (Deuteronomy, 22:23–24)

The next few verses in the surah briefly cover the attitude of the People of the Book towards legislation relating to capital punishment and penalties for illicit and extramarital sex. They point out that these were first given in the Torah to the Jews and were later corroborated by the Christian Gospel. Those who ignored, avoided, or violated that legislation are condemned as unbelievers, transgressors, and sinners. The Torah, according to the Qurʾanic outline, was in force until the arrival of the Gospel of Jesus which had come into effect after it. When the Qurʾan was revealed, both Jews and Christians were expected to take heed of it and update whatever legislation they had already received. The surah is quite unequivocal about this:

101

And to you [Muhammad] We have revealed the Book with the truth. It confirms other books that have come before it and prevails over them. Therefore rule over them according to God's revelations and do not follow their whims and fancies in deviation from the truth that has come to you. We have ordained for each [community] a system of laws and assigned them paths to follow. (48)

Two important points emerge from this passage. The first one is that God's religion and legislation for humankind have been perfected and concluded with the message of Prophet Muhammad. This is true for matters of doctrine and belief, where the Qur'an and the Prophet endorsed and revitalized the essence of earlier revelations received by all the prophets and messengers who preceded him. As for divine legislation, God has sent down the basic and fundamental principles, and left the interpretation and application of those principles to people's mental and intellectual capability of deduction, rationalization, and wisdom. It is people's responsibility to decide how to use God's revelation to serve the needs and interests of the human community. Religion is indeed one, but the details and scope of legislation in the different religions vary. This leads us to the second point, mainly that Muhammad's mission is distinguished by containing within it the essential elements that make it universal and durable for as long as humankind continues to exist on this earth. The teachings of Islam are compatible with common sense and are totally harmonious with the needs and limitations of human nature. It is also destined to remain valid and relevant for all stages of human material and intellectual development. Other monotheistic legacies were relevant to and applicable within particular communities and for finite periods.

In his commentary on the Qur'an, the renowned Muslim scholar, Shaykh Muhammad Rashīd Riḍā, points out that Judaism was noted for being such a severe and stern religion because it was addressed to people who had for generations lived in slavery and subjugation, and who had hardly any independent existence of their own. This had caused many of them to grow obstinate and unyielding. This is quite evident from even the most cursory reading of the first five books of the Old Testament, which take the reader into a cruel and claustrophobic authoritarian world. Christianity, when it came later, did not override earlier laws and teachings, and was more inclined towards conciliation. It steered well away from confrontation with the ruling Byzantine emperors, choosing instead to "turn the other cheek." Under the Byzantines, though, Christianity was turned into a conquering, belligerent, and vindictive force. Islam, however, came to restore the balance between the material and the spiritual, between the rational and the intuitive, between this life and the life that is yet to come. It has accorded humans a special and unique status in the world and laid the solid foundations for their relationship with God and the relationships among human beings themselves. Shaykh Riḍā goes on to say:

> The essence of the universality of Islam and the mission of Prophet Muhammad, God's peace and blessings be upon him, does not become evident until we live and establish Islam on the basis of rationalism, and understand its laws and imperatives through active and incisive interpretative work [ijtihad], and by taking a lead from bona fide and competent scholars and legislators. Those who oppose this rational free-thinking approach put themselves in opposition to God and completely undermine the essence of the Shariʿah of Islam and its relevance and effect. Through their ignorance they do a great disservice to Islam.

God then says in this surah: "Believers, do not take Jews or Christians as protectors" (51). The pertinent question here is: Does this apply to all, or only some Jews and Christians? For a satisfactory answer, one has to read the foregoing and the following verses as one whole passage and put the various ideas in context. Looking at it this way, one can perceive three distinct categories of Jews and Christians.

The first are those who are so extreme in their opposition to the Islamic Shari'ah that they will accept any other system in its place, no matter how alien to their beliefs. Although they know that Islam guarantees them full religious freedom, they continue to harbor a fear of Islam and a hatred towards the Muslims. The way the Prophet was recommended to treat these was to:

> Judge among them according to God's revelations and do not be led by their desires, and make sure they do not distract you from some of what God has revealed to you. If they reject your judgment, be sure that God wishes to punish them for some of their sins. A great many people are evil-doers. Is it un-Islamic laws they accept? Who is a better judge and law-giver than God for people with true faith? (49–50)

This group is so blinded by hatred and jealousy, that there is no longer any hope in persuading them to see any sense or in winning their friendship.

The second category comprises those who live among the Muslims but their hearts are with the enemies of Islam. It is of course vital for Muslims to ensure that their ranks are not infiltrated or weakened by people who may let them down at the crucial moment, were they to engage in a defensive war with an outside enemy. This did happen in the past, as the following verse relates:

> You see the faint-hearted hasten to woo them [the infidels], saying, "We fear lest fortune might turn against us." But God may well bring about victory or some other event of His own making,

whereupon they would be smitten with remorse for what they had been hiding within their hearts. (52)

In the early days of Islam, religious minorities were to be found all over Muslim lands. However, when Muslims had to fight against outside enemies, such as the Byzantines, non-Muslims were never recruited into the fighting force in order not to strain their consciences nor create any religious or moral dilemmas for them. The Muslim authorities were happy to receive their financial support, hoping that the least they could do was not to side with the enemy or betray the Muslims.

The third group of Jews and Christians the Muslims were instructed not to take as protectors were those who ridiculed and belittled Islam and its teachings and practices, such as prayer or the call to prayer, the *adhān*. The surah refers to them in the following manner:

Believers, do not take as protectors those who were given the Book before you or the infidels who mock your religion or tinker with it. Fear God, if you are true believers. When you raise the call to prayer they take it as a joke or a sport. It is because they do not understand. (57–58)

Religion is a serious matter and has to be treated with dignity and respect. It is difficult to see how anyone who does not show such respect can be treated as a friend or an ally.

Islam is a tolerant and accommodating religion, and when it comes to religious conviction and matters of belief it specifically forbids coercion and compulsion. Muslims are permitted to go into business and trade partnerships with non-Muslims on the basis of mutual honesty and trust. Muslim men are permitted to marry non-Muslim women and raise families built on mutual love and affection. Positive and constructive interreligious dealings and cooperation in all fields are to be encouraged to avoid intercommunal strife and promote tolerance, trust, and respect among all people. Islam has clearly defined the circumstances in which Muslims can shun followers of other religions or boycott them, because differences between various religions are inevitable. Nevertheless, Muslims are also taught to respect their religion and reflect that respect in dealing with others on an equal basis. That should not be very difficult, except for some, such as those fanatics who consider other people inferior to themselves, or bigoted agnostics and cynics who cannot tolerate people with convictions and strong beliefs different from their own. This is what the following verse refers to: "Say, 'People of the Book, is it that you find fault with us only because we believe in God and in what has been revealed to us and in what was revealed earlier...?'" (59). These are the basic principles that decide a Muslim's relations with   and attitude towards followers of other religions. These are reasonable and sensible principles, free of hatred, prejudice, and vindictiveness.

God comforts the Muslims in the following verse by assuring them that they are never short of friends and allies:

> Your allies are God, His Messenger and other believers who observe prayer and give the alms in humility. Those who ally themselves with God, His Messenger, and the believers are of the party of God that are sure to triumph. (55–56)

One of the basic teachings of Islam is to love or hate for God's sake; love that is pure and unselfish and a rejection that is free of malice and injustice and bears no grudges towards those who are rejected. Islam also teaches forbearance and the need to overlook the minor mistakes of others and their shortcomings, while being firm and severe when the situation demands it.

Reflecting on the case of Māʿiz, who insisted to the Prophet that the punishment for adultery be administered to him, I found that the

Prophet tried very hard to dissuade him and make him change his mind, and was ready to forgive him since he had repented. However, Mā'iz was adamant in wanting to cleanse himself by dying and he was granted his wish.[14] The attitude of Jesus when faced with a similar situation, was also to react in a similar way, as in the case of the adulteress who was brought to him for stoning. God has no grudges against anyone, nor is He wantonly waiting to take revenge on sinners and people who commit misdemeanors; nor are God's prophets bloodthirsty hangmen but reformers and fair-minded leaders.

No doubt there is a big difference between a casual unintentional error and a premeditated deliberate violation or rejection of God's laws. All prophets were stalwart in their stand against all forms of crime, especially when it became a normal acceptable practise in society. The Jewish and Christian establishments, over the generations, have grown lenient towards criminal and immoral behavior; so much so that they have been rendered totally helpless and ineffective in fighting it. Evidence for this shameful state of affairs can be seen in today's western societies, a by-product of the lapsed Judeo-Christian tradition, where most religious leaders are strangely indifferent to the deterioration of social and moral behavior in their midst. More shamefully, they have turned a blind eye to the abuse of human rights in many countries as well as to political, social, and economic exploitation of other races.

This surah has devoted long passages to exposing the paradoxes and the contradictions in the thinking and behavior of Jewish and Christian spokesmen and leaders, calling for their actions to be condemned: "Why do the rabbis and the elders not dissuade [their people] from saying what is evil and acquiring what is unlawful? Wicked indeed is what they do!" (63). How can Jews and Christians preserve their religions without adhering to the true teachings of

---

[14] Narrated by Muslim and al-Tirmidhī.

their prophets and complementing them with the guidance that Islam has come to offer them? God directs the Prophet thus:

> Say, "People of the Book, you shall achieve nothing until you implement the Torah and the Gospel and all that is revealed to you from your Lord." What has been revealed to you [Muhammad] from your Lord will only increase the high-handedness and unbelief of many of them, but do not grieve for the unbelievers. (68)

To defend the integrity and the truth of God's teachings and guidance is an essential duty of all believers. This should become a central dimension of their consciousness and existence. It is ironic how the supposedly pious priests among Jews and Christians could afford more respect and support to agnostics or pagans or advocates of corruption rather than to believing Muslims, who shared with them a vast common ground of faith and belief. This attitude brought severe criticism:

> Those Israelites who disbelieved were cursed by David and Jesus, son of Mary, because of their disobedience and transgression. They never used to censure one another for any wrongdoing. (78–79)

It was followed by instructions to the Muslims not to befriend or appease them:

> You [Muhammad] can see many of them making alliance with the unbelievers. What they lead themselves to do is condemned. They have incurred the wrath of God and shall endure eternal torment. Had they believed in God and the Prophet and what has been revealed to him, they would not have taken them [the unbelievers] as allies. But many of them are wrong-doers. (80-81)

When reprimanding such groups for their laxity and tolerance of evil and immorality in society, it was essential to emphasize and redefine some of the basic and fundamental principles of religion.

People usually tolerate injustice or immorality for fear of the consequences of standing up to them. Some are even keen to appease tyrants and despots for purely materialistic reasons of worldly gain and privilege. Standing up for one's principles can indeed be extremely costly. Nevertheless, it is the collective outcome of this brave and selfless stand that really counts in the end. Betraying the truth and abandoning the fight for what is right may bring short-term gains, but the consequences in the long run can be disastrous and humiliating. Real success and true happiness can be achieved only when God becomes the central criterion for one's preferences and alliances. God says:

> If the People of the Book had believed and feared [God], We would have pardoned them their sins and admitted them to the gardens of delight. If they had observed the Torah and the Gospel and what has been revealed to them from their Lord, they would have enjoyed abundance from above and from beneath them. (65–66)

This should not be taken as addressing Jewish and Christian savants only, for it applies equally to Muslim scholars and leaders who have taken custody of God's word. Correct and proper behavior can only be a product of true belief, and that is the reason the discussion goes back again to fundamentals, the pure unadulterated belief in the oneness of God (*tawḥīd*).

The rabbis confess monotheism, but are their perception and understanding of that principle correct? Do they accord God the unique and venerated status of perfection He deserves? Do they consider themselves above His will or subject to the same laws and standards as the rest of humanity? Such are the criteria by which they—as well as others—are to be measured. When in the past some of them chose to monopolize God's religion for the sole advantage of their own positions or national goals and objectives, God's displeasure was evident enough.

The surah expresses disapproval of their record and treatment of their prophets. It says:

> We [God] made a covenant with the Israelites and sent forth to them messengers. But whenever a messenger came to them with a message that did not suit their fancies, some of them they branded as liars and others they put to death. (70)

The Church, on the other hand, adheres to beliefs and doctrines that are paradoxical and totally self-contradictory. Jesus is God, and Mary is the mother of God. But God is the Eternal Father, who sent His son, Jesus, to save the human race, and Jesus is therefore the son of God. However, there is also the Holy Spirit who is also God. So, although there are three Gods, they are in fact one God, or rather God is three-in-one, a Trinity, and so on. The surah says:

> Unbelievers are those who say, "God is one of three," for there is but one God. If they do not desist from what they are saying, those of them that disbelieve shall be severely chastened. (73)

The great religious debate in the world today is in essence between Islam, which upholds the absolute oneness of God, the one and only creator and controller of the whole of life and the universe, on the one hand, and a brand of Christianity with illogical, inconsistent, and incomprehensible doctrines that are being modified and remodified by self-serving institutions, on the other. God advised

Prophet Muhammad to say to the People of the Book: "'Do not transgress the bounds of your religion, do not yield to the desires of those who erred before and had led many astray and had themselves strayed from the right path'" (77). The Christian world is hopelessly divided, and this division has been the underlying cause of many religious wars in the world, some of which went on for decades, claiming millions of innocent victims. It was only when the powers of the Church were separated from those of the state that the infighting abated. However, the Church, with newly acquired allies, has now turned to fight Islam and the Muslims. It is Islam that is being branded retrogressive, fundamentalist, anti-modernist, and violent. Still, the conciliatory tone of the Qur'an should remain relevant for all time:

> The closest and most affectionate towards the believers are those who have said, "We are Christians." That is because among the latter there are priests and monks and because they are not conceited. When they listen to what has been revealed to the Messenger, you see their eyes fill with tears for recognizing the truth. They say, "Lord, we believe and so count us among the witnesses." (82–83)

History tells us that the early Muslims were hoping for the support of the Christians of Abyssinia and Byzantium. They were looking forward to the triumph of the Byzantine Christians over the Persians, because they saw that as a victory for their own cause. Christian delegations began to converge first on Makkah and then on Madinah to listen to what Muhammad had to say, and many of them converted to Islam, believing it to be a fulfillment of the prophecies of their own books and prophets. Later, with the decline of Byzantine power, Islam spread widely over the whole of Asia Minor and North Africa, whose inhabitants, the overwhelming majority of whom had been Christian, adopted Islam. As the verse puts it, they were saying: "'Why should we not believe in God and in the truth that has come to us, and hope our Lord will admit us among the righteous?'" (84). However, this was brought to a halt by the vicious and relentless Crusades waged against the Muslims. They started over one thousand years ago, and do not seem to have come to an end yet. These wars have shaken the very foundations of the world of Islam and have done incalculable damage to the spirit and the unity of the Muslims. Still, there must definitely be people in Europe and America, the bastions of Christianity today, who are looking for the truth although they are discouraged from accepting Islam because of the pathetic and miserable state of the Muslims today. Nevertheless, only time will tell.

In this brief discussion of the relationship between Islam and the People of the Book, we are informed about the bases and principles upon which the Muslim community is built. Muslims are strongly warned about leaning too far towards either materialism or monasticism, and that they should not forbid themselves the good and wholesome things that God has provided and made lawful for them.

> Believers, do not forbid the wholesome things which God made lawful to you. But do not transgress, because God does not love the transgressors (87).

They are also warned against all forms of extremism in behavior and conduct. This is followed by verses giving clear-cut rulings forbidding the taking of intoxicants, which today's so-called Christians consume normally every day. There are also rulings on protecting the sacred Muslim lands in Makkah and Madinah, refraining from fruitless and abstract religious polemics, and on the need for Muslims to abide by the Qur'an and the Sunnah. They are also warned not to take the route of the unbelievers and bigots:

> When it is said to them, "Come to that which God has revealed and

to the Messenger," they say, "Sufficient for us is the faith we have inherited from our fathers," even though their fathers were so ignorant and misguided. (104)

The surah ends with two topics: a call to the Christians to be sincere in their faith and to clean up and purify their doctrines and beliefs, and a reminder to the Muslims of their covenant with God and their need to respect and fulfill that covenant. We read God's solemn questioning of Jesus: "Did you say to people, 'Take me and my mother as two gods besides God?'" (116), to which Jesus would naturally reply:

I told them only what You ordered me to say. I said, "Worship God, my and your Lord." I was their witness as long as I had stayed with them, and when you took me to You, You have been the one watching over them. (117)

The truth of the matter is that there is only one God, to whom all else submit in total humility. The Christian Churches have over the years tampered with the teachings of Jesus and contrived alien doctrines that do not reflect the spirit or objective of those teachings. Only pride and self-interest drive them to insist on adopting these erroneous and false doctrines as part of the original and authentic Christianity.

As regards humankind's covenants with God, it is made clear that no special relationship exists between God and any particular human group. On the Day of Judgment, everyone shall meet his or her Lord and Creator alone to account for his or her deeds and actions.

This is the day when their truthfulness will benefit the truthful. They shall dwell forever in gardens with rivers running underneath. God shall be pleased with them and they with Him. That is the supreme success. (119)

No one else but God commands sovereignty over this world, for "God has sovereignty over the heavens and the earth and all that is in them, and He has power over all things" (120).

Al-Mā'idah contains some of the very last statements of legislation revealed to Prophet Muhammad.

SURAH 6

*Al-An*ᶜ*ām*
(The Cattle)

THIS IS THE FIRST MAKKAN surah of the initial seven long surahs of the Qur'an. The Book itself was addressed in the first instance to the religiously ignorant pagans and polytheists of Arabia, who worshiped idols, were hopelessly unenlightened, and clung slavishly to the beliefs and religious traditions they had inherited from their ancestors. They were typically bigoted and narrow-minded. In talking to them, the Qur'an adopted a rigorous, patient approach, amassing all possible evidence and using all methods of persuasion to make them see the truth. It spoke at length about God, His omnipotence, and the proof for His existence and power, manifest in their own creation and their life, and in the natural world around them. It challenged, teased, and cajoled their basic human nature and common sense, tapping their latent spiritual instincts and urging them to shake off the fetters of paganism.

The surah is distinguished for the recurring affirmations and direct instructions addressed to the Arab mind of the seventh century AC, that was reveling in religious ignorance and backwardness. This is clear right at the start as the opening verse says: "Praise be to God, who has created the heavens and the earth and ordained darkness and light. Yet the unbelievers set up other gods as equal with their Lord" (1). Despite God's incredible and unique power, however, the ignorant and unenlightened continue to take other objects as gods besides Him, ascribing to them a comparable status. Following the opening verse, we find an emphasis on the fact that humankind's life span on earth is finite, and a day will come when all shall return to face God and account for their actions. God shall then stand as the judge of all. The praise due to the Almighty is enforced by the affirmation: "He is the God in the heavens and on earth. He knows what you conceal and what you reveal and He knows all that you do" (3).

The surah also has a distinct feature in that God is frequently referred to in the third person singular, He, for example, in verses 97 and 98. This has the immediate result of capturing one's attention very effectively, and one can feel the overwhelming and imposing presence of God, which invokes recognition of, and total submission to, His majestic power. The Qur'an speaks of God with pure, direct awareness, and with unparalleled sincerity and reverence. It tries to pluck people out of the traditions they have adopted, shake them up, and rid them of the ignorance in which they have wallowed. In addition to these affirmations, we find explicit, precise, and direct instructions and briefings from God to His Prophet, Muhammad, on how to educate, inform, and argue with the unbelievers. The instructive word, "Say," appears frequently; it is in fact repeated in the surah forty times, sometimes occurring as often as twice or four times in the same verse:

> Say, "To whom belongs all that the heavens and the earth contain?" Say, "To God. He committed Himself to mercy and shall gather you all on the Day of Resurrection; a day about which there is no doubt." (12)

> Say, "What could be the greatest testimony?" Say, "God. He bears witness for me and for you. This Qur'an has been revealed to me that I may thereby warn you and all whom it may reach. Do you really believe that there are other gods besides God?" Say, "I do not so believe." Say, "He is but one God, and I am totally guiltless of your polytheism." (19)

The argument is eloquent, sincere, clear, straightforward and extremely powerful. It is being conducted by God on behalf of His Prophet. Clearly the surah was revealed at a time of tense and heated confrontations between the Prophet and the unbelievers of Makkah.

Scholars are agreed that the surah, despite its length, was revealed in its entirety on one occasion. Although some doubtful and unsupported reports point out that parts were revealed in Madinah, this is due to a misconception that all Qur'anic passages relating to the People of the Book, Jews and Christians, belonged to the Madinah period. Likewise, some scholars are mistaken in claiming that zakah was implemented at Madinah, whereas in fact its implementation started with verses revealed at Makkah and the details of its application followed in verses received in Madinah. However, this surah was revealed on one occasion and the illiterate Prophet committed it to memory immediately and recited it to the scribes and other notable Companions who recorded and memorized it.

We shall now continue to review the main issues raised in this surah, the first of which is the inevitable fate of transgressors and those who offend God, no matter how long that fate takes in coming. The actions of this type of people usually begin with their refusal to listen to the truth, and once they have listened to it they begin to deny it. When that fails they turn to trivializing and mocking it until they eventually have to make an all-out attack on it and on those who uphold it. All this with God choosing to allow things to take their natural course as a test of the tenacity and endurance of the believers, and to see how far the unbelievers are prepared to go in their transgression. Regarding the unbelieving Arabs, God says:

Can they not see how many generations We have destroyed before them? We gave them more power in the land than We have given you [the unbelievers], and sent down for them abundant water from the sky, and gave them rivers streaming beneath them. Yet We destroyed them for their sins and raised up other generations after them. (6)

Thus, when nations and civilizations grow arrogant and oppressive, they fall apart, decline, and degenerate. The question here must be whether this divine law applies to those human societies that totally deny God and ignore His power, or is it also true for those human groups which in their way of living mix and confuse the truth with falsehood? The answer, according to the surah, is that the law holds for both. Let us read carefully the following words:

We sent forth apostles before you to other nations, and afflicted them [the nations] with calamities and misfortunes so that they might humble themselves [to God]. If only they had humbled themselves when Our scourge overtook them! No, their hearts were hardened and Satan praised their deeds for them. (42–43)

They misunderstood God's grace and assumed that they had succeeded in deceiving Him. However, before they could congratulate themselves for their hollow victory: "We suddenly struck them and they were plunged into utter despair, and thus was the power of the transgressors annihilated. Praise be to God, Lord of all creation" (44–45).

Having studied the state of our Muslim nation throughout its history, I find that the threats directed in this surah against the unbelievers are just as valid and real in the case of those who deviate from the truth:

Say, "He has the power to afflict you with suffering from above your heads or from beneath your feet, or split you into factions causing the one to overpower the other." Look how We demonstrate the signs so that they may understand. Your people [Muhammad] have rejected it [the Qur'an] although it is the truth. Say, "I am not your guardian. Everything shall come to its end and then you shall realize." (65–67)

A person can indeed, at times, be benevolent and patient for much longer than necessary but when it is time to react, the reaction can be swift and devastating, and so it is with God when He decides to punish oppressive nations and redress injustice and wrongdoing.

Some people, when reminded of a weak trait or a certain flaw in their character or behavior, rather than taking note, try to find faults with others. It is also true that when some people are advised to apply their own mental and intellectual faculties to understand and verify certain basic facts, they turn to asking for concrete proof or miracles. However, what good are magic and miracles if the mind itself is not receptive or if it is reluctant to appreciate the truth? This has been the cause of the difficulty believers come up against when dealing with cynics, agnostics, or unbelievers, past and present. They are simply not prepared to see beyond what they know already. The verse that follows puts it very well:

> If We were to send down to you [Muhammad] a book inscribed on paper and they touched it with their own hands, the unbelievers would still assert: "This is but plain sorcery." (7)

Another preposterous proposition they made was that Muhammad should have been accompanied by an angel to attest to his fidelity: "They also say, 'Why was an angel not sent to him?' But if We had sent down an angel, their fate would have been sealed and it would have been too late for them" (8). The point here is that if such an angel had been sent down to support the truth of the

119

Prophet's mission, and they still refused to believe, their end would then have been decided and their annihilation would have been inevitable. Although others before them had asked for miracles of this kind, when they were given them, they persisted in their rejection of God's apostles and prophets. God goes on to assert that for a human to see an angel in physical form is impossible, because the human vision is limited to a certain range of electromagnetic waves beyond which no human can see. Indeed, even if angels were to appear in a form that humans could discern, doubt and uncertainty would always remain as to whether what was seen was human or angel. The verse puts it thus: "If We had made him [the apostle] an angel, We would have given him the semblance of a man, and would have thus added to their confusion" (9).

However, despite the vehemence of their rejection of Islam, their hostility towards the Prophet, and their determination to dissuade or even destroy him, the divine advice to Muhammad was always to persevere and continue with his own positive work to win more followers and supporters and persuade more of them to accept Islam. The assurance is: "Other apostles before you have been scorned, but those that scoffed at them were overtaken by the very scourge they had derided" (10). Being human, the Prophet was nevertheless disappointed and saddened by some of that behavior, and was always hoping for divine intervention to ease his burden. God again reassured him: "We know well that what they say grieves you. It is not that they do not believe you, but transgressors always deny God's revelations" (33). The unbelievers were, in reality, guilty of offending against God more than they were against the Prophet, and by denying the truth of God's revelation, they were being more hostile towards Him than they were towards His Messenger. The latter was being told to persevere because:

Other apostles have been disbelieved before you, but they patiently bore up and endured persecution until We granted them victory.

None can change the edicts of God, and you [Muhammad] have already heard of the experiences of other apostles. (34)

Nevertheless, the Prophet was hoping for an act of God, an extraordinary event that would confound his detractors and strike them dumb. However, God's reply was: "But if you [Muhammad] find their aversion hard to bear, then seek a tunnel into the ground or a ladder through the sky by which you can bring them a sign" (35). Naturally, this was a challenge which could not be met. These were matters for God to decide, and He is the ultimate judge, who, if He wished, "would have given them guidance, so do not be foolish" (35).

After reading these words, it would indeed be absurd and foolish to suggest that the Qur'an was not a divine book received through revelation by Muhammad, who had no hand whatsoever in its composition or authorship. God rules this world according to set laws and norms that no one else can influence or change. God's prophets and messengers had to carry out their missions to the full, no matter what opposition or hostility they had to contend with. People have a certain defined space of time during which they are free to react to God's commands and decide whether to adopt them or not. Once that time has passed, however, it is God's prerogative to act and deal with those people in the appropriate manner.

The verses continue to explain to the Prophet that his people's problem is with their minds that have led them to turn away from the truth. "Those that can hear will surely respond. As for the dead, God will bring them back to life, and to Him they shall all return" (36). Yet the unbelievers continue to flaunt their ignorance:

They ask, "Why has no sign been sent down to him [Muhammad] from his Lord?" Say, "God is perfectly capable of sending down a sign." But most of them are unable to understand. (37)

It is indeed curious how these people think. If the intricate and boundless systems of the universe and life are not sufficient evidence for the existence of God, how can such evidence be obtained by breaking the very natural laws themselves and performing so-called miracles that contradict them? How can the incredibly accurate physical laws governing the movement of the galaxies and their countless planets and stars not be sufficient proof for God's existence?

When one looks at life in all its forms—human, animal, and plant—one can only be astounded and overwhelmed by the phenomenon itself and by the fact that it has endured for all these millions of years. The following verse gives the answer:

> All beasts roaming the earth and all birds flying with their wings are but communities and nations like you are. We have omitted nothing in the Book, and they shall all be gathered before their Lord. (38)

Look at the amazing bird kingdom, for example, and how the mothers fly around the fields and forests gathering food in their own bellies to go back and feed their fledglings waiting in the nest. God has indeed perfected creation at all levels, but cynics, unbelievers, and agnostics continue to deny His existence and worship idols and other false manmade gods, while asking for fantastic proof of God's existence. The surah comments: "Those who controvert our revelations are deaf and dumb; they are in total darkness" (39). The irony of the unbelievers' attitude is that they claim they will believe the Prophet when the evidence they ask for is produced.

> They solemnly swear by God that if a sign is given to them they will believe it. Say, "Signs are up to God." And how can you [believers] tell that even if a sign came to them [the unbelievers] they would not disbelieve? We turn away their hearts and their sight, just as they

refused to believe the first time round, and then We let them blunder about in their wrongdoing. (109–10)

The unbelievers went even further in their folly by asking the Prophet to rid himself of the weak and humble among his followers in order for them alone to have the privilege of being around him. On this point God tells the Prophet: "Do not drive away those who pray to their Lord morning and evening seeking His favor" (52), but tell them the good news that God is on their side and will grace and honor them:

When those that believe in Our revelations come to you [Muhammad], say, "Peace be upon you. Your Lord has committed Himself to mercy. Any one of you who commits evil out of ignorance and then repents and mends his ways, God shall be Forgiving and Merciful [towards him]." (54)

With these assurances, the Prophet was able to carry on with his task of spreading Islam and calling people to God. He also received instructions on how to refute the slanders and lies the unbelievers were spreading about him personally.

Say, "I am forbidden to worship the gods whom you invoke besides God." Say, "I will not yield to your wishes, for then I would have strayed and become misguided." Say, "I have received the veritable truth from my Lord, yet you refuse to believe it. I do not have what you urge me to give you; judgment is entirely up to God only. He declares the truth and He is the best of arbiters." (56–57)

Indeed, one cannot help but feel sympathy and admiration for the Prophet for the patience and strength of character with which he faced his staunch detractors. One could also feel that Muhammad was displaying genuine and true leadership qualities in wishing for his people the same guidance, honor, and well-being he was wishing for himself. He is instructed to make it clear to his people: "Say, 'Were I capable of giving you what you urge me to give, matters between me and you would have been settled once and for all, but God is best aware of the evil-doers'" (58). With this calm, persistent, and persuasive approach, the Prophet continued to execute his universal mission.

A close and careful reading of this surah, its assertions, and instructive exhortations, has led me to ask: What more could miracles do to convince people of God's existence and power? If all the miracles cited in this surah are compared with the positive and rational arguments and reasoning put forward in it, they cannot be more persuasive. Let us read, as an example, the following passage:

> He [God] has the keys [of knowledge] to all that is unknown; none knows them but He. He knows all that is on land and all that is in the sea, and every tree leaf that falls is known to Him. Every seed [growing] in the deepest recesses of the ground and every soft or hard element is recorded in a perspicuous Book. (59)

The unknown, which mainly includes things and events in the future, but a great deal of the present and the past as well, is totally obscured from our view, although fully accessible and exposed to God Almighty. One meets other people every day, works with them, and talks to them about all manner of things. Nevertheless, what do we really know about one another's personalities or what goes on in one another's minds?

God, however, is Omniscient; He has total and conclusive awareness of the inner and outer truth about every human being as well as overall knowledge of past, present, and future events. There are simply no limits or bounds to His knowledge, or, as the Qur'an puts it, "He is aware of everything" (*al-Mulk*: 19). God is also omnipresent; He is everywhere all of the time, but not merely as an observer or a spectator. Indeed, God acts, and directs and controls creation in accordance with His wisdom and purpose. He is not an abstraction, a theoretical concept, or an isolated notion of the imagination, but is proactive and in full charge of the affairs and destiny of creation.

Now let us read on. "It is He that causes you to sleep at night and knows what you have done during the day, and he causes you to rise again [the next day] to fulfill your allotted span of life..." (60). Whether deeply asleep at night or working during the day, our lives and destinies are in the hands of God, with whom rest the final decisions. One day the end shall arrive for every one of us, and that is when we move closer to the Day of Judgment: "To Him you shall all return, and He will reveal to you all that you have done" (60). More fundamental truths are still to come.

> He reigns supreme over His servants. He sends forth guardians [angels] who watch over you until it is time for you to die when Our messengers [the angels] take your souls away, without fail. (61)

We humans have no initial control over our lot: we can have no choice as to where and when to be born. We cannot determine the level of our intelligence, talent, and fortune. Even God's prophets vary with respect to these endowments—some being more illustrious than others. However, when it comes to accountability, every one is judged according to his or her limits and capabilities. Then, "Our messengers [the angels] take your souls away, without fail. All shall then be returned to God, their true Lord. His is the judgment, and His reckoning is most swift" (61–62). Those ominous and foreboding words are, however, immediately followed by the most courteous and heart-warming ones:

Say, "Who protects you against the dark perils of land and sea, when you humbly pray to Him openly and in private saying, 'Save us this time, and we shall be ever thankful?'" Say, "God delivers you from them and from all other afflictions, yet you still take other gods [besides Him]." (63-64)

The Qur'anic style taps people's hopes and fears, their worries and their aspirations, in order for them to maintain a balanced view of life, their experience, and status in this world. The logical incisive arguments advanced in the Qur'an are far more persuasive and effective than any other pleading or polemic. The matter is quite serious and should not be taken half-heartedly or treated with frivolity, so:

When you meet those who scoff at Our revelations, turn away from them until they engage in other talk. Should Satan cause you to forget, take leave of the wrongdoer as soon as you come to remember. (68)

Similar instructions to the Prophet and his followers were repeated in verse 70, all of which remain valid for Muslims everywhere. Once conversations or discussions of God and religion turn frivolous or derisive, a Muslim should make his or her point in earnest and then withdraw. God shall be the ultimate judge.

More instructions are given to the Prophet:

Say, "Are we to pray to gods, other than God, who can neither benefit nor harm us, and relapse into unbelief after God has guided us, like someone lured by devils, bewildered, whose friends call him to the right path, saying: 'Come with us.'" (71)

The note of sincerity, earnestness, and concern is quite impressive. "Say, 'God's guidance is the only guidance, and we [the believers] have been commanded to surrender ourselves to the Lord of all creation'" (71).

The surah then takes us back to the past, recounting prophet Abraham's encounter with the star-worshipers and how he tried to steer them gently to believing in the one God. Abraham went along with those people's thinking and looked at a bright star in the night sky and said: there was the Lord, as they claimed. But the star faded away. He then turned to the moon and said the same, but soon it also disappeared below the horizon. He saw the bright shining sun and said, as they would say, that must be God, since it was bigger and stronger, but before long it likewise set and darkness fell again. Abraham thought that surely the real God would not disappear and leave the world or parts of it behind. If God were to abandon the planet Earth for only one instant, its orbital movement would get out of control and the oceans, which constitute three quarters of its area, would overflow, killing all land creatures. God controls the whole of the physical world and all of the forces that govern it. Any slight changes that could upset the delicate balance of these forces would spell the end of the world and life as we know it. God says elsewhere in the Qur'an: "It is God who keeps the heavens and the earth from collapsing, and if they were actually to collapse none would ever be able to hold them back in place except Him" (*Fāṭir.* 41).

God can never be conceived to forget or relinquish His control of existence, nor would He abandon or neglect His creation, whose existence and continuity are totally and completely dependent on Him. It is also God who ordains the destiny of every soul and coordinates relations among all elements of creation. The Qur'an, citing Abraham's experience of his search for the one true God, sealed the account with this conclusion: "I have turned my face to Him who has created the heavens and the earth, and to no one else, and I take no other gods besides Him" (79). It was left to unbelievers, skeptics, and agnostics to ponder these truths and accept or reject them. God could not be made any fairer or clearer to them. Still, the success of God's messengers in persuading their people and winning them over to their side varies from one messenger to another, as indicated in the following verse:

> And such was Our valid argument which We gave Abraham to use against his people. We raise whom We wish to higher levels, and your Lord is Wise and All-Knowing. (83)

The roots of the Islamic faith go deep into history. The version delivered by Prophet Muhammad was not a new religion that had suddenly emerged in the Middle Ages, but a representation of the messages of all the earlier prophets who identified the one God and called on their people to obey and worship Him alone. Noah, for example, also advanced the same message, saying: "'I have been commanded to be among those who surrender [to God]'" (*Yūnus*: 72). Such prophets and messengers are mentioned in the Qur'an with the greatest of respect and reverence, and their experiences and examples are related with praise for their sincerity, hard work, and total devotion to God. Their central imperative was: God is true; God is one; all must surrender to Him. Verses 83 to 86 of *al-Anʿām* mention by name eighteen of those prophets, followed by this comment:

> All these [prophets] We exalted above all nations, and We guided many of their fathers, their children, and their brothers. We selected them and guided them to a straight path. Such is God's guidance; He bestows it on whom He pleases of His servants. Had they taken other gods besides God, all their labors would have been in vain. Those are the men on whom We bestowed the Book, wisdom, and prophethood. If these people [the Arabs] reject them, We will entrust them to others who will not deny them. (86–89)

And so it was. All the Arabs of Makkah embraced Islam while Prophet Muhammad was still alive, and within a relatively short period it was to reign supreme over the whole of Arabia. From there, Islam spread rapidly along the Nile valley and through North Africa in the west, to Syria and Iraq in the north, and to Asia Minor in the east, liberating and enfranchising. Whole communities embraced Islam en masse and became its most stalwart defenders and proponents. The surah asserts the fact that Islam was an extension of and a complement to the messages received by earlier prophets:

> Those were the men whom God guided, and so [Muhammad] follow their guidance and say [to your people], "I do not ask of you any recompense for this. It is a reminder to all humanity." (90)

It is thus clear from these verses that Muhammad's followers are the legitimate beneficiaries and the bona fide heirs of Abraham, Moses, and Jesus. They are the true challengers to the unbelievers and they are the ones to be relied on to establish God's order on earth and spread His message to all humankind.

Unbelief, past and present, is the outcome of ignorance and arrogance, while religion entails proper and sober understanding of the reality of the true and only God, His power, and total submission and obedience to His order. This characteristic remains uniquely true of the followers of Islam. There are yet those who deny God's revelation, which is not altogether surprising since they deny God's own existence. This was the belief held by heathens and pagans in the past, and is today held and advocated by secularists, agnostics, skeptics, and atheists of all schools and description. Nevertheless, God is too merciful and benevolent to leave the human race drifting aimlessly without guidance or direction. Prophets and messengers are sent to show humanity the true way in life. However, the surah says that the unbelievers, "have not truly appreciated God when they have said, 'God has never revealed anything to a human being'" (91).

The retort follows swiftly: "Say, 'Who, then, revealed the Book which Moses brought as a light and a guide for people?'" (91). The reference here to Moses rather than to Muhammad emphasizes Islam's universal nature, asserting the belief in all God's messengers and Books. As mentioned earlier Islam is the religion of eternal and universal truth, which the People of the Book, Jews and Christians, were incited to forsake and neglect. Their scholars and elders did not look after God's revelation properly, some of which they had lost, some they concealed, and some they unashamedly violated. "You [the rabbis] transcribe it [the Torah] on scraps of paper, of which you show some and conceal most" (91). Furthermore, and as if that was not enough, they were determined to oppose Muhammad relentlessly, and fight him and his followers with such aggression and vehemence.

The surah then turns to address the Arabs, telling them that they have been taught things that neither they nor their forefathers knew before. They have now been chosen to bear the responsibility of upholding God's revelation on earth, and it is they who are now being tested and challenged.

All three divinely revealed Books: the Torah, the Gospel, and the Qur'an, are accessible to us today and can be studied and scrutinized as closely as one would wish. All that is required is that people should study them with open and fair minds. My own reasoning has led me to believe that the world has a Master and that this Master enjoins upon human beings fairness and benevolence and inspires them to avert oppression and transgression. I further believe that God will bring all people back to life in the hereafter to account for their actions and behavior in this life. The question that immediately springs to mind is: Which of the three divinely revealed Books has best expounded these truths and has more soundly defended them? Which of them has been most effective in winning the hearts and minds of people all through the ages? To help us answer these questions, let us refer to the following verse:

Who is more of a transgressor than the one who ascribes lies to God or says, "Something has been revealed to me," when nothing has been revealed to him, or the one who says, "I will reveal the same as God has revealed"? (93)

This is followed by an account of what those transgressors will face when they die and before they are even brought back to life in the hereafter.

If only you, [Muhammad], were to see the transgressors while in the throes of death and the angels stretching their hands out to them saying, "Give up your souls; today you shall be rewarded with a shameful punishment in return for the falsehood you were uttering against God and for the arrogance you have shown towards His revelation." (93)

Can any fair-minded person really doubt that the Qur'an, with such an approach and style, is a genuine divine revelation or claim that it is false or that it is the work of the human mind?

Having sharply reprimanded the unbelieving ignorant people, the surah returns to affirm and assert God's glory and power. It puts forward a series of fundamental questions. How does the soil acquire its fertility? How do trees grow and bring forth their fruits? How do crops and vegetation come about? And it goes on to give the answers. "It is God who splits the seed and the fruit-stone. He brings forth the living from the dead, and the dead from the living. Such is God, so how then can you turn away?" (95). This is true also for other phenomena in the wider universe: "He kindles the light of dawn. He made the night for rest, and the sun and the moon for reckoning. Such is the ordinance of the Mighty, the Omniscient" (96).

The verses continue to elaborate on this theme, describing the various physical phenomena that point to God's power and wisdom, concluding that He alone deserves to be worshiped, glorified, and obeyed. Those who can see that will do well for themselves, but those who cannot will be much worse off:

> Enlightening signs have come to you from your Lord. He that sees the light shall benefit himself, but he who is blind would incur harm to himself. [Say, O Muhammad], "I am not your keeper." (104)

What good will miracles do when the issue is so compellingly clear and simple? The sole objective of God's messengers all through the ages has gone no further than trying to bring about this rational and sensible belief. Prophet Muhammad is then cited as saying: "Should I then seek a judge other than God who has revealed to you the Book [the Qur'an] fully explained?" (114). Indeed, the learned elders among the People of the Book, within their hearts, realize and appreciate the power of the Qur'an and the veracity of its proponent: "Those to whom We gave the Book know well that it [the Qur'an] is revealed by your Lord with the truth, and you should therefore have no doubts" (114).

⚜

To cement the relationship between the Ummah and the Qur'an, we read in this surah:

> Follow what has been revealed to you from your Lord; there is no God but He, and avoid the polytheists. (106)

> And thus is your Lord's path a straight path. We have made all signs plain to those who think and learn. (126)

> This [the Qur'an] is a blessed Book which We have revealed, confirming what came before it, that you may warn the mother city [Makkah] and its environs. Those who believe in the life to come will believe in it too. (92)

The Israelites, after the decline and destruction of the earlier Arab communities of ʿĀd, Thamūd, Madyan, and others, inherited the custodianship of God's revelation. However, with the advent of Muhammad and Islam the task fell back onto the Arabs, who are told: "This is a blessed Book We have revealed. Observe it and fear God, so that you may find mercy" (155). This should urge the Arabs to understand fully and appreciate the responsibility they are shouldering, having received the Qur'anic revelation. God rewards people according to their efforts, without any compulsion or coercion: "Your Lord would not destroy nations without just cause and due warning" (131). Even so, people will continue to argue and try to find excuses for and ways around their faults and misdemeanors, falsely and erroneously ascribing them to the will of God. God puts it in the following way:

The idolaters will say, "Had God wished it, neither we nor our fathers would have taken other gods besides Him; nor would we have made anything unlawful." Those who had come before them did likewise reject [the Truth] until they had a taste of Our scourge. Say, "You have no proof that you can put before us, you have nothing but conjecture and you are nothing but perjurers." (148)

Before that, God made it clear that He would further guide and help those who opened their hearts to the Truth and believed in it, but those who did not would be downcast and dejected, and, "thus shall God bring punishment on those who do not believe" (125). The inference is that God will not offer guidance to those who reject faith outright, but will help those who are receptive and willing to be guided. This was put very graphically and succinctly as follows:

He whom God wishes to guide, He opens his heart to Islam, but he whom He wishes to confound, He will make his heart narrow and restricted as though climbing up into heaven. (125)

133

God's will in this context does not preempt one's choice to believe or not to believe, because the verse continues to say: "Thus shall God bring punishment on those who do not believe" (125).

Every man and every woman shall stand up to be judged, to review their record in this life and account for their actions. Even so, this accountability will have no meaning or justification if the person was helpless, powerless, or restricted. Belief and faith, however, are not merely to be proclaimed. Believers are required to give their beliefs real expression in their obedience to God's commands in all walks of life. The surah points out that the ignorant pagans invented certain forms of religious practise and worship that had no basis of truth or logic. They created the very gods to whom they turned for guidance and judgment, and they built their arguments and religious doctrines on false and nonsensical premises. God has warned against this very strongly in the surah, saying: "The devils will inspire their cronies to argue with you, but if you obey them you shall also become idolaters" (121); also: "Who is more wicked than the one who invents lies about God in order to mislead others through sheer ignorance? God does not guide transgressors" (144).

We notice that people in various societies quite often develop religious practices and traditions of their own to decide what is good and what is bad, thereby confusing the true original religion with alien teachings and laws that can in many cases distort and obliterate it. Thus the surah delivers clear and strong directives:

Say: Come, I will tell you what your Lord has ordained for you.

a. You should not take other gods besides Him.

b. Show kindness towards parents.

c. You should not kill your children for fear of destitution, because We provide for you and for them.

d. Avoid foul sins, overt and covert.

e. Do not kill a soul that God has forbidden to be killed,

134

without the right justification to do so. This is what He urges
you to do, so that you may understand.

f. You have no right to any of an orphan's possessions, except
what is required for his [her] own wellbeing, until he [she]
comes of age.

g. Observe fairness and justice in weights and measures; We
never burden a soul with more than it can bear.

h. Judge fairly and testify to the truth, even against your own
kinsmen.

i. Be true to the covenant of God. This is what He urges you to
do, so that you may take heed.

j. And, this is My path, a straight one. Follow it and do not follow other paths, for these shall lead you away from it. This is
what He urges you to do, so that you may be fearful of God.
(151–53)

On hearing these verses, an Arab elder is reported to have commented, "Even if this were not a religion, then it is certainly highly
ethical and fair." False religious belief is usually the product of
fatuous ideas and absurd myths presented as supernatural and mysterious.

Reflecting closely on these ten directives or "commandments,"
one cannot fail to see the underlying logic, wisdom, and common
sense. There is none of the superstitions, mysticism, or wizardry
that are so typical of pagan belief and worship, past and present.
Before Islam, the Arabs used to claim to be purer and much more
intellectually endowed than the People of the Book, and that if
they were, like them, to receive divine revelation, they would out-
shine them completely. God addresses this claim thus:

Or you would say, "Had the Book been revealed to us, we would
have been better guided than they." A veritable sign has now come
to you from your Lord as a guide and a mercy. Who is more wicked

than he who has denied the revelations of God and turned away from them? Those who turn away from Our revelations shall be sternly punished for their antipathy. (157)

The cautionary threat imparted in this verse is not addressed to seventh-century AC Arabs alone, but to all modern-day Ba'thists, Arab nationalists, and secularist Arabs, among others, who oppose Islam.

Are they [the unbelievers] waiting for the angels [to come and take their souls] or for your Lord [to carry out His threat against them], or for some of your Lord's [extraordinary] signs to come? The day these come, faith shall not benefit a soul that had no faith hitherto. (158)

The Prophet is reported to have spoken of cataclysmic events to occur in the universe towards the end of the world, which will cause the sun to rise in the west. At that moment it will be too late for regrets and repentance. What use is it for unbelievers to declare their faith when they are drowning or when they are in the throes of death? The question still remains whether the Arab nation of today will revert to Islam and save itself before it is too late. The Arabs are notorious for internecine conflict and division. Their appetite for such strife seems to be insatiable, thus inviting weakness and dissolution upon themselves. The surah warns the Prophet that he should: "Have nothing to do with those who have split up their religion into sects. Their fate is up to God, who will show them what they had been doing" (159).

The surah ends with three of the forty-four direct instructions addressed to the Prophet, which are as follows:

Say, "My Lord has guided me onto a straight path, to an upright religion, the faith of Abraham, the devout." (161)

Say, "My prayer and my devotions, my life and my death, are all devoted to God, Lord of all creation." (162)

Say, "Should I seek a lord other than God, when He is the Lord of everything?" (164)

These verses point to the fact that Muhammad had led a life of total devotion and dedication to God and His message, and that he had done his utmost to deliver, uphold, and disseminate it faithfully and diligently.

The last statement in the surah is an affirmation of the nature of life in this world as a trial, a continuous test, from beginning to end. Human beings are being challenged and tested in their relations with other fellow humans as well as in their behavior towards and treatment of all that is around them. The result of this grand test shall be revealed later in the hereafter. Life here is a passing phase; it has no permanency. Nevertheless, what happens in this life is crucial for the final judgment.

He has made you the inheritors of the earth and raised some of you in rank above others, in order to test your gratitude. Swift is your Lord's retribution; yet He is certainly Forgiving and Merciful. (165)

Al-Aʿrāf
(The Heights)

THIS SURAH BEGINS with an overview of two main issues: one relates to the Qur'an itself, and the other to those who deny or reject divine revelation as a whole. About the first issue, we read God's words saying:

> This is a Book that has been revealed to you [Muhammad]—let there be no distress in your heart because of it—so that you may warn thereby, and as an admonition to the believers. Observe what has been revealed to you from your Lord and do not take other deities besides Him. (2–3)

The "distress" in the Prophet's heart would be a result of the negative reception with which the unbelievers would greet God's revelation and His Messenger, while the "warning" is in fact an integral aspect of the proclamation of the message. The people Muhammad was addressing were being called upon to obey the teachings of the Qur'an and abandon all other pagan religious practices and traditions, regardless of their origins. These "other deities" and traditions would bring them no good whatsoever. The surah refers to the "Book" on several occasions such as:

> We have given them a Book which We have imbued with knowledge, a guidance and a blessing to those who believe. Are they [the unbelievers] waiting but for its fulfillment? (52–53)

Once the Book's prophecies and warnings are fulfilled, the believers would be successful but the unbelievers would be frustrated and chastised. We also read: "My guardian is God who has revealed the Book, and He takes good care of the righteous" (196). These words were said on behalf of the Prophet asserting that God would support him and protect him until he had delivered God's message in full and conveyed His guidance to humankind. On the need to study God's Book and comprehend its teachings and wisdom, we are instructed thus: "When the Qur'an is recited, listen to it and observe silence so that you may be blessed" (204).

The second issue with which the surah opens, those who deny God's revelation, is also addressed in several verses right from the beginning of the surah when it says: "We have destroyed many a city, striking it at night or by day. Their only cry, when our punishment befell them, was to say, 'We have indeed transgressed'" (4–5). The rise and fall of states, nations, and civilizations have been a prominent feature of human history all through the ages. The surah speaks at length of specific ancient Arabian tribes such as 'Ād, Thamūd, and Madyan, to whom prophets and messengers were sent, as well as the people of Noah and Lot. We gather from these accounts that God's revelations and messengers had in the first instance been directed towards communities in southern and northern Arabia. However, when those communities reneged and opposed the messengers, God punished them severely, destroying them and their cities and towns.

This is then followed by an extensive account of the mission of Moses, who emerged with divine revelation aimed first at the Pharaohs and later on at the Hebrew Israelites of Egypt. When these also deviated, neglected God's guidance, and refused to submit to His will, they too were punished and their power was destroyed. Subsequently, God's revelation was again addressed to the inhabitants of central Arabia, where Prophet Muhammad was able to lead the Arabs in setting up a righteous and enlightened society that was to become a model for humanity and the world for many centuries to come. Through this process, the Arabs inherited the responsibility for divine revelation, and the Book they received, the Qur'an, has endured intact. It stands today as, and will continue to be, a beacon of virtue for all humanity and a guidance for all aspects of human life.

The Arab nation has to realize and appreciate the importance of the task it has undertaken, and understand well that it will be accountable to God for the way it handles it. The surah emphasizes:

> We shall question those to whom the messengers were sent, and We shall question the messengers themselves. With full knowledge, We shall recount for them all they have done, for We have never been absent. (6–7)

God affirms right at the beginning of the surah that accountability and judgment will be comprehensive and fair:

> On that Day, truth shall be the criterion. Those whose good deeds tip the scales shall be successful, but those whose deeds are of little weight shall lose their souls, because they denied our revelations. (8–9)

This is followed by a detailed account of the history of other groups and nations that dissented and quarrelled over God's revelation and an assessment of the outcome of their experiences. Eventually we are given a glimpse of a dialog that takes place in the hereafter between the believers, the unbelievers, and a third group of people who occupy a place on an elevated wall (Arabic: *al-A'rāf*, the heights, or raised decks) separating the other two groups. Those who enter Paradise are portrayed as enjoying a life of boundless love, magnanimity, and peace. Their sole preoccupation is to glorify and venerate God, thanking Him for His generosity and grace, saying: "Praise be to God who has guided us to this. Were it not for Him we should have never been rightly guided" (43). They are greatly humbled by God's overwhelming grace, which they consider is more than they have earned or actually deserve. However, God reassures them: "'This is a Paradise you have earned with your labors'" (43). Once they have settled down, they become curious about what has become of their former antagonists and oppressors.

Then those in Paradise called out to those in the hellfire, saying, "We have found what our Lord promised us to be true. Have you, too, found what your Lord promised to be true?" They said, "Yes." A voice will then declare to them both, saying, "God's curse be upon the transgressors." (44)

The transgressors will be those who deny life in the hereafter and their accountability to God for their actions here in this life. Among them will be tyrants, persecutors, and despots as well as people who distort divine truth and lead others away from God's straight path. The surah refers to, "those sitting on the raised decks" (Arabic: *aṣḥāb al-a'rāf)*, who are generally identified by Qur'anic scholars as people whose good and bad deeds have balanced each other, and who are awaiting God's word that will decide their fate. In my opinion, however, these comprise pious people and martyrs who, all through the ages, have complemented the good work of God's prophets and messengers and carried forward His messages, leading others and humanity as a whole to God's straight path and to the righteous life the prophets have advocated. Their position indicates an elevated and lofty status, looking with grace and amity towards those in Paradise, and with scorn at those in the hellfire. This is also borne out by the tone and nuance of the Qur'anic expressions. They are described as self-confident individuals who are strongly critical of God's detractors and berate the position in which they have ended. This could not be a description of people whose good deeds have simply balanced their bad ones or who are not sure of their destiny.

It is also unlikely that they will be unaware of God's decision on their fate.

A final cry is heard from those in the hellfire, calling for help: "Those in the hellfire cry out to those in Paradise, saying, 'Give us some water, or some of that which God has bestowed upon you'" (50), but to no avail! How can they be saved now, since, when they were given the chance, they refused to believe in God and denied they would ever be accountable to Him? The Day of Judgment was never on their minds, nor had they prepared themselves.

It is important to point out here that the Qur'anic style makes use of the interchange and blending of ideas, metaphors, and images within the same coherent context, to drive home the meanings and reach the heart and the mind at the same time. It is not made up of clearly defined or conventionally structured sentences and passages as those with which we are familiar in ordinary prose or composition. The Qur'anic style and approach reflect the diversified, complex, and intricate though essentially unified nature of the world around us. It is a world that is made up of millions of elements encompassing an unlimited number of manifestations, themes, and images.

There is also an intriguing interchange of reference in the surah to Adam, the father of the human race, and to humankind as a whole. Towards the beginning the surah says: "We have created and shaped you [humankind] and then said to the angels, 'Prostrate before Adam'" (11), whereas towards the end it says: "He created you of a single being and from that being He created a mate to seek comfort and peace with her" (189), until it says:

Yet, when He granted them a goodly child, they set upon taking other gods besides Him. Exalted be God above their gods. Will they worship those that can create nothing, but are themselves created? (190–91)

The reference here is of course to the offspring of Adam and Eve, especially those human groups and generations that had gone astray and deviated from the messages God revealed to the human race from time to time. People in this world are vulnerable to Satan's insinuations and temptation. Satan, as we learn from the Qur'an, has the means and the ability to influence people's behavior and choices in this life. Yet he is able to succeed only with those who are receptive to his suggestions and are willing to go along with him. For, no matter how effective or advanced the means of persuasion used, no one can really force another person to accept a particular idea or belief.

People seem to forget what happened between Adam and Satan, leading to Adam's expulsion from Paradise, nor do they seem to have learned the lessons of that encounter. Furthermore, Satan has taken it upon himself to humiliate and denigrate the human race, which he sees as a rival and a foe. The surah says:

> He [Satan] replied, "Reprieve me till the Day of Resurrection."
> God said, "You are reprieved." He [Satan] declared, "Because You
> have confounded me, I will lay in ambush for them [humankind] all
> along Your straight path. I will spring upon them from the front and
> from the rear, from their right and from their left, and You [God]
> will find the majority of them ungrateful." (14–17)

Should people not have taken note and prepared themselves well for the battle with Satan? Even more surprising, Satan's ruse which succeeded in deceiving Adam was so blatant and should have been easily discovered. He told Adam that he had been forbidden the fruit of the tree only to prevent him from becoming an angel or enjoying immortality. Was Adam not able to resist that temptation and blunt Satan's efforts to mislead him? After all, what does immortality really mean? Or, for that matter, what does death mean but a short transitional phase leading to a life of eternity? Satan, however, is a deceitful, unscrupulous creature, capable of employing all devious means of deception to achieve his ends. Nevertheless, he can hardly be held responsible; those who listen to him or fall for his stratagems will have only themselves to blame.

Adam was deprived of the life of bliss, comfort, and peace he had enjoyed in Paradise. He and his wife Eve were sent down to make their living on earth by the sweat of their brows. Despite that, the episode with Satan in Paradise keeps recurring with their offspring all the time. God said to Adam and Eve, and to Satan: "'Go down [to earth], enemies one to the other. On earth you will have a brief sojourn and enjoyment'" (24), after which they will all return to God Almighty to account for their actions and behavior in this life. Thus, all human life shall be played out in full on this earth: "He [God] said, 'On it [the earth] you shall live and on it you shall die, and out of it you shall be raised to life again'" (25).

This narrative is rounded off with proclamations addressed to humankind as a whole on certain important issues relating to human behavior. They are all aimed at steering people's lives towards righteousness and common sense; and it is indeed quite appropriate for us to look closely at these exhortations, because today's life has become so materialistic, immoral, and permissive, dragging human societies to moral degradation and a miserable living.

The surah also dealt with the issue of dress. Humans are unique among all creatures in that they wear clothes to cover their bodies and enhance their appearance. Clothes have become cultural symbols of class and status, as well as an expression of inner desires and feelings. The type of clothes people wear make powerful statements about them. Some clothes are worn to reflect worth and wealth, while some are worn for aesthetic reasons, to attract and seduce; and they are worn tight or thin to show body form. In the end, though, one's worth or status cannot be decided by what one wears. The surah refers to what might be called, "the garb of piety," that internal and intangible personal quality, which reflects one's true value and character:

Children of Adam! We have sent down to you garments to cover your nakedness, and garments for adornment, but the garb of piety is best. These are some of God's signs, so that they [the unbelievers] may remember. (26)

We can see that this is linked to what we find at the beginning of the surah when it says: "Follow what has been sent down to you from your Lord and do not follow others besides Him. But you seldom bear this in mind" (3). It is linked to what we read later on when the surah says:

He [God] sends forth the winds as a harbinger to precede His mercy, and when they have gathered up heavy clouds, We then drive them to a barren land and let water fall upon it, bringing forth all manner of fruit. Thus We shall raise the dead to life, so that you may bear all this in mind" (57).

Although there are indeed numerous reasons to make people keep these matters in mind, people are forgetful, and their memories are short.

Another topic explored in this passage is the need for Adam's offspring to avoid the mistake he had made in succumbing to Satan's suggestions: "Children of Adam! Let Satan not deceive you, as he deceived your parents, causing them to be driven out of Paradise" (27). Having succeeded in this objective, Satan's attention was then turned to whether he could prevent their offspring from returning to Paradise. As the human race's staunchest enemy he would seek to achieve his goal by exposing and exploiting people's weaknesses as he had done with their forebears. He has the advantage of being able to see people without being seen himself. Nevertheless, Satan cannot delude or deceive a true believer because belief in God is itself a shield that protects against Satan's intrigues. There can be no excuse for falling into the traps laid by Satan. It is a feeble argument that some people put forward when they say that they are following in the footsteps of their forefathers, and have to honor their old traditions or practices. On the other hand, we find that many people confuse their religious beliefs with superstitions and nonsensical practices and rituals, claiming that these are part of divine religious teachings. God could never condone or endorse vile practices or any behavior that is in contradiction to people's basic nature and common sense. God says:

> When they commit an indecent act, they say, "This is what our fathers used to do, and God has commanded us to do it." Say, "God never enjoins what is indecent. Would you ascribe to God things of which you are ignorant?" Say, "My Lord has enjoined justice." (28–29)

Justice and fairness are the best guarantee for peace and harmony among all members of the human race, and no one could have any reason to disregard or belittle the merits of these qualities. For success and salvation everyone should turn to God and obey Him.

> Say, "My Lord has enjoined justice, and ordered you to turn your faces to Him wherever you prostrate in prayer and to call on Him with true devotion. As He created you before, you shall return to Him; some [of you] He has guided and some go astray." (29–30)

False religious orders and teachings often advocate austerity, asceticism, obscurantism, and harsh disciplines in order to gain control over their followers and instill kindness and the love of God in their hearts. They encourage the tattered appearance and stern boorish ways of living. However, the teachings of Islam are a clear departure from this because they aim, first and foremost, at a person's heart and soul. They purify people's inner being, suppress their greed and selfishness and instill in them humility and kindness through pure unadulterated belief in and total submission to the one God. It is far more respectable that one should dress decently and appropriately for prayer, for example, than appear in tattered clothes. The surah endorses that, saying: "Children of Adam, dress well when you attend your places of worship. Eat and drink without excess, for God does not love the extravagant" (31). The Prophet is reported to have advised: "Eat what you wish to eat, and wear what you wish to wear, but avoid excess and ostentation."[15]

Excessive consumption and extravagant living and appearance lead to vice and encourage overindulgence. Religion ought not to become a game of sport or a means for showing off one's wealth or possessions. In seeking success in the life hereafter, one would be much better off not to allow oneself to be so strongly attracted or attached to worldly enjoyment and aggrandizement. On the other hand, austerity and the wearing of rags for their own sake will not bring one any closer to God either. God questions the wisdom and use of these misplaced austere tendencies, saying: "Say, 'Who has forbidden wearing the decent clothes or eating the good things which God has provided for His servants?'" (32). God, in other words, has provided these good things and it pleases Him that people should enjoy them and use them for their happiness and pleasure. This is further emphasized by:

Say, "These are for the enjoyment of the believers [and others] in this life, but shall be theirs alone on the Day of Resurrection." Thus We make our revelations plain to people who understand. Say, "My Lord has forbidden all indecent acts, overt and covert, sins and wrongful transgression." (32–33)

So there we have it. God has allowed humans the use and enjoyment of all He has created in this world, but has forbidden

---

[15] Narrated by al-Bukhārī, Ibn Mājah and Imam Aḥmad.

excessiveness and acts that are harmful to people personally and collectively, or to the environment around them. We have seen people wearing certain types of clothes to show piety and religious rectitude but who are very haughty and arrogant, even rude, in their behavior and attitudes. The Prophet has pointed out that God dislikes a person who displays arrogance and conceit. The emphasis, in Islam, is on purity of heart and sincerity of motives that drive us to selfless action. These, to millions of people, can come only as a result of unwavering belief in the one God and total devotion and submission to Him alone. Left to their own religious instincts and common sense, people would not seek to worship several gods. Polytheism is the by-product of ignorance and lack of religious maturity and enlightenment. Thus, we read that the things God has forbidden include taking, "as gods besides Him others that have no legitimacy or authority, and to say about God that of which you are ignorant" (33).

The surah makes it clear that people's instinctive religious tendencies have been instilled in them ever since they were created.

> Your Lord brought forth descendants from the loins of Adam's children, and made them their own witnesses, asking them, "Am I not your Lord?" They replied, "Yes, to that we bear witness." This He did lest on the Day of Resurrection you should say, "We had no knowledge of this," or say, "Our forefathers were idolaters, and we followed in their footsteps. Would You, then, destroy us because of what they, the wrong-doers, had done?" (172–73)

This indicates quite clearly that one cannot blame one's society or environment, no matter how overpowering they might be. When it comes to belief and faith, one must listen to one's own inner feelings and instincts which will lead one to believe in the one God and reject all other false creeds and ideologies. Rational thinking and common sense reject the idea that something can exist or come about without an instigator or initiator behind it. A "zero option" of creation, that the world is created out of nothing, simply does not add up or make sense. People have always felt a need to know where they have come from and how, and to identify the origins of life and the world around them. Their feelings and their minds have always led them to long for the "Supreme Power" which commands and controls all. But who or what is this "Supreme Being?"

In the Qur'an, God strongly reprehends those who seek to identify God through pure speculation and conjecture: "Who is more wicked than those who invent lies about God or deny His revelations? They shall receive their destined share" (37) of boon and attainment in this life,

> until the moment Our angels come to take away their lives and ask them, "Where are those gods whom you invoked besides God?" They will answer, "They have forsaken us," and they will admit they were unbelievers. (37)

Habit and social or cultural conditioning can be responsible for one's confusion and perplexity over the recognition and appreciation of God. A well-fed person living in luxury can forget the pain of hunger and starvation just as easily as a healthy person forgets the suffering of illness or disease. Both fail to appreciate the harsh realities of life and become self-satisfied and complacent. Modern-day strident existentialist-positivist-empiricist civilization, which is the legacy of past God-denying cultures, has led people to ignore past human experience and pretend that existence is a self-generating phenomenon in which there is no place for a Creator or a supreme Omnipotent God.

Hence the need for divine revelation. Its role has been to remind people of God and steer their thinking and their lives back on the tracks of His path. God says:

Your Lord is God, who created the heavens and the earth in six days and then ascended His throne. He throws the veil of night over the day, swiftly following it. The sun, the moon, and the stars are all subservient to His will. He has full authority and command over all creation. Glorified be God, Lord of all creation. (54)

As people go through life, they will experience happiness and grief, success and failure. They will ever be in need of God's help and sustenance and support. The surah calls to humankind thus:

Pray to your Lord with humility and in private. He does not love the transgressors. Do not corrupt the earth after it has been set right, and call on Him, with fear and hope. God's mercy is close at hand for the righteous. (55–56)

Promise and threat, fear and hope are some of the most powerful forces in human behavior. How often do we experience that certain feeling within our hearts that only God can give us what we aspire to achieve and only He will relieve our burden and alleviate our misery. To underline this, the surah says:

He [God] sends forth the winds as a harbinger to precede His mercy, and when they have gathered up heavy clouds, We then drive them to a barren land and let water fall upon it, bringing forth all manner of fruit. Thus We shall raise the dead to life, so that you may bear all this in mind. (57)

Thus we have seen how certain themes and ideas are given first in headline form and then as we proceed with the surah, details of each theme begin to emerge. They are not separate from or independent of one another, but are brought together and interwoven in a harmonious mosaic of concepts, exhortations, and imperatives to inspire, teach, and show the way to God. The vital element in this process is, of course, people's receptive ability. Torrential rain falling on rocks would yield no growth and no crop: "Good soil yields its fruit by God's will, but defiled soil will give only poor and scant fruit. Thus do We make plain our signs to those who are thankful" (58).

The surah has given much coverage to the history and experiences of earlier nations and human groups that rejected God's revelation and bore dire consequences for their conduct. Most of these groups appeared in or around the Arabian peninsula. Noah's people lived in Iraq, ^cĀd in the Yemen, Thamūd in northern Arabia, Madyan between Sinai and the river Jordan, and Lot's people in eastern Palestine. All these nations resisted God's messengers and rejected their teachings. The accounts of these peoples' experiences were preceded with the story of Adam and his encounter with Satan, which highlights an aspect of particular significance to us here. Satan did not stop at deceiving Adam and having him expelled from Paradise, but continued to pursue his offspring, generation after generation. The Qur'an relates to us in detail the experiences of earlier human societies with God and with Satan.

We may ask ourselves: How many years does this history span in the annals of time? My study of the subject leads me to estimate that Noah's Flood occurred about eight thousand years ago. The interval between Adam's arrival on earth and Noah's Flood would not be much longer than that. The Qur'an does not say anything about the human generations that lived before Noah. This leads me to suspect the accuracy of archaeological and geological findings of a human skull tens of millions of years old. Having studied the Qur'an very carefully, I find that the history of earlier generations did not simply go through such mechanical phases of receiving God's warnings, ignoring them, and then being punished. The reality would have extended into succeeding generations which inherited these phases, one after another. This is clear in these verses:

Whenever We sent a prophet to a city We afflicted its people with
calamities and misfortunes so that they might submit to Us. Then
We replaced adversity with good fortune, until they multiplied and
became prosperous and said, "Our fathers, too, were afflicted with
adversity and good fortune." Thus We smote them suddenly without them realizing it. (94-95)

People grew complacent and believed that what had befallen them
was normal, since it had already happened to their ancestors. What
had God to do with the cycle of history? The reply is:

Had the people of those cities believed and feared God, We would
have showered upon them riches and blessings from heaven and out
of the earth. But they disbelieved, and We destroyed them as punishment for what they had done. (96)

Succeeding human generations should therefore learn from preceding ones:

Is it not plain to those who inherit the earth from their predecessors
that if We wished We could punish them for their sins and set a seal
upon their hearts that they would remain bereft of hearing? (100)

Thus the earlier inhabitants of Arabia and their contemporaries
disappeared into history. God's revelations were then directed
towards another Semitic branch, the Israelites. God says: "After
them We sent Moses with our revelations and signs to the Pharaoh
and his people, but they too disbelieved them. Look what fate
awaited the evil-doers" (103). The Israelites, descendants of Jacob,
were originally Hebrew bedouins who inhabited the Syrian desert.
They went to settle in Egypt in response to a call by Joseph, a son of
Jacob. Their way of life flourished for some time and their numbers
multiplied. Refusing to assimilate into Egyptian society, they held

their own religious beliefs and observed their own religious practices, which did not endear them much to the Egyptians. They came
into bitter conflict with the indigenous population, which led to
their being brutally persecuted at the hands of the Pharaoh.

After a long period of unrelenting suffering and perdition, salvation came at the hands of the prophet Moses who promised them:
"Your Lord may well destroy your enemies and make you inherit
their power, and then see how you will manage" (129). Moses
seemed to fear the worst, and his premonitions were accurate. As
soon as the Israelites, by the grace of God, were safe from Pharaoh's
abuse and persecution, their first undertaking was to indulge in idol
worship.

> We led the Israelites across the [Red] sea, and they came upon a
> people who were worshiping idols they had. They said, "Moses,
> make us a god like the gods they have." He said, "You are indeed an
> ignorant people. These people are doomed, and their actions are
> damned." (138–39)

Sadly, they were captivated by paganism and idol worship, which
seemed to have taken hold of all their senses and consciousness.
Hardly had Moses departed from them for prayer when they
embarked on making a calf out of their women's jewellery, as an
object of worship instead of God. God says: "Those who worshiped
the calf shall incur anger from their Lord and disgrace in this life.
Thus We reward the liars" (152).

A large section of the fugitives held false or confused beliefs, and
were more susceptible to following their whims and desires. They
would deceive God and try to circumvent the teachings and disciplines of their religion. When, for example, they were forbidden
fishing on the Sabbath (Saturday), they would throw their nets into
the sea but not collect the fish until Sunday. Naturally, some of them
had the sense to warn others and give advice, but to no avail.

Therefore, when they forgot the warnings they were given, We delivered those who had warned against evil and inflicted a stern punishment on the transgressors for their wrongdoing. (165)

History tells us that the kingdom of the Jews was destroyed and ransacked by many enemies over successive generations, and the surah confirms that, saying: "We dispersed them in groups and colonies throughout the earth; some of them were righteous and others were not" (168).

Prophet Muhammad is reported to have been asked, "Will God destroy us while good people are still living amongst us?" His reply was, "Yes, when most of you are wrong-doers."[16] For such reasons God dispersed the Israelites and subjugated them to the rule of other nations. In this case, however, human transgression and disobedience had not come about as a result of ignorance or lack of prior warning, but had been a calculated and deliberate stance: "Every time a messenger came to them with something they did not fancy, they either rejected or killed him" (al-Mā'idah: 70). As cases of overweening pride and insolence accumulated, there came a time when God's patience with them would run out, and their state is described by this parable:

> Tell them of the man to whom We vouchsafed Our revelations but he turned away from them, and Satan overtook him and he was led astray. Had We wished, We would through Our revelations have given him a lofty status, but he clung to worldly life and succumbed to his desires. He is like the dog that pants if you chase it and pants if you leave it alone. (175–76)

This of course is true for individuals as well as nations who receive guidance, underestimate its value, or reject it altogether. Today, the

---

[16] Narrated by al-Tirmidhī.

opponents of Islam are facing "Muslims" who, unfortunately, are far more negligent of God's revelations and guidance than they are. Sadly, many of today's "Muslims" are people who have violated God's laws, cast aside the banner of Prophet Muhammad, and adopted systems that are alien to their religion and their culture. It would come as no surprise, therefore, that they too should be included with Moses' recalcitrant followers in the general meaning of the verse which says:

> We have allotted to hell many jinn and humans possessing hearts they cannot comprehend with, and eyes they cannot see with, and ears they cannot hear with. They are like animals, or even more heedless. (179)

Next we come to two very thought-provoking verses. One says: "He whom God guides is rightly guided; but those whom He confounds are the losers" (178), while the second asserts: "He whom God confounds, none can guide him; and He leaves them blundering about in their wickedness" (186).

Let me say right at the outset that there is no way that these verses, and others like them in the Qur'an, can be interpreted to indicate predestination. The human quality of free will is beyond question; otherwise responsibility and accountability would be null and void and the whole of existence turn into a meaningless farce. Guidance or lack of it can come about either by personal choice, that is, self-induced, or by the action of an outside agent. God leads astray or confounds only those who have already by their own choice taken that route. God says elsewhere in the Qur'an: "Those who persist in the error of their ways, the Merciful shall leave [them] to their own devices" (*Maryam*: 75).

The ending of these two verses confirms our view that a person's free will is inviolable. The one ends with the phrase: "...those He

confounds are the losers," while the other ends with the words: "...
and He leaves them blundering about in their wickedness," indicating in both cases that the underlying reason for their condemnation
stems from their own choice. Furthermore, the inimitable style of
Qur'anic language is an important factor in this regard. We may care
to refer back to verse 179, which talks of the "hearts that cannot
comprehend," "the eyes that cannot see," and "the ears that cannot
hear." The meaning here is that such "hearts," "eyes," and "ears"
will lead those who possess them to hell, but these people ought to
open their hearts and eyes and ears to the truth—something which
they are perfectly capable of doing. For the same reasons, we find in
the surah expressions such as: "Will they not reflect? Their man
[Muhammad] is no madman" (184), and: "Will they not ponder
upon the universe of the heavens and the earth, and all that God created?" (185). The point is that those who are not able to study,
reflect, or ponder, shall only have themselves to blame.

To avoid the fate of earlier generations, Muslims are urged to
ensure that their relationship with God is always at its best, and that
they should shun the idea of resorting to anyone else other than God
for help or support: "God has the most excellent names, so call on
Him by these names" (180). God alone is the most Perfect, most
Glorious, and most Self-Sufficient. When we are lost we call on
Him to guide us back to the right path; when we are in the dark we
call on Him for light; when we are in need we call on Him for help
and support. Under similar circumstances, the unbelievers would
resort to other powers, which is an insult to God and a grave offense
against His magnificence and glory. The foremost characteristic of
the Ummah is its pure monotheism and its total devotion to the
one God.

Among those whom We created there are people who guide others
to the truth and act justly by it. As for those that deny Our revelations, We will lead them, unawares, to ruin, step by step. (181–82)

God's wrath and punishment can sometimes be obscured by short-lived prosperity or illusions of triumphs and success, or petty achievements. This is part of the way in which God normally deals with transgressors. He gives them the freedom and chance and the time to decide and choose, but when He strikes, He strikes hard and suddenly: "I [God] give them a chance, but my retribution is severe" (183). The believers, when they are struck by disasters, defeats, or calamities, are expected to be resilient and persevere, no matter what, until things change for the better and God's help arrives, which it is sure to do.

Belief in the hereafter is an essential element of the Islamic faith and complements the belief in God. However, it belongs to the realm of the unknown. No matter how curious and eager we are to know its whys and wherefores, it remains God's own privilege. God says: "They ask you [Muhammad] about the Last Hour, 'When will it come?' Say, 'It is known only to my Lord; He alone will reveal it at its appointed time'" (187). Knowing this great secret can be relevant only for its contemporaries. As for the rest, their hour ends when they die. It is only then that we realize how short and trivial this whole life has been.

Another feature of Muslim belief is the assertion that Muhammad was a prophet of God, but totally human. He was no god, nor semi-god, nor partially god. He was a mortal, subservient to God like all other mortals, with no exceptional or extraordinary powers of his own that could be used to benefit or harm anyone. And so are all the angels and the rest of humankind. Any claim to the contrary is false.

The surah rounds off with reference to Adam in the context of talking about his offspring. Here the tone is one of reproach and anger. God has blessed Adam's children, the human race, with plenty of favors and goodness, but instead of being thankful, some take other gods besides, or instead of Him. To this God says: "Will they take other gods that can create nothing but are themselves created; gods that can give them no help, nor can they even help themselves?" (191–92).

The speech is then directed to the Prophet and his followers, condemning the pagan polytheists and their failure to avail themselves of God's guidance that was being revealed to them. It says: "If you call them to the right path they will not follow you. It is the same whether you call them or remain silent" (193). It was indeed a strange reaction on the part of those unbelievers, but the Prophet had to stand firm and hold fast to the revelation he was receiving and assert: "'My guardian is God, who has revealed the Book, and He is the guardian of the righteous'" (196). This "Book" was more sound and effective than the "miracles" they were demanding. "Say, 'I follow only what is revealed to me by my Lord. This [Book] is veritable proof from your Lord, a guide and a blessing to those who believe'" (203). However, the Prophet was told to be patient and tolerant, no matter how stubborn and arrogant his detractors were: "Be lenient, show magnanimity, and shun the ignorant" (199).

At the beginning, the surah relates how Satan succeeds in having Adam thrown out of Paradise and indicates that Satan's efforts to mislead and confound Adam's children, humankind, will never cease. However, Satan can only suggest and insinuate. Those who hold the right belief will be able to resist and overcome those efforts: "When those who fear God are tempted by Satan, they remember [God] and they are immediately fully alert" (201). Those bereft of this faculty will be taken in by Satan's deception and lose out. Remembering God and invoking His name, especially by the recitation and study of the Qur'an can be an effective protective shield against Satan's attempts. Therefore the believers are told: "When the Qur'an is recited, listen to it in silence so that you may be shown mercy" (204). However, remembering God is not merely a mechanical activity but a function of the heart and the mind, requiring full attentiveness and concentration. It should be done regularly, in public and in private, and should inspire one and spur him or her onto higher things and more fruitful and constructive pursuits. "Remember your Lord within your self in humility and reverence and in a moderate voice, in the morning and in the evening and do not be negligent" (205). Remembering God thus brings human beings into harmony with the physical world around them in a rhapsody of praise for God, Lord of all creation.

Al-Anfāl
(The Spoils of War)

THE MUSLIMS' DEFEAT at the battle of Uḥud in 625 AC, like their victory a year earlier at Badr in 624 AC, was not expected. Nevertheless, unexpected events are often the best means to test the caliber and tenacity of people. This surah was revealed in the wake of the Muslims' triumph at Badr to explain and identify the influence of God and the role of people in the victory achieved in that battle. It makes it clear that the victory awarded to the Muslims on that occasion was God-sent, in return for their steadfastness and perseverance all through the previous years. It further affirms that those valiant men who fought so hard were an instrument of God in fulfillment of the Qur'anic prophecy: "God has decreed, 'I and My messengers will surely triumph.' God is Powerful and Mighty" (al-Mujādilah: 21). The surah confirms that in this battle God sought, "to establish, through His words, the truth, and to rout the infidels" (7).

The surah therefore opens with a statement affirming that the spoils of the war are not the property of individual fighters, and that their distribution is up to God and His Messenger. This immediately overrules the need for any dispute or disagreement over how they are to be used or distributed. The battle's foremost objective was to establish that there were brave and selfless men among the Muslims willing to stand up for the truth.

The true believers are those whose hearts fill with awe at the mention of God, and whose faith grows stronger as His revelations are recited to them, and those who put their trust in their Lord. They observe prayer and give of what We have bestowed upon them. Such are the true believers. (2–4)

These, then, are some of the features of true faith: remembering God, fearing Him, reciting His words, trusting Him, giving of one's wealth. But, towards the end of the surah, we are informed of yet more of these features. The faithful are also

> those who have believed, emigrated [from Makkah to Madinah] and fought for the cause of God, and those who have sheltered and supported them—they are all true believers. (74)

True faith, therefore, also entails protecting one's religion by escaping to safety if and when necessary, fighting for the cause of God, and giving shelter and support to fellow believers. Elsewhere in the Qur'an, God says:

> True believers are those who believed in God and His Messenger and never wavered, and those who fought with their wealth and their lives for the cause of God. Such are the truthful. (*al-Ḥujurāt*: 15)

It is deep-seated sincerity, firm unshakable trust, and boundless generosity and sacrifice, giving up the dearest things any person can possess and cherish: wealth and life. In yet another surah, God says:

> The true believers are those who believed in God and His Messenger, and who, when gathered with him [Muhammad] over an important matter, would not leave without his permission. (*al-Nūr*: 62)

These verses collectively indicate clearly that true faith has many manifestations. It has no rigidly fixed definition, but is displayed in various actions and traits that are determined or dictated by circumstance. To prove their true faith, believers are accordingly required to rise to each occasion as it occurs. Thus, when the Muslims were told to leave aside the spoils they gained in the battle and await God's decision, they accepted and obeyed. They knew for certain that whatever God was to decide would be in their best interest.

When the Muslim expedition arrived at Badr, the Prophet issued his orders to the Muslims to prepare for battle against the unbelievers. The original purpose of the expedition was to intercept the Arab trade caravan, but now they found themselves preparing for a confrontation that was not of their own making. The reaction he received was mixed. Some thought that armed conflict would not be advisable since the Muslims had not been adequately prepared for it. They recommended waiting until other Muslims in Madinah had been mobilized and were able to join them at Badr, several kilometers south of Madinah. But the Prophet's opinion was that to decline the challenge of the Makkan Arabs at that particular moment would undermine the Muslim standing and demoralize their young community. He felt that God would not let him down at such a critical moment in the history of Islam, and so he consulted his Companions and his final decision was to go ahead and fight. We read in the surah:

As when your Lord rightly brought you out of your home to fight, but some of the believers were reluctant [to join you], arguing with you about the truth after it had become manifest, as though they were being led to death with their eyes wide open. (5–6)

The Prophet's hope for victory was justified by the words:

God promised you victory over one of the two groups [the Makkan trade caravan or the non-Muslim fighters], but your wish was to take possession of the one that was unarmed [the trade caravan]. (7)

The Muslims obviously wished for the easy prey, the soft target. But God had other plans for them, which became clear only after the battle was over and victory was secured. God's aim was to "establish the truth and demolish falsehood, in spite of the evil-doers" (8). The normal human reaction of believers in such critical circumstances would be to resort to calling on God for help and support. As the Muslims came to realize the strength and superiority of their enemy they turned to God: "When you [the Muslims] pleaded with your Lord to help you and He responded to your call, saying, 'I am sending you a thousand angels, one after the other'" (9). Although one angel would have been enough to rout the unbelievers, God wanted to reassure the Muslims by mentioning the number: "God made it so to give you good tidings, and so that your hearts are assured by it, for victory comes only from God. God is Mighty and Wise" (10).

Just before the fighting commenced, the Prophet is reported to have prayed long and hard, entreating God to grant him and the Muslims the victory he had been promised. He is said to have gone as far as saying: "If this group of Muslims [at Badr] are defeated You shall never be worshiped again on this earth."[17] With arms stretched high in the air and eyes fixed at the infinite skies, the Prophet was engrossed in earnest prayer. He saw Badr as a decisive battle, a last chance for Islam to triumph and spread. Abū Bakr, Muhammad's close confidant and a senior Companion, was standing behind him, allaying his fears and assuring him of God's certain victory. However, the Prophet persisted with his pleadings until God's words were revealed informing him of the outcome of the battle before it had even begun. In passing one may note that scholars have been intrigued by the contrast in Abū Bakr's confident attitude at Badr, reassuring the Prophet and calming him, and his anxiety when they were together inside a cave just outside Makkah, being pursued by Arabs who were trying to prevent them escaping to Madinah. The

---

[17] Narrated by al-Bukhārī and Muslim.

explanation lies in the fact that the Prophet's love of and devotion to God are supremely profound and deep—more than anybody else's. During the escape to Madinah, the Prophet was totally helpless and could, therefore, rely solely on God's aid and protection. But at Badr, he was in charge of an army possessing worldly means of material force. The Prophet's feeling was that despite the men and the force he had under his command, he was still in need of divine aid and support. No matter how strong or well-equipped a fighting force may be, victory would come only by the will of God.

And so it was. Divine intervention was evident. The rain fell to keep the ground firm under the Muslim fighters' feet. The Muslims were at one point overcome by sleep, as a token of God's protection, and all their apprehensions had evaporated. They experienced total inner peace and an overwhelming power to fight and fight well, while the enemy's camp fell into disarray, sustaining a most devastating defeat. "It is because they defied God and His Messenger. Those who defy God and His Messenger shall receive stern punishment" (13). Even so, God's aid can come only to those fighters who have already made all the possible preparations and taken all the necessary measures to ensure victory. The first of these were the brave fighters themselves who were ready to give up their lives for the cause of God and the magnificent rewards in the hereafter.

Human nature tends to favor life over death, and prefer the safety of comfort to hardship and deprivation. Nevertheless, the surah urges the believers by saying: "When you advance to engage the infidels in battle, do not give them your backs" (15). The fear within must be defeated first, and the value of one's life should be placed in a proper perspective. At Badr, a handful of brave and dedicated Muslims were able to demonstrate that numbers and size are not the most decisive factor when it comes to war between infidels and true believers in God. God explains how this is possible:

It was not you [Muslims] who slew them [non-Muslims] but it
was God who slew them. It was not the dust you [Muhammad]
threw at them but it was God who threw fear in their hearts, in
order to richly reward the believers. God is All-Hearing, All-
Knowing. (17)

God's plan led the Makkans to be lured into their downfall at Badr,
regardless of their larger numbers and superior force. The few who
had trusted in God and sought His aid and support were the ones to
deserve and reap the fruits of victory.

The surah addresses "the believers" directly six times in a very severe
manner over six crucial matters. Rather than allow the Muslims to
gloat over their victory or congratulate them for it, the surah tends
to opt for reprimand and suppression of any potential feelings of
euphoria or arrogance. On the first two occasions, verses 15 and 20,
God directs the Muslims to hold their ground and not to run away
from the battlefield. None of Prophet Muhammad's men did in fact
run away or has been reported to have even contemplated withdrawal from battle. However, it seems that in the wake of such a
clear victory, more emphasis had to be placed on God's role in that
victory and on dissuading the Muslims from ever looking to make
material gain out of it. Furthermore, there was a need to preempt
any inclination to quarrel over the spoils of the battle. Indeed, there
is constant prompting in the surah to the Muslims not to behave in a
way similar to their enemies, who were described as animal-like,
living for their desires and their self-satisfaction, and incapable of
comprehension or understanding. Indeed, the surah points out that
even if they were to comprehend, their arrogance and conceit
would prevent them from seeing the truth and submitting to God,
who tells them:

Believers, obey God and His Messenger, and do not turn away from Him, now that you have heard His revelation. Do not be like those who say, "We hear," but in fact they do not. (20–21)

Such a strong reprimand for a victorious army! And having likened the infidels to deaf and dumb animals, the surah turns to exhort the Muslims to: "Respond to God and the Messenger when he calls you to what gives you righteous life" (24), and continues to caution and forewarn:

And know full well that God can stand between a man and his heart, and before Him you shall all be assembled. Guard yourselves against a cataclysm of temptation that shall affect not only the wrong-doers among you, and know well that God is severe in punishment. (24–25)

This ominously stern statement is most astonishing, coming as it did after fifteen years of persecution, trepidation, and hard struggle. What could be the meaning behind it? Undoubtedly, God wanted to teach the Muslims a lesson in humility and warn them against becoming euphoric or overbearing as a result of their great victory over the non-Muslim Arabs of Makkah. He urges them to recall what things had been like for them before:

And remember how, when you were few and vulnerable in the land [of Makkah] and frightened that others would cut you off, He provided you with sanctuary [at Madinah], bolstered you with victory [at Badr] and gave you the good things of life, so that you might be thankful. (26)

In reminding the Muslims of their humble beginnings and the state they had been in before their glory, God would ensure that they would not be unduly disposed to amass material gains or turn to tyranny. Then comes another dire warning:

Believers, do not betray God or the Messenger, nor knowingly violate your trust. Know well that your wealth and your children are given to you as a means to put you to the test, and that God's reward is great. (27–28)

Victorious warriors everywhere return home jubilant and proud, and are met with garlands, drums, and celebrations before they receive their medals and decorations. But the Qur'an greets the triumphant Muslims of Badr, the first major battle between Muslims and non-Muslims, with criticism, advice, and instructions for moderation and humility. Western scholars and students of Islam, the so-called orientalists, should perhaps take note and review their assessment of the battle of Badr, which they have portrayed as the first tangible evidence for the militancy and the violent and aggressive nature of Islam.

The surah then recalls the early history of Islam and the Muslims before the Prophet had emigrated to Madinah:

Remember [Muhammad] how the unbelievers plotted either to take you captive or kill you or drive you out [of Makkah]. They scheme but God also schemes, and God is the more successful schemer. (30)

The non-Muslim Arabs were so blindly misguided that they challenged God: "...if this [the Qur'an] is Your revealed truth, rain down upon us stones from the sky or inflict upon us grievous punishment" (32). Disbelief can certainly be manifested and expressed in many ways. Without a doubt, the most vile type of disbelief is atheism or total denial of God, followed by polytheism where other gods are recognized and worshiped besides God or when God is claimed to have offspring that share His divinity. There are those, of course, who claim divine attributes for themselves. However, the vast majority of unbelievers are ordinary people who follow blindly and think that what they are doing is right and pleasing to God. Among the pagan Arabs of Makkah there were some who genuinely believed that idols could harm and benefit them and that they were the key and the way to the "Greater God."

The task of the prophets and messengers was to reinstate and reestablish the creed of pure monotheism, a task which required a great deal of time and effort. God says to the Prophet: "God would not punish them while you are still among them, nor would God punish them as long as they seek forgiveness" (33). Yet would this absolve them of punishment altogether? No, as they were still guilty of transgression and oppression:

> Why should God not punish them, since they debar others from the Sacred Mosque [the Ka'bah], although they are not its custodians. Its true custodians are those who fear God, but most of them [the unbelievers] do not know this. (34)

Their claim to the Sacred Ka'bah and their worship around it were to prove false and of no merit whatsoever. The true guardians who can claim the right of worship at the Ka'bah are believers in the one God who submit to Him alone. Not only did the unbelievers deny Islam but they also spent their wealth on the persecution and oppression of its followers. God says: "The unbelievers spend their wealth on debarring others from the path of God. They will spend it, but they shall regret that, and still be routed" (36). That was what happened to them at Badr. Even so, would that be the end of the road for them?

God directs the Prophet to offer them a chance to abandon their false ways and join the Muslims: "Tell the unbelievers that if they desist, their past deeds shall be forgiven, but if they renege, let them reflect upon the fate of earlier generations" (38). They should know then that those who persist in sin and oppression shall end in sorrow and grief. Far better for them to have learnt from the history of other nations and mended their ways, or else force shall continue to be used against them to subdue them and eradicate their false beliefs: "fight them until idolatry is eradicated and the religion of God shall reign supreme" (39).

Now the surah lashes out at those Muslims who had their eyes on the spoils at Badr, urging them not to fight over them and to preserve their faith and dignity, as dictated by the occasion and the noble task they had come out to undertake in the first place. We read that the spoils were to be divided into five portions, one of which would be spent on general public causes and the rest would go to the fighters. "Know that one fifth of the spoils you acquired goes to God, the Messenger, his kinsfolk, the orphans, the needy and the traveler" (41). We learn from the Prophet's own practise, and that of his successors that this arrangement was temporary and that other schemes were adopted in the allotment and distribution of the spoils of war under Islamic law, as happened during the reign of the second Caliph, ʿUmar ibn al-Khaṭṭāb. However, this subject requires some explanation. Muslims during the early days of Islam used to volunteer for fighting and received no wages in return for their efforts. Each fighter had to acquire his own weapons and make provision for his wife and children during his absence at war. They received no financial support or compensation from the state whatsoever. This made it quite fair and sensible that volunteer fighters should receive some compensation from the spoils they took in battle. When the state was able to organize its own regular army, pay the soldiers, provide weapons and equipment, treat the wounded, and look after the families of those who died, the spoils would then go directly to the state which would allocate them as it saw fit.

Note that the spoils issue is sandwiched in the surah between two other topics. One is the belligerence of the unbelievers who divert their wealth to oppose Islam, persecute the Muslims, and thwart their efforts to spread the faith; and the other is the divinely aided victory the Muslims had achieved at Badr. On the second subject, the surah says:

> When you [the Muslims] were on the near side of the valley and they [the unbelievers] were on the far side, with the caravan below you, had you agreed an appointment [to meet and fight] beforehand, you would have both failed to arrive in time; but God was to accomplish a purpose He had ordained, so that those who perished would perish for an evident reason, and those who survived would survive for an evident reason. God is All-Hearing, All-Knowing. (42)

It is clear that their defeat at Badr was a devastating blow for the non-Muslim Arabs of Makkah and their allies, while at the same time it boosted the status and morale of the Muslims and compensated them for fifteen years of hardship and suffering. Without a doubt, Badr represents a decisive and critical moment in the history of Islam.

And here comes the final proclamation that the surah conveys to the Muslims. It comprises six pieces of advice that would help them achieve victory. To rise to the top undoubtedly requires hard work, but to stay at the top would most certainly need an even greater effort. God says to the Muslims:

> Believers, when you meet an enemy, be firm and remember God in abundance, so that you may succeed. Obey God and His Messenger, and do not dispute with one another, lest you weaken and lose your strength, and remain steadfast because God is with those who persevere. Do not be like those who departed from their homes vainglorious in pursuit of vanity, and debar others from the path of God. (45–47)

To achieve victory, Muslims must therefore constantly remember God, seek His help, and know well that it is all for His sake. God will always look after and care for those that the fighters leave behind. Obedience and submission to God and His Messenger are vital elements in gaining victory. The unbelievers deny God because they have no true perception of or respect for Him, whereas Muslims are more likely to show God the reverence and esteem He deserves. Addressing his army before going into battle against the Persians, the second Caliph, 'Umar ibn al-Khaṭṭāb pleaded with them to shun sin and wrongdoing. He told them that he was more worried about them for the consequences of their misdemeanors than because of the strength of their enemy. Once the two warring camps were equally sinful, Muslims would be no match for their enemy and would stand no chance of victory because they were smaller in numbers and had inferior equipment.

It pains me when I look at the Muslim nation today and see how weak its moral and social fabric has become, and how disunited its peoples are. Our credentials for victory and success seem to diminish every time we take on an aggressor; we have become the world champions of lost causes. Although Muslims today comprise one fifth of the world population, their countries are divided, with some of them constantly at loggerheads with one another. Their enemies, however, have united their forces and consolidated their efforts, and have been giving the Muslims one beating after another. They are now in control of Muslim lands and capital while we are squabbling among ourselves and pursuing our petty wars against each other. We need the steadfastness and the perseverance referred to in the surah to maintain our devotion and loyalty to God and to face up to all temptation and hardship. Decadent, pleasure-seeking, and corrupt societies are not capable of mastering these qualities.

As for Islam's view on engaging in war and taking up arms, these are legitimate causes provided they are undertaken for reasons that satisfy God and serve the interests of Islam. Wars fought by Muslim governments these days can hardly be considered legitimate "Islamic" wars, because they are fought for nationalistic or partisan reasons. In most instances, they lead to further entrenchment of dictatorship and oppression. The fate of those who fight in wars not undertaken for the cause of God and Islam is described in the following verse:

> If only you could see the angels [at Badr] when they were taking the souls of the unbelievers! They were striking them on their faces and their backs, saying to them, "Taste the torment of the fire! This is the punishment for what your hands committed. God is not unjust to His servants." (50–51)

Tyranny and tyrants all through history have displayed similar traits and shared a similar fate. The unbelievers of Arabia who fought the Muslims had followed in the footsteps of

> Pharaoh's people and those who had gone before them. They disbelieved the revelations of God, and so God smote them for their sins. God is Mighty and stern in His retribution. (52)

Times may change, but the norms and laws set out by God remain valid for all time.

A non-Muslim Arab who had lost his sons in the battle of Badr was quoted to have said: "Were it not for Badr, these people [the Muslims] would have never prevailed." He was right. Badr marked a turning point in the history of Islam and the Muslims. Their power and influence received a strong boost, whereas it was the beginning of the end for their enemies, whose power and influence retracted as they began to lose control over Arabia. The writing was on the wall for the non-Muslim Arabs, whereas all the signs pointed to a great future for Islam in Arabia and beyond. God says:

> God relates to you the story of the city which was once safe and tranquil; its provisions came to it in abundance from every quarter, but its people denied God's favors. Therefore God afflicted it with famine and fear as punishment for what they did. (*al-Naḥl*: 112)

God would indeed deal with societies and nations according to the same criteria: "Because God does not change a favor He has bestowed on a people until they change their own situation" (53). Gratitude for and appreciation of God's favors are therefore essential and vital elements in ensuring the continuation and growth of divine favors. This was made very clear with respect to the Arabs taken prisoner by the Muslims at Badr. God says:

> Prophet, say to those who have been taken prisoner, "If God finds goodness in your hearts, He will compensate you with better than what you have lost, and He will forgive you. God is Forgiving and Merciful." But if they seek to betray you [Muhammad], remember that they had betrayed God earlier, and so He made you triumph over them. God is All-Knowing and Wise. (70–71)

The same goes for all who deny God's favors and spurn His commands and teachings. They will continue to be faithful as long as it serves their interests, otherwise they will just as easily and quickly renege and deny any obligation or responsibility. They are described thus: "The most evil creatures in the sight of God are the faithless who will not believe; those who break their agreements every time and have no fear of God" (55–56). Only the readiness to use force against force can make such people see sense. The Prophet was therefore instructed to hit back hard at his belligerent enemies to deter those following them. God commanded the

Prophet: "Therefore, whenever you overwhelm them in battle hit hard at them, as an example to those who are waiting behind them so that they may take warning" (57). If injustice and aggression can be stopped or deterred only by the use of force, then Muslims have no alternative but to resort to force. Muslims normally prefer peace and strive to preserve it, because it enables them to build and promote their Islamic way of life freely and openly. However, when they are prevented from pursuing their normal everyday Islamic obligations and duties, or subjected to suppression and persecution for their beliefs and opinions, then they have no alternative but to resist and fight back by all necessary and available means.

The interesting point here is that in the struggle between right and wrong, between the Muslims and their enemies, numbers, size, and material force do not matter because Muslims have God on their side. This is endorsed by the following verses:

> Prophet, urge the believers to fight. Twenty steadfast people of you will defeat two hundred [of the enemy], and a hundred will defeat a thousand unbelievers because these are devoid of understanding. (65)

The next verse, however, reduces the odds from one to ten to one to two, as follows:

> God has now lightened your burden, for He knows that you have some weakness. Therefore, a hundred steadfast people of you will defeat two hundred [of the enemy], and a thousand will defeat two thousand, all by God's permission. God is with those who are steadfast. (66)

This has, understandably, given rise to some debate among Muslim scholars and disagreement over which of the two ratios is the rule and which is the exception. My personal view is that the higher one is the rule, because the lower ratio applies at times of temporary weakness or in exceptional circumstances in which a Muslim fighting force is disadvantaged for reasons beyond its control. In modern warfare, it is perfectly possible for one foot soldier to hold up a whole battalion, or a few highly motivated, well-trained and well-equipped fighters to play havoc with an armored division. Examples of this have been witnessed in all recent wars. As God says elsewhere in the Qur'an: "Many a small band has, by the grace of God, defeated a mighty one; and God is with those who are steadfast" (*al-Baqarah*: 249).

Before coming to a close, the surah has one more topic to deal with concerning the force of brotherhood and fraternity that cement a Muslim community together, allowing it to act and grow as one whole. Such a bond is instigated by and devoted to the love of God and the advancement of His cause. Religious fraternity and ties bind people more strongly than any other, and Islam has made the Muslims, with all the numerous features and factors that discriminate and distinguish among them, into one unique entity, the like of which has not been seen throughout human history.

God says in the closing verses:

Those who have believed, emigrated [from Makkah to Madinah] and fought, with their wealth and their lives, for the cause of God and those who have sheltered and supported them [at Madinah], are allies one to another. But those who have believed but have not emigrated [to Madinah], you shall have no obligations towards them until they emigrate. (72)

It is because those Muslims had stayed behind in Makkah, at such a crucial time in the history of Islam, that they forfeited any help or support that would otherwise have been due to them from their fellow Muslims. As for the unbelievers, they were also allies one to another, and were to be accorded the same treatment:

Those who disbelieved are allies one to another. If you fail to distinguish in your alliances between the believers and the unbelievers, there will be disorder on earth and great corruption. (73)

The tragedy we face today is that the nation of Islam, which ought to be one and united, is in reality divided and fragmented into nations, nationalities, and states. At a body such as the United Nations, Muslims have no unified voice. In fact, some so-called leaders of Muslim countries have said openly that they did not consider Islam as a significant factor with any influence on their relations and alliances with other countries. In the constitutions and policies of Muslim countries, nationalist and ethnic prejudices take precedence over the brotherhood and fraternity of Islam. Worst of all, "nationalisms" such as Arab nationalism are championed and advocated by secularist groups such as the Arab Ba'th Socialist party and others. However, the Arabs are not viable as a nation without Islam, to which they owe their glory and place in the history of human civilization. The only way for us to emerge safely out of our contemporary predicament is to open the way for Islam to resume its proper role in our thinking and behavior, shape our internal and external relations, and control all aspects of our life.

SURAH 9

Al-Tawbah
(Repentance)

THIS SURAH, also known as *al-Barā'ah*, was revealed fifteen months before Prophet Muhammad's death in 632 AC, or twenty-two years after he began to receive the first revelations of the Qur'an. All through those twenty-two years, the Prophet's policy towards Islam's antagonists was dictated by the Qur'anic statement:

> If they disbelieve you [Muhammad] say, "My deeds are mine and your deeds are yours. You are not accountable for my actions, nor am I accountable for what you do." (*Yūnus*: 41)

It is a policy that any fair-minded person can see as nonbelligerent. However, some of Islam's detractors were determined that it should not take root or find its way into the rest of Arabia. They instigated a series of military expeditions and incursions against the Muslims, most of which resulted in their forces being routed and finally totally overwhelmed by Islam. Nevertheless, they did not learn the lesson, and as soon as one skirmish or battle was over, they would prepare for the next one. Eventually, they ended by becoming marauding hordes and raiders threatening the stability and security of the young state in Madinah, which made it necessary for the Muslims to fight them and take decisive action against them.

This is the aim of and the justification for the "disclaimer," given at the beginning of this surah, which was made on behalf of the Prophet through the Qur'anic revelation. Unfortunately, this has been generally misinterpreted and maliciously misconstrued by some scholars to show that the surah was in effect a "declaration of war" on all non-Muslims without exception. Phrases such as "... and fight the unbelievers altogether" have been culled from the text and taken to mean *all non-Muslims, without exception*, omitting the rest of the sentence which says, "as they too fight you altogether." Some also understood the word "people" in verse 3, which says "this is a proclamation from God and His Messenger to the people on the day of the greater pilgrimage..." to refer to all humankind, overlooking the exceptions and the comments that follow in the same verse. The exceptions are: "...those idolaters who have honored their treaties with you in every detail and have not aided anyone else against you" (4). The meaning could not be clearer or more unequivocal. The war, for which no apology should be made, was to be prosecuted specifically against those groups who had aided the enemies of Islam or violated the rights of Muslims.

The comments that follow are even more significant. In every conflict there are innocent people who have no inclination to support either of the fighting sides. The Prophet was instructed to guarantee such people safety and security and secure for them right of passage until they reached their safe lands. God says:

> And when an unbeliever seeks asylum with you, give him protection so that he may hear the words of God, and then enable him to reach his place of safety, because such people have no knowledge. (6)

How can this be an advocacy of aggression or warmongering? This misunderstanding seems to have arisen when some commentators and historians stretched the surah's statements to cover Muslim conquests which took place in later years in Egypt, Syria, and Iraq, and which were to allow the Muslims to sweep over the whole of the Persian and a large part of the Byzantine empires. However, this is a totally unjustified interpretation, since the Muslim armies did not target the capitals of those empires but moved over lands usurped by them to address those communities they had dominated by force. The armed conflicts that took place between these two powers or their proxies came about as a result of Muslim response to aggression and intimidation along with the desire to free those communities and release them from the grip of Byzantine or Persian political, cultural, and religious control. Only then were those communities able to learn about Islam and adopt its culture and way of life. The surah is therefore free of any charges of inciting Muslims to war, or of laying down religious or legal justifications for hostility or aggression against innocent or peaceful people. Let us have a closer look at its main themes and arguments.

The surah begins by directing the Prophet to give his enemies in Arabia, who were at war with the Muslims, a four-month grace period, a cessation of hostilities, during which they could review their attitude and plans towards Islam and the Muslims. God says to those enemies: "You shall go unmolested in the land for four months, but be warned that you shall not escape the reach of God and that God will bring humiliation on the unbelievers" (2). That concession was not in any way made out of weakness, and they should not, therefore, have been deceived by any strength they may have had or by any temptation to exploit the situation. The announcement was made during the pilgrimage to Makkah, in which, at that time, both Muslims and non-Muslims from all over the Arabian peninsula were able to participate. It was therefore made publicly and to the widest possible audience in Arabia at the time.

The surah continues to elaborate on that decision, putting an end to all possible charges and accusations of aggression leveled against the Muslims, saying:

How could God or His Messenger have any trust in the unbelievers, except those with whom you made treaties at the Sacred Mosque [at Makkah]. So long as they keep faith with you, keep faith with them. (7)

The distinction is very clear. Commitments and obligations must be respected and honored by all sides. However, the surah continues to warn:

How can they [the unbelievers] be trusted? If they prevail over you they will respect neither agreements nor obligations. They seek to appease you with their words only, but their hearts spurn you, and most of them are evil-doers. They exchange God's words for a pittance and debar others from His path, and their actions are damned. They respect no agreements with or obligations towards any of the believers, because they are transgressors. (8–10)

No aggression was committed by the Muslims, nor were they planning any aggression or breach of agreements. One detects, in fact, a certain degree of fear and apprehension on the part of the Muslims, who felt that those acts of intimidation indicated confidence and strength in the enemy camps. God sought to allay that fear by urging the Muslims to keep up the struggle and face the enemy head-on: "fight the leaders of unbelief because they are untrustworthy, so that they may desist" (12). Trust and honesty spring from faith and commitment to principle; the unscrupulous and devious cannot be trusted. The urging and prompting continue:

Would you not fight against those who have breached their agreements and were determined to drive the Prophet out, and who had attacked you first? Do you fear them? Surely, it is God you should fear most, if you are true believers. (13)

As we read on, it becomes clear that the groups singled out for attack were neither men of peace, nor people who could be trusted.

Rather, they were people with deep-seated grudges who had been agitating and instigating aggression and ferment against Islam and Muslims for a considerable time. As these are further exposed, the surah's tone becomes even more forceful:

> fight against them and God will chastise them at your hands and humiliate them. He will grant you victory over them and heal the spirit of the believers. He will take away the rancor that is in their hearts. (14–15)

Not a trace of warmongering or aggression against innocent or peaceable people is to be found in this passage. The fact is that to describe this surah as the turning point in Islam's attitude towards war is a gross misunderstanding. Muslims have always been and will continue to be peace-loving people, using open debate and persuasive peaceful means to introduce their religious beliefs and the principles of their way of life, and refusing to be intimidated or coerced.

Before the revelation of this surah, Arab paganism had been tolerated for twenty-two years. Even so, the non-Muslim Arabs continued to treat Islam as an outlawed religion in Makkah. They refused to recognize the new Muslim state emerging in Madinah and insisted on waging war against it, which resulted in some thirty battles and skirmishes. Arab casualties in all those long years of confrontation did not exceed two hundred; a figure that cannot be compared with the number of Protestants slaughtered by the French Catholics in the famous 1572 St. Bartholomew's Day Massacre in Paris. Indeed, over those twenty-two years, the Muslims were guided by the Qur'anic instructions that said:

> Now then, for that [reason], call [them to the Faith], adhere as commanded to the straight path and do not be led by their [the unbelievers'] desires. Say, "I believe in all the Books that God has

revealed and I have been commanded to exercise justice among you. God is our Lord and your Lord. We are accountable for our actions and you are accountable for your own actions. There is no [need for any] argument between us and you. God will bring us all together, and to Him we shall return." (*al-Shūrā*: 15)

Unfortunately, it all proved to be in vain. The motto of "you keep your religion and I shall keep mine," which the Muslims raised, had been rejected. The Arabs insisted on armed confrontation, and that was when the Muslims gave them four months to decide either to change their opinion and refrain from fomenting trouble or leave the region which had by then become a Muslim domain. The only other law set out by Islam at that time was that unbelievers should no longer be allowed to perform the pilgrimage to Makkah and no one should worship naked at the Ka'bah, as was the custom of pagan Arabs. All the idols around the Ka'bah were destroyed and Makkah purged of all forms of idol worship once and for all. This was affirmed in the surah thus:

It is no longer proper for the idolaters to attend God's mosques, since they have admitted to unbelief. Their works are in vain and in hellfire they shall abide for ever. God's mosques should be attended only by those who believe in God and the Last Day, who observe prayer and give alms and fear none but God. (17–18)

God was of course aware that Muhammad's life was drawing to an end. He went on to live for only fifteen months after this surah was revealed. It was time to prepare the Muslims for that tumultuous event and the grave consequences that were to follow it. So, although Arabia had been secured for Islam, the Byzantines were still posing a threat in the north. Some non-Muslim Arabs had fled there, still harboring grudges and aggressive designs against the Muslims. The potential for trouble was very real indeed. As soon as the news of Muhammad's death in 632 AC spread, rebellion broke out in various places around the fringes of the Arabian peninsula. It was left to the Prophet's first successor and Caliph, Abū Bakr, to put down the rebellion before the Muslims were able to feel completely secure and confident to take on the Byzantines, whose domination of Syria and Palestine represented a real obstacle to the northward spread of Islam.

Muslims are therefore basically opposed to war and are never the ones to start it. By the imperative of their own religion, they are taught not to impose their beliefs on others by force. Their mission is to impart and communicate God's message, leaving people free to decide whether to believe or reject it. Those who refuse to believe are free to pursue their lives in peace as long as they do not pose any obstacle or threat to Islam and the Muslims, who perceive their faith as the strongest and most vital binding relationship between God and humankind and that it is their responsibility to make others aware of it and provide them with the opportunity to understand and appreciate it. This is the basis of the relationship between Muslims and non-Muslims in Islamic society. God says elsewhere in the Qur'an: "Therefore, if they [the unbelievers] do not trouble you and cease their hostility towards you and offer you peace, God gives you no authority over them" (*al-Nisā': 90*). Those who take up arms against a Muslim state or parts of it must be met with force, and if they are overcome, they should be disarmed. Once that is achieved, they are free to lead their own lives and practise their beliefs in peace and security under the protection of the Muslim authorities, in return for which they have to pay a levy.

This is the background against which prescription of the *jizyah*, or exemption tax, came into being. It is not due from those who are neutral and have never taken up arms against the Muslim state. The surah gives ample explanation for the reasons behind the establishment of this tax, for it stipulates who should pay it. They are those who do not believe in God and the Last Day, who do not forbid what God and His Messenger have forbidden, and who do not follow the true religion, until they pay the exemption tax unreservedly and with humility. (29)

Those liable to pay such tax are described further as those who "wish to blow God's light out, but God insists on making His light prevail" (32). Some of their religious leaders are described as greedy and fraudulent people. On a closer look at how this exemption tax or *jizyah* was implemented, it becomes clear that as a result of the early huge waves of converts to Islam in countries such as Egypt, Persia, and Asia Minor, funds collected from this type of tax had greatly diminished—doubtless to the delight of Muslims! The aim of Muhammad's mission had never been to amass wealth but to spread God's guidance and mercy.

Abū Bakr, a senior Companion of Muhammad, led the Muslims during the pilgrimage to Makkah in the ninth year AH, 631 AC, in which non-Muslim Arabs were also allowed to participate. The pilgrimage organized a year later was led by the Prophet himself and was restricted to Muslims only, since God had declared in the Qur'an that "the idolaters are unclean, and should not, from this year onwards, approach the Sacred Mosque [at Makkah]" (28). Non-Muslim resistance to Islam in Arabia all but collapsed. All treaties and agreements hitherto in force came to an end, and the Prophet assumed total religious, political, and administrative sovereignty over the whole region. Idol worship was wiped out. And as a result of a series of confrontations with the Muslims, the last one of which took place during the sixth year after the Hijrah, 628 AC, at Khaybar in north-central Arabia, Jewish power and influence had also been shaken. Certainly Jews continued to live (and thrive) in peace as farmers and tradesmen in Madinah and various parts of Arabia, although they no longer had any organized military presence. Their religious and personal freedom was nonetheless fully guaranteed and protected. When the Prophet died, a shield of his was found in trust with a Jewish citizen of Madinah. Christian delegations were arriving at Madinah in droves, as they had done at Makkah previously, from various parts of Arabia and the surrounding regions to learn about the new religion, debate with the Prophet, and compare what they heard with their own beliefs and scriptures. Some of them of course converted to Islam. The Muslims saw no threat in any of that. The one major threat that was seen looming on the horizon was coming from forces of the Byzantine empire who were in control of Syria and Palestine in the north. The Byzantines were growing weary of Islam and began to take measures to curb its spread into their territories.

Here we must highlight the two following important facts:

1. Islam showed a great deal of amicability and warmth towards the Christians. When the Muslims of Makkah first thought of escaping the persecution of the Arabs, Prophet Muhammad instructed them, in 615 AC, to take refuge with the Negus, the Christian king of Abyssinia, whom he described as "a just and benevolent king." The Qur'an, in the surah entitled *al-Rūm*, or *The Romans*, expressed strong sympathy with the Christians in their war against the Persians in 615 AC in Syria and predicted that they would triumph in the following round of fighting.

2. In spite of this amity and sympathy, Islam was very clear in its rejection of the doctrine of the Trinity and the divinity of Jesus or the Holy Spirit. The Qur'an, first at Makkah and later on at Madinah, continued to emphasize these views and call upon Christians to review their doctrines and correct their beliefs. The last statement to be revealed in this connection appears in this surah condemning misguided Jews and Christians for taking:

their rabbis and monks, as well as the Messiah, son of Mary, as gods instead of God. They were commanded to worship but one God; there is no god but Him. Exalted be He above those they take as gods besides Him. (31)

In Islam God is one, without ancestry or offspring, supreme in His control over all creation. For religious leaders and clerics to set out laws and enforce religious practices and edicts of their own is nothing but heresy according to the Qur'an. Churches in America and Europe have blessed colonial wars and, more recently, sanctioned depraved practices such as homosexuality, without proper reference to authentic revelation.

The Byzantines had entrenched their power in regions north of the Arabian peninsula, and were known to resort to the use of force to prevent Islam from making inroads into their territory. Byzantine armies began to move southward to enforce Byzantine authority over the region, clashing with the Muslims twice, at Mu'tah in 629 AC, and at Tabūk in 630 AC. There is no doubt, however, that the Muslims wanted to have access to the populations of Byzantine territories to introduce them to Islam, a task they perceived to be their right. However, those early Muslims were also mindful of the fact that they could not use force or coercion to impose their religion on others. The Byzantines resisted that effort and appeared determined to advance their version of Christianity and impose it on their subjects. Their emperors had long rejected the Arius doctrine that Jesus was human and not divine. They had barred the eastern churches who differed with them radically over the nature of Christ, detained the Patriarch of Egypt, and killed his brother. However, the Muslims were fighting for freedom of religion. They entered Egypt and Syria, offering security and immunity from persecution and guaranteeing freedom of worship.

In anticipation of Byzantine resistance, the Prophet devoted much attention to removing the barriers placed in the way of Islam north of Arabia. He embarked on the mobilization of Muslim forces to enable them to deal with Byzantine intimidation. When the moment of confrontation arrived, the Byzantines were the most powerful nation on earth. They had defeated the Persians and become the dominant superpower in the area. No wonder, then, that some faint-hearted Muslims were shaken when war with the Byzantines became imminent. Yet another, more sinister, danger was also in evidence—the hypocrites or fifth-columnists working from within the Muslim community.

Thus the second half of the surah is devoted to exposing these hypocrites and waverers, while at the same time mobilizing loyal and sincere Muslims and spurring them to action. These are addressed in no uncertain terms:

> Believers, why is it that when it is said to you, "Go forth and strive for the cause of God," you drag your feet? Are you content with this life in preference to the life to come? The joys of this life are paltry compared with those of the life to come. If you do not go and strive, He will punish you sternly and replace you with others, and you shall do Him no harm whatsoever. (38–39)

The time had come to free the Muslim community and Muslim lands from the hypocrites, just as they had been emancipated from idolaters and traitors. The realm of Islam had to be defended and consolidated.

This surah comes as a series of intensive drills, a rich and powerful mixture of instructions and confidence boosters to prepare the Muslims to face the world without the divinely inspired leadership of Prophet Muhammad. The first drill was to be the confrontation with the Byzantines. It was to expose the strengths as well as many of the weaknesses of the Muslims on both the individual and collective levels.

People who strive for a just cause can triumph only when their loyalty to God is stronger than their enemy's loyalty to their aims and their leaders. God says: "Some people take other gods besides God and accord them adoration equal to that due to God, but the believers have stronger adoration for God" (*al-Baqarah*: 165). This becomes clearer at the critical times of conflict between true believers and ardent infidels. Hence we read in this surah the following:

> Say, "If your fathers, your sons, your brothers, your wives, your clan, the property you have acquired, the merchandise you fear may not be sold and the homes you love, are dearer to you than God, His Messenger, and the struggle for His cause, then wait until God's retribution arrives. God does not guide the evil-doers." (24)

When the time came to issue the orders to confront the Byzantines, the main factors prevalent at the time can be summarized as follows:

1. The Byzantines were the undisputed superpower in the region, especially after their decisive victory over the Persians.
2. The Muslims comprised a small section of the Arabs who had embraced the new religion, while the majority of the Arabs continued to be clients or subjects of either the Byzantine or the Persian empires.
3. The Muslim fighting force was relatively limited and lacking, as shown at the Mu'tah and Thātu al-Salāsil battles.
4. The young Muslim community was plagued from inside by the intrigues of the hypocrites and a handful of disgruntled groups who had not fully integrated into the new society and were prey to rumors, conspiracies, and outside influences.

The surah came at the right moment to overhaul the Muslim community and expose its weaknesses before it was too late. It lashes out at those who refuse to join in the fighting for the cause of Islam, saying:

Why is it that, when it is said to you, "Go forth and strive for the cause of God," you drag your feet? Are you content with this life in preference to the life to come? The joys of this life are paltry compared with those of the life to come. (38)

It rejects the absurd and false excuses given by the cowardly and the lazy:

Those who believe in God and the Last Day will not beg you [Muhammad] to exempt them from striving with their wealth and their lives. God best knows the righteous. Those who seek such exemption are people who disbelieve in God and the Last Day, whose hearts are filled with doubt and are left wavering. (44–45)

Further on in the surah we read:

Those Arabs turned up with excuses, asking to be exempt [from helping in fighting off the Romans], while those who denied God and His Messenger actually stayed behind. Those of them who disbelieved shall be afflicted with a terrible anguish. (90)

Indeed, most of those who had chosen to stay behind and refused to join the fighting were the faint-hearted and the skeptics who had no confidence in Islam. One such person had the temerity to beg the Prophet to allow him to remain at home because he feared the temptation, as he put it, of beautiful Byzantine women. He would only go and fight, he said, if the Prophet were to guarantee him that he would not fall for them:

Some of them say, "Give me leave to stay behind, and do not expose me to temptation." Surely they have already succumbed to temptation. Hell shall engulf the unbelievers. (49)

It is only natural that those who go and fight should meet with many challenges, tests, and temptations, including the possibility of defeat, which is a severe test in itself. Nevertheless, the surah reassures the Prophet and the Muslims:

If you [Muhammad] meet with success, it grieves them [the unbelievers], but if a disaster befalls you, they say, "We have already taken our precautions," and they turn away rejoicing. Say, "Nothing shall befall us except what God has predestined for us. He is our Guardian. Let the believers put their trust in God." (50–51)

The battle of Tabūk in 630 AC brought down God's wrath upon the hypocrites within the Muslim community. It uncovered their intrigues and completely exposed them to the rest of the community. This, as stated earlier, was necessary to purge the Muslim ranks and clear the way for a new phase in history and the spread of Islam. Hypocrites and traitors could destroy any society, no matter how politically and economically powerful. God says in the surah: "Do not be taken in by their wealth or their [numerous] offspring. God only seeks to punish them in this life, and they shall die unbelievers" (55). The hypocrites came in many disguises. There were the greedy self-centered ones who were happy only if they received financial gifts from the Prophet, or else they would curse and complain. These the surah describes as follows: "Some of them speak ill of you [Muhammad] with respect to the alms. If they are given of them, they are contented, but if they are not they grow resentful" (58). Some of them spread rumors and invented malicious lies about the Prophet personally, but then would go and swear to him that they never said such things. They would take advantage of the Prophet's magnanimity and benevolence. The surah exposes that aspect of their conduct too:

> Some of them speak ill of the Prophet, saying, "He believes every-thing he hears." Say, "He hears only what is good for you. He believes in God and trusts the believers. He is a blessing to those of you who have believed, but those who harm the Messenger of God shall receive stern punishment." (61)

These hypocrites had their own supporters and special groups who used to meet privately. As a phenomenon, they grew gra-dually from a series of different situations and developments, and for varying reasons. Although the Qur'an has referred to them on many occasions, the present surah has gone all the way in expos-ing them and condemning their aims and activities. This was dictated, as already mentioned, by the decisive and critical phase reached by Islam when the surah was revealed. The Muslims had just established their religious and political hegemony over the Arabian peninsula and were preparing to face the strongest super-power of the time, the Byzantine empire. If Prophet Muhammad were to waver at that moment, the very existence and the whole future of Islam would have been put in jeopardy. Indeed, the hypocrites and the non-Muslim Arabs were looking forward with hope to the Muslims being routed by the Byzantines and that would have been the end of Islam. However, the Qur'an was assuring Muhammad and the Muslims: "It is He who has sent forth His Messenger with guidance and the religion of truth to make it prevail over all religions, even though the idolaters may not like it" (33).

Events began to move very fast, contrary to the expectations of the hypocrites whose activities reached a climax as the Muslims were preparing for battle.

Whenever a chapter [of the Qur'an] was revealed, saying, "Believe in God and strive behind His Messenger," the rich ones among them [the hypocrites] would ask your permission, saying, "Let us remain with those who will stay behind." They were content to be with those who stayed behind, and their hearts were sealed, and so they shall not understand. But the Messenger and those who believed with him strove with their wealth and their lives. They shall have all the good things, and they shall be successful. (86–88)

The phenomenon of the hypocrites first appeared after the Muslims emigrated to Madinah in 622 AC. It had by then become clear that Islam was more than just a system of beliefs, it was a political entity also, severely reducing the chances of any tribal or religious personalities in Arabia who were aspiring to political or religious leadership and power. Some had simply found it too much to abandon their paganistic and promiscuous way of life to which they had been accustomed. In the initial stages, Islam's approach in dealing with this problem was soft and tolerant. As the threat from the hypocrites, which is well documented in those surahs revealed in Madinah, started to grow, it became apparent in this surah that the Qur'an was adopting a more unequivocal approach towards them, which culminated in the showdown portrayed in this surah. Indeed, the Qur'an's remarks about the hypocrites, in the aftermath of the Muslim defeat at Uḥud, were quite mild:

The disaster that befell you on the day the two camps clashed was by the will of God, in order to identify the true believers. It was also to identify the hypocrites who, when it was said to them, "Come and fight for the cause of God, or lend support," they said, "We would have gone with you, had we known that there would be real fighting." On that day they were closer to unbelief than to belief. (*Āl ʿImrān*: 166–67)

But, the tone of the Qur'an was distinctly different regarding those who refused to join the fighting at Tabūk. God says admonishingly:

> They swear by God that they had said nothing [against the Prophet].
> Yet, they uttered the word of unbelief and renounced Islam after
> embracing it. They also sought to achieve what they had failed to
> achieve [killing the Prophet]. Are they resentful only because God
> and His Messenger were generous to them? (74)

Some of the hypocrites pledged that if they became rich they would be kind to others and contribute to the war effort, but they went back on their promises. The surah again exposes them:

> Some of them made pledges to God, saying, "If He gives us of His
> bounty we will give in charity and be righteous." But when God
> bestowed upon them of His grace, they became niggardly, turning
> their backs, and they recanted. He [God] then allowed hypocrisy to
> set in within their hearts until the day they meet Him. (75–77)

And so it became inevitable that the Muslim society should be protected against the hypocrites. They were becoming too cynical and unfairly critical of those good and sincere Muslims who were trying to do their best for Islam and the Muslims. This was threatening to undermine the unity and welfare of the whole community:

> Those that censure the believers who volunteer to give for charity,
> and scoff at those who give according to their means, shall have God
> scoff at them. A woeful chastening awaits them. (79)

The hypocrites had been growing in power and in numbers. They had embarked on building a mosque of their own as an alternative to the mosque of the Prophet, where they could recruit supporters, hold meetings, and plan their campaigns. The surah again exposes these plans mercilessly:

> And there are those [hypocrites] who built a rival mosque to promote unbelief and cause divisions among the believers, and in anticipation of the coming of him [an Arab monk called Abū 'Āmir] who had declared war against God and His Messenger. They swear that they mean well, but God bears witness that they are lying. (107)

This provided the Prophet and the Muslims with tangible proof of their evil intentions and their determination to sow division and discord in the heart of the Muslim community. However, the Muslims, led by the Prophet himself, decided to demolish that alternative mosque in obedience to the Qur'an:

> You shall never worship in it. The mosque that was from the first day founded on piety is best suited for you to worship in. It is attended by men who love to remain pure, and God loves those who remain pure. (108)

The surah continues relentlessly with its confrontation of the hypocrites to ensure that the Muslim community is free from their influence as from that of the idolaters. Eventually, the Muslims were ready to undertake the bigger and more important task of taking Islam out of Arabia and into the rest of the world, as "a mercy and a blessing to all humanity" (*al-Anbiyā'*: 107) as the Qur'an put it.

The surah then makes it very clear to the Muslims that in order to carry out that great task, they will be required to make vital and substantial sacrifices. It says: "God has offered to trade the lives and wealth of the believers for Paradise" (111). What does this solemn transaction entail? Why does the trade-off include such valuable possessions? The reward is obviously commensurate with the sacrifices being made. The enormity of the task ahead and the vehemence of the opposition with which Islam would be resisted and fought justified the high price. If God's cause was to be upheld and defended, vital preparations needed to be made. God says: "Believers, bear arms against the unbelievers dwelling around you, and let them feel your strength, and be sure that God is with the righteous" (123).

Who were those neighboring infidels against whom the Muslims were commanded to wage war? The overall drift of the surah indicates that they were the Byzantines. They had come from imperial Constantinople, sweeping across Anatolia and Syria, settling right on the edge of the Arabian peninsula. They were the masters of their time; their aims were to usurp, colonize, exploit, and dominate. They had no respect for the beliefs or lives of other nations, while their own beliefs were false and distorted.

The deal that emerges concerns the followers of Moses, Jesus, and Muhammad, whose part is to work together for the advancement and enforcement of God's messages and cause. The surah says:

God has offered to trade the lives and wealth of the believers for Paradise. They fight for the cause of God, slay, and are slain. It is a true promise He has made in the Torah, the Gospel, and in the Qur'an. And who is more true to his promise than God? (111)

The contrast between the opening passages of the surah and its ending cannot be more striking. It begins with a "disclaimer" and stern warnings to those who have breached their treaties and agreements with God and the Muslims, but ends with assurances from God that He has sent Prophet Muhammad, out of mercy and care for humanity, as a blessing to all. Muhammad was a prophet and a leader working for peace but if fighting was unavoidable, then so be it! His objective was to establish justice, remove oppression, and alleviate suffering. The surah ends with calm reassuring words:

There has now come to you a Messenger from among yourselves who grieves for your predicament and who cares for you, and who is kind and merciful to the believers. If they turn away, say, "God is All-Sufficient for me. There is no god but Him. I put my trust in Him. He is the Lord of the Glorious Throne." (128–29)

Muhammad went to war only to eradicate oppression and injustice. Once basic rights and freedoms are guaranteed and protected, war becomes an abominable crime. This is a fact established in this surah which puts war and peace in a clear and proper perspective, and can in no sense therefore be described as a "declaration of war."

SURAH 10

Yūnus
(Jonah)

THIS SURAH WAS REVEALED at Makkah and it shares many of the features we have seen in *al-Anʿām* and *al-Isrāʾ*. Like them, its main theme is to guide man to his Creator by means of observation, contemplation, and reflection upon God's vast creation. In my view, the Makkan approach which was, in the first instance, directed at the pagan Arabs who were mainly idol-worshipers, and which proved very effective in stimulating their minds and reviving their dormant intellectual instincts that would lead them to believe in God and put their trust in Him, would be just as effective today in dealing with agnostics, secularists, and other atheists.

One of the general features of the Qur'an, both Makkan and Madinan sections, is that it is a Book about and for humanity which appeals in earnest to the human mind and soul to wake up, seek God, and prepare for meeting Him. As a matter of course, the Qur'an had also to address the People of the Book, the Jews and the Christians, and deal with the various issues and disputes they raised. This is most apparent during the Madinan period.

Idol-worshipers were overwhelmed by materialistic logic, which relied entirely on the senses, and were totally preoccupied by worldly gain. This is reminiscent of what we observe in many contemporary societies. In these societies, the majority of people have no interest in God or any yearning to know Him. Established religion has no lasting impact on these people, because they live for the moment and have no cause to look beyond the life they live here on earth. They leave matters of faith to the church and its clergy who perpetrate and promote largely outdated, lifeless rituals and practices, based on dogma and doctrines which are devoid of common sense and rational appeal.

A loyal student of Orientalism advanced the ludicrous idea that the Qur'an's approach in Makkah had been emotional, but had turned rational in Madinah as a result of influence from the Jewish community there. But, when the same scholar came to point to the use of scientific logic in the sections of the Qur'an revealed in Madinah, he quoted: "Were there other gods in them [the heavens and the earth] besides God, they would have been ruined; exalted be God, Lord of the Throne, above their claims" (*al-Anbiyā'*: 22), which is in fact a Makkan one.

The Qur'an constantly emphasizes the fact that our existence in this life is no more than a prelude to another one, and that those who recognize God and acknowledge Him here shall have the privilege of knowing Him there as well. We may conclude that existence is a continuum, part of which is experienced here in this life, the realm of obligation and responsibility, while the rest is experienced in the life hereafter, the realm of accountability and reward. Yet, modern thinking rejects such notions and concepts. In this world, we are required to praise God, thank Him, and carry out the obligations and duties with which He has charged us. But in the hereafter, all that shall be done instinctively and without any effort or struggle on our part:

> Those who believe and do good works, their Lord shall guide them through their faith. Rivers will run at their feet in gardens of delight. Their prayer therein will be, "Glory to You, Lord" and their greeting, "Peace," and their closing prayer will be, "Praise be to God, Lord of all." (9–10)

Those who enjoy the worship and company of God in this life shall also enjoy complete happiness in His company in the hereafter. But those who reject Him now shall have nothing pleasant to look forward to in the life to come. Total preoccupation with the 'here and now' and the deliberate neglect of what might lie beyond the present is a distinguishing feature of contemporary Western civilization. Advocates of traditional religions in the West repeatedly defend ideas and dogma which have no influence whatsoever on the direction in which this civilization is heading: "Those who entertain no hope of meeting Us, being pleased and contented with the life of this world, and those who are heedless[18] of Our revelations, shall have the fire as their abode in return for their deeds" (7–8). Because it relies on the senses alone, materialist logic finds the Qur'an, and divine revelation as a whole, eccentric and incomprehensible. It is an arrogant and pretentious approach which only recognizes empi-rical evidence for everything! *Yūnus* opens with a depiction of this attitude:

> These are verses of the Book overflowing with wisdom. Does it seem so strange to [your] people that We have revealed to one of them [Muhammad] that he should warn people and give good tidings to those who believe that they shall have a privileged status with their Lord? The unbelievers say, "This man is a skilled sorcerer." (1–2)

Religious belief (*imān*) is an instinctive and natural human inclination. It is only blurred or obscured by dogmatic 'professional' clergy or dogged ignoramuses.

This surah highlights the close and direct link between belief and good deeds (*al-ʿamal al-ṣāliḥ*). The one, *inter alia*, necessitates

---

[18] *Ghāfil* is usually translated as "oblivious" which means "unaware": one cannot be held responsible for something one is unaware of. We feel that "heedless" is better as it means one is aware of something, but chooses to ignore it. Therefore, one has responsibility for that decision. (Ed.)

the other. God says: "So that He may equitably reward those who believe and do good works" (4), and: "Those who believe and do good works, their Lord shall guide them through their faith" (9). Therefore, *imān* and *al-ʿamal al-ṣāliḥ* go hand-in-hand. Several verses later, God says: "For those who do good there is a good reward and more besides" (26). The Arabic term used here is *iḥsān*, which denotes the combination in life between pure and sincere faith and righteous deeds within the framework of God's guidance and under His care. The surah also offers a definition of *awliyā' Allah* meaning "the friends of God" or "the men of God" as those who have faith and fear God. It says: "Men of God have nothing to fear or to regret; they are those who have faith and are God-fearing" (62–63).

It is fitting to recall here what Prophet Muhammad is quoted in the surah as saying: "...Were I to disobey my Lord, I fear the punishment of an awesome day" (15). One may also recall God's words: "Those who have done evil, it shall be rewarded with like evil, and humiliation shall overwhelm them. They shall have no protection against God," (27) and: "God does not put right the deeds of those who perpetrate corruption" (81).

Muslims are treated as any other religious community by being told that, when it comes to judgment, they shall not be afforded any special concessions. For them, as for all mankind, rewards shall be commensurate with deeds and actions. Since earlier communities and nations had no special treatment and were rewarded in line with their activities, the Muslims would be no exception. The surah says:

> We have destroyed generations before you when they indulged in wrong-doing. Their Messengers came to them with veritable signs but they would not believe. Thus shall We recompense the guilty. Then We appointed you their successors on earth, so that We might see how you would fare. (13–14)

From beginning to end, the surah stresses the following simple fact:

> Say, "People, the truth has come to you from your Lord; whoever is rightly-guided it is for his own good, and whoever goes astray would do so at his own peril. I [Muhammad] am not your guardian." Observe what is revealed to you [Muhammad], and be patient until God's judgment is passed... (108–109)

By comparing this fair statement, which comes at the end of the surah, with what Prophet Muhammad is told at its beginning, that he should "warn people and give good tidings to those who believe that they shall have a privileged status with their Lord" (2), it becomes clear that the essence of the Prophet's mission was to establish justice, affirm what is right, and eradicate evil. It is further clear from the surah as a whole that the Muslim community he was to establish would be a fair and virtuous one whose members acknowledge God, call on others to recognize Him, follow His path, and look forward to meeting Him in the hereafter.

Such a community is incorruptible by wealth and power and is free of oppression. It is a community that rejects and opposes tyrants and dictators and calls on the Lord, as Moses is quoted in the surah to have done, to "destroy their wealth and harden their hearts so that they would never believe until they face the harrowing punishment" (88).

In this surah we also find a satisfactory answer to that perennial question: Who is this God whom human beings are obliged to worship and shall face in the hereafter? It says:

> Your Lord is He who created the heavens and the earth in six days and then ascended the Throne. He takes charge of all affairs; none has power to intercede with Him except with His permission. Such is your Lord, therefore worship Him. Will you not take heed? (3)

This brief and concise answer is expanded further by other verses in the surah. There are in this world thousands upon thousands of creatures and living things that are in constant need of food and sustenance. Who provides for them and who helps them grow and develop? Who gave these creatures eyes with which to see and ears with which to hear? These and other organs are in fact infinitely intricate and complex systems working together in total harmony within one body. But how was it possible that the same intricate system is being duplicated in millions upon millions of creatures?

> Ask them, "Who provides for you out of the heavens and the earth? Who holds control over hearing and sight? Who brings forth the living from the dead and the dead from the living? Who is in charge of all affairs?" They will reply, "God." Say, "Will you not fear God, then?" (31)

A farmer plants a single seed in the soil out of which a thousand other seeds are produced. Who transforms the pungent inedible soil into a cereal with a pleasant aroma and an appetizing taste? Who transforms organic waste and dead matter into sugar-cane, and into roses and flowers reflecting thousands of the most exquisite shades and colors and emitting a vast array of delectable scents and smells? "Such, then, is God, your true Lord. What is there beyond the truth but error? How then can you turn away?" (32).

What is even more baffling is that, rather than reflecting upon creation and trying to understand how it came about, some people have opted to look into the identity and the nature of the Creator Himself. There can be nothing more wasteful or futile. This retrogression in human intellectual pursuits has been one of the main causes of the decline of Islamic civilization as well as the universal setbacks it has suffered. While we would not indulge in giving specific and precise interpretations to Qur'anic verses describing the attributes of God, we believe with certainty that God Almighty ascended the Throne in a manner befitting His might and glory. We further believe that God rules over the whole cosmos, which He alone had created without precedent or the help of a partner, and that He continues to have control over all its affairs. God, as such, would not be in need of help from any of His creation; He is Mighty and Self-Sufficient. This is a fact which all human beings must acknowledge and understand so that they would need to turn to no one else for help except to God Almighty. The Qur'an strongly censures those who neglect this truth, as it says:

> They worship instead of God others that can neither harm nor benefit them, and say, "These are our intercessors with God." Say, "Do you presume to inform God of what He knows to exist neither in the heavens nor on earth?" Glory to Him, and exalted be He far above the gods they take besides Him. (18)

Human beings, not least the prophets themselves, and the angels, not least Gabriel, are servants of God who recognize His authority and bow to His power.

> They do not speak till He has spoken and they act by His command. He knows what is before them and what is behind them. They intercede for none save whom He accepts, and they are in awe of His fear. (*al-Anbiyā'*: 27–28)

Once faith is built on a sound basis, man's relationship with God develops along proper lines, and he is rewarded with eternal life in the hereafter, where this life becomes a pleasant memory. Decades of a lifetime and the millennia of human history pass like hours,

...and the day He brings them [the unbelievers] all together again, as though they had sojourned [in this world] but for a day's hour, they will get to be acquainted with each other...(45)

But that day always seems so far in the future, leading some people to conclude wrongly that it will never in fact come.

Elsewhere in the Qur'an, we are told how in the early days of Islam at Madinah, the Israelites used to greet the Muslims with offensive words.

> When they [the Israelites] come to you, they salute you in words which God does not greet you with, and ask themselves, "Why does God not punish us for what we say?" Hell shall be punishment enough for them; they shall burn in it, a wretched fate. (al-Mujādilah: 8)

They ask for their punishment to come and the longer it is delayed the more doubtful they become. The polytheists would also be so confident and convinced of their belief that they would deny God's existence, reject His Messenger and oppose him, and insist on daring God to punish them.

> They challenge you [Muhammad] to hasten on the scourge. Had the time for it not been already appointed, the scourge would have long since overtaken them. It will come down upon them suddenly, and catch them unawares. They challenge you to hasten the scourge, but hell shall encompass the unbelievers. (al-ʿAnkabūt: 53–54)

This tendency to challenge God is what *Yūnus* refers to in the following verse:

> Were God to hasten to bring upon men what is evil the way men hasten in seeking what is good, their term would have long since

expired. Therefore We allow those who entertain no hope of meeting Us to wallow blindly in their transgression. (11)

This warning echoes that given in verse 58 of *al-Kahf* that:

were your Lord, the Merciful, to punish them [the unbelievers] for what they had done, He would have inflicted punishment on them sooner; but they have a pre-set appointment which they can never avoid.

Would it not be more appropriate for the unbelievers to take advantage of the delay in bringing punishment upon them to repent and make up for their misdeeds?

Say, "Do you see if His punishment should come to you by night or by day, what portion of it would the sinners wish to hasten? Would you then believe in it at last, when it actually comes to pass?" [It will be said:] "Ah! now? and you wanted [aforetime] to hasten it on!" (50–51)

Would any human being be able to avoid God's punishment when its appointed time comes? How could they, when God Almighty is in control of everything? "Indeed, to God belongs all that is in the heavens and the earth. God's promise will certainly be fulfilled, though most of them [the unbelievers] are oblivious" (55). That is said with respect to all creation, but as for rational beings, God specifically says: "Indeed, to God belong all who are in the heavens and the earth. Those they worship besides God are not real gods and they are only following their fancies..." (66).

Since the whole universe and all creatures in it, human and otherwise, are subservient to God and are fully obedient to His will, how can anyone or anything escape His power or punishment? "They ask you [Muhammad], 'Is it [the punishment] really true?' Say, 'Indeed, by my Lord, it is true, and you are completely powerless'" (53). What causes some people to think that it is so strange or extraordinary that God should choose a man to receive His revelation and convey it on His behalf to others? One reason could be sheer envy, as we are told in verse 8 of surah *Ṣād*. Another could be angry reaction at criticism of pagan practices and traditions. Naturally, those who inherit polytheist or material beliefs, rituals or traditions are loath to accept monotheism (*tawḥīd*). *Yūnus* is one of the surahs that champions the concept of *tawḥīd*, and it goes to elaborate lengths to explain and define it. It puts forward evidence from the natural world to demonstrate the existence of God and His unparalleled power, saying:

> It was He that made the sun to shine and the moon to brighten up and ordained her phases so that you may learn to compute the seasons and the years. God has created all this only for a purpose. He expounds His signs for those people who understand. (5)

The Arabs rejected divine revelation and the surah cites three instances of their denunciation of the Qur'an. first: "When Our clear revelations are recited to them, those who entertain no hope of meeting Us say, 'Bring us a different Qur'an, or make some change in this one...'" (15). What they really wanted was that Muhammad and the Qur'an should praise and honor their gods and endorse their erroneous beliefs and bogus religious traditions. But, the Qur'an instructs him: "Say, 'It is not for me to change it of my own accord. I follow only what is revealed to me...'" (15). The Prophet was also directed to point out to his people that he had already lived among them up to the age of forty years before he received any revelation or criticized their religious beliefs. He was only prompted to do so when God's revelation had been communicated to him, and he could not possibly disobey God's commands. "Say, 'Had God so willed, I would have never recited it to you, nor would He have made you aware of it. I had spent a whole lifetime among you before it was revealed. Do you not understand?'" (16) Second:

> This Qur'an could not have been composed by anyone other than God. It is a confirmation of the revelation received before it and a full exposition of the Book. Beyond doubt it is from the Lord of all creation. (37)

No fair-minded person reading the Qur'an with an objective mind would fail to realize immediately that Muhammad could not have made up a single word of it. It is also evident that the main thread going through all of its text is that of the truth. Were the Qur'an to be the work of anyone else, some of its contents would not have made any sense at all. Were we to accept those allegations, it would imply that the human mind was more capable, as it were, of producing divine revelation than even God Himself! For, the Qur'an puts forward the strongest possible defense of the principle of *tawḥīd* and is the most eloquent and convincing exposition of its meaning and ramifications. If the Qur'an was the work of a human mind, however, what would stop its detractors who make that claim from producing works similar to it?

> Or do they [the unbelievers] claim that he [Muhammad] had invented it [the Qur'an] himself. Say, "Bring me a single surah that matches any of it, and call on whom you may besides God to help you, if you are truthful." (38)

The Qur'an challenges the Arabs to seek the help of anyone, human or otherwise, who would be skilled or knowledgeable enough to compose something similar to the Qur'an or even a single short surah. Centuries have now passed and the challenge remains. No one has yet been able to take it up. "Indeed, they disbelieved it before they were able to comprehend it, and before its prophecy has been fulfilled..." (39). Because of their ignorance, God has delayed their punishment in case they might retract their claims and come to their senses. The surah explains that "some of them believe in it, while others do not; but your Lord best knows the evil-doers" (40). What attitude should then be adopted towards the skeptics and the cynics? "If they do not believe you, say, 'My deeds are my own and your deeds are your own. You are not accountable for my actions, nor am I accountable for what you do'" (41). No other book has been open to so much scrutiny, criticism and free debate. The Qur'an has been presented to humankind under no duress or coercion. Those with honest and open minds can only respond to it positively; others who reject it are blinded with ignorance and prejudice.

> Some of them listen to you; but you cannot make the deaf hear while they are incapable of understanding. Some of them look at you; but you cannot make the blind see [the truth] while they are bereft of sight. (42–43)

Third: God says in this surah: "People, an admonition has come to you from your Lord, a panacea for the ailments of the heart, a guidance and a mercy for those who believe" (57). Indeed, the Qur'an is all of this. It nourishes and cultivates the soul. It acts as a deterrent against sinful behavior. It shields the heart and the mind against doubt, cynicism and uncertainty. In short, it provides those who accept it with material as well as psychological and spiritual advantage and enrichment. No one who understands the Qur'an and opens his/her heart and mind to it should ever feel that anyone else is happier or more fortunate. "Say, 'Let them [the believers] rejoice in the grace and mercy of God, for these are far better than all the riches they [the unbelievers] may accumulate.'" (58) With the Qur'an as his reference and guide in every situation, Prophet Muhammad was able to fight and overcome all the foes who rose up against him and was able to refute and rebut their arguments. The surah echoes this, saying:

> No matter what you [Muhammad] may be engaged in, however much of the Qur'an you recite, and whatever anyone else may be doing, We shall be there to witness it as you embark upon it. Not an atom's weight on earth or in the heavens escapes your Lord, nothing smaller or bigger than that, but is recorded in a comprehensive book. (61)

The ending of the surah reinforces its opening statements that *tawḥīd* is the essence and the cornerstone of belief and faith in God. As the opening verses of the surah refer to people's surprise at the fact that God had chosen to send His revelations to an ordinary human being, the last verse reassures Prophet Muhammad, directing him to: "Follow what has been revealed to you and be patient in adversity until God passes His judgment. For He is the best judge" (109).

The dispute over the Qur'an has been very intense, and we as Muslims have no doubt whatsoever that it is the incontrovertible Truth. The meanings of some of its linguistic constructions and expressions are sometimes not immediately clear to those not sufficiently versed in the Arabic language and its rhetoric, and some have misunderstood or misinterpreted them. In everyday language, you may urge someone not to be lethargic or to maintain certain standards of character or behavior, without him being lazy or showing a decline in behavior. Your objective would be to provoke, encourage and stimulate that person to move forward and improve. Similarly, God urges His Prophet, saying: "If you doubt what We have revealed to you, ask those who have read the scriptures before you..." (94). Would this be a recommendation that Muhammad should seek counsel with, or direction from, those who advocate the doctrine of the Trinity or who claim that God appeared in human form? The answer must be a resounding 'No!' Such queries by the Prophet as cited in the Qur'an are either rhetorical or polemical or for reasons of instruction and education.

Tawḥīd, from the standpoint of Islam, is beyond dispute: God is one, eternal, He begot none nor was He begotten, and there is none equal to Him. Likewise, the contentious allegations made by the Israelites with respect to God and His Messengers, as cited in the surah, are refuted. Hence the Prophet is told:

> The truth has come to you from your Lord; therefore do not doubt it. Do not be among those who deny the revelations of God or else you shall be with the losers. Those on whom your Lord's judgment has been passed shall never believe, even if they were to be given every possible sign [of the truth], until they come face to face with the woeful punishment. (94–97)

Simple honest logic and common sense dictate that God can never be two or three or more, nor could He be in any way likened to a human being.

Humans are vulnerable and weak. When faced with hardship, they can easily feel completely helpless, despondent and exposed. Crises can overwhelm and subdue them. It is at such moments that many people seek God and plead for His support and assistance. However, in some cases, as soon as the difficulty is overcome and the ordeal is over, people's faith dwindles and their yearning towards God fades away. The surah tells us:

> When misfortune befalls man, he pleads to Us lying on his side, sitting or standing. But as soon as We lift his affliction, he goes on as if he had never sought Our help. Thus their misdeeds are made to appear fair to the wrong-doers. (12)

This is indeed a scurrilous and disgraceful trait. One ought always to remember who had come to one's rescue when needed, and to acknowledge the favor one owes God Almighty and be loyal to Him under all circumstances. The surah depicts this type of behavior in more detail, saying:

He it is who enables you to travel on land and sea. And [behold what happens] when you go to sea in ships: [they go to sea in ships,] and they sail on in them in a favorable wind, and they rejoice thereat—until there comes upon them a tempest, and waves surge towards them from all sides, so that they believe themselves to be encompassed [by death; and then] they call unto God, [at that moment] sincere in their faith in Him alone, "If You will but save us from this, we shall most certainly be among the grateful!" Yet as soon as He has saved them from this [danger], lo! they behave outrageously on earth, offending against all right! O men! All your outrageous deeds are bound to fall back upon your own selves! [You care only for] the enjoyment of life in this world: [but remember that] in the end unto Us you must return, whereupon We shall make you truly understand all that you were doing [in life]. (22–23)

It is a psychological fact of human behavior that when one is drowning or surrounded by danger, one turns to no one else but God Almighty. He is the only resort and the real savior. The vexing question here is why, once saved, does humankind immediately forget the hand that saved it and deny the favor extended to it? It is indeed a serious and disturbing defect of human nature that needs urgent and constant attention. Those who at times of triumph and prosperity forget everything else deserve whatever punishment they may receive. Such punishment is usually swift and comes when it is least expected. God says:

Life in this world is like the water We send down from the sky which is absorbed by the earth's plants, crops and vegetation which are consumed by men and beasts. As the earth flourishes and becomes adorned luxuriantly, and as people begin to feel they have full control over it, Our judgment falls upon them by night or during daylight and We turn it into stubble as if it had never blossomed hitherto. Thus do We expound the signs for people who reflect. (24)

Sudden and severe disasters are painful and devastating to individuals as well as to society as a whole. Calamities usually strike the crops shortly before the harvest and just as the owners begin to feel confident that it is within their grasp to gather it. This makes the impact that much more calamitous. As humans, every one of us is entitled to call upon God's help and support when hardship strikes, but when God comes to our help, we are expected to show gratitude and to continue to do so even after the ordeal is over. Humanity cannot stand alone and shall always be in need of God's help and support. The example given in the surah applies in many different situations in human life. Humankind's arrogance and conceit provoke God's anger which can strike suddenly and with devastating consequences.

Before the surah is brought to a close, God Almighty, in a few tender, gentle words, instructs His Messenger to address humankind with the following reassuring advice:

Say, "People! If you are still in doubt about my faith, I am not going to worship what you worship besides God. I will but worship God who will cause you all to die. I have been commanded to be with the believers." Dedicate yourself to the true faith and do not be one of the polytheists. You shall not call upon anything besides God which can neither benefit nor harm you, for, if you do, you shall be one of the wrong-doers. If God afflicts you with misfortune none can lift it but He; and if He wills you something good none can take it away. He bestows His favor upon whom He wills of His servants. He is Forgiving and Compassionate. (104–107)

This strong and direct link between humans and God is the very essence of the faith of Islam. Other "gods" or powers, if any, are worth nothing. Humanity's fears and hopes are all dependent and focused on and directed towards God alone. This fact forms the solid foundation upon which everyday relations and dealings between humans are based.

In this surah we also encounter several brief accounts of earlier nations and religious communities such as that of prophet Yūnus whose name gives the surah its title. The implication here is that the Arabs of Makkah, whom Prophet Muhammad was addressing with the new faith of Islam, might receive the same pleasant fate as that of Jonah's people. The Makkan Arabs, in fact, had in the initial stages fiercely and relentlessly opposed Islam. They resisted and fought against it for close to twenty years. Eventually, however they embraced it and devoted all their energies and resources to defending and spreading it. The people of Jonah fared much better than other communities, such as the people of Hūd. God says:

> For, alas, there has never yet been any community that attained to faith [in its entirety,] and thereupon benefited by its faith, except the people of Jonah. When they came to believe, We removed from them the suffering of disgrace [which otherwise would have befallen them even] in the life of this world, and allowed them to enjoy their life during the time allotted to them. (98)

Whenever these narratives are cited in the Qur'an they usually reflect situations and experiences faced by Prophet Muhammad himself, in order for him to draw lessons from them. Hence the similarity in dealing with such situations, despite the time-space factor. The prophet Noah (Nūḥ), we are told, faced his people's resistance and opposition for nine and a half centuries, but he persisted steadfastly with his mission of calling them to God. The surah tells us:

> Tell them [the Arabs] of the story of Noah who said to his people, "If it offends you, my people, that I should live among you and remind you of God's revelations, let me tell you that I have put my trust in God. Decide upon your course of action and call forth all your gods, declare your intentions and take whatever action you want to take towards me without delay. If you turn away from me, remember that I demand nothing from you in return. I seek my recompense from God alone. I am commanded to be one of those who submit to God..." (71–72)

What Noah had told his people was the same as Muhammad would tell his people. God's prophets and messengers are honest individuals devoted to the service of God. They seek no personal gain, material or otherwise, in carrying out their missions and obligations towards God and their fellow men. The surah cites experiences of other messengers and their communities, with extensive coverage of episodes from the history of the Pharaoh of Egypt and the Israelites and their prophets and leaders. The Pharaohs were destroyed as a result of their arrogance, oppression and exploitation of their people, while the Israelites took advantage of the privilege of receiving divine revelation and abused the favor and trust God had invested in them. In this context God says:

> We settled the children of Israel in a blessed land and provided them with all manner of good things. They came to disagree among

themselves only after knowledge was given to them. Your Lord will judge between them on the Day of Resurrection concerning their disputes. (93)

These words are a warning to the Muslims to avoid the pitfalls which had plagued the Israelites. Muslims are required to shoulder the responsibility of carrying God's message with honesty and dedication.

Hūd
(Hūd)

LIKE SEVERAL QUR'ANIC surahs, *Hūd* opens with a reference to the Qur'an as "a Book, whose verses are well expressed and made plain, from the All-Wise and All-Knowing" (1). This should cause no surprise because the Qur'an contains proof of its veracity, universality, and everlasting qualities. It was delivered to Prophet Muhammad to pass on to all humankind with the aim of saving them from the dire consequences and the wilderness of polytheism (*shirk*), and lead them into the enlightened realm of *tawḥīd,* the bed-rock of salvation. The surah continues: "Worship none but God. I come to warn you and give you good tidings on His behalf" (2).

The task Muhammad had been charged with was not an easy or ordinary one. When his trusted friend and Companion, Abū Bakr, pointed out to him that his hair was going gray, Muhammad was reported to have said: "Indeed! *Hūd* and its sister surahs [reportedly *al-Wāqiʿah, al-Mursalāt, al-Nabaʾ* and *al-Takwīr*] are the cause of my graying hair."[19] I have always been intrigued by this comment and this spurred me to try and find out what it is about this surah that would cause the Prophet's hair to go gray. Would it be the trials and ordeals suffered by earlier nations? But these have been cited in other surahs too. Could the cause be the stubbornness and dogged attitude of some of his own people towards him? The surah says:

---

[19] Narrated by al-Tirmidhī in his *Sunan.*

They conceal what is in their hearts to hide it from God, but when they cover themselves up with their clothes He still knows what they conceal and what they reveal. God knows what is in the deepest recesses of their hearts. (5)

However, I discounted that as the reason for the troubling impact the surah had on the Prophet because he was too strong for that. I therefore decided to look for another reason.

The surah has one outstanding feature which distinguishes it from the rest. It is full of intensely personal, direct and indirect instructions addressed to Prophet Muhammad, using the first personal pronoun, emphasizing the weight and the significance of the mission he had undertaken. Consider the following words:

You [Muhammad] may be contemplating to omit some of what is being revealed to you or feeling distressed by it because they [the unbelievers] say, "If only he was given a treasure or had an angel sent down to him!" But you are merely a warner, and God has control over everything. (12)

Such instances recur scores of times, as we shall see, throughout the surah. Here is another example:

God alone has knowledge of the unseen in the heavens and the earth. All things shall be referred to Him for judgment. Serve Him, and put all your trust in Him. Your Lord is never unaware of what you do. (123)

Commenting on the fate of Noah's people following the Flood, God says to Muhammad:

217

These are accounts from the past We reveal to you. Neither you nor your people have hitherto known of them. Have patience, the God-fearing shall have a joyful end. (49)

Half way through this narration, Muhammad is again directly addressed with the following words:

Or do they [the Arabs] say, "He [Muhammad] had made it [the Qur'an] up himself"? If so, say to them, "If I had made it up, the consequences of my crime shall fall on me; but I plead innocence of your crimes." (35)

How could Muhammad have invented the Qur'an himself or interfered with its authorship when he had had a solid, untarnished reputation for honesty and truthfulness all his life?

The surah goes on to relate the encounter of the people of ʿĀd with their messenger Hūd and their mistreatment of him. God says: "When Our judgment came to pass, We delivered Hūd through Our mercy, together with those who believed with him, and We spared them a horrifying scourge" (58). This is followed, yet again, with a comment directed at Muhammad, saying: "Such were ʿĀd. They denied the revelations of their Lord, and disobeyed His Messengers and followed the words of every headstrong tyrant" (59). Thamūd, the people of the prophet Ṣāliḥ, had met with a similar fate. God informed Muhammad: "When Our judgment came to pass, We delivered Ṣāliḥ, through Our mercy, and those who followed him from the ignominy of that day. Your Lord is Mighty, All-Powerful" (66). God then tells the Messenger of the end of the people of Lot, whose city was totally destroyed and submerged underground, saying:

When Our judgment came to pass, We turned the city upside down and rained on it a torrent of stones of baked clay, especially marked

from your Lord. Such punishment is never far off from the transgressors. (82–83)

The last sentence is meant as a warning to the Arabs who were bent
on repudiating Muhammad and his message.

Commenting on the destruction of the Pharaohs and the people of
Madyan, God informs the Prophet, saying: "We have recounted to
you the annals of these nations; some have survived, while others
have ceased to exist" (100). Towards the end of the surah we note
that God addresses Muhammad directly on not less than eighteen
occasions, in addition to the accompanying instructions, which goes
to explain the enormity of the impact the surah must have had on
Prophet Muhammad personally. This section starts from verse 101,
which says:

> We never wronged them, but they wronged themselves. When
> your Lord's judgment came upon them, the gods they called upon
> besides God availed them nothing; they only added to their ruin.

The words "your Lord" are repeated three times in two consecutive
verses, thus:

> The damned shall be cast into the fire, where, groaning and
> moaning, they shall abide as long as the heavens and the earth
> exist, unless your Lord wills otherwise. Your Lord accomplishes
> whatever He wills. As for the blessed ones, they shall abide in
> Paradise for as long as the heavens and the earth continue to exist,
> unless your Lord wills otherwise. They shall enjoy endless bounty.
> (106–108)

Then God says to Prophet Muhammad: "Have no doubts about what these people [the Arabs] worship" (109). He reminds him of the fact that God's judgment of humankind shall be deferred till the appointed day, saying: "And but for a word from your Lord, already decreed, their fate would have long been sealed" (110). Until that day should come, Prophet Muhammad was obliged to endure and persist with his mission, facing whatever hardships and tribulations arose in the meantime. Those who follow Muhammad would also be expected to do likewise: "Follow then the right path as you have been commanded, together with those who have repented with you, and do not transgress" (112). He was further instructed to: "Attend to prayer, morning, afternoon, and during the earlier part of the night. Good deeds make up for evil ones. This is an admonition for thoughtful people" (114). Personal speech does not end there. Let us read on.

> Your Lord would never wrongfully destroy towns while their inhabitants are righteous. Had your Lord so willed, He would have made all humankind as one nation, but they continue to differ among themselves, except for those towards whom God has shown mercy. It is to this end that He has created them. The word of your Lord shall be fulfilled, "I will fill hell with jinn and humans, altogether." (117–119)

Would not Muhammad be justified, after all this, in saying that surah *Hūd* had given him gray hairs?

Casual misdemeanors in one's life are not necessarily detrimental, as they can be mitigated by repentance. As a matter of fact, these could very well act as a kind of "vaccine" that immunizes a person against committing similar offenses against God, and hence they may be of benefit. Evil actions that bring about the destruction of

SURAH II • *Hūd*

nations and communities are those which set in and take root within the fabric of society as a whole. In certain societies, evil and seditious behavior become the accepted norm, protected by and incorporated into their laws and conventions. The opposite is then seen as odd, unconventional, and out of the ordinary. Morality, decency, and righteousness are frowned upon and branded eccentric and reactionary.

Prophet Lot spent a great deal of time and energy trying to persuade his people to desist from the practise of sodomy, but they ignored his advice. Let us look at what they had to say to him. "His [Lot's] people's only answer was, 'Banish them [Lot and his followers] from your city, because they are chaste people'" (al-A'rāf: 82). Indecency, perversion, and immoral practices had become the norm. Usually, corrupt civilizations first sink into decadence and then decline. Symptoms of such decline have now become visible in several aspects of contemporary Western civilization. Today's humans need to be addressed again with the opening verse of this surah:

> Serve none but God. I [Muhammad] have come to you to warn you and give you good tidings on His behalf. Seek forgiveness of your Lord and turn to Him in repentance and He will provide well for you until an appointed time. He will reward each one on merit. But if you give no heed, I fear for you the punishment of an apocalyptic day. (2–3)

The immediate promise for those who repent is 'a good and decent life'. Human nature being what it is, people prefer comfortable living, and since life is a trial, God reassures human beings that as long as they believe and submit themselves to Him, He will provide them with comfort and enjoyment in this life and enable them to progress and improve their lot. The surah tells us that the same promise was made to the people of Hūd, when he said to them:

221

"My people, seek the forgiveness of your Lord and turn to Him in repentance and He will bring incessant rain upon you from the sky and add strength to your strength. Do not turn away from Him and become transgressors." They said, "Hūd, you have come to us with no clear proof. We will not forsake our gods at your behest, nor will we believe in you." (52–53)

On the face of it, their argument appears to have a ring of rationality to it, but in reality it is devoid of all sense. When Hūd called upon them to believe in the one God, their reaction was one of total astonishment, saying: "'We can see you are a foolish man, and, what is more, we think you are lying'" (*al-Aʿrāf*: 66). He patiently persisted, saying: "'My people, I am not foolish; I am a Messenger sent by the Lord of all creation to convey to you the messages of my Lord and to give you honest counsel'" (*al-Aʿrāf*: 67–68).

Each account related in the Qur'an highlights certain aspects of the history of the nations and communities concerned. When these narratives are put together, a full picture emerges. This in itself is a specialist feature in the interpretation and understanding of the Qur'an. *Hūd* relates such accounts in a rather similar way to *al-Aʿrāf*, but on Noah (Nūḥ), for instance, we find in this surah certain details, extending over almost two pages, that are not given in *al-Aʿrāf* which devotes only a few lines to the same story. Noah's pleading with God to save his own son from drowning in the Flood cannot fail to move one's emotions and sympathy. "Noah called out to his Lord, saying, 'Lord, my son is of my kith and kin. Your promise is the truth, and You are the best of judges'" (45). Noah was asking God to keep His promise to save him and his family from the Flood, but God's swift reply came saying:

"Noah, he is certainly not of your kith and kin; he is of unrighteous conduct. Do not ask me about matters you have no knowledge about. I warn you not to be like the ignorant ones." (46)

Some scholars have erroneously interpreted these statements to mean that Noah's wife had been unfaithful and the son was the result of an illicit relationship. This cannot be farther from the truth. Noah's wife only betrayed him in as much as she had joined those of her people who rejected Noah's prophethood and opposed his mission, thereby allying herself with his enemies. Her son also took a similar stand which stripped him of affinity to Noah, as God pointed out to him, according to the surah. The son was swept away by the flood like all the others, and that is what the surah refers to in saying: "God said, 'Noah, he does not belong with your people; his actions are not virtuous. Do not ask Me about matters you know nothing of...'" (46). Noah's response was as to be expected: obliging and compliant. He said:

"I seek refuge in You, my Lord, for asking You about matters of which I have no knowledge. If You do not forgive me and have mercy on me, I shall certainly be a loser." God said, "Noah, come ashore with peace and blessings from Us upon you and upon some of the nations who are with you." (47–48)

God's revelation to all prophets and messengers since Noah and Abraham right up to Moses, Jesus and Muhammad has always given precedence to ties of faith and religion over those of blood and ancestry. To love or to hate, for the sake of God, has always been the basis for agreement or disharmony, respectively, among individuals and communities.

Having given us an account of Noah's experience, the surah moves on to relate how Hūd's people reacted with such hostility and opposition to his efforts to guide them to God. His only solace was to say: "'I have put my trust in God, my Lord and your Lord. There is not a single living creature whose destiny He does not control. My Lord's path is right and straight'" (56). When divine retribution fell upon those people it was swift and decisive. Those mighty and powerful, giant-like people were overwhelmed by gales that snatched them off: "like trunks of uprooted palm-trees..." (*al-Qamar:* 20). Hūd and his followers were rescued. "When Our judgment came to pass, We delivered Hūd through Our mercy, together with those who believed with him, from a horrifying scourge" (58). The depressing episode is concluded with the following damning comment:

> Such were ʿĀd. They denied the revelations of their Lord, disobeyed His Messengers and followed the lead of every headstrong tyrant. They were cursed in this world and cursed they shall be on the Day of Judgment. ʿĀd had rejected their Lord. ʿĀd, the people of Hūd, are damned for ever. (59–60)

Once God's judgment is passed on those communities that reject Him and oppose His will, no matter how powerful and strong they might be, they would stand no chance in the face of God's mighty punishment. It remains an historic mystery why the ancient Arabized tribes such as ʿĀd and Thamūd were so unanimously headstrong in opposing God's prophets and persecuting their followers. It had brought them nothing but destruction and annihilation.

The surah then moves on to relate accounts of the tribe of Thamūd and their response to prophet Ṣāliḥ. The caste system which had emerged during the time of Noah seems to have become even more entrenched in the Thamūd society. Most of Ṣāliḥ's followers, however, seem to have come from the lower and less powerful classes. In another surah, we read that:

The haughty elders of his people said to the believers from among the oppressed ones, "Do you really believe that Ṣāliḥ is sent by his Lord?" They answered, "We believe in the message with which he has been sent." The haughty elders said, "We totally reject that in which you have believed." (*al-Aʿrāf*: 75–76)

For individuals to choose to destroy themselves is reproachable enough, but when whole communities opt for mass self-destruction the crime becomes compounded. Racial discrimination stems basically from blind arrogance, and it is the underlying cause behind all the ethnic strife seen in the world, past and present. Racial prejudice was rife among the Arabs before Islam, and it is particularly deeply ingrained in many societies of today. A pre-Islamic Arab poet, ʿAmr ibn Kulthūm, put it rather arrogantly when he said:

> When we go to fetch water,
> We draw the purest and the sweetest.
> Others drink muddy and soiled water.

Even though the spread of ethnocentric tendencies such as fascism and Nazism has been relatively curtailed in recent times, national bigotry, chauvinistic scientific and scholarly research and self-centered personal greed remain the collective backbone of "modern nationalism." All other loyalties have been swept away. But humanity has not been created to further such bigoted, narrow-minded causes. God says:

And to Thamūd We sent their compatriot Ṣāliḥ. He said, "My people, worship God; you have no god but Him. He brought you into being out of the earth and established you on it. Seek His forgiveness, and turn to Him in repentance. My Lord is near and answers all." (61)

This statement is not addressed to Thamūd alone, but rather to all generations of humankind whom God had charged at various stages of human history with cultivating the earth and developing it, and who have an obligation to worship God and serve Him until such a day that they will all return to Him for accountability and final judgment. One can only feel a sense of frustration and despondency at the prevailing state of affairs in the world today. It is torn between two camps. One, the Muslim camp, upholds and represents authentic religious faith but has no say in, or influence on, world affairs or destiny. The other, the materialist power-hungry West, and its allies all over the world, is effectively the dominant culture in today's world. It has harnessed the earth's energies and resources and ventured to conquer outer space, but has no room for God in its philosophy or way of life.

Thamūd were closer to the latter type, powerful but faithless. Their prophet Ṣāliḥ advised them to:

> "Remember when God made you inherit ʿĀd and placed you in a high position on earth and enabled you to build palaces and carve dwellings in the mountains. Remember God's favors and do not go about ruining the earth." (al-Aʿrāf: 74)

But, blinded by arrogance and corrupted by power, Thamūd proved ungrateful and showed no respect for their obligations towards God, and so: "When Our judgment came to pass, We, through Our mercy, spared Ṣāliḥ and those who believed with him from the ignominy of that day of doom. Your Lord is All-Powerful and Mighty" (66).

Thamūd were succeeded by Madyan who combined political deviation with economic corruption. In *al-Aʿrāf*, as we had seen earlier in this work, a relentless campaign was waged on political corruption and oppression, but in *Hūd* the attack is directed against economic corruption. In the former, God appeals to the people of Madyan to tolerate and open their minds to views opposed to their own, and to examine notions and concepts before rejecting them or persecuting those holding them. They were told by prophet Shuʿayb:

> "Not to stand in every street threatening and debarring from the path of God those who believe in Him, nor seek to distort the truth. Remember when you were few and He increased your number, and consider the fate of the wrong-doers." (*al-Aʿrāf*: 86)

Madyan broke up into two camps: one believed and embraced the faith and the other refused and rejected it, waging war on the believers. Shuʿayb believed that time would settle the issue and that the truth would come out and falsehood be exposed. He asked for the believers not to be harassed or intimidated, saying:

> "And if a group of you believes in the message with which I have been sent and another does not, be patient until God judges this issue between us, for He is the best of judges." (*al-Aʿrāf*: 87)

But Madyan also opted for refusal and confrontation with Shuʿayb and his followers. "The haughty elders of his people said, 'Return to our fold, Shuʿayb, or we shall banish you and all your followers from our city'" (*al-Aʿrāf*: 88). In *Hūd*, however, the emphasis, together with the condemnation of polytheist belief, is on fighting economic corruption. It says:

> And to the people of Madyan We sent their compatriot Shuʿayb who said to them, "My people, worship God, for you have no god but Him. Do not give short weight or measure. I can see that you are in good prosperity, and I fear for you the scourge of a calamitous day. My people, be fair and give just weight and measure, do not defraud your fellow men and do not spread evil in the land..."
> (84–85)

Madyan's response to their prophet was a mixture of disdain and mockery:

> They said, "Shuʿayb, do your prayers teach you that we should abandon what our fathers and forefathers have worshiped, or not use our wealth in whatever way we please? Tell us, you are the wise and sensible one!" (87)

Effectively, they had rejected the belief in one God, *tawḥīd*, and consequently failed to live a clean, moral and just way of life. As Shuʿayb continued to advise and guide them, they said: "'We see you as very weak among us, and were it not for your tribe we would have stoned you, as we have no respect for you'" (91). Their end was just as tragic and catastrophic as that of their predecessors: "Like Thamūd, gone are the people of Madyan" (95).

Then comes an account of the Pharaohs, who suffered a similar fate, whose story we shall encounter in more detail in later surahs. Having related these accounts, God says to Muhammad: "We recount to you the history of these Messengers in order to put courage in your heart. Through this you are given the truth, as well as lessons and admonitions for the believers" (120). Surah *Hūd* has given extensive coverage to episodes from the history of earlier nations in order to show Muhammad that there was nothing new about his own people's rejection of his call. The battle between right and wrong, truth and falsehood, would never cease, but the final triumph shall be to the believers' side.

These days, we hear a great deal about the "Big Bang" theory which tries to explain the origins of our vast infinite universe and how the galaxies, stars and planets came to assume their present shapes and positions within it. The time span taken by this process and the distances between these terrestrial bodies are yet to be determined and understood fully. The question that arises when thinking about these phenomena is: What about the Creator who brought all this about? His attributes and powers can only be limitless and beyond definition or comprehension; with no beginning or end. More astounding than the creation of the universe is the ability to maintain its stability and keep it going as an amazing dynamic and harmonious system. Similarly, more incredible than the creation of a single fetus is providing it with the environment and all the elements necessary for its growth and development. The whole question becomes even more difficult to fathom and comprehend when we think of the countless multitude of creatures that exist and have existed in this world. The surah asserts that:

> There is not a single creature on earth but God provides its suste-
> nance. He knows its dwelling and its resting-place, all of which is
> recorded in a comprehensive book. (6)

When it comes to the question of scale, humans represent a very small and insignificant part in this world, and the size of our planet Earth is negligible compared to the rest of this vast universe. Science has not been able to determine the limits of the universe. But faith and belief tell us that to God, dimensions of time and space have no meaning and that He is Omnipresent; He is everywhere at all times. One may very well wish to reflect deeper on this question and try even to understand how God might "sit" on His throne, which is said in the surah to exist "on water," but how can we visualize or comprehend this concept when we are not able to understand or decipher a great deal else of what exists and happens in the natural world much closer to us?

It is far more productive and conducive for man to concentrate on understanding the purpose of his existence in this world and work towards fulfilling it. The surah says: "It is He who created the heavens and the earth in six days, while His throne was on water, in order to find out who are the most righteous among you" (7). Notwithstanding the ignorance of many people, this life is but a prelude to a far better and everlasting one: "When you [Muhammad] say, 'After death you shall be raised to life,' the unbelievers say, 'This is nothing but plain sorcery'" (7). Due to their ignorance, the counter argument of the ingenuous and foolish skeptics usually is: "If punishment is true, let it happen sooner rather than later. If it really happens, then we will believe". But what use would their belief in punishment be after it comes? "If We defer their punishment till the appointed time, they ask, 'What is delaying it?' When it arrives nothing would ward it off them, and the consequences of their mocking would overwhelm them" (8).

One of the most serious flaws in human nature is that of hastiness and impetuosity. Many humans live for the moment. They turn to God for help and support in the face of adversity and affliction, but as soon as these are alleviated or lifted, they behave as if they had never occurred.

> If We show man Our mercy and then take it away from him, he yields to despair and becomes ungrateful. And if after adversity We let him taste good fortune, he would say, "I am no longer in danger," and grows jubilant and proud. This is always the case, except for those who believe and do good works. They shall be forgiven and receive a rich reward. (9–11)

Human beings need divine revelation to explain to them where they have come from and where they are going. This is at its most effective when it comes with such force and eloquence as the Qur'an did when it was first introduced to the Arabs. It posed a challenge to its detractors. In *Yūnus*, the Arabs were invited to produce even a single passage or chapter comparable to the Qur'an, but in *Hūd*, the challenge is raised, and they are asked to produce ten chapters of a similar quality as the Qur'an. It is certainly more demoralizing and humiliating to be asked to take a test when one has already failed an easier one.

> Would they say, "He [Muhammad] has invented it himself"? Say to them, "Produce ten invented chapters like it, and call on whom you will besides God, if you are truthful." But if they fail to respond to you, then be certain that it has been revealed with God's knowledge and that there is no god but Him. Will you then submit and be Muslims? (13–14)

When Muhammad introduced Islam to people, he had the support of God behind him. Prior to that there were the prophecies of earlier Scriptures which anticipated his coming. With such support he would have nothing to fear.

> Are they [the unbelievers] to be compared with those who have received evident revelation from their Lord, supported by a witness from Him and heralded by a predecessor, the Book of Moses, a guide and blessing? These believe in it, but the factions who do not accept it shall certainly end up in the fire. Therefore, do not have any doubts about it. It is the truth from your Lord; yet most people have no faith (17).

Muhammad and the prophets and messengers before him could not have fabricated the revelation they received. All they advocated was that there was only one God whom men would meet for judgment; those who do good deeds would reside in Paradise and those who transgress would end up in hell. How could this be taken as a lie and why would those good and trustworthy men fabricate such ideas? Earlier communities who denied and rejected such beliefs had met their destruction, for which archaeological and historic evidence can still be found today. The Qur'an brings the attitudes and reactions of those generations into question, wondering why none of their people had been honest and brave enough to stand up and defend the truth and warn their own people. The surah says:

> Were there, among the nations that have gone before you, any upright men who stood against evil, except the few We delivered from among them? The transgressors pursued their worldly pleasures and thus became guilty. Your Lord would never destroy towns while their inhabitants are righteous and upright. (116–117)

To discharge his obligations towards God, Prophet Muhammad had adopted a proper and clear approach. Many continue to argue among themselves. Controversy and disagreement continue to plague mankind and tear it apart. God was then, and is now, perfectly capable of making the whole of mankind live as one peaceful and harmonious nation, believing in the same faith, but He has elected, in His transcendent wisdom, to give human beings the freedom to choose and to use their own perceptions and powers of discernment. "Had your Lord so willed, He would have made the whole of mankind as one nation, but they shall continue to differ among themselves" (118). Strife, competition, and rivalry are inherent features of human nature and behavior, and they are essential for human progress and development. The next verse, however, qualifies the statement by adding:

> ...Except for those whom your Lord blesses with mercy. It is for this end He has created them. The word of your Lord shall be fulfilled, "I will fill hell with jinn and humans, all together." (119)

God could have easily created humankind with totally different faculties and features, like the angels, for instance, who have no power to disobey, or like the animals who behave instinctively and are not accountable for their actions. However, He gave humankind the ability to differentiate between right and wrong and the freedom to choose between them. The consequences of that choice are therefore paramount in causing humankind either to sink to the depths of despair or rise to the stratosphere of happiness and progress.

SURAH 12

Yūsuf
(Joseph)

IT IS POSSIBLE that, from a very early age, young Joseph felt that he had a special position in God's estimation. He had clearly shown certain qualities of leadership. For, although he was the youngest of his brothers, his personality had stood out amongst them and he won their father's love more than any of them had done. Jacob (Yaʿqūb), Joseph's father, inherited religious leadership from his own father, Isaac (Isḥāq), who had inherited it from his father, Abraham (Ibrāhīm). Would it be unreasonable to deduce that Joseph would expect to inherit that legacy from his father, Jacob?

Joseph related to his father a dream he had, saying: "'Father, [in a dream] I saw eleven stars and the sun and the moon; I saw them all prostrate themselves before me...'" (4). Jacob understood the meaning of that dream and was filled with apprehension over his young son's future: he feared his brothers' jealousy, and so said to him:

> "My son, do not relate your dream to your brothers, lest they plot to harm you; for, Satan is man's sworn enemy. Thus your Lord has chosen you and will teach you the interpretation of dreams, and He will bestow the full measure of His favor upon you and upon the house of Jacob..." (5–6)

Jealousy drove Joseph's brothers to collude to take him out to the fields one day with the intention of harming him or, somehow, intentionally losing him so that his father would never see him again.

234

They put their plan into action and Joseph found himself at the bottom of a dark pit in the middle of a wilderness. The young Joseph remained calm and confident that he would be saved and would one day face his brothers and make them ashamed of what they had done to him. His brothers had left him for dead, but God had other plans for him:

> And when they took him with them and decided to throw him into the bottom of the dark pit, We revealed to him that, "You shall tell them of all this at a time when they would not know who you are." (15)

As Joseph was left behind by his brothers, he was overwhelmed by the feeling that somehow they, and not he, would be the losers in that dangerous game they were playing. A few decades were to pass before Joseph's dream would come true. They were not to know it, but his brothers were to go and beg him for food, after he had become an important official in the government of Egypt.

> As they [his brothers] entered, they said to Joseph, "Noble prince, we and our people have been afflicted by famine. We have brought but little money. Be generous and charitable to us; God rewards those who are charitable." He [Joseph] said, "Do you remember what you recklessly did to Joseph and his brother?" (88–89)

God's infinite wisdom had seen to it that Joseph's ordeal at the bottom of that dark and desolate pit would become the first step on the road to power and glory. When his brothers arrived home after leaving him for dead in the pit, they said to their father:

> 'We went off racing with one another, and left Joseph behind to look after our things, but the wolf came and attacked him. We know you will not believe us, though we do speak the truth.' (17)

235

Their father's reply was: "'No. Your hearts have tempted you to do something evil to Joseph. Sweet patience! God alone can help me bear what you are telling me'" (18). It was, indeed, sweet patience which eventually paid off for Joseph and his father.

The Qur'an here presents factual details from an episode of human history rather than a mere work of fiction. Human society has always known literary works of fiction, which are in the main a product of their writers' rich, but sometimes contrived, imagination. fiction writers create situations and characters, modeling and manipulating them in a fashion and for a purpose that would make the story interesting, compelling, and complete. The author takes full responsibility for the ideas and the aims of the story. Some authors use symbolism and allegory, and some use animal rather than human characters.

But relating real historic events is a different matter altogether because it involves the identification and understanding of God's laws and how they operate in life and society, as well as the interpretation of certain facts and truths that affect human life and behavior. God says to Prophet Muhammad: "In revealing this Qur'an, We will recount to you the best of narratives of which you were hitherto completely unaware" (3). Muhammad had no hand in the articulation or authorship of the revelation he received. Towards the end of the surah we read: "This is part of what is unknown to you which We reveal to you. You were not present when they [Joseph's brothers] conceived their plan and schemed against him" (102). The surah closes with a comprehensive and definitive statement that applies to all historic narratives given in the Qur'an. It says:

In tales of peoples gone by there is a lesson for men of understanding. The Qur'an is no fabrication, but a confirmation of previous scriptures, a detailed exposition of everything, and a guidance and a mercy for those who believe. (111)

Joseph's model for diligence and devotion in the service of God and His message, no matter how great the obstacles might be, is an honorable and commendable one. The surah tells us that his prophethood began as soon as he had come of age: "And when he reached maturity We bestowed on him wisdom and knowledge. Thus do We reward the righteous" (22).

Wisdom and knowledge are the two main essential constituents which God grants His prophets. In *al-Anbiyā'*, verse 74, God says: "And to Lot We gave wisdom and knowledge and delivered him from the city whose inhabitants were committing vile acts...," while in *al-Qaṣaṣ*, verse 14, God says of Moses that: "When he had reached maturity and grown to manhood We bestowed on him wisdom and knowledge. Thus do We reward the righteous."

However ironic it may seem, despite his noble lineage, Joseph was sold into slavery by people whose main concern was the price they would get for him, and "the Egyptian who bought him said to his wife, 'Be kind to him. He may prove useful to us, or we may adopt him as our son'" (21). Thus a prophet's son found himself serving in a king's household, where he was to face another type of temptation. Even at that ripe young age, Joseph was very conscious of God and well-known for his piety. God says in the surah: "Thus We established Joseph in the land, and taught him to interpret dreams. God has power over all things, though most people may not realize it" (21).

Joseph respected the man who had taken him into his own household and became exceptionally loyal to him. He was not of the despotic and arrogant type of Egyptian chiefs, but a decent and honorable one. A friendly and sincere relationship had developed between the two men, as Joseph continued to uphold and observe the religious beliefs and traditions of his ancestors as well as their belief in the one God, preserving at the same time his personal virtue and upright conduct. Being accepted into the ruler's family and treated as a son, however, did not stop the lady of the house from

237

coveting to win Joseph's emotional and sensual attention. She could not resist his charm and beauty and pursued him for the satisfaction of her pleasures. But Joseph was beyond temptation, and as soon as the lady began to coax him into seduction his virtuous instincts were alerted. He recalled the honor he had inherited from his forefathers as well as the trust placed in him by the master of the household, and decided that under no circumstances could he betray either of them. The scene was set:

> The lady of the house where he [Joseph] was living then tried to seduce him. She bolted the doors and said, "Come to me!" He said, "God forbid! He [her husband] is my mentor who has welcomed me into his home. Transgressors shall never succeed." (23)

Being who he was, Joseph could not but refuse such an invitation and pass that severe test. Prophet Muhammad is reported to have said that among the seven people God Almighty would confer special favor upon on the Day of Judgment is "a man seduced by a woman of beauty and power but refuses her advances, saying, 'I fear God...'."[20] Joseph, more than anyone else, would be expected to take precisely that stance. His resolve was confirmed by the lady herself who admitted: "'I attempted to seduce him, but he held back'" (32).

As a virile, fully developed man in the prime of his youth, Joseph's desires would under such circumstances be quite naturally aroused, but at that very moment he would also be aware that he could not allow himself to be led by those desires. Personal honor, religious faith, and fear of God would all combine to control the carnal passions and sensual feelings he must, as a human being, have experienced. Were he bereft of these natural human emotions and feelings, were he passionless or inadequate, he would merit no credit for resisting this lady's amorous advances.

---

[20] Narrated by al-Bukhārī and Muslim.

She advanced towards him, and he, too, was inclined towards her, and had he not seen a sign from his Lord he [would have succumbed]. Thus We shielded him against evil and indecency, for he was one of Our select servants. (24)

Faith triumphed over temptation, and Joseph's integrity and chastity were preserved intact. As Joseph turned away, making his way towards the door, the Egyptian chief's wife ran after him, grabbing his shirt and tearing it as he dashed away from her towards the door. The drama reached a fever pitch when the husband appeared on the scene and the wife, spurned and driven by rage and guilt, immediately retorted by accusing Joseph of attacking her, demanding that he should be punished. She said: "'A man who wished to violate your wife should be imprisoned or severely punished'" (25). Convinced of his own innocence, Joseph said without hesitation: "'It is she who attempted to seduce me'" (26). There was no video or voice recording, and no material evidence to support either claim, but the circumstantial evidence was overwhelmingly in Joseph's favor. Simple logic and common sense pointed to the fact that since his shirt was torn from the back, Joseph must have been innocent.

One of her own people said, "If his shirt is torn from the front, then she is speaking the truth and he is lying. But if his shirt is torn from behind, then she is lying and he is speaking the truth." And when her husband saw that Joseph's shirt was rent from behind, he said, "This is typical female cunning; women's guile is great indeed!" (26–28)

Such circumstantial evidence is admissible in Islamic courts, and so is that obtained through the analysis of fingerprints, blood samples and other modern forensic techniques. The Egyptian chief's wife persisted in protesting her innocence, but as the rumors spread outside her household she could no longer hide her infatuation with Joseph while at the same time seeking justification for her behavior. Her plea to other women who blamed her would have been: If you were in my position you would have done exactly what I did! The narrative continues: "In the city, women were saying, 'The chief's wife has sought to seduce her servant. She is passionately infatuated by him. We believe she is totally misguided'" (30). To prove her point, the chief's wife invited a group of women to a banquet and gave each one of them a sharp knife with which to cut the food and then asked Joseph to appear before them. They were totally enthralled with his charm and were so taken by how handsome he looked that they unconsciously cut their hands with the knives they were holding, and said: "'This is no mortal human. This is a gracious angel'" (31). At last, as the women's emotions ran high, enraged with frustration and fury, she had no choice but to admit: "'I seduced him, but he held back. And if he does not do as I order him, he shall be thrown into prison and shall be terribly humiliated'" (32).

It is clear that this admission on her part had come as a result of her realization that the evidence against her was overwhelming. Her guilt became established. Freudian and other modern schools of human psychology have sought to find justification for permissiveness, indecency, and illicit sexual behavior. Perversion is portrayed as "normal" and moral discipline as repressive. But history tells us that immorality and promiscuity undermine societies and can indeed destroy whole civilizations. Joseph's reaction was the epitome of integrity, manliness, and humility when he said:

"My Lord, I would rather go to prison than give in to their advances. Unless You shield me from their cunning, I shall succumb to them and lapse into folly." His Lord answered his prayers and warded off their wiles from him. God is All-Hearing, All-Knowing. (33–34)

He was rescued from his lady's scheming and, notwithstanding his honesty and trustworthiness, was put in prison. "Yet, for all the evidence they had seen, they decided to jail him for a while" (35).

In this surah, we are told of three different dreams, all of which had come true. The first was when Joseph himself saw a vision of the sun, the moon, and eleven stars prostrating themselves before him. He related that dream to his father, as we have seen at the beginning of the surah, and we are yet to be told of its meaning. The second occasion was during his imprisonment.

> Two young men entered the prison with him. One of them said, "I dreamt that I was pressing grapes." And the other said, "I dreamt I was carrying bread upon my head and the birds were eating of it. Tell us the meaning of these dreams, for we can see that you are a man of virtue." (36)

The third one was the Egyptian king's dream which will be discussed later. Dreams are psychic phenomena related to the spiritual side of human behavior. Despite their visionary and premonitory attributes, dreams of themselves cannot be taken as omens of good or bad fortune. They are an indication of a quality of an extraordinary perception in the human disposition which enables certain individuals to see things in the future, with such clarity and in such detail, that others can not. I have personally known of a man who, before traveling from Cairo to his home town in the Egyptian countryside, had a vivid dream of the funeral of one of his relatives. When he arrived there he witnessed the scene in real life exactly as he had seen in the dream. I have known people who have had premonitions of all kinds without any apparent reason or explanation. The German philosopher, Kant, is said to have seen a fire more than a hundred miles away, while the following story involving the second Caliph, ʿUmar ibn al-Khaṭṭāb, and one of his army leaders, Sāriyah, is well known and fully documented in Islamic history books. While ʿUmar was once giving a speech at a mosque in Madinah he was heard calling in a loud voice: "Sāriyah! Watch the mountain!" He was reported to have seen the enemy fighters poised to launch a surprise attack against the Muslim army from behind a mountain, and involuntarily warned his commander. The commander, a long distance away, was able to hear ʿUmar's voice and take appropriate action to stave off the attack.

These phenomena are neither predictable nor governed by fixed rules. Suffice it to say that they do exist and that they did indeed occur with respect to Joseph. Having listened to the dreams of his two fellow prisoners, Joseph reassured them saying:

> "Whatever food is provided for you, I am able to describe it for you before it arrives. This is part of the knowledge my Lord has given me, for I have left the faith of those who disbelieve in God and deny the life to come. I follow the faith of my forefathers, Abraham, Isaac and Jacob. We take no one as gods besides God..." (37–38)

Joseph was proud of the faith he had inherited from his forefathers. It was that faith which had sustained him through the ordeals and the temptations he had had to face in his life, including his unjustified imprisonment. He could not let the opportunity go by, though, without telling those two inmates something about his beliefs. He said: "'Fellow prisoners! Are sundry gods better than God, the One, the Omnipotent?'" (39). Any other so-called god is but a figment of imagination and a hollow entity, adding up to nothing.[21] Joseph

---

[21] Modern science has unravelled numerous mysteries of life and the universe, and has made tremendous advances that lead to the recognition of God and acknowledgement of His power. Nevertheless, modern man remains heedless, preoccupied with satisfying his material needs, and almost totally oblivious to his obligations and accountability towards God. (Author)

interpreted the dreams of his two fellow prisoners as indicating two different fates, saying:

> "Fellow prisoners, one of you will serve his master with wine, but the other will be crucified and the birds will peck at his head. That is the answer to your questions." And Joseph said to the prisoner whom he knew would be set free, "Remember me to your master." But Satan made him forget to mention him to his master and so Joseph stayed in prison for several years. (41–42)

Once that prisoner was released, he became immersed in the life outside and forgot the innocent man he left behind languishing in the prison.

In the third dream the king had a disturbing vision and urgently sought its interpretation. Joseph's former prison companion remembered him and asked to be taken to him in prison to have the king's dream interpreted. He asked him:

> "Joseph, man of truth, tell us the true meaning of the dream in which seven fat cows are devoured by seven lean ones; and in which there are seven green shoots of corn and seven dry ones, so that I may go back to my people and inform them." (46)

Joseph obliged, and the king was informed of the meaning of his dream and asked for Joseph to be brought to him. Joseph, however, refused to go to see the king before his own innocence was established and he was completely cleared of the crime for which he had been wrongly accused and imprisoned. Joseph's case involving the Egyptian chief's wife was thus reopened and her lady friends, who were privy to what really happened, were called in to answer the king who asked them:

"What made you attempt to seduce Joseph?" They replied, "God forbid! We know of nothing bad against him." The chief's wife said, "Now the truth must come to light. It was I who attempted to seduce him. He has indeed told the truth." (51)

At that point, Joseph turned to the king to assert his innocence, saying: "'From this the chief will know that I had not betrayed him in his absence, and that God does not fulfill the work of the treacherous'" (52). Upon hearing this the Pharaoh immediately decided that Joseph would be the right man to put in charge of some of the state's affairs during the difficult economic period awaiting his kingdom, as his dream had indicated.

The king said, "Bring him before me. I will choose him for my own service." And when he had spoken to him, the king said, "You are henceforth established in a secure position, honored and trusted by us." (54)

Joseph was offered an important public position in the Pharaoh's government, and chose to take charge of its treasury affairs.

Joseph said, "Give me charge of the treasures of the realm; I am trustworthy and competent." Thus did We establish Joseph in the land [of Egypt], with full authority to do as he pleased. We bestow Our mercy on whom We will, and never deny the righteous their reward. (55–56)

It is important to note here that Joseph had pointed out both the moral as well as the corporeal qualities that were necessary to qualify him for the post he had agreed to accept. In other words, he was not merely a virtuous and trustworthy man, but was also competent and capable of assuming fully his responsibilities over the state's resources. Moreover Joseph was able to propose himself for a role in public office because there was no other person in Egypt at the time as suitable and qualified for the post as he was. The public interest could only be best served by appointing a strong and honest person to take up the responsibilities that the position demanded.

※※

Examining the early history of Islam, we come across the case of the well-known Muslim soldier, Khālid ibn al-Walīd, who put himself forward to lead the Muslim troops in the battle of al-Yarmūk in 635 AC. Khālid had seen that none of the other warriors present at the time possessed his qualities and combat experience and he therefore chose to command the troops himself, leading them to numerous successive victories. Throughout history, experience has shown that placing the wrong men at the head of important military expeditions almost always leads to disastrous results in the field of battle. On the first day he took command, Khālid drew up a fresh plan of attack, reorganized the Muslim army, rallied all available forces and went on to achieve a resounding victory against the Byzantines, driving them out and spearheading the Muslim conquest of the whole of the Fertile Crescent.

Seeking leadership or public office is a grave matter if undertaken for reasons of self-aggrandizement and greed for power, privilege or domination. History is replete with the examples of many great nations that have been led to ruin and humiliation by despotic and power-hungry individuals.

※※

The seven lean years foretold by the king's dream finally arrived and the famine which resulted swept well beyond Egypt to reach Syria and Mesopotamia whose inhabitants were forced to travel all the way to the more affluent land of Egypt in their search for food.

Among them were Joseph's own brothers who, several years earlier, had conspired to kill him and presumed him dead. Joseph welcomed his brothers into Egypt but would not agree to give them any provisions until they brought their younger brother back with them on their return visit. So the brothers returned home and informed their father of Joseph's request. Jacob did not welcome the idea, saying: "'Am I to trust you with him as I had once trusted you with his brother? But God is the best of guardians and He is the most merciful of all'" (64). However, as the conditions of the family were so dire, Jacob finally gave in to his sons' persistence and saw them off a second time saying:

> "My sons, do not enter from one gate; enter from different gates. In no way can I shield you from the might of God; judgment is His alone. In Him I have put my trust, and in Him all should put their trust." (67)

The reason behind this curious piece of advice seems to be Jacob's anxiety that a group of ten, united men seen entering the gates of the city could be seen as a threat by its inhabitants. He clearly feared for their safety.

The brothers appeared before Joseph a second time and on meeting them he gave his younger brother a special welcome. "When they entered before Joseph, he embraced his brother and said to him, 'I am your brother, so do not worry over what they do'" (69). The verse indicates that Joseph must have had some inclination about his brother's plight to console him in that manner. Joseph then devised a plan by which he could detain his younger brother and force his brothers to return to their father without him. He asked his aides to conceal the royal measuring cup, usually studded with precious stones, in his brother's luggage and, once they had done so, announced that it had been stolen. It was agreed that whoever had stolen it should be detained by the king.

Meanwhile in Palestine, on learning that he had been deprived of a second son, Jacob said: "'God may bring them all back to me. He alone is All-Knowing and Wise'" (83). It was no doubt a traumatic experience for Jacob who had yet to recover from the ordeal of losing Joseph. His grief was compounded and he "turned away from them, saying, 'How grieved I am over Joseph!' His eyes went white with grief and he was choked with melancholy" (84). However, in a desperate snatch at hope he told his sons to "'go and seek news of Joseph and his brother and do not despair of the mercy of God. Only the unbelievers despair of God's mercy'" (87). Thus, Joseph's brothers returned to Egypt for a third time. Looking dejected and miserable, on their arrival they went to see Joseph and said to him: "'Chief! We and our people have been scourged with hardship. We have brought you a few goods. Give us some corn, and be generous to us. God rewards those who are charitable'" (88).

At this point Joseph suddenly revealed his true identity and spoke to them sternly and effectively, saying: "'Do you remember what you recklessly did to Joseph and his brother?'" (89). Only then did it dawn on them that this man might be their brother Joseph and they immediately asked: "'Are you really Joseph, then?' He said, 'I am indeed Joseph and this is my brother. God has been gracious to us. Those that fear God and persevere, God will not deny their reward'" (90). With these words, Joseph reminded his brothers, and thereby all humankind of a fundamental principle of faith and a fact of life: fear of God and patient perseverance are rewarded with success. It is a principle as valid as any scientific or physical law.

Several decades after Joseph's first dream, everyone around him began to realize the truth of God's will, and his brothers said:

"By the Lord, God has exalted you above us all, for we have indeed been guilty." He said, "This day, you are free of reproach. May God forgive you. He is the most merciful of all." (91–92)

A man with a generous and kind heart has no room for vengeance or malice, and at the moment of triumph he shows greater benevolence towards others and more humility towards God. Joseph then said to his brothers: "'Take this shirt of mine and throw it over my father's face. He shall recover his sight. Then bring me all your people'" (93). Well into his journey from Palestine to Egypt, Jacob cried: "'I can sense the scent of Joseph, although you may refuse to believe me'" (94). This verse again brings us face to face with the mysteries of premonition and the world of the unseen.

We are left wondering as to how Jacob could have felt Joseph's existence? How could he have perceived of events that had taken place hundreds of miles away? "And when the bearer of good news arrived, he threw Joseph's shirt over Jacob's face, and as he regained his sight, he said, 'Did I not tell you that I know from God things that you do not?'" (96). A few days later Joseph's first dream was also to come true, as did the other two he had interpreted in the course of this surah.

When they went in to see Joseph, he embraced his parents and said to them, "Enter Egypt where, God willing, you shall be safe." He then sat his parents on the [royal] bench where they all prostrated themselves before him. He said, "Father! This is the meaning of my old dream; my Lord has made it come true. He was gracious to me as He had me released from prison, and brought you here out of the desert after Satan created discord between me and my brothers. My Lord is subtle in fulfilling His will. He is All-Knowing, Wise." (99–100)

Having related these parts of Joseph's story, God turns to address Prophet Muhammad, saying: "What We have here related was unknown to you. You were not present when Joseph's brothers conceived their devious plot" (102). Besides the obvious fact that the Prophet had not been present during those events, the Qur'an confirms that he had no knowledge of them prior to receiving the Qur'anic revelation. It was in effect warning his detractors that Muhammad's knowledge of all such matters had come from God. Such rejectionists and cynical critics can still be found today, but God urges His Prophet to: "Say, 'This is my way; I call people to God; both I and my followers have a clear perception [of where we are going]. Glory be to God! I take no gods besides God'" (108). But such doubters are negligent and totally oblivious of the evidence pointing to God and the truth of His revelation: "Many are the marvels of the heavens and the earth which they pass by and to which they pay no heed" (105).

SURAH 13

Al-Ra^cd
(Thunder)

IN THE OPENING VERSE of this surah, God addresses Prophet Muhammad saying: "What has been revealed to you from your Lord is the truth, but most people do not believe" (1). Yet those who disbelieve and reject the truth have no reasonable argument to support their attitude. Even if no revelation had been sent from God to humanity, there is ample evidence in the universe around us to prove God's existence and sovereignty. Reflection and intelligent observation of the physical and cosmological phenomena of the universe would reveal that denial of God is neither a rational nor a reasonable position to take. It would also lead to the conclusion that submission to or worship of other man-made gods is a nonsensical and absurd practise.

As we look closer at this verse, we find that it is complemented by another: "Is then he who knows that what has been revealed to you [Muhammad] by your Lord is the truth equal to one who is blind?" (19).

The surah tells us that those who acknowledge and appreciate the value and meaning of revelation are rational and honest people. The following verses go on to describe them saying: "Only the wise will take heed; those who fulfill their covenant with God and do not break their pledge; who join what God has bidden to be joined, fear their Lord and dread the terrors of an evil reckoning..." (19–21). These verses list ten virtues which, if acquired, lead to great and generous rewards. The first is mature thinking and the second is fulfillment of the greatest covenant of all: to believe in the One God and never to take other gods for worship besides Him. The surah affirms:

> These shall have a blissful end. They shall enter the gardens of Eden, together with their righteous fathers, spouses and descendants. The angels shall come to them from every door, saying, "Peace be unto you for all that you steadfastly endured." How excellent is the ultimate abode! (22–24)

The theme of revelation and Muhammad's responsibility for conveying it to humankind recurs again in the surah when it says:

> Thus We have sent you [Muhammad] to a nation before whose time other nations had passed away, so that you may recite to them what We have revealed to you. Yet they deny God, the Merciful. Say, "He is my Lord. There is no God but Him. In Him I have put my trust, and to Him I shall return." (30)

The ignorant pagan Arabs who had strongly resisted the message of the Qur'an used as their main alibi a request for Prophet Muhammad to perform a miracle or produce some extraordinary sign to prove the truth of what he was telling them. Elsewhere in the Qur'an, we are told that even if he had been able to satisfy their demands they would not have believed him. In this surah we read of more such demands, including the following:

> The unbelievers say, "If only a sign had been given him by his Lord!" But you are only to give warning and every nation has its mentor. (7)

The unbelievers say, "If only a sign had been given him by his Lord!" Say, "God confounds whomever He wills, and guides to Him those who repent." (27)

The unbelievers follow their inverted logic to its natural conclusion: "The unbelievers say, 'You have not been sent by God.' Say, 'God is sufficient witness between me and yourselves, and so are those with knowledge of the scriptures'" (43). People, including those assumed to be religious or believing, cannot be expected to develop or nourish a faith in God unless they are willing and capable of using their minds and intelligence to study their own physiological and mental faculties and capabilities, as well as the systems operating in the universe around them.

Prophet Muhammad had been urged many times to recite the Qur'an, as in *al-ʿAnkabūt*: 45, *al-Naml*: 91–92, and in this surah, verse 30. These and other instances show that recitation is more than just a simple reading of Qur'anic passages. It means the study, interpretation, and understanding of the principles, ideas and concepts that the Qur'an is putting forward. It also means the translation of those ideas into laws, actions, relationships, programs, and practical systems that help uplift the human situation and improve the quality of life.

The recitation of the Qur'an also protects it against tampering and distortion. The Arabs, in whose language it was revealed and to whom it was initially addressed, are especially urged in the first place to undertake this honorable responsibility. If they falter, they are warned to take note that: "The unbelievers, because of their misdeeds, shall not cease to be afflicted by disaster or see it fall close to them until God's promise is fulfilled. God never fails in His promise" (31).

Although scholars and commentators commonly hold the view that this surah is a Madinan one, revealed after *Muhammad*, I am of the opinion that it is a Makkan one. This is borne out by its style and its preoccupation with the unbelievers' incessant demands for miracles to prove Muhammad's prophethood which is a recurring theme in Makkan surahs such as *al-An'ām*, *Yūnus*, *al-Isrā'* and others. The surah opens with the words: "What has been revealed to you from your Lord is the truth" (1) and towards the end of it God says:

> Those who were given the scriptures [Jews and Christians] rejoice in what is revealed to you [Muhammad] while some factions deny parts of it. Say, "I am commanded to worship God and to associate none with Him. To Him I pray and to Him I shall return." (36)

These words conveyed a prophecy which has in fact been fulfilled. When Islam started to spread into Egypt and Syria, people, especially Christians, embraced it en masse. They willingly and easily adopted the new faith and passed it on to others further afield. History illustrates that the Muslim public treasury began to dry up as more and more people converted to Islam and were no longer paying non-Muslim duty to the state. The Muslim governor of Egypt decided to impose such taxes on new converts to maintain the province's income. The Caliph 'Umar ibn 'Abd al-Azīz is reputed to have written to him saying: "May Allah curse you! The Prophet Muhammad was sent to guide people to God, not to collect taxes. Repeal the taxes you imposed on new converts."

The overwhelming majority of those who converted to Islam in Egypt, Syria and other parts of the world became Arabized, ethnically, culturally and in terms of their religious beliefs and practices. This process of "Arabization" has been a source of vitality and continuity for the Arab nation which forms the backbone of the Muslim world community. The surah says:

Thus We have revealed it [the Qur'an] as a code of judgment in the Arabic tongue. If you [Muhammad] succumb to their desires after all the knowledge you have been given, you shall have none to save or protect you from God. (37)

The Qur'an thus establishes and represents political authority and stands both as a source and a reference for literary, moral, and social guidance. Islam initially spread in the outer fringes of the Arabian peninsula, while the people of Makkah maintained their old beliefs. It was not until late in Muhammad's lifetime that the Makkan population turned completely to Islam. This is what is referred to in the following verse which says:

Do they [the people of Arabia] not see how We advance in the land [Arabia] and close in on them from around its borders? God decides and no one has the power to reverse His judgment, and He is swift in reckoning. (41)

The Qur'an is the written Book that guides man to God, while nature and the physical universe are manifestations pointing towards His power and existence. Both require alert minds and sensitive hearts to be understood and appreciated. The Qur'an stresses this point by its frequent reminder: "Do you not understand?", "Do you not remember?" and similar phrases. In this context we cite the following verse:

And there are on earth [many] tracts of land, close by one another [and yet widely differing from one another]; and [there are on it] vineyards, and fields of grain, and date-palms growing in clusters from one root or standing alone, [all] watered with the same water: and yet, some of them have We favored above others by way of the food [which they provide for man and beast]. Verily, in all this there are messages indeed for people who use their reason! (4)

It is indeed a matter for reflection how, from the same piece of land, a variety of produce can be grown: grapes, lemons, colocynth, and nettles. How can plants irrigated by the same water emerge with different tastes, textures, colors, and smells? Is it not also amazing how the silkworm feeds on mulberry trees and produces silk, whilst bees which feed on pollen produce honey, and sheep which feed on the same plants produce dung? However, despite the astonishingly infinite variety of creatures and substances found in this world, some people continue to question the existence of God, while others demand miracles or supernatural feats to be convinced.

The surah speaks of God's infinite power, evident in the breeding and reproduction of living creatures: human, animal, bird and reptile. Millions upon millions of beings, organisms and living systems grow and multiply in a continuous life cycle on land, under the sea and in the earth's atmosphere. Each organism goes through an intricate perfectly-timed cycle of its own. All the phenomena and processes encountered in the macro- as well as the microcosmic worlds form one harmonious, well-integrated structure which smoothly lends itself to the full power and control of God who

> ...knows what every female bears: He knows of every change in her womb. He has set everything according to a fixed measure. He knows both what is hidden and what is manifest. He is the Supreme One, the Most High. (8–9)

The Creator is also responsible for the design of the grand cosmological system and the order sustaining the whole physical universe, with all its countless planets, stars, galaxies, and other formations. Nothing distracts Him, and in His scheme nothing takes precedence over anything else. The surah continues in a unique manner pointing out and explaining the manifestations of God's supreme power and grace before it puts forward certain rhetorical questions for which it supplies its own answers.

Say, "Who is the Lord of the heavens and the earth?" Say, "God." Say, "How is it then, that you have taken other gods besides Him, who can bring neither good nor harm even unto themselves?" Say, "Are the blind and the seeing equal? Is darkness the same as light?" Or have they assigned partners to God that have brought into being creation like His, so that they have become confused? Say, "God is the Creator of everything, and He is One and He has power over all things." (16)

As mentioned above, the surah opens by referring to the physical universe as evidence for the existence and power of God, and then turns to man's response to the Qur'an which presents this evidence and elaborates on it. I chose to deal with the latter subject first because I wanted to devote more space to the first one.

Muslims live almost as non-participants in today's world. Their contribution to science is almost negligible, although nothing could be more conducive to the understanding of the Qur'an than the study of the physical world. I once imagined myself positioned a hundred miles away in space, and wondered: what would I see on earth? Would I see a thick cloud of smoke and smog that has polluted the earth's atmosphere? Would I hear the cacophony and the dissonance of factory and plant noise which has drowned all other sounds? I believe that the world has a finite life-span, but is it prematurely and inexorably driving itself towards that end? Another question: What is man's position and role in this vast cosmos? We have read that a new black hole has been discovered in outer space which is a hundred times larger than any other black hole known to man. It has been reported that scientists believe that the colossal new black hole contains around one thousand million active stars, that it is exerting a tremendous amount of gravitational pull which prevents even light from escaping out of it! I thought to myself: this is only one black hole, so what if we are to look wider into other parts and aspects of our universe? Let us do that through the surah.

> It was God who raised the heavens, as you can see, without pillars. He then ascended His throne and ordained the sun and the moon each to run their respective appointed term. He governs all matters, and makes all signs clear so that you may be firmly convinced of your meeting with your Lord. (2)

We look at our own bodies every day. Man is a whole intricate universe in his own right. Within our bodies thousands of organs, systems, and processes exist and operate together in harmony and with efficiency. Look at how hundreds of thousands of hairs grow again and again on the human body; billions of red cells are found in the blood stream, reproduced within the body as and when necessary. The human nerve system constantly receives signals from the brain which man has yet to fathom, or understand precisely how it works and how it carries out its numerous and complicated tasks day and night. God has always been and ever shall be in charge of maintaining the function of all these systems and deciding their fate and destiny. Elsewhere in the Qur'an, we read: "All things shall return to your Lord. He is the one who makes people laugh or cry; He takes life and He gives it..." (*al-Najm*: 42–43).

Science has established that our universe is vast beyond our comprehension, but what scientists ought to acknowledge is that God is much greater. In human terms, people can only concentrate on a finite number of tasks for a given period of time, but God is never distracted and is always aware of everything, from the plaintive moaning of a tortured animal to the mass cries of victims of human oppression. Moreover, He duly gives the oppressors their just reward. God can hear a leaf falling from a tree and He hears the roaring of thunder. He can see the clotting of blood inside veins, as clearly and as easily as He sees the trail of a shooting star. Nothing escapes Him.

Ibrāhīm
(Abraham)

THE SURAH OPENS with the following words:

We have revealed to you [Muhammad] this Book [the Qur'an] so
that you may lead humankind out of darkness into the light, by the
will of their Lord, and to the path of the Mighty, the Glorious; the
path of God to whom belongs all that is in the heavens and the earth
(1–2).

Darkness is manifested in this world in many different forms:
ignorance, conceit, corruption, tyranny, disobedience to God, and
so on. God revealed the Qur'an to Muhammad, the seal of the
prophets, in order to lead people out of all kinds of darkness and to
teach them that this life is a prelude to another one yet to come; that
those who give priority to this life over the next are doomed to failure and that those who oppose God's revelations and resist His will
are odious and corrupt.

Long before the advent of Prophet Muhammad, God had sent
Moses to lead the people of Israel out of the darkness of slavery and
humiliation and secure their freedom of mind, conscience, and
movement, and the privilege to enjoy God's kindness and generosity. All Moses asked of his people was for them to appreciate those
favors and acknowledge God's grace.

We sent Moses with Our revelations, saying, "Lead your people out of the darkness into the light, and remind them of God's favors." Surely in this there are signs for every steadfast, thankful man. (5)

All religions aim to transport man from a state of ignorance and perversion to one of knowledge and uprightness. The Book that Prophet Muhammad was given, the Qur'an, is well-equipped to guide man and save him from error and loss. However, throughout human history, humankind has always resisted divine revelation and stood in opposition to God's messengers seeking to thwart and frustrate their missions. Many have exploited their power, wealth and influence to entice those who believe away from the truth but the believers have on their part persevered in their faith, saying: "Why should we not trust in God, when He has already guided us to our paths [of truth]? We will endure your persecution patiently. All those who have to trust should place their trust in God" (12).

The process of religious, moral, and social reform of human communities does not bear fruit overnight. It requires diligence, dedication, and relentless effort. Muhammad spent twenty-three long years instructing his people and schooling them in the teachings and principles of the Qur'an in order to discipline their pedestrian uncultured attitudes, eradicate their ignorance and backwardness in the fields of science and civilization, and prepare them for the leadership of humankind. The Qur'an took the Arabs on a huge quantum leap—culturally, politically, intellectually, and morally. When they took on their opponents they triumphed, thereby earning a distinguished and established place in human history. The surah alludes to these concepts when it says:

And the unbelievers said to their Messengers, "Return to our religion or we will banish you from our land." But their Lord revealed to them, saying, "We will destroy the transgressors and give you the land to settle in after they have gone. That is the reward for him who dreads standing before Me [in judgment] and fears My threat." (13–14)

Weak, aimless, and neglected nations cannot rise to positions of leadership unless they are revitalized by the power and rigor of faith. When a nation believes in God, submits its energies and resources to Him and adopts His messages, it is transformed into a force to be reckoned with. Through this process, God decides the destinies of nations and communities: "As they [the Messengers] sought Our help, every hardened tyrant came to grief" (15). Muslims today who are resisting change all over the world should take note!

Social differences have existed in all human societies. There have always been masters and slaves; leaders and followers; elites and masses; heroes and their admirers who look up to them and emulate their example. But although all of these different groups are normally brought together by a unity of purpose, the difference is that the one group usually reflects or expresses the convictions, feelings, and aspirations of the other, just as often the admirers of a particular author or novelist come from those who share the ideas he articulates in his work. The relationship between leaders and followers is evident in many walks of life. We note that during the Battle of Badr the non-Muslim Arab leader, Abū Jahl, a foremost opponent of Islam at the time, was being protected by his followers who were determined to defend him. But this did not prevent some young Muslim fighters from reaching and killing him!

It is ironic, therefore, to note that on the Day of Judgment the unbelievers will fall back on some of the bonds that bind them to one another, but to no avail.

They shall all appear before God. The weaker will say to the haughty ones, "We were your followers. Will you then save us from any of God's punishment?" They will reply, "Had God given us guidance, we would have guided you. It is now all the same whether we despair or remain patient; there is no escape for any of us." (21)

These concepts were explained by God to people well in advance so that they would not be misled by bogus leaders. Nevertheless, many still continue to be exploited and misguided by those they trust and look up to. "Have you not seen those who repay the grace of God with unbelief and lead their people to utter perdition? They shall abide in hell—such a wretched place!" (28–29). Leaders and followers shall meet with the same miserable fate.

Like *al-Raʿd* before it, this surah affirms the fact that besides being logical and natural, truth is a positive, beneficial, and constructive concept, while falsehood is harmful and destructive to society. In the surah we read: "Thus God depicts truth and falsehood. The froth disappears into thin air, but what is of use to humankind remains firmly established on earth..." (*al-Raʿd*: 17). In the present surah we read:

Can you see how God compares a good word to a wholesome tree? Its root is firmly in the ground and its branches reach up to the sky; it yields its fruit every season by God's leave... (24–25)

Societies and nations fare differently according to the beliefs, ideals, and values by which they live. These, naturally, relate to religious, ethical, civil and cultural factors. As for Islam, *tawḥīd* is the essence and the root of its civilization, and the most fundamental source of all its tenets and principles. *Tawḥīd* encompasses and defines the whole ethos of the Islamic way of life and is the fountain from which all aspects of its civilization spring. On the other hand, the surah affirms that falsehood, being rootless and bogus, only leads to misery and frustration: "An evil word is like an evil tree which is uprooted from the earth and shorn of all its roots" (26). The contrast is stark and the choice glaringly clear. The surah goes on to outline two main features required of a believing nation. The first is that it should be a believing nation, preoccupied with the observance of religious duties such as prayer; the redistribution of wealth through zakah; and the welfare of its citizens. It should not be concerned with advancing its own ethnocentric or national interests at the expense of other nations or communities. A godly nation uses its power and dominance to further God's word in the world:

> Tell My servants, those who are true believers, to be steadfast in prayer and to spend, in private and in public, of what We have bestowed on them before a day comes when all trading and mutual friendship shall cease. (31)

History tells us that the communities set up, or led by, God's prophets were raised on obedience to God and diligent adherence to His commands. As some of them abandoned those messages, cast them aside, or obliterated them, they went into decline and degenerated into selfish materialism and the pursuit of short-term worldly aggrandizement. The inevitable disintegration of economic and material life in those societies, and the shortage of material resources and consumer goods would be the sole focus of their lamentation and sorrow. Today's world is in need of a role-model nation that would reflect God's will and implement His word. This would be the nation of Islam. However, it would have to be a leading nation that stands head and shoulders above all other nations and provides a true and viable example to the rest of the world in all aspects of life. This leads us to the second feature of the "believing nation": that it must be powerful, self-reliant, and in full control of its own destiny and resources. This is made clear in the following three verses:

> It was God who created the heavens and the earth. He sends down
> water from the sky with which He brings forth fruits for your suste-
> nance. He has harnessed for your service the ships sailing in the seas
> by His leave. He harnessed the river for your service, and the sun
> and the moon discharge their functions without fail, and He has
> constrained to your service the night and the day. He has given you
> of everything you have asked; and if you were to list the favors of
> God you would never be able to list them all... (32–34)

Believing communities have existed throughout human history, but
some of them went astray, lagged behind, and became marginalized.
Instead of being masters on earth they found themselves helplessly
controlled by their own worldly pursuits. They wavered in their
loyalty and submission to God and were thrown off course, leaving
the door open for their rivals and enemies to take the lead and plunder humanity's soul and dignity, ravage the world's resources, and
threaten life and the future of the whole planet.

Jihad in our time encompasses a whole range of activities including inventiveness, development, and construction on land, in the
sea, and in outer space. It implies research in all fields to gain wider
and deeper understanding of the world around us and all the phenomena associated with it. It pains me to think how little the
Muslims have contributed to human progress in recent times whilst
other nations have forged ahead making tremendous achievements
of which they will be proud for many generations to come. By making a comparison between the Jews and the Arabs, two Semitic
nations descending from a common Abrahamic lineage and heirs to
a common religious heritage, one can immediately see the former
are in possession of power and influence, whilst the latter, entrusted
with God's message, have fallen far short of their obligations to
uphold it and have become backward and defeated.

Abraham, the epitome of righteousness and piety, traveled far and wide to spread the doctrine of *tawḥīd* and to fight paganism and idol-worship. When he decided to settle briefly in the Hijaz in western Arabia, he made a prayer:

> "Lord, I have settled some of my offspring in a barren valley near Your Sacred House, that they may observe prayer. Lord, make people's hearts yearn with kindness towards them and provide them with fruits of all kinds that they may be grateful." (37)

This branch of Abraham's progeny can be traced back to Ishmael, his son from his second wife Hagar, whilst the other branch can be traced back to Isaac, father of Israel, who was Abraham's son from his first wife Sarah. The surah informs us that both sons were born during Abraham's old age, for which he was very grateful, saying:

> "Praise be to God who has given me Ishmael and Isaac in my old age. My Lord hears all prayer. Lord, make me and my descendants steadfast in observing prayer and, our Lord, accept my prayer." (39–40)

It is ironic that the Jews consider themselves descendants of the master wife and the Arabs descendants of the slave wife giving the latter an inferiority complex. The whole issue is absurd. Human beings are all equal, and are only distinguished by their closeness to, and fear of, God. Abraham's legacy belongs to all his offspring, and it is simply below God Almighty to designate a particular piece of land as the sole property of Jacob's children in perpetuity. We read in *al-Aʿrāf* that: "Earth belongs to God; He bequeaths it to whom He wills of His servants. The righteous shall have a happy end" (*al-Aʿrāf*: 128).

In the perennial fight between good and evil, many helpless people will endure pain and suffering, and may say to their oppressors: "'We shall meet your persecution with patience'" (12). Oppression can never prevail and retribution can easily occur in this life here on earth. In the end, no matter how long it may be delayed, justice will be done. The surah affirms this, saying: "Never think that God is unaware of what the wrong-doers do. He only gives them respite till a day when their eyes are fixed wide open in horror and shock" (42).

History illustrates that oppressors are ruthless, barbaric people and as God's enemies, are utterly merciless in their war against believers. But their power and ferocity cannot alter the course of divine justice. The surah says:

> They [God's enemies] would have devised their plans, but God is able to deal with their plotting even if it could move mountains. Never think that God would break the pledge He gave to His Messengers. God is Mighty and capable of revenge... (46–47)

The surah opened with a statement to the effect that God had revealed the Qur'an to Muhammad, the seal of the prophets, in order to lead people out of darkness and into the light. It closes with another statement, no less forceful or definite, that: "This is an admonition for humankind, that they may be warned thereby and that they may know that God is the One and Only God and that wise people may take heed" (52). "The wise people" ought to give credit to their own intelligence by not taking other gods besides the one God. They ought to study God's revelation very closely and hold fast to the beliefs and principles that will ensure their success and salvation.

Al-Ḥijr

"ALIF, LĀM, RĀ. These are the verses of the Book and a perspicuous Qur'an" (1). God's revelation to humankind, referred to here
as the Book, is written and communicated by word of mouth. The
Arabic words, *al-Kitāb* and *al-Qur'ān*, are both used to identify God's
revelation to Muhammad. "The disbelievers would often wish they
were Muslims" (2). As the truth becomes clearer and God's words
are fulfilled, the cynical and the negligent amongst humankind wish
they had taken heed. But the Qur'an directs the Prophet to: "let
them feast and enjoy themselves and hanker after their delusions;
they will soon realize the futility of their endeavors" (3). Pursuit of
worldly pleasures has been a constant feature of human history. In
today's civilization, however, it seems to have been elevated to the
status of religion, and people have all but forgotten about accountability in the hereafter. But the Qur'an emphatically instructs the
Prophet not to: "yearn for the enjoyments We have made available
to some of them, nor grieve over them" (88).

The interesting point to note here is that the surah opens with
statements which are endorsed and echoed by similar ones towards
the end of it. When talking about people who challenged earlier
prophets and hampered their work, we read at the beginning of the
surah: "Never have We destroyed a nation before its appointed
time. Men cannot forestall their doom, nor can they delay it" (4–5).
Further elaboration is given towards the end of the surah, with the
citing of case histories such as those of the peoples of prophets Lot,

Shuʿayb and Ṣāliḥ. Failures and mistakes of transgressor nations grow and accumulate up to the point when divine punishment becomes inevitable and unavoidable. On the instance of Lot's people, God says:

> By your life, they were blundering and intoxicated. They were struck at sunrise as We turned their land upside down and hailed upon them a shower of clay-stones. Surely in that there are signs for those who reflect. Their ruins are still there for all to see. (72–76)

Concerning prophet Shuʿayb's people, God says: "The forest dwellers were also guilty and We took vengeance upon them. They all stand out as a manifest example" (78–79). Then the surah talks of Ṣāliḥ's people, identified here as the people of al-Ḥijr, a valley in north-west Arabia known today as the cities of Ṣāliḥ, which gives the surah its title. Ṣāliḥ's people:

> denied the messengers and were given Our signs, but they ignored them. They hewed out their dwellings into the mountains and lived in safety therein. But one morning they were struck down and nothing they had gained could avail them. (80–84)

These verses which appear at the end of the surah explain and complement the ones appearing at the beginning, starting with verse 4, which says: "We [God] have sent messengers before you to earlier nations, but they scoffed at each messenger who had come to them..." (10–11). The Arabs also scoffed at the Qur'an and at Muhammad. "They said, 'You to whom the Qur'an was revealed, you are surely possessed. Bring us the angels, if what you say is true'" (6–7). The Arabs were not alone in making this demand, for other nations before them had also asked for the same, but God had ignored such trivial and frivolous demands. These societies seemed to consider revelation as some kind of game in which the winner would be the crudest and the most vulgar. But God replies: "We send not the angels down except for just cause: if they came [to the ungodly], behold! no respite would they have" (8).

At this stage God mentions that the Qur'an, as the final divine revelation, will be preserved for eternity and no matter what its detractors may do, they shall not succeed in destroying or obliterating its message. "We [God] have revealed this Qur'an, and We shall preserve it" (9) and: "We have given you [Muhammad] seven oft-repeated verses [*al-Fātiḥah*] and the great Qur'an" (87). Some people reject the Qur'an out of prejudice and sheer pigheadedness. The more, and the stronger, the evidence they are presented with the more adamant they grow in their effrontery and opposition: "If We opened for them [the unbelievers] a gate in heaven through which they ascended higher and higher, they still would have said, 'Our eyes are shut; we must be under a spell!'" (14–15)

The surah also contains a fascinating account relating to the universe, its secrets and forces, which point to the power of its Maker. As one looks up into the infinity of the heavens, one cannot help but be captivated by the multitude, distribution, and movement of the planets and stars in this vast universe which knows no boundaries. Likewise, as one gazes at the wonders scattered all across the earth, both on land and sea, one is immediately amazed by how God sustains and provides for all the millions upon millions of creatures and living organisms that exist upon it. God says:

And indeed, We have set up in the heavens great constellations, and endowed them with beauty for all to behold; and We have made them secure against every satanic force accursed so that anyone who seeks to learn [the unknowable] by stealth is pursued by a flame clear to see. And the earth We have spread it out wide, and placed on it mountains firm, and caused [life] of every kind to grow on it in a balanced manner, and provided thereon means of livelihood for you [O men] as well as for all [living beings] whose sustenance does not depend on you. (16–20)

While the surah goes into some detail in the opening part relating to the wonders and marvels of the universe, it gives a statement of a more general nature towards the end:

We have created the heavens, the earth and all that lies between them for the sake of universal truth. The appointed Hour is sure to come, and so forbear and show sweet magnanimity. Your Lord is the All-Knowing Creator. (85–86)

Science has shown that the human body is made up of the same elements as the earth's soil. But how do flesh and bones turn into dust, and how does the dust turn back into flesh and bones? Genes carry hereditary information, but are they responsible for the design and the origination of that information, or for the human character that emerges as a result? Are we to believe that it is the human brain and other bodily organs, complex and ingenious as they are, which in fact determine man's character and destiny? With closer scrutiny, it becomes clear that these amazing organs are only a means, or tools, by which divine power is manifested enabling man to know God and acknowledge Him as the Giver of life and death and the Originator of creation. God "holds abundant stores of all things and gives of each according to a predetermined measure" (21).

God's knowledge is instantaneous and comprehensive; all reality is totally and simultaneously accessible to Him. Dimensions of time and space lose all their properties. God alone knows the 'how,' 'what' and 'when' of the future: "We know those of you who have already gone by as well as those who are yet to come. Your Lord will gather them all together; He is Wise and All-Knowing" (24–25).

The life-cycle of living organisms is a wonder to behold! Living creatures breed, multiply and die in endless numbers. A parasite feeding off the back of a larger animal may, in turn, become a meal for a bird. By eating the insect, the bird provides relief for the mammal. In this way the life-cycles of the animal kingdom are interlinked.

Humankind is a marvel of divine creation. Made "from parched dark clay" (26) people die and return to earth and turn into dust again. But what makes them such distinguished creatures? What sets them apart from the rest of creation? The answer is the divine spirit which has been breathed into them, and which gives them the qualities and status unique to humans in the divine world order. It was this streak of divine spirit which made *Iblīs*, or Satan, envious of man, causing him to refuse to recognize man's superiority. As a result, Satan vowed to seek revenge against Adam and his offspring. The surah informs us that Satan said:

> "Lord, as You have let me go astray, I will tempt them [humankind] on earth and will lead them all astray, except those of Your servants whom You have favored." God said, "The final word on this is that you shall have no power over My servants, except the nefarious among them who follow you." (39–42)

The story of Adam and his arch-enemy, Satan, is recounted in the Qur'an on several occasions. In this instance, the main emphasis is on the very nature of the raw material from which man is made: parched dark clay!

This life is transient, a mere bridge to another permanent world where everyone will receive his or her due reward in accordance with their performance in this life. The losers will be those who denied God's sovereignty and neglected His guidance. As Satan himself has no real power over human beings, those who allow themselves to be misled by him will only have themselves to blame for falling into error; as the saying goes, "ignorance of the law is no excuse." All that Satan can do in this life is to tempt and mislead humankind through the power of suggestion. Individuals who, having received ample warning of Satan's methods, choose to listen to and follow his suggestions, will have no one to blame but themselves for the consequences. People have to be ever alert and vigilant, realizing that as long as God's laws are not abandoned, He will be forgiving and generous, otherwise His wrath can be overwhelming. The surah says: "Tell My servants that I alone am Forgiving and Merciful; and that My punishment is a woeful punishment" (49–50).

This strong admonition is followed with an illustration involving an episode from the life of prophet Abraham. His wife, as the angels had told him, was pregnant and about to give birth to a son, and the town, whose inhabitants engaged in the abhorrent practise of sodomy, would soon be destroyed. The Qur'an makes no mention of the Old Testament account referring to God as eating at a feast hosted by Abraham, because this is an act which does not become God and by ignoring the tale the Qur'an strips it of credence. Prophet Lot's people were abominable and although he tried very hard to dissuade them from their vile practices they failed to change. Consequently, God destroyed them, turning their city upside down. Sodomy and homosexuality are a curse and an affliction which spread as a result of promiscuity and sexual depravity amongst mankind. Although legalized in some contemporary societies, these acts have always been considered in the past as morally unacceptable. However, these have not been the only perversions that modern western civilization has legitimized through its legal system.

We have already seen how the opening and closing statements of the surah skillfully complement one another, separated by passages relating episodes from the lives of the prophets Adam, Abraham and Lot to reinforce the principles conveyed by those statements and thereby enhance their impact. Thereafter the surah picks up the thread of giving further instructions to Prophet Muhammad, who had been honored by receiving God's revelation, on how to respond to that honor: "Do not yearn for the enjoyments We have made available to some of them, nor grieve over them, but show kindness to the faithful, and say, 'I am he that gives plain warnings'" (88–89).

The surah then links this approach with earlier Israelite and Christian responses to revelation which had, on the whole, been schismatic and cynical: "Just as We had sent revelation to the schismatic, who break the Qur'an into separate parts, believing in some and denying others" (90–91). Israelite and Christian contemporaries of Prophet Muhammad treated the Qur'an in a manner similar to the way their predecessors had treated their own scriptures. They accepted what suited them and refused to believe in the rest. In the case of their own scriptures this had led them to tamper with their texts, altering some of the principles and rules which were expounded therein. The surah warns: "By your [Muhammad's] Lord, We will question them all about what they had done" (92–93). Meanwhile, God consoles Prophet Muhammad with the fact that his unbelieving detractors would not be able to thwart his mission for too long: "We [God] will protect you [Muhammad] against the cynics who mock you and take another god besides God. They shall soon come to know their fate" (95–96).

During the early days of Islam, the Arabs of Makkah had staged a relentless campaign of mockery and ridicule against the Prophet as well as the revelation he was receiving. They spared no effort in widening their campaign of psychological warfare, in an attempt to win other tribes in Arabia over to their side. Naturally, this left the Prophet distressed and despondent. However, God directed him to pay no attention to this crusade and not to allow it to dishearten him. The surah directs the following comforting words to the Prophet: "We [God] know you are distressed by what they say. Extol the glory of your Lord. Prostrate yourself before Him and worship Him until death overtakes you" (97–99). These closing words conveyed an implicit divine promise that Islam would prevail in the world. History has shown that this has been the case.

SURAH 16

Al-Naḥl
(Bees)

THIS SURAH was clearly revealed during the latter part of the
Makkan period, 610 to 622 AC, when the confrontation between
the Muslims and the pagan Arabs of Makkah had reached such a
fever pitch that despair had begun to creep into the hearts of the
Muslims as they could see no signs of the victory promised by Allah
for their new religion. In contrast to this desperation, the non-
Muslims were beginning to gloat and feel self-confident in their
position as none of the threats made against them in the Qur'an
and by the Muslims had seemingly materialized. It is within this
context and historical setting that the surah opens with the promise:
"The judgment of God will surely come to pass: do not seek to
hasten it..." (1).

Islam eventually triumphed over those who persisted in opposing
it causing them to suffer in defeat. Although the non–Muslims may
have perceived the time-scale involved for this to have been
achieved to be a lengthy and protracted one, on the divine scale of
things, however, it could not have occurred any sooner. The Muslims were required to show patience and not lose heart and, indeed,
the surah ends with these sober instructions to the Prophet:

> Be patient, then, and God will grant you patience. Do not grieve for
> the unbelievers, nor distress yourself at their intrigues. God is with
> those who fear Him and seek excellence in what they do. (127–128)

The Muslims had already suffered and persevered a great deal. At the height of their distress the following two verses were revealed to console and comfort them, giving them the moral support they so desperately needed:

We will provide those who had migrated for God's cause after they had been persecuted, with a good abode in this life; and the reward in the life to come is even better, if they but knew it. (41)

Your Lord is forgiving and merciful towards those who had migrated, after they had been persecuted, struggled hard and persevered. (110)

The 'migration' (*hijrah*) referred to here is one which was undertaken by some scores of Muslims, travelling in small groups, during the first seven years of Muhammad's call to prophethood. No longer able to withstand the persecution and victimization of the Makkans they emigrated to Abyssinia, hoping to find safety and shelter there. Al-Bukhārī reports that Asmā', daughter of ʿUmays, who was among the party of Muslims who first emigrated to Abyssinia then to Madinah, was once visiting Ḥafṣa when ʿUmar ibn al-Khaṭṭāb entered the room. He turned to Asmā' and said: "We have a greater right to God's Messenger because we migrated before you did." Asmā' became angry and retorted: "Never, by God. Whilst you were with the Prophet and he was feeding your hungry and teaching your ignorant, we were in that appalling and strange land during which time we came under persecution and threat; and all for the cause of God and His Messenger. By God, I will not rest until I have informed him of what you have said to me." True to her word, when the Prophet next visited Ḥafṣa's house, Asmā' related the incident to him and upon hearing ʿUmar's comment and Asmā's reply he remarked: "They have no more right to me than you. ʿUmar and his Companions have the honor of a single migration (*hijrah*), while you, the 'people of the boat' [having returned from Abyssinia by boat], have the credit of two."[22]

At the beginning of the surah, revelation is referred to as 'the Spirit' because of its capacity to revive and rejuvenate nations and individuals.

> By His will He sends downs the angels with the Spirit to whomsoever of His servants He chooses, bidding them to warn that there is no god but Me: therefore fear Me. (2)

Elsewhere in the Qur'an, Allah has stated: "Thus have We revealed to you [Muhammad] a Spirit of Our will when you knew nothing of the Book or of faith..." (*al-Shūrā*: 52). It is this spirit of the Qur'an which inspired the Arabs and transformed them from a nation of marauding tribes, with a marginal place in history, into a dynamic and vigorous social force that went on to lead the world.

The surah then takes up the discourse along two main themes, one dealing with revelation and the other with the wonders of nature and the physical world, alternating between them to convey to humankind instructions, explanations, examples, and evidence for the existence of God and His grace to humankind. In the first theme, we are told of the two different responses given by man to the Qur'anic statement that, by His will, God: "sends downs the angels with the Spirit to whomsoever of His servants He chooses" (2). The first response is that of the rejectionists and the hopelessly lost people for:

> When they are asked, "What has your Lord revealed?" They say, "Myths of old!" They shall bear their own burden in full on the Day

---

[22] Narrated by al-Bukhārī.

of Resurrection, together with part of the burden of those they had, in their ignorance, led astray. (24–25)

In everyday society this kind of rebuttal normally comes from the elite or the leaders and opinion-formers who influence the masses and mislead them. The Prophet is reported to have said: "Whoever advocates a wrong or misleading idea shall bear the accumulative burden of all those who are influenced by it."[23] The responsibility for disseminating false and insidious ideas among common people should not simply stop at the act of promoting and spreading such information without an examination of or care for its repercussions. Philosophers, thinkers, and writers must be prepared to bear the burden resulting from the effect which their ideas may have on other individuals and on society as a whole.

On the other hand, people themselves should also think critically and be ever vigilant and discerning with regard to the principles and ideas they choose to accept and believe in. In other words, they should not allow themselves to be led like sheep. The surah says:

And those endowed with knowledge will say, "Shame and affliction shall this day befall the unbelievers. Those upon whom the angels will bring death while they are wronging themselves…" (27–28)

In contrast to this attitude verse 30 points to the stance of the God-fearing, who display a much more intelligent, considered, and sensible response.

But when the God-fearing were asked, "What has your Lord revealed?" They replied, "He revealed the best!" Those who do good will be well-rewarded in the present life, although the life to

23 Narrated by Muslim, Abū Dāwūd, al-Nasāʾī, al-Tirmidhī, Ibn Mājah and Imām Aḥmad.

come will be even better. Blessed is the dwelling place of the righteous. (30)

The surah goes on to elaborate further on the qualities of these people stating: "Those pure ones to whom the angels, when they come to take their lives, would say, 'Peace be upon you. Enter Paradise in reward for what you had done'" (32). The verse is referring to people who will have striven to keep their hearts clean and their lives pure and devoted to the cause of Allah, seeking to serve Him to the best of their ability and do good till the moment of death overcomes them. Faith and righteousness require cultivation and caring, and are strengthened by incentives and discipline, and with the exercise, application, and enhancement of a host of human instincts, talents, habits, and skills.

The surah then turns to the second theme, that of the physical world and the clear effects of God's hand in its structure and existence:

He created the heavens and the earth in accordance with the universal truth. Exalted be He above all they associate with Him! He created man from a drop of fluid: yet man has clearly emerged as an open adversary. (3–4)

Man's intransigence is indeed bewildering. No other creature is so well aware of its weaknesses and frailties, yet dares to challenge the authority of God and deny His grace and favor. The surah illustrates this by pointing to one of the great favors of God to humankind in the verses: "He created beasts for you which give you warmth and food and other benefits. You enjoy their grace and beauty when you bring them home and when you take them out to graze" (5–6).

Profiling the relationship between humans and animals, the Qur'an presents a picture that is free of dominance and exploitation. Man, as the master and keeper of animals, is taught to live in harmony with them and treat them with respect. The human and animal roles in this world are complementary and inter-dependent. Animals are a source of comfort for humans, and should be treated with care and kindness for they are a blessing and a gift from God.

The surah then goes on to detail other divine favors of God to humans:

> He sends down water from the sky, of which you drink and irrigate the pasturage on which you feed your animals. And with it also He brings forth crops, olives, palm trees, grapes, and fruits of every kind. Surely in this there is a sign for those who reflect. (10–11)

What causes the rain to fall, and the earth to produce plants, crops and flowers which blossom and appear in such amazing and beautiful colors? It never ceases to amaze me how, from the same soil and using the same rain water, different varieties of plants and crops grow to provide food and nourishment for animals and humans alike whilst thick forests and expansive empty plains exist side by side. How does all this come about, and what power lies behind it all?

> He [God] harnessed for you the night and the day, and the sun and the moon; the stars are also subservient to His command. Surely in this there are signs for men of understanding. (12)

The planet on which we live, and which sustains us, is but a speck in a vast complex universe with countless planets and stars, and we are but a mere drop in an infinite ocean! Although our universe is undoubtedly vast, the power of its Creator is even more immense and awe-inspiring. Nevertheless, despite these overwhelming realities, there are in every generation people who remain ignorant of

God and/or who imagine Him to be a piece of rock or a plank of wood and worship Him as such.

> Is He, then, who creates, the same as him who cannot create? Will you not take heed? If you were to reckon up God's blessings you could not count them. God is Forgiving and Merciful. He is aware of what you conceal and what you reveal. Those taken as gods beside Him can create nothing; they are themselves created. They are dead, not alive; nor do they know when they will be raised to life again. (17–21)

This surah is also known by the title "*al-Ni'mah*", meaning "bounties" or "favors", as it calls on man to remember and value an impressive host of gifts and blessings which God has provided to humans for their use and benefit. As noted earlier, the evidence for God's power and sovereignty as manifested in the wonders of the silent physical world is supported by that which is eloquently articulated in the Qur'an. The two are complementary and used interchangeably to lead mankind to the universal truth and acquaint them with God Almighty.

Nonetheless, and despite the signs, skeptics and disbelievers have existed throughout human history. They have slandered God's prophets and branded them liars, rejecting belief in life after death. "They solemnly swear by God that He will never raise the dead to life. But God's promise shall be fulfilled, though most people may not know it" (38). The truth is that this life, with all its enjoyments, is transient and will be followed by an eternal and far richer one. This was the message that no Messenger had ever failed to convey to his people.

> All those We had sent before you [Muhammad] were men to whom We had sent revelation. If you do not know, refer to those with knowledge [of earlier revelation]. We had sent them with

strong evidence and scriptures, and to you [Muhammad] We have sent the Qur'an, so that you may explain to people what is sent down for them, and that they may give thought. (43–44)

Materialists, secularists, and animists do not believe in divine revelation. The Arabs of Makkah were idol-worshipers who did not believe in a life to come. When the Prophet told them that he had received divine revelation which taught that the physical, as well as the metaphysical, world was bigger and more sophisticated than they had come to realize, they turned against him. The Qur'an advised them to refer to the Israelites and the Christians, earlier recipients of divine revelation whom the Qur'an refers to as 'People of the Book,' and learn from their experience. This leaves us wondering as to what happened to the revelations which Moses and Jesus had brought to their respective followers?

The Old and New Testaments contain statements which are strange and inaccurate. Who, for instance, can believe the Old Testament account that God grew jealous of Adam after he had eaten from the tree of knowledge, and, fearing that he would eat of the tree of eternity and become His contender for power, had him expelled from the Garden of Eden and sent down to earth as a punishment for him and his offspring? Is it conceivable that God 'killed His only son, Jesus, or allowed him to be killed as atonement for Adam's sin and to facilitate his salvation'? These and other myths are among some of the many fabrications which are to be found in the Old and New Testaments, books claimed to be the word of God, such that whoever rejects them "shall never enter the Kingdom of God"!

The reason that the Qur'an referred the Arabs of Makkah to the People of the Book was only because these had had an experience of divine revelation, and not in order for them to learn from their scriptures. Indeed, the Qur'an corrected certain claims of earlier revelations:

By God, We have sent Messengers before you to other nations, but Satan made their vile deeds seem fair to them. He is now their patron, and a woeful punishment awaits them. We have revealed to you the Book so that you may resolve for them their differences, and as guidance and mercy to those who believe. (63–64)

The Qur'an is an elucidation of the truth propounded by earlier revelation and a means of salvation for man's soul and sanity. The revelation brought by Prophet Muhammad purified and reconciled man's thinking with earlier religious thought and closed the gap between purely materialistic belief and the belief in the unknown. The surah defines Muhammad's mission thus: "We have sent the Qur'an, so that you may explain to people what is sent down for them, and that they may give thought" (44). Reflection is a healthy function of a sound and vigorous mind, and rational thinking is an essential feature of a sensible mentality. Any system of religious belief which does not address man's rational faculties, or is not in tune with the requirements and limits of human nature, can claim no divine origins.

God has said, "You shall not serve two gods, but one God, so fear none but Me." His is what the heavens and the earth contain, and to Him all should undoubtedly submit. Would you then fear anyone else but God? (51–52)

The surah then returns to citing more of God's favors to mankind. "God sends down water from the sky with which He nourishes the soil after it was dead. In that there is a sign for people who pay attention" (65). As a result of this process, cereal, crops, and fruits of different kinds grow out of soil, manure, and fertilizing substances. Who controls and regulates the relationship between such paradoxes? "In animals too, there is a worthy lesson for you. We give you out of what is inside their bellies of food and blood, pure milk which is pleasant for all those who drink it" (66). Cows do not manufacture the milk they produce, nor is a cow's body the real or ultimate source of her milk. Likewise, chickens lay their eggs without having any idea of what minerals and other nutrients are contained therein. All this begs the question: who is behind this grand and marvelous design? Who makes it all work in such harmony, compatibility, efficiency, and balance? The answer is God Almighty, yet, alas, how few of us appreciate this tremendous fact or reciprocate it with any real show of obedience and gratitude to Him.

Your Lord inspired bees to dwell in mountains and trees and man-made hives, and to feed on every kind of fruit, and to seek the routes their Lord made easy for them to find. Out of their bellies comes a syrup of different hues, therein a cure for men. Surely in this there is a sign for those who ponder. (68–69)

Volumes have been written about the nutritional and medicinal values of honey. These tiny insects are able to extract nectar from flowers and plants everywhere. They group together in intricate and well-ordered kingdoms or colonies to produce this unique and fascinating substance which has provided man with nutrition, remedy, and enjoyment throughout the ages.

The surah goes on to cite a number of other favors of God to man spanning the length and breadth of his life: "God has created you and He will cause you to die, though some of you shall reach the senility of old age and forget all they had known hitherto…" (70). Life itself is a gift bestowed on man to enable him to fulfill his intended mission in this world. In return, man is obliged and expected to show gratitude and appreciation to God Almighty. God has allotted to people varying degrees of prosperity and fortune in their lives as a means of testing them, both in times of prosperity and in times of adversity. Will the wealthy be able to conquer their greed and selfishness and look with mercy and compassion towards the deprived, and care for them?

Marriage is yet another of God's great gifts and is a means for the preservation of the human race. But, how deeply have people truly valued its sanctity and preserved it from the crippling and unnecessary traditions, rituals, and demands of human society?

> God has provided you with spouses from among yourselves and, through your spouses, sons and grandchildren, and He has provided you with the good things. Would they then believe in falsehood and deny God's favors? (72)

One of the most intriguing features of human beings is their capacity to manufacture and believe in falsehoods. Instead of serving the One true God who has bestowed all manner of blessings upon them, they would rather turn their attention to the worship of concocted gods, both animate and inanimate:

> Rather than God, they worship others which cannot, nor will ever, confer on them any benefit from the heavens or the earth. Compare none else with God; God knows and you do not. (73–74)

Judgment is a certainty which every single human being will face. They will have to stand alone before God and be a witness to what they had done in this life, and for Allah this will occur in the twinkling of an eye: "The coming of the final Hour shall happen in a twinkle, or even faster. God has power over all things" (77).

The surah continues in a similar vein: "God brought you out of your mothers' wombs knowing nothing, and He gave you senses of hearing, vision, and feeling, so that you may be thankful" (78). The process of growth from babyhood to manhood is an amazing and fascinating one. Man's transformation from a small, vulnerable, and defenseless creature into a grown, mature, and independent adult is a magnificent manifestation of God's immense power and creativity.

From the secrets of the womb to the functions of the planet and the universe, God is fully aware and in control of everything. Nothing exists or happens on land, sea, or air without His knowledge, command, or power: "Do they not see the birds that fly in the vast skies, and nothing but God sustains them in flight? Surely in this there are signs for the believers" (79). Unfortunately, familiarity has blunted our fascination with the mysteries of God's creation and dulled our senses to the signs of His existence everywhere.

> God has made your houses places of shelter for you, and of animals' hide and skin He provided you with homes which are light to carry when you travel and easy to erect when you camp. From their wool, fur, and hair you can make furniture and other utility items for enjoyment during your short lives. Of what He has created God has provided you with shelter from the heat of the sun, and He has given you dwelling places in the mountains... (80–81)

Reading *ayah* after *ayah* one is quickly and deeply led to understand and appreciate that the number of favors bestowed by God on mankind is as vast as the stars in the sky and that: "If you reckoned up God's blessings you could not count them all. God is Forgiving and Merciful" (18).

At this point the surah turns to talk about the Qur'an itself but with reference to the Day of Judgment.

On the Day of Judgment We shall call a witness from every nation to testify against it. We shall call you [Muhammad] as witness against these people [the Arabs of Makkah]. We have revealed to you the Book manifesting all things and as guidance and mercy and good news for the Muslims. (89)

The same scene is cited in *al-Nisā'* which says:

How will it be then when We call forward a witness from every nation and call upon you [Muhammad] as witness against these people [the Arabs of Makkah]? On that day those who disbelieved and disobeyed the Messenger shall wish that they were reduced to dust, and they shall not [be able to] conceal anything from God. (*al-Nisā'*: 41–42)

It is reliably reported that when this verse was revealed to the Prophet he was driven to tears, suddenly understanding the weight of the responsibility placed upon his shoulders. The revelation received by Prophet Muhammad contained within it the key to understanding everything in this world. He delivered it intact and with honesty, and raised a nation which would go on to create a civilization that would change the whole course of human history and lead humanity along the true path to God. Today, this same revelation lies abandoned and the Muslim people, once the creators of empires, now do no more than pay lip service to its message and as a result languish in a climate of backwardness, defeat, apathy, and humiliation. What can the possible reasons for such failure be? Are the Qur'an's instructions so difficult to implement that we fail to execute them? The answer is an emphatic no. Those who find such lofty principles difficult to live by have only themselves to blame for living in misery and suffering. For Allah says: "God enjoins justice, kindness and charity to one's own kindred, and forbids indecency, wickedness, and oppression..." (90).

The surah then turns to a slander perpetrated by the enemies of Islam against the integrity of the Prophet during the early stages of his mission. The Arabs used to say that Muhammad had been taught the Qur'an by Jewish and Christian elders, or someone well-versed in the knowledge of earlier scriptures. The implication was that these mysterious mentors were non-Arab. However, they had explained why none of them had come forward to claim credit for their alleged contribution. "We know very well that they [the Arabs] say, 'Someone is teaching him.' But the man they allude to is non-Arab, while this [the Qur'an] comes in pure Arabic speech" (103).

The Qur'an immediately points out the absurdity of the accusation and the fallacy of the argument, for how could a non-Arab, no matter how skilled and versed in the knowledge of earlier scriptures, be able to compose a religious text of such utter beauty, perfection, and purity as to be considered by all literary experts as a unique masterpiece of Arabic prose unmatched to this day, without speaking a word, or very little, of the language itself? Moreover, if such a mentor did happen to exist, why on earth would the Arabs keep his identity a secret? Surely, the obvious action would have been to confront Muhammad with him in order to discredit his mission and expose him as an impostor? The accusation becomes more ludicrous if we take a closer look at the Torah, the Gospel and the Qur'an, an exercise which would reveal serious and fundamental differences between them.

The Torah speaks of a 'personal god' whom it presents in extremely derogatory and demeaning terms, for instance in the account of God's alleged defeat in a wrestling contest with Israel, or Jacob, father of the Jews. Furthermore, on several occasions God is made to appear in human form, and invariably described as 'ignorant,' 'reckless,' and 'remorseful'! There is no room for comparison between the contents of the Torah and those of the Qur'an. By what stretch of the imagination can the Torah be considered a source of inspiration or a reference for the Qur'an which bases faith on abso-lute monotheism and the total and absolute perfection, uniqueness, and sovereignty of God? It describes God as:

> ...the Merciful who sits majestically on the throne. He has full command over all that is in the heavens and on earth, and all that lies between them as well as underneath the soil. Whether or not you speak aloud, He knows the most hidden of secrets. (*Ṭā Hā*: 5–7)

The Qur'an says: "Everyone in the heavens and on earth shall return to the Merciful in utter submission. He has a complete record of them all, and one by one, they shall all return to Him on the Day of Judgment" (*Maryam*: 93–95).

Likewise, the Gospel also differs dramatically from the Qur'an in its conception of God. It says nothing even remotely resembling the above verse, and talks instead of "the Holy Spirit" (a probable reference to the Archangel Gabriel) and of Jesus, the son of Mary, as "God the Son" and "God the Father." In other words, that all three are, in essence, one, and that God is a trinity in which the father, the son and the holy ghost are one and the same!

This is poles apart from the Qur'anic conception and admits of no reconciliation between them for Allah says: "Say, 'God is One, the Eternal God. He begot none, nor was He begotten, and there is none that is equal to Him'" (*al-Ikhlāṣ*: 1–4).

In light of the above, how can one possibly conclude that Prophet Muhammad borrowed from the Torah or the Gospel, especially bearing in mind the fact that nothing in these scriptures comes even close to the unique style, diction, and presentation employed by the Qur'an? Its linguistic, literary, and stylistic merits, as well as its content and structure are without parallel, either in the language in which it is preserved, Arabic, or in any other language known to man. The Qur'anic concept of God is rich with reverence and veneration. It inspires man to be fully aware and appreciative of His absolute power and control over the whole of creation. God is Omnipotent, Omnipresent and Omniscient. The Qur'an invokes in the human mind immediate and spontaneous submission and obedience to God Almighty. Any attempts to undermine the origins and integrity of the Qur'anic text will always prove groundless.

> God shall not guide those who do not believe His revelation, and a grievous punishment awaits them. Those who disbelieve God's revelation invent lies, and they are indeed liars. (104–105)

Although the Qur'an does not spare such liars, for their crime is serious, it does show clemency and compassion towards those who are misled or who succumb to temptation due to weakness or duress.

> As for anyone who denies God after having once attained to faith—and this, to be sure, does not apply to one who does it under duress, the while his heart remains true to his faith, but [only to] him who willingly opens up his heart to a denial of the truth—upon all such [falls] God's condemnation, and tremendous suffering awaits them: all this, because they hold this world's life in greater esteem than the life to come, and because God does not bestow His guidance upon people who deny the truth. (106–107)

As Muslims, we believe that the Qur'an shall continue, unrivaled and unchallenged, till the very end of time, to be the unparalleled phenomenon it has always been.

As mentioned earlier, this surah is mainly dedicated to pointing out the numerous and wide-ranging bounties and blessings that God has granted to humans. Foremost among these is the Qur'an itself, as a guide and a beacon. Several communities throughout human history, however, have chosen to ignore or not to acknowledge these favors, refusing to show any gratitude to God.

God gives the example of a once peaceful and safe village whose provisions came to it in abundance from every quarter, but it denied God's favors. Therefore, God afflicted it with famine and fear as a punishment for its people's deeds. (112)

In cases where people have changed course after having been misled, and have come to recognize and reciprocate God's blessings with gratitude, God will always forgive them and take them back into the fold. It is comforting to know that His door is always open for those who repent and want to make a fresh start. "Your Lord is always forgiving and merciful towards those who commit evil through ignorance, and then repent and mend their ways" (119).

The surah then goes on to speak of Abraham, who was the elder of all God's prophets and 'a nation unto himself,' a paragon of piety and steadfastness in the service of God and His message. Prophet Muhammad was instructed to follow in his footsteps. The surah then makes a fleeting reference to the fact that the imposition of the Sabbath on the Israelites had been as a punishment for their internal wrangling, and internecine conflicts.

The surah closes with a profound statement addressed to Prophet Muhammad emphasizing the fact that Islam is a faith built on understanding, reasoned discussion, intelligent argument and amicable persuasion. It is never to be spread by force or compulsion.

Call others to the path of your Lord with prudence and gentle exhortation, and argue with them in the most courteous manner. (125)

Mastering this approach in *daʿwah*, or propagation of Islam, requires not only a deep and earnest knowledge of the Qur'an and the Sunnah of the Prophet but also a good understanding of the intricacies of human nature.

SURAH 17

Al-Isrā'
(The Night Journey)

THIS SURAH IS KNOWN by the two titles: the Israelites and *al-Isrā'*, the Night Journey. Its opening verse refers to Prophet Muhammad's remarkable night journey from Makkah to Jerusalem in 621 AC. The following verses then immediately turn back in history to relate some important episodes from the Israelites' first sojourn in Palestine. The Torah had firmly and conclusively established the religious and political identity of the Israelites. However, although they had initially emerged as a model community, promoting order, cohesion, and fairness, their behavior soon changed and began to resemble more that of the Pharaohs, their arch oppressors. In the end they created chaos and havoc.

The Qur'an explains how administrative incompetence and moral corruption within the leadership of a community can be eradicated by simply removing the base and inept authority perpetrating them. Reform may also be achieved through an outside force, where foreigners intervene to take control, restore order, and punish those responsible for the situation:

We revealed to the Israelites in the Book [the Torah]: "You shall commit evil in the land twice, and you shall commit great oppression." When the first round of your oppression will come to pass, We shall send formidable loyal servants of Ours to ravage your lands in fulfillment of Our command. (4–5)

Once nations lose control over their own affairs, they become open to outside control and domination, forfeiting their rights to independence of thought and freedom of action. Moreover, corruption and oppression are incompatible with a system based on divine revelation, and, for this very reason, the punishment for its negligence is usually very severe as otherwise the community can easily fall prey to foreign control and suffer indignity and humiliation. Once the lessons are learnt and the community's true and original spirit is awakened, its sense of dignity and self-esteem is restored. This was the experience of the Israelites, for God says: "We allowed you [the Israelites] to prevail against them once again, and aided you with wealth and offspring, and made you more numerous [than ever]" (6). The cycle of progress continues as victory merely ushers in a new phase of trials and appraisal procedures. "If you persevere in doing good, you will but be doing good to yourselves; and if you do evil, it will be [done] to yourselves…" (7).

The Qur'an foretells that the Israelites would soon renege and deviate, incurring yet more divine displeasure and punishment. "…If you [the Israelites] revert [to sinning], We shall revert [to chastising you]. And [remember this:] We have ordained that [in the Hereafter] hell shall close upon all who deny the truth" (8). The Israelites were first ravaged by the Babylonians under Nebuchadnezzar in 586 BC, when the Temple of Solomon in Jerusalem was destroyed and they were taken into captivity. The second time was in 70 AC at the hands of Titus, later to become Roman Emperor, who razed the Temple to the ground (after which it was never rebuilt) and scattered the Israelites throughout the world.

In recent times, however, it has been the turn of the Muslims to neglect their obligations towards the establishment of God's order in this world and as a result incur His displeasure. The great irony of the current situation is, however, that it is the Israelites, previously condemned for the same misdeeds, who have overwhelmed the

Muslims. Since the Muslims, in possession of authentic and impeccable revelation, have regressed into bigotry and ethnocentricity, they have been humbled by the Israelites, a condemned and censored people, who have in contrast rallied around their religious laws and traditions to overcome the Muslims.

A unique feature of this surah is the direct use of the word 'Qur'an' which is employed around eleven times, a characteristic not found in any of the other surahs. These references occur in the following verses:

(9)   This Qur'an guides to that which is most upright...

(41)   We have made plain Our revelations in this Qur'an so that they [the unbelievers] may take warning...

(45)   When you [Muhammad] recite the Qur'an, We place between you and those who deny the life Hereafter a hidden barrier.

(46)   ...and when you mention your Lord, Him alone, in the Qur'an, they [the unbelievers] turn their back in flight.

(60)   We have made the vision which We showed you [Muhammad], as well as the [*zaqqūm*] tree cursed in the Qur'an, but a test to men's faith.

(78)   Observe the prayers [salah, at their appointed times] from the time the sun rises in the meridian and through the night. Recitation of the Qur'an at dawn is particularly celebrated.

(82)   Parts of the Qur'an which We reveal are a panacea and a mercy to the believer...

(88)   Say, "If all mankind and the jinn conferred to produce the like of this Qur'an, they would surely fail…"

(89)   We have set forth for humankind in this Qur'an all manner of arguments, yet most of them persist in denial.

(106) We have divided the Qur'an into parts so that you [Muhammad] may deliver it to people with deliberation…

It is also referred to indirectly in the following verses:

(86)   If We wished We could take away what We have revealed to you [Muhammad]…

(105) We have revealed it [the Qur'an] with the Truth, and with the Truth it has come down.

It appears that the reader's attention is being drawn to the fact that the Qur'an is the most effective instrument that can unite the Muslims and make them into a great world power again. In contrast, the abandonment and negligence of its message by its followers will be considered inexcusable and unjustifiable.

In the story of the Israelites we have a clear lesson and a warning. They were dominated and defeated by pagans and fire worshipers because they did not respect their divine scripture. Looking at the dismal history of the Muslims, is it any wonder that, having been guilty of a similar infringement, they are also being humiliated by the worst and most lowly of enemies? All is not lost however and this downward trend can be reversed in order to surmount and overcome the situation. The Muslim nation's ethical, social, political, and economic life, its laws, practices, and relations with the outside world should stem from the Qur'an and be guided by its principles. In short, Muslims must learn to live every aspect of their life by the Qur'an. This process cannot be completed overnight and will be an ongoing and gradual development, governed by the laws of human nature and the imperatives of social change. Unfortunately, man is impatient and can easily be driven to despair: "Man prays for ill as fervently as he prays for good; truly, man is ever impatient" (11).

✖✖

The surah establishes the God-ordained patterns that govern man's world:

> We made the night and the day as signs; We enshrouded the night with darkness and made the day bright, so that you may seek the grace of your Lord and learn the calculation of the seasons and the years. We have made all things manifestly plain (12).

As time goes by the cycle of human progress and decline is repeated, as indicated in the surah; civilizations rise and fall, and communities dominate and become dominated. The single common element in this process is man himself; his behavior and judgment decide his destiny and future. "He that seeks guidance shall be guided to his own advantage, but he that errs shall err at his own peril. No man shall bear another man's burden..." (15).

This principle is universal, and equally applicable to individual as well as collective human behavior. However, the Qur'an points out that affluence and economic injustice are the first symptoms of corruption in a nation. The ascendancy of those who hoard wealth and exploit others is usually the main reason, and the first sign, of a nation's downfall.

> When We decide to destroy a city [a nation], We address the affluent of its people. If they persist in their corruption and disobedience, [Our] judgment becomes irrevocable and We shall raze it to the ground. (16)

Implicit in these statements is the fact that nations and civilizations are liable to be weakened and undermined by affluence and extravagance. Their fate is also linked to their people's attitude towards the hereafter and the judgment that is sure to come. "He that opts for this fleeting life We shall give him of it whatever We will" (18). Affluence and prosperity are bestowed on nations and individuals according to God's will, and they do not necessarily entail obedience and submission to Him.

The surah sounds a stern warning: "We have destroyed many nations since Noah's time..." (17) for their corruption and transgression, and "...no [such] nation shall be spared destruction or stern punishment, before the Day of Judgment. That is permanently recorded in the [eternal] Book" (58).

By way of advice, the surah recommends, in verses 23–39 inclusive, a list of social, moral, and economic practices and measures which, if adopted, would strengthen the fabric of society and maintain justice, balance and cohesion within it. The section begins thus: "Your Lord has enjoined that you worship none but Him, and to show kindness to parents..." (23) and ends with the statement:

These injunctions are but a part of the wisdom which your Lord has revealed to you [Muhammad]. Serve no other god besides God, lest you should be cast into hell, remorseful and despised. (39)

We note that the section opens and closes with an emphasis on *tawḥīd*, indicating that it is the backbone of righteousness and true submission to God. Along with *tawḥīd* comes respect and kindness towards one's parents. To appreciate the value of this, one need only look at how parents and old people are treated in today's Western materialistic societies. Once they reach a certain age, parents and grandparents are committed to old people's homes and institutions that are devoid of love and kinship, abandoned by their sons and daughters and left to die in loneliness and desolation. Despite the hard work and effort put into raising their children, parents in this society receive very little in return and nothing reflects more disloyalty and selfishness than uncaring, ungrateful offspring. Furthermore, the general trend in many societies today is to raise children with the idea that they should break away from their families at the earliest possible age. In the West, for example, they meet only, if at all, once a year at Christmas, or at family weddings and funerals.

In Muslim societies, children should have a different relationship with their parents. God says: "Treat them with humility and tenderness and say, 'Lord, be merciful to them, for they nurtured me when I was in childhood'" (24). Regarding other family relations, He says: "Give to the near of kin their due, and also to the destitute and to the wayfarer. Do not squander your wealth wastefully…" (26). I understand this to mean that one should not live in luxury when one is surrounded by others in desperate need of the basic necessities of life. This is further stressed in the verse which says: "Be neither miserly nor extravagant, lest you would become despised or destitute" (29). Alluding to the pre-Islamic Arab custom of burying alive unwanted new-born girls, the surah goes on to point out that such methods of birth control are not the best solution for the world population problem. People must seek fair and equitable means of distribution of wealth and resources among all members of society: "Do not kill your children for fear of want" (31).

Increasingly, illicit sexual relations, including extra-marital sex, or adultery, have become the norm in modern society. Free indulgence in promiscuous sex is seen as a healthy alternative to the so-called sexual repression associated with morality and family-based societies. But God says: "Avoid illicit sexual relations, for they are foul and indecent" (32). Murder, that is to say the *unlawful* killing of one human being by another, is recognized as a crime in all societies. However, the *lawful* killing of a human being for the commission of a crime, that is to say capital punishment, has been made illegal in several countries today, and this has led to the spread of insecurity and crime, resulting in the loss of innocent lives. The Qur'an exhorts:

> And do not take any human being's life—[the life] which God has willed to be sacred—otherwise than in [the pursuit of] justice. Hence, if anyone has been slain wrongfully, We have empowered the defender of his rights [to exact a just retribution]; but even so, let him not exceed the bounds of equity in [retributive] killing. [And as for him who has been slain wrongfully] behold, he is indeed succored [by God]! (33)

The Qur'an also enjoins man to protect the property of the orphan, honor pledges, covenants, and contracts, and exercise justice and fairness in using weights and measures. Every individual bears responsibility for what he hears or sees or feels. As humans, our lives have a purpose, our senses and actions carry liabilities and we are answerable for all our experiences. The Qur'an tells us: "Do not follow what you do not understand. All shall be accountable for what their ears, eyes, and hearts do" (36). A little reflection and discretion with respect to our thoughts and to what we hear and learn can help us avoid a great deal of misunderstanding and ill-feeling. The section is rounded off with the profound advice: "Do not walk haughtily on the earth. You shall neither split the earth nor rival the mountains in their height" (37). These valuable exhortations are vital ingredients for the development of morally and spiritually balanced individuals and are, moreover, indispensable building blocks for the development of strong and enlightened societies.

The surah then turns to an inspiring and reassuring discussion about God Almighty and His power and affinity with the believers. It touches on the natural physical world around us and the amazing harmony and rapport which distinguish its systems, movement, and existence. The infinite and incredibly complex universe, with its millions upon millions of stars, planets, and galaxies, is in constant motion, but this motion is so smooth and tranquil that every second that passes provides additional proof of the power and might of its Creator. Another marvel of creation is the human body composed of hundreds of millions of cells which form a number of complex systems performing a wide range of vital well-integrated functions that make man a central and effective force in shaping the destiny of the world. Does each of these cells realize the purpose of their existence or comprehend the functions they carry out? Do 'white cells' or 'red cells' have brains of their own that tell them what to do or how to behave? No, it is Allah who controls them and who has programmed them to perform a specific set of functions lasting for a determined period of time which could extend to a whole generation. This marvel is duplicated, with the same efficiency and precision, in thousands of millions of human beings and has been done so for hundreds of thousands of years.

Every atom in this vast cosmos, every cell, every human being, and every creature is a testament to God's predominance and authority. Is this not proof enough of His incontestable supremacy and unparalleled power? This world cannot exist on its own, nor could it have come into existence of its own free will or volition. It is totally and completely dependent on the power and grace of God. Skeptics who choose not to believe in God or acknowledge His authority do Him no harm whatsoever.

> We have made plain Our revelations in this Qur'an so that they [the unbelievers] may take note, but it only adds to their deviation. Say, "If, as you affirm, there were other gods besides God, they would surely seek to dethrone Him." Glory to Him! Exalted be He, high above their false allegations! The seven heavens, the earth, and all that dwell in them extol His glory. All creatures celebrate His praises. He is Magnanimous and Forgiving. (41–44)

The surah goes on to address and educate the unbelievers about God, accusing them of preferring to live in darkness rather than to accept the truth of God's existence. By refusing to accept His message, the unbelievers of Muhammad's time suspended their rational intellectual faculties and thereby denigrated themselves to a level lower than the animals which only live life on a day-to-day basis and see nothing beyond their immediate material existence. Their excuse was that Muhammad must have been a victim of incantation, influenced by a magic spell, and that what he was saying to them was absolute nonsense for there could be no life after death.

It is interesting to note here that modern civilization also adopts the exact same logic, with reference to life after death, as reflected clearly in its art, literature, law and philosophy. Ancient and modern skeptics would say in disbelief:

> "What! When we are turned to bones and dust, shall we be restored to life?" Say, "You shall; whether you were made of stone or iron, or any other substance which you may think can never be given life." They would ask, "Who will restore us to life?" Say, "He who created you the first time round." They would shake their heads and ask, "When will this be?" Say, "It may be quite soon. On that day He will summon you all, and you shall answer Him, praising, and you shall think that you have only lived for a little while...." (49–52)

This is the second time this argument appears in the surah, indicating that human beings are raised above the animals by virtue of their free will and intellectual capabilities, but that once these capabilities are relinquished, their senses lose their human functions and begin to resemble more those of the animals—they look without seeing, hear without understanding, and speak without knowledge. More ominously, however, as man openly denies the existence and sovereignty of God and refuses to believe in his accountability to Him, he forfeits the right to and privilege of God's guidance.

> Those whom God guides would be rightly guided; but those whom He confounds shall have no ally besides Him. On the Day of Resurrection they shall be dragged on their faces, blind, dumb and deaf. Hell shall be their abode: whenever its fire dies down We shall bring them a fiercer one. Thus shall they be rewarded: because they disbelieved Our revelations and said, "Shall we be raised to life after we are turned to bones and dust?" Do they not see that God, who has created the heavens and the earth, is capable of creating their like? The times of their death and resurrection are fixed with certainty. Yet the wrong-doers persist in unbelief. (97–99)

Verse 83 of *al-Baqarah* cites God's advice to the Israelites to: "Be courteous to others," emphasizing the point that politeness and civility are necessary features of the believers. Echoing this counsel verse 53 of this surah also directs Muslims, through Prophet Muhammad, to be courteous and pleasant to one another: "Tell My servants to be courteous in their speech, for Satan sows discord among them. Satan is the sworn enemy of man" (53). This is followed by an assertion that Islam, and the Muslims, shall eventually triumph. "Your Lord is best aware of all who dwell in the heavens and on the earth. We have exalted some prophets above others, and to David We gave the Psalms" (55). Elsewhere in the Qur'an, the Psalms of David are said to include this promise: "We ordained in the Psalms, as in the Book previously, that My righteous servants shall inherit the land of Paradise" (*al-Anbiyā'*: 105). Taken together, these statements affirm the continuity of God's message throughout human history. This continuity is based on the concept of *tawḥīd*, the distinguishing and most fundamental principle that binds the community of believers together and links them firmly to God.

Say, "Pray to whomever you wish besides God. They cannot relieve your suffering, nor end it." Those to whom they pray themselves seek God's grace, vying to be close to Him, pleading for His mercy, and fearing His punishment. Your Lord's punishment is ever fearful. (56–57)

Following these verses the surah moves on to give a most profound statement concerning Adam and his offspring. "We have placed Adam's offspring in high regard, facilitated their travel on land and by sea, provided them with good things, and exalted them significantly above many of Our creatures..." (70). But Adam himself proved lacking in will-power, whilst some of his offspring showed and have continued to show a remarkable lack of gratitude for the generosity extended to them. The Qur'an relates some astonishing instances of human disrespect of, and indifference towards, God and His kindness to humankind. Humankind have been especially favored with intellectual powers which enable them to discern, reflect, rationalize, and judge values, objects, ideas, behaviors, and principles. However, once they begin to disregard or defy the logical foundations of the world in which they live, their rationalization and, subsequently, communication with it break down.

Prophet Muhammad spared no effort to present the principle of *tawḥīd* in the simplest and most intelligible and forceful manner possible. Although miracles were demanded of him, and he was challenged to present extraordinary material evidence to support his arguments, there were no indications that his detractors would have believed him anyway. At one stage the Makkans demanded Muhammad to turn the hill of Safa, in Makkah, into gold before they would give any credence to what he was telling them.

However, there was no guarantee that they would have believed him, even if he had done as they asked, for God says: "And we refrain from sending the signs, only because the men of former generations treated them as false. We sent to Thamūd the she-camel as a clear sign, but they disregarded it. We give signs only in order to frighten [the unbelievers]" (59). The unbelievers of Quraysh were quite specific:

> They said, "We will not believe you until you make us a spring, gushing out of the ground, or have for yourself a garden of Eden with palm-trees and grapes and rivers flowing through it, or bring the sky down upon us, as you have threatened to do, or bring God and the angels before our very eyes, or have built for yourself a house of gold, or ascend to heaven; but we shall not believe you until you bring down for us a book which we can read." Say, "Glory to my Lord! Am I anything but a [humble] human Messenger?" (90–93)

The truth of the matter, reiterated again and again, is that even if God had acceded to their demands, they still would not have believed in Him. The Qur'an says:

> If We opened for them [the unbelievers] a gate in heaven through which they ascended higher and higher, they still would have said, "Our eyes are dazzled; we must be under a spell!" (*al-Ḥijr* 14–15)

The unbelievers are saturated with obstinacy and disbelief (*kufr*), an overwhelming persistent state of envy, stupidity, selfishness and greed. Freedom from *kufr* requires enlightenment, fair-mindedness and high moral standards. The conflict between *kufr* and faith (*imān*) is a continuing one in the history of man and its outcome will not become apparent until the hereafter, and then:

he whose record is placed in his right hand, will read it, and shall not be wronged a wick's width. But he who has been blind in this life shall be even more blind in the life to come and will be in a worse state of loss. (71–72)

However, the rejection of his people was not going to deter Muhammad from the task with which he had been entrusted; the timeless message had been addressed to all mankind and so was destined to spread to the far corners of the world. Muhammad's mission was made all the more difficult by the fact that, apart from the help and blessings of God, his methods had to rely on persuasion, education, and reform alone. Some prominent Makkan leaders demanded to be given special concessions and insisted on being treated differently from the rest. A similar situation had been faced by prophet Noah when the more powerful members of his community had asked him:

> "Are we to believe in you when your followers are but the lowest of the low among us?" He [Noah] replied, "How do I know what they may have done? My Lord alone can bring them to account, if you would but understand! I am not about to drive away the believers…" (*al-Shuʿarā'*: 111–114)

If Muhammad could have been swayed into paying more attention to the demands of the influential people this would have been at the expense of the lesser, more ordinary folk who had just as much right to learn and understand about the religion. The surah tells him, however:

> They [the unbelievers] sought to entice you from Our revelations, hoping that you might invent some other scripture in Our name. Indeed, you would have been their trusted ally. Had We not strengthened your faith, you might have inclined to their way

slightly. In that case, you would have incurred a double punishment: in this life and in the life to come. You would have found none to protect you from Us. (73–75)

Whatever means one adopts to spread the message of Islam, it must be in accordance with the principles of the faith and cannot deviate from them. This is why the Prophet was reprimanded for giving more attention and energy to the pursuit of rich and influential individuals whilst neglecting the needs of the poor and ordinary ones. In any case, there was no way of ensuring that the powerful were simply not deceiving him in their continuous scheming to undermine the Muslims. "They sought to intimidate you and drive you out of your home town. Had they succeeded, they would have scarcely survived your departure" (76). Makkan Arabs resorted to persecution and conspiracy in order to intimidate the Prophet and his followers, and force them out of Makkah. At one point, they were poised to kill him, but God led him to safety. Prophet Muhammad emigrated to Madinah and, within a few years, Islam had prevailed and he returned to Makkah triumphant.

Once the external material struggle had been overcome and the Muslims had achieved victory, a new internal struggle took prominence as the self learned to do battle with its ego, pride, and desires. Muhammad was taught that to become closer to God he should perform extra prayers and devote more time to personal, spiritual regeneration and development.

Observe the prayers [at their appointed times] from the time the sun rises in the meridian and through the night. Recitation of the Qur'an at dawn is particularly celebrated. (78)

In the course of my research on the Prophet's personality and spiritual devotion to God, I was overwhelmed by the feeling that humanity has never known a more devout and pious worshiper than

Muhammad. This is firmly supported by the Qur'an and amply documented in the Prophet's recorded sayings and biographies.
Muhammad was the last of the illustrious chain of prophets sent by
God to mankind, and he was the seal of prophethood. His coming
had been alluded to in the scriptures of the Jews and Christians and
they were aware of his imminent arrival. When the impending
event occurred, the true believers among them accepted him without hesitation. God says:

> We have revealed the Qur'an with the universal Truth, and it has
> been revealed with the Truth. We have sent you [Muhammad]
> only as a Messenger to deliver good tidings and to warn. We have
> revealed the Qur'an in stages, piece by piece, so that you may recite
> it to people with deliberation. Say, "It is for you to believe in it or to
> reject it." Those endowed with knowledge prior to its revelation
> prostrate themselves when it is recited to them, saying: "Glorious is
> our Lord; our Lord's promise has been fulfilled!" (105–108)

History informs us that as the Roman empire began to decline, the
Christians of Syria and Egypt accepted Islam willingly and en masse,
and, together with the Arabs, they carried it forward to all corners of
the globe. This is a vindication of the truth of the above verses and a
strong indication of the true and genuine faith of large sections of
pre-Islamic Jewish and Christian communities.

Al-Kahf
(The Cave)

THE COSMOS REPRESENTS the physical evidence for the existence of God, and revelation is the guide to that evidence. True and sincere belief in God (*imān*) grows out of studying and understanding the evidence and the guiding light leading to it. We read in the opening verse of *al-Anʿām*: "Praise be to God who has created the heavens and the earth and ordained darkness and light...". *Al-Kahf* opens with the words: "Praise be to God who has revealed to His servant [Muhammad] the perfect Book [the Qur'an] free of all blemish" (1).

In the Qur'an, God urges man to be curious about life and the world around him, to study every phenomenon he comes across, and, at the same time, to study the Qur'an and reflect on its concepts and meanings. Without this reflection and the will to learn and discover, man will be bereft of guidance and understanding.

> Will they [the unbelievers] look at the universe of heavens and earth, and all that God has created, and [consider] that their appointed hour might be nigh? What other book than this one shall they believe? (*al-Aʿrāf*: 185)

The physical world is teeming with evidence for *tawḥīd*. Everything in the world points to one universal indubitable truth: that there is but one Creator, who has no ancestry or offspring, and to whom all creation belongs. The Qur'an has made this clear and beyond question. Even Muhammad himself, who received the revelation and relayed it to humankind, is a servant of God like everyone else. Any argument to gainsay these facts is simply futile and untenable.

And admonish those who say that God has begotten a son. Neither they nor their ancestors have any knowledge of such claims. It is a monstrous claim that they utter; they are saying nothing but sheer falsehood. (4–5)

Reflection on the wonders of the cosmos enhances one's faith in God and leads one closer to Him. The Qur'an has very clearly established the link between intelligent study and contemplation and the development of a strong and rational faith.

The Qur'an, as the quintessential reference source for *tawḥīd*, is perfect, untampered with, and free of distortion. This assurance is in itself a divine favor which deserves praise. The surah thus opens with the words:

Praise be to God who has revealed to His servant [Muhammad] the perfect Book [the Qur'an] free of blemish, so that he may give warning of a dire scourge from Him, and give good news to the believers who do good deeds that a wonderful reward awaits them, which they will enjoy endlessly... (1–3)

The surah cites episodes from the chronicles of history to illustrate the veracity of the concept of *tawḥīd* and its value to human society. It narrates the stories of the young men of the cave, the rich man of the orchard and the pauper, Moses and the pious man, and the well-known account of Dhū'l-Qarnayn. Each account is followed by an enlightening commentary designed to instill in the mind a recognition of the existence of God and the need to prepare for our accountability to Him.

Before this, however, a few words of comfort are given to alleviate Muhammad's despondency at his people's negative response to the Qur'an. "You may destroy yourself with grief over their rejection, sorry that they do not believe in this revelation" (6). Muhammad was told not to overburden himself because his main task was to deliver the message, and that he would not be held responsible for the people's reactions to it. Human beings are rational creatures, well equipped mentally and intellectually to discern ideas and judge actions and consequences. Every individual shall be accountable for the life he or she has spent on this earth. Divine justice shall be done, and none shall be wronged.

The Cave Youths, or the Sleepers, were young men who lived in a polytheist community but embraced *tawḥīd* and rejected all other ideologies, thereby earning the anger of their own people. This is made clear in the verse that says: "'Our people serve other gods besides Him, though they have no convincing proof of their divinity. Who is more wicked than him who invents lies about God?'" (15) Their belief had made them a target for mounting persecution by their people and their lives were in danger. They decided to seek safety elsewhere. This led them to a cave on the outskirts of the town, where they remained for a considerable period of time, unaware that they would go down in history as a paragon of faith and devotion. Political and religious bigotry and persecution are known to exist in every human society: "Did you [Muhammad] think that the Youths of the Cave and *al-raqīm* [the writing tablet] were the most extraordinary of Our signs?" (9). Naturally, they were not!

The sun is 150 million kilometers away from the earth and its rays take eight minutes to reach us. Bearing these facts in mind, it is a miracle that, to protect the innocent youths, sunlight fell on the entrance of the cave at such an angle that it obscured its occupants from the unwelcome gaze of any passers-by.

You [Muhammad] would have seen the rising sun inclined to the right of their cavern and, as it sets, it passes them to the left, while they are inside it. That was one of God's signs... (17)

God's signs abound everywhere, in the history of humankind and all around us today, but most people are blind to them.

Three hundred years later, unaware of how long they had been asleep, the youths awoke. The first thing they felt was hunger, and one of them went to the market to fetch some food. The others urged him to be careful and ensure that no one recognized him. "For if they find you out they will stone you to death, or force you back into their religion and then you shall never succeed" (20). They were so innocent and sincere that their only concern was for their faith and how they could protect it. Their account, therefore, is rather appropriately concluded with the words:

Say, "None but God knows how long they stayed [in the Cave]. He knows the secrets of the heavens and the earth. He sees and hears best. Man has no other ally besides Him. He shares His sovereignty with no one else." (26)

The next verse reasserts the principle of *tawḥīd*, already emphasized in the opening verse of the surah: "Proclaim what has been revealed to you of your Lord's Book. His words are immutable. You shall have no protection other than with Him" (27).

The Qur'an provoked two distinct reactions amongst the people of Muhammad; some believed it and its teachings, whilst others rejected it outright. God directed the Prophet to side with the former, showing support and affinity towards them, but to keep away from the latter, saying:

Discipline yourself to remain with those who pray to their Lord morning and evening, seeking His pleasure…and never obey him

311

whose heart We have rendered oblivious of Our remembrance; who follows his desires and whose lot is utterly hopeless. (28)

In this life man is free to believe or not to believe: "Say, 'The Truth comes from your Lord. Whoever wishes to believe, let him believe, and whoever wishes to deny, let him deny'" (29). On the Day of Judgment, justice shall be fully done towards both parties: "For the wrong-doers We have prepared a fire which will surround them like a formidable wall..." (29), while "those who believe and do good works, We shall not deny them their reward" (30). Having clarified the position, the surah directs Prophet Muhammad to address the whole of humankind, saying: "'This is the truth from your Lord. You are free to believe it or reject it'" (29).

A believer recognizes the existence of God and, conscious of this reality, dedicates his life to the pursuit of His pleasure and the hope of meeting Him in the hereafter, for he is fully aware that death does not signal the end of existence but is simply the staging post for a journey into another life. In contrast, however, a non-believer is firmly rooted in this life and spends it entirely in pursuit of his personal pleasures, needs, and desires. In the expectation that his existence will end at death, with no prospect of a life to come, the non-believer views the present and whatever remains of his life as the only reality.

The surah then moves on to examine features of this principle and formulates it through a discussion between a wealthy non-believer and a believer of rather humble means. "Tell them, by way of example, about the two men, to one of whom We gave two lush vineyards surrounded by palm-trees and joined by cornfields..." (32) while the other was of meager possessions. Gloating in his opulence, the affluent non-believer boasted: "'I am richer and more powerful than you'" (34). Rather than showing consideration towards his less fortunate neighbor and offering to share some of his possessions with him, he chose to exult in his position judging himself solely on the basis of his material wealth. There is no knowing who is best in the sight of God for Islam teaches that wealth and material possessions are gifts from God, and not criteria for judging whether a person is good or bad. Whatever God gives, He can just as easily take away and if some wealthy people believe that they have come by their wealth through their personal skills and dexterity alone, they should ask themselves the question: Who gave them these qualities in the first place? It was left to the poor believer to put the facts across:

> Why, when you entered your garden, did you not say: "This is of the grace of God! There is no power except with God!"? And if you think that I am poorer than yourself and with fewer offspring, God may yet give me a garden better than yours, and send down thunderbolts from the sky upon your vineyard, making it [but] slippery sand... (39–40)

This prophecy was fulfilled, and the green and fertile fields of the wealthy owner were indeed turned into a barren and arid waste. The rich neighbor was grief-stricken and lamented his fate, saying: "'I wish I had not served other gods besides my Lord!' No allies had he to protect him other than God, nor was he able to defend himself" (42–43). He had been too proud, complacent, and self-satisfied, and although self-preservation usually does drive human beings to place their personal interests before those of others, in many cases people become self-possessed anyway and are totally overtaken by their own self-interests. God no longer holds a place in their hearts and their consciences and they become completely self-centered.

In fact our own modern materialistic civilization has produced generations of self-seeking and greedy individuals. Modern culture has completely removed the issue of life-after-death from its agenda, and any discussion of it is seen as meaningless and futile, to be indulged in only by intellectual imbeciles, religious "fanatics" or the superstitious. To such people God says:

Cite for them the simile of this life. It is like earth's vegetation which thrives when the rain falls on it from the sky, but it then dries and is strewn away by the winds. God has power over all things. (45)

This is not to say that life, though transient and brief, is all evil or that affluence and prosperity are bad. Wealth and power are bestowed on many people as a blessing and a mercy from God. We have already seen how Joseph came to be appointed to a high position of power in Pharaoh's kingdom. "Thus We established Joseph in the land to rise therein as high as he pleased. We bestow Our mercy on whom We will, and shall never deny the righteous their reward" (*Yūsuf*: 56). Indeed power and wealth are necessary to establish God's universal truth on earth and support and perpetrate good and useful causes.

Wealth and affluence are not the prerogative of the non-believers only. The wealthy landowner in the above tale was not condemned for his affluence but for his crass attitude and fatuous justification, expressed as follows:

"I do not believe this will ever come to an end, and I do not believe the Last Hour will ever come! But even if it were to come, I am sure to find an even better replacement for this wealth!" (35–36)

But what caused him to arrive at this conclusion or reach such levels of arrogance and irascibility? The surah comments: "Wealth and children are the ornament of this life. But deeds of lasting merit are better rewarded and hold greater hope with your Lord" (46). Although wealth and offspring add to the happiness and the enjoyment of this life, they are also sources of power and influence. In *al-Isrā'*, verse 6, God said to the Israelites: "Then We granted you victory over them and multiplied your numbers and your resources, and caused you to outnumber them." Prophet Muhammad was quoted as saying: "Clean wealth befits the righteous."[24] When the spirit of altruism and self-sacrifice is suppressed or defeated, man's infatuation with material wealth becomes an obsession; and if wealth is combined with greed and stinginess, the results can be disastrous. However, when wealth is underpinned with faith in God and is utilized for good causes, it becomes an asset and earns God's pleasure.

Prophet Muhammad was reported to have said:

God will strengthen and enrich the heart of a man for whom success in the hereafter is the sole preoccupation; wealth shall come to him in spite of himself. But a man preoccupied with worldly matters shall only see poverty and deprivation; he shall only receive his pre-destined share but will suffer poverty day and night. Whoever turns his heart to God, others shall turn towards him with kindness and friendship, and God would bring him quicker success.[25]

These wise words are deeply reassuring, evoking a sense of contentment and inspiring us to free ourselves from the scourges of greed and self-indulgence. However, they should by no means be taken as an excuse for apathy and a reason to avoid the lawful and clean pursuit of wealth and material prosperity. The threat to man's humanity and future happiness arises when he neglects God, discounts his accountability to Him, dismisses the reality of life after death, and surrenders his soul to the pursuit of material worldly interests and desires. Because of the catastrophic effect of this moral and religious amnesia on man and society as a whole, the surah reminds us of:

the day when We shall cause the mountains to move and the earth to appear barren and plain; when We shall gather them [humankind]

---

24 Narrated by Imām Aḥmad.
25 Narrated by al-Tirmidhī.

all, leaving not a single soul behind. They shall be lined up before your Lord. (47–48)

Most people are negligent and forgetful. Conveniently, the present in their lives overshadows and obliterates the past and ignores the future. But this only makes facing God a more frightening and traumatic experience.

The record book will be laid open and you shall see the transgressors dismayed at its contents. They will say, "Woe to us! This book has omitted nothing small or great but noted it down!" They shall find all their deeds recorded, and your Lord will wrong no one. (49)

The Day of Judgment is a day of shocks and surprises. It is only then that the transgressors and wrong-doers will realize the extent of their folly and their despair. But it seems that man will continue to be complacent and indifferent to God's warnings, and will mainly see the truth when it is too late. "Look at all the previous nations. We destroyed them for their wrongdoing, at the appropriate and predestined time" (59).

The next story to be told in the surah is that of Moses and an unnamed pious elder, identified by the Prophet's hadith as al-Khiḍr. The moral of this story, in my view, reinforces the popular wisdom expressed in sayings such as: 'a blessing in disguise' and 'where ignorance is bliss, it is folly to be wise.' We act on what we consider to be right and beneficial, but we are often presented with contrary results which are sometimes disappointing or even tragic. What are we to do? The Qur'an teaches us to accept God's will as expressed in the following verse: "You may hate a thing and it is good for you, and you may love a thing and it is bad for you. God knows but you do not" (*al-Baqarah*: 216). But does this mean that we should lose faith in our actions and our judgment and allow ourselves to be consumed by cynicism? The answer is, of course, no. We are required to plan to the best of our ability, use all available means of success, take all precautions against failure, and leave the rest to God. This does not mean that we should allow ourselves to act against God's laws or contrary to decent human behavior and common sense. Our ignorance of the future does not justify the use of harmful or improper means. The case of Moses and al-Khiḍr is, of course, a special one, because both men were receiving separate revelations from God and were trying to discharge their separate responsibilities within the context of their shared experience.

After Muhammad, there was to be no further revelation, and no one can, therefore, claim to have access to divine direction, other than the Qur'an, or be 'charged' with a divine mission. No longer can anyone justify wrongdoing of any kind. Moses' experience was also designed to impress certain personal principles upon him. He had once denied that anyone else had more knowledge than he, and as a result God decided to take him through this episode in order to show him the error of his thinking.

The story begins by highlighting two moral qualities required of a leader: confident determination and stamina. The second Caliph, ʿUmar ibn al-Khaṭṭāb, complained of two types of people: a weak pious man and a treacherous powerful one. Leaders need to have strong personalities but to be God-fearing as well; weak leaders are ineffective, no matter how pious they may be.

It befitted Moses, as a leading prophet of God, to be in possession of both these qualities essential for leadership. "Moses said to his young aide, 'I shall go on traveling until I reach where the two seas meet, even if I have to travel for a long time'" (60). He would not rest until he caught up with al-Khiḍr, no matter how long his journey might last. They met, and Moses very humbly asked: "'May I accompany you, so that you could teach me some of the wisdom you have been taught?'" (66) Al-Khiḍr replied curtly: "'You will not be able to bear with me; for how can you bear with what is beyond your knowledge?'" (67–68) Moses promised to be patient and obedient, but his patience ran out when he saw the man making a hole in a boat belonging to a group of innocent fishermen, which meant that they would not survive their voyage. He protested vigorously, but the pious man unraveled the mystery, saying: "'The boat belonged to some poor fishermen. I damaged it because they were being chased by a king who seizes every boat he sees'" (79). Damaging the boat therefore would have deterred the pirate king from seizing it, thereby ensuring that the fishermen did not lose their boat to him.

However, Moses' objections grew still stronger when he saw al-Khiḍr doing even stranger things which did not seem right or fair to him. As the story unfolds, however, we begin to see the reasons and wisdom behind al-Khiḍr's mysterious behavior. The boat was made defective in order to save it, and its passengers, from the pirate king. A young man al-Khiḍr killed was wicked and had intended to kill his parents. By killing him al-Khiḍr had saved them. However, al-Khiḍr makes it clear to Moses that: "'I have not done all this on my behest. That is the meaning of what you were not patient enough to understand'" (82). Al-Khiḍr's behavior was inspired by God Almighty, or else it would have been totally unacceptable. Only God knows in advance the outcome of every action and al-Khiḍr was merely acting on His instructions.

As regards comparisons between Moses and al-Khiḍr, it must be made clear that Moses, along with Noah, Abraham, Jesus and Muhammad, is one of the most senior and leading prophets of God. Al-Khiḍr's privileged knowledge does not afford him a status higher than Moses. A patient on his sick bed can have better sight or hearing than his visitors, but this does not make him a healthier man.

Religious faith is often associated with asceticism and renunciation of worldly power and possessions. However, in fact, this is a mistaken image of true faith and religious life since reclusive, inward-looking faith is usually of little benefit to society.

The fourth and final story in this surah involves an historical figure identified as Dhū'l-Qarnayn (the two-horned one). His career combined knowledge with power, and he is introduced in the Qur'an as a model for strong faith and genuine humility. Regardless of whether he was Greek, Persian, Chinese or Yemeni, we are told that God had given Dhū'l-Qarnayn substantial means and considerable power. He was knowledgeable, sincere, wise, and fair, and was clearly in charge of a vast kingdom.

> They will ask you [Muhammad] about Dhū'l-Qarnayn. Say, "I will give you an account of him." We established him in the land and provided him with all means of success and he pursued them. (83–85)

God opened the door of victory for him and he used it to good advantage. His conquests took him to the remotest coast in the west where he came across a people of mixed faith. God said to him:

> "Dhū'l-Qarnayn, you may either punish these people or show them kindness." He said, "We shall surely punish the wicked, and they shall return to their Lord for a stern punishment. As for the believers who do good works, their reward shall be good" (86–88).

A fair and benevolent treatment.

Dhū'l-Qarnayn then went eastward where he encountered primitive communities living on the open land and wearing no clothes. Another expedition took him to a place between two mountain chains inhabited by similarly primitive and helpless people, continually being raided by their marauding neighbors. They sought his help to protect them and keep their predators at bay. "They said, 'Dhū'l-Qarnayn! Gog and Magog are ravaging this land. May we pay you tribute to build a rampart between us and them?'" (94) Recognizing God's generosity towards him, he told them that he needed no payment, but requested that they lend him their labor to construct a barrier that would keep their plundering neighbors away. He said: "'Lend me your manpower and I will raise a rampart between you and them'" (95).

Dhū'l-Qarnayn's engineering genius is demonstrated by the way he constructed the dam. He used a molten mixture of iron, brass and rock to erect a massive wall, rising to the mountain tops. "They [the enemies] could neither scale it nor dig their way through it. He [Dhū'l-Qarnayn] said, 'This is of the grace of my Lord...'" (97–98).

It saddens me to see that Muslims today have not carried on this tradition of engineering and technical skill. When it comes to scientific and practical innovation and application, the Muslims have been left far behind. Unfortunately, our energies and skills are wasted in 'innovation' in religious matters which has brought us confusion and discord and hampered our material progress and scientific advance.

Verse fifty-nine of this surah and verse 58 of *al-Isrā'* speak of widespread cataclysmic events towards the end of time which will cause the destruction of the world and civilization itself and we may well ponder the question whether this will coincide with the re-emergence of such pillaging and terrifying hordes as Gog and Magog, reference to whom is made also in the Torah. Furthermore, we read in *al-Anbiyā'*, verses 96 and 97, that:

> When Gog and Magog are let loose again, emerging from every corner; when the true promise nears its fulfillment, the unbelievers' eyes shall be left staring in bewilderment...

Al-Kahf concludes in a similar vein to that with which it opens:

asserting and enhancing the principles of *tawḥīd* and refuting all allegations subscribing offspring or partners to God. Towards the end it says: "Do the unbelievers think that they can take My servants as patrons beside Me? We have prepared hell as an abode for the unbelievers" (102). In the opening passages, it was indicated that human beings were created to excel in their work and that this would be their main purpose in life:

We have made all that is on the earth an adornment for it to test them [humankind] and see whose deeds would fare best. (7)

Nearer the end of the surah Allah says:

Say, "Shall we tell you of those whose labors are in vain? They are those whose endeavors in this world are misguided but they think that what they do is right. They are the ones who disbelieved in the revelations of their Lord and denied that they shall ever meet Him…" (103–105)

This is followed by a verse referring to the infinite nature of 'the words of God' which contain and express His infinite knowledge and wisdom. God is the Creator who exercises absolute and incontrovertible authority and control over the whole cosmos, deciding every action and determining the outcome and behavior of every single movement in this timeless and infinite world He created. Elsewhere in the Qur'an, we read that: "Every day He is engaged in a different task" (*al-Raḥmān*: 29). How can anyone master 'the words of God'?

Say, "If the waters of the sea were ink to write the words of my Lord, the sea would surely dry up before the words of my Lord are exhausted, even if we brought another sea to replenish it." (109)

Since God is One, He is the only resort for help, mercy, and protection and it would be futile to turn elsewhere.

> Say, "I am but a mortal like yourselves, to whom it is revealed that your Lord is but one God. Whoever is seeking to meet his Lord, let him do good works and never worship anyone else besides his Lord." (110)

Maryam
(Mary)

THIS SURAH CONSISTS of ninety-eight verses. Its most striking feature is that seventy-two of them end with the same two Arabic letters, producing a unique and distinctive rhythm. Another feature is that the Arabic word, *Raḥmān*, the Merciful, one of God's most exalted names, appears in the surah sixteen times as in the following verses:

(18) She said, "I seek the *Raḥmān's* protection that you may desist, if you are really God-fearing."

(26) "Eat and drink and rejoice; and should you meet anyone say, 'I have today vowed to the *Raḥmān* that I shall not speak with anyone.'"

(44) "Father, do not worship Satan; for he has rebelled against the *Raḥmān*."

(45) "Father, I fear that a scourge will fall upon you from the *Raḥmān*..."

(58) ...For whenever the revelations of the *Raḥmān* are recited to them, they fall prostrating and weeping.

(61) The gardens of Eden which the *Raḥmān* has promised His servants...

(69)   From each group We shall wrest those most rebellious against the *Raḥmān*.

(75)   Say, "The *Raḥmān* will bear long with those who are in error..."

(78)   Has he been made aware of the unknown? Or has the *Raḥmān* given him a promise?

(85)   The day when We shall gather the righteous in multitudes before the *Raḥmān*.

(87)   None shall have the benefit of intercession save those with a pledge from the *Raḥmān*.

(88)   They said, "The *Raḥmān* has begotten a son."

(91)   That they should ascribe a son to the *Raḥmān*...

(92)   ...when it does not become the *Raḥmān* to beget a son.

(93)   All that is in the heavens and on the earth shall return to the *Raḥmān* in submission.

(96)   The *Raḥmān* shall endow with love and endearment those who believed and did good works.

It is also interesting to note that the surah mentions the word *raḥmah*, mercy, in its opening verses, and on three other occasions. Further-more, the surah is dominated by accounts of God's grace and good- ness, which stem from His infinite mercy.

Surah *Maryam* was revealed in Makkah, probably during the earlier part of the Makkah period and before the first wave of Muslim emigration to Abyssinia, circa 615 AC. It gives an account of the birth of Jesus, son of Mary, which it presents as an extraordinary act of

God. This account is preceded by that of the birth of John (Yaḥyā), son of Zachariah, which was just as remarkable. Despite the fact that Zachariah and his wife were old and frail, and his wife moreover infertile, God had graced them with a son. In these two instances God demonstrated that He was not only capable of allowing an infertile elderly wife to conceive from her elderly and frail husband and give birth, but He had also the power to cause a young virgin to conceive and have a baby without being touched by a man. The two accounts also appear in the same sequence in *Āl ʿImrān*, which was revealed at Madinah.

What happened in these two cases is quite extraordinary from a human point of view, and makes one stop and reflect on God's power. Being the originator of the laws of cause and effect, and by having control over them, God is not bound by the logic and the dynamics of those laws. He is above physical and other laws that govern the whole cosmos. Indeed, Jesus himself acknowledged that: "'I am the servant of God. He has given me the Book and ordained me a prophet. His blessings are upon me wherever I go...'" (30–31).

Why was Zachariah eager to have a son, while many people would have been quite happy by this stage in life to be without any children? The answer is that he was concerned about the Israelites' spiritual leadership and the continuity of their religion. There were many among them who were pretenders to that leadership and who were not capable of it. As a result, Zachariah could do no more than to turn to God to give him a son who would save the Israelites, preserve their religion, and lead them along the right path. He said:

"I now fear my kinsmen who will succeed me, and my wife is barren. Grant me a son who will be my heir and an heir to the house of Jacob, and who will find grace with You, my Lord." (5–6)

He was given John and, as a token of gratitude to God, he was commanded to spend three days and nights in continuous prayer and devotion.

> He [Zachariah] looked at his people from the *miḥrāb* [sanctuary] and signaled to them to pray to the Lord morning and evening. To John We said, "Hold onto the scripture with a firm resolve," and We bestowed on him wisdom while still a child. (11–12)

The surah also relates the extraordinary story of Jesus and his mother, Mary, and what it quotes of Jesus' statements to the Jews is sufficient proof for the innocence and integrity of his mother.

> He [Jesus] said, "I am a servant of God. He gave me the Book and ordained me a Prophet. He has blessed me wherever I go, and He has commanded me to observe prayer [salah] and to give alms [zakah] as long as I shall live." (30–31)

The unusual manner of Jesus' conception and birth eventually gave rise to a new religion which was built on the mistaken premise that since Jesus had no human father, then his father must have been God, and that therefore like his father, he must also be divine. This logic led to the introduction of a third "god": the "holy spirit" who blew into Mary's womb so that she could conceive. Thus emerged the so-called doctrine of the "holy trinity," as a fundamental Christian dogma.

Such a doctrine was unprecedented in earlier religious belief, and had never been proposed or introduced by any Messenger or Prophet of God. It has been documented in what is known as the 'New Testament.' This begs the question: Do the words 'father,' 'son' and 'holy spirit' denote one and the same entity, or essence, or are they the titles of three separate and distinct entities? They are, rather ambiguously, said to identify three separate entities, which are in fact one! Some say it is one 'essence,' identified by two titles. But if the essence is one, how can a 'title' assume another entity, become flesh, be crucified and raised to heaven, while the 'father,' i.e. the 'essence,' looks on? Are the 'titles,' in fact, three different aspects of one whole 'essence'? No satisfactory answer can be found and none of the foregoing hypotheses and formulae are logical.

The simple truth is that God is one, and Jesus was but a mere mortal servant of His, one of millions who obey Him. This is affirmed many times in the Qur'an, as in this surah:

> God is my [Muhammad's] Lord and your Lord: therefore serve Him. This is the straight path. Yet the various sects are divided among themselves [over Jesus]. But the unbelievers shall suffer on that great Day [of Judgment]. Their sight and hearing shall be sharpened on the Day when they appear before Us. Today, however, these evil-doers are obviously lost in error. (36–38)

Schism and division are destined to continue to plague mankind until the Day of Judgment, when the truth shall be made manifest for all to see. There is but one God; He begets not; all else is created by Him and submits to Him; God alone shall judge everyone on the Day of Judgment. Many of those involved in these schisms have eyes but cannot see; they have ears but cannot hear. They will follow blindly, until that Day when all shall be revealed and they will be able to see and hear.

The account of Jesus is followed by an episode taken from the story of Abraham and his many encounters with idol-worship throughout his life. The dialogue, which revolves around him and his father, epitomizes the nature of the unending struggle between Islam and other hostile ideologies witnessed in every generation. In a very earnest and poignant manner, Abraham pleads with his father on four separate occasions to abandon the pagan worship of idols which he indulged in and submit to the one true God. Eventually he says to him: "'Father, I fear that a scourge will fall upon you from the Merciful, and you will become a minion of Satan'" (45). In contrast to the earnest entreaties of his son, the father replies harshly and with severity: "'Abraham! Do you dare renounce my gods? If you do not desist I shall have you stoned, and you can stay away from me'" (46).

Abraham's father threatened to have his son stoned and banished if he continued to insist on upholding the true faith. In reply Abraham cut himself off from his unbelieving father and people to find solace and spiritual companionship with God. In return for his loyalty and sincerity of faith, he and his offspring were chosen by God to carry out His mission to all humankind. "And when Abraham deserted his people and the idols which they worshiped, We gave him Isaac and Jacob, both of whom We appointed as prophets" (49).

The surah then proceeds to list the names of a number of prophets, to whom the favors of God had been granted. These men are the true leaders of humankind and worthy role models for the rest of humanity. Those who had lived amongst the prophets of God and had been taught directly by them were undoubtedly influenced by them on the personal, psychological as well as mental levels. Those generations would certainly occupy a much more revered status in the history of humankind. No wonder that Prophet Muhammad was reported to have said: "The best generation is my generation, followed by their successors and their successors, and so on...".[26] As

---

[26] Narrated by al-Bukhārī.

generations succeed one another, faith in God and adherence to His message become progressively diluted, and people become more vulnerable to deviating from His true path. The surah alludes to this fact by saying: "But the generations who succeeded them neglected their prayers and succumbed to their desires. These shall certainly meet with doom and loss" (59).

In Islam, salah is a form of worship which represents a direct link between man and God. It lifts man's spiritual awareness, cleanses his soul, and gives him the necessary immunity against evil and temptation. Abandoning this vital means of communication with God opens the door for Satan to creep in and sow his insidious seeds of corruption. Corrupt and depraved behavior in humankind inevitably leads to a gross distortion in man's understanding of the meaning and purpose of God's message to him. In *al-A'rāf*, verse 169, God says: "Other generations succeeded them [the Israelites] who inherited the Book and satisfied themselves with what this transient life offers them, saying, 'We shall be forgiven!'" The tendency to settle for short term rewards, accepting the here-and-now and expecting one's misdemeanors to be forgiven, is a feature of fraudulent religious thought, whose upholders are doomed: "Except those who repent, believe and do what is right; they shall be admitted to Paradise and shall not be wronged one iota" (60).

The degeneration of religious belief became even more pronounced in later human generations such that there have been, and still are, communities in the world today whose people do not recognize God or believe in a life after death. The Qur'an cites these communities, saying:

> Man asks [with skepticism], "When I am dead, shall I be raised to life again?" Does man forget that We have created him when he was nothing. By your Lord, We will call them all together and drag them together with the devils on their knees around the fire of hell.

Then, from every community We will take out those most ardent in their disobedience to God... (66–69)

All those who have not believed in God and have refused to acknowledge His sovereignty and guidance will, on the Day of Judgment, face the prospect of dwelling in hell for ever. They will find themselves helpless before God and their fate will be entirely in His hand. "We know best who among them deserves to be burnt therein..." (70). These words are addressed to those who deny the life Hereafter. In contrast, those who have believed in God will never have to suffer the torment of hell in any sense or degree, and of these some of the most devout will not even be questioned at all, as a reward for their sincerity and devotion. "We shall then deliver those who had been God-fearing, and abandon the wrong-doers therein on their knees" (72).

The surah then goes on to cite some of the more futile arguments of the Makkan Arabs when they were first presented with Islam. It points out that they were more concerned with the superficialities rather than the substance of the argument. "When Our clear revelations are recited to them the unbelievers say to the believers, 'But which of us enjoys a better status and is more affluent?'" (73) The answer comes thus: "How many a generation have We destroyed before them, who were far greater in riches and in splendor!" (74) The argument of the unbelievers betrays a clear bankruptcy of ideas. Here is another more revealing example:

Mark the words of the one who refused to believe in Our revelations, yet he says, "I will surely be given wealth and children!" Has he been privy to knowledge of what is to come? Or has the Merciful given him such a pledge? (77–78)

We have encountered this kind of attitude before in the story of the two companions in *al-Kahf*, verses 32–46. Such people delude themselves into believing that they are getting the best of both worlds, thinking that they have no obligation to believe in God or worship Him in this life, but at the same time assuring themselves of a better status in the life to come. "No! We shall record his words and make his torment long and terrible. He shall leave all his wealth behind and face Us on his own" (79–80). He shall be stripped of all riches and power and will have to face God with his deeds.

During the Makkan period, the Qur'an launched a relentless campaign against the idea of God having offspring. This campaign was directed against idolaters and other religious groups who assigned a kinship between God, the Creator, and His creation, human or otherwise. The Qur'an emphasizes that none of God's creation can have the power to supersede or override His power. All creation is subservient to God Almighty.

> They say, "the Merciful has begotten offspring!" You have made a monstrous claim, at which the heavens would crack, and the earth split asunder, and the mountains crumble to pieces. They ascribe offspring to the Merciful, but it is inconceivable that the Merciful should beget offspring... (88–92)

This idea is referred to as *shirk,* or in essence the association of other deities with God in worship. It is a crime which God abhors and will not forgive. God does, however, applaud the true belief in *tawḥīd* and rewards those individuals as well as communities who uphold it and build their life on it. "The Merciful will reward those who believe and do good works with love and affection" (96).

331

Prophet Muhammad is reported to have said:

> When God loves a person He would call the Archangel Gabriel and say to him, "I love so and so, and you should also love him." Gabriel would then love that person and announce all across the heavens that God loves so and so. All creatures in the heavens would then love that person and he or she would then be granted a higher status on earth.[27]

It has been said that when a man gives up his heart to God, God causes other believers to love him and he earns their affection. God tells Prophet Muhammad: "We have made the Qur'an easy [and revealed it] in your tongue so that you may give good tidings to the God-fearing and warn the ardent skeptics" (97).

---

[27] Reported in *Al-Lu'lu' wa al-Marjān*.

Ṭā Hā

THERE IS NOTHING in the Hadith which confirms that the title of
this surah is one of the names of the Prophet. 'Ṭā' and 'hā' are simply
two of the letters found in the Arabic alphabet with which the surah,
like several others in the Qur'an, begins. A satisfactory explanation
for this is yet to be put forward. Some commentators believe that it
may be a cryptic message to the Arabs telling them that although the
Qur'an was composed in their own language using an alphabet they
recognized, they would not be able to match its power and beauty.
Its divine features are unmistakable. No other Book advances the
principle of absolute *tawḥīd* with such force. Anyone approaching
the Qur'an with an open mind can see that it drives man's sense of
reason towards this concept with strong and decisive determination.
It overwhelms the heart with the awesome power and light of God,
and describes the life hereafter in such graphic and realistic detail, it
is as if it were in front of us.

The man to whom the Qur'an was revealed was well-known to
his own people for his insight, honesty, and trustworthiness and
not even his fiercest enemies could deny him these qualities.
Muhammad, who had never been known to lie to his people or
deceive them, thought that as soon as he conveyed God's revelation to them, they would believe him without hesitation. He was
sadly mistaken, since prejudice and bigotry drove some of them to
reject the Qur'an and accuse Muhammad of lying and brand him a
madman. Nothing is more hurtful to an honest man than to be

falsely accused. In the case of Muhammad, it pained him deeply, prompting God Almighty to comfort him and raise his spirits by assuring him that he was only a Messenger conveying God's revelation to the people; those who believed would benefit and those who rejected would be doomed.

> We have not revealed the Qur'an to distress you, but only as an exhortation to all who stand in awe [of God]. It is a revelation from Him who created the earth and the high constellations, the Merciful who sits in command on the throne... (2–5)

The description of God's glory and splendor adds to the greatness and special status of both the Qur'an and the Prophet to whom it was revealed.

To be a Messenger of God is no easy task, and perhaps the most trying aspect of it is having to face up to skeptics, dissenters, and detractors. To console Muhammad and allay his fears, the Qur'an informs him that he was not the only one to have undergone that experience. Before him, there was Moses who had to stand up to the might of the Pharaoh and lead the Israelites, a most stubborn and obstinate nation, if ever there was one.

> Have you heard the story of Moses? When he saw a fire [in the distance], he said to his wife, "Wait here, for I have seen a fire. Perchance I might bring you a torch from it or find someone to show me the way..." (9–10)

The story of Moses can be found in several parts of the Qur'an. But each account of it is related in a different way and style, with various details appearing exclusively in each account. This account relates Moses encounter with the Pharaoh and the episode with the sorcerers, whom Moses confounded. It occupies a major part of the surah, and covers the hardships Moses had to endure while trying to lead the Israelites out of Egypt and into the Promised Land. In this surah we have a unique description of Moses' staff, not found anywhere else in the Qur'an. Moses says: "'I lean upon it, and [use it to] beat down fodder for my flocks, and it has many other uses besides'" (18).

Moses' earnest and impressive speech before the Pharaoh is also unique to this surah. "The Pharaoh said, 'Moses! Who is your god?'" Moses replied:

"Our God is He who created everything and gave it its right bearings." Pharaoh then asked, "What of the bygone generations?" Moses said, "My Lord knows best. He has a full record of their history. He neither errs nor forgets. It is He who has made the earth a proper place for you to live in and has traced out for you ways to walk on. He sends down water from the sky to bring forth plants of all kinds..." (49–53)

The surah also gives a detailed account of the confrontation between Moses and the Pharaoh's sorcerers, and how as a result they were confounded and deserted the Pharaoh, putting their own lives in danger. They said to the Pharaoh:

"We have believed in our Lord so that He may forgive our sins and the sorcery you have forced us to practise. Our Lord's reward is far better and more lasting. Whoever comes before his Lord with wrongdoing shall be consigned to hell, where he shall neither live nor die. But he who comes before Him having believed and done good works shall be exalted to the highest of ranks..." (73–75)

This account of Moses is rounded off with a chilling description of the Day of Judgment. It begins: "They ask you [Muhammad] about the mountains, say, 'My Lord will annihilate them and raze them to the ground, reducing them to level plains'..." (105–107) and continues, saying: "Heads shall be bowed before God, the Living, the Everlasting, and those bearing injustice and wrongdoing shall come to grief..." (111).

These powerful passages are bound to shake the unbelievers and invoke faith and fear in the heart.

Scholars of the Qur'an have noted a systematic reference to the notions of awareness and forgetfulness in this surah. This occurs on the following ten occasions:

1. "We have not revealed the Qur'an to distress you, but only as an exhortation to all who stand in awe [of God]" (2–3). Revelation is a reminder and a leading light to overcome negligence and forgetfulness.

2. "I am God. There is no god but Me. Serve Me and observe salah to remain mindful of my remembrance" (14). Observance of salah means preparing for it, physically as well as spiritually, and performing it in orderly congregations where worshipers stand in straight rows.

3. Having requested God that his brother Aaron should accompany him to the Pharaoh, Moses says: "...let him share my task, so that we may glorify You and remember You a great deal. You are surely watching over us" (32–35).

4. God then says to Moses: "Go, you and your brother, with My revelations, and do not cease to remember Me" (42).

5. The objective of the mission of Moses and Aaron was to inform the Pharaoh and raise his awareness of God. They

were instructed to: "Speak to him with gentle words; he may take heed and fear Us" (44).

6. When Moses describes God's boundless knowledge of the affairs of His creation he says: "'My Lord knows best. He has a full record of their history. He neither errs nor forgets'" (52).

7. When the Sāmirī, an Israelite elder, describes the calf he made for the Israelites to worship, he says to them: "This is your god, and it is the god of Moses whom he has forgotten" (88).

8. At the end of the story of Moses and his people, God says to Muhammad: "Thus We do recount to you the history of past events. We have given you a Book (a reminder): those who turn away from it shall bear a heavy burden on the Day of Judgment" (99–100).

9. When describing the Qur'an and the reasons for its revelation, God says: "Thus We have sent it down: a Qur'an in the Arabic tongue, and proclaimed in it warnings and threats so that they [the unbelievers] may fear God or it might revive faith in their hearts" (113).

10. When talking about the expulsion of Adam from Paradise, God says: "We made a covenant with Adam, but he forgot, and We found him lacking in determination" (115).

There then comes a general warning to individuals and communities alike that:

He that rejects My revelation shall lead a wretched life and, when We bring him before us on the Day of Judgment, he shall be blind and will ask, "Lord! Why have You brought me blind before You when hitherto I was able to see?" God says, "Just as Our revelations came to you and you forgot them, so on this Day you shall be forgotten." (124–126)

The above verses clearly indicate that the whole surah revolves around the dangers implicit in forgetting one's obligations to God or forsaking His guidance. Involuntary casual forgetfulness is normal and harmless, because one usually remembers afterwards and quickly acts to redress the situation. The danger, however, is greater when lack of consciousness of God becomes the norm in one's life, making one blind to the truth and an easy prey to the influences of temptation and deviation.

⁂

The other account the surah covers is that of Adam. It begins by giving the reasons for Adam's weakness before Iblīs and how he came to be expelled from Paradise. The wool was pulled over Adam's eyes, and his will-power wilted. The Qur'an expresses it in these words: "He forgot, and We found him lacking in steadfastness" (115). When God ordered Adam not to eat the fruit of the tree, Adam understood the instructions quite clearly, but as time went by began to lose consciousness of them. Consequently, when Iblīs, or Satan, said to him: "Shall I show you the tree of immortality and everlasting prosperity?" (120), Adam's curiosity and desire to eat of the fruit grew stronger. As his defenses crumbled, Adam rushed to eat from the forbidden tree, persuading his wife to do likewise, which led to their expulsion from Paradise. The Qur'an is very specific here; Adam bears full responsibility for this decision and its outcome, and his wife's only fault was not to try to deter or prevent him from eating the forbidden fruit. Thus, Adam and his wife forfeited a blissful life in Paradise and were brought to earth to start a new life full of hardship and suffering.

338

Carelessness and forgetfulness have become a part of man's nature and a daily occurrence in human behavior. Paradise is therefore reserved for those who are alert and conscious of God, and who are resolute in their resistance against temptation. But God, in His grace and mercy, has allowed for this weakness and provided room for redress and correction. Those who remember will always be offered the chance to make good their misdemeanors, but those who persist in their heedlessness: "shall lead a wretched life and, when We bring him before us on the Day of Judgment, he shall be blind..." (124).

This life is a period during which man acts and behaves as he chooses, with accountability or answerability deferred to the life hereafter. Nevertheless, God may choose to reward some people during their lifetime in this world.

As we approach the end of the surah, we find that it links back to its beginning by consoling the Prophet and lifting up his spirits.

Do they [the unbelievers] see how many generations We have destroyed before them? They can still walk amidst the ruins of their dwellings. Surely in this there are signs for men of good judgment. (128)

The battle between good and evil is eternal. Despite the fall and destruction of many heedless civilizations and communities, and despite the fact that truth has not been obliterated, human societies continue to deviate and rebel against God and challenge those who believe in Him.

In my own short lifetime, I have seen people pay with their lives to uphold the truth, and I have seen tyrants hold sway in defiance of God and His guidance. The ebb and flow of victory and defeat is part of the nature of life on earth and only the fittest will survive. "The froth will disappear into thin air, but what is beneficial to man shall remain behind" (*al-Ra'd*: 17).

This battle between good and evil takes place according to certain fundamental objective laws and rules that favor neither tyrants not martyrs. The surah conveys this fact by saying: "Were it not that your Lord has long since decreed to defer their destruction until an appointed time, it would have certainly taken place" (129). The surah goes on to offer solace and comfort to the Prophet urging him to show resilience and devotion to God, glorify Him and appeal for His help and support. Occupying one's life in service to God leaves little time to be wasted on futile or trivial activities.

In words reminiscent of those in verses 97–98 of *al-Ḥijr* ("We know you [Muhammad] are distressed by what they [the unbelievers] say. Praise the glory of your Lord and prostrate yourself to Him"), and to enable him to withstand the agony and pain of the treatment he was receiving from his people, the Prophet was instructed to:

> Bear with what they [the unbelievers] say. Praise the glory of your Lord before sunrise and before sunset. Praise His glory during the night, and in the morning and later in the day, so that you may find fulfillment. (130)

Successful leaders (like the prophets who had a mission to carry out) overcome opposition by rising above material gain, enhancing their relationship with God and drawing strength from worshiping Him. "Do not regard with envy the worldly benefits We have bestowed on some of them, for We seek only to put them to the test…" (131).

Although unbelievers often appear to gain a far greater share of wealth and material prosperity in this world, this holds little real value in the sight of God and, one day, it will all come to nothing.

We saw this in verses 73–74 of *Maryam* which say:

> When Our clear revelations are recited to them the unbelievers say to the faithful, "Which of us two will have a finer dwelling and better companions?" Look how many generations have We destroyed before them, far greater in riches and in splendor!

ʿUmar ibn al-Khaṭṭāb, a senior Companion of the Prophet, was reported to have expressed pain and bitterness at seeing the Prophet sitting on a straw mat while Persian and Roman emperors lived in opulence and luxury. The Prophet however informed him that these rulers were receiving their rewards in this life while he was working for the rewards of the hereafter. "The reward of your Lord is far better and more lasting" (131).

Muhammad was then directed to:

> …bid your people to pray, and persevere therein. [But remember:] We do not ask you to provide sustenance [for Us]: it is We who provide sustenance for you. And the future belongs to the God-conscious. (132)

Muslim homes are places where God is constantly praised and remembered. They provide an atmosphere of love, devotion to God and decency where families can be raised to serve God Almighty and please Him. While most people vie for material pursuits and self-aggrandizement, and are prepared to risk their honor and sanity for trivial and puerile objectives, believers strive for spiritual fulfillment and a higher quality of human life.

Finally, the surah rounds on the Makkan opponents of Islam, recalling their demand for a miracle to prove Muhammad's truthfulness in what he was preaching. "They say, 'Why does he not bring us a sign from his Lord?' Have they not been given a Book with a full record of previous scriptures?" (133). However, they failed to recognize that they had been given the Qur'an, which is not only a comprehensive record of wisdom and guidance, but an unparalleled and indubitable miracle in its own right. What more proof did they need? Nevertheless, some of them chose to reject it and cast doubt over its authenticity and integrity. Had they been struck by divine punishment before Muhammad came to warn them and show them the truth, they would have appealed for guidance and direction. But, since a Prophet had been sent to them, they no longer had an excuse. "Say [to them], 'All are waiting; so you wait. You shall soon know which of us have taken the right path and have been rightly guided'" (135).

SURAH 21

Al-Anbiyā'
(The Prophets)

THIS SURAH WAS REVEALED towards the end of the Makkan
period and takes its title from the fact that sixteen prophets are mentioned in it by name, with brief accounts of parts of their history.
More space, however, is devoted to the story of the prophet
Abraham. There are indications in the surah that the prophets were all
male, possibly because as men they would be stronger and more suited
to deal with the realities of hardship and persecution. "The Messengers We sent before you were all men to whom We gave revelation. If
you [Makkans] do not know, then ask those who do" (7). Some
scholars include Mary and Moses' mother among God's prophets,
although they had received no revelation as such.

The opening verses of the surah indicate that the Arabs of Makkah
were, to a great extent, religiously illiterate and totally bound to
materialism. Their knowledge of God was, to say the least, confused. They believed in polytheism and worshiped numerous
deities. They held no belief in a life hereafter or accountability for
their actions after death. They lived for the present alone. This is
expressed in the following verses:

> The day of reckoning for humankind is drawing near, yet they
> blithely persist in unbelief. They listen with contempt to every fresh

343

warning that comes to them from their Lord. Their hearts are totally oblivious [of God]… (1–3)

The surah then advances several rebuttals against the arguments of those who deny the existence of life after death and accountability in the hereafter. "We have not created the heavens and the earth and all that lies between them in vain"(16). The Qur'an gives intuitive common sense reasons to show that life after death is a real prospect. Having created the world the first time, God is surely able to bring it to an end and recreate it a second time. "Are the unbelievers unaware that the heavens and the earth were one piece and We split them, and that with water We made every living thing?…" (30).

A majority of physicists and cosmologists today subscribe to the so-called 'Big Bang' theory to explain the beginning and formation of the universe as we know it. Moreover, we know that the earth's core is molten and exists at extremely high temperatures, that the crust, the part on which we live, is solid and that three-quarters of the earth's surface is covered with water, which sustains life on this earth. God says: "We set firm mountains upon the earth to maintain its stability, and We made on it roads and plains so that [people] may find their way around it" (31).

But denial of life after death is not simply restricted to ancient generations. Modern man is also intoxicated with the love of this life and material gain, and modern civilization has no room for a belief in the hereafter. Like their predecessors, people today scoff at the very idea:

They say, "When will this promised punishment befall us, if it is true at all?" If only the unbelievers knew the Day when they shall strive to shield their faces and their backs from the fire flames, and there will be no one to help them! It will suddenly overwhelm them and stupefy them. They shall not be able to ward it off, nor shall they be reprieved. (38–40)

The surah points out that accountability in the hereafter will be meticulous and completely fair:

We shall set up just scales on the Day of Judgment, and not a single soul shall be wronged. Actions weighing as little as a grain of mustard seed shall be taken into account. We will be the ultimate competent judge. (47)

In addition to their denial of life after death and accountability to God, the unbelievers also doubted the integrity and honesty of Muhammad, accusing him of lying and sorcery. "The wrong-doers whisper to one another, 'Is this man not a mortal like yourselves?'" (3) by which they meant to undermine Muhammad's status with God and the authenticity of the revelation he was relaying to them. Prophets and Messengers had to be human, since only by experiencing human feelings and emotions could they be able to communicate with their fellow men, allowing people to understand them and acknowledge their leadership. It was also necessary for them to face physical and moral hardships in discharging their missions to provide genuine and worthy role models for their people. Being unable to share human sensibilities, passions and perceptions, angels would not have been effective for such a task.

In order to accept Islam, the unbelievers asked for a physical miracle, saying: "'Let him [Muhammad] give us a sign, as did Messengers in days gone by.' The communities before them did not believe either, so We destroyed them. If We show them a sign, will they believe?" (5–6). However, the reality is that they would not have believed anyway no matter how many signs were brought before them. Elsewhere in the Qur'an, we read: "If We opened for the unbelievers a gate in heaven and they ascended through it higher and higher, still they would say, 'Our eyes were dazzled, truly we must have been bewitched'" (*al-Ḥijr.* 14–15).

God also points out to the Arabs that the choice of Muhammad as their Prophet and Messenger would elevate their status in the history of mankind and transform them from heathen bedouin tribes to a civilized and leading nation. He says: "We have revealed for you [O men!] a Book in which is a message. Will you ever understand?" (10).

The Arabs accepted Islam with great difficulty, but once they embraced it they promoted and defended it with all their power and will, devoting themselves to spreading it all over the world. Their faith was based on a pure unadulterated *tawḥīd*, in contrast to the prevalent Christian belief that Jesus was God and that the Archangel Gabriel was also God, leading to the emergence of the Christian doctrine of the "trinity" which remains in existence to this day. The Qur'an rejected these notions and refuted them by asserting that Jesus and Gabriel were

> …but His servants. They do not speak till He has spoken, and they act according to His command. He knows what is ahead of them and what is behind them. They would only intercede for those whom He accepts, and they are fearful of Him. If any of them says, "I am a god besides Him," We shall reward him with hell. (26–29)

The irony in these words is unmistakable. No genuine God can be threatened in this way and remain passive. But none of the so-called gods had come up to defend their integrity, because none existed.

There can only be one supreme omnipotent God in this world, with total and absolute sovereignty and authority over all its affairs. The surah says:

> To Him belongs all that is in the heavens and on earth. The angels who are in His presence do not disdain to worship Him, nor do

they ever weary. They glorify Him day and night, relentlessly. Have they [the unbelievers] taken earthly deities that can restore the dead to life? Were there other gods in the heavens and the earth besides God, the heavens and the earth would have been ruined. Exalted be God, Lord of the Throne, far above their false allegations. (19–22)

All of the prophets advocated *tawḥīd*: "We had revealed to all the Messengers We had sent before you [Muhammad] that there is no God but I, and therefore serve Me" (25). Where are the alleged gods? What signs or proof are there for their existence? The fact is that there are none but God Almighty.

When it comes to relating various episodes from the history of some earlier prophets, the surah does not adopt a chronological or geographic pattern. We saw in *Maryam* that Abraham is mentioned before Moses, whereas this surah begins with the story of Moses and his brother Aaron and then turns to Abraham, though he was their predecessor. The reason for this seems to be the fact that Moses had been given the Torah which gave him prominence and distinction. The reference to the Torah serves as a prelude to the reference to the Qur'an itself which is described as: "a blessed admonition We have revealed. How could you then reject it?" (50).

We get a glimpse of Abraham as a staunch young believer, challenging the idolaters and threatening their gods. "They said, 'We have heard a young man called Abraham speak [ill] of them (the idols)'" (60). Abraham had in fact destroyed some of their stone idols, except for the biggest one, and placed a hatchet around its neck, saying to the idolaters, mockingly: "'No. It was their chief idol who did it! Ask them, if they can speak'" (63).

The surah then talks of Lot, Abraham's nephew and partner in fighting the unbelievers. It says:

Then We delivered him [Abraham] and Lot, and brought them to the land which We had blessed for all humankind. We gave him Isaac, and then Jacob as well, all of whom We made good righteous men. (71–72)

The surah goes on to talk of Noah, then of David and Solomon relating the episode when they differed over a judgment in a certain dispute. It says: "We gave Solomon insight into the case, and We bestowed upon both of them wisdom and knowledge" (79). The moral of this story is that legitimate differences of opinion are healthy and acceptable, and both sides, regardless of which is right or wrong, receive credit for their endeavor as long as their efforts are genuine and sincere. Many Muslims see differences of opinion as a threat and a reason for division and condemnation, which is contrary to the spirit and approach of the Qur'an.

The surah makes mention of Job, telling us that he was once a healthy and wealthy man with many children but had lost all his wealth and power, and resorted to God for help.

And tell them of Job as he called on his Lord, saying, "I am sorely afflicted; but You are the most Merciful of all." We heard his prayer and relieved his affliction. We gave him back his family and as many more with them, a blessing from Us and an admonition to devout worshipers. (83–84)

Other prophets, such as Ishmael, Idrīs [probably Enoch], Dhū'l-Kifl [probably Ezekiel], Jonah, Zachariah and John, also suffered ordeals of various kinds and were put to the test, but they turned to none but God for solace and help. When affliction strikes a man he should seek strength and courage from God rather than from other helpless mortals, no matter how strong or powerful they may be.

These accounts tell us that life does not come easy. Hardship and tribulation are essential ingredients of human endeavor in this world. Those who persevere and resort to God's help are bound to receive it. The trials the prophets had to undergo were part of their training and enhanced their own standing in history and constituted a means of education for their followers. One of the best illustrations of this is to be found in the life of Prophet Jonah who

> ...went away in anger, thinking We have no power over him. He called out in the darkness, "There is no god but You. Glory be to You! I have been a wrongdoer." We answered his prayer and delivered him from distress. Thus shall We save the true believers. (87–88)

The majority of the prophets known to man have emerged from the eastern and southern Mediterranean regions, scenes of great ancient civilizations. They have all advocated and taught the same message which is now fully contained in the Qur'an.

The accounts of these prophets have been sandwiched in the surah between two passages on the Day of Judgment. The first one says:

> We shall set up just scales on the Day of Judgment, and not a single soul shall be wronged. Actions weighing as little as a grain of mustard seed shall be taken into account. We will be the ultimate competent judge. (47)

The second passage is more detailed and starts with verse 93 which condemns the fragmentation, schisms and religious divisions which had beset the followers of those prophets. Although these followers were expected to show greater tolerance for one another, history tells us that the opposite was the case. Two thousand years later, the Israelites continue to reject Jesus. When Muhammad emerged as a prophet, the Christians rejected him and united with the Israelites against him and his followers.

Sadly, it seems that these divisions and conflicts are set to continue until a time in the future when, according to the surah, hordes from the eastern part of the globe, who had never received divine revelation, would sweep across the civilized world, plundering and pillaging everything in their way. The surah says:

> But when Gog and Magog are let loose and rush headlong from all sides; when the true promise draws near to fulfillment, the unbelievers shall stare in bewilderment... (96–97)

Some scholars are of the opinion that this is a reference to the Mongols and the Tatars who invaded Baghdad in the thirteenth century AC. They ravaged Baghdad and brought down Muslim rule there. But this is incorrect, because the surah clearly indicates that the eruption of Gog and Magog would usher in the Day of Judgment and represent a sign of its imminent arrival.

Having spoken about the happy people of Paradise and the wretched ones of hell, the surah says: "On that Day We shall roll up the heavens like a scroll of parchment. As We first created man, so will We bring him back to life..." (104). Thus human history and life on earth shall be brought to an end.

The surah goes on to say: "We wrote in the Psalms [of David] after we recorded it in the Book, 'The righteous among My servants shall inherit the land'" (105). Elsewhere in the Qur'an we read: "They [the faithful] will say, 'Praise be to God who has made good to us His promise and given us the earth to inherit, that we may dwell in Paradise wherever we please'" (*al-Zumar.* 74). The reference here could be to 'the land' of Paradise or to land here on earth, in the sense that supremacy and domination on earth will ultimately be given to those who deserve them as a result of their moral and humanitarian qualities.

The Psalms are cited here because David was leading a persecuted community, striving to protect their beliefs and freedom. In these words, God tells us and David that supremacy and sovereignty come with certain qualities and qualifications.

The surah closes, as it began, with a call to the Arabs, whom Muhammad was addressing with the Qur'an, to uphold *tawḥīd*, prepare for life in the Hereafter and adhere to God's revelation. It says: "Say, 'It is revealed to me that your God is one God; will you then submit to Him?'" (108). It is up to God to judge people's performance and the reward due to each one: "Say, 'My Lord, judge between us according to the truth. Our Lord is the Merciful, whose help we seek against all your blasphemies'" (112).

Al-Ḥajj
(The Pilgrimage)

THIS SURAH OPENS with an emotional appeal, highlighting the terrifying aspects of the Day of Judgment, designed to shock humans and shake their consciousness.

> Humankind, have fear of your Lord. The shuddering on the Day of Judgment shall be tremendous. When that Day comes, every nursing mother shall forsake her infant, every pregnant female shall deliver her burden, and you shall see people reeling like drunkards although they are not drunk... (1–2)

We learn from the Prophet that the advent of the Day of Judgment will be accompanied by tremendous cataclysmic disturbances such as volcanic eruptions when the earth will be gripped in the throes of death.

This initial shocking appeal is followed immediately by a rather sober and rational one:

> Humankind, if you are in doubt over resurrection remember that We first created you from dust, then from a drop of fluid, then from a clot of blood, then from a lump of flesh, developed and not fully developed, so that We might manifest to you Our power... (5)

Skepticism over the resurrection is a direct outcome of ignorance and lack of understanding of how life came into being. Skeptics tend to believe that resurrection is a completely isolated event, bearing no relationship to the whole cycle of creation and life on earth. We see life and life-forms being created every second, which should tell us that a second cycle of life or a new creation of the same life-form is plausible and, indeed, feasible.

This leads us to ask: Who is responsible for the creation of the male sperm? Under what power does this sperm develop and find its way to the female egg to produce a fetus, carrying all the vital genetic information that will shape its future and eventually develop it into a fully formed human being? How is this creature able to leave its mother's womb and adapt almost immediately to the new environment outside where, for the first time, its lungs have to breathe in air and its eyes have to cope with powerful light rays? Who has endowed human beings with these amazing genetic features and inherent capabilities?

The creation of life is not a freak accident, brought about by blind chance or by some obscure laws of probability. It is a phenomenon that has been occurring an infinite number of times, in an infinite number of ways, over an incredibly long period of time. The surah turns to yet another marvel of creation.

Look at the soil when it is dry and barren; but no sooner do We send down rainwater upon it than it is revived and begins to swell and bring forth radiant and blooming plants of every kind. (5)

This again leads us to ask: how does all this come about? How can we observe this revival taking place before our very eyes and yet fail to accept that life can be resurrected? Out of dead soil grow crops and plants providing staple foods for animals and humans, containing starch, sugar, fats, salts, minerals, and vitamins, all of which constitute the very essential elements for sustaining life. We are bound to enquire about the power that lies behind all this. These phenomena are indisputable. Since we believe what we can see and observe, we ought not to doubt that the dead can be brought back to life again. The surah gives the only possible logical explanation:

> That is because God is the ultimate truth; it is He who resurrects the dead; it is He who has power over all things; the hour of resurrection is sure to come; and God will raise the dead in their graves to life again. (6–7)

A great number of people accept these facts by intuition and common sense, but there are also a great number who reject them, believing that life is an act of blind chance and death is the end of everything. It would be wrong to give any credence to this notion, and it would also be wrong to accept the false belief that most philosophers and scientists are agnostics or unbelievers. In fact, many studies have shown the opposite to be the case. Rejection of God's existence, though widespread, does not stand upon sound scientific grounds. It often stems from sheer ignorance, arrogance, or defective and bogus ideologies. The attitude of Satan, or Iblīs, is a case in point; he rebelled against God precisely because he recognized His existence.

The surah goes on to talk about disbelief (*kufr*), saying: "Some wrangle about God, though they have neither knowledge nor guidance nor divine revelation. They turn away in scorn and lead others astray from God's path..." (8–9). In persisting to deny God's existence, unbelievers are contradicting their own human nature and challenging the revelations sent down by God. The outcome of their attitude is bound to be appalling. There are also people who link their belief in God to what befalls them here in this life; that is, if they are prosperous and happy they believe, if not, they rebel. The surah puts it thus:

Some people serve God half-heartedly and remain on the fringe of true faith; when blessed with good fortune they are content, but when an ordeal befalls them they turn upon their heels. These forfeit deliverance in both this life and the life to come. That would be a real and total loss. (11)

This life is a term for testing, trials, and tribulation, during which man is free to choose and decide the direction he wishes to take in life. He meets with good as well as bad fortune, and his ability to cope with both is put to the test. To simply shrug off one's responsibilities and explain away these trials and ordeals as 'predetermined' and therefore 'pointless' would be foolish and disgraceful. The essence of Islam is submission to God and total acceptance of His will, whether good or bad. Success lies in the recognition of God's will; otherwise, man is welcome to challenge that will and see how far he can go.

If anyone thinks that God will not succor him in this world and in the life to come, let him reach out unto heaven by any [other] means and [thus try to] make headway: and then let him see whether this scheme of his will indeed do away with the cause of his anguish. (15)

All matters shall be settled before God, who is equitable and fair, to whom all humankind shall return.

God will judge fairly the believers [the Muslims], the Jews, the Sabians, the Christians, the Magians, and the polytheists on the Day of Resurrection. He bears witness to all things. (17)

Following this extended introduction, the surah turns to describe man's long-standing conflict between belief (*īmān*) and disbelief (*kufr*); between carrying the banner of truth (*ḥaqq*) and raising the banner of falsehood (*bāṭil*). There is no love lost between those who believe in God and those who deny His existence and sovereignty; reconciliation appears to be impossible. But, does this mean that conflict and bloodshed are inevitable? The answer must be in the negative. Believers are obliged to reason and argue with non-believers and show them the truth. In this task, they are bound by the constraints of wisdom, mutual respect, and reasonable argument, for both camps are equally under probation. The truth needs to be explained and made easy to understand. If people refuse to accept it today they must be given another chance to consider, and must in all circumstances be treated fairly and without coercion.

It was this patient approach which brought victory to Prophet Muhammad. Opponents of Islam may possess the material power to hurt the Muslims, but their arguments are shaky. There have always been efforts to silence or suppress God's Messengers because they speak the truth, and the truth has its own power behind it. In another surah, the Qur'an says:

> The unbelievers said to their Messengers, "Return to our religion or we shall banish you out of our lands." Their Lord revealed to the Messengers, "We shall destroy the wrong-doers, and establish you in the land after them..." (*Ibrāhīm*: 13–14)

In this surah, the perennial confrontation between those who uphold the faith and those who reject it is covered in the passage which begins: "Here are two antagonist camps who are in conflict over their Lord" (19). These words are said to have been revealed in reference to the Battle of Badr in 624 AC between the Muslims and the Arabs of Makkah. It was the first major armed clash between the Muslims and the non-Muslims and it came after fifteen years of peaceful dialogue and patience on the part of the Muslims.

The verses that follow point out that prophets of every generation had experienced similar hardships. The establishment of their religion required a great deal of patience and relentless hard work. The verses affirm that:

> God stands in defense of the believers. God does not love the treacherous and the ungrateful. Permission to take up arms is hereby given to those who have been attacked, because they have been wronged. God has the power to grant them victory: those who have been unjustly driven from their homes, for no other reason than their saying, "Our Lord is God." Had God not enabled people to struggle against one another, monasteries and churches and synagogues and mosques, in which God's name is much invoked, would have been destroyed. (38–40)

Prophets and their followers never incite wars of aggression and never condone bloodshed or unjustifiable war-making. They do, however, try to oppose and suppress tyranny. God gives the believers victory because of the principles and values they uphold and represent, and not for their personal glorification. Verse 41 explains these principles:

> Those who, once We give them supremacy in the land, will establish salah, give zakah, promote all that is good and proscribe all that is evil. All matters will ultimately rest with God. (41)

The main objective of the work of God's prophets and their disciples is to acquaint people fully with God and teach them how to extol and worship Him, and how best to serve Him.

Within the context of justifiable war and self-defense, comes a passage introducing the topic which gives the surah its title: Hajj, or pilgrimage to Makkah. The surah gives a description of the main rituals of Hajj with the aim, it seems, of showing the Arabs how much they had distorted and deviated from the true religion of Abraham which they had professed to follow. How could they make such a claim when Abraham epitomized *tawḥīd* and they were practising sheer unmitigated paganism? The truth is that, despite their assertions to be its custodians, the Arabs had betrayed their religious heritage. This was made worse by their vicious hostility and opposition to the new call of *tawḥīd* proclaimed by Muhammad.

> Those who refuse to believe, and debar others from the path of God
> and from the inviolable mosque [the Kaʿbah at Makkah] which We
> have set up for all humankind, the natives and the visitors alike, and
> all those who seek to profane it with evil or wrong-doing, shall be
> sternly punished. (25)

To fight against such aggressors and violators would be considered justified and laudable.

When one looks closely at the rituals of Hajj, performed once a year, it becomes immediately clear that it is a magnificent and inspiring demonstration of man's devotion to God. It is a mass celebration of *tawḥīd*, held at a time and in a place designated by God Almighty Himself, bringing people together from all corners of the globe. This excellent and worthy tradition was established many centuries ago by Abraham. The surah says: "We guided Abraham to the site of the mosque [the Kaʿbah] and said to him, 'Never take other gods besides Me...'" (26). It has been suggested that the Hajj is no more than a set of irrational and chaotic rituals that are meant to test people's stamina and endurance and do not call for any understanding. This is a gross misapprehension. There is nothing in the Hajj rituals that is without a purpose or religious significance.

Let us take the *ṭawāf*, or circumambulation of the Kaʿbah. It is a form of prayer and an occasion for praising and glorifying God Almighty. Tradition and convention in religious practise, like in anything else, have their own intrinsic value and significance. Rationality and logic are not the only factors that determine such value and significance. The Kaʿbah is venerated for its universal symbolism as the first house built on earth exclusively for the worship and praise of the One God. It is the citadel of *tawḥīd*.

The surah goes on to introduce the Hajj rituals in more detail.

Call on all people to make the pilgrimage. They will come on foot and on the backs of swift camels from every far-away place. They will come to avail themselves of many benefits, and to invoke the name of God, over a set number of days, and thank Him for the animals He provided for them to slaughter. Eat of their meat and feed the poor and the unfortunate... (27–28)

Modern technology and advanced means of meat processing and distribution have made it possible today to feed millions of people in Makkah and all over the world with the meat of animals slaughtered during the Hajj.

We have made the well-fed camels a part of God's rites [during the Hajj]. There is much goodness in them for you. Invoke the name of God when you draw them up in line to slaughter them; and when they are dead, eat of their meat and feed the poor and the needy... (36)

These rituals have a very real and strong human side to them. They are a festival for the celebration of *tawḥīd* on a communal scale.

> Avoid the profanity of idol-worship and avoid perjury. Dedicate yourselves to God, and serve none besides Him. He who serves other deities besides God is like a man who falls from heaven and is snatched by vultures or thrown away by the wind to a God-forsaken place. (30–31)

A strong community must be built on a powerful mix of history and religious practices which combine nostalgia, emotions, and sound cultural roots. "Those who observe and revere the rituals God has enjoined, reflect God-consciousness that is in their hearts" (32).

The perennial struggle between good and evil is complex and difficult to comprehend fully. Whenever an individual or a community undertake to promote the good and uphold it, they are bound to provoke hostility and opposition. Gradually the differences turn into fierce confrontation, draining the energies and resources of both sides. It is quite possible, for reasons known only to God Almighty Himself, that evil prevails causing mosques to be turned into museums, stables or warehouses. We have seen this happen in Spain, Turkey, the former Soviet Union, India, Bosnia Herzegovina, and many other parts of the world. Many Muslims have been slaughtered defending their mosques and other religious monuments.

No one knows what the future holds, but Muslims will have to continue to struggle on behalf of their religion and way of life, because divine justice will be done. The Qur'an reassures Prophet Muhammad, saying:

If they refuse to believe you, remember that before them the people of Noah, ʿĀd, Thamūd, the people of Abraham, the people of Lot and the inhabitants of Madyan had refused to believe, and Moses was also rejected. I [God] had given the unbelievers ample time, but then struck at them. How severe was My punishment! (42–44)

The surah continues in the same tone to establish that to God time is measured on a different scale. While some human generations suffer defeat, others triumph and enjoy supremacy. "They [the unbelievers] bid you [Muhammad] hasten the threatened scourge, but God will not fail His promise. A day to your Lord is like a thousand years in your reckoning" (47).

A messenger's task is to deliver God's message clearly and fully, so that no one shall have an excuse for not being made aware of it.

Say, "People, I have been sent but to give you clear warning; those who believe and do good works shall be forgiven and richly rewarded, but those who deliberately seek to deny and discredit Our revelations shall reside in hell." (49–51)

We learn from the Qur'an that while God's messengers devote all their energies to establishing the truth and defending it, there are other Satanic forces that work against them. Some people are unfortunate in that although they profess belief initially, they are later prevailed upon by insidious forces to say: "'Had we not stood firm, he [the Messenger] would have turned us away from our gods...'" (*al-Furqān*: 42).

Elsewhere in the Qur'an, we read: "Thus We have assigned to every prophet an enemy: the devils among humans and the jinn, who inspire each other with vain and varnished falsehood"

361

(*al-Anᶜām*: 112). In *al-Ḥajj*, we are clearly told that these 'varnished falsehoods' are the insinuations of Satan for:

> Whenever any of the messengers and prophets We had sent before you expressed a wish, Satan would interfere with their wishes. But God would remove Satan's insinuations and confirm His own revelations. God is All-Knowing and Wise. (52)

Satan's insinuations are efforts made to obliterate and pervert the truth, keeping people ignorant of it. In every community there are hordes of people who will say and do the most outrageous and disgraceful things in order to distort the truth and confuse the masses about it. But the surah reassures us that God watches over His revelation and will protect it against such harmful and destructive activities. Satan's efforts will also appear in the form of distortions, misinterpretations, and fabrications which are introduced over time into God's messages, causing people to reject, destroy, mistrust, and ridicule them. Be that as it may, the truth as advocated by God's prophets and messengers will be protected and its followers will ultimately prevail.

One of the essential qualities of those who uphold and advocate God's truth is full awareness and knowledge of whom they represent and work for. The motives and aims of those who are working to establish God's order and way of life on earth are totally different from those whose selfish aims are worldly gain and enjoyment. Knowing this we can therefore appreciate why God so urged the Prophet to press ahead with explaining the fundamentals of His mission, in the reassurance that He has power and control over all things.

Do you not see how God sends down water from the sky and forthwith the earth turns green? God is Gracious and All-Knowing. To Him belongs all that is in the heavens and the earth. He is Self-Sufficient and Praiseworthy. (63–64)

The surah goes on to draw attention to the power and glory of God and the marvels of His creation, pointing out that He alone deserves to be glorified, served, and worshiped by everything and everyone in this world. "They worship besides God that which He never sanctioned and that of which they are ignorant. The wrong-doers shall have none to support them" (71).

God addresses the Prophet:

We have ordained for every nation a way of life which they will observe, so do not let them [the unbelievers] dispute with you concerning your way of life. Call people to your Lord; you are truly well-guided and on the right path. (67)

The Ḥajj, as a fundamental obligatory religious duty, is a good case in point. When the Muslims were first directed to perform it, the Prophet instructed them on how to do so, saying: "Take your [Ḥajj] rituals from me."[28] He showed them what they were required to do and how they were to do it, and he also explained the significance of the rituals, thus establishing the Ḥajj as an ordered and precisely timed and coordinated event composed of a set of actions and undertakings that translate the principle of *tawḥīd* into practise.

An important ritual during the Ḥajj is the slaughter of animals on the tenth day of the month of Dhū'l-Ḥijjah, to which the surah refers: "Their meat and blood are of no benefit to God; it is your piety that will carry weight with Him" (37). The Ḥajj is a perfect

---

[28] Narrated by Muslim.

manifestation of Islamic values based on equality and lack of discrimination between people. Accordingly, the Prophet denied the tribe of Quraysh any special privileges or concessions in performing the Hajj, such as taking an exclusive route from 'Arafāt to Mina. The surah says: "If they [the unbelievers] argue with you, say to them, 'God knows best all that you do'" (68).

❊❊

Another manifestation of *tawḥīd* is given in the example of creation in the animal kingdom:

> Humankind, listen carefully to this example: those whom you invoke besides God could not create a single fly, even if they had joined all their powers together. In fact, they cannot retrieve anything that a fly may take away from them. Both worshiper and worshiped are hopelessly powerless. (73)

❊❊

The surah closes with a statement expressing the essence of the overall task of the world's Muslim community. This task was handed down from God to the Prophet, who faithfully passed it on to the Muslims, who then assumed the responsibility of passing it on to the rest of mankind. Thus the Prophet stands witness to the Muslims, and they in turn stand witness to everyone else. Nations and communities strive for ethnic supremacy, material progress, or domination. The Islamic nation carries the awesome responsibility of up-holding God's universal order and advocating submission to Him. And, even though Muslims have been defeated and subjugated, and the whole world has for many centuries endured injustice and tyranny, Muslims are obliged to fight on and deliver humanity from evil and oppression.

364

Believers, bow down and prostrate yourselves, worship your Lord, and do good works, so that you may gain success. fight for the cause of God with the devotion due to Him... so that the Messenger [Muhammad] becomes your witness and you the witness of humankind. (77–78)

If only the Muslims recognized and appreciated their real mission and responsibility!

SURAH 23

Al-Mu'minūn
(The Believers)

THERE IS A STRONG and definite relationship between actions and results. A good act will yield a favorable outcome, whilst an evil act, no matter how slick or suave it may look today, will lead to a lamentable end. Most people are preoccupied with the here-and-now, with quick and spectacular results, and are completely oblivious of the future. This surah is dedicated to drawing our attention to the life hereafter. It reassures the believers with the promise of a happy and rewarding future, and warns cynics and skeptics that, for them, the worst is yet to come. The surah opens on a promising note: "Blessed are the believers, who are humble in their prayers; who avoid profane talk, and give zakah…" (1–4).

'Umar ibn al-Khaṭṭāb reported that when Prophet Muhammad received a Qur'anic revelation, his Companions could hear buzzing sounds around him. One day Muhammad went into this state for a while and when he came round he read the first ten verses of *al-Mu'minūn*. 'Umar went on to say that the Prophet had told them that whoever heeded those verses would enter Paradise. Then, he said, the Prophet turned towards the Ka'bah, raised his hand in the air and said:

> God, please increase our share [of goodness] and do not reduce it; be generous to us and do not humiliate us; give to us and do not deprive us; favor us and do not favor others more than You favor us; and give us contentment and be pleased with us.[29]

---

29 Narrated by Imam Aḥmad.

The opening verses cover an important and wide range of religious and moral principles and instructions. The same ideas are reiterated, with minor alterations, half-way through the surah.

> Those who are in fear of their Lord; who believe in the revelations of their Lord; who worship none besides their Lord; who give to charity with their hearts filled with awe, knowing that they will be returning to their Lord: these vie with each other to do good works and they will be winners. (57–61)

The two passages are clearly complementary and combine to give a fuller description of the character of the believers.

A description of the unbelievers is given towards the end of the surah, highlighting some of their features. The surah also relates examples of the end that awaits the wrong-doers. The reward, or punishment, promised by Allah is given after a certain period of time spent here on earth, after people's faith and sincerity have been tested and tried and their deeds noted for judgment hereafter. This interim period is described in vivid and graphic detail in the surah: "We first created man from an essence of clay, then out of him We created the sperm and made it rest in a secure place [the womb]..." (12–13).

The question that immediately springs to mind is: How did all this happen? Other questions also arise: How did the clay turn into a living body? How did the genes form and become encapsulated in the sperm? By what system or logic or law do these genes recognize their course and function, turning a helpless lump of flesh into a full-grown adult, with amazing talents and capabilities? The whole universe attests, in the loudest possible way, to the power of God. Yet, many people continue to dismiss the truth and disbelieve in Him. The surah goes on: "Then you shall surely die, and on the Day of Resurrection you shall certainly be restored to life again" (15–16).

※※※

The surah then takes us back in history, citing communities who had rejected their prophets and rebelled against God, turning their backs on His guidance. It mentions the people of Noah and those of Hūd, and then says:

> After them We raised other generations. No people can hasten their appointed hour or delay it. Then We sent Our Messengers in succession, yet time after time people disbelieved their Messengers, so We destroyed them one by one and made them tales of history. May the disbelievers be always in ruin. (42–44)

All the communities which the surah mentions lived in what is known today as the Middle East. Noah lived in northern Iraq, Abraham came from Iraq and traveled through the Hijaz in western Arabia, Egypt, and Palestine. Moses was born and raised in the Nile valley, whence he tried to escape with his people, the Israelites, and then died in the Sinai desert. Jesus was born in Palestine and visited Egypt. Ṣāliḥ and Shuʿayb lived in northern Arabia, and Hūd in the Yemen. We may conclude from this that people in this part of the world have always been more aware, or have had a richer experience, of heavenly revealed messages than people in other parts of the world. Therefore, those of them who rejected these messages or opposed them stand to sustain heavier divine punishment.

God's messengers were wise, reasonable and considerate leaders and teachers, never over-burdening their followers or coercing them to believe. God has directed His prophets thus: "Messengers! Eat of that which is wholesome, and do good works, for I am well aware of your actions. Your religion is but one religion, and I am the

Lord of you all, and so fear Me" (51–52). A few verses later we read: "We burden no soul with more than it can bear. Our Book records the truth, and none shall be wronged" (62).

Those localized missions were completed with the revelation of God's universal and final message to Muhammad. The Book he received, the Qur'an, was addressed primarily to the inhabitants of the Arabian peninsula, as it was revealed in their language, but its message was universal and intended for the whole of mankind. The Arabs had initially refused to accept Islam and rejected Muhammad despite their knowledge of his integrity and honesty. The surah refers to this by saying:

> Should they not reflect carefully over the Qur'an? Was what has been revealed to them different from what was revealed to their forefathers? Or do they deny their Messenger because they do not know him well? Or do they think he is possessed? He has come to them with the truth, but most of them do not like the truth. (68–70)

However, the price of their arrogance was high. Those who opposed Islam suffered a humiliating defeat at Badr in 624 AC, and their leaders were humbled forever. The surah says: "But when We visited Our scourge upon the opulent ones among them, they cry out in supplication" (64).

The non-believing Arabs used all means at their disposal to try to suppress Islam and undermine its veracity, growth, and influence, yet they failed to do so. The surah tells us:

> Surely he [Muhammad] has come to them with the truth, but most of them do not like the truth. Had the truth coincided with their desires and aspirations, the heavens, the earth and all that dwell in

them would have surely been corrupted. We have given them a Book that would raise their self-pride, yet they turn away from it. (70–71)

Hardship and tribulation are a necessary means of purification and refinement for human society. Prophet Muhammad was reported to have said: "Nothing befalls a Muslim, whether anxiety, depression, hardship, or illness, even if a thorn pricks his skin, but would be taken into consideration by God in forgiving his sins."[30] Power and wealth are liable to drive men to arrogance and oppression of those less fortunate than them. This is exactly what happened to the Prophet's people during the early part of his commission; so much so that he was heard asking God: "Help me against them as You helped Joseph: send them seven lean years."[31]

In some cases, the curse or punishment is prolonged, or recurs, because the people have not heeded the call: "If We showed them mercy and alleviated their misfortune, they would still blunder about in their evil ways" (75). The Arabs of Makkah resisted Islam for almost twenty years. Their opposition to it drained their resources and brought about their disintegration as a power in the region. It affected all aspects of their society and caused them to suffer politically, socially, and economically. This surah, which was revealed in Makkah, continues to threaten the Arabs with the aim of dissuading them from perpetrating hostility towards Muhammad and his followers. It says:

We punished them, but they neither submitted to their Lord nor appealed to Him for rescue. Let them wait for the time when We

---

[30] Narrated by al-Bukhārī.
[31] Narrated by Imam Aḥmad.

shall send a torrent of punishments upon them and leave them in utter despair. (76–77)

The surah then returns to exhort and educate man and appeal to his human intellect. It reminds people of God's infinite favors to them: the creation of human beings, the provision of natural resources for them, the night and the day, the sun and the moon, and so on. He has also endowed man with hearing, sight, and feeling and understanding. The surah then addresses the skeptics with the following three hard-hitting questions:

1.   Say to them [Muhammad], "Who controls the earth and all it contains and to whom does it all belong? Tell me if you know for sure." They will say, "It belongs to God." Say to them, "Then will you not take heed?"
2.   Say to them, "Who is the Lord of the seven heavens and the magnificent Throne?" They will say, "God." Say, "Will you not then fear God?"
3.   Say to them, "Tell me if you really know: who has sovereignty over all things and gives protection, but against whom there is no protection?" They will say, "God." Then ask them, "How then can you be so confused?" (84–89)

These questions were not being addressed to the idol-worshipers alone who knew that their gods had neither created the world nor controlled it, but also to some People of the Book who had tampered with the tenets and doctrines of their faith and therefore distorted the concept of true *tawḥīd*. The Qur'an sets out the solid foundations of pure *tawḥīd* which establish God as the sole Creator of, and Sovereign over the whole universe and everything within it. We read:

371

Never has God begotten a son, nor is there any other god besides Him. If there were, each god would have broken away from the others and they would have sought to overpower one another. Exalted be God above what they [the unbelievers] say. He knows what is beyond human perception and that which is manifest. Exalted be He above the gods they take besides Him. (91–92)

Tawḥīd is based on rational insight and sound reflection, whereas all contrary beliefs are based on pure fantasy, conjecture, and idle speculation.

This surah points out that man's life in this world is short, and that he must always seek the truth and fight temptation and misleading beliefs. It reminds the reader of death and how he might react to it:

When the moment of death arrives for a wrongdoer, he will say, "Lord, let me go back, that I may do good back there!" Never! These are just words he is uttering. Behind them [the unbelievers] there shall stand a barrier till the day they are restored to life again. (99–100)

This scene, where people, having died, ask to be returned to the world a second time to mend their ways appears in the Qur'an about ten times. This shows very clearly that as death approaches, the wrong-doers own up to their misdeeds and beg to be given another chance to live a clean life. In the surah we are given two scenes; one at the moment of death and one at the moment of judgment. On the latter occasion, wrong-doers will be reproached with the question:

"Were not My revelations recited to you, and did you not deny them?" They would say, "Our Lord, we were betrayed by our misfortune; we had gone astray. Lord, deliver us from hell. If we return to our bad ways, then we shall indeed be transgressors." (105–107)

These repeated appeals might help clarify matters for those who believe that man's fate in the hereafter is predetermined and that his pleading will have no influence on it. Islam has been grossly misunderstood on this point. To answer these cynics, the surah rounds off with a passage asserting that God Almighty is fair towards all men. He has equally blessed all human beings with the gift of life and given them senses and perception and intellectual faculties to distinguish between good and bad, right and wrong. The surah asks: "Did you think that We have created you in vain and that you would never be recalled to Us? Exalted be God, the true Sovereign!" (115–116)

God has made promises and sent warnings; He has given some people good health and inflicted others with ailments; He made life a mixture of happiness and suffering: all of this in order to enrich the human experience and make people recognize the reality and value of God. People can choose either to be vigilant and prepare for their encounter with God, and invest for life in the hereafter, or they can choose to reject God and dismiss any accountability to Him. God will judge both with fairness and justice; but when it is too late, excuses will avail no one. The surah tell us that as the time for accountability draws near, the skeptics will be flustered and will lose all sense of time:

God will ask them, "How many years did you live on earth?" They will reply, "A day, or possibly less. Ask those who kept count." He will say, "You stayed for a brief period, if you but knew it!" (112–114)

The surah concludes by stressing, yet again, the value and role of enlightened faith, pointing out that authentic religious belief is not built on mythology, folklore, and superstition. True religion respects rational thought and accords the human mind its rightful place in understanding the world and shaping it. Without their power of thought and free will, humans would not be accountable for their actions.

> He who invokes another god besides God—a god of whose divinity he has no possible proof—will have to account to God. The unbelievers shall never succeed. Say, "Lord, forgive and have mercy. You are the best of those who show mercy." (117–118)

Al-Nūr
(Light)

AL-NŪR, the title of this surah, is one of God's exalted names and appears in verse thirty-five. Just as God is the source of all life and creation, He is also the source of light, physical as well as metaphorical. The universe is like a shadow that cannot exist without a body; if the latter goes the former fades away or disappears altogether. The universe only exists because God is there, controlling it and running its affairs. The light which enables life to continue originates with God Almighty. Hence, all that we know and see and feel in this world is, in its own right, living proof of the existence of God.

The Arabic term *nūr* can be found in several sayings of Prophet Muhammad. When, in 619 AC, he was rejected by the people of Ṭā'if, east of Makkah, he turned to God for help, saying:

> I take refuge in the light of Your face which has illuminated the darkness and put right the affairs of this life and of the life to come. I appeal to You that You shall not send Your wrath upon me or be angry with me. The pleasure is Yours until You are well pleased. There is no power without God.

When the Prophet used to get up to pray during the night, he was known to recite the following prayer: "Lord, praise be to You. You are the Light of the heavens and the earth and all that is in them. Praise be to You. You are the Sustainer of the heavens and the earth and all that is in them."[32] He was also reported to have said: "Your Lord knows no night or day; the light of the Throne comes from the light of His face."[33]

We shall return to this topic shortly, but let us first look at the opening verse of the surah: "This is a surah which We have revealed and sanctioned, and We have proclaimed in it clear revelations, so that you may take heed." Unique to this surah, this is a solemn opening statement which underlines the seriousness of the injunctions and instructions that are to follow. Attention to this fact is drawn twice more in verses 34 and 46:

> We have sent down to you revelations showing you the right path, and examples of those who have gone before you, and an admonition to the God-conscious. (34)

> We have sent down revelations showing the right way, and God guides whom He wishes to the right path. (46)

The special attention accorded seems to be due to the subject-matter of the surah itself which deals with relations between men and women in society; introduces penalties for some sexual crimes and a number of social rules and regulations for mixed-sex environment and behavior; establishes some of the lawful and the unlawful modes of social behavior in Muslim society and contains a whole host of instructions relating to personal privacy and the etiquette governing behavior not only in other people's homes but inside one's own as well.

The aim of these social and personal rules and regulations is to maintain the integrity and decency of Muslim social life and to protect society against corruption and disintegration. Islam has been

---

[32] Narrated by al-Bukhārī.
[33] Ibid.

remarkably successful in achieving this goal and one has only to look at modern societies to see to what extent promiscuity and lack of moral cohesion have eaten into its fabric giving indecency and immorality a different and more acceptable status. Coupled with this, religion has been completely sidelined, leaving the door wide open for social ethics and norms that attach no importance to honor or moral integrity to creep in without effective challenge.

The surah begins by setting out the punishment for illicit sexual relations (*zinā*) between men and women and declares unlawful marriage to adulterous women. It also emphasizes the gravity of offenses such as slandering virtuous women. It explains the rule for what is known in Islamic law as 'mutual cursing' between husbands and wives who accuse each other of adultery. As the surah sets out these principles and regulations, it also explains that they have been laid down as part of God's grace, wisdom, and mercy to man and not as a set of isolated orders without purpose.

In this context the surah refers to the occasion during the Prophet's life when his wife ʿĀʾishah was slandered in an incident, known as *ḥadīth al-ifk*, involving a Muslim called Ṣafwān ibn al-Muʿaṭṭal. This incident served to expose the hostile undercurrent which had permeated throughout the early Muslim community, and against which the Qurʾan had warned when it said: "You shall certainly hear a great deal which is hurtful coming from those who had received the Book before you [Israelites and Christians], and from the polytheists" (*Āl ʿImrān*: 186).

There is nothing more abhorrent or socially damaging than the spreading of rumors against honorable and decent women and as such rumor-mongers are a real threat to society. On this particular occasion, a prominent opponent of Islam named ʿAbdullah ibn Ubayy, perpetrated the monstrous lie that the Prophet's wife,

'Ā'ishah, had been intimate with one of her fellow Muslims during a journey. This slander caused her untold distress.

The Prophet was utterly dumbfounded by this accusation and spent several days in complete bewilderment, believing in his wife's innocence but unable to prove it. The matter was finally and decisively put to rest (until the end of time no less) by the immortal and powerful words of the following surah which not only exonerated 'Ā'ishah from this evil crime but also chastised those who had seemingly doubted her innocence.

The story evoked several lessons for the Muslims, expressed in the following verses:

> When you heard it [the scandalous rumor], why did the faithful, men and women, not think better of themselves...? (16);

> Those who relish in spreading corruption among the believers shall receive stern punishment in this life and in the hereafter... (19)

and;

> Those who defame honorable and innocent believing women shall be cursed in this world and in the hereafter... (23)

Thus the controversy was laid to rest, but not before it had left some scars.

The surah then goes on to outline some of the rules of social etiquette which the Muslims should observe, not only in their daily interactions with members of the external community but also within their own homes as well. One of these areas of etiquette concerns the protocols which should be observed by Muslims when entering the homes of other people for, as places of rest and privacy, their sanctity should be respected. The surah teaches that among the first things one must do upon entering someone's house is to announce one's presence, greet those inside it and obtain permission to enter and that these formalities should not only be observed when entering the house from the outside but also when moving from room to room within it.

With a similar rationality for preserving decency and discouraging corruption and promiscuity in society, the surah also urges modesty and a strict sexual morality in the relationship between men and women. Although these rules and regulations were not new to Islam (as earlier religions had also advocated and promoted them), the difference was that Islam set them out more succinctly and elaborated on them in more detail. Islam also provided rulings on various aspects of dress, personal hygiene, and the wearing of jewelry as well as guidelines on the use of such things as perfume and cosmetics, and the subtle features that make a person adorable or attractive. In contrast to these high standards of decency and morality, some cultures, which profess to be religious, stand for the extreme opposite, exporting permissive sexual morality, vulgarity, nudity, pornography, indulgence and perversion.

Indeed, one has only to look at the role played by the mass media today to understand how it is being used as a powerful tool to promote indecency and encourage loose standards of morality such that it strongly threatens to destroy not only the very foundations of the family but also society as well. This scenario is not only confined to the West but is happening all over the world.

Islam looks at marriage as a religious obligation, and directs members of society to seek lawful and decent relationships, avoid the breakdown of the family and, more generally, to protect society from social disintegration. It is comforting and reassuring to know that the Qur'an gives such care and attention to these basic aspects of human social life, subjects which occupy more than a third of the surah (see, especially, verses 27–34 and 58–61).

☒☒

The surah takes its title from the following:

> God is the Light of the heavens and the earth. His Light may be compared to a niche that houses a lamp, the lamp is in a crystal of star-like brilliance. The lamp is fueled by the oil of a blessed olive tree, neither eastern nor western, which radiates almost spontaneously without it being lit by fire... (35)

Scholars, such as the eleventh-century philosopher al-Ghazālī, understood this "light," or *nūr*, to be the true quintessential light or the definitive source of all light in the universe. He goes on to explain that to describe God as Light puts Him above everything else in existence and points to His power to create living matter out of dark nothingness. The evidence of God's existence and power is so overwhelming and pervasive in the physical universe as well as in our own everyday lives, that only the ignorant or the arrogant can be blind to it. Others interpret 'light' as the guidance God infuses into the hearts of believers that gives them the ability to discern right from wrong, good from evil, and gives them a strong belief and confidence in their faith and what they profess to be true.

The Qur'an is one aspect of that *nūr* which illuminates man's way towards God. It has been described as such on several occasions. We read in the Qur'an: "Believe in God and His Messenger and the *nūr* We revealed..." (*al-Taghābun*: 8); and: "Humankind, a proof has come to you from your Lord, and We have revealed to you a clear *nūr*" (*al-Nisā'*: 174).

On closer reflection, the two meanings of the word *nūr* will be found to be complementary. As one marvels at the light observed in the physical world, it leads to guidance being imbued inside one's heart, drawing one closer to God. Those who fail to be aware of God and deny or ignore His power and role in the world will be deprived of the privilege of God's Light and guidance, no matter how materially fortunate or advanced or successful they may be. The surah asserts that: "He from whom God withholds light shall find no light at all" (40).

The surah goes on to speak about God's power and splendor, as manifested in the physical world, urging intelligent and discerning people to study these manifestations and reflect upon them in order to gain a deeper understanding of God and of themselves. We read:

> Do you not see how God is praised by all that is in heaven and on earth? The birds, as they spread their wings in the air, praise Him. All creatures have been taught how to praise and glorify God and He has full knowledge of all their actions. God has sovereignty over the heavens and the earth and to Him all things shall return. (41–42)

No believer can fail to be moved by such powerful and reassuring words. Reflecting on the subject matter of the surah, one would be justified in wanting to know and understand the relationship between family etiquette and moral and social conduct (which earlier passages had covered) and the greatness and omnipotence of God. The answer is that Islam recognizes a close link between law (sharīʿah) and faith (ʿaqīdah) which are two interrelated and complementary concepts. In *al-Baqarah*, verses 226–227, for example, we read:

> Those who renounce their wives on oath must wait four months. If they change their minds, God is Forgiving and Merciful; but if

they decide to divorce them, remember that God is All-Hearing, All-Knowing.

We notice that four of God's attributes are mentioned in this short passage dealing with divorce.

In the Qur'an, faith and belief, or ʿaqīdah, are linked to actions, or aʿmāl. Man's ordinary, mundane affairs and behavior are linked to his awareness of, and faith in, God. This inseparable bond between sharīʿah and ʿaqīdah is fundamental to Islam. Some people in the Muslim world are trying to separate the two and compartmentalize them, thereby proposing and seeking sources of law to govern Muslim societies other than those of Islam itself.

Al-Nūr, in particular, has established the means by which illicit sexual activity, promiscuity, and loose moral behavior are to be curtailed and prohibited in Muslim society. It hits hard at those who wish to undermine the moral fabric of society, saying:

> They say, "We believe in God and the Messenger, and we obey."
> But some of them immediately turn their backs. Surely these are not
> believers. And when they are called to God and His Messenger to
> judge between them, some of them turn away. (47–48)

It is curious to note that those who refuse God's teachings and the leadership of the Prophet in political, legal, and economic matters are usually non-practising Muslims who do not observe their basic Islamic obligations. Yet it is these same people who are most adamant in opposing Islam and undermining the very foundations of Muslim society and civilization. No wonder that the surah goes on to say:

The answer of the believers, when summoned to Allah and His Messenger, in order that He may judge between them, is no other than this: they say, "We hear and we obey." It is such as these that will attain felicity. It is such as obey Allah and His Messenger, and fear Allah and do right, that will win [in the end]. (51–52)

This is yet another form of the perennial conflict between those who reject religion in its totality and champion every possible cause to destroy it, and those who defend religion and devote their energies to bringing people closer to God and to the way of life He has ordained for humankind.

Muslims today are dispirited, divided, and weak. But this surah brings them hope:

God has promised those of you who believe and do good works that He will make them masters on earth as He had made those who came before them. He will establish firmly the faith He has chosen for them and replace their fear with security... (55)

This victory, however, does not come easily. It has to be earned with hard work, sacrifice, and devotion. Muslims today will have to learn from the example of the Prophet and his Companions. They spent almost a quarter of a century fighting Arab paganism and polytheism before they were able to establish Islam as the dominant force in Arabia. From there, and within a phenomenally short period of time, they emerged to take on the Roman and the Persian empires and it was not very long afterwards that the Muslims came to be the most powerful and dominant force in the world. Within thirty years of the first words of the Qur'an being revealed to Muhammad, a single man from a poor family in the heart of Arabia, a powerful nation was established with influence extending to all corners of the globe: a nation brought up under the watchful eyes of God to uphold His laws and establish His way of life on earth.

But what are the conditions that the Muslims must satisfy to assume the leadership of the world again? The surah replies: "Let them worship Me and no one else besides Me" (55) and "Attend to prayer [salah], render the alms [zakah], and obey the Messenger, so that you may be shown mercy" (56). Cynics and unbelievers will say that this is naive and idealistic, pie-in-the-sky thinking, but God says: "Never think that the unbelievers can stand up to God in this world. The fire of hell shall be their final abode: an evil end" (57). It is not surprising that skeptics and doubters are unable to understand this rationale or appreciate its gravity. They would rather dismiss the whole argument. To the believers, however, it is a certainty that stems from their unshakable faith and trust in God Almighty.

SURAH 25

Al-Furqān
(The Criterion)

WE OWE IT TO OUR CREATOR, God Almighty, to recognize and acknowledge His existence without having had to have messengers sent to guide us. The world around us is full of evidence for His existence and grace and, left to its own pristine nature and undefiled instincts, humankind's intuition should have eventually led them to God.

Although we do not know the total number and names of all the divine messengers sent by God to humankind over the generations, what we do know for certain is that Muhammad was the last of them and that the Qur'an is the final and complete version of all their messages. It was God's will that Islam should be the final and universal message. "Glorified be He who has revealed *al-Furqān* [the Qur'an] to His servant [Muhammad], that he may be a warner to all humankind" (1). Muhammad was an ordinary human being but with exceptional qualities. His mission epitomized the glory of all humanity, his experience marked the cross-roads of history, and under his leadership humanity entered its great phase of maturity. He was chosen and charged with this great historic task by God:

> The Sovereign of the heavens and the earth, who has begotten no offspring and whose Sovereignty is shared by no one; who has created everything and assigned everything to its proper function. (2)

These divine attributes had been debated by ignorant and unbelieving people for far too long, but Muhammad had come to

385

establish a society and a whole nation that would be dedicated to upholding their existence and fighting to preserve belief in them.

The surah lists a whole set of objections raised by Muhammad's detractors and undertakes to discuss and refute them, one by one:

1. The rejection of God's prophets and messengers by their own people is an age-old stance, and it was, therefore, not surprising that Muhammad should receive the same treatment. "The unbelievers say, 'It [the Qur'an] is nothing but prevarication of his own invention, and others are helping him to fabricate it.' They are being unjust and fraudulent in what they say" (4).

    Who were those 'others' who have supposedly helped Muhammad fabricate the Qur'an? And if indeed they had been capable of such a commendable feat, why had they not claimed prophethood for themselves?

2. "They said, 'It [the Qur'an] is fables of the ancients which he [Muhammad] has written down himself and it was being dictated to him morning and evening'" (5).

    This was a reference to the Jews and Christians whom the Arabs claimed were teaching Muhammad his religion. But would the Christians have taught him to reject the trinity or refute it? Or, would the Jews have approved of the ferocious criticism leveled against them in the Qur'an? Such allegations simply do not stand up to scrutiny.

3. "They said, 'How is it that this Messenger eats and walks about in the markets? Should he not have had an angel sent down with him to warn the people?'" (7).

Eating of course would not demean the Prophet in any way for it was natural for him to do so. As for the allegation that an angel should have come with him, one can retaliate with the question: What would its supposed role have been anyway? Would it have stood in for the Messenger? Moreover, if the Prophet was in need of an angel's support, why would he be charged with a task he was not capable of performing himself?

4. "The transgressors say, 'You are following a bewitched man.' Look at their ghastly allegations towards you [Muhammad]. They have gone astray and have completely lost their way to the true path. Glory be to Him who, if He wills, can give you better than that; He can give you gardens with rivers flowing through them and He can give you palaces too" (8–10).

5. The surah goes on to list more objections and allegations made by the unbelievers. "Those who entertain no hope of meeting Us ask, 'Why have no angels been sent down to us? Why can we not see our Lord?' They have overreached themselves and have gone too far in their transgression. On the day when they see the angels, the transgressors will not receive glad tidings as the angels tell them, 'You are barred from God's favor'" (21–22).

This will be the kind of reception they will be accorded. They will not be welcome, and whatever they might have done during their lifetime in this world will be thrown to the wind. It is curious to note that the objections put forward by the Arabs of Makkah were the same as those expressed by earlier communities who rejected previous prophets and messengers.

6. The next objection is: "The unbelievers ask, 'Why was the Qur'an not revealed to him [Muhammad] altogether in one go?'" (32) the answer to which is: "We have revealed it gradually and in installments in order to strengthen your heart with it" (32).

    In other words, the Qur'an was deliberately revealed over a period of time and on specifically selected occasions for a deeper impact on Muhammad and his followers, and for better results. It is a misconception that this was unique to the Qur'an. The Old and New Testaments were also collated and written over several years, indeed centuries.

7. The objections continue: "Whenever they see you they sneer at you and say, 'Is this the man whom God has sent as a Messenger? Had we not held firm to our gods, he would have turned us away from them'..." (41–42).

These objections are a clear indication that the Qur'an had shaken the religious foundations of Makkan society and exposed the fraudulent beliefs of its inhabitants. They were losing heart as the veracity of the Qur'an became more and more evident to them. This was similar to what had happened to the people of Abraham when they saw their idols smashed and "reconsidered, saying to each other, 'Surely you are the ones who have done wrong'" (*al-Anbiyā'*: 64).

Nevertheless, the Arabs of Makkah persisted with their refusal to acknowledge the truth of the Qur'an and continued with their sneering, "But when they face the scourge they shall realize who has been more grossly misled" (42). The surah then makes a more general criticism of those who ignore the truth and hanker after their whims and desires. It says:

Look at those who worship their own desires! Would you [Muhammad] be held responsible for their actions? Do you think that most of them can hear or understand? They are like cattle, though they are more heedless. (43–44)

Thus the Qur'an hits back with strong words at those who had scoffed at the Prophet and the Muslims. The Arabs made the mistake of judging the Prophet and his followers by their meager wealth and insignificant material power. But these are hardly the criteria by which truth and integrity are judged. An individual or a community can be as wealthy or materially advanced as possible, but all this comes to naught if the same community is not built on authentic and sound beliefs and guidance. The surah cites more of the Arabs' objections to Islam:

When it is said to them, "Prostrate yourselves before the Merciful," they ask, "Who is the Merciful? Would you have us prostrate ourselves on your orders?" And they grow even more rebellious. (60)

The epithet "the Merciful" (*al-Raḥmān*), like *Allah,* is one of God's most exclusive and exalted names. The unbelievers refused to accept Muhammad's teachings and advice because they were too proud to abandon their idols to worship *al-Raḥmān.*

When debating with the unbelievers two different approaches have been adopted in this surah. In one approach the unbelievers are warned and threatened with a fate similar to that of the rebellious communities who preceded them, such as the Pharaohs, ʿĀd, Thamūd, among others. In this vein the surah recalls the destruction of Lot's people, saying: "The unbelievers must surely have passed by the city [of Sodom] which was destroyed by the fatal torrent; or have they not seen it? But they do not believe in the resurrection" (40).

The second approach, which is even more effective, resorts to reasoned argument, addressing man's intellect and presenting facts and evidence as a means of persuasion. This is particularly evident in this surah. It points man's attention to the amazing natural phenomena existing in the vast cosmos, the heavens and the earth, and intriguingly begins by referring to the existence of shadows: "Do you not see how your Lord extends the shadow? He could have made it static, if He so wished. But We made the sun a sign for it" (45). Light and shadow are indeed extraordinary phenomena. Everything has its own shadow and shades come in all shapes and sizes, but nothing is more magical and fascinating than the shadows formed by the eclipse of the stars and planets. Not only are these amazing marvels a source of great pleasure and beauty but they are also vital for the development and continuation of life on this earth.

Consider the phenomena of night and day and their role in the sustenance and preservation of life. What controls their precise and carefully regulated cycle? Take the function of sleep and its importance in revitalizing the body, assisting growth and promoting sanity and good health. It is amazing how, during such a state of unconsciousness, some metabolic activities, such as breathing and digestion, continue to function while others come to a complete stop. These and other manifestations, both within ourselves and in the world around us, should serve to spur us on to seek God, and praise and thank Him constantly.

One can go on to look at the perpetual movement of the wind, the development of clouds and the resulting rain which forms lakes and rivers serving to fertilize the soil, causing in turn the growth and development of all kinds of living matter. A beautiful cycle of nature generating and permeating life far and wide. The surah puts it beautifully when it says:

It is He who sends the winds as harbingers of His mercy; We send down pure water from the sky to give life to the dead land and quench the thirst of countless beasts and humans of Our creation. (48–49)

The manifestations that encourage faith and support it are many and close at hand. Wherever we care to look there is evidence pointing towards God.

Having pointed out some of these manifestations, God says: "Blessed is He who decked the sky with constellations and set in it the glowing sun and the illuminating moon" (61). From this verse it is possible to infer that galaxies and universes, other than our own, do indeed exist. Modern astronomy and physics have shown that the cosmos contains millions of galaxies and star formations, and that our solar system occupies but a tiny fraction in this vast, limitless space.

Relative to this, man becomes an increasingly insignificant creature. This reinforces the fact that we are here to be tested and that our deeds and activities are assessed against certain well-defined principles and criteria. Will we take notice and heed God's instructions or will we neglect and rebel against them? As the surah points out, we are also being tested in our relationships with one another: "We make some of you a means to test others in order to try your endurance. Your Lord is aware of all" (20).

This never-ending trial is crucial, and success or failure determines our position in the hereafter. The surah implies that true believers who serve God and worship Him well are the ones who will pass the test of this life and achieve Paradise in the hereafter. The final passage in the surah presents a portrait of true believers, identifying ten of their essential qualities. These qualities are as follows:

1. "True servants of the Merciful are those who walk humbly on the ground and who say, 'Peace!' when the ignorant accost them" (63). This modesty should not be mistaken

for weakness or inadequacy. It is a sign of moderation and lack of ostentation. Believers refuse to be diverted or intimidated by the ignorant and the mischievous.

2. "Those who spend the night prostrating and standing in praise of their Lord" (64). This does not mean the whole of the night, but part of it, because the human body needs to rest to resume its duties on the following day. In the Muslim daily routine it is important that one does not retire before performing the night (ʿishāʾ) prayer or wake up too late the following morning for the dawn (fajr) prayer. The reward for performing these two prayers in congregation (jamāʿah) or in the mosque is equivalent to praying all through the night.

3. "Those who say, 'Our Lord, ward off from us the punishment of hell, for its punishment is everlasting" (65). This is a fate that every Muslim must try to avoid and can only do so by diligence and freedom from greed and materialistic indulgence.

4. "Those who are neither extravagant nor niggardly, but are moderate in their spending" (67). Both these extremes are abhorrent and harmful.

5. "Those who invoke no other deity besides God..." (68).

6. "And do not destroy life, which God has forbidden, except for a just cause..." (68).

7. "Do not engage in illicit sexual relations" (68).

These are three of the most vile crimes perpetrated in human societies, "and whoever commits any of them shall on the Day of Judgment receive compounded punishment which he shall suffer in humiliation forever" (68–69).

Nevertheless, the door for correction and reform in this life is always open. Once a wrong-doer decides to change and mend his ways, he will receive God's help and support.

8.   "Those who do not bear false witness and shun profanity with dignity and grace" (72).

9.   "Those who, when reminded of their Lord's revelations, attend with open ears and eyes" (73). This reinforces the idea that the study of the Qur'an should be accorded full attention and respect; otherwise one will not reap the full benefit from it.

10.   "And those who say, 'Our Lord, give us joy in our spouses and our children, and make us a model for those who fear You'" (74). This is a plea from the believers to God to nourish their sense of family feeling and to strengthen the ties of love, emotional stability, and solidarity among their family unit.

These true believers: "shall be rewarded for their fortitude with the loftiest places in Paradise. That is the best abode, and there they shall abide for ever" (75–76).

Al-Shuʿarā'
(The Poets)

WHEN IT FIRST EMERGED in the seventh century AC, Islam was greeted with strong hostility and resistance by the idol-worshiping Arabs of Makkah. They rejected its two fundamental concepts, that there could be only one God, and that Muhammad was a Messenger sent by Him to humankind.

The idea of revelation (*waḥī*), as a means of communication between God and man, had never been known to the Arabs before and prior to the advent of the Prophet. They had also not believed in the ideas of resurrection and accountability in a life hereafter. In fact, their view of whatever remnants of Jewish and Christian religious beliefs and practices were left among them was characterized by indifference and derision. For these and other reasons, the Makkan Arabs initially showed very little interest in Muhammad or what he was trying to teach them, and the harder he tried to explain his mission the more hostile and rebellious they grew. In the end they came to cherish the distress that he and his followers were suffering and did their best to prolong their misery and anguish. This surah came to Muhammad with reassuring and soothing words advising him that he should not encumber himself by worrying about his people. It says:

These are the verses of the indubitable Book. You will perhaps overstrain yourself for the fact that they do not believe. If We will, We can send them a sign from heaven, before which their heads would be bowed in humiliation. (2–4)

394

In His infinite wisdom, however, God chose that the sign Muhammad would present to the world would be the Qur'an, a book to be recited and handed down from one generation to the next, which would appeal to man's mind and address above all else his intelligence. The Makkans, however, were demanding miracles, stunning indications or signs which would convince them once and for all that Muhammad was telling them the truth. The irony was that such signs were in existence all around them, both in the realms of place and of time, and if they chose to they could observe them any time of the day or night. As far as place is concerned, the surah draws attention to the barren earth which, in one season, can be arid and lifeless and yet, in another, can be green and fertile. It says:

> Do they not see the earth and how We have brought forth from it all kinds of beneficial plants? Surely in this there is a sign; yet most of them do not believe. Your Lord is the Mighty one, the Merciful. (7–9)

The last two verses recur in the surah eight times; once following a reference to a place and the rest following a reference to an event in time. These latter occasions are related to episodes in the history of earlier communities who had been destroyed as a result of their hostility towards, and rejection of, the divine revelation conveyed to them by Messengers with similar experiences to that of Muhammad. Those episodes were cited to warn the Arabs against meeting with a similar fate.

God's prophets were individuals who had commendable leadership qualities such as integrity, honesty and selflessness. They were, moreover, teachers rather than egotistic profit-seekers. What the surah tells us about Noah can be applied, in general, to them all.

> The people of Noah, too, rejected their messengers. Noah, their compatriot, said to them, "Do you not fear God? I am your true messenger. Fear God and follow me. For this I ask no recompense from you, for none can reward me except the Lord of the whole universe." (105–109)

None of the prophets asked anything of their people except that they should submit to God and fear Him, neither did they seek any material remuneration or power. But despite these selfless motives many were treated harshly and unfairly with a large number being slain by their own people: a tragic outcome. The surah says:

> Tell Me! If We had let them live in ease for several years and then the promised scourge fell upon them, what good would their past prosperity do them? Never have We destroyed a nation without sending them warners. This is a reminder to others. We are never unjust. (205–209)

The surah recalls the encounters between Moses and the Pharaoh and those between Abraham, Lot and Shuʿayb and their respective peoples, as well as episodes from the experiences of ʿĀd and Thamūd. All these accounts are presented lucidly with clear language and good effect. The debate between Moses and the Pharaoh revolved around the subject of the true identity of God. The Pharaoh wanted to know who or what God really was, a question that even Moses could not answer, for to identify and define the essence or nature of God in terms that we can understand is beyond human intelligence.

> The Pharaoh asked, "And who is the Lord of the universe?" Moses replied, "He is the Lord of the heavens and the earth and all that lies

between them. If you would only believe!" Pharaoh said to those around him, "Did you hear what he said?" Moses said, "He is your Lord and the Lord of your forefathers." Pharaoh said, "This Messenger who has been sent to you is certainly insane..." (23–27)

This argument is similar to the one we saw in Surah *Ṭā Hā*. Nevertheless, the Pharaoh refused to recognize the God of Moses and said to him: "'If you serve any god other than me, I shall throw you in prison'" (29).

A day was agreed for a public duel between Moses and the Pharaoh's sorcerers, organized to expose the fraudulence of what Moses was preaching and put an end to his mission and teachings. The stage was set "and the people were summoned, 'Assemble, so that we can follow the sorcerers if they win the day!'" (39–40). To Pharaoh and his entourage, it was a foregone conclusion that Moses would be publicly defeated and humiliated and as such the sorcerers' triumph was never in doubt. However, events took such a turn that not only were the sorcerers spectacularly defeated, but they also renounced their faith in the Pharaoh and accepted the religion of Moses instead. As expected, this sent the Pharaoh into a terrible rage and he turned on them and said,

> "Do you dare follow him [Moses] without my consent? He must be your master who taught you sorcery. But you shall see! I will cut off your hands and legs on alternate sides and will crucify every one of you." (49)

This sudden but complete change of attitude by the sorcerers never ceases to amaze. Almost at a stroke, they turned from abject servitude to the Pharaoh to the deepest and most sincere faith in God. The Pharaoh persisted in his arrogant refusal to accept the truth and condemned his courtiers for changing their convictions without waiting for his permission. Like all tyrants everywhere, the Pharaoh believed that he was in command of his followers' consciences as well as their livelihood.

The days went by and Moses decided to lead his people out of Egypt to escape the Pharaoh's wrath and persecution. When the Pharaoh heard of this he gathered his army and went after them. As they drew nearer, Moses' followers became alarmed and said to him: "'They are catching up with us'" (61). The Torah records this episode in graphic detail and gives a description of the panic and fear which had struck the Israelites. But Moses said to them: "'No, my Lord is with me, and He will guide me'" (62). As they reached the Red Sea, God intervened and directed Moses to strike the water with his staff, and, lo and behold, the water receded on both sides leaving a dry pathway across the sea for Moses and his followers to cross safely to the other shore. The Pharaoh and his army duly followed through, but once they had progressed well along the sea bed, the water flooded over them from all sides and they were drowned. Thus ended one of the most infamous episodes of man's disingenuous attempts to challenge the sovereignty of God Almighty in the world.

As we read the story of prophet Abraham, we can clearly see how simple and straightforward were the teachings imparted to him by God. The more one reads the philosophers' attempts in trying to explain and understand life and existence, the more one is struck and impressed by the simplicity of divinely-revealed religious belief. Listen to how Abraham expresses his faith in God:

> "He is the One who created me and He gives me guidance. He is the One who gives me food and drink. When I am sick He restores my good health; He will cause me to die and He will bring me back to life. I also hope that, on the Day of Judgment, He will forgive me my misdemeanors." (78–82)

As pointed out on several occasions, the establishment of *tawḥīd* as a fundamental foundation of human life has been a common denominator for the missions of all prophets. Prophet Muhammad was the rightful heir to Abraham's legacy. Some of the communities which refused to believe in the concept of *tawḥīd* professed that they had only worshiped idols in order to bring them closer to God. They had recognized the existence of a master God but in reality saw minor gods as a link to Him. The only problem with this kind of belief was that the differentiation would soon disappear and all the gods become equal. In this part of Abraham's story we read the following:

> As the idolaters argued with their idols in hell, they said to them, "By God, we were in great error when we equated you with the Lord of the universe. It was the evil-doers who led us astray. We have no intercessors now, nor a single loving friend." (96–101)

A feature of contemporary civilization is that it marginalizes God and drives people away from Him and into the arms of materialism and agnosticism.

We note that the story of Abraham follows on from the story of Moses and precedes that of Noah because the chronological order is not of importance in this context. In the story of Noah, attention is drawn to the degrading and demeaning treatment which the rich and strong mete out to the poor and weak. This tells us that discrimination and class distinction in society have been known since the dawn of human history. It is not surprising, therefore, to find that it is the poor, the under-privileged, and the weak who are the first social groups to come to the support of the prophets and Messengers. What they seek is justice and equality and the restoration of their dignity and self-pride. Noah was told:

"Are we to believe in you when you have attracted only the most abject of people?" He said, "I have no way of knowing what they have been doing. My Lord will bring them to account. Would that you understand! I will not drive away the believers. I am sent only to give clear warnings." (111–115)

The idolaters of Makkah made similar objections to Muhammad but he rebutted them and God instructed him that he should not: "Drive away those who invoke their Lord morning and evening, seeking His pleasure..." (al-Anʿām: 52). Elsewhere in the Qur'an this affinity in attitude between the unbelievers is highlighted: "Have they inherited this, one generation from another? Surely, they are transgressors. Turn away from them; you shall incur no blame!" (al-Dhāriyāt: 53–54). However, the history of religion is not a simple conflict between the poor and the rich, for both the rich, as well as the poor, supported Muhammad when he called them to the faith and embraced Islam. Moreover, they would all stand side by side during the prayers and were equally happy to accept the tribulations they collectively had to face.

Perhaps no community has as much in common with contemporary civilization as the ʿĀd and Thamūd. The ʿĀd were a nation of giant-like people, endowed with a strong and imposing physique. They were also very clever and resourceful. Their power and material superiority led them to believe that they were invincible. They lived extravagantly, spent their wealth lavishly, gave no consideration to weaker communities or individuals, and exercised power with complete arrogance and insolence, thinking that no force in the world could stand in their way. Prophet Hūd was sent to them by God and is quoted here as saying:

"You have erected tall edifices as landmarks on every hill, just for vanity; you have built strong fortresses, hoping that you may live for ever; and when you exercise power you act like tyrants. Fear God and follow me." (128–131)

They had constructed splendid buildings as symbols of their vanity and power, and although construction and building are in themselves not a crime—indeed, rather the reverse, for they are commendable activities—what was being condemned here was the extravagance and wastage of the wealth and resources involved, especially when these edifices and monuments were erected for nothing other than ostentation and vainglory. These same features are only too conspicuous in the greed-motivated, lust-driven Western civilization of today which is beset by consumerism, narcissism, and arrogance. Whenever the United States or Europe went to war against weaker nations they played havoc with their culture, history, and resources, totally ignoring all considerations of humanity, justice, and respect of human rights. It was this ungodly attitude which had incurred God's wrath upon the ʿĀd, Thamūd and their like.

The surah then goes on to cite the story of the people of Lot, who were indulging in depraved and perverted practices. These very same actions are fast becoming acceptable in today's contemporary Western civilization, and instead of fighting against their immoral and destructive nature and guarding society against their evil, contemporary society is in fact doing the reverse, naturalizing, legalizing, and accepting them, with an end to incorporating them into the life of the society itself. This is a recipe for disaster. Lot's people were destroyed because they ignored his warnings to them: "You have [sexual] relations with males and abandon your wives whom God has created for you. Nay, but you are people who transgress [all bounds of what is right]" (165–166).

Finally, we are told of the story of Shuʿayb and his people, the forest dwellers (*aṣḥābuʾl aykah*), who were advised to:

"Give just measure and do not defraud others. Weigh with even scales and do not defraud your fellow men of what is rightly theirs; nor should you go about spreading corruption." (181–183)

The people of Shuʿayb did not heed their prophet's call and they were also destroyed. The Muslim community is required to learn from the lessons and experiences of past communities, and as the rightful heir of all the goodness and achievements of past generations and civilizations, it leads humanity by virtue of the obligations imposed on it by God.

Muslims must remember that Muhammad's mission was a universal and eternal one; that they are the custodians of the Qur'an which represents the definitive and conclusive message that God has conveyed to humanity and which is designed to govern and organize life on this earth.

Al-Naml
(The Ants)

THIS SURAH, which was revealed in Makkah, introduces a number of intriguing aspects taken from the animal kingdom, some of which are yet to be discovered by man. The last verse in the surah affirms this fact, saying: "And say, 'Praise be to God. He will show you His signs and you will recognize them. Your Lord is never unaware of what you do'" (93). The early parts of the surah give the reader glimpses of the fate that will befall both the believers and the unbelievers (the former being successful and rightly-guided while the latter are destined for ignominy). This brief introductory passage is elaborated upon in more detail towards the end of the surah following a review of four episodes taken from the earlier histories of Moses and the Pharaoh, Solomon and Sheba, Thamūd, and the people of Lot. The surah also refers briefly to the 'beast' which it says will appear towards the end of time. Let us first look at the historical accounts cited in the surah.

When Moses saw his staff turn into a serpent, he was alarmed and ran away, but God addressed him:

"Moses, do not be alarmed. Messengers have nothing to fear in My presence. As for those who do wrong and then replace the evil with good deeds; in that case I am Forgiving and Merciful…" (10–11)

These words were designed to reassure Moses that God had forgiven him for the killing of the Egyptian man as specified in *al-Qaṣaṣ*: 15–21. Following this incident, Moses had said: "'My Lord, I have wronged myself, so please forgive me.' God forgave him, for He is the Forgiving and Merciful" (*al-Qaṣaṣ*: 16). The surah affirms that the Pharaoh and his people had persistently and deliberately rejected God, despite their belief that Moses was truthful and right and that their hostility to him was unjustified. It says: "They wrongly and arrogantly denied our signs although in their hearts they knew them to be true. Look what fate meets those who perpetrate corruption" (14).

Before proceeding to the case of Solomon, we should recall the verse in *al-Anʿ ām* which says: "All the beasts that roam the earth and all the birds that fly with their wings are nations like you…" (38). Members of these kingdoms live and communicate among themselves using special languages which are possible for man to discover and understand. God had endowed prophet Solomon with the gift of understanding animal communication methods and the ability to communicate with them: "He [Solomon] said, 'My people, we have been taught the language of birds and endowed with all good things. Surely this is a signal favor'" (16).

In one incident cited, Solomon could hear what a particular ant was saying when it tried to warn its fellow ants:

> "Ants, enter your dwellings, lest Solomon and his warriors should unwittingly crush you." He [Solomon] smiled at her words, and said, "Lord, please inspire me to give thanks for the favors You have bestowed on me and on my parents, and to do good works that will please You, and admit me, through Your mercy, among Your righteous servants." (18–19)

The surah also refers to a hoopoe which had brought Solomon the news that Bilqīs, the Queen of Sheba, and her people were sun-worshipers. The hoopoe had been astonished to see them worshiping something else other than God and he had exclaimed to Solomon:

"But I found her and her people prostrating themselves before the sun, instead of God. Satan has seduced them and turned them away from the right path and they have gone astray. Should they not prostrate themselves before God who knows all the secrets that are in the heavens and the earth, and who knows what you conceal and what you reveal..." (24–25)

Solomon dispatched a message to the Queen of Sheba which said: "'In the name of God, the Compassionate, the Merciful. Do not be supercilious, and come to me in total submission'" (30–31).

Islam, the essence of which is *tawḥīd* and submission to God, is the religion taught and advocated by all prophets without exception. Abraham, Moses, Jesus, and Muhammad have preached, upheld, and propagated one and the same religion. The Queen of Sheba took time to consider Solomon's invitation and to consult her advisors. Above all, she was anxious to establish whether Solomon was like all the other sovereigns she had known who had only been interested in wealth and power. When her delegation arrived at Solomon's court with expensive gifts and precious souvenirs, he immediately realized what she was after. Solomon said to the delegation: "'Is it wealth that you bring me? What God has given me is far better than what He has given you. You seem to rejoice in your gifts'" (36).

Solomon was prompted to present the Queen of Sheba with a feat that would convince her of his truthfulness. He said to his courtiers: "'Which one of you can bring me her throne, before they sue for peace?'" (38) In an instant, the surah tells us, the Queen of Sheba's throne was miraculously transported from Yemen to Jerusalem. When Solomon saw it he was overawed and said:

"This is of the grace of my Lord. He is testing me to see whether I will be thankful or deny His favor. The thankful shall reap the benefit of their gratitude, but those who deny the favor should know that God is Self-Sufficient and Generous." (40)

Although we cannot be certain how this happened, modern science has shown us today that mass and energy are only different states of the same matter, and that both can be made to travel at incredibly fast speeds. When Bilqīs arrived in Jerusalem she was completely amazed at seeing the throne there and when asked if her own throne was like the one she was looking at, was not certain, but replied: "'It is as though it were the same'" (42). She was to learn more from Solomon to convince her that he was a messenger from God, and finally said: "'My Lord, I have wronged myself, but I now submit with Solomon to God, Lord of all creation'" (44).

The surah then moves on to narrate the story of the Thamūd, another example of a people given to stubbornness and arrogance. As soon as a prophet named Ṣāliḥ emerged amongst them to lead them to God and to a better life, they embarked on a scheme to kill him saying: "'Let us swear in the name of God to kill him in the night, together with all his household, and then say to his next of kin that we had never witnessed their killing...'" (49). However, it seems that instead of killing Ṣāliḥ they decided to kill the she-camel which God had sent to them as a sign of Ṣāliḥ's credentials. Their end was tragic.

Thus they plotted, but We too have plotted, without their knowledge. Look at the consequences of their plotting! We destroyed them and all their people. Their dwellings are desolate ruins, as a result of their transgression... (50–52)

The surah continues citing the story of the prophet Lot and the town of Sodom whose inhabitants practiced perversion in their public places of gathering. Lot was an Israelite who had emigrated to Sodom only to discover shockingly that open homosexuality was being practised by the men of the place as a matter of course. When he objected to this abomination the people decided to expel him, his family, and the small group of followers who supported him. The surah says:

> And tell of Lot. He said to his people, "Do you commit indecency with your eyes open? How can you lustfully seek men instead of women? Surely you are an ignorant people." His people replied only by saying, "Banish the house of Lot from your city, because they are virtuous people." (54–56)

The people of Lot were also destroyed and their city turned upside down. Although these vile practices were well known to the Jewish and Christian communities, whose books severely condemned them, they have come to be accepted today in the modern Judeo-Christian societies of America and Europe. Right from the beginning of this surah, we note that these practices and the people who promote them have been implicitly condemned to severe punishment. The surah says:

> We have made the foul deeds of those who deny the life hereafter seem attractive to them, so that they go on blundering about in their folly. Such are those who shall be sternly punished and in the hereafter shall be the worst losers. (4–5)

Having related these episodes from the experience of earlier prophets, God turns to address Muhammad with these words: "Say, 'Praise be to God, and peace be upon His servants whom He has chosen!...'" (59). God is praised for thwarting the transgressors and cleansing the earth of their vile practices. Elsewhere in the Qur'an we read: "Thus the transgressors were thwarted. Praise be to God,

Lord of all" (*al-An'ām*: 45). The defeat of corruption and tyranny is a triumph for truth and decency and a favor for which God deserves to be thanked and praised. Credit is also due to the prophets and messengers for their patient struggle and relentless fight for a better and cleaner life on earth.

The surah then poses the following rhetorical question: "Which is more worthy of worship: God or the idols they serve besides Him?" (59). This is reminiscent of Joseph's plea to his prison mates when he said to them: "'Fellow prisoners! Are sundry gods better than God, the One who conquers all?'" (*Yūsuf*: 39).

This is yet another assertion that *tawḥīd* is the common denominator of all heavenly revealed religions. Polytheism, or *shirk*, is an aberration that occurs in societies that have had no genuine guidance or have lost their way. The Arabs practised more than their fair share of *shirk*, and this surah gives five basic arguments for *tawḥīd*, which no sensible and rational human being can fail to understand and appreciate.

1. "Surely worthier to be worshiped is He who has created the heavens and the earth and sent down to you water from the sky, with which We bring forth gardens of delight. Try as you may, you cannot make the trees grow. What? Another god besides God? They are nothing but blatant idolaters" (60).

    Not even the most ignorant person would agree that an idol or a man-made deity is capable of creating the heavens or the earth, or that it can cause the rain to fall from the sky or the plants to grow out of the soil!

2. "Surely worthier is He who has firmly established the earth and made rivers run through it; who has set mountains upon it and separated salt water from sweet water. What?

Another god besides God? Indeed, most of them are ignorant" (61).

The balance and stability of the earth and its orderly movement are a fascinating feat. The earth is not only moving around its own axis but it is also moving around the sun as part of a very complex and intricate system. Nevertheless, the earth retains its stability and perpetual equilibrium, and nothing 'falls off' its surface.

The earth is a sphere with eighty per cent of its surface covered with sea water. Rivers and lakes form all over the land, but due to different chemical and physical properties their clean water is never soiled by sea water. Do these observations not lead one to search for their Creator?

3. "Surely worthier is He who answers the afflicted when they cry out to Him, and relieves their pain. He has made you the inheritors of the earth. What? Another god besides God? How little you reflect!" (62)

This verse points to God's grace towards humans, and to their need for God's help and care when they are hit by disasters or afflictions they cannot cope with. God is always there to alleviate the pain and relieve the suffering.

4. "Surely worthier is He who guides you in the darkness on land and in the sea, and He sends the winds as harbingers of His mercy. What? Another god besides God? Exalted be He above all their idols" (63).

God has provided man with the means of navigation for use on the land, air, and sea. He has also harnessed the wind for man's benefit. Which of the other alleged gods is capable of any of this?

5.   "Surely worthier is He who created and is capable of creating anew; He who provides you with sustenance from heaven and from earth. What? Another god besides God? Say, 'Show me your proof, if you are truthful'" (64). No such proof has been forthcoming.

To deny the existence of God is a syndrome, not a philosophy or a science. It is a by-product of arrogance and fanciful theorization, and cannot be accredited with any logic or intellectual respectability. Contemporary scientific materialism is a rehash of ancient pagan philosophies. Its danger lies in the fact that it has come to be considered as science, purported to be based on evidence and tangible proof. This thinking is the underlying cause behind today's global malaise which is leading humanity to disaster. The ancient unbelievers said:

"When we and our fathers are turned to dust, shall we be raised to life? We were promised this once before, and so were our fathers. It is nothing but a myth of the ancients." Say to them, "Look around you in the world and see what was the end of the wrong-doers." (67–69)

Muhammad was instructed to rebut such arguments and to bring people face to face with the reality of the hereafter. His mission was to give the world a civilization with a strong faith in God, built on authentic revelation, whose people are taught and prepared to face accountability in the hereafter. Islam has established a society whose laws, relationships and behavior are shaped by the belief in the hereafter. It is not for nothing that Muslims stand up to face God in prayer five times a day every day of their lives.

This surah contains a verse which speaks of a mysterious creature which will appear on earth towards the last days, and which will, by God's permission, speak to humans and severely reprimand them for their laxity, negligence, and failure to recognize God and serve Him as He should be served. It will condemn a great deal of the corruption, injustice, and evil which many individuals and societies have perpetrated on this earth. There has been a great deal of speculation with respect to the real nature and identity of this beast, but most of it is mythical and none of it carries any credibility. We need not go further than what the surah tells us: "When the Hour draws near, We shall bring for them out of the earth a beast that shall speak to them and say, 'People have had no faith in Our revelations!'" (82).

The surah concludes with a few words on the hereafter and the Day of Judgment. On this terrible day, accountability will be in accordance with the following principle:

> Whoever earns good shall be rewarded with what is even better. These shall be secure from the terror of that day. But whoever earns evil shall be hurled headlong into the fire and shall be asked, "Are you not being rewarded according to what you have earned?" (89–90)

The closing verses remind Muhammad and his followers of their mission in this world: to lead humanity and guide people to their Lord in the light of Qur'anic revelation. They are also reassured about the future.

> I [Muhammad] have only been instructed to worship the Lord of this city [Makkah], which God has made sacred. All things are His alone. I am instructed to surrender to Him, and to proclaim the Qur'an... (91)

Time shall be the judge, both in this life and in the life to come, between those who believe and those who do not. "Say, 'Praise be to God! He will show you His signs and you will recognize them.' Your Lord is not unaware of what you do" (93).

SURAH 28

Al-Qaṣaṣ
(The Story)

THIS SURAH CONTINUES from where the preceding one, *al-Naml*, left off and opens with reassuring words for the believers about the future as well as asserting the dark and gloomy end awaiting the transgressors and unbelievers. It affirms that patience shall be well rewarded, and that the oppressed and persecuted shall be set free and their shackles broken.

The surah relates an episode from the story of Moses and his people as an illustration that the laws of history retain their validity despite the passage of time. It says: "These are the verses of the perspicuous Book. We truthfully recount to you tales of Moses and Pharaoh for the benefit of those who believe" (2–3). The Pharaoh referred to here is most likely to be Ramses II who ruled Egypt around the thirteenth century BC and whose kingdom extended to the Danube river in south-east Europe. The surah says of him:

Pharaoh ruled with tyranny in the land and divided its people into castes, one group of which he persecuted, killing their sons and sparing only their daughters. Truly, he was an evil man. (4)

Killing the male and sparing the female children was indeed a vile and criminal method of ethnic cleansing, but despite these measures the Pharaoh was not to achieve his goal of annihilating the Israelites. The surah asserts that: "It was Our will to favor those who were

413

oppressed in the land, to make them leaders, to bestow on them a noble heritage and to give them power in the land..." (5–6).

These words came to be a great consolation for the early Muslims who were being hounded and persecuted by the Makkan Arabs, giving them confidence and hope in the future. Towards the end of the surah, Muhammad and his followers were promised that they would return to Makkah triumphant. The surah says:

> He who has revealed the Qur'an to you will surely bring you home [to Makkah] again. Say, "My Lord best knows those who are rightly-guided and those who are hopelessly led astray." (85)

This is reported to have been revealed to Muhammad whilst he was on his way from Makkah to Madinah, in 622 AC. Ten years later Muhammad was to lead the Muslims in triumph back to Makkah, with all its inhabitants embracing Islam.

The following episodes from the history of Moses and the Israelites narrated in this surah were not covered in the previous two. These are:

1.   The birth of Moses and the difficulties he encountered during his early life.

> We guided Moses' mother saying, "Nurse him, but if you are concerned about his safety, then cast him into the river. Have no fear and do not worry; for We shall bring him back to you and We shall choose him as a messenger." (7)

> Needless to say, for a mother to place her baby in a river is not an easy thing to do, but with much trepidation Moses' mother obeyed the instructions given to her because she had faith and trust in God:

An aching void grew up in the heart of the mother of Moses, and she would indeed have disclosed all about him had We not endowed her heart with enough strength to keep alive her faith [in Our promise]. (10)

2. The reception Moses was given when he was picked up from the river by the Pharaoh's household. Moses had enough charm and promise to beguile the Pharaoh's wife who took an immediate liking to him, saying to her husband: "'This child may bring joy to me and to you. Do not kill him, he might be of use to us, or we may adopt him as our son'" (9).

Thus Moses was spared, and as soon as his sister, who was following the news of his progress, found out that he had been picked up, alive and well, by the Pharaoh's household, she offered to find him a suitable nurse to look after him. It came to pass that as Moses refused the breasts of the palace nurses a suitable nurse was found for him, who, by the will of God, happened to be his natural mother. Moses' secret remained intact.

3. Moses grew up among the Pharaoh's household. Not only had his life been spared, but he had also been brought up in comfort and freedom, to prepare him for the hard task that lay ahead. "When he came of age and had grown to manhood We bestowed on him wisdom and knowledge. Thus We reward the righteous" (14).

At this stage in his life, Moses had an unfortunate experience which made his existence in Egypt very difficult. One day, as he entered the town, he saw an Israelite being forced by an Egyptian to carry a load which was far too heavy for him. A quarrel ensued between them, and: "The one who was of his [Moses'] own race appealed for help against his enemy, so Moses struck him and rendered him dead" (15).

Moses was a strong man, but had not intended to kill the Egyptian. He realized his mistake and appealed to God, saying: "'My Lord! I have wronged myself, so please forgive me.' And God forgave him" (16). When Moses felt that God had forgiven him, he was grateful and vowed to fight tyranny and defend the oppressed.

It appears that the Pharaoh's men came to know of the incident and began to hatch a plot to kill Moses in revenge for the death of the Egyptian. However, he was informed of the plan by a sympathizer and, realizing that his life was in danger, decided to flee Egypt to travel to Madyan in north-west Arabia.

4.   In Madyan, Moses met with a hospitable man who, on learning of his ordeal, gave him a place to stay and said to him: "'Fear nothing. You are now safe from those wicked people'" (25). He offered Moses employment and gave him his daughter's hand in marriage. The Israelites have yet to forgive Moses for marrying a non-Hebrew woman.

The identity of Moses' host has not been revealed, and I do not believe, as has been suggested by others, that he was the prophet Shuʿayb. The man said to Moses:

"I will give you one of my two daughters in marriage, provided you stay eight years in my service. If you stay ten years that will be up to you. I do not wish to overburden you; God willing, you will find me an upright man." (27)

From a young man growing up in a Pharaoh's palace, Moses ended up as a shepherd in the Arabian desert. But such tribulations did nothing to diminish his stature. Great men are never affected by material or social status; their integrity, honor, magnanimity and quality of character are established by their actions and behavior rather than by their position. The years Moses worked as a shepherd must have given him a chance to think and reflect on what he had been through. They must also have enabled him to think about his people and what would become of them. It was a period of mental preparation for the task that lay ahead. The surah tells us that:

> When he fulfilled his term and was journeying with his wife, Moses saw a fire on the side of Mount Ṭūr. He said to his wife, "Stay here. I can see a fire. Perhaps I can bring you news." (29)

This fire was the beacon that was to lead him to greatness. "When he arrived close to it, a voice called out to him from a tree in a blessed spot on the right-hand side of the mountain, and said, 'Moses, I am God, Lord of all creation...'" (30). This was another great turning point in Moses' life for, having been working as a humble shepherd, he now became a messenger of God with a mission to free a whole nation from slavery and lead them to glory. At this moment Moses remembered what had happened to him in Egypt and so asked God to provide him with manpower for support. God said: "'We shall give you your brother to help you, and will give both of you such power that no one shall be able to harm you. Supported by Our signs, you, and those who follow you, shall triumph'" (35).

Moses went back to Egypt and, as we learnt in more detail in *al-Aʿrāf*, *Ṭā Hā* and *al-Shuʿarāʾ*, spectacularly prevailed over the Pharaoh's sorcerers in the famous public duel that took place between them. The surah affirms that: "When Moses came to them with Our clear signs, they said, 'This is nothing but contrived sorcery; we have never heard of anything like it from our forefathers'" (36).

The surah also relates another confrontation between Moses and the Pharaoh. The latter ordered his chief right-hand man, Hāmān, to help him find the God to whom Moses had referred:

And Pharaoh said, "Nobles, you have no other god that I know of except myself. Hāmān, build me a tower from bricks of clay that I may climb and see the god of Moses. I suspect that he is definitely lying." (38)

The foolish Pharaoh believed that God resided in the sky or somehow sat above the clouds. Although this notion may sound comical or silly, it is a belief still held surprisingly by some people today. On returning from a space voyage, a Soviet cosmonaut was quoted as saying that he had looked for God in space but had not found Him. The only thing he had seen was his fellow cosmonaut! How can people be so naive and absurd? Who has claimed that God is restricted to the heavens or the skies? God is the Creator and Governor of the whole universe, and His power and signs are evident everywhere for all to see. The Pharaoh and his like, who deny the existence of God shall: "Lead others to the fire, and on Resurrection Day shall have none to help them. In this world We laid Our curse on them, and on Resurrection Day they shall be held in dishonor" (41–42).

The fact that Prophet Muhammad was relating these details of Moses' life and the Israelites' history to the Arabs should have been sufficient proof that what he was telling them had come from another source. Muhammad was an illiterate man who had grown up in an idol-worshiping environment. How could he have come by all these historical accounts and details? The surah says:

You [Muhammad] were not present on the western side of the mountain when We charged Moses with his commission, nor did you witness the event. We raised many generations thereafter but time has caused them to forget. You were not among the people of

Madyan, reciting to them Our revelations, but it was We who have chosen you as a Messenger. (44–45)

God gave Muhammad a Book which revived earlier messages and restored their credibility, but many people refused to accept it. They asked for miracles like the ones Moses performed. But what good did these miracles do? The unbelievers persisted in their refusal, even after witnessing them. About these people God says:

> When the truth had come to them from Us, they said, "Why is he not given the same as was given to Moses?" But do they not deny what was given to Moses? They say, "Both [the Qur'an and the Torah] are works of sorcery complementing one another!" And they say, "We will believe in neither of them." (48)

As for those who followed Moses out of Egypt, having been saved by God from drowning in the Red Sea, they had the audacity to ask Moses to make them a god to worship and certainly seem to have lost the point of his message altogether.

The believers among the Arabs opened their hearts to the Qur'an and benefited from it in understanding their role in the world and in charting their way through history, leading humankind to God and His guidance.

When a community loses its direction in life and is ruled by whims and desires, it can only fail and disintegrate. Islam faced strong resistance from the pagans of Arabia and only a small minority saw the truth from the very beginning and embraced the new faith. The Jews and the Christians, however, were another matter. The Qur'an treated them with utmost fairness and courtesy, and those of them who embraced Islam were welcomed with open arms. God says:

Those to whom We gave the Book before believe in it [the Qur'an]. When it is recited to them, they say, "We believe in it. It is the truth from our Lord. We submitted ourselves to God even before it came." These shall be given their reward twice, because they have endured with fortitude. (52–54)

In the same context, the Prophet was reported to have said that God would double the reward of three types of people including: "a Jew or a Christian who believed in his prophet and lived to believe in me and follow me."[34]

When Islam began to spread outside Arabia, Western Asia and North Africa were largely populated by Jews and Christians living under Roman rule and large numbers of these embraced Islam as soon as they were introduced to it. However, in contrast, the pagans of Arabia put up a strong resistance to the new faith and waged war against its followers. This hurt the Prophet and caused him a great deal of pain and anguish, but God consoled him saying: "You cannot guide whomever you please: it is God who guides whom He will..." (56). This verse is believed to refer to Muhammad's uncle, Abū Ṭālib, who, despite his nephew's sincere wishes, had not embraced Islam. He acknowledged the efficacy and the truth of Islam, and the integrity of Muhammad, but remained strongly attached to the traditions and religious beliefs of his forefathers. Reports also speak of some Makkan Arab dignitaries expressing concern that, were they to embrace Islam, the rest of the Arab tribes would drive them out of Makkah. To this God replied:

And they say, "If we accept your guidance, we shall be driven from our land." But have We not given them a sanctuary of safety where fruits of every kind are brought as a provision from Us for them? Indeed, most of them are ignorant. (57)

---

34 Narrated by al-Bukhārī.

But as the Arabs persisted in their resistance to Islam, the Qur'an warned them, saying: "Many a rebellious and ungrateful nation We have destroyed! The dwellings they left behind are almost deserted; We have outlived them" (58).

The surah continues in a similar vein, promising and warning: "All that you have been given is trivial worldly enjoyment and God's reward is better and more lasting. Do you not understand?" (60). The truth is that most people are reckless and do not heed such advice. The Pharaohs could have ruled with justice and benevolence and could have added to their achievements and glory. On the other hand, their subjects could have resisted and refused to submit to their tyranny. The Qur'an deplores the attitude of both camps, saying:

> On that day God will call them and ask, "Where are the gods whom you alleged to be My partners?" The condemned masters will reply, "Lord, these are the people we misled; we led them astray as we our-selves were led astray. We plead innocence before You; it was not us they worshiped." And the others will be told, "Call on your idols!" And they will call on them, but they shall get no answer. As they see the scourge, they will wish they were rightly guided. (62–64)

The surah then introduces more scenes from the Day of Judgment, emphasizing the fact that God has created people with different capabilities and aptitudes, and that it is He who decides the fate appropriate for everyone. It says: "Your Lord creates and chooses as He will. No one else can choose. Glorified and exalted be He above their false gods!" (68). The surah then briefly draws our attention to God's power as manifested in the natural world. "Say, 'If God should extend the night for you until the Day of Judgment, what other god could give you light? Will you give heed?'" (71). God has made light and darkness for a purpose, and every human being, rich or poor, master or slave, who has ever lived shall be accountable for his or her life on this earth. From political tyranny, the surah goes on to deal with economic oppression, making it clear that every human society should be free from both these evils.

The following passage recounts the story of Korah (Qārūn), a contemporary of Moses who was an extremely wealthy man. But wealth in itself is neither good nor bad. It is simply a means to an end and can be beneficially used or abused. Korah is described as owning treasure chests stacked with gold and silver, but he was warned not to:

> exult in your riches; God does not love the exultant. Seek, by means of what God has given you, success in the hereafter but do not neglect your share in this world. Be good to others as God has been good to you, and do not strive to perpetrate evil in the land. God does not love the evil-doers. (77)

The generosity of some rich people knows no bounds and they seek to help others in every possible way, without flaunting their wealth or being ostentatious. They would give before they are asked and acknowledge God's kindness towards them by not using their wealth to abuse or exploit others. But, as we see in this surah, Korah decided that he had earned his wealth by sheer genius and personal hard work alone, and that he was therefore justified in doing with it as he pleased. "He said, 'I have been given all this on account of the knowledge I possess.' Does he not realize that God had destroyed before him generations of people who were mightier and more avaricious than he? The transgressors shall not even be asked about their sins" (78).

The temptation of wealth has been a crucial test in every human civilization, including the contemporary one. Whole political, economic, and social systems have been based on class and discrimination between rich and poor and have brought nothing but injustice and misery to the world. Differences in wealth and fortune are natural and necessary in human society. Even prophets enjoyed different fortunes: some were well off whilst others lived on the edge of poverty; some were kings in their own right and had great wealth under their control whilst others had next to nothing. However, the ones who were poor never despaired or complained of their situation and the ones who were rich never abused their wealth for personal enjoyment or used it to gain power illegally over others.

Islam strikes a balance and regulates the earning and spending of wealth in such a way that benefits society as a whole. The key principle is expressed in the surah thus:

The hereafter We assign to those who do not seek to perpetuate tyranny or corruption in this world. The God-fearing shall meet with ultimate success. Whoever does good shall receive a better reward; and whoever does evil shall only be requited according to his deeds. (83–84)

Society cannot be organized properly without authentic religious guidance. Man-made laws and regulations can never ensure justice and equal opportunity for all, or prepare people well enough for accountability before God in the hereafter. Passive religious belief, or lip-service to Islam, is of no consequence. It is not enough to believe and keep one's faith to oneself. Islam is not a philosophical idea or an intellectual concept, but it is a holistic and comprehensive system covering every aspect of human life.

The surah closes with a few strong words addressed to Prophet Muhammad himself. They stress the weight of his responsibility and point him in the right direction to help him succeed in shouldering it. It says:

You never hoped that this Book would be revealed to you. Yet through your Lord's mercy you have received it. Therefore lend no support to the unbelievers. Let no one turn you away from God's revelations, now that they have been revealed to you. Call others to your Lord, and serve none besides Him. Invoke no other god with God; there is no god but He. All things shall perish except Him. His is the judgment, and to Him you shall all return. (86–88)

Theoretical knowledge and scientific information by themselves are not sufficient to guarantee order and justice in society. Satan was fully cognizant of God, but still refused to submit to Him and obey His commands, leading him to be condemned and damned for ever. A truly Islamic society must nurture among its members a deep and enlightened faith in God as well as the will and the desire to act according to the imperatives of that faith, and to prepare for the life hereafter.

SURAH 29

Al-ʿAnkabūt
(The Spider)

LIFE IS A TEST, a trial, which we all have to undergo. Once we pass from this life into the next we will find out how we have fared and whether we have passed the test or not. Those who pass will go to Paradise and those who fail will go to hell. The terms and the severity of the trial vary from one person to another, depending on many factors. This is because our obligations vary according to our aptitudes, capabilities, intelligence, resources, and willingness to exert ourselves and make sacrifices.

When Muhammad first addressed humankind with the message of Islam, the world was in a state of loss and bewilderment. The Arabs were idol-worshipers with no religion of their own. The Israelites had become an ethnocentric community who thought of themselves as the chosen people of God, and claimed true religion as their exclusive prerogative. The Christians had also radically changed and distorted the message of Christ and transformed him from a mere mortal into the son of God, the Archangel Gabriel and God himself. God had become one in three and then three in one.

In a *ḥadīth qudsī*, God is reported by Prophet Muhammad to have said:

> I have created all my servants in a pristine state, but devils have turned them away from their original religion, telling them what is right and what is wrong, and commanding them to take false gods besides Me.[35]

---

35 Narrated by al-Bukhārī.

425

We are also told that God was displeased by most of humankind except a remnant of Jews and Christians. God said to Muhammad: "I have sent you to be tested, and to test them…". It was to this rudderless world that Muhammad was sent.

The Prophet was charged with the great task of leading mankind back to God and steering it onto the right path to restore its sanity and balance. How could one man possibly change the whole world? Of course it would have been impossible without the help and guidance of God. With the odds seemingly greatly stacked against him Muhammad embarked on his difficult mission. He initially built a small group of sincere and dedicated followers around himself and, with this early group of Muslims, struggled to break away from Arab paganism and to take on the two most powerful and antagonistic forces in the world at the time: the Roman and the Persian empires. That first generation of Muslims never rested or let up until Islam had prevailed across the whole of Arabia, and were in the end poised to take on the Roman and the Persian empires on their own territories. Such a heavy burden was bound at times to raise despair and frustration. As things became harder and more demanding, some Muslims were liable to give up and retreat.

This surah came to put all these matters in a proper perspective. It opens by saying:

> Do men think that once they say, "We believe," they will be left alone without being put to the test? We tested those who have gone before them. God will come to know the truthful, as He will come to know those who are lying. (2–3)

The world today seems to have come full circle. There is no place or role for God in contemporary civilization. Muslims today find themselves on the verge of undergoing the same test that Muhammad and the early Muslims had undergone, and it is being expected of them to repeat their successes.

In the opening passage God says: "He who strives in God's cause strives for his own good. God is Self-Sufficient and needs no help from anyone" (6). Towards the end God gives this profound pledge: "Those who strive in Our cause We will surely guide to Our paths. God is always with the righteous" (69). For any nation to assume the leadership of mankind legitimately, hope and trust in God's support and guidance are vital requirements. The surah says:

> Some people profess to believe in God, yet when they undergo any suffering in His cause they use their persecution to turn away from faith. But when your Lord gives you victory, they will say, "We were on your side." Is God not well-aware of the thoughts in men's breasts? (10)

Some believers grow impatient and demand God's support and victory prematurely. Others give up and lose heart. But the surah reminds them of the stoicism of Noah who spent nine hundred and fifty years striving to teach and discipline his people. Some of them lose sight of reality and grow impetuous and irrational in their representation and defense of Islam. Such people should reflect on the approach of prophet Abraham, as given in this surah. He relied on persuasion and rational argument, saying to his people: "'...Those whom you serve besides God cannot give you sustenance. Therefore seek sustenance with God, worship Him, and give thanks to Him...'" (17). The surah adds:

> Do they not see how God brought this whole world into being in the first instance and how He then recreates it all? That is an easy matter for God. Say, "Go forth all over the earth and see how God brought about this existence and ponder how He will bring it back to life a second time. God has power over all things." (19–20)

In some societies, people allowed their animal instincts to rule over them and became obsessed with sexual and sensual gratification to the point of perversion. The people of Lot, for instance, for whom sodomy was a common public practise, are a case in point. The surah tells us that Lot had tried very hard to dissuade his people from pursuing these vile practices:

> Lot said to his people, "You commit indecent acts which no other nation has committed before you. You lust after males, and commit highway robbery, and you practise vile acts in your public gatherings." (28–29)

It is interesting to note how fast contemporary civilization is going down the same road. Sexual morality in the West is in complete chaos. Permissiveness and promiscuity have become the norm. The status and role of the family and the institution of marriage are being seriously eroded and the repercussions of this state of affairs for Western civilization as a whole are ominous.

The surah goes on to talk of the fate of other nations who had rebelled against God and rejected His guidance saying: "We punished every nation according to their sins. On some We sent violent storms, some were seized by a dreadful catastrophe, some We made to disappear into the ground, and We caused some to be drowned..." (40). Human power cannot stand up to the might of God; just as a spider's web has no chance of resisting a strong wind. "We present these parables to humankind, but only the wise ones will grasp their meaning" (43). The dedicated believers must show tenacity and trust in the future, whether it is this life or the life to come.

The surah identifies two distinct reactions from the People of the Book towards Islam and the Muslims. The first reaction is to recognize Islam and tolerate the Muslim way of life; to these the Muslims are instructed to reciprocate the respect and tolerance shown them. The second reaction is antagonism and the Muslims are taught to beware such aggressive attitudes to Islam and to take care in dealing with those who hold them, not taking their sincerity and trust for granted. The surah gives the Muslims a general direction as to how to deal with these two groups. It says:

> Do not argue with the People of the Book except with courtesy, apart from those among them who transgress. Say to them, "We believe in that which is revealed to us and which was revealed to you. Our God and your God is one and the same, and to Him we all surrender ourselves." Thus We revealed the Book to you. Those to whom We gave the Book previously believe in it, and so do some of your own people. Only the unbelievers deny Our revelations. (46–47)

Any objective and fair study of the relationship between the world of Islam and the world of the Judeo-Christian religions over the last fourteen centuries should be able to identify the causes of the hostility and bloody confrontation that have existed between them. It should be possible to apportion blame for the antagonistic and aggressive realities that have dogged their relationship. Before the emergence of Islam the Romans, as bearers of the Cross, had swept across the lands of western Asia and north Africa. However, on learning of Islam, large parts of the same area came under its influence with very little resistance. Four centuries later, the Crusaders of southwestern Europe initiated fresh hostilities against the Muslim world, prosecuting a futile campaign which ran for more than two centuries.

In modern times, it was Christian Europe again which embarked on a large-scale colonization of Muslim lands and territories, bringing about the destruction of the Islamic nation and the fragmentation of the Muslim world. This began with the British domination of the Indian subcontinent, followed by the French invasion of Egypt and Algeria (to be followed later by the rest of the Arab Maghrib) in the early nineteenth century. By the turn of the twentieth century, Britain was occupying Iraq, the eastern and southern Arabian coasts, Palestine, and Egypt whilst Italy had invaded Libya and Abyssinia. Well into the twentieth century the Europea domination of the Muslim world was almost complete. Who has been the aggressor and who has been the victim in all these unfortunate and deplorable confrontations? Which has been the aggrieved party?

Today, Muslims are reasserting themselves and are striving to rediscover and establish their true Islamic identity. Why should they be deprived of their rights or prevented from determining their own future? Why should they be labeled 'militant' or 'fundamentalist' or 'retrogressive'? Muslims believe that the words of the Qur'an are the literal words of God and convey the truth. They wish to abide by God's rules and laws as expounded by the Qur'an and Prophet Muhammad. Why should this be a cause for concern or alarm to any other group or society? There is no justification for the vilification of Islam and the derision and abuse that is directed at the Qur'an and the Prophet both in the West and by its "comrades" and "supporters" in the Muslim world. God says to Muhammad:

> You have not been reading any books before the Qur'an, nor have you ever transcribed one with your right hand. Had you done either of these things, the unbelievers would have had more reason to doubt you. No! It [the Qur'an] contains clear signs to be preserved in the breasts of the learned. Only the transgressors deny Our signs. (48–49)

Islam is again today the target of much misunderstanding, misinterpretation, and opprobrium. There is no doubt that there are powers in the world today that do not wish for Islam to prosper or spread.

The surah cites criticisms by the idolaters who asked Muhammad to perform miracles to support his claims. It says:

They ask, "Why has no sign been given him by his Lord?" Say to them, "Signs are in the hands of God; my mission is only to give clear warning." Is it not proof enough for them that We have revealed to you the Book to recite to them? Surely in this there is mercy and an admonition to those who believe. (50–51)

The Qur'an itself is Muhammad's enduring miracle. Its influence and impact on man and human civilization have been, and will continue to be, profound. The Qur'an has been the mainstay of the Muslim world community. It represents a unique link between the human and the divine which makes life in this world meaningful and worth living and striving for.

Qur'anic observations with respect to scientific and physical phenomena have astonished scientists and scholars throughout history. The Qur'an is a book that has produced a fresh and energetic civilization which has restored to humankind its dignity, purpose, and honor. It charts a way of life that has given humanity real and profound hope, as well as the will to explore, build, produce, and advance in order to improve the quality of human life on this earth and ensure man's salvation in the hereafter. The conflict between good and evil is a long drawn-out struggle. The lack of faith in God spurs the impatient unbelievers to precipitate His punishment. The surah says:

They challenge you [Muhammad] to hasten on the scourge. Had there not been a time appointed for it, the scourge would have long overtaken them. Indeed, it will come down upon them without warning, and catch them unawares. (53)

The early Muslims were driven from Makkah and had to leave all their possessions behind. But God compensated them in full and gave them a new homeland. The surah affirms that: "Countless are the beasts that cannot fend for themselves. God provides for them, as He provides for you. He is the All-Hearing and All-Knowing" (60). Modern civilization is built on materialism which rejects religion and denies accountability in the hereafter. This is the exact opposite of what true Muslims believe, because to them the hereafter is as real as the life they live today, if not more so. The surah says: "The life of this world is but a sport and a pastime. It is the life to come that is the true life; if they but knew it" (64). The surah ends on a warning and a promise.

Who is more wicked than he who invents falsehoods about God and denies the truth when it is declared to him? Hell shall be the appropriate home of the unbelievers. But those who strive for Our cause, We will surely guide them to Our paths. God is with the righteous. (68–69)

SURAH 30

Al-Rūm
(The Romans)

IN DEFINING THE RELATIONSHIP between Islam and Christianity, one notices that the Qur'an never obfuscates or compromises on the principle of *tawḥīd*, absolute monotheism. God is but one, with no offspring or ancestry; He is unique and undivided, nor is He made up of several elements. To refer to God as the Father and the Son, all rolled into one, is totally unacceptable. The Qur'an asserts: "God is but one God" (*al-Nisā'*: 171).

This statement essentially means that the second and third elements of "God," were they to exist, would not be divine, but created mortals. The Qur'an states:

> Say, "Are you asking me to worship someone else other than God, you ignorant people?" It has been revealed to you and those before you that if you were to associate others with God your actions shall come to nothing and you will be a loser. Rather you should worship God and remain grateful to Him. (*al-Zumar*: 64–66)

These are all Makkan verses, indicating that Islam was very clear on the Trinity issue right from the outset. Nevertheless, politically and historically, Islam proceeded to maintain amicable relations with Christendom. When persecuted and harassed by the Arabs of Makkah, Prophet Muhammad advised his followers to emigrate to Abyssinia, now Ethiopia, in the Horn of Africa, which was then a Christian land. They went there professing that Jesus and his mother were ordinary pious human beings.

433

The defeat of the Byzantine Christians at the hands of the Persians, in Syria in 615 AC, heartened the idolatrous Arabs, but was met with sadness and grief by the Muslims. It was quite an extensive defeat in which the Byzantine Christians had lost Egypt, the Yemen and the whole of Mesopotamia, and paid a heavy and humiliating price. The world was convinced that it was the end of the Romans who no longer had a future as a world power.

The only exception to this viewpoint was to be found in the Qur'an. At Makkah, it boldly declared that the defeat would be short-lived. It said:

> The Byzantines have been defeated in the near lands, but after their defeat, they shall prevail within a few years. God has control over things before and after. On that day believers will enjoy victory from God, who supports whom He will. He is Powerful and Merciful. This is a firm promise from God who never breaks His promises, even though most people are not aware of it. (2–6)

The Qur'an directly challenges the conventional wisdom of the time and, in no uncertain terms, affirms that within a few years things would change completely. This prophecy was fulfilled and vindicated by events on the ground. The irony is that some Christians, instead of applauding Islam's stance, had claimed that Muhammad had only made that declaration because of his hatred of the Persians. They refused to accept the prophecy as proof of Muhammad's credentials as a genuine prophet commissioned by God.

Christians are seen as being closer to adopting monotheism, as advocated by Islam, than other religious groups. This has been borne out in history, as large communities of Christians converted to Islam during the Muslim conquests of the early centuries. Common sense had prevailed as people abandoned the self-contradictory teachings of some Christian doctrines and opened their hearts and minds to the pristine teachings of Islam.

The basic qualities of the sound human nature (Arabic: *al-fiṭrah*) are expounded in *al-Aʿrāf*, but they receive a more extensive treatment in this one. It declares that Islam is the religion of sound common sense and wholesome human nature. It moves in harmony with free thinking, in pursuit of the truth, without prejudice or predisposition. The surah urges Prophet Muhammad, saying:

> Therefore stand firm in your devotion to the true Faith, the natural and upright Faith which God created humankind to embrace instinctively. God's design should not be altered. This is the right religion, although most people do not realize it. (30)

God, as the object of veneration and worship, is above all abuse. He is glorious and praiseworthy, and humans, jinns and angels should submit and surrender to Him alone. He has no equal or matching rival anywhere in the whole universe. The surah says: "Glory be to God in the evening and the morning. Praise be to Him in the heavens and the earth, at twilight and at noon" (17–18).

Tawḥīd is also a purifying belief. It purges the faith of the influences of polytheism and idolatry. It identifies God as the supreme power to whom all else submit and against whom no one dares to rebel.

The surah says: "He brings forth the living from the dead, and the dead from the living, and He puts life back into the earth after it had been lifeless. Likewise you shall be raised to life" (19).

God has willed that life in this world shall be an occasion to test human beings. They shall then die, and after a certain predetermined time they shall be brought back to life to account for their actions during the period spent in this world. To help people lead a righteous life and find their way to Him, God has set up numerous signs all over the universe as witness to His existence and power. The surah draws our attention to seven of them:

1. One of His signs is that He has created you from dust, and made you into human beings, dispersed everywhere. (20)

2. One of His signs is that He created for you spouses from among yourselves, so that you may seek peace and comfort with them. He has planted affection and mercy between you and them. In this there are signs for people who think. (21)

3. One of His signs is the creation of the heavens and the earth and the diversity of your tongues and colors. In this are signs for all intelligent men. (22)

4. One of His signs is that you sleep by night, and by day also seek His bounty. In this there are signs for those who listen. (23)

5. One of His signs is that He sends lightning flashing before your eyes, inspiring you with fear and hope; He sends down water from the sky to revive the soil after it had been lifeless. In this there are signs for those who understand. (24)

6. One of His signs is that the heavens and the earth exist by His will and command, and that whenever He summons you, you shall immediately come out of the ground. (25)

7. One of His signs is that He sends the winds as bearers of good tidings, to let you have a taste of His mercy, and so that ships may sail by His command and you may gratefully seek His bounty. (46)

The Qur'an urges the pursuit of knowledge in order to enhance faith and eradicate the poison of skepticism and agnostic tendencies. Nevertheless, there will always be people who would "appreciate only the outer facade of worldly life, but of the life to come they are heedless" (7).

This type of person is widely familiar in today's society, the main reason being the marginalization of God's revelation due to the incompetence of its inheritors and their inability to promote and deliver its message to the rest of the world. Materialistic philosophies and ideologies dominate man's thinking today but they have failed to satisfy his intellectual curiosity or fulfill the demands of human nature.

A healthy human person would recognize God and be ever drawn towards Him. Even when distracted he would endeavor to return to the proper track. However, human beings are liable to be overcome by selfishness, dissension, and negligence and thrown off course, but the Qur'an would not leave them to their own devices.

On the contrary, the Qur'an repeatedly calls on human beings to return to their pristine human nature. It says:

Turn to God and fear Him. Observe the prayer [salah] and do not be of those who take partners with God; those who broke up their religion and were split into sects, each being self-satisfied and complacent in their own beliefs. (31–32)

Dissension is a human characteristic induced by the desire for self-expression and dominance, and is often associated with pride and complacency. It occurs among religious as well as secular communities and groups. It is a phenomenon known throughout human history, past and present. However, this should not be confused with differences and disagreements arising from the exercise of ijtihad by scholars, experts, and practitioners of Islamic law, or among the various schools of fiqh which have emerged within Islam.

Differences of interpretation should not necessarily lead to rancor and division. Those who adopt differing approaches and formulate divergent views on matters which are open to debate should be credited for their efforts, whether their conclusions are right or wrong.

Taking such legitimate differences further by fuelling schism, factionalism, and dissension can only lead to weakness and destruction.

In an extended passage, the surah dwells on the crucial effects of good and bad fortune on individuals and communities. At times of crisis, people may become closer to God, but as soon as the ordeal is over, many forget and deny God's grace.

> When misfortune befalls human beings, they turn in prayer to their Lord, meek and repentant. But when He then gives them a taste of His mercy some of them take up other gods besides their Lord. They show no gratitude for what We have bestowed upon them. Enjoy yourselves awhile; you will come to know the truth. (33–34)

This could only be repugnant neglect or shameful treachery. When blessed with good fortune, some people take it for granted and neglect to use it for a good purpose, but as soon as they are disadvantaged, through ill-health or decline of wealth, they fall into despair and lose hope completely. They feel they have lost something which is theirs by right, forgetting that the apportionment of fortune is up to God Almighty. The surah says:

> When We give people a taste of mercy, they rejoice in it; but when misfortune befalls them through their own fault, they grow despondent. Do they not know that God grants abundant sustenance to whom He wills and can also withhold it? Surely there are signs in this for true believers! (36–37)

Human beings are required to show gratitude for the good they receive and perseverance during times of hardship. They should accept God's judgment willingly and behave towards others accordingly. God says:

> Therefore give the near of kin, the destitute and the traveler in need

438

what is due to them, respectively. That is best for those striving to please God; such people will surely prosper. (38)

Poverty and wealth have been the scourge of humankind since life began. The drive for capital accumulation in a world of finite resources together with the political realities of today's modern societies is causing extraordinary pressures to be placed upon them such that humanity is being pulled apart in extreme directions not only by an inevitable class struggle but by volatile forces beyond its control. The surah continues:

> Corruption occurs on land and sea in consequence of people's misdeeds. God has ordained it so that they may have a taste of the fruit of their own works and perchance desist. (41)

Fraternity, cooperation, and mutual kindness, induced by faith in God, are the best safeguards against the arrogance of wealth and the degradation of poverty. The surah urges Prophet Muhammad and all humankind with him:

> Therefore turn firmly towards the true faith before the day, predetermined by God, arrives and no one will be able to delay it. On that Day, mankind shall be split into two camps. The unbelievers will bear the consequences of their unbelief, while the righteous would have made goodly provision for themselves. (43–44)

Within this context, the surah goes on to talk about the perennial struggle between right and wrong, belief and unbelief. As Muhammad had embarked on delivering God's message, and was facing up to the obstacles created by his enemies, the surah told him: "We sent before you apostles to their people, and they showed them veritable signs, but We took vengeance on the offenders, while it was our duty to support the true believers" (47).

With this clear assurance, how can the Muslims, who account for over one fifth of the world population, sustain all these military, cultural, and moral setbacks and humiliations? Why have they come to this low point?

The fact is that Muslims have been acting in contravention of the basic laws of human nature and society. They have all but lost their unity, civilized comportment, and self-confidence. In contrast to many other societies, Muslims appear the more lethargic and backward. The solidarity brought about by Islam has been fading away and remains mostly superficial. Such a community would hardly merit promotion and support. In ancient history God scattered the Israelites and made them subservient to idolatrous communities. False and hollow faith does not earn God's succor, but things could change; the more the Muslims improve their lot the sooner they would meet with that elusive victory.

Muslim societies today are the archetype of political, economic, and social chaos and confusion. Success would not come to such a disorganized and fragmented nation. But Islam shall endure.

This surah contains a most profound statement asserting that Islam will endure until the end of time, and that it would do so through a community of human beings who would uphold and defend it. It says: "Those who have been given knowledge and faith will say, 'You [humankind] have lived, as God ordained, till the Day of Resurrection. Today is the Day of Resurrection, but you had no knowledge of it'" (56).

The Muslim nation will, therefore, endure for as long as mankind exists in this world. Its setbacks will be temporary. We ought to be certain that, as the nation upholding God's final message, ours shall ultimately prevail, and this thought should spur us on to consolidate our resources, resume our prominent position in the world and restore our nation's former glory.

That would be a most appropriate ending for humankind's existence on earth, as the surah's closing statement to Prophet

440

Muhammad seems to suggest: "Therefore have patience. God's promise is true. Let not those who disbelieve drive you to despair" (60). Perseverance is required to sustain victory, and cultivate and nurture its dividends.

Luqmān

THIS SURAH OPENS WITH A REFERENCE to the righteous and the rewards awaiting them, which is followed by an allusion to the mischief makers and their evil designs against Islam. It says:

> There are some people who would indulge in frivolous talk in order to lead others away from God's path, without justification, and hold [God's words] up to ridicule. They shall meet with shameful punishment. (6)

We are told in literary circles that this is a reference to the Arabian bard and storyteller al-Naḍr ibn al-Ḥārith who used to collect tales of ancient Persian royalty and relate them to Makkan audiences as a form of public entertainment. He would impress on them that his narrations were far more educational and entertaining than the Qur'an which Muhammad was delivering to them.

Some commentators take the view that the verse refers to the vocation of public singing. The consensus is that indecent, provocative, or licentious singing, and singing that aims to titillate are strongly censured by Islam. Likewise, any activity that distracts people from their proper and honorable duties and responsibilities is similarly discouraged.

The surah elaborates further on the reward awaiting the righteous. It says: "Those that have faith and do good works shall enter the gardens of delight, where they shall dwell forever. God's promise shall be fulfilled; He is the Almighty, the Wise" (8–9).

It goes on to extoll the Creator, as He deserves to be extolled, questioning the identity and efficacy of the false gods worshiped besides Him. They are merely a figment of the unbelievers' imagination. These ideas are conveyed in a slightly different style later on in the surah, where we read: "He that surrenders himself to God and leads a righteous life stands on the firmest ground. To God shall all things return" (22).

In contrast, wrong-doers are addressed with dire warnings: "Do not be grieved by those who disbelieve. To Us they shall return and We will reveal to them all that they had done" (23).

The surah speaks at length of God's power and glory. As Creator and Provider, He takes full charge of world affairs, directly governing the lives, fortunes, and destinies of all creation. He guides and controls the activities of billions of human beings, multitudes of animals, plants, and other creatures, and countless numbers of planets, stars, and other mysterious heavenly bodies floating in space. The surah says: "If all the trees on earth were pens, and the ocean, replenished by seven more oceans, were ink, they would run out before God's words run out. God is Almighty, Wise" (27).

None of that is beyond God's power. "The creation and rebirth of all of you [humankind] is as easy for Him as the creation and rebirth of a single soul. God hears all and observes all" (28).

Those who submit to God and venerate Him deserve full commendation for recognizing the truth and differentiating between God's power and the powers of His subservient creation.

The surah derives its title from a sage mentioned by name in verse 12. We learn that when Prophet Muhammad was asked about Luqmān he gave the Arabs of Makkah an account of a set of succinct but powerful instructions Luqmān had given his son, which are rich in wisdom and sensible advice. Luqmān's sagacity stands in total contrast to ancient Greek philosophy which was shrouded in ambiguity and idle speculation.

Luqmān's account begins with God urging him to be thankful

to Him. Human beings tend not to appreciate the good things they receive and always crave for more. Many a person would accept what one does for them but turn away without even a word of thanks. They are just as ungrateful towards God Almighty, the origin of their existence and sustenance!

The surah says: "We gave wisdom to Luqmān that he should be thankful to God. He that is thankful shall reap the fruit thereof, but whoever denies God's favors [should know that] He is Self-Sufficient, Praiseworthy" (12). God has no need for man's praise or glorification; those who acknowledge God's grace and give thanks do so for their own benefit, otherwise they would lose out.

Luqmān's advice to his son begins thus: "'My son, serve no other deity besides God, for polytheism (Arabic: *shirk*) is a grave transgression'" (13). This is followed by a bidding to be kind to one's parents who are, apart from God, immediately responsible for one's existence. It is interesting to note that modern society does not care very much for the welfare of parents. The majority of them in their old age find themselves leading lonely lives in old people's homes. But this is to expected in a society which has all but forgotten God altogether.

The advice continues: "'My son, observe the prayer, enjoin what is good and forbid what is evil. Endure with fortitude whatever befalls you. That is a duty incumbent on all. And turn not your cheek away from people in [false] pride, and walk not haughtily on earth: for, behold, God does not love anyone who, out of self-conceit, acts in a boastful manner'" (17-18).

It closes with the statement: "'Be modest in your bearing and lower your voice: the harshest of voices is the braying of the ass'" (19). The testament is a wonderful collection of profound wisdom and high religious and moral principles, which people of all generations ought to learn and observe.

The surah goes on to expound God's grace for which humans should be grateful. It says:

Do you not see that God has harnessed for you all that the heavens and the earth contain, and lavished on you His favors, visible as well as invisible? Yet some still argue about God, without knowledge or guidance or enlightening scriptures. (20)

It continues in this vein until it says:

Do you not see how the ships sail upon the ocean by God's grace, so that He may reveal some of His signs to you? Surely there are signs in this for every steadfast, thankful person. (31)

The surah ends with an affirmation of individual human accountability. It says:

Humankind, fear your Lord, and fear the Day when no parent shall benefit his child nor a child shall be of any benefit to his parent. (33)

The fact of the matter is that every man is a maker of his own destiny; if saved it will be because of his good deeds, or else his evil deeds will bring about his downfall. We read elsewhere in the Qur'an that: "No soul shall bear another's burden. If a laden soul calls on another to share its burden, none would respond, not even the nearest of kin" (*Fāṭir* 18).

The surah then goes on to deny that any soothsayer or oracle can see into the future or have prior knowledge of what is to come. It says:

God alone has knowledge of the Hour of Doom. He sends down rain and knows what every womb contains. No mortal knows what he will earn tomorrow, or where he will meet with death. Verily God is Knowledgeable, Aware. (34)

Weather forecasting, for example, would not be classified as sooth-saying because it is the result of inferences based on the intelligent study of certain physical and meteorological phenomena. Neither would other scientific and medical processes such as ultrasonic scanning to determine the sex of a baby during pregnancy. What the surah refers to is the ability to encompass full and total knowledge of what female creatures all over the world are likely to carry in their wombs, for all time everywhere.

SURAH 32

Al-Sajdah
(The Prostration)

THIS IS A MAKKAN SURAH whose opening verses announce the birth of the Muslim nation. The Qur'an, being the incontrovertible word of God, had been revealed to an illiterate community, which as a result had been totally transformed and charged with a universal mission. It refutes the arguments of its detractors:

> Do they say, "He [Muhammad] invented it himself"? It is the truth from your Lord, so that you may forewarn a nation whom no one had warned before you, and that they may be rightly guided. (3)

Before Islam, missions had been assigned to certain groups and communities, but they were short-lived and remained localized. The mission which galvanized the Arabs into a global force for change, however, was the one brought by Muhammad.

It was a universal message befitting its origin: the Creator and the universe.

> God created the heavens and the earth, and all that lies between them, in six days and then ascended the Throne. You have no guardian or intercessor besides Him...(4)

The surah then goes on to elaborate on how the Creator of the vast cosmos is also the force that is in charge of its affairs and controls its destiny.

Our universe is a wonderful, complex and awe-inspiring system. The earth revolves around its own axis once every twenty-four hours and takes 365 days to complete its orbital journey around the sun. The Milky Way, of which our solar system forms but a small part, is a galaxy consisting of millions of stars, floating with millions of other galaxies in an expansive, boundless space about which we know only very little. Light travels the vast distance from the sun to earth in a matter of minutes.

The task of controlling and running such a complex structure would require, from our limited human perspective, hundreds and thousands of years, but for God Almighty it all happens in a flash. God wills and God acts, and accordingly things come about in this world of ours. God installs and removes; causes life and causes death; provides victory and inflicts defeat. The surah says:

> He governs all, from the heavens to the earth, and all shall ascend to Him on a Day, a thousand years long by your reckoning. He knows the unknown and the manifest. He is the Almighty, the Merciful. (5–6)

The Muslim nation has its own distinct characteristics. Unlike today's Western civilization which worships its own achievements, the Muslim nation adopts a life order based, first and foremost, on *tawḥīd*, the Oneness of God whom it reveres and to whom it exclusively directs and dedicates all its actions and activity. Muslims believe in a Day of Judgment and prepare themselves for it, unlike most people today who are totally oblivious to this belief, as the surah points out:

> They say, "Once we have dissolved into the soil, shall we be brought to life afresh?" Indeed, they deny they will ever meet their Lord. (10)

When the time comes, they shall regret these claims:

> Would that you could see the wrong-doers when they hang their
> heads before their Lord! They would say, "Lord, we now see and
> hear. Send us back and we will do good works. We are now sincere
> believers." (12)

However, it would be too late, and it would be time for them to
reap the harvest of their deeds. Only those who believed and did
good works would be successful.

One of the practices that distinguish the Muslim community is
the observance of the daily prayers, salah, which are performed at
various times of the day and night. Night-time, especially in modern
society, is traditionally the time for self-indulgence and illicit behavior of all kind, while modern life leaves no time for worship or
prayer during the day. But in Muslim societies there will always be
believers who: "forsake their beds [during the night] to pray to their
Lord in fear and hope; who give in charity of that which We have
bestowed on them" (16).

The surah asks whether there could be a more contrasting picture
of the two camps: "Can he, then, who is a true believer, be compared to him who is an evil-doer? Surely they are not alike" (18).

Islam teaches that time must be organized and managed efficiently. Elsewhere in the Qur'an, God says: "We made your sleep a
means of rest, and the night a cover, and daytime a period for earning your livelihood" (al-Naba': 9–11). Human beings need to rest as
much as they need to work, and they must constantly remember
God in both states. For, we read elsewhere in the Qur'an that:
"Prayer, salah, is a duty incumbent on the faithful, to be conducted
at appointed hours" (al-Nisā': 103).

One of the problems which modern societies face today is that
prayer is not only neglected but actively discouraged and ignored.
The Qur'an refers to this, saying: "Do you see he who prevents/

rebukes a worshiper when he [turns] to pray? Do you see whether he follows guidance or enjoins true piety?" (*al-ʿAlaq*: 9–12).

The early Muslims had to contend with ignorant and vulgar enemies who had no respect for religious worship and would never appreciate its value. Today, however, they face people with similar inclinations but who hide behind the arrogance of industrial power and military superiority. There is no avoiding the challenge and facing the consequences, for: "who is more wicked than he who, when reminded of his Lord's revelations, turns away from them? We will surely take vengeance on the guilty" (22).

God then reminds His Messenger, Muhammad, that his predecessors had suffered much hardship and rejection. He should persevere as they had persevered.

> We gave the Book to Moses, never doubt your meeting him, and We made it a guide for the Israelites. And, as they showed steadfastness and had firmly believed in Our revelations, We appointed leaders from among them who guided others at Our bidding. (23–24)

The import of this statement is that leadership is granted only to those who combine steadfastness with unflinching faith. Such was the example set by the Prophet Abraham who earned the title 'leader of humankind' when he passed the test of prophethood on all counts. Attaining greatness demands great sacrifices.

The surah tells us with certainty that Muhammad would meet Moses, but we cannot be definite whether that meeting had taken place after Muhammad's death or during his life on the night when he ascended to heaven, *lailat al-isrā'*. All we can say is that the meeting has taken place.

The Tunisian scholar, Fāḍil ibn Ashur, interprets the meeting of Muhammad and Moses as a reference to their sharing a similar experience in delivering God's message. God is saying to Muhammad that his enemies and detractors would strongly resist his call, just as Moses had been rejected and opposed. The good news is, however, that God's faith would prevail. The surah asserts:

Are they not aware of how many generations We have destroyed before them? They can still walk among their ruined dwellings. Surely in this there are veritable signs; will they not, then, listen? (26)

Muslims today are subjected to insufferable injustices in various parts of the world. No fair-minded person would fail to sympathize with many of today's Muslims.

Qur'anic laws and teachings have largely been ignored and put away on the shelf. Small groups of dedicated Muslims are still fighting here and there in the face of enormous odds. There is still hope that God will intervene and put things right, and that justice will be done.

The surah concludes by saying:

They ask, "When will this victory come, if you are truthful?" Say, "When that day comes their faith shall not avail the unbelievers, nor shall they be reprieved." Therefore turn away from them, and wait as they are waiting. (28–30)

Al-Aḥzāb
(The Confederate Tribes)

THIS SURAH ADDRESSES Prophet Muhammad in his capacity as the guide and leader of the Muslim nation, on five occasions, giving him instructions on specific matters relating to his personal conduct as well as to the overall organization of the community.

On the first occasion, the surah says:

Prophet, have fear of God and do not yield to the unbelievers and the hypocrites. God is All-Knowing, Wise. Obey what is revealed to you from your Lord, for God is cognizant of your actions. Put your trust in God, for God is the best Protector. (1–3)

The import of these instructions is to reassure the Prophet of his position and reassert his loyalty to God and his steadfastness in conveying His message to the world.

But there was, however, a personal matter to which he had to see. Before he received God's revelations, the Prophet had, as was the Arab custom in those days, adopted a son by the name of Zayd ibn Ḥārithah. Islam did not approve of adoption, and hence God's words:

God has never given any man two hearts in his bosom; nor has He made the wives whom you divorce your mothers, nor your adopted sons your own sons. These are mere claims which you utter, but God states the truth and guides to the right path. (4)

The question then arises as to what is to be done regarding existing adoptions? The surah answers:

> Call them [adopted children] after their own fathers; that is more just in the sight of God. If you do not know their fathers, regard them as your brothers in faith or your companions... (5)

Natural parents have the sole parental rights over their children, but if the parents are unknown or cannot be traced, then the kinship of Islam takes the place of blood relationship. A Muslim society embraces and provides care for all foundlings, whether orphans, abandoned children, or children with unknown parents.

Muslims today are guilty of neglecting this vital practise. Indeed, it is shameful to see certain Muslim countries' orphanages, refugee centers and similar institutions that cater for children, set up and run by foreigners and non-Muslims.

The surah emphasizes the value and superiority of religious bondage by saying: "The Prophet has a closer affinity with the believers than they have even with themselves, and his wives are like mothers to them" (6).

Muhammad is a spiritual father-figure for the whole nation of Islam; no one is keener to guide this nation and lead it to safety. Muhammad is the symbol of Islam and Islam is the religion which has taken the Muslims from darkness to light. Accordingly, Muhammad himself is reported to have said:

> I take responsibility for every Muslim in this life and in the hereafter. Read, if you please, God's words that, "the Prophet has a closer affinity with the believers..." The wealth of any believer who dies shall be inherited by his next of kin, whoever they are, but whoever leaves any debt...let him come to me [in the hereafter] and I shall act as his guardian.

Prior to the revelation of verse 6 mentioned in the above hadith, the Prophet was reluctant to give a full Muslim burial to those who died leaving behind unpaid debts. After this revelation, however, and with the growth of the community, the situation changed and he was able to pay such debts and provide for orphans and the homeless.

This made the Prophet a father-figure for the believers and his wives were accorded the same status as that of mothers in both the legal and spiritual sense. They were a vital link between the Prophet and the rest of the community, conveying the revelation he received and acting as teachers and role models. Accordingly, none of them was eligible to marry anyone else after the Prophet's death.

The second set of instructions concerns the behavior of the Prophet's wives and the general conduct of his household. The surah says: "Prophet, say to your wives, 'If you are seeking the pleasures of this life, come, I will give you your dues and release you honorably.'" (28)

Unlike a royal household, the Prophet's was modest, decent, respectable, and totally unpretentious. However, while the Prophet himself led a simple and dignified life, his wives, having come from wealthy and noble families, had been brought up in comfort and opulence. As the fortunes of the Muslim community markedly improved, it was not very long before those wives started to make demands on the Prophet.

However, the revelation came to establish the fact that, although he was the undisputed leader of Arabia and God's messenger to all humankind, the Prophet's household was to remain one of humble means and humble appearance. His wives were expected to support him in his mission and observe all the requirements of the religion he was advocating. The Prophet's family could not be given special protection if the Muslim community were to come under threat or had to live under siege.

The Prophet was instructed to give all of his wives an ultimatum: to stay with him and suffer what he and the rest of the Muslims were suffering or to be granted a divorce by him. They were given a choice: "'…if you seek God and His Messenger and the abode of the hereafter, know that God has prepared a rich reward for those of you who excel in their actions'" (29).

Despite the potential hardship, all of the Prophet's wives chose to remain part of his noble household, thereby meriting their highly-regarded, dignified, and special status among Muslims and within Islam as a whole.

On the third occasion the surah says: "Prophet, We have sent you forth as a witness, a bearer of good tidings, a warner, as one who shall call men to God by His leave, and as a guiding beacon" (45–46). Whereas earlier prophets and messengers were sent to specific communities, Muhammad was the first prophet to be sent to the whole of humankind. His was the final and universal message.

The Qur'an forms the foundation and backbone of Muhammad's message as well as the proof of its veracity. It addresses every human being individually, until the end of time. The Qur'an is without doubt the veritable word of God, to which Muhammad contributed nothing other than to deliver it and to follow its teachings faithfully.

Muhammad is also a witness before God for delivering His message to his own people, and similarly, his followers will also be called to witness for its conveyance to the rest of humanity. However, it remains to be seen how good a witness the Muslims will prove to be! Earlier generations of Muslims performed this task admirably; taking Islam to all corners of the globe, they fulfilled their duty of facilitating its growth and understanding among other communities. However, with the advent of time, a climate of apathy and malaise crept in with the inevitable consequence that a wretched and sick humanity became deprived of God's gift and guidance. Furthermore, Muslims have themselves become a liability and an obstacle to the spread of Islam. The message that Muhammad brought to mankind is today in dire need of competent and talented people to convey it to the rest of the world.

The fourth message brought by this surah to the Prophet concerns his choice of spouses. Not all women would have been suitable for the great honor and title of "Mothers of the Faithful." A wife must provide support for her husband in the task with which he has been charged, or at least she should not stand as an obstamcle in his path. In the case of Prophet Muhammad, it must be acknowledged that his wives were most faithful, understanding, and supportive.

God says in the surah:

Prophet, we have made lawful to you the wives to whom you have granted dowries and those in your custody from those captured in war, whom God has given you as booty. We have also made lawful to you daughters of your paternal and maternal uncles and of your paternal and maternal aunts who had emigrated with you [from Makkah to Madinah], and any other believing woman who gives herself to the Prophet in marriage and whom the Prophet wishes to marry. This privilege is exclusively yours, being granted to no other believer... (50)

Islam allows a man to marry not more than four wives at any one time. When a man who had ten wives converted to Islam, the Prophet ordered him to keep only four and release the others.

The question can be raised here as to why this did not apply to Muhammad as well. The answer is twofold: firstly; once a wife had agreed to stay with him, despite the humble and austere life he was leading, it would not have bern fair to divorce her, and secondly; what would have become of the women he would divorce since they were forbidden from marrying anyone else? The only sensible decision was for them to remain in his custody, even if they were advanced in age.

The Prophet was then told:

> It shall be unlawful for you to take more wives or to change your present ones for other women, though you may be attracted by their beauty, except those you obtain as booty in war. God takes cognizance of all things. (52)

Polygamy is acceptable as an integral part of a moral social system. It is justifiable by the differences in human nature and the need for offspring. It was the norm in the lives of many earlier prophets, although one should be skeptical regarding the accuracy of the Old Testament story that Solomon had a thousand women, which is clearly an exaggeration. As for modern civilization, it should be the last to condemn polygamy since it allows it under many different guises. Today a man may have more women than Solomon was said to have had, without having to bear the responsibility of marrying them!

The fifth and final instruction the surah brings to the Prophet relates to his wives' dress. It says:

> Prophet, tell your wives, your daughters, and the wives of the believers to pull their cloaks close round them. That is more appropriate, so that they are recognized and would not be molested. God is Forgiving and Merciful. (59)

The next two verses put this instruction in a proper perspective. They say:

> If the hypocrites and those with sick minds and the scandal-mongers of Madinah do not desist, We will incite you against them, and they will not remain in it for much longer. Cursed wherever they are found, they will be seized and totally destroyed. (60–61)

In modern-day cities there is hardly any room for virtue; vice and moral corruption are neatly packaged to become attractive and more easily available to everyone. Promiscuity, and salacious and prurient behavior are the order of the day.

❊❊❊

Besides the instructions to the Prophet, the surah addresses the Muslims on six occasions.

The first relates to the concerted war campaign staged by the Arab tribes on Madinah, the capital of Islam, in 627 AC. It was a crucial episode. Non-Muslims, gathered from all parts of Arabia, and supported by some Jews and groups of fifth-columnists, homed in on Madinah with the intention of overrunning it. The Muslims found themselves trapped between an enemy from outside and the enemy within. The surah describes the scene:

> They surrounded you from the top [the east] and the bottom of the valley [the west], so that your eyes were blurred and your hearts leapt to your throats, and conflicting thoughts about God passed through your minds. At that point the faithful were put to the test and were severely shaken. (10–11)

The Muslims had dug a ditch around the city of Madinah, and were scurrying around, trying to fill the gaps and reinforce the defense line. Their faith in God, though shaken, remained strong. The surah tells us the sight of their enemy approaching invigorated their sense of defiance and gave them more courage to resist. It says:

> When the believers saw the confederates, they said, "This is what God and His Messenger have promised us; surely the promise of God and His Messenger has come true." And this only strengthened their faith and submission. Among the believers there are some who have been true to what they pledged to God. Some of these have fulfilled their pledges [and passed away] while others

are still awaiting their turn, never wavering an iota from their positions. (22–23)

The logic of faith differs vastly from that of self-interest. The Muslims of Madinah, to their credit, defended it well and preserved its territorial integrity, leaving the attacking invaders despondent and frustrated. Inclement weather prevailed and strong winds forced them to depart empty-handed. The surah takes up the story: "God turned back the unbelievers full of rage, and they went away empty-handed, and the believers were spared the fighting. God is Mighty, All-Powerful"(25).

The Prophet had reportedly commented with this prayer: "Thanks be to God alone. He has fulfilled His promise, supported His fighters, and has alone routed the confederates." The non-Muslim invaders were lucky to be able to return safely to their homes, and from that point on they were convinced that Madinah had become invincible and abandoned all plans to invade it.

The second set of instructions says: "Believers, remember God a great deal and praise Him morning and evening" (41–42). This seems to be a collective call rather than an individual one. The Muslims are a nation entrusted with a universal message they must protect and preserve. Their message is founded on affiliation with God, upholding His religion and affirming the ultimate accountability to Him, concepts to which present-day society is totally oblivious.

Man's sole preoccupation today revolves around 'the standard of living' and the advancement of his material welfare. Ancient religions have failed to inculcate in man a genuine belief in God and how to prepare to meet Him. When the Muslim community becomes a true champion of submission to the One God, it would then deserve His blessings, as the surah says: "He and His angels bless you, so that He might lead you out of the darkness and into the light. He is merciful to the believers" (43).

This honor can only be extended to a community that remembers God and undertakes to spread His message. When the Muslims were true to that message, they did attain a position of world leadership, but as they neglected their obligations towards God, they have lagged behind and become downtrodden.

The third instruction relates to matters of etiquette when entering the Prophet's home. The Muslims loved the Prophet more than they loved themselves. Many of them, especially those without work, liked to congregate at his house and spend as much time in his company as possible. But this had to be regulated and the Qur'an conveyed the instruction saying:

> Believers, do not enter the Prophet's dwellings unless you are given leave; [and when invited] to a meal, do not come [so early as] to wait for it to be readied: but whenever you are invited, enter [at the proper time]; and when you have eaten, disperse... (53)

It was essential to lay down these rules because, unlike palaces of kings or other rulers, with reception facilities and several wings, the Prophet's home consisted of a limited number of small rooms attached to the mosque.

In such confined space the Prophet's wives would be liable to lose their privacy and become a target for the gaze of strangers. The instruction continues:

> If you [the believers] ask them [the Prophet's wives] anything, speak to them from behind a curtain. That would leave your and their consciences much clearer. You must not speak ill of God's Messenger, nor shall you ever wed his wives after him; that would be a grave offense in the sight of God. (53)

This was also the basic reason behind the institution of *ḥijāb* for Muslim women. Inside their own home, women usually dress lightly and less formally, and they are therefore entitled to full privacy and protection against stray or prying eyes.

Such behavior by some Muslims used to annoy the Prophet, and those with evil intentions used to do it deliberately. Among these were rumor-mongers and people who spread vice and corruption in Madinan society. The surah tells us:

> God well knows those of you who undermine your morale and say to their fellow-subversives, "Join our camp," and only a few of them fight on your side, ever reluctant to support you. At times of adversity they would look to you [Muhammad] for help, their eyes rolling as though they were on the point of death. But once they are out of danger they unleash their sharp tongues against you [the believers]... (18–19)

Such subversive elements did exist in Madinah, and God warned His Messenger against them in a fourth set of instructions, saying: "Do not listen to the unbelievers and the hypocrites; disregard their insolence and put your trust in God" (48). God also said:

> Those who speak ill of God and His Messenger shall be cursed by God in this life and in the hereafter. He has prepared for them a humiliating punishment. Those who cause harm to the believing men and believing women, for no fault of their own, shall bear the guilt of slander and a gross sin. (57–58)

The fifth set of instructions concerns the moral integrity of prophets and their reputation. The surah says: "Believers, do not behave like those who slandered Moses. God cleared him of their calumny, and he remained highly respected by God" (69).

This is further affirmed on the sixth, and last, occasion when God says: "Believers, fear God and speak the truth, and He will bless your works and forgive your sins" (70–71).

As the surah reviews the hardship and the intimidation the Prophet had to put up with, it brought him great solace and much comfort by reassuring him that: "God and His angels bless the Prophet. Bless him, then, you that are true believers and greet him with a worthy salutation" (56).

The surah concludes with a brief account of mankind's task on earth. Man has been distinguished with free will and a sense of responsibility that discerns good from evil. Man is neither an animal controlled by his instincts and desires nor an angel living in an ideal world. Man is a unique creature, capable of the most sublime as well as the most debased behavior; he can choose to take one direction towards Paradise and eternal bliss, or take another one leading to hell and damnation.

God has entrusted His message to man because man is capable of bearing the responsibility and fulfilling the task required of him, towards both God Almighty and his fellow human beings. Equally, he has the capacity and the potential to betray both.

The surah then refers, in a succinct verse, to the great task entrusted to humankind, saying:

We have offered the task to the heavens, to the earth and to the mountains, but they refused to undertake it because they were afraid of it, yet man agreed to bear it, betraying his arrogance and ignorance. (72)

SURAH 34

Saba'
(Sheba)

THIS IS THE FOURTH SURAH in the Qur'an which opens with praise to God, glorifying and thanking Him, the other three being *al-Fātiḥah, al-Anʿām* and *al-Kahf*. He is the Creator of the whole universe and all that is in it, and He is the ultimate judge and arbiter of all its affairs which He does with fairness and compassion. The surah also asserts that God is Omniscient and "knows of all that goes into the earth and all that comes out of it; He knows all that comes down from heaven and all that ascends to it" (2).

God has knowledge of every single grain planted in the soil and every crop that grows out of it; He knows of every drop of rain that falls from the sky and of every breath of air that rises towards it. The whole cosmos is an open book before God Almighty and nothing escapes His notice. When a storm breaks, God is aware of the movement of each grain of dust, in whichever direction it moves. God is also in control of the forces of nature, such as heat, radiation, and electric and solar energy.

Beyond the physical world there is another, invisible to the human eye and imperceptible to the human mental or physical senses. But God "knows all that is hidden. Not an atom's weight in heaven or earth escapes Him; nor is there anything smaller or greater but is recorded in a perspicuous register" (3).

This surah shares many of the features of *al-Furqān* by answering blow for blow the objections of the unbelievers to religious faith. The first of these objections is their denial of the Day of Judgment, a stance common to unbelievers of the past as well as those of the present. The surah says: "The unbelievers say, 'The Hour of Doom will never come.' Say to them, 'By my Lord, it is surely coming!...'" (3).

The refusal to believe in resurrection is indeed an absurd attitude. What prevents the Creator from creating a second time? Since He was able to do it in the first place, how could He not do it again? Is it not obvious that God has full control of man's destiny, day in and day out, and that man is in real need of God, whether awake or asleep, hungry or well-fed? Man is, indeed, capable of overlooking the plainest and most evident of facts!

A second life is vital in order for differences to be settled, balance restored and justice to be done by all. Some shall be rewarded and others punished. Jews and Christians who contended with Muhammad and obstructed Islam, a message they were expected to endorse and support, shall face the consequences of their actions.

People today, like the unbelievers of the past, are overwhelmed by materialism and pay no attention to the Day of Judgment. But this is really a sign of folly and self-delusion. Hence the surah dwells on this subject, saying:

> The unbelievers say, "Shall we show you a man [Muhammad] who claims that when you have disintegrated into dust you will be raised to life again? Is he telling lies about God, or is he mad?" Truly, those who deny the life to come are doomed and have gone hopelessly astray. (7–8)

The surah questions the very logic of this argument on several occasions, saying:

> When our revelations are clearly recited to them, they say, "This is but a man who would turn you away from the gods your fathers worshiped." They say, "This [the Qur'an] is nothing but an invented falsehood." Yet as the truth is presented to them, the unbelievers say, "This is but plain sorcery." (43)

The surah relates two accounts which have direct relevance to the above debate. The first one refers to the prophet David (Dāwūd). God Almighty says:

On David We bestowed Our favor. "O mountains, and you birds, echo his songs of praise [to God]." We made iron pliant to him. [And we said], "Make coats of mail armor, and do what is right. Verily I am watching over what you do." (10–11)

The parable of David belies the ignorant belief of some religious people that backwardness is the way to success in the life to come. This is a gross misconception. The route to religious faith is through the mastery of useful knowledge rather than sloth and indolence. The lesson that millions of Muslims have to learn today is that they cannot simply borrow technology and industrial know-how from other nations. David was able to combine two achievements in his life-time: to use his elegant voice—which even the birds appreciated and admired—to venerate, praise, and worship God; and to apply industrial skill to make military as well as civilian tools and utensils for everyday use.

In order to appreciate and comprehend the life to come, one has to understand and fully experience life here and now. Faith can never be upheld or promoted by imbeciles or lethargic people. Muslims have only become a liability to Islam and an easy target for their enemies since they lost their enthusiasm for life and their ardor for success and achievement.

We are told in verse 13 that Solomon, the son of David, had shrines and statues built for him, which indicates that such art and architectural forms were permissible at that time. They have subsequently been prohibited by Islam, however, because they were frequently turned into deities and objects of worship. Knowing how susceptible human nature can be to abusing such forms of art, we are of the opinion that their use should continue to be prohibited. In some

Christian churches, statues and icons are indeed treated as sacred objects, a practise which the Protestants had abolished by banning their use in their churches.

David and Solomon were kings as well as prophets, but their state duties never prevented them from fulfilling their religious obligations. The surah says: "...Give thanks, House of David; few of My servants are truly thankful" (13).

The second account refers to the community of Sheba. It says:

> For the natives of Sheba there was indeed a sign in their metropolis: they had two gardens, one on each side. [We said to them,] "Eat of what your Lord has provided you and render thanks to Him. Pleasant is your land and forgiving is your Lord." (15)

Some people are under the wrong impression that wealth is always a blessing and that those who are less endowed are somehow denied God's pleasure. They seem to forget that God tests people through wealth and fortune as much as He tests them through hardship and suffering. Success and salvation are contingent on how one fares in coping with one's destiny and the will of God Almighty. Elsewhere in the Qur'an, God says: "We test all of you with good and evil, and to Us you shall all return" (*al-Anbiyā'*: 35).

By denying God's favor and abusing the wealth they had been given, the community of Sheba had failed the test. The surah says:

> But they gave no heed. So We let loose upon them the waters of the dam and replaced their gardens by two others bearing bitter fruit, tamarisks, and a few lote-trees. Thus did We punish them for their ingratitude: do We punish any but the ungrateful? (16–17)

Once God's grace and blessings are withheld from a community, disunity, depravity and insecurity set in, but people only have themselves to blame, because:

They did themselves an injustice; so We made their fate a byword and scattered them throughout the land. Surely, in this there are signs for every steadfast and thankful person. (19)

The surah points out that numerous individuals and groups had failed the grace test, and that some had been arrogant and ungrateful. They had opposed God's revelation, claiming their beliefs and traditions to be superior, and had been hostile to His prophets and messengers. It says:

Whenever We sent a warner, the affluent in the community would say, "We refuse to believe in what is sent with you; we have greater wealth and more offspring, and we shall not be punished." (34–35)

Affluence, in the main, has been a cause for social strife, decline, and disintegration in contemporary as well as past human generations. Those who are well-off tend to indulge in their wealth and exploit the poor and the weak. This has given rise to social theories and ideologies aimed at the eradication of the right of ownership which, in turn, has led to war and conflict among various social groups and classes. A closer examination of social conflict reveals that what lies behind it is greed for worldly gain. Religion is being gradually eroded and the life hereafter is fading into insignificance, giving way instead to ideologies and political and economic systems that worship materialism and material aggrandizement. Nevertheless, religion remains the only way out of this malaise. Referring to the people of Sheba, the surah asserts:

Satan has judged them rightly; they followed him all, except for a band of believers. Yet he had no power over them: We only wanted to discern between those who believed in the life to come and those who were in doubt of it. Your Lord takes cognizance of all things. (20–21)

With these accounts in mind, the surah goes on to examine more of the unbelievers' objections to religion, adopting a most unique debating style. The Prophet is instructed to appeal directly to these objectors: "Say, 'Who provides for you from heaven and earth?' Say, 'God. We cannot both be right: either you or we are in evident error'" (24).

Indeed, who is more worthy of veneration and worship: the provider or the receiver? How could the stone deities the unbelievers worshiped be invoked to provide for the living? Whose belief was closer to the truth?

Having been so generous to the unbelievers in this debate, the argument is taken further to show them up and totally refute their allegations. Prophet Muhammad was instructed to: "Say, 'You are not accountable for our sins, nor are we accountable for your actions.' Say, 'Our Lord will bring us all together, then He will rightly judge between us. He is the All-Knowing Judge'" (25–26).

In human societies, there are always those who lead and others who follow. The former are usually driven by ambition and greedy self-interest, while the latter tend to be submissive and easily led. Factors such as wealth, power, and status come into play in defining the relationship between the two groups, which is best exemplified by the relationship between Pharaoh and the sorcerers who "…said to Pharaoh, 'Shall we be rewarded if we win [over Moses]?' He said, 'Yes. And you shall gain a higher status'" (*al-Shuʿarāʾ*: 41–42).

In this surah we come across a scene from the Day of Judgment, frequently encountered in the Qur'an, in which those who advocate disbelief and those who are willing to obey and support them engage in argument, exchanging abuse and accusations, and blaming each other for the fate they would suffer in the hereafter. A close examination of the opposition to religious faith, past and present, would reveal that it is almost always motivated by greed and selfish desires.

The surah depicts the scene so vividly.

When the wrong-doers will be brought before their Lord, they will be throwing the blame on one another, and the powerless ones say to the arrogant ones: "Had it not been for you, we would have been believers!" The arrogant ones will then say to the powerless ones: "Was it we who debarred you from God's guidance when it was presented to you? No! Verily you yourselves were wrong-doers." (31–32)

The debate continues until it is swiftly brought to an end by the keepers of hell.

Towards the end of the surah, God instructs the Prophet to reveal to his people the true nature of the message of Islam, decisively and convincingly refuting the arguments of the unbelievers. He says:

Say, "I shall give you one piece of advice. Face God and think very carefully, in pairs and singly, whether your compatriot [Muhammad] is in any way inflicted by insanity." He [Muhammad] is but a warner sent to forewarn you of a grievous scourge. (46)

Rational profound thinking, whether undertaken individually or collectively, is an essential requirement for understanding Islam. Gods calls on man to be mentally and intellectually alert, to ponder and reflect on God's creation all around him. Muhammad was the harbinger of this call and the herald who came to shake mankind into alertness and active awareness of God. He did his duty for no personal financial or political gain. He honestly and sincerely devoted himself to the task and withstood all the hardship and persecution it inflicted upon him. The surah says: "Say, 'I demand no recompense from you; keep it for yourselves. My reward shall come from none but God. He is the witness over all'" (47).

It goes on to affirm that those who deny God's universal truth today will come to see it for themselves face to face: "If you could only see the unbelievers when they are seized with terror! There shall be no escape for them; they shall be seized from close by" (51).

They will declare their faith in God, but it would be too late. They should have shown more wisdom and prudence while they had the chance. "They will say, 'We now believe!' But how will they attain to faith when they are so far away from it? They had already denied it and ignorantly refused to believe in the unseen" (52–53).

SURAH 35

Fāṭir
(The Creator)

THIS IS THE FIFTH AND FINAL SURAH opening with praise to God, a commendable and worthy act. The Qur'an is full of praise to God which can be found in various places in its surahs. Praise is due to God at the beginning as well as at the end of every action.

The surah opens thus: "Praise be to God, Creator of the heavens and the earth! He appoints the angels as messengers, with two, three or four wings..." (1).

Angels are luminous, charming, and genial creatures, capable of assuming various forms. They reside in the heavens and are well-disposed to goodness, obedience, knowledge, and the ability to undertake onerous tasks. They are at the ready to carry out God's commands affecting the rest of His creation. They are charged with a wide range of responsibilities such as administering death, life, birth, or recording facts and figures, as well as supervising or overseeing particular events or individuals.

While the surah indicates that angels can have as many as two, three or four wings, we learn from Prophet Muhammad that some of them could have hundreds or thousands. The surah adds that God "...multiplies His creation as He wills. God has power over all things" (1).

This surah, like *al-Naḥl* before it, catalogs God's favors towards His creation and the grace He bestows upon everyone and everything at the point of creation as well as during their respective lives. It opens with this definite and universal truth: "The mercy God bestows on people none can withhold; and what He withholds none can provide, apart from Him. He is the Almighty, the Wise One" (2).

Human beings are in urgent need of understanding this universal law of creation, since many of them are under the illusion that what nature provides bears no relation to God Almighty whatsoever. Some have the audacity to eliminate God completely from the equation of life, giving the most wild explanations for the nature and purpose of existence.

That profound statement is followed by this appeal:

> Humankind, bear in mind God's goodness towards you. Is there a creator, other than God, who would provide for you from the heavens and earth? There is no God but Him. How then can you turn away? (3)

God is the origin of all the goodness in this world. The Prophet is reported to have prayed, saying: "God, whatever goodness I, or anyone of Your creation, receive this day, is from You alone. There is no partner with You. Praise and thanks be to You."

This deep-seated conviction is an essential element of faith. God is the provider and the guardian of all goodness. Neglecting this reality and believing that a power other than God, or besides Him, can provide for creation can only lead to the extinction of religious faith. This deviation has led some people to be more fearful of God's creatures, human and otherwise, than of God Himself, paving the way for despotism and oppression.

The surah re-emphasizes the point, saying:

> Humankind, the promise of God is true. Let the life of this world not deceive you, nor let Satan delude you about God. Satan is an enemy of yours: therefore treat him as an enemy. He only tempts his followers so that he can lead them to hell. (5–6)

God has revealed the Qur'an to Muhammad in order that he may lead humankind out of the darkness and into the light. His main aim is that they should become righteous and those who respond would be successful. The surah says: "If they deny you, other messengers have been denied before you. To God shall all things return" (4).

A little further on, the surah restates this fact with reference to the stubborn stance taken by the people of Arabia who rejected Muhammad and persecuted him. It says:

> If they deny you, others before them had also denied their messengers who had come to them with veritable signs, with scriptures and with the light-giving Book. But in the end I struck down the unbelievers. Terrible indeed was My repudiation of them. (25–26)

God's retribution, however, does not usually come at once. People are always given ample time to ponder, wake up, and mend their ways. The surah points out that:

> If God were always to punish people for their misdeeds, not a single creature would be left alive on the surface of the earth. He grants them respite till an appointed time. When their hour comes, they shall realize that God has been watching over all His servants. (45)

God would be aware of those who had taken advantage of that respite and those who had not. The surah also points out that some people mistake God's generosity for indifference and take even wider liberties. It asks:

> Is he whose foul deeds seem fair to him like the person who is rightly guided? God leaves in error whom He wills and guides whom He pleases. Do not [Muhammad] feel any grief for them; God has knowledge of all their actions. (8)

Muhammad used to experience a great deal of sorrow and pain on account of the intransigence of some of the people he was addressing with Islam. These verses brought reassurance and consolation.

The surah makes another powerful statement.

Humankind, it is you who stand in need of God. God is the Self-Sufficient and the Worthy of praise. He can eradicate you if He so wills and replace you with a new creation; that would not be a difficult thing for God to do. (15–17)

There are no bounds to God's power. He is capable of obliterating the whole world and recreating a new one, more obedient and better disposed to glorifying and worshiping Him.

People are fundamentally free to choose between justice and injustice, and whether to fulfill their obligations towards God or not. The surah asserts:

Those who seek glory should know that glory is God's alone. The good word reaches Him and He graciously rewards good deeds. But those who plot evil shall be sternly punished; their scheming shall come to nothing. (10)

The surah goes on to elaborate its central theme: that it is God who creates and it is He who provides. He sends the wind to form clouds, and He created rivers with fresh, sweet water and oceans whose water is salty and bitter.

Read, if you would, the passage which begins as follows: "God created you from dust, then from a tiny sperm, and then He made you into males and females..." (11). Nevertheless, people continue to lead heedless lives, completely oblivious of God and negligent of their obligations towards Him.

There is an almost universal agreement among religious scholars that the Islamic faith is based on intelligent observation of life and the physical world around. Islam is an earnest call to enlightened reflection on nature, its various manifestations and forces, and an invitation to unravel its laws and secrets.

Reflection on the very essence of God Almighty is unfeasible and futile. His power and glory are only discernible through the marvels of His creation, which stand as incontrovertible proof for His omniscience, omnipotence, majesty, and splendor.

One has only to look around to find an amazing array of vegetation and life forms, with a variety of color, taste and smell, growing over the same, small area of land. If one looks up towards the sky, one will see the resplendent sun, the luminous moon and the shining stars scattered over a wide horizon, thousands and millions of kilometers across a vast, splendid universe.

All this is but part of the grace and blessings of God Almighty. The surah points out:

Can you not see that God sent down water from the sky with which We brought forth fruits of different hues? There are mountains streaked with various shades of white and red, and dark black rocks. People, beasts and cattle are of different colors, too. Only those of God's servants that have knowledge truly fear Him. Verily God is Almighty, Forgiving. (27–28)

In addition to scientists in medicine, geometry and cosmology, it can be confidently said here that "those who have knowledge" include botanists, biologists, geologists, and scientists of physics and chemistry. The accumulative result of scientific work in all these fields points to the majesty and splendor of the Maker of this magnificent universe. He can only be One, deserving of all praise and gratitude.

The Qur'an's main thesis revolves around the following truth: faith and belief can only be attained by intelligent, inquiring minds

475

and by hearts which are totally devoted to God. It is within this intellectual framework that the Muslim nation has been charged with carrying God's message to the rest of humankind. God says:

> Then We made those of Our servants whom We have chosen the inheritors of the Book. Some of them have done themselves injustice, some have been temperate, and some, by God's leave, vie with each other in doing good: this is the supreme virtue. (32)

Several communities had been charged with carrying God's message, the Israelites being the last of them immediately to precede the Arabs. The Israelites, however, proved self-centered, and exploited God's revelations to further their selfish whims and feed their arrogance, thereby offending God and incurring His displeasure. They were forever to forfeit that honor, which the Arabs then came to inherit.

The surah points out that the Arabs themselves had divided into three categories: those who rejected God's revelation, those who accepted it but did not fully observe its teachings, and those who adopted Islam and totally dedicated themselves to it.

Future generations will be judged according to which of these three groups is the dominant one. If either of the first two prevails in a society, the omens for its salvation would not be very good. The whole of the community might, in such a case, incur God's displeasure or punishment.

The surah poses a challenge for Muslims today. Would they, as they read these words, really feel up to the task? There is an erroneous saying attributed to Prophet Muhammad in which he is alleged to have said: "The Ummah has inherited all the Books revealed by God. Those who transgress, their sins shall be forgiven; those who are moderate, their questioning shall be mild; and those who strive for the best shall enter Paradise without accounting for anything."

Such misleading statements can only make the Muslim public more complacent and encourage Muslims to remain backward and insignificant. While noting this, one is encouraged by what the closing verses of this surah say:

> They [the Arabs] solemnly swore by God that if a prophet should come to warn them, they would accept his guidance more readily than either of the two other nations [Jews and Christians]. Yet when someone did come to warn them, they showed even more rejection. Arrogance on earth and evil tendencies drove them to that. But evil shall rebound only on those who plot it. Would they be awaiting the fate of those before them? God's will is unalterable and unavoidable. (42–43)

The ideas conveyed by the above passage occur in the Qur'an on two other occasions, in *al-Anʿām* and *al-Ṣāffāt*. On all three occasions the objective is to denounce the pre-Islamic Arabs for their arrogance and rejection of earlier revelation, and their claim that, had they received revelation from God, they would do better than the Jews and the Christians. Hence, they were put to the test!

We must fully credit the earlier generations of Islam for their sincere effort towards the establishment and propagation of Islam all over the world. However, we must also recognize that the Arabs were soon to relapse and revert to their old habits, deviating from God's true path and neglecting their obligations towards Islam. More recently, some Arabs have replaced Islam with Arab nationalism, abandoning their loyalty to God. The surah warns:

> Have they never looked around and seen the fate of those who went before them, and who were more powerful than they? There is nothing in the heavens or earth beyond the power of God. Verily He is All-Knowing, All-Powerful. (44)

Will the Arabs then take heed?

Yā Sīn

YĀ AND SĪN ARE TWO LETTERS of the Arabic alphabet and do not, as commonly assumed, denote a name of Prophet Muhammad. God swears by the Qur'an itself, saying: "I swear by the impeccable Qur'an that you [Muhammad] are a messenger, leading to a straight path" (2–4).

Besides being in itself a self-evident marvel, the Qur'an is supporting proof of Muhammad's truthfulness in his claim to be God's messenger, calling to God's straight path without any pretense or contrivance. The Qur'an: "is a revelation sent by the Almighty, the Merciful, so that you [Muhammad] may forewarn a heedless people, whose fathers had not been warned" (5–6).

Physical miracles are seldom intellectually enlightening. The people of Arabia inherited a deep-rooted tradition of idol worship, and were deemed unlikely to be persuaded to abandon it through spectacular feats. They needed elaborate revelation that would stimulate and challenge their minds and shake off their ignorance, as some of them were in total darkness. "We have bound their necks with chains reaching up to their chins, so that they cannot bow their heads" (8). The picture is of a people overwhelmed by ignorance that had bound them rigid and stiff so that they were not able to see the truth or recognize it. "We have put barriers before them and behind them and covered their vision, so that they cannot see" (9).

This is the outcome of blind and ignorant following which renders people insensitive and unresponsive to the truth.

You [Muhammad] shall only admonish those who believe in the Qur'an and fear the Merciful without having seen Him. Give these the good news of forgiveness and a rich reward. (11)

The surah is usually referred to as the "heart of the Qur'an." Its main theme is the assertion of the principle of *tawḥīd*, Oneness of God, and its objective is to draw attention to God's magnificent creation and to call people to prepare for accountability to Him. It can be divided into an introduction followed by three distinct parts.

The introduction, as we have seen, speaks of the nature and the status of the Qur'anic revelation, addressing both its believers and detractors alike. The three parts provide historic, rational, and moral arguments respectively for the veracity and authenticity of the Qur'an.

The historic argument comes in the form of a tale relating the fate of a small village, not unlike Makkah of the sixth century AC, whose people had rejected God's revelation. The rational argument centers around the universe, with its order and intricate systems, as living physical proof for God's omnipotence and dominance over the whole of creation. The third argument revolves around the resurrection and man's accountability to God in the hereafter with the aim of convincing the Qur'an's recipients of the truth of God's revelation.

The first part of the surah starts with the words: "Relate to them, as a case in point, what happened to the people of a township when messengers came to them..." (13). The actual identity of the town in question is hardly of concern to us here. What really matters is the encounter and the events that ensued from it.

Ever since the time of Noah, the detractors of revelation believed that God's messengers had come to usurp their power and property, and so they met them with rejection and threats. The unbelievers in this town said to the messengers:

479

"Your presence bodes for us nothing but evil. Desist, or we will stone you and inflict on you a painful scourge." The messengers said, "The evil you forebode can come only from yourselves. You reject us only because we have come to admonish you. Surely you are true transgressors." (18–19)

Elsewhere in the Qur'an we read what Noah's people had said to him:

"We see you but a mortal like ourselves. Nor do we see you followed by any but the lowliest among us, those who are rash and undiscerning. We see no superior merit in you: indeed we think that you are lying." (*Hūd*: 27)

The detractors notwithstanding, there will always be people who will recognize the truth and uphold and defend it. In this town, the duty fell to one man who stood up and asserted the following two facts:

1. The messengers were sincere individuals who sought no wealth or status.

2. They were calling to the true and only God, besides whom there is no other power capable of causing anyone any harm or any good.

The pious man is reported to have said: "'My people, follow the messengers, who ask no reward of you and are rightly-guided. Why should I not serve Him who has created me and to whom you shall all be recalled?'" (20–22).

The surah does not tell us whether the man was killed for the stand he had taken, or died naturally, but we learn that he failed in persuading his people to follow God's messengers. We are, however, told of what he had to say after his death, having seen the rich rewards awaiting him. He said: "'Would that my people knew how my Lord has forgiven and honored me'" (26–27). Nevertheless, the ungrateful inhabitants of that town received their due punishment:

> After him, We did not send [any armies] from heaven to destroy them: nor did We need to send down any. A single blow and they were lifeless! (28–29)

Arrogance can end in total annihilation. The price of rejecting God's messengers and humiliating them can be very high indeed, and the more serious the crime the greater the punishment. God says: "Alas for these wretched people! They scorn every messenger that comes to them. Do they not see how many generations We have destroyed before them? They shall never come back to this world" (30–31).

This brief, but profound, tale makes one wonder about the future and fate of contemporary civilization which totally rejects God and dismisses His eventual judgment. Could it be inducing its own self-destruction?

The second part of the surah offers evidence for God's omnipotence and magnificence. It starts with the statement:

> One of [Our] signs is the infertile soil which We bring into life and let the grains grow out of it for their [humankind's] sustenance. We furnish it with gardens of palm-trees and vineyards, and cause springs to gush out of it. (33–34)

Human beings are notorious in abusing the natural environment which is essential for their survival. There is a tradition among farmers that the best melons are grown on pigeon droppings. Nature turns human and other remains and excrement into fertilizer, facilitating the growth of all kinds of crops and countless types of fruit and vegetables. The question then arises: who has made all this goodness possible and abundantly available? The surah answers:

Glory be to Him who created males and females of the plants that grow out of the soil, of humankind themselves, and of numerous living things they know nothing of. (36)

The surah turns our attention to the heavens and their fascinating constellations. The world is covered in darkness, but as the rays of the sun fall on the earth it brightens up into a sheet of light. When the rays disappear, darkness returns. The surah describes this process in these words: "The night is another sign for humankind. We withdraw from it the [light of] day, and they are plunged back into darkness" (37).

The sun and the moon might seem to be moving in the same orbit, but that is not the case; they move in two completely separate orbits and they are destined never to meet. When one reflects on the universe, one wonders what keeps these thousands upon thousands of stars and planets in their respective orbits? What energy drives them? Who constructed this amazingly stable and intricate system? Who determines the positions, speeds, orientations and directions of each and every one of them?

As humans we occupy a very tiny corner of this vast universe, and with our own eyes we can observe God's marvelous signs. Some of us believe in God and others refuse to believe.

The surah takes us back to earth to point us towards the seas and oceans and the ships that sail in them. It says: "Another sign We gave them when we carried their offspring in the laden ark, and We have made them similar vessels to sail in" (41–42).

The sea is four times as large as the land and constitutes a far bigger world. We now know that matter floats on water according to an exact scientific law; it floats or sinks according to precise equations. Will people not acknowledge that when they are faced with danger at sea, only God can rescue them?

Further supporting testimony is given towards the end of the surah. God says:

> Do they not see that, among the things that Our hands have fashioned, We created for them beasts of which they are masters? We have subjected these to them; they use some for transport and they feed on some others. (71–72)

People in their millions eat and enjoy the flesh of animals every day, but are they aware of who had envisaged that and made it available?

The final part of the surah deals with two of the most fundamental religious principles: resurrection and judgment. Modern society ignores these two vital tenets and looks upon them with disdain. Modern culture teaches that a person's life, just like that of an animal, ends here in this world; there is no judgment or accountability.

The Day of Judgment, like death, is not possible to predict and will take people by complete surprise. The surah refers to this by saying:

> They say, "When will this promise be fulfilled, if what you say be true?" There will be only a single blast which will overtake them while they are still arguing. They will have no time to make a will, nor shall they return to their kinfolk. (48–50)

The meaning here is that when the Hour of Truth arrives, it shall be swift and decisive. It will happen while people are going about their normal business, in markets and other places. The Prophet is reported to have said:

> The Hour would fall sooner than two traders in the market close a deal; it would fall within the time a man milks his she-camel and tastes the milk; it would come sooner than a man carries food to his mouth...

The Hour will come at such a speed that there will be no time left for making a will or doing anything else. Once life stands still all over the earth, God will command all human beings to rise and be ready to face the judgment.

> ...They will rise up from their graves and hasten towards their Lord. They will say, "Woe to us! Who has roused us from our resting place? This is what the Merciful had promised: the messengers have indeed told the truth." (51–52)

The surah gives a brief account of the happiness and tranquil life the believers will enjoy in Paradise. Those condemned to the hell-fire will be scolded and berated. God will admonish them:

> Children of Adam, did I not charge you never to worship Satan, your declared foe, but to worship Me? Surely that was the right path. He has led a multitude of you astray. Have you no sense? (60–62)

Although the main theme of this part of the surah is the resurrection and judgment of humankind, it touches on other aspects of God's power and majesty, and His special magnanimity and generosity towards humankind.

By way of illustration of the resurrection, the surah gives a brief but extremely instructive example. It says:

Is man not aware that We created him from a little sperm, and yet he stands flagrantly contentious? Forgetting the example of his own creation, he asks, "Who will give life to decayed bones?" Say, "He who had first brought them into being; He has knowledge of every creature." (77–79)

It stands to reason. He who had created once can certainly create a second time.

The Qur'an then draws attention to an important phenomenon observed in nature every day which is the result of a biological fact. Human beings breathe in oxygen and breathe out carbon dioxide, while the reverse takes place in trees and plants. Carbon then becomes the main element that turns trees and plants into fuel. The surah says: "He [God] who gives you from the green trees fire that you use as fue." (80).

God brings the living out of the dead and the dead out of the living, and these natural processes are marvels attesting to His majesty and glory. Hence a fitting close: "Glory be to Him who has control of all things. To Him you shall all be recalled" (83).

Al-Ṣāffāt
(The Ranks)

THE SURAH OPENS WITH a description of the angels, led by the Archangel Gabriel, carrying God's words that were being revealed to the seal of the prophets, Muhammad. "[I swear] by those who range themselves in ranks, by those who cast out demons, and by those who recite the Word" (1–3). This is an affirmation of Islam's most fundamental principle: *tawḥīd*, the unity and Oneness of God Almighty.

Gabriel had the unique privilege of being in charge of conveying God's revelation to Muhammad, but many other angels had the honor of partaking in that highly regarded task. Elsewhere in the Qur'an, God says: "By His will He sends down the angels with the Spirit to those among His servants whom He chooses, bidding them proclaim, 'There is no god but Me; therefore fear Me'" (al-Naḥl: 2). The angels also fulfill the task of warding off intrusive devils who try to intercept revelation and tamper with it.

The Prophet was reported to have said that revelation emanated from God Almighty, in the first instance; then, once He had decided in heaven what would be revealed, the angels beat their wings in submission to His command, [making a clatter] akin to that made by hitting metal chains on stone. Then, when the terror has left their hearts, they would ask each other: "'What has your Lord said?' 'The truth,' they would reply. 'He is the Most High, the Supreme One'" (Saba': 23).

God is described here as "the Lord of the heavens and the earth, and all that lies between them: the Lord of the eastern regions" (5). The eastern regions is a reference to the places where the sun rises, which vary throughout the year.

The opening passage contains two facts: the oneness of God, *tawḥīd*, and the resurrection. Both are rejected by the unbelievers, who "...when it is said to them, 'There is no god but God,' they turn arrogant and say, 'Are we to renounce our gods for the sake of a mad poet?'" (35–36). It is futile to try to deny the truth, for truth shall prevail.

The surah describes two scenes from the Day of Judgment in the hereafter as if they were unfolding before our eyes. It says:

> Call the transgressors, their wives and the idols they used to worship besides God, and lead them to the path of hell. Hold them there for questioning. What has come over you that you are not able to help each other? Today, they shall surrender with humiliation and reproach one another, saying, "You have forced us to deviate." Others would reply, "No! It was you who were not believers. We had no authority over you; you were indeed transgressors..." (22–30)

The leaders and their disciples are at loggerheads; each is blaming the other for their miserable fate. The weaker accuse the rich and the powerful of leading them astray and coercing them into temptation, while the latter retort by describing their detractors as stupid and inane and calling on them to face up to their responsibilities. The surah says: "On that Day they will all share in the punishment. Thus shall We deal with the evil-doers" (33–34).

In the other scene we are told:

> They will turn to one another asking questions. One will say, "I had a friend who used to ask [me]: 'Do you really believe? When we are dead and turned to dust and bones, shall we really be brought to

judgment?'" And then he will say to his fellow-believers, "Would you come and have a look?" He will look and see his friend in the very midst of hell, and say to him, "By God, you almost ruined me!..." (50–56)

Such an encounter is a familiar everyday occurrence. Every one of us tries to bring others round to our beliefs and way of thinking. Had the believer not been strong, he would have slipped up and lost his way. The surah describes his relief in the hereafter as he continues to confront his former friend:

"...But for the grace of God I too should have surely been where you are. Shall we only die once, and shall we never be punished at all?" Surely that is the supreme triumph. To this end let everyone strive. (57–61)

As frequently seen in the Qur'an, such as in *al-Aʿrāf*, scenes from the hereafter are presented as though they are happening here and now, in order to achieve a greater impact.

One can feel the believer's joy as he realizes that his faith has saved him from the misfortune consuming his former friend. As he joins the faithful in Paradise, basking in its comfort and abundance, the believer remembers a friend who used to deny the existence of God and the Day of Judgment. He is curious to find out what had become of him. On seeing him wallowing in hellfire, he cannot but appreciate his own good fortune.

God then says: "Is this not a better welcome than the *zaqqūm* tree? We have made this tree a scourge for the transgressors. It grows in the nethermost part of hell, bearing fruits like devils' heads" (62–65).

This tree has been mentioned a few times in the Qur'an. Here are some instances: "As for you sinners, you shall eat the fruit of the *zaqqūm* tree and fill your bellies with it" (*al-Wāqiʿah*: 51–53), and:

"The fruit of the *zaqqūm* tree is the food of the sinner. Like dregs of oil, like scalding water, it shall simmer in his belly" (*al-Dukhān*: 43–46), and: "...the tree cursed in the Qur'an" (*al-Isrā'*: 60).

The nearest thing to this tree has been described as a poisonous desert plant that grows on barren ground, bears small leaves and gives out a foul smell. It produces a kind of milk which causes swelling of the skin and could lead to death. The trees of hell are far more loathsome and hideous. Attractive plants, once dry, can be used as fuel; their trunks and branches are repositories of energy. Such are the marvels of God's creation that even green trees and plants are turned into fire.

God made the *zaqqūm* tree the food of people of hell, saying: "They [the unbelievers] will eat from it until their bellies are full, and then they will mix it with scalding water" (66–67). But why this severe punishment? "They found their fathers erring, yet they eagerly followed in their footsteps" (69–70). They incurred such punishment because they blindly followed the practices, traditions, and conventions of their forefathers.

Most people, in fact, are guilty of similar behavior, denouncing the views and ways of others without due examination or scrutiny. People may even wrongly kill one another out of sheer bigotry or take it upon themselves to suppress their opponents and annihilate their ideas. The surah says: "Most of the ancients before them went astray, though We had sent them apostles to warn them. But take note of the fate of those We had warned..." (71–73).

The surah relates episodes from the experiences of six different messengers by way of encouragement and reassurance to Muhammad.

The first comes from the life of Noah, one of the most resolute of God's messengers, who withstood untold hardship. Then it talks of Abraham, the founding father of the nation of Islam who established the first beginnings of Islamic life on this earth. It recalls Moses, who brought the Torah, a book not unlike the Qur'an, that introduced religion as faith and a code of law for temporal as well as spiritual life. These were three of the most senior messengers, followed by three others: Lot, a nephew of Abraham and one of his followers; and Elijah (Ilyās) and Jonah (Yūnus), two Hebrew prophets who expounded the Torah, the Book of Moses.

Curiously enough, Noah's story is told here from the end. He spent nine and a half centuries teaching his people but received nothing in return except rebuke and distress. As he lost all hope, he called upon God to come to his assistance and received the support he needed. He made a passionate plea and received the appropriate response:

Noah called upon Us, and We were the best to respond. We delivered him and his clan from a mighty scourge, and made his descendants the sole survivors. We bestowed on him the praise of later generations. Peace be upon Noah among all mankind. (75–79)

Thus Noah has been credited with eternal praise, as affirmed elsewhere in the Qur'an: "We [God] said to Noah, 'Go ashore in peace from Us. Our blessings are upon you and upon some of those who are with you'" (*Hūd*: 48).

Noah was a messenger to his own people and the flood that occurred during his time was a local one which did not extend to places such as Egypt, Persia, Europe, or Africa.

Abraham was a prophet who staunchly upheld the principle of *tawḥīd* which was as steadfastly advocated by Noah before him. The surah relates his quest for the truth and his struggle to dissuade his people from idol-worship. It says: "He looked up towards the stars and said, 'I am not well!' His people turned away from him and, once they had departed, he furtively set upon their gods, asking them, 'Will you not eat your offerings? Why do you not answer?...'" (88–92).

The narrative relates that Abraham sought to discredit his people's pagan practise and so pretended to be unwell in order to be left alone. Once his people were preoccupied elsewhere he set upon the idols, smashing them into pieces, sparing only the most supreme god, so that the people might refer to it to find out what had happened (see *al-Anbiyā'*: 58). He placed the pickaxe around the neck of the surviving idol to indicate that it had obliterated the rest!

It is obvious that Abraham resorted to such a ruse in order to expose the stupidity of his people and the absurdity of their religious beliefs and practices. It has been argued that this episode shows that Abraham had lied on three occasions. But this is nonsense! Such a false interpretation had been interpolated into the *tafsīr* literature and has, quite rightly, been dismissed by all serious research. Abraham's integrity is beyond reproach, and such an interpretation would be sheer balderdash!

One of the most celebrated events of Abraham's life is the encounter with his son, Ishmael (Ismāʿīl), who had been born during Abraham's old age. As the boy grew before his father's proud eyes, God, in His wisdom, ordered Abraham to slay his son as an offering to Him. The surah takes up the story:

> And when he [Ishmael] reached a working age, his father said to him, "My son, it has been revealed to me in a dream that I should sacrifice you, so tell me what you think?" (102)

One could imagine Abraham's predicament: a father ordered by God to sacrifice one of his most precious possessions in the world, the son he treasured and loved. Were the son to have been harmed in any other way the father would have been stricken by grief, so how deep his distress must have been when he was the one ordered to kill him!

Abraham, being the loyal and obedient servant and messenger he was, could not imagine ignoring an order from his Lord and so he told his son what was required of him. The son, being a truthful and pious believer, responded by saying: "'Father, do as you are bidden. God willing you shall find me steadfast'" (102).

The moment arrives when both would give themselves up to their respective fates. As the father takes out the blade and puts it to the son's throat, they are both rescued:

> We called out to him, saying, "Abraham, you have fulfilled what you were ordered in the dream." Thus do We reward the righteous. That was indeed a bitter test. We ransomed his son with a noble sacrifice and bestowed upon him peace for all generations to come. (104–109)

The parable is another example that God's testing of mankind is grave and extensive, and that true faith is more than mere lip service, but entails perseverance and total submission to God.

The surah directs Muhammad to ask the unbelievers: "...if it be true that God has only daughters while they themselves have male offspring?" (149). The Arabs were loathe to have baby daughters, considering it a sign of weakness and misfortune, and would bury them alive at birth, but they believed that the angels were daughters of God. The surah ridicules their practise and dismisses their allegation, implying that they had no understanding of, or respect for, God Almighty. It asks sarcastically: "Did We create the angels female, and did they witness their creation?" (150).

Earlier in the surah, Muhammad was directed to ask the unbelievers: "...if they deem themselves a more formidable creation than the rest of Our creation. We formed them out of malleable clay" (11). That argument came in the context of God's great and tremendous power.

On both occasions, the aim is to expose the shallowness and the absurdity of the unbelievers' concept of godhead and their inane image of God. God has no offspring of any kind: jinn, human, or angelic; nor is there any such concept as a god of goodness and a god of evil. Such beliefs can only find favor with ignorant and superstitious people. There is but one God.

The Arabs would also claim that, had they been given a heavenly Book like the Jews and the Christians, they would have proved more loyal and devout. The surah tells us: "They say, 'Had we received Revelation as the ancients had done, we would have become true servants of God'" (167–169).

Some earlier communities had come to believe only after much persuasion, and Revelation brought them power and dominance, but some of the Arabs rejected God's word when it was revealed to them. Many communities, however, deviated and had to face the consequences. The surah says: "We have long promised Our Messengers that they would prevail. Our armies shall be victorious" (171–173). The victory promised by God Almighty only comes after much travail and exertion, and after the people have proved their entitlement to it. The surah says:

> So allow them some respite, and wait to see their downfall as they face the consequences of their disbelief. How dare they provoke Our scourge! Dismal shall be the morning when it falls upon those who had been forewarned. (174–177)

The instruction to persevere and await the outcome is repeated once more before the surah is concluded.

Ṣād

THIS SURAH OPENS WITH ACCLAMATION for the Qur'an and the high position and honor it commands in this world. It says: "By the highly acclaimed Qur'an" (1).

As we read elsewhere in the Qur'an, such high status would also be granted to its followers: "We have revealed to you a Book in which there is a reminder for you. Will you not then take heed?" (al-Anbiyā': 10).

The Qur'an also acts as a reminder, evoking awareness and attention, as borne out by the Qur'anic statement: "We have made the Qur'an easy to remember, but will any take heed?" (al-Qamar: 40). There are always those who are too proud to accept the truth, but they face a dismal end, sooner or later!

Muhammad was met with rejection and abuse:

> They were surprised that a warner should arise among them. The unbelievers say, "This is a sorcerer and a liar. He claims that the gods are but one God. This is indeed a strange notion." (4–5)

Nevertheless, Muhammad was told to: "Bear with what they say, and remember Our servant David (Dāwūd), who was a strong man; he always turned [to God]" (17).

It is interesting to note that Muhammad was being comforted by the example of David and Solomon, two prophets who were also powerful kings of their people. To dispel the misconception that

494

only the poor and weak prophets experience trouble and hardship, Muhammad is told that powerful and wealthy ones also faced difficulties in fulfilling their divine mission.

The surah then goes on to relate an episode from David's life, saying:

> Have you heard the story of the two disputants who climbed the wall into his place of worship. He was alarmed as they entered, but they said, "Have no fear. We have a dispute: one of us has wronged the other. Judge equitably between us and do not be partial..." (21–22)

The injured party explained his case saying: "'This is my brother. He owns ninety-nine ewes, but I own only one. He demanded that I should entrust it to him, and got the better of me in the dispute.'" (23) The culprit maintained a guilty silence as David spoke, saying: "'He has certainly wronged you in seeking to add your ewe to his flock. Many partners are often unjust to one another...'" (24)

David soon realized that it was he who was the target of this lesson. For it happened that David, who had several wives, had cast his eyes on another woman already spoken for by one of his subjects. And what chance would a commoner have against a prophet king?! David had simply overruled his subject.

To draw David's attention to that grave error, God Almighty sent him those two brothers seeking his arbitration. The surah continues:

> David realized that We had put him to the test, and so he sought his Lord's forgiveness, and fell down prostrating and repented. We forgave him that misdemeanor. He shall be close to Us and in the hereafter he shall be well received. (24–25)

Although a wealthy man, David, in my view, was also grateful. I believe he did indulge his personal enjoyment of the vast wealth God had given him. He should, however, have known better than to covet a woman already spoken for by someone else; even if he had approached her first, he would have been expected to show more magnanimity by giving precedence to the other contender. Whatever the case might have been, the point was made and David had been forgiven by God, and so the surah goes on to speak highly of him. It says:

> David, We have appointed you a master in the land. Rule with jus-tice among the people and do not yield to caprice, lest it should turn you away from God's path. (26)

The prophet king had committed an error. It was a grave mistake that could have been his undoing, but he had felt the pain and turned quickly to God for forgiveness. His power and wealth did not shield him from being made accountable and put to the test.

The rejection and the reversals Muhammad was experiencing in Makkah weighed less heavily, and God had honored him with the Qur'an as the final and all-embracing Book of Revelation. He was also given the profound knowledge that would help him avoid falling into error and would lead him to the truth and to God Almighty. God says:

> Would We equate the believers who do good works with those who spread corruption on earth? Would We equate the righteous with the ungodly? This is a blessed Book that We have revealed to you [Muhammad], so that they might contemplate its verses and the wise might take heed. (28–29)

The Jews accused their prophet David of committing adultery and murder. They claimed that he was intimate with Uriah's wife and had conspired to kill him so that he could have her for himself. The Qur'an, however, speaks very highly of this honorable man and clears him of all the obscenities associated with him.

The king prophets were by no means indulgent, wasteful people. They did strive hard to employ their wealth and power for the service and pleasure of God.

The surah tells us about Solomon and says: "We gave Solomon to David, and he was a good and faithful servant" (30). Solomon was mobilizing his army to send them to the people of Yemen and their sovereign, the Queen of Sheba, who were sun-worshipers, inviting them to believe in the One God. His message to them, as we read elsewhere in the Qur'an, was: "Do not exalt yourselves above me, and come to me as Muslims" (al-Naml: 31).

Solomon mobilized an army of horsemen and took pride in inspecting them and appreciating their beauty for considerable periods of time. He was fond of raising warhorses and considered a vocation that would give him favor with God Almighty. The surah says:

> When, one afternoon, his prancing steeds were ranged before him, he said, "My love for good things has distracted me from the remembrance of my Lord." By then the sun had gone down. "Bring them back to me," he said, and started stroking their legs and necks. (31–33)

He was clearly in awe of the horses. Some commentators understood the Arabic original to mean that when the steeds were brought back to Solomon he fell to hacking their legs and necks. But this would be an absurd interpretation.

The surah then says: "We put Solomon to the test and placed a body upon his throne, and then he repented" (34). This is clearly a reference to some event, which I have not been able to verify, which caused Solomon to turn to God in repentance and ask His forgiveness. It is reported that Solomon insisted one day to sleep with a hundred—or one thousand, according to the Old Testament version—of his wives in a single night, who would conceive and give birth to a hundred knights to defend the cause of God. The result was, according to the reports, only one stillborn baby whose body was brought to Solomon on his throne!

I find this story rather fantastic, for Solomon would neither have had the stamina nor the time to accomplish such a feat. Nor could he have been certain that conception would have taken place in every case or that every offspring would have been a knight.

Solomon was a great king of his people, but it is noteworthy that he was also diligent, pious, repentant, and deeply knowledgeable. God described him as "a good and faithful servant" (30). Out of his faith in God and in acknowledgment of His generosity, Solomon asked for greater wealth and power. He saw that God had bestowed favors on all kinds of people, and he felt the urge to receive more and prayed to God saying: "'My Lord, forgive me and bestow upon me such power as shall belong to none after me. You are the Granter of Bounties [without measure]'" (35).

God's bounty is indeed boundless, and Solomon, it appears, wanted to be more powerful than all his rivals, of whom there were several who wished him no good at all. He could have also wished for a degree of power and dominance higher than everyone else for all time to come.

God says: "We harnessed for him the wind, blowing softly at his bidding wherever he directed it; and the devils, every builder and diver, as well as others bound with chains" (36–38).

Despite all this opulence and splendor, Solomon died sitting on his throne while issuing orders to his army of jinn and humans. This surah confirms that he had been assured a better life in the hereafter: "He shall be close to Us and in the hereafter he shall be well received" (40).

The surah talks of another wealthy prophet, Job (Ayyūb), who was stricken by a debilitating ailment, and says: "Remember, too, Our servant Job. He called out to his Lord, saying, 'Satan has afflicted me with hardship and misfortune'" (41). Satan does not cause physical harm, and the meaning here is that Satan was throwing doubt and despair into Job's mind as a result of the suffering and anguish he was experiencing. Elsewhere in the Qur'an we read: "And [mention] Job when he called out to his Lord, saying, 'I am sorely afflicted. But You are the Most Merciful of all'" (*al-Anbiyā'*: 83).

He was praying that his physical ailment might be alleviated to enable him to regain his strength and confidence and overcome those doubts. He was instructed thus: "Stamp your foot, and a cool spring will gush forth. Wash yourself and drink of it." (42) Job was cured and, "We gave him his people and as many more with them: a blessing from Us and an admonition to those who reflect." (43) The thinking people are those who learn the lessons of history and strive to strengthen their trust in God.

The surah goes on to refer to six other prophets including Abraham, his son Isaac (Isḥāq) and his grandson Jacob (Yaʿqūb), describing them as men of might and vision. This is an indication that religious faith signifies strength, perception and understanding, and a higher level of human experience. The surah says:

We made them [the prophets] pure in their devotion to the hereafter. And verily they were, in Our sight, among the elect and the truly good. (46–47)

The other three prophets are Ishmael [Ismāʿīl], Elisha [al-Yasāʿ] and Dhū'l-Kifl, all of whom are described as righteous.

Verses 17 to 54 indicate that a good reputation, which merits a mention in God's Book, is a blessing from God to His deserving servants, elevating their status, granting them a new lease of life, and assuring them of generous rewards. A Muslim dedicates all his

actions and works to the pleasure of God rather than the appeasement of fellow humans. Once God approves of those actions, one
would receive love and praise from others. Furthermore, there is the
reward in the hereafter. The surah says:

> This is but an admonition. The righteous shall return to a blessed
> retreat: gardens of Eden, whose gates shall open wide to receive
> them. They shall sit reclining there and will be served plenty of fruit
> and drink. (49–51)

In contrast, the enemies of God who set themselves up to resist
His revelation shall receive a different treatment. The surah says:
"But the end of the transgressors shall be doleful. They shall burn in
hell, a dismal resting place" (55–56).

The Qur'an takes us to the scene of another exchange between
leaders and their followers. The leaders who are already in hell will
be told: "'Here is another group being thrown into hell with you.
No welcome shall await them; they shall be promptly cast into the
fire'" (59).

The second group are from the followers, but their leaders refuse
to welcome them although they had supported them in this world.
They shall reply saying: "'No welcome for you either! You brought
this upon us, a gloomy end for us all'" (60).

One can only be amazed at what the transgressors would say in
the hereafter when they recall life in this world. They would remember what they had done to those they tormented and persecuted, and
ask: "'Where are those people we used to think were evil? We used
to laugh at them. Why can we not see them?'" (62–63). These would
be the believers whom the unbelievers used to scoff at, and they
would be in Paradise. That is one example of: "the wrangling of the
people of hell" (64).

Towards the end, the surah reverts to the main theme, introduced at the beginning, where the unbelievers accuse Muhammad

of being a sorcerer and denounce his declaration of *tawḥīd* (verses 4 and 5). In response, Prophet Muhammad is instructed to: "Say, 'I am but a warner. There is no god but God, the One, the Supreme'" (65).

The essence of Muhammad's mission is that there is only one God in this world. He is the Master and all else are His subjects. Muhammad made that principle very clear, but some people remained blind to it. The surah says:

> Say, "This [the Qur'an] is a great message, to which you take no heed. I had no knowledge of the arguments among the angels. It has been revealed to me that I am only an honest warner." (67–70)

Muhammad made very clear to his people that he had no previous knowledge of the arguments and disputes taking place among the angels, and that he only knew what was revealed to him from God. Elsewhere in the Qur'an, we read: "You were not present on the western side of the mountain when We charged Moses with his mission, nor did you witness the event" (*al-Qaṣaṣ*: 44).

Muhammad was chosen to receive the Qur'an and explain the essence of *tawḥīd* to his followers, rejecting all types of polytheism and bringing humankind in touch with the one God, to whom everything submits. The surah closes saying:

> Say, "For this I ask no recompense from you. Nor do I pretend to be what I am not. This is but an admonition to humankind, and you shall before long know its truth." (86–88)

SURAH 39

Al-Zumar
(The Crowds)

THE ARABIC TITLE OF THIS SURAH means 'groups' or 'hordes' or 'crowds' of people. This word is used in no other surah of the Qur'an. The surah deals with the behavior patterns and conditions of various human groups, and presents approximately ten ways of comparing them. These revolve around the principle of *tawḥīd*, its features and its influence on human life.

Polytheism, the allegiance to and recognition of more than one god, has plagued human history and disgraced the behavior of humankind, past and present.

How could intelligent, sensible human beings prostrate before a statue made of stone, or fear it? How could an airplane pilot believe that his safety and that of his plane are determined by a horseshoe that would bring him luck? Humankind have a lot to answer for in their behavior, but their abject ignorance of God must be the first and foremost.

Human beings would do well to have faith and trust in the Creator and recognize His absolute perfection, but some have taken other gods beside Him, in the form of statues, purported to be symbols of the Divine Being. They justify that by saying: "We worship them only that they may bring us nearer to God" (3).

These man-made deities mean nothing; they are figments of man's imagination and should be discarded. The issue of godhead is far more crucial and serious, and if God Almighty wished to have mediators between Him and His creation, He would have chosen a more superior means. The surah says: "Had it been His will to adopt a son, God would have chosen whom He pleased out of His creation. Glorified is He, the One, the Almighty" (4). Had God ever wished to have offspring, he would have selected the best human or angelic creature, which would still have been a created entity, not a creator, and a servant of God, abiding by His commands.

God's power is above all powers, and all creatures should serve and submit to Him alone. Polytheists, pagans as well as others, overlook this basic fact and confuse the Creator with His creation. *Tawḥīd* is only valid with the belief in one God, and one God only; all else is subservient to Him.

The Qur'an is at the forefront of religious books that have established this truth and have gone a long way to affirm its principles. In this surah, we have a consistent assertion of the concept of *tawḥīd*.

This Book is revealed by God, the Almighty, the Wise. We have revealed the Book to you [Muhammad] with the truth: so worship God, offering Him sincere devotion. (1–2)

God has revealed the best of scriptures, in the form of a Book, consistent with itself, [yet] repeating [its teachings in different ways]. The skins of those who fear their Lord tremble thereat, then their skin and their hearts soften to the remembrance of God... (23)

We have given humankind in this Qur'an all manner of parables, so that they may take heed. (27)

We have revealed the Book to you [Muhammad] with the truth, for the benefit of humankind. Those who take heed shall do so for their own good... (41)

Follow the best of what has been revealed to you from your Lord before punishment befalls you, when you are unaware. (55)

Verily, My revelations did come to you, but you denied them and were arrogant; you had no faith at all. (59)

At the beginning of the surah, there is a lengthy passage dealing with the attributes of God, especially His attribute as Creator and the manifestations of His power as seen in the heavens and on the earth, and in man and the animals. This forms a fitting prelude for the portraits of the behavior and features of various groups of humankind that follow. In the first of these portraits we are told:

If you deny God, know that He is in no need of your recognition, and that He does not approve of ingratitude in His servants. God does not wish ingratitude for His servants. If you are thankful, however, God would be pleased with you. No soul will bear another's burden... (7)

Human beings, in fact, are overwhelmed by God's grace and generosity. They live off the earth He has created; they breathe the air He has made available; they eat the nutritious food He has provided. Many, of course, forget all this and behave towards God as if He does not exist at all. Nevertheless, these very people would run to God in times of hardship, but as soon as they are out of danger, they revert to their disgraceful attitudes. The Qur'an tells us elsewhere:

When the waves, like giant shadows, engulf them, they pray to God in all sincerity and devotion. But no sooner does He bring them safe to land, some of them hold back their belief. None will deny our revelations except the treacherous and the ungrateful. (*Luqmān*: 32)

Gratitude is a sign of common sense and an honorable nature. When God praised Noah, He described him as "a thankful servant" (*al-Isrā'*: 3), and He praised Abraham as "grateful for his Lord's favors. He has chosen him and guided him to the straight path" (*al-Naml*: 121).

When Prophet Muhammad was asked why he devoted so much time to prayer and dedication to God, he replied: "Should I not be a grateful servant of my Lord?" People must be made aware of these facts and exhorted not to abuse the favors God has bestowed upon them. The surah presents another portrait of contrasts, directing Muhammad to ask his audience:

"...Can he who spends the night in adoration [of God], prostrating and standing, in dread of the terrors of the life to come and pleading for the mercy of his Lord, [be like him who sleeps all through the night]? Are those who know the same as those who are ignorant?... " (9)

The hours of the night are a time for reflection and devotion to God (Arabic: *qiyām al-layl*), and should not be spent in pursuit of frivolous or self-indulgent activities. The Prophet is reported to have said:

Devote some hours during the night in prayer, because it was the habit of the pious people before you and it endears you to your Lord. It is a chance to remember your misdemeanors, keeps you away from wrongdoing and protects your body against ailment.

He went even further in extolling the virtues of prayer by night when he said: "Any one of you who goes to bed at night intending to wake up later to pray and fails to do so before the morning, he shall be rewarded, and the sleep he had would be a gift from his Lord!"

Qiyām al-layl is a highly recommended act of worship. What we read in this surah would, to my understanding, most likely refer to the observance of the obligatory prayer. Nevertheless, it could also be understood to mean that one ought to devote certain nights in the week to study, prayer and the recitation of the Qur'an, while giving one's body its full share of rest on the other nights.

It is only natural that people vary widely in their aptitude and stamina, and while some can go without sleep for the whole night and be satisfied with just one or two hours' rest, others are not able to function without a full night's sleep.

The next contrast is between the pious, charitable people who have full faith and trust in God and His Messenger, and who have reined in their whims and desires and surrendered their will totally to God Almighty, and those who are consumed by worldly pleasures and their own desires, totally oblivious of God and His judgment. The former follow the example of the Prophet, who said: "I fear, if I disobey my Lord, the torment of a fateful day" (13). The latter are reassured that: "The real losers are those who forfeit their souls and all their kinfolk on the Day of Resurrection. That shall be the ultimate loss" (15).

Multitudes of people struggle very hard in this world to live in affluence with their families and kinfolk, and amass as much wealth and influence as they can, but on the Day of Judgment they shall meet their Lord stripped totally of all their power and wealth. The surah captures this example in these words:

Let those who shun idol-worship and turn to God in repentance rejoice. Give good news to My servants, who listen to what is said to them and follow the best of it... (17–18)

In the next portrait, the Qur'an offers a comparison between those who are guided and those who are destined to hellfire, where the first group is mentioned implicitly. God asks the Prophet Muhammad, rhetorically: "Can you rescue those condemned to hellfire?" (19).

The meaning here is that the wrong-doers have earned their humiliation and cannot be judged similarly to those who fear God and deserve His generosity. Those condemned by God can only be saved by Him.

Then the surah tells us about the rewards awaiting the God-fearing:

But it is for those who fear their Lord, that lofty mansions, one above another, have been built: Beaneath them flow rivers [of delight]: [such is] the Promise of Allah: Never does Allah fail in [His] Promise. (20)

In the next portrait, God says:

He whose heart God has opened to Islam shall be guided by light from his Lord. But woe to those whose hearts are hardened against the remembrance of God... (22)

Once one's heart opens up to Islam, one's body and soul willingly rise to the service of God. The other side of the portrait is represented by those whose hearts are closed to the truth and refuse to heed the call of God. These would be loathe to meet their obligations towards God, such as salah, zakah and jihad. The next verse affirms this fact by saying:

God has revealed the best of scriptures, in the form of a Book, consistent with itself, [yet] repeating [its teachings in different ways]. The skins of those who fear their Lord tremble thereat, then their skin and their hearts soften to the remembrance of God... (23)

The Qur'an is the source of wisdom and guidance, a protection against wrongdoing, and a certain means of adherence to God's universal truth.

In the next portrait, the surah draws a contrast between him who is safe from punishment on the Day of Judgment and:

He who shields himself from the horrors of the Day of Judgment with his own face. To the wrong-doers We shall say, "Taste the punishment which you have earned." (24)

507

They are definitely not the same! The wrong-doers are so over-whelmed by punishment that they will not have time to protect their faces, the first part of the body one normally tries to protect.

The surah goes further to hint that the punishment might even come in this life:

> Those who have gone before them also disbelieved, so the scourge overtook them unawares. God made them live in disgrace in this life, but the punishment in the life to come shall be more terrible, if they but knew it. (25–26)

The comparison in the next portrait revolves around the principles of *tawḥīd* and loyalty. It is a comparison between those who seek the pleasure of God and those who seek the appeasement of other deities, be they human or otherwise. One could say with certainty that there are people in this world whose hearts and minds are totally devoid of the love and respect of God, and are preoccupied instead with loyalty and devotion to others, including the so-called 'heroes' and 'stars,' following their desires and their greed to amass wealth or 'win votes'!

A true believer prays to God, gives for the sake of God, and fights for the cause of God. He is consistent and well-focused. The surah says:

> God makes a comparison between a man with several masters who are at odds with one another, and another who has one master, to whom he is devoted. Are these two to be held alike? God be praised! But most of them are ignorant. (29)

Yet another comparison is made:

> Who is more wicked than a man who invents a falsehood about God and denies the truth when it is declared to him? Is there not

a home in hell for the unbelievers? Those who proclaim the truth, and give credence to it, are surely the God-fearing. (32–33)

Truth is precious, and those who are able to recognize, embrace, and proclaim it are rare, and deserve all praise and admiration. The wicked, on the other hand, fabricate lies about God, and when directed to the truth they turn away and refuse to accept it. Those who uphold the truth are promised that:

> Their Lord shall give them all that they desire. Thus shall the righteous be rewarded. God will absolve them of their foulest deeds and reward them according to their noblest actions. (34–35)

What a wonderful, beneficent, heart-warming gesture from God Almighty for those who believe!

Then the surah poses an intriguing question: "Is God not all-sufficient for His servant? Yet they threaten you with those they serve besides Him..." (36). God can lift people high or take them to the lowest depths; He can bring them harm or great fortune; He can raise their status or leave them in the gutter, and no power in the world can overrule Him, or revoke or countermand His decision. No one who seeks refuge with God will be left unprotected.

This is the essence of the next portrait of contrast: those who cannot defend themselves are not capable of protecting others. The surah expresses it thus:

> Say, "Do you think that, if God wishes to cause me harm, those you worship besides Him would be able to relieve my affliction; or that if He favored me with mercy, they would be able to withhold His mercy?" Say, "God is sufficient for me; in Him do the faithful put their trust." (38)

Muhammad, and the believers with him, are advised to face those who deny God with the words: "My people, do as best you can and so will I. You shall soon know who will be seized by a scourge that will disgrace him, and be smitten by an everlasting scourge" (39–40).

The next example portrays the huge gap separating the believers from the unbelievers. The truth of the matter is that most wrong-doers are not aware that they are on the wrong path; some are even under the misconception that they are righteous and are ready to justify and defend their position. With reference to such people, the surah says:

> When God alone is mentioned, the hearts of those who deny the hereafter shrink with aversion; but when those they worship besides Him are mentioned, their hearts are filled with joy. (45)

What was the Prophet to do with such people? God tells him to: "Say, 'Lord, Creator of the heavens and the earth, who has knowledge of the unseen and the manifest, You alone can judge between Your servants in their disputes'" (46).

Since the majority of people are usually led by their own whims and desires, the responsibility falls upon those who recognize the truth and believe in it. They ought to be grateful to God for showing them the right path. The surah gives yet another portrait:

> When misfortune befalls man he calls out to Us, but when We bestow favor upon him, he says, "I have earned it myself." By no means! It is but a test; yet most men do not know it. The same was said by those before them: what they had earned did them no good. (49–50)

This attitude seems to be part of man's nature. When he is despairing, he acknowledges his helplessness, repents, falls back on prayer, and resorts to God for help. When his circumstances change for the better, however, and he begins to feel more secure, he forgets his weaknesses and begins to take the credit for regaining his strength and well-being. He should ask himself why he could not conquer the despair and overcome the weakness at the time!

Man's arrogance and lack of faith in God can only lead him to total bankruptcy. As a servant of God, man should know his limits, repent and correct his mistakes as soon as possible. To procrastinate is a sign of impotence and want of will.

The Prophet is reported to have said: "If you commit a transgression, cancel it with a good deed." In this life, a person might reach a point of total despair, surrender to Satan and all his schemes and temptations, and pile up the mistakes and misdemeanors. But no matter how dark the picture may become, this surah tells us that there is always room for hope and salvation. It says: "Say, 'Servants of God, you that have sinned against your souls, do not despair of God's mercy, for he forgives all sins. Verily, He is Oft-Forgiving, Most Merciful'" (53).

The surah presents another portrait, comparing those who never lose hope in God and persist in their pursuit of His pleasure, with those who are consumed with apathy and lag behind. On the Day of Judgment, the latter would say: "'Alas! I disobeyed God and scoffed at His revelations'" (56). God would remind him: "'Yes, indeed. My revelations did come to you, but you denied them. You showed arrogance and were one of those who disbelieved'" (59).

The surah continues to contrast the beliefs and behavior of those who profess faith in God and those who deny Him, and gives more illustrations for both. It says:

On the Day of Resurrection you shall see the faces of those who uttered falsehoods about God blackened. Is there not in hell a home for the vainglorious? But God will deliver those who fear Him, for they have earned salvation. No harm shall touch them, nor shall they grieve. (60–61)

Elsewhere in the Qur'an (*al-Mā'idah*: 119 and *al-Baqarah*: 177), God refers to "those who are truthful" to describe "those who are God-fearing," indicating that truthfulness and fearing God are synonymous in the Qur'anic vernacular.

The surah closes with a vivid portrait, describing how the believers and the unbelievers are respectively treated on the Day of Judgment. The people of hell shall come to realize when it is too late that, since they had neglected God, He will give them no attention. But the people of Paradise shall resume life in comfort, in recompense for their devotion and dedication to God in this life. Elsewhere in the Qur'an we are told: "Their prayer in Paradise shall be, 'Glory be to You, Lord.' Their greeting will be: 'Peace,' and their final praise [will be] to God the Lord of all creation" (*Yūnus*: 10).

In that atmosphere of abounding tranquillity and infinite happiness, the angels also join in praising God Almighty:

You shall see the angels circling round the Throne, praising the glory of their Lord. They shall all be judged with fairness, and shall all say, "Praise be to God, Lord of all creation!" (75)

SURAH 40

Ghāfir
(The Forgiver)

THIS SURAH IS ALSO KNOWN by the title *al-Mu'min* (The Believer). It is the first of a group of seven surahs opening with the two Arabic letters *ḥā'* and *mīm*. ʿAbd Allah ibn ʿAbbās, the prominent Companion, was reported as having said: "Everything has a heart, and *ḥā' mīm* is the heart of the Qur'an."

One is immediately overwhelmed and impressed by the surah's relentless and consistently forceful exposition of the Islamic concept of *tawḥīd*. The surah opens with: "*Ḥā' mīm*. This Book is revealed by God, the Almighty, the Omniscient" (1–2). *Al-ʿAzīz* (the Almighty) and *al-ʿAlīm* (the Omniscient) are two of God's glorious names whose meanings are reflected in the Qur'an that originates from Him. Ibn Kathīr, the classic commentator, points out that this is a confirmation that the Qur'an is protected by God's awesome power and that it can never be obscured or obliterated.

One characteristic of the Qur'an's unique style is that, when addressing humankind with its teachings, it often combines promises with warnings, in order to instill the feelings of fear and hope that balance man's behavior and attitudes. The surah goes on to describe God, saying: "He forgives sins, and accepts repentance; His punishment is severe and His bounty is infinite" (3).

Elsewhere in the Qur'an, we are told: "Know that God is stern of punishment, and that He is Oft-Forgiving, Most Merciful" (*al-Māʾidah*: 98). Man is constantly in need of incentives and deterrents,

513

because his failures can often drive him to despair and bankruptcy, while his arrogance may lead him to apathy and complacency.

Ibn Kathīr reported that an influential man from Syria used to visit ʿUmar ibn al-Khaṭṭāb, the second Caliph, in Madinah regularly; then, one day, having been away for longer than usual ʿUmar enquired after him and was told that the man had taken to drinking heavily. ʿUmar wrote him a letter saying:

> For your sake, I praise God, there is no God but He. He forgives sins and accepts repentance; His punishment is severe and His bounty is infinite. There is no God but He, and all shall return to Him.

He then turned to those around him and asked them to pray that God might accept the man's repentance. When the letter arrived, the man kept repeating the words: "He forgives sins and accepts repentance; His punishment is severe." He was heard saying: "I am being warned of God's punishment and promised His forgiveness," until he broke down sobbing, and from that day he abstained from drinking for good. When the news reached ʿUmar, he said: "This is what you should do when someone commits a misdemeanor. Advise him, reassure him gently, never let him lose his self-confidence, pray to God for his sake, and do not help Satan to mislead him." I cite this incident because today there are professed Muslims who have all but given up on God's mercy, and whose sole preoccupation seems to be to castigate and belittle others.

It is quite interesting that a surah with a title like "The Forgiver" should condemn futile argumentation, arrogance, and the persistence in refusing to accept the truth. It says:

> None but the unbelievers dispute the revelations of God. Do not be deceived by their ostentatious posturing in this life. Long before them the people of Noah denied Our revelations, and so did other

factions after them. Every community strove to slay their messenger, seeking with false arguments to refute the truth; but I seized them, and how severe was My punishment! (4–5)

Such condemnation occurs in the surah on five different occasions, and on each occasion the surah exposes the false attitudes and methods of the unbelievers in dealing with the truth, describing them as stubborn, irrational, unfair, and autocratic. God says elsewhere in the Qur'an:

I will turn away from My revelations the arrogant and the unjust. Whatever sign they witness, they will deny it; even if they see the right path, they will not take it. But if they see the path of error, they immediately choose to walk it, because they have denied Our revelations and completely neglected them. (al-Aʿrāf: 146)

Aggression and injustice are often supported by false contrived argument. All prophets suffered abuse and ill-treatment, and so did their followers in every generation and society.

However, life is a period of trials and appraisals, and sincere people ought to persevere and bear up no matter how oppressive and demanding life may be. The surah reassures the believers that God's angels are watching over them and praying for their guidance and salvation. It says:

Those angels who carry God's Throne and those who stand around it give glory to their Lord and believe in Him. They implore forgiveness for the believers, saying, "Our Lord, You embrace all things with Your mercy and Your knowledge. Forgive those who repent and follow Your path, and shield them from the scourge of hell." (7)

The surah tells of an unidentified Egyptian follower of Moses who embraced his teachings and urged people to abide by them. He reminded the Egyptians, saying: "Joseph had previously come to you with veritable signs, but you persisted in doubting them" (34).

As a faithful proponent of *tawḥīd*, Joseph, in his time, expounded the fundamentals of God's religion and denounced idol-worship. During his period in government, justice prevailed and Egypt was prosperous. Nevertheless, its people never ceased to reject his teachings and cast doubts over them.

Moses, when he was commissioned by God to address the Pharaoh and his people, was greeted with a harsher attitude. The surah comments:

> Thus God confounds every doubting aggressor. Those who dispute God's revelations without any perceived authority, are held in deep abhorrence by God and by the faithful. Thus God seals up the heart of every conceited tyrant. (34–35)

The unidentified 'believer' in this surah comes across as an extremely effective advocate of the truth. At times he appeals to his people, and at others he leans hard on them. He warns them directly, and uses subtle phrases and metaphors, mindful all the while that he needed as much time as possible to elaborate the ideas and principles he was advocating, before alerting Pharaoh's repressive machine. His words have gone down in history as some of the most eloquent ever spoken in defense of God's message to humankind. They have inspired many a believer, not least Abū Bakr, the first Caliph, who quoted them when he decided to take on some of the Arabian tribes who reneged on Islam, following the death of Prophet Muhammad.

Ignorance combined with bigotry and caprice are a great misfortune. The best way to deal with them is through the pursuit of knowledge which is liable to widen one's horizons and strengthen one's resolve and will-power. This is equally true for individuals as well as communities. This surah urges traveling far and wide, in time and space, to learn from history and gain a wider perspective of life and the world. It says:

> Have they [the unbelievers] not looked around them in the world and seen what was the end of those who had gone before them? They were far greater nations than them in prowess and influence on earth. God scourged them for their sins, and they had none to protect them from God. (21)

Human history is full of examples and lessons, and man's progress is governed by laws not unlike the laws of nature that govern the physical world. The study of the history of other communities is essential and can be extremely educational. The surah reiterates the same idea, saying:

> Have they [the unbelievers] not looked around them in the world and seen what was the end of those who had gone before them? They were far more numerous than them and of far greater prowess and influence on earth. Yet all they had achieved was of no avail to them. (82)

The Qur'an explains that this catastrophic outcome was the result of arrogance, a lack of knowledge, and self-satisfaction. It says:

> When their messengers brought them veritable signs they proudly boasted of the knowledge they had; but soon the scourge of their scoffing engulfed them. (83)

Many misguided people persist in their errors and refuse to recognize their mistakes until they are struck with some calamity that brings the truth home to them. The surah says:

Those who dispute the revelations of God, without any perceived authority, nurture in their hearts ambitions they shall never attain. Therefore seek refuge in God; it is He who hears and sees all [things]. (56)

To face the arrogance and intransigence of the unbelievers, one needs to persevere and seek God's assistance, as the surah tells Muhammad and his followers:

Therefore have patience; God's promise is true. Implore forgiveness for your sins, and celebrate the praise of your Lord evening and morning. (55)

Patience should not be restricted to a specific time frame, since the punishment of the wrong-doers may be deferred to beyond the individual's own lifetime. The surah makes it clear that justice is up to God's own judgement, and emphasizes the need for dedication and persistence:

Therefore have patience; God's promise is true. Whether We let you [Muhammad] witness some of the punishment We have promised them [the unbelievers] or cause you to die beforehand, to Us they shall all return. (77)

In the early part of the surah we find instructions to the believers to seek help from God alone and to dedicate their religious veneration to Him only, discounting all other presumed deities, no matter how popular or influential. It says:

Pray, then, to God with sincere devotion, however much the unbelievers may dislike it. He is the Exalter of ranks [of being], Possessor of the Throne, He bestows His inspiration by His own command to those of His servants whom He chooses, as a warning of the impending arrival of the Day they are all gathered for judgment. On that Day they shall all rise up fully laid open before God. (14–16)

The words reverberate with praise for God. They leave an unmistakable feeling of awe and dread towards resurrection and judgment in the hereafter, of which the coming of God's messengers is a sign and a warning.

The same ideas are reiterated later on in the surah, saying: "Your Lord said, 'Call on Me and I shall answer your call. Those that disdain My service shall enter hell in total disgrace…'" (60). The service of God is not even a secondary objective of modern society. It is no more than a faint feeling in the hearts of a religious few.

The surah directly affirms God's power and control over the world on three separate occasions:

1. God made for you the night to rest in and the day to give you light. God has been kind to humankind, yet most of them are ungrateful. (61)

Prophet Muhammad was reported to have taught his followers to thank God on waking up in the morning, saying: "Thanks be to God who gave me back my life and my health and enabled me to remember Him." Every new day is an affirmation of God's abundant grace, and one must make proper use of one's life in this world.

2. God has made the earth a stable place for you, and the sky a canopy to protect you. He has created you in the best form and provided you with the good things of life. God is your Lord. Glorified be God, Lord of all creation. (64)

Is it not remarkable how the earth can revolve around its own axis and travel around the sun, and yet maintain stability and balance?

Only if you have experienced earthquakes would you know how devastating an unstable earth can be. God's power of control over the solar system enables all creatures, great and small, to go about their lives in serenity and perfect order.

> 3. God has provided you with beasts, that you may ride on some and eat the flesh of others. You put them to many uses; they take you where you wish to go, carrying you by land as ships carry you by sea. (79–80)

I was listening to a nature programme on the radio once, and it said that a scientist estimated that there were hundreds of thousands of different kinds of insects in a forest. I was stunned just thinking of how many species there were all over the globe. What natural laws govern the life of these creatures and maintain equilibrium in their relationship to man? As the surah says: "He displays His signs clearly before you. Which of God's signs do you deny?" (81).

Human beings are vain and self-possessed creatures. We are proud of our intelligence and skills, because we are not able to appreciate the whole phenomenon of creation. However, this surah tells us clearly that: "Surely, the creation of the heavens and the earth is far greater than the creation of humankind, but most people do not know it" (57). Really, we ought to show more humility and contain our pride.

Some people have a tendency to believe in something and be happy, and steer away from arguing or justifying their beliefs to others or trying to persuade them of what they believe to be the truth. There might have been relatively more people like that in the past. In today's world, however, it is no longer possible for people to be immune to outside influences. Modern means of mass communication and interdependence have, for example, left ordinary people fully exposed to the eyes and the power of the state.

Modern states possess a complex cobweb of material and moral means that no longer allow people to live in isolation from the rest of society. Dialogue, exchange of ideas, cultural cross-fertilization and opposition, have all become established features of life in the global village. Islam urges constructive dialogue and discourages wrangling and acrimonious disputes. Elsewhere in the Qur'an, God advises Muhammad to: "Requite evil with good. We are fully aware of all their slanders" (*al-Mu'minūn*: 96).

Freedom of thought must be universally respected. Intimidation, arrogance, slander, coercion, and repression must be condemned and rejected by all civilized men. Ever since its inception, Islam has faced all these negative attitudes, and has been opposed and rejected by people who deny the existence and authority of God and submit themselves to undeserving deities of their own creation.

This surah roundly deals with those who favor futile argumentation, and considers the rejection of Islam to be a rejection of all revelation, including the teachings of Moses and Jesus. It says:

> Could you not see how those who dispute the revelations of God turn away from the truth? Those who have denied the Book and the message We sent through Our messengers will one day realize their error. (69)

Many people in the West who profess to be religious detest Islam for the only reason that their fathers and forefathers had opposed it. But how genuine is their belief in Moses and Jesus? Do they really believe in life after death and judgment in the hereafter? They are the product of a materialistic civilization that believes in the here-and-now, and belong to a society that is founded on a morality of permissiveness, injustice, and the superiority of the white race over the rest of humankind.

There is no denying that the Muslims have neglected their heritage and noble mission in this world, but they should do better than to allow themselves to be led blindly into the abyss by this ungodly, heedless civilization.

SURAH 41

Fuṣṣilat
(Revelation Well-Expounded)

THE SURAH OPENS with the words:

> A revelation from the Compassionate, the Merciful. A Book whose
> verses are well expounded; a Qur'an in Arabic for men of under-
> standing. It proclaims good news and gives warnings... (2–4)

Revelation originates with God, the spring of mercy, as guidance to
humankind and protection against the evil of their thoughts, desires,
prejudices, and deeds. It is the source of all the goodness and justice
in this world.

Sensible discerning people appreciate the benefits and the love
these words convey to the true believers, and the warning they make
to the foolish who are oblivious of the truth, but who are often a
majority in society. The surah stresses this fact, saying: "Yet most
men turn their backs and give no heed" (4).

One major feature of the Qur'anic revelation, is that it was
received in the Arabic language. Translations in other languages do
not have the same status as the Arabic original, because God, in His
infinite wisdom, chose the Arabic language to be the medium for
Qur'anic revelation and honored the Arab people with the task of
conveying it to the rest of the world; also, because the translations
only convey the meaning of the Qur'an, they will not have the same
impact as the Arabic version.

In the early days of Islam, the Arabs were reluctant to embrace it, with some of them showing tremendous resistance to it. Prophet Muhammad had to work very hard to persuade them to identify with Islam, defend it with their lives and wealth, then proceed to overrun some of the most powerful and tyrannical empires in history.

Today's Arabs have inherited two of the most vile characteristics: the traditions of their forefathers during the decline of Islamic civilization, and the habits and illusions of today's materialistic and pleasure-seeking Western culture.

There is nothing worse than an agnostic Arab. They are most irrational, bigoted and unjust. The surah could not be more accurate when it quotes their ancestors, saying:

"Our hearts are sealed against that to which you [Muhammad] are calling us. Our ears are blocked, and there is a huge divide between us and you. Do as you see fit, and so will we." (5)

Nevertheless, God has chosen them and their language for the unique honor of conveying His message to the world. God says:

Had We revealed the Qur'an in a language other than the Arabic tongue they would have said, "If only it were clearer! How could an Arab [Muhammad] convey a revelation in a foreign tongue?" Say, "To true believers it is a guide and a panacea. But those who deny it are deaf and blind. It is as if they are being addressed from a distant place." (44)

Arabism is not determined by race alone; anyone who has mastered Arabic, the language of the Qur'an, would become Arab. Numerous converts to Islam of Persian and Roman ancestry have rendered far more valuable services to the Qur'an and the Arabic language than many who were born in the heart of Arabia. As long as people's hearts and other faculties are free to receive Muhammad's message, they would be able to understand and appreciate it. He is instructed to proclaim:

> Say, "I am but a mortal human being like you, and it is revealed to me that your Lord is the One God. Therefore submit directly to Him and implore His forgiveness. Woe to those who serve other gods besides Him; who give no alms and deny the life to come." (6–7)

Such moderate duties: to submit to the One God, seek His forgiveness, and be charitable towards the poor and the needy. But for arrogant and selfish people, they seem difficult tasks, and their end would, therefore, be bleak.

The Qur'an warns the Arabs, then as now, that the more they persist in their rejection of God's universal truth and His Messenger, Muhammad, the more certain it is that they would meet the end of their ancestors, ʿĀd and Thamūd. The surah says: "If they turn away say to them, 'I warn you of a thunderbolt, like that which struck ʿĀd and Thamūd'" (13).

Why were the people of ʿĀd destroyed? "They were unjustifiably arrogant in the land, and would say, 'Who is mightier than us?'" (15). Why were the people of Thamūd destroyed? "As for Thamūd, We offered them guidance but they preferred to remain blind rather than be guided" (17).

ʿĀd's ingratitude towards God and their contempt for their fellow human beings, and Thamūd's deviation from the true path and their preference for falsehood were the causes for their downfall. Other nations that follow in their footsteps shall face a similar fate, because God never allows corrupt works to bear fruit, and a look at the attitude of today's Arab nations towards Islam can, alas, inspire only pessimism!

The punishment that God's enemies may receive in this life would not suffice: "As God's enemies are brought forth altogether and led into the fire, their ears, eyes and their skins shall testify against them..." (19–20). Sight and hearing have been bestowed upon human beings to enable them to recognize and appreciate God's marvels of creation and use their intellect to seek God's greatness in this vast universe. If man suspends these faculties and does not use them as a means to seek God, they shall be the first to testify to that before God on the Day of Judgment, and he shall face a despicable end.

We note a long pause between the presentation of the message and the fate promised to its detractors, during which the surah talks about creation and the vast system of the cosmos. It says:

> Say, "Do you deny the Lord of all creation, who created the earth in two days, and make other gods His equals?" He set upon the earth mountains to stabilize it, bestowed His blessings on it, and in four days equitably apportioned its means of sustenance to all who seek it. (9–10)

Man was created out of clay and lives off the earth's goodness and resources. God has appointed him a representative and a custodian on earth to serve God who had blown life into him. Nevertheless, man tends to disregard his responsibilities and exceed his limits.

Science tells us that the solar system was created first, while the Qur'an says: "God created the heavens and the earth and then made darkness and light" (*al-Anʿām*: 1). Mankind came much later, once the earth was prepared and made habitable and adequately provided with all the necessary means that would sustain life on it. Man is often reminded in the Qur'an to consider this earth upon which he is living and make his choice whether to believe in God or not. The contemplation of material and physical phenomena that exist on this earth is conducive to bringing man closer to belief in God.

Halfway through the surah we are told about worlds of other creatures, such as jinn and angels, that can influence man's life and behavior, for better or for worse. Advocates of materialism deny the existence of these creatures simply because of lack of material evidence, but Muslims appreciate matter as well as an existence beyond the material world leading them to acknowledge, in addition to the human world, the worlds of jinn and angels.

Among the jinn, we believe, there are righteous individuals as well as ones we know as satanic that seek to mislead humans and influence them to disobey God and neglect their obligations towards Him.

The most well-known of the jinn is Satan (Iblīs) who took advantage of Adam's weakness and deceived him by persuading Adam to eat of the forbidden tree and be expelled from the Garden of Eden. Adam's first failing was his forgetfulness and the weakness of his will-power, which were both quickly exploited by Satan.

Satan and his supporters adopted a similar approach in their fight against Islam when it first emerged. God says:

> We have assigned to them [the enemies of Islam] companions to encourage and abet them. They well deserve the fate of earlier generations of jinn and humans, and they would certainly be losers. The unbelievers say, "Do not listen to the Qur'an, and talk aloud when it is being recited, so that you may gain the upper hand." (25–26)

The unbelievers rejected the Qur'an and refused to listen to it, following Satan's insinuations to heckle and interrupt every time it was recited so as to prevent others from being influenced by it. Such an attitude represents the epitome of cowardice on their part, an indication of their inability to argue their case and defend their beliefs.

This is a characteristic of all who turn away from the truth, and the surah affirms that they shall regret their behavior:

The unbelievers say, "Our Lord, show us the jinn and the men who led us astray and we shall crush them beneath our feet so that they become the vilest (of all)." (29)

On the other hand, the people who had opened their hearts and minds to God's universal truth and rallied around it, shall be welcomed and well looked after by the angels:

Those who say, "God is our Lord," and behave righteously, the angels shall descend upon them, saying, "Fear nothing, do not grieve, and rejoice in the Paradise you have been promised..." (30)

Most commentators are of the view that the dying are reminded of this verse as they prepare to depart to the next world, in order to reassure them about those they are leaving behind, as well as the happiness that is awaiting them.

We find no objection to this interpretation which seems to go with the context that the angels descend on the believers at times of struggle and inspire and assist them to seek and find the truth. The Prophet was reported to have told someone who had praised God well that he had been assisted by a benevolent angel, and he would tell the renowned Muslim poet, Ḥassān ibn Thābit, that the Archangel Gabriel (Jibrīl) was lending him support.

Whereas devils encourage evil, the angels, however, assist with good and righteous acts, but in the final analysis, men are judged by their attitudes and actual behavior.

Satan is undoubtedly shrewd and resourceful in his main task of misleading humans and turning them away from God's true path, which makes the need to remind people of God and educate them to seek Him all the more urgent. This consciousness of God and His message is liable to uphold the truth, promote it and counteract the efforts of Satan and his cronies. The surah says: "Who speaks better than he who calls others to God, acts righteously and says, 'I am a Muslim'?" (33).

God's messengers have provided the universal role-model in this regard, whose struggle has been the cornerstone for righteous belief in this world. Their most effective approach was to acquaint people with their God and endear Him to them. The surah contains a host of verses that urge people to draw closer to God.

And among His signs are the night and the day, and the sun and the moon. But do not prostrate yourselves before the sun or the moon; rather prostrate yourselves before God who created them both... (37)

And among His signs is that you see the earth dry and barren, but no sooner do We send down the rain upon it than it is revived and flourishes... (39)

With Him rests knowledge of the Hour. No fruit is borne, no female conceives or delivers except with His knowledge. (47)

Regrettably, our efforts to propagate Islam are lacking, and in parts of the world are sometimes non-existent. The Arabs' neglect of their special obligation in this respect is completely indefensible. They have become preoccupied with their selfish pursuits and petty squabbles, thereby losing their power and undermining the message of Islam. The following verses might very well have been meant for them:

Those who deny Our signs are well-known to Us... (40)

Those who deny Our message when it comes to them [shall meet a stern punishment]. It is an exalted scripture that could not, nor shall ever, be corrupted... (41–42)

The universal message of Muhammad embraces all other revealed messages, and Muslims thereby are the custodians of God's revelation for all time to come. This is implied in the statement: "Nothing is being said to you that has not been said to the messengers before you..." (43). The surah tells us that the Israelites neglected their religious responsibilities:

We have given Moses the Book, but his people were divided over it. Had you, Lord, not deferred their judgment, He would have settled their fate there and then. (45)

Nevertheless, the Jews today remain far more active in the service of their heritage and culture than the Muslims, allocating vast facilities and resources for that purpose. The surah closes with statements specifically addressed to the Arabs, past and present:

Say, "Have you considered how heedless you would be if this Qur'an is indeed from God and you reject it? None is more heedless than he who is deeply in the wrong." (52)

And:

We shall manifest Our signs for them all over the cosmos and in their own souls until they see clearly that this is God's universal truth. Does it not suffice that your Lord is witness unto all things? (53)

With every day that passes, more aspects of the Qur'an's veracity and power are revealed and further proof emerges for the integrity and authority of Muhammad's message of pure *tawḥīd*. Mankind has yet to come up with a god other than the One God who has sent the Prophet we know and laid down laws and rules for the organization of individual and social life that have yet to be challenged and fully implemented.

No! They remain in doubt that they will meet their Lord, but He encompasses all things. (54)

SURAH 42

Al-Shūrā
(Counsel)

THE SURAH OPENS WITH five separated letters of the Arabic alphabet, an indication that the Qur'an is composed of these familiar letters, in pure and lucid Arabic style. It then goes on to say: "Thus God, the Almighty, the Wise, reveals to you as He has revealed to others before you" (3). God commissioned prophets who spoke the language of their respective peoples, and Muhammad conveyed God's message faithfully as it was revealed to him and was the role-model *par excellence* for its understanding and implementation.

His Companions and followers emulated his example with diligence, but evil and wrongdoing continue to flourish in this world because people tend to neglect God's revelation or ignore it, proving that, of all God's creation, man continues to be the single most rebellious and insubordinate being. "[While] the angels sing the glory of their Lord and beg forgiveness for those on earth. God is Oft-Forgiving, Most Merciful" (5).

Reference to revelation is made at the beginning as well as at the end of this surah, while in between it presents the essence of God's final message to humankind whose promotion and propagation was entrusted to the Arab nation, explaining the relationship between it and earlier communities who were given the scripture.

Thus We have revealed to you [Muhammad] the Qur'an in Arabic in order that you may warn the people of the mother-city [Makkah] and their neighbors of the impending day when all are brought forth, some would go to Paradise and some to hell. (7)

Islam is an everlasting, universal and comprehensive message, addressed to all humankind, with a definite beginning in time and a birthplace in Makkah in Arabia, and the whole world as its domain. Muhammad and his generation fulfilled their obligations admirably so that, within less than fifty years, Islam had conquered two of the most powerful empires and was challenging the supremacy of powers in Asia and Africa.

But what of the earlier bearers of God's revelation? The Jews had turned religion into an ethnocentric heritage to cherish and take pride in, while under the Christians, the true principles of religion were overtaken by the doctrines of the Trinity, salvation, and the endless arguments over Jesus as the son of God.

Islam announced its close relationship to Moses and Jesus right from the outset, affirming that its message was a revival and an endorsement of theirs. The surah tells us:

He [God] has ordained for you [the believers] the faith He enjoined on Noah, and what We have revealed to you [Muhammad], that which We had enjoined on Abraham, Moses, and Jesus, that you should uphold the true faith and preserve its unity. The polytheists will find it hard to respond to your call. God brings closer to Him whomever He wills and He guides those who turn to Him in repentance. (13)

The truth of the matter is that God's religion is one universal message, the same ever since man set foot on this earth, and it shall remain so until the end of human life. The seven heavens, the earth, and all that is in them praise God's glory. God created the human race and bestowed upon them endless bounties; all humans are servants of the Almighty. The closest of them to His domain are those who worship and submit with diligence and humility. These concepts, the essence of Muhammad's message, are clearly expounded throughout the Qur'an.

Man's rational and intellectual faculties have led him to recognize God, who has been highly revered, praised, and exalted in the Qur'anic revelation received by Muhammad, which, in turn, substantiates the truth and authenticity of his message. What Muhammad said and taught about God, His power and attributes, is fully corroborated by rational and intellectual argument.

Those who accuse Muhammad of being a liar and an impostor are, in fact, offending against God as well. The surah says:

> They [the followers of earlier revelation] became divided, out of aggression towards one another, only after the truth had come to them. Had it not been for a word already given by your Lord to defer their punishment to the set date, matters would have been settled forthwith. Those who have inherited the Book from them are now in grave doubt over it. (14)

Muhammad was very firmly directed to ignore the jealousy and spite some Jews and Christians harbored against Islam and Muslims and to go ahead with his mission:

> Therefore call men to the true faith and follow the straight path as you are bidden. Do not be led by their whims and desires, but say, "I believe in all the revelation that God has sent down, and I have been commanded to establish justice among you. God is our Lord and your Lord. We are accountable for our deeds and you are accountable for your deeds; let there be no contention between us. God shall bring us all together, and to Him all shall return." (15)

Nothing could stop the spread of Islam which continued, by peaceful and civilized means, and was welcomed by Jews and Christians in Central Asia and North Africa as well as by pagans in Persia, Azerbaijan, India, and China.

Others, in Europe and America, continue up to the present day to resist Islam and undermine the integrity of Muhammad, but their opposition is not likely to hamper God's will. The surah assures the Muslims that:

> The wrangling of those who argue about God, after His message has been widely accepted, shall have no weight with their Lord; His wrath shall fall upon them, and a grievous punishment awaits them. (16)

The surah resumes its account of more of the arguments put forward by God's enemies and Muhammad's detractors. It says:

> Or do they say, "He [Muhammad] has fabricated lies and attributed them to God"? But if God wished, He could seal your heart, and wipe out falsehood, and establish the truth by His words. God knows what the innermost hearts contain. (24)

If Muhammad were an impostor, God would have exposed him and obliterated all traces of his vile works. Elsewhere in the Qur'an, God says:

> Had he [Muhammad] invented lies about Us, We would have seized him by the right hand and severed the veins of his heart, and none of you could have protected him. (*al-Ḥāqqah*: 44–47)

Islam found its way to many parts of the globe and became a way of life for people worldwide. The Islamic daily call to prayer can be heard in almost every country, proclaiming the Oneness of God and the truthfulness and honesty of the Prophet Muhammad. Throughout history, many have tried to emulate the Qur'an and fabricate 'revelation,' but their endeavors were a target of ridicule and their influence is scarcely felt anywhere today.

Islam builds a community whose members are totally devoted to God and preoccupied with revering Him and preparing for their meeting with Him in the hereafter. However, this does not mean that the Muslim community is a community of dervishes and naive people. The Muslim community is an active and dynamic community whose members strive for success in this life and the life to come, in equal measure. While Muslims live and work they are aware of God's watchful eye over them and are mindful of their duties and responsibilities and the reward awaiting them. The surah says:

> He is the One who accepts the repentance of His servants and pardons their sins. He is aware of all their actions. He responds to those who believe and do righteous deeds, and bestows more of His grace upon them. (25–26)

The surah goes on to remind humankind of the greatness and glory of the Creator, who created the heavens and the earth. It cites certain marvels of God's creation that would inspire awe and bring human hearts closer to God:

> He sends down the rain after people have almost lost all hope and spreads His mercy everywhere... (28)

> Some of His signs include the creation of the heavens and the earth and the various living creatures He has dispersed all over them... (29)

> And among His signs are the ships that sail like mountains upon the ocean... (32)

These are references to natural laws that govern the movement of the sea and the ships that sail in them; to gravity which governs the stars and planets. We are told that the heavens are inhabited by multitudes of angels who ceaselessly praise the glory of God Almighty, and by the jinn who are, like us, accountable species.

For all we know, there could be other forms of life and other creatures that we may one day come to know about. Man's foremost responsibility is to build civilized life on this earth with which he has been entrusted.

Modern civilization, although far more advanced than previous ones, suffers from the same fundamental defects which had beset earlier civilizations. It has singularly failed to establish sound systems of morality and justice.

As a prerequisite to averting social decay, and to ward off God's wrath, the surah lists nine qualities that must be fulfilled by the community:

> Whatever has been bestowed upon you is but for enjoyment in this
> fleeting life. Better and more enduring is God's reward to those
> who: believe, and put their trust in God; who avoid gross sins and
> indecencies and, when angered, are willing to forgive; who respond
> to the call of their Lord, observe the prayers [salah], and conduct
> their affairs by mutual consultation, and give of what We have
> bestowed upon them and, when oppressed, resist and fight back.
> Let evil be rewarded with like evil. But the reward of those who
> forgive and seek rapprochement is with God who does not love the
> wrong-doers. (36–40)

Life may well smile on tyrants and criminals; they may have the upper hand in this world and enjoy all kinds of comfort and opulence. But, what good is it all, when: "The real losers are those who shall forfeit their own souls and their kinfolk on the Day of Resurrection. That shall be the ultimate loss" (*al-Zumar*. 15).

The Arab nation was honored in receiving God's final revelation and in being its custodian and mentor, and deserved to lead the rest of mankind. However, as time went on, Arabs neglected and gradually forsook their responsibility towards God's revelation. Worse still, we have today come to see Arabs discarding Islam altogether

535

and taking pride in a presumed nationalism that seems to mean the abandonment of Islam and Arabic, the language of the Qur'an. Under the banner of Arab nationalism, other languages, including local and regional dialects and colloquialisms have been advanced at the expense of the Arabic lingua franca. The effects of this mutilation can be felt in the culture, values, and literature of the wider community which is being separated from its history and its religious and legal character and heritage.

The cultural and religious struggle for the spirit and the soul of the Arab Muslim nation goes on at a feverish rate, and is yet to be decided. The surah conveys a poignant and timely warning to the Arab nation, saying:

> Respond to your Lord before that day comes which none can put off against the will of God. On that day, you shall have no refuge, nor can you retract any of your deeds. If they turn away, know that We have not sent you [Muhammad] to be their guardian. Your duty is to convey the message. (47–48)

What is even more exasperating is that while Arabs dissociate themselves from Islam, other groups and communities all over the world are actively reviving and restoring their religious and cultural heritage. Are they seriously prepared to allow the disintegration of their Islamic legacy and character?

The surah closes, as it started, with a reference to revelation, indicating how it might come about, saying:

> God would not speak to any mortal except by revelation, or from behind a veil, or through a messenger sent to reveal, by His leave, whatever He wills. He is Most High, Wise. (51)

Not all humans are suited to receiving divine revelation. Those selected for the task have to be of certain caliber and disposition; and even they, like the stars in the sky, vary in their qualifications for this selection. Some are sent to single communities, while others are sent to larger ones, or to all humanity.

Muhammad was sent with a Book containing a universal panacea for man's ills for all times and places. He admirably conveyed the message verbally, established its principles in society, and translated them into a living and vigorous civilization. Islam stands today as a pillar of strength for the salvation of the whole of humankind.

> Thus, of Our will, We have revealed to you [Muhammad] a living
> message; you hitherto had no knowledge of revelation or faith, and
> We made it a light whereby We guide those of Our servants whom
> We please. You [Muhammad] do indeed guide people to the
> straight path of God, to whom belongs all that is in the heavens and
> the earth. Surely to God all things shall in the end return. (52–53)

SURAH 43

Al-Zukhruf
(Ornaments)

THIS SURAH OPENS with an affirmation of the Arabic character of the Qur'an as the message with which the Arabs have been charged. This reminder could not be more appropriate or more timely for those Arabs who today believe that their nation can live and progress without Islam. The surah says: "By the glorious Book, We have revealed the Qur'an in the Arabic language so that you may understand its meaning" (2–3). The day the Arabs abandon the Qur'an and its teachings, they would forfeit the prospect of any prestige or good standing in the world.

The Qur'an is rich in wisdom and unique among all the revealed Books, which it easily surpasses. Like earlier recipients of revelation, the Arabs would be lost if they were to dismiss it and forsake the knowledge and guidance it has brought them.

The surah exposes the contradiction in the unbelievers' stance. They acknowledge the existence of God, but persist in worshiping idols and other deities besides Him.

If you [Muhammad] ask them [the Makkans] who created the heavens and the earth, they are bound to say, "The Almighty, the Omniscient, created them." (9)

If you ask them who created them, they would readily say that it was God. How then can they turn away from Him? (87)

If this was the case, what would they think was the role of the idols they worshiped? What possible justification could there be for revering helpless images carved out of stone? They would do far better to seek the One God and appeal to Him.

Who paved the earth for you and opened in it for you routes and avenues that you may find your way? Who sends down water from the sky in due measure to revive the barren ground, and thus you shall be raised to life? (10–11)

The surah refutes the allegation that God begets offspring, affirming His Oneness and singularity:

Say, "If the Merciful had a son, I should be the first to worship him." Exalted be the Lord of the heavens and the earth, Master of the Throne, above all their allegations. (81–82)

The people of Arabia, paradoxically, used to despise having female offspring, but that did not stop them from alleging that God had them.

They purported that the angels, who are in fact God's servants, were [His] daughters. Had they witnessed their creation? Their allegation shall be recorded and they shall account for it. (19)

Elsewhere in the Qur'an, God says:

Has your Lord favored you with male offspring and had for Himself daughters from the angels? You are indeed making such a grotesque allegation. (*al-Isrā'*: 40)

The unbelievers did not stop at that! They went further to claim that God had willed them to disbelief and led them to take other gods besides God. The surah says:

Thus, no messenger did We send before you [Muhammad] to warn other communities, but the complacent among them would say, "We are merely following in the footsteps of our forefathers." Their messenger would ask them, "What if I offer you a faith more enlightened than that which you have inherited from your forefathers?" They would say, "We simply refuse to believe in what you have brought." So We took vengeance on them, and you have seen the fate of the disbelievers. (23–25)

Rejection of the truth is often motivated by whims and prejudices rather than by substantial rational argument, and people's puerile fancies often drive them to reject the most elementary truths.

The Qur'an illustrates this elsewhere when it says:

[The tribe of] Thamūd rejected the warnings. They said, "Are we to follow a mere mortal? We would surely be wrong or insane. Did he alone among us receive the revelation? He is indeed a malicious liar." (*al-Qamar*. 23–25)

The experiences of all God's messengers testify to this phenomenon; the unbelievers' base desires all get the better of them. In *Ṣād*, verse 8, the unbelievers are reported as saying:

"Has the revelation been sent down to him [Muhammad] alone out of us all?" They are in doubt about My revelation, but let them await My punishment.

In the present surah, they say: "'If only this Qur'an was revealed to an eminent man from either of the two towns [Makkah or al-Ṭā'if]'" (31). This statement betrays a society built on an entrenched caste system. They are not able to perceive religious leadership as being separate from class and status.

The Israelites also objected to Ṭālūt, or Saul, being made their ruler. "They asked, 'How could he be our king when we are more deserving of kingship than he? Besides, he is not rich at all'" (*al-Baqarah*: 247). The reply was: "God has chosen him over you, and has given him wide knowledge and a strong body. God bestows His sovereignty on whom He wills" (*al-Baqarah*: 247).

Communities are made up of individuals with different skills, professions, and aptitudes that complement one another, and human societies require men of high caliber and moral integrity to lead them, establish freedom and equality, and lift the spirits and the living standards of their people. Overindulgent individuals who prefer a life of comfort and affluence would not normally make good candidates for such a demanding task.

The answer to the Makkans' request that a prominent figure, rather than Muhammad, should be given the Qur'an comes in these words:

> Is it they who apportion your Lord's blessings? It is We who deal out to them their livelihood in this world. We have made them of different ranks, some higher than others, so that some may serve under others. Your Lord's blessings [towards you] are far greater than all their possessions. (32)

This distinction among people in their various professions and vocations is essential, but God's prophets and messengers are chosen by God to teach and lead others to a better and more enlightened life.

Material riches and wealth are no indication of one's goodness, decency, or integrity. Many a rich person will end up as fuel for the fire of hell, while, in contrast, many poor and meek people, who undergo hardship and suffering in this life, shall enjoy endless bliss in Paradise. God further affirms that:

> But for the fear that all humankind might have become a single nation of unbelievers, We would have given those who deny the Merciful dwellings with silver roofs, and silver staircases. We would

have given them silver gates for their houses and silver couches to recline upon, and ornaments of gold. Yet all these would have been fleeting enjoyments of this life. It is the life to come that your Lord reserves for those who fear Him. (33–35)

The surah further affirms that corrupt and destructive elements of society shall always find sponsors and supporters: "He who turns a blind eye to God's revelation shall have a devil for a constant companion" (36).

These are the people who make up groups and parties that oppose Islam and put obstacles in its way. Muhammad and his followers are urged to stand up to these groups and defend the revelation which they have the honor to protect and uphold. The surah says: "Therefore hold fast to that which has been revealed to you; you are on the right path. This Qur'an is an admonition to you and to your people, and you shall all be accountable for it" (43–44).

Islam is the *raison d'être* of Arab civilization and standing in the world; it has been revealed in their tongue and they were given the unique honor of passing it on to the rest of humanity.

The Qur'an presents to all humankind a way of life that guarantees success both in this world and in the hereafter. It has restored the reputation and the integrity of earlier revealed scriptures, such as those received by Moses and Jesus, confirming their basic tenet that there is only one God. The surah says: "Ask those of Our messengers whom We sent before you [Muhammad] whether We ever appointed gods to be worshiped besides the Merciful" (45).

By way of illustration of how corrupting wealth and power can be, the surah relates an encounter between Moses and one of the Egyptian Pharaohs, the supreme ruler of that magnificent kingdom of the Nile. Moses made a passionate appeal to Pharaoh to believe in the One God and desist from oppressing the people.

But Pharaoh was arrogant and refused; and he

> declared to his people: "O my people! Is the kingdom of Egypt not mine, and are these rivers not flowing at my feet? Can you not see this? Am I not better than this despicable powerless man [Moses] who can scarcely express himself clearly? Where are his golden bracelets, and why are no angels sent down to accompany and support him?" (51–53)

Pharaoh rejected Moses' call and chased him and his Israelite followers out of Egypt. They fled eastward, and Moses led them across the Red Sea where Pharaoh and his men were drowned. As he was drowning, Pharaoh said: "'I now believe that there is no god other than He in whom the Israelites believe; I am of those who surrender themselves unto Him'" (*Yūnus*: 90).

His golden jewelry was not able to save Pharaoh, whose power and false claim to godhead were sunk in the sea with him. Real strength and influence are not derived from opulence and material riches. Worse still, severe punishment awaits the arrogant in the hereafter.

The surah then turns to the controversy regarding Jesus, son of Mary, which had raged on in Arabia when the Qur'an was being revealed. Some Arabs retorted that they would not mind if Jesus too, whom the Christians believed to be God, would go to hell with those who revered him, as asserted elsewhere in the Qur'an:

> You [the Arabians] and those you worship other than God, shall be the fuel of hell where you shall all eventually go. Were they [the idols] true gods, they would not have to end up there. (*al-Anbiyā'*: 98–99)

When the Qur'an made references to Jesus, the people of Arabia were ruffled and protested vehemently, as the surah points out, saying:

When Mary's son [Jesus] is cited, you people scoff and jeer loudly, and say, "Which is better, he or our gods?" They cite him merely to provoke you, for they are contentious people. (57–58)

Jesus is undoubtedly one of the most revered individuals, but the peculiarity of his birth without a father had led many people to believe he was the son of God. This false belief gained widespread acceptance, and to disprove it, God has promised to bring Jesus back to earth a second time to testify that he is a mortal and a messenger of the One God.

This is the purport of the statement that: "He [Jesus] is a portent of the Hour. Therefore have no doubts regarding its coming and follow Me; for this is the straight path" (61). There have been nume-rous theories on the second coming of Jesus and his vindication of the message of Islam, as delivered by Muhammad.

Mankind is divided into two main camps: those who recognize God and those who distort His identity, and Jesus had come to declare:

"God is my Lord and your Lord, therefore worship Him. That is the straight path." Yet the people divided into groups, wrangling among themselves, and the wrong-doers shall suffer the anguish of a woeful day. (64–65)

When the Hour comes, the believers will be invited to: "Enter Paradise, you and your spouses, for infinite happiness" (70). The unbelievers, on the other hand, shall face a gloomy end: "The evil-doers shall endure forever the torment of hell, which shall never be alleviated, and they shall have no hope therein" (74–75).

The unbelievers in this world seek to undermine Islam and over-whelm its followers, but God has His own scheme to vindicate His message and avenge the believers. The surah says: "If they are resolved to scheme against you, We also have Our plan" (79). This

brings to mind another Qur'anic assertion that: "They [the unbe-
lievers] scheme and I, too, scheme; so bear with the unbelievers and
let them wait a while" (*al-Ṭāriq*: 15–17).

Among many peoples, misguidance has been passed down from
one generation to another, and many people have chosen to persist
in their foolish ways. But the believers should persevere in their task
of teaching people about God and His message. The surah closes
with these poignant words:

> The messenger pleads, "Lord, these people would not believe."
> Bear with them and wish them peace. They shall come to know the
> error of their ways. (88–89)

SURAH 44

Al-Dukhān
(Smoke)

THE SURAH OPENS WITH GOD testifying that the Qur'an is "the clear Book" (2), "sent down on a blessed night" (3), which is certainly the night in the month of Ramadan, the ninth month in the Islamic calendar, known as the 'Night of Power' (*Laylat al-Qadr*). Commentators who maintain that this night could fall in the middle of Shaʿbān, the month preceding Ramadan, are definitely mistaken.

That night was blessed with the revelation of the Qur'an, this rich treasure of wisdom, enlightenment, and goodness. Elsewhere in the Qur'an we read that it was: "A blessed Book revealed to you [Muhammad] from your Lord, so that they may reflect on its signs..." (*Ṣād*: 29) and: "This is a blessed Book We revealed, so obey it..." (*al-Anʿām*: 155).

The honor and grace of the Book come from the fact that it purifies and improves human beings, as it managed to transform the nomadic Arab hordes into a nation with a civilization and an empire on which, at one time, the sun would never set.

The Book was revealed "to warn humankind" (3), against tyranny and injustice as a prelude to establishing a new order in the shape of Islam, based on *tawḥīd*, submission to the One and only God, which humanity desperately needs.

We know that initially the Arabs resisted the call of Islam and harassed its followers and drove them out of their homes. Prophet Muhammad is reported to have asked God: "help me against them

[the Arabs] with seven [lean years] like those of the prophet Joseph."
Subsequently, Makkah was hit by a severe drought and was covered
in a cloud of dry dust. A number of Makkan citizens went to the
Prophet and pleaded with him to ask God to alleviate their people's
situation, but when that happened, the unbelievers reneged. The
surah refers to this in saying: "We shall indeed ease the punishment
somewhat but you shall revert [to your old ways], and on that day
We shall deal you a supreme blow and exact retribution" (15–16).

Retribution came upon the unbelieving Arabs at the Battle of
Badr (624 AC) when, in a confrontation with the Muslims, they were
soundly defeated and lost a number of their most prominent leaders.

This interpretation is the one most widely held by commentators, but there is another one which I find more convincing. The
'smoke' the verse refers to could be some yet unknown natural phenomenon, on the scale of the hole in the ozone layer, that would
befall our planet with such catastrophic effects, as a result of human
corruption and wrongdoing. It would come in response to worldwide hostility to Islam and to the person of Prophet Muhammad.
When that happens, many people would be shaken and come to
realize the consequences of their betrayal of God's trust, and would
seek His mercy and forgiveness.

In any case, a full and final decision shall be made on the Day of
Judgment, when every soul shall receive its just recompense.

The surah points out that earlier recipients of divine revelation
had undergone trials and tribulations. Moses pleaded with Pharaoh
to release the Israelites and allow them to leave Egypt with him, but
the Pharaoh insisted on keeping them under his control and on
subjecting them to persecution. Eventually, the Pharaoh and his
entourage perished. They left behind numerous "gardens and
springs, cornfields and noble palaces, and abundant wealth and
affluence in which they took great delight. Nevertheless, We passed
it all to another people" (25–28).

The cycle of civilization is ever turning; history often repeats itself. In the fullness of time, wrong-doers of every generation shall have their comeuppance, while believers are expected to rise to their ideals and support their words with action and be role models for fairness and honesty.

Unfortunately, as time goes on, most religious communities tend to drift away from the original teachings of their prophets. God says of the Israelites: "We chose them knowingly above all nations and We sent them signs which rigorously tested them" (32–33).

But how did the Israelites fare after their deliverance and liberation? They reneged and became corrupt, and so they were punished.

Then it was the Arabs' turn who inherited the Qur'an and led the spread of Islam for several centuries. However, most of them were later to desert the teachings of Islam and have since lost their place in the world, having become divided and fragmented, and having fallen prey to the domination and exploitation of other nations.

God has promised true believers who uphold His revelations faithfully and sincerely that they shall be generously rewarded with power and influence, and happiness in this world and in the hereafter.

Modern societies are highly developed and intelligent although they assign no importance to the hereafter and are totally oblivious to the fact that they shall one day account for their actions to God. Their position is not very much different from that of pre-Islamic Arabian society who scoffed at life after death and thought it was a myth. The surah points out that:

These people say, "We shall die but one death, nor shall we ever be raised to life. Bring back our [dead] forefathers, if what you say is true." (34–36)

God will indeed bring all people to life for judgment, and everyone shall account for their deeds. Without this fact, life would be meaningless and a total waste of effort. The surah affirms:

> We did not create the heavens and the earth and all that lies between
> them for idle sport. We created them but in truth, though most of
> them [humankind] do not know. The Day of Judgment is a time
> appointed for them all. (38–40)

The universal and ultimate truth in which the heavens and the
earth were created is manifested in the intricate physical laws that
govern atoms and galaxies, ants and elephants, plains and forests, the
land and the sea. Science and scientific research have uncovered
many astonishing facts that testify to the power of the Creator. This
veritable truth shall also be revealed at the time of the final reckoning in which conscientious and sincere believers are set apart from
the intransigent unscrupulous people.

The Qur'an's warnings relating to the Day of Judgment and its
ramifications are clear and incisive. Its accounts of the hereafter and
life after death leave no room for arrogance or infatuation with the
transient pleasures of this life.

The surah closes with such a scene, saying: "The Day of
Judgment is a time appointed for them all; the Day when no ally
shall be able to help another ally and none shall be saved except those
to whom God shows mercy" (40–42).

What awaits the wrong-doers?

> The fruit of the *zaqqūm* tree shall certainly be the food of the
> sinful. Like molten alloy, boiling inside their bellies like scalding
> water. (43–46)

And what awaits the believers? "The believers will find themselves
in a secure state amid gardens and springs, wearing [garments] of silk
and brocade, facing one another" (51–53). The Day of Judgment is
a time appointed for them all.

The Qur'an has been revealed to Muhammad in order to awaken

the heedless from their torpor and to establish a great community and civilization with a momentous mission to carry to the rest of humankind.

> We have made it [the Qur'an] lucid, in your own tongue [Arabic] so that they may take heed. So wait, then, and watch, for they, too, are waiting. (58–59)

SURAH 45

Al-Jāthiyah
(The Kneeling One)

THIS SURAH OPENS WITH an exhortation to study and con-
template the physical world around us and to discover and identify
the signs and marvels that testify to the existence and power of
God. It says:

> The revelation of the Book is from God, the Almighty, the Wise.
> Surely, in the heavens and the earth there are signs for the believers.
> And in your own creation and in the beasts that are scattered far and
> near, there are signs for those with certain faith. And in the alter-
> nation of night and day, and in the sustenance God sends down
> from the sky with which He revives the earth after its death, and
> in the controlling of the winds, there are signs for those who under-
> stand. (1–5)

We have already come across similar Qur'anic passages in such
surahs as *al-Baqarah*, *Āl 'Imrān* and others, whose main import is to
establish a rational basis for religious faith so that it can be built on
clear and logical principles.

However, contemplation and theoretical study are not by themselves sufficient to bring about happiness and prosperity for mankind.
The powers and energies of the physical world have to be harnessed
and deployed for the good of man. The surah elaborates on this
theme, saying:

God has subdued the sea for you, so that vessels may sail on it, by His leave, and so that you may seek His bounty and be thankful to Him. He has placed under your control all that is in the heavens and the earth. Surely, in that there are signs for those who reflect. (12–13)

Not only does this control over the physical world enhance man's material life in this world, but it also enables him to reinforce and preserve his faith in God. Indeed, Muslims have declined mainly as a result of their negligence in this regard.

The Qur'an guides mankind with its principles and teachings while the physical world provides the tangible evidence for God's existence and power. It is, indeed, difficult to understand why people should ever deviate. The surah says: "Such are the signs of God which We reveal to you [Muhammad] in truth. What evidence other than God and His signs would they accept? Woe to every sinful liar!" (6-7).

Nevertheless, and despite this double-edged admonition, God, in His infinite mercy, chooses to defer punishment in order to give people greater opportunity to reflect and reconsider. The surah advises the Muslims to present their religion with courtesy and care and not to pressurize the unbelievers into submission. It says:

Tell the believers to forgive those who do not believe in God's punishment and God will reward people according to what they have earned. Those who do what is right do so for their own good, and those who perpetrate evil do so at their own peril, and to your Lord you shall all be recalled. (14–15)

Besides the sciences of philosophy and physics there are traditional and religious sciences, all of which are required to lead mankind to happiness and prosperity. In many instances, however, this has not been the case. The study of physical sciences has not always been put to good use; man has conquered space and is now almost fully able to see creation in action, as in the case of conception and the growth of human fetuses and embryos, but many people continue to deny God and insist that there is no creator.

This is a salient feature of modern civilization in the East as well as in the West, and this anomaly we see with respect to empirical scences can also be found among students of religious sciences. Becoming rigid and fossilized, they have lost their appeal and ability to influence human thought and world events. Religious books have become hollow tomes and most of the regression and corruption we witness in the world can be blamed on institutionalized religion and religious leaders and their followers.

As a result of their corruption, the elders of Israel could be said to have been the first to belie Socrates' assertion that 'virtue is knowledge' because, as the surah points out, they abused and misrepresented the knowledge they had been given. It says:

> We gave the children of Israel the Book and We gave them power and prophethood, and We provided them with many a good thing, and We favored them above all nations, and We gave them perspicuous signs of the religion, yet it was not until knowledge had been vouchsafed to them that they disagreed through transgression one against another... (16–17)

So long as religious knowledge does not lead to purity, honesty, and justice, it is of little use or value. Today, there are men of religion as well as men of secular sciences who are totally unscrupulous but who might otherwise have served humanity very well indeed. The surah continues:

> Look at him who is knowingly worshiping his own whim, whom God has let go astray and has set a seal upon his ears and his heart and drawn a veil over his eyes! Who else other than God shall guide him?... (23)

To show intelligence in understanding the world and, at the same time, to display a total lack of sense in appreciating the truth regarding the hereafter inevitably causes one to submit to the dictates of the material world of the here and now. It makes one see nothing beyond the temporal life of this world and causes one to lose the initiative to prepare for life in the hereafter, and thus one becomes a total and hopeless agnostic. The surah says:

They say, "There is nothing for us but this life; we die and we live and we are only destroyed by time." In fact, they have no certain knowledge of this; they are merely guessing. (24)

In response to such a preposterous claim, the surah closes with resounding admonitions relating to resurrection and accountability, recalling the time in the future when people will face the judgment of their Lord. It says:

God is in total command of the heavens and the earth, and when the Hour comes, those who had denied shall lose out. And you shall see every nation down on its knees. Every nation shall be called to face its record and be told, "Today you shall reap the rewards of your deeds. Here is Our book that speaks the truth about you, for We had been recording what you were doing." (27–29)

Modern scientific progress has indeed brought unprecedented affluence and prosperity, and has made pleasure and indulgence much more easily available and accessible. But this has also led to people becoming preoccupied and intoxicated by material and sensual enjoyment. They have no interest or concern for life in the hereafter. Earlier recipients of divine revelation, Jews and Christians, had failed in maintaining the momentum of faith and belief in God and had in the main turned against Islam and sought to stem its spread and progress. The outcome has been counter-productive and has served to marginalize religion and its role in society. It should be no wonder that on the Day of Judgment they will be confronted with the statement:

"We shall today forget you as you were heedless of your encounter with this day; the fire shall be your abode and there shall be no one to help you." (34)

Unbelievers may very well gain some benefit over the short term, but that would not bother God for, eventually, they shall end up as losers.

The surah ends, as it began, with praise and glorification of God, stressing the same two attributes of His mightiness and wisdom:

And so praise to God, Lord of the heavens and the earth, the Lord of all the worlds. Glory be to Him in the heavens and the earth. He is Almighty, the Wise. (36–37)

SURAH 46

Al-Aḥqāf
(Sand Dunes)

THIS IS THE LAST of the group of seven surahs that open with the individual Arabic letters *ḥā'* and *mīm*. In all cases, this is followed with the assertion that the noble Qur'an is a direct revelation from God, the Lord of all creation, to which mankind should submit and refer for wisdom and guidance.

It further asserts that this world in which we live is finite and that human life on earth shall one day come to an end, following which there will be another life and a time for just retribution. It says: "We have not created the heavens and the earth and all that lies between them except in truth and for an appointed term. Yet the unbelievers turn away from the warnings they receive" (3).

The unbelievers, in effect, reject the evidence inherent in the physical and material world and deny man's accountability before God in the hereafter.

The surah then presents a debate between Prophet Muhammad and the unbelievers over their beliefs and behavior. This begins with a reference to their deities and their failure to create anything, saying:

Say, "Show me what parts of the earth these idols you invoke besides God have created! Or, did they perhaps partake in the creation of the heavens? Bring me a [revealed] book before this one [the Qur'an] or some other vestige of knowledge, if you are really truthful." (4)

No one in their right mind would claim that Asia was created by one god and Africa by another, or that the sun is the work of one god and the moon is of another. It would be sheer nonsense to hold such a belief, and so it is futile to invoke or resort to any other deities besides God, the Creator. The surah affirms:

> Who is farther astray than one who calls, besides the One God, upon others who would not respond till the Day of Judgment and who are in fact unconscious of their call? (5)

The unbelievers claim that the Qur'an is the work of Prophet Muhammad.

> Or do they claim that he [Muhammad] has conceived it [the Qur'an] himself? Say, "If I had invented it, then there is nothing you can do to protect me from God. He knows best what you say. He is sufficient witness between me and you... " (8)

Certainly, Muhammad could not be castigated for preaching the Qur'an and calling people to submit to God, to devote their lives to His service, and to seek His pleasure. Furthermore, he was a living example of such submission and devotion. No other revealed book could be compared to the Qur'an in its emphasis on the glorification of God and submission to His will and power. How could Muhammad be censured for advocating any of that?

The view, widely held by unbelievers who deny divine revelation, that the Qur'an is the work of Muhammad does not withstand scrutiny. The surah retorts:

> Say, "I am not the first messenger [to emerge]; nor do I know what will be done with me or with you. I only follow what is being revealed to me, and my only task is to give clear warnings." (9)

When the Prophet embarked on his mission he could not have known that it would lead to confrontation with his people or what the outcome would be. Nevertheless, he put his trust in God and persisted with the task until he prevailed. Despite the suffering and the tribulation, Muhammad remained devout and loyal to God, to the last breath of his life. Could this possibly have been the manner of an impostor?

The Arabs of Makkah had very little excuse for denying Muhammad's prophethood because the Jews of Madinah were followers of Moses and the pious among them were sure that Prophet Muhammad would be coming. The surah castigates them, saying:

> Say, "What if it had indeed come from God and you rejected it, and a witness from the Israelites has vouchsafed for it and believed in it while you deny it with disdain? Truly, God does not guide the wrong-doers." (10)

Today, there are many people who reject the prophethood of Muhammad, many of whom do not believe in God anyway, and these have, first of all, to recognize God as the supreme Creator.

As for Jews and Christians or "People of the Book", as the Qur'an calls them, their view of their own revealed scriptures is rather ambiguous, and if they really and sincerely believe in the One God, they would have no cause to reject Muhammad's message which maintains that:

> Those who say, "God is our Lord," and follow the straight path shall have nothing to fear or to regret. They are the people of Paradise, wherein they shall dwell forever as a reward for their labors. (13–14)

Muhammad did no more than call upon people to believe in God and hold fast to the straight path, and he was there to lead them along that path.

It is not uncommon for families to split up, with some members choosing to believe and others not; a father may accept the faith while his son rejects it, and vice versa. No one should be compelled to embrace the faith. Hence that plaintive and heartfelt prayer by the believer:

"Inspire me, Lord, to give thanks for the favors You have bestowed on me and on my parents, and to do good works that will please You. Bless my offspring, as I turn to You and surrender myself." (15)

The surah gives the example of children who refuse to believe in the resurrection and in accountability despite the advice of their parents. It says:

And he who curses his parents saying, "Shame on you! Do you promise me that I shall be resurrected when many generations have already passed before me?" They beg for God's mercy and plead with him, "Woe to you! Believe! The promise of God is true," but he replies, "These are merely legends of old." Those are the ones whose fate has been sealed, from among previous generations of jinn and men; they are truly the losers. (17–18)

It is not unusual for unbelievers in God to spend their whole lives indulging themselves and seeking to satisfy their carnal pleasures and desires. In this respect the surah says:

The unbelievers shall one day be brought before the fire of hell and be told, "You have squandered away the good things in your worldly life and enjoyed them to the full and today you shall be rewarded with ignominious punishment..." (20)

It is reported by Ibn ʿAṭiyyah that this verse had left a strong impression on ʿUmar ibn al-Khaṭṭāb, the second Caliph. As the head of an expanding Muslim state, ʿUmar was a model of simplicity and austerity. On entering Syria with the victorious Muslim army, he was greeted by the leader of the expedition, Khālid ibn al-Walīd, who offered him a sumptuous meal. His immediate response was: "If this is what we eat, what about the destitute Muslims who died without having had their fill of barley bread?"

Khālid replied: "They shall have Paradise!" ʿUmar, it was said, broke down crying, saying that in that case the poor Muslims were the winners!

It is true to say that God does not forbid the enjoyment of the good and lawful things, but seeking luxury and affluence could lead to a life of extravagance and overindulgence resulting in preoccupation with one's pleasures and desires and negligence of one's duties and responsibilities.

The opposition to Islam and its followers was vicious and relentless but the Muslims, under the guidance of the Qur'an, persevered and defended their position well. In order to raise Muslim morale, the Qur'an would cite episodes from the history of earlier believers, saying:

> Recall ʿĀd's compatriot [the prophet Hūd] who warned his people [who lived] among the sand dunes, who had been warned before and after him, saying, "Worship none but God. I fear for you the punishment of a momentous day." (21)

The tribe of ʿĀd, were a powerful people, with a semi-gigantic, strong physical disposition, who lived near Hadramawt in the south of Yemen. They showed shameless contempt and intransigence towards the prophet Hūd who was sent to them. The warning here could be in reference to punishment on the Day of Judgment or to a severe drought they suffered, lasting for two years, which threatened to annihilate them. Their response was: "'Have you come to turn us away from our own gods? Then bring us the scourge you threaten us with, if you are truthful'" (22).

There was no escape for them. As they looked up to the horizon one day they saw huge clouds approaching, which they had mistaken for rain, but:

When they saw the clouds heading for their valleys, they said, "Here comes the rain!" He said to them, "By no means! It is what you have been urging: a wind bringing a woeful scourge. It will, with God's leave, destroy everything." When morning came, there was nothing to be seen except their dwellings. (24–25)

No one was left alive, and there was nothing to be seen except the ruins of their deserted dwellings. The ʿĀd were a much stronger people than the Quraysh, so would the Arabs learn from their example and heed Muhammad's call? Nevertheless, people, at times, have the tendency to suspend all their faculties and show complete indifference to their own future salvation.

The surah continues to address the Makkan unbelievers:

We had established them [ʿĀd] firmly and made them more powerful than you are; and We gave them ears and eyes and hearts. Yet nothing did their ears or eyes or hearts avail them since they denied the revelations of God; and the scourge at which they scoffed enveloped them. (26)

Living in the heart of Arabia, the Arabs of the Quraysh were quite familiar with the history and remains of earlier communities of prophets such as Ṣāliḥ and Lot and peoples such as those of Himyar and Sheba, all of whom had chosen to reject their messengers and worship idols who had: "Utterly forsaken them: such were their lies and such their false inventions" (28).

The more intransigent the Makkans were, the more examples and warnings were cited to them. In the meantime, numerous accounts appear in the Qur'an that are meant to alleviate the

Prophet's anxiety and raise the awareness and morale of believers in every generation.

The surah then goes on to mention how the jinn would listen to the Qur'an and accept its teachings, in the hope that their example might inspire human listeners to do the same. The question of jinn is a vexatious one. The Qur'an says of Satan, who hails from the jinn, that: "He and his minions can see you whence you cannot see them." (*al-Aʿrāf*: 27)

Superstitious people, however, have gone to extreme lengths to project a bizarre picture of these creatures and their relationship with humans, claiming that they can be controlled by humans and intermarry with them.

While the ignorant pursue these mythical fancies, they neglect to observe and appreciate the marvels of creation evident in the universe. It is the investigation and study of these phenomena, rather than preoccupation with the jinn, that have made the greatest contribution to human progress and civilization.

Regarding the jinn, however, the Qur'an says:

> We dispatched a band of jinn to listen to the Qur'an being recited, and as they heard it they said to each other: "Listen carefully!" As the recitation was finished they rushed back to warn their own people. (29)

While the jinn appreciated the Qur'an and listened to it with respect, we read elsewhere in the Qur'an that the unbelievers among humans say: "'Do not listen to this Qur'an and raise your voices to drown its recitation, so that you may indeed prevail'" (*Fuṣṣilat*: 26).

We note that the jinn, according to the surah, also said: "'We have heard a Book revealed since the time of Moses, confirming what had been revealed before it...'" (30). This clearly indicates that the Injīl, the book revealed to Jesus, was complementary to the

Torah, while the Qur'an is a separate scripture introducing new laws and principles superseding what had come before it.

The surah continues in its reporting of what the jinn had said: "'Our people! Respond to the Messenger of God [Muhammad] and believe him, and God will forgive your sins and deliver you from a woeful scourge'" (31).

It continues to renounce the Arabs of the Quraysh and threaten them with punishment in the hereafter:

> Do they not see that God, who created the heavens and the earth and was not troubled by their creation, is able to raise the dead to life? Indeed, He has power over all things. (33)

If only the arrogant could realize that the tribe of ʿĀd was mightier than that of the Quraysh, and the jinn were more powerful than both of them, but their power and might could not save them.

The surah closes by exhorting Muhammad to follow the examples of earlier senior prophets—Noah, Abraham, Moses and Jesus—in persevering against his people. It says: "Bear up patiently, as did those venerable messengers of old and do not seek to hasten their [the unbelievers'] end…" (35). The struggle for the truth is never easy and calls for patience and hard work, and when the time comes, victory shall be sweet.

The surah ends ominously by saying:

> The day they see what they had been threatened with, it would seem that they had lived for a mere hour of a day. This is [Our] proclamation. Shall any be destroyed but the evil-doers? (35)

SURAH 47

Muḥammad

THIS SURAH, WHICH IS ALSO KNOWN by the title "fighting," testifies to the fact that Prophet Muhammad was a prophet of mercy as well as combat; he is with the oppressed against the oppressor, and with the victim against the wrongdoer, and he stands up to tyranny and injustice.

In order to appreciate the context of this surah, one has to think how oppressed people, in Bosnia or Palestine or anywhere else in the world, feel towards their oppressors who have usurped their land, slaughtered their men, raped their women, and trampled on their human rights. Oppression and cruelty breed hatred and animosity.

Islam does not pander to tyranny or appease powerful oppressors, while the Qur'an urges its followers to oppose evil and stand up to injustice. We read:

> fight them so that God may chastise them at your hands and humiliate them and grant you victory over them, and thereby heal the spirit of the believers. God will remove all rancor from their hearts. (*al-Tawbah*: 14–15)

The present surah indicates that war and armed struggle are necessary solutions for a much worse evil. It addresses the believers, saying:

When you come face to face with the unbelievers on the battlefield, strike at their necks until you weaken them and then bind the captives firmly. Thereafter you may release them magnanimously or for a ransom, till the war comes to an end. For, if God had wished, He would have vanquished them, but He wanted to test you by means of one another... (4)

The surah opens with a declaration of certain universal truths that are valid for all time. It says:

Those who disbelieve and obstruct God's path, their works shall come to nothing. But as for those who believe and do good works and believe in what was revealed to Muhammad, which is the truth from their Lord, God will forgive them their sins and better their condition. That is so because those who disbelieved have followed falsehood while those who believed have followed the truth from their Lord. Thus God gives examples to mankind. (1–3)

The same concepts and principles are highlighted towards the end of the surah when it says:

Those who disbelieve and obstruct God's path and opposed the Messenger [Muhammad] after the guidance became manifest to them, shall not cause God any harm and He will frustrate their actions. (32)

Muslims used to recite passages from this surah during combat as it has a special pounding rhythm that aroused fear in the hearts of their enemy. As God exhorts the believers to defend the faith, He makes an earnest promise, saying:

Believers, if you support God, He will support you and steady your feet on the ground. But the unbelievers shall be consigned to perdition and their actions shall come to nothing. (7–8)

Among these promises and exhortations, the surah refers to the fate and rewards of those who give their lives for the cause of God, saying:

> Those who are slain in God's cause, He shall never waste their works. He will guide them and better their condition and admit them to Paradise which He had already made known to them. (4–6)

It then gives a glimpse of what awaits the believers in Paradise, saying:

> Paradise, which the God-fearing were promised, has rivers of pure water and rivers of fresh milk and rivers of wine, delectable to those that drink it, and rivers of refined honey... (15)

In appreciation of these and countless other luxuries, and of God's boundless generosity, the believers praise and glorify and give thanks to their Lord.

To protect the unity and integrity of the Muslim community, the surah exposes the behavior and sneaky methods employed by the hypocrites in the community. These untrustworthy individuals would attend meetings with Prophet Muhammad and listen to his teachings and instructions, and they may even have joined the Muslims in certain religious rites and rituals, but with doubt in their hearts. Many of them would report on what they had seen and heard to others hostile to the Prophet and the Muslims. The surah expresses it thus:

> Some of them would listen to you and as soon as they depart they turn to those who are knowledgeable and ask, "What did he say just now?" Such are those upon whose hearts God has set a seal and who follow their whims and desires. (16)

Their inquiry conveys both a lack of respect and a sense of sarcasm towards what the Prophet was saying, but their cowardice and insincerity are soon exposed when they are ordered to take up arms in defense of the faith. Their lack of faith, their infidelity, and their love for worldly things make them flinch and recoil with horror. The surah says:

> And when a powerful surah is revealed and fighting is mentioned in it, you see those with ill will in their hearts looking at you with a fainting look as though they were in the throes of death. (20)

There are people who do not believe in Islam and oppose it out of sheer ignorance and simple-mindedness, but hypocrites have no comparable excuse. They live among the Muslims and listen to the same teachings revealed to the Prophet and they observe his actions and behavior firsthand. Affirming that their penalty would be more severe, the surah says: "Satan has insidiously enticed those who reneged on their faith after the guidance had been revealed to them, and he has deluded them" (25).

Today, there are hypocrites whose deviousness and intrigue surpass that of their predecessors. These pursue their dastardly activities through the education system and the mass media and by undermining the religious and cultural character and integrity of Muslim societies, and they serve the interests and aims of those hostile to Islam and Muslims everywhere. The surah goes on:

> That is because they say to those who abhor what God has revealed, "We shall obey you in some matters." God is aware of their secret intrigues. What will they do when the angels take their lives away, beating their faces and their backs? It is because they followed what incurred God's wrath and they detested His pleasure, and so He made their works come to nothing. (26–28)

Such hypocrites cannot perpetrate their nefarious pursuits unde-
tected for ever; if God does not expose them, their behavior and
their demeanor will invariably give them away. God says:

Had We wished, We would have pointed them out to you
[Muhammad] and you would recognize them by their expressions.
But you will know them by their words. God knows all that you
do. (30)

The surah closes with strong exhortations to the believers not to
capitulate in the face of their detractors no matter how long or arduous the struggle may be. They must overcome their weaknesses and
persevere in combat. It says: "Therefore do not falter or sue for
peace when you have gained the upper hand and God is with you,
and He will not begrudge the fruits of your works" (35).

But to those who withhold their support and refuse to join in the
defense of the faith, the surah says:

Behold! You are called upon to give in the cause of God but some
of you are tightfisted; they are only niggardly towards themselves.
God is Self-Sufficient but you are destitute. If you turn back, He
will replace you with others who shall not be like you at all. (38)

Miserly societies whose members are not prepared to sacrifice for
each other do not deserve to flourish or prevail.

Al-Faṭḥ
(Victory)

HAVING CONCLUDED the Treaty of Ḥudaybiyyah with the
Makkans in 628 AC, the Muslims, under the leadership of Prophet
Muhammad, returned to Madinah nursing deep disappointment.
They had hoped to visit the sacred mosque to worship at the Kaʿbah
and perform the rites of pilgrimage at Safa and Marwa, but their
plans failed. Their negotiations with the Makkans had been arduous,
at times acrimonious, and could have easily degenerated into armed
conflict were it not for the Prophet's shrewdness and foresight.

On the way back to Madinah the present surah was revealed to
Muhammad, full of promise and good tidings:

> We [God] have given you [Muhammad] a glorious victory, so that
> God may forgive you your past and future sins, and complete His
> blessings upon you and lead you unto a straight path; and so that He
> may grant you a decisive victory. (1–3)

The Muslim withdrawal from Ḥudaybiyyah was indeed a victory
and marked the beginning of a great and crucial triumph for Islam.

With those events all obstacles had been removed and the
onward march of Islam had begun in earnest. The truce forced upon
the Prophet by the Makkans and grudgingly acceded to by the
Muslims was to prove a turning point in the history of Islam. News
of the truce and its ramifications spread all over Arabia and earned
the Muslims wider respect and recognition. They emerged as a
strong and cohesive political entity with a clear purpose and with

their prestige enhanced. Less than two years later Makkah fell to the Muslims and ten thousand of them marched into it, destroying the pagan idols and raising the banner of Islam. Bilāl, the Abyssinian, called the Muslims to prayer for the first time from the roof of the Kaʿbah.

The Prophet's genius at Ḥudaybiyyah bore fruit and, by way of reward, God promised him forgiveness and ultimate triumph, which was to extend to the rest of the believers. The surah says:

> It was He who filled the believers' hearts with peace of mind to further strengthen their faith. God commands all forces in the heavens and on the earth, and God is All-Knowing and Wise, so that He will admit the believers, men and women alike, into gardens through which rivers flow... (4–5)

As for their enemies, in spite of their professed power and strength, they could hope for nothing but grief and failure, both in this life and in the life to come.

The essence of Muhammad's mission was to eradicate pagan and ignorant religious practices, establish the truth and build a community that declares allegiance to God and glorifies Him alone. The Prophet's generation of Muslims, the Companions, were the pioneers of that community who devoted themselves to the service of God in the mosques as well as on the battlefield. They promised their support to the Prophet to the death. They lived for God and died for God:

> Those who swear allegiance to you [Muhammad] are in fact swearing allegiance to God; God's hand is above their hands, so whoever breaks his oath breaks it at his own peril, but he that fulfills what he has pledged to God shall be richly rewarded by Him. (10)

Muhammad's first followers were all true to their word, and in this surah, God declares His pleasure with them all and promises them great rewards. The surah says:

God was well pleased with the believers as they swore allegiance to you [Muhammad] under the tree [at Ḥudaybiyyah]. He knew what was in their hearts and he therefore filled them with peace of mind and rewarded them with a speedy victory and with abundant spoils to take with them... (18–19)

While the Muslims were on their way back to Madinah, this surah was revealed to reassure them and put their minds at rest. It also exposed those who chose to stay behind in Madinah in the first place and indicated how they should be dealt with. When the Muslims decided to go to perform the ʿUmrah at Makkah, the hypocritical cynics were saying that they would never be coming back and that the Quraysh would annihilate them!

These cynical fifth-columnists had not learned the lessons of previous episodes, especially the one involving the abortive siege of Madinah by Makkan tribes in 628 AC. Their hostility to the Muslims was well-entrenched, and they would look for every opportunity to make mischief and perpetrate sedition and instability within the Madinan community. The surah points out:

Those Arabs who stayed behind would say to you [Muhammad], "We were preoccupied with our possessions and our families, so ask forgiveness for us." They say with their mouths what they do not feel in their hearts. Say, "Who can give you any protection if God wanted to harm you or do you some good? No, God is fully aware of what you do." You thought that the Messenger and the believers would never return to their families, and your hearts delighted in that belief, and you thought the worst for them and, thus, you were totally damned. We have prepared a blazing fire for the unbelievers who disbelieve in God and His Messenger. (11–13)

The hypocrites of Madinah were certain that the Makkan Arabs would prevent the Muslims from entering Makkah and, if armed confrontation broke out, the Muslims were sure to be defeated because they were smaller in number. So when the Muslims changed their plan and deferred their ʿUmrah for another year and returned safely to Madinah, the hypocrites were shocked and enraged.

The surah reassures the Muslims saying: "To God belongs all that is in the heavens and on earth; He forgives whomever He will and He punishes whomever He will, for God is Oft-Forgiving, Most Merciful" (14).

It is a sign of God's infinite mercy that He has left the door forever open for those who repent and seek forgiveness as long as they abandon their self-interest, duplicity, and infatuation with worldly gain. To test their loyalty, the surah calls upon them to fight with the Muslims against the unbelievers, saying:

> Say [Muhammad] to those Arabs who stayed behind, "You shall be called upon to fight a mighty people, unless they submit. If you obey, God will reward you well, but if you turn away as you have done before, He will inflict upon you a painful punishment." (16)

Who are these 'mighty people' the surah refers to? Some commentators say they were the tribes of Hawāzin and Thaqīf who clashed with the Muslims at Ḥunayn on the outskirts of Makkah; some say they were Banū Ḥanīfah, the tribes of Musaylimah the imposter, while others said they were the Romans. Be that as it may, they were a formidable opponent whom only a sincere believer would dare fight.

Some deserters, driven by sheer greed, decided to join the Muslims in their battle against the Jews of Khaybar, in northern Hijaz, because they knew that the spoils would be rich, but God advised the Prophet not to give them that privilege. The surah says:

As you proceed to take the spoils, those who stayed behind will say, "Let us come with you." They seek to change God's words. Say, "You shall not accompany us; thus God has already spoken." They will say, "You are jealous of us!" No, how little they understand. (15)

The triumph at Khaybar, coming only forty days after the return from Ḥudaybiyyah, and the rich spoils the Muslims acquired as a consequence, were God's reward for the tenacity and courage they had displayed at Ḥudaybiyyah.

The fall of Khaybar, the richest and staunchest Jewish stronghold in northern Hijaz, came almost twenty years after the advent of Islam. It marked the end of the Jewish settlements and their role in that part of Arabia.

The Jewish tribes who settled in Arabia did not serve the monotheist religion at all well in that land. They were never keen to educate their Arab neighbors or help them abandon pagan worship which was rife among them. Rather, they sided with the pagans against Prophet Muhammad and his followers and did their utmost to thwart the growth and spread of Islam.

The Israelites look upon religion as a national heritage, giving them a distinct identity that separates them from the rest of mankind. God, in their view, is the God of Israel and not the God of all humanity. To compound this erroneous belief, the Israelites claimed for themselves a unique and privileged status with God without fulfilling the obligations of such a status. Rather, they promoted greed and rivalry for worldly things and considered religion their exclusive prerogative that would set them apart from other nations.

On his arrival in Madinah, Muhammad, the Arabian prophet, showed a great deal of respect and courtesy towards his Israelite neighbors, but they responded with treachery and intrigue. This is referred to elsewhere in the Qur'an which says:

Many from amongst the People of the Book [Jews and Christians] wish to turn you away from your religion, out of sheer deep-seated envy, after the truth has become clear to them. So pardon and forgive until God's judgment comes, for God has power over all things. (*al-Baqarah*: 109)

God's will was fulfilled in His punishment of the Israelites, time and time again, in the hope that they might desist. However, they did not, and their last stronghold at Khaybar was overrun by the Muslims in the seventh year of the Hijrah. They lost all the power and wealth they had previously gained and were stripped of the means that might enable them to cause mischief for the Muslims. The surah says:

God has promised you [the Muslims] abundant spoils to take with you and has granted you these spoils [of Khaybar] right away. He has stayed your enemy's hands, as a sign to the believers and in order to guide you to the straight path. (20)

This rich reward was for those who gave their allegiance to the Prophet 'under the tree' at Ḥudaybiyyah and those who joined him on the Khaybar expedition.

The surah points out clearly that if the Prophet were to engage the Makkans in battle, they would be routed. It says: "Were the unbelievers to fight you, they would have gone into abject retreat, and would have no one to protect or support them" (22).

Why, then, did the Prophet not fight the Makkans? Firstly, it was important that the age-old dignity and integrity of the Kaʿbah as a place of peace and worship should be preserved and respected, and secondly, there were by then people inside Makkah who had accepted Islam but, fearing persecution by their own people, chose not to declare their allegiance to the Prophet's authority at Madinah. These would have been under a greater threat of being killed in the cross fire if fighting had broken out.

God says in the surah:

> But for the fear that you might unwittingly put in danger believing
> men and believing women unknown to you, God would have
> ordered you to fight; but God would extend His mercy to
> whomever He wills. Had the believers stood apart, We would have
> inflicted upon the unbelievers a stern punishment indeed. (25)

The Muslims, nonetheless, were able to worship at the Ka'bah
the following year and, with the minimum of casualties, Makkah fell
to them in the eighth year of the Hijrah.

Islam urged the saving of human lives on both sides and the number of people killed in fighting in those earlier expeditions was very
small and could not be compared to the enormous human cost of
many comparable wars.

The surah continues to recall the events of Ḥudaybiyyah and
after, saying:

> God has in all truth fulfilled His Messenger's vision that you [the
> Muslims], God willing, shall enter the sacred mosque [in Makkah]
> in complete security, with your hair cropped or shaven and without
> any fear. God knew what you did not and moreover granted a
> speedy victory. (27)

Then comes a statement that merits long and careful consideration. The surah says: "It is He who sent His Messenger with guidance and the religion of truth, so that it may prevail over all religions, and God is a sufficient witness" (28). This clearly affirms that
Islam shall triumph and that its banner and influence shall never
wane. Prophet Muhammad confirms this assertion by saying: "My
nation is like the rainfall: no one can tell whether it is best at the
beginning or at the end." Nevertheless, the triumph of Islam in any
one generation is contingent upon that generation living up to the

task of upholding the faith and fulfilling the conditions and prerequisites of success. Unless those conditions are satisfied, the Muslims would not prevail and shall, subsequently, have only themselves to blame.

The closing verse of the surah elaborates on the characteristics and qualities of the successful Muslim community. It begins: "Muhammad, the Messenger of God, and those with him are steadfast against the unbelievers and kind towards one another..." (29).

It is a telling passage that draws our attention today to a comparison between how Muslims are treated in Muslim countries and under Muslim governments and how other countries, such as Israel or Britain or the United States for instance, treat their own citizens. Human life and the dignity of man appear to have a much lower value and command less respect in Muslim countries. There was a time when Muslims behaved towards one another with honor, respect, and compassion, but today this seems to be the case in non-Muslim societies while Muslims squabble and fight among themselves. It is difficult, under current conditions, to see how Muslims can expect to earn God's support and fulfill their task as leaders of mankind.

Al-Ḥujurāt
(The Chambers)

ONE OF THE ESTABLISHED ASPECTS of Muslim social behavior is the deference and respect shown by the younger towards the senior, or elder, members of the community. Complementary to that, younger members are treated with sympathy and kindness. Prophet Muhammad was reported to have said:

> He who does not respect our elders or show compassion towards our young ones or does not venerate our learned people, does not belong with us.

The present surah introduces certain aspects of Islamic social etiquette that enhance and preserve the dignity and probity of Muslim society. These include the appropriate manners which Muslims should adopt in the presence of Prophet Muhammad and other manners to be observed by Muslims towards one another, as well as those recommended in dealing with people from other nations and communities. Regarding the Prophet, the surah says:

> Believers, do not behave presumptuously in the presence of God and His Messenger, and fear God, for God hears all and knows all. Believers, do not raise your voice above that of the Prophet and do not speak loudly to him as you would do to one another... (1–2)

Elsewhere in the Qur'an, we read: "Do not address the Prophet in the same manner you address one another..." (*al-Nūr*: 63).

The Prophet, as God's spokesman, should have been accorded special deference, approached with humility, and addressed with utmost courtesy. As it was, he received more than his fair share of abuse and insults from his detractors. The surah further emphasizes that showing respect towards the person of Prophet Muhammad would earn one favor and great rewards with God Almighty.

Muslims are urged to verify the truth and accuracy of what they hear; rumor and fabricated reports could cause irreparable damage to the fabric of society. The surah exhorts: "Believers, if a scoundrel brings you news, examine it carefully, lest you should unwittingly wrong others and then regret your actions" (6).

Islam teaches that Satan is capable of insinuating antipathetic ideas into people's minds. He is ever eager to fan the flames of discord and would exploit any small disagreements and turn them into huge conflicts. This is the insidious and unseen cause behind many a destructive and divisive confrontation. Within a Muslim community, any such hostile scheming must be pre-empted and such antagonistic situations must not be allowed to arise. Instead, the community must promote harmony and concord and stand united against those who persist in aggression and threaten the unity and cohesion of Muslim society.

Throughout their history, Muslims have faced wars in which they sustained heavy setbacks and the reason has invariably been their lack of courage to defend the truth and stand up to oppression. The result has been humiliation for Muslims everywhere and yet more daring aggression on the part of their enemies. The surah directs that:

> If two parties of believers take up arms against each other, then make peace between them. If either of them commits aggression against the other, then fight the aggressors until they submit to the will of God. Once the aggressors desist, reconcile the two parties with equity and justice, for God loves those who exercise justice. (9)

The weakening of the ties of brotherhood among Muslims is a bad omen and provides non-Muslim enemies with a pretext to interfere and exploit the situation to their advantage. In all cases, Islam shall be the prime loser!

The surah draws our attention to a number of vile aspects of behavior that we must avoid. It is vulgar and foolish to mock or ridicule other people or be condescending towards them. Only God Almighty knows the true worth of every individual. A person's status is determined by several factors, some of which are inherited characteristics and others that are attributable to the environment in which he or she grows up. You may deride someone, yet he may prove more worthy and successful than yourself. The surah says:

> Believers, let no man mock another man, who may perhaps be better than himself. And let no woman mock another woman, who may perhaps be better than herself... (11)

Islam condemns slandering others or scoffing at them. It denounces snooping, maligned suspicion, backbiting, and defamation. Regrettably, these are widespread in human intercourse, and if people were to avoid these negative traits in their dealings with one another, they would spend half their lives in silence!

Muslims must understand that they have no right to look down upon other people. Muslims have a duty to convey their beliefs and morals judiciously, courteously, and in a spirit of kindness and love. One fears that the failure to spread the word of Islam more widely is largely attributable to a failure in approach and communication. The surah asserts:

> People, We have created you from a male and a female, and made you into nations and tribes, that you might come to know one another. The noblest of you in God's sight are those who are most deeply conscious of Him. (13)

The surah closes with an elaboration of the status of those Arabs who had embraced Islam without adopting its personal and social manners or its laws and regulations. They are an example of those who inherit their belief in Islam in name only and fail to carry it forward with conviction. Their hearts are devoid of faith and their actions are useless and meaningless.

It says: "The Arabs say, 'We believe.' Say, 'You are not believers, and you should rather say, 'We accept Islam,' since faith has not settled in your hearts'" (14). It goes on to explain that they would be judged by their deeds, saying: "If you obey God and His Messenger, He shall deny you none of the rewards of your labor..." (14). If they betray Islam or neglect its teachings or turn their backs on it in times of crisis, they cannot profess to be true Muslims. True believers, "Are those who believe in God and His Messenger and never falter; those who give up their wealth and their souls for the cause of God. It is they who are genuine believers" (15).

Today, there are many Muslims of the former type. They claim allegiance to Islam while they ignore its teachings and disregard its ethics and commands, and fail to support or defend its cause.

SURAH 50

Qāf

THE SUBJECT OF THIS SURAH is the resurrection and judgment in the hereafter. This is preceded by a series of indications and signs pointing to God's omnipotence and omniscience and the rationale behind that awesome phenomenon.

In our daily life we come across many miracles which, although we can understand, we are not able to explain. We know that the food we eat turns partly to energy and partly to bones and living body tissue. We also know that these bones and tissue carry genes which pass on traits and characteristics from generation to generation. However, how does all this come about?

Surplus or unwanted food is discarded and goes back into the soil where crops and plants grow in an amazing and wonderful cycle to feed living creatures and perpetuate life. Life and death occur inside every living body, every minute of the night and day. Is it any wonder then that God should assert in the Qur'an that humans shall be resurrected and brought back to life, and judgment, after death?

The surah denounces those skeptics who dispute this fact, saying:

They are surprised that a warner from among themselves has come to them. The unbelievers say, "This is indeed a strange thing! [Would we be brought back to life] once we have died and turned into dust? Such a return is far-fetched!" We know how much the earth consumes of their bodies, and We have a book in which all is recorded. (2–4)

This interaction between the dead and the living takes place every moment before our very eyes. How can the doubters be so stupid?

The Qur'an bases faith on sound rational argument and expresses it in the most powerful and lucid language. It is reported that a Muslim lady memorized this whole surah after hearing it recited once by Prophet Muhammad. The words were engraved in her memory to be preserved and translated into action.

To the Muslim mind, resurrection is not idle theory, but a vibrant belief that overwhelms the individual as he acts and goes about his life. The surah says:

> We created man and We know the innermost of his thoughts, and We are closer to him than his jugular vein. Two guardian angels, one on the right and one on the left, watch over him, and every word he utters is noted and recorded by a vigilant observer. (16–18)

There is a huge difference between a life based on skepticism and one based on sound, unshakeable belief in the resurrection, accountability to God, and final judgment.

Many religious systems and beliefs have failed to invigorate man's conscience and instill a fear of God within it. Many people today regard death as the end and the conclusion of all life on this earth, but the surah points out that these will be taken aback when they face a second life. It says:

> And on that promised Day, the trumpet shall be sounded, and every soul shall be ushered in, accompanied by a guide and a witness, and it shall be told, "You were oblivious of all this and now We have removed your veil and you shall now have a keen vision." (20–22)

Regrettably, many Muslims are nowadays attracted by such erroneous beliefs, refusing the idea of the ultimate divine judgment, and see life after death as a mere illusion. But life shall undoubtedly come to an end, and every man shall reap the fruits of his actions.

SURAH 50 · *Qāf*

The surah presents two contrasting scenes; in the first we hear the testimony of the devil assigned to the unbeliever saying: "'Here is my charge and here is his record.' [And God shall say], 'Cast into hell every hardened unbeliever, every obstructionist of good deeds, every doubting transgressor...'" (23–25).

The devil will try to extricate himself by saying: "'Lord, I did not mislead him, but he had already gone far astray'" (27). But such protestation is of no avail, as the surah says: "God says, 'Do not dispute in My presence, as I gave you warning beforehand. My word cannot be changed and I am not unjust to My servants'" (28–29).

This scene recalls to mind a similar situation mentioned in verse 128 of *al-Anʿām* which says:

"Jinn, you have misled humans in great numbers." Their human votaries would say, "Our Lord, we have enjoyed each other's fellowship, and now we have reached the end of the term You appointed for us." He will say, "The fire shall be your abode and there you shall remain forever..."

The second scene is that of the fate of the faithful. The surah says:

And Paradise is brought closer to the God-fearing, [and it will be said to them:] "This is what you were promised; it is for every penitent and faithful man who fears the Merciful without seeing Him and who comes before Him with a contrite heart. Enter it [the Garden] in peace. This is the day of Eternity." (31–34)

Although this life is a time for action rather than reward, God sometimes chooses to punish certain groups as an example and a deterrent to others. The surah says: "We have destroyed many a generation before them, far more powerful than themselves [the Makkans] who roamed the land but to no avail" (36).

583

As the surah draws to a close, it returns to its opening theme of creation, reaffirming that God had created the world with ease and of His own power and accord. It says: "We created the heavens and the earth and all that lies among them in six days and without experiencing any weariness" (38). God remains in total control of the world and all its affairs and He is the source of life and livelihood for the vast multitudes of creatures that have lived in it for all these millions and millions of years. God sustains the movement of the galaxies and the planets and the stars of this vast universe without experiencing tedium or fatigue. Were He to cease for even a single moment, the whole cosmic order would collapse!

To accuse God of weakness is, in fact, a folly many senseless people have committed, and here we find the Qur'an strongly refuting this absurd concept and reaffirming God's absolute glory and power over all things.

The Qur'an uses reason and rational argument in addressing the human mind and appeals to man's natural and instinctive inclination to reject such nonsense. The surah concludes by saying:

We well know what they [the unbelievers] say. You [Muhammad] cannot force them [to believe], so admonish with the Qur'an whoever fears My warning. (45)

Muhammad was not a despot who had come to change people's beliefs by force. He was a genuine pioneer, a true herald, and an honest and trustworthy teacher.

SURAH 51

Al-Dhāriyāt
(The Dust-Scattering Winds)

THE SURAH OPENS WITH A SERIES of attestations that merit closer study. It begins by mentioning the wind which is a vital element for life on earth as it carries clouds that bring rain to thirsty people and animals, as well as to the land for tilling and cultivation.

Wind is a force that binds all living creatures together as it travels over the whole surface of the globe. Who controls such a force and charts its course of movement at every moment? Even those parts of the world with low rainfall benefit from this phenomenon by way of rivers and natural reservoirs or lakes thousands of kilometers away from where the rain falls.

The surah encapsulates this delicately integrated picture in a few well-chosen words, as it says:

> By the dust-scattering winds and the cumulus clouds and by the swiftly-gliding vessels and by the angels who deal out the fortunes of men, what you are promised shall be fulfilled and final judgment shall surely come to pass! (1–6)

Just as it is possible that a gentle breeze is capable of moving huge clouds, heavily-laden with rainwater, it is possible for God Almighty to bring about the final judgment and make men accountable for what they have done in this life.

Other attestations follow: "By the heaven and its marvellous structures, you [the unbelievers] are in total confusion!" (7–8).

The sky and its countless constellations are so finely and meticulously built into one harmonious system. Every movement takes place according to a set pattern and well-integrated system.

From the heavens, the surah turns to the earth, saying: "And on earth there are signs for the undoubting believers" (20). Indeed, is not the earth itself a marvel to behold? Science says that it, like all other planets and stars, is held in orbit by the force of gravity, but what is gravity and how did it come about?

The surah continues:

And in yourselves [there are signs]. Can you not see? In heaven is your sustenance and all that you are promised. I swear by the Lord of heaven and earth that it is true, as sure as you are speaking now! (21–23)

The human body, with its various faculties and systems of sight, hearing, sensation, mental power, and so on, is another intricate and complicated wonder. Nonetheless, there are those who would claim that God does not exist, and that life is but matter! But even if life were pure matter, how did it come about and who laid down the laws and rules by which it is sustained, regulated, and controlled? The answer comes towards the end of the surah when it says:

We [God] built the heaven with a mighty hand and gave it vast expanse, and We spread out the earth well and created a pair of everything, so that you may remember. (47–49)

Those who deny the existence of God are taking a tremendous risk and expose themselves to an awesome threat. The surah warns:

Therefore, take refuge with God without delay. I [Muhammad] bring to you from Him certain warning. Do not take other gods besides God. I bring to you from Him compelling warning. (50–51)

Despite the warnings, obstinate unbelievers persist in their rejection of God, accusing His messengers of sorcery and madness. The surah says: "Thus whenever a messenger came to those before them [the Makkans], they cried, 'Sorcerer!' or 'Madman!' Have these inherited the same attitude? Surely all of them are transgressors" (52–53).

It was that stubborn attitude that had brought about the destruction of many communities in the past. The surah cites several telling examples. It tells of the episode of Abraham's 'guests' which indicates how his people misunderstood the concept of godhood and how much they were influenced by pagan beliefs. The 'guests' were a number of angels who had brought Abraham's wife, Sarah, the good news that she was going to have a baby son. They also told him that God would destroy the towns of Sodom and Gomorrah where acts of wickedness and perversion were being practiced.

The Old Testament version of this episode is significantly different. It says that God came down to Abraham who had prepared a huge feast of roasted calf meat and bread, on which God gorged Himself. The Qur'an, however, which Jews and Christians view with much suspicion, treats the subject with evident reverence and respect.

The surah speaks of Pharaoh and his army who had oppressed the Israelites and mistreated them. "We seized him and his warriors, and cast them into the [Red] Sea. He deserved much blame" (40). They vanished and no tears were shed for them.

Of the tribe of ʿĀd, who considered themselves invincible, the surah says: "In the fate of ʿĀd there was another sign, as We let loose on them a sterile wind that turned everything in its path into rubble and dust" (41–42).

Many once mighty and powerful nations and communities have disappeared. God sent to them messengers and teachers to guide and advise them but they stubbornly refused to heed their warnings and persisted in their transgression and wrongdoing.

God is in no need of people's help or service: all they are asked to do is to glorify and praise Him for His grace and generosity. The surah says:

> I created mankind and the jinn but to worship Me. I demand of them no sustenance, nor do I need them to feed Me. God alone is the Provider; He is the Mighty One, the Invincible. (56–58)

Ingratitude towards God Almighty shall not go unpunished, as the surah confirms:

> The wrongdoer shall meet a doom similar to that of their predecessors. Let them not be so hasty and challenge Me. Woe to the unbelievers when their threatened day arrives. (59–60)

SURAH 52

Al-Ṭūr
(The Mount)

THIS SURAH HAS A GENTLE and soothing effect on the human spirit. It brings light into a believer's life like that which comes with the dawn at the end of a long dark night.

Jubayr ibn al-Muṭ'im was one of the Makkan delegation who had gone to Madinah to negotiate the release of prisoners of war following the Arab defeat at Badr in 624 AC. While the Muslims were performing the prayer, he heard the Prophet leading the prayer and reciting *al-Ṭūr*. He was captivated by what he heard and began to question his own pagan beliefs.

He was later to recall the incident and said that his heart almost jumped out of his body when he heard the words:

Were they created out of nothing or were they their own creators? Did they create the heavens and the earth? Surely they have no faith. Or, do they hold the treasures of your Lord, or have control over them? (35–37)

He added that he was shaken by the words:

By the Mount [Mount Sinai] and by the Book that is inscribed on a spread parchment; and by the oft-frequented House [the Ka'bah] and by the elevated ceiling [the sky], and by the swelling sea, your Lord's punishment shall surely come to pass and no power shall be able to ward it off. (1–8)

He said that they had such a terrifying impact on him that he thought he was going to be struck by divine retribution at that very moment. Thus it was that Jubayr embraced Islam, by virtue of hearing the Qur'an and reacting to its simple but powerful message.

The link between Qur'anic revelation and previously revealed books is obvious. Moses received the Torah at Mount Sinai while Muhammad received the Qur'an near the Ka'bah, both of which conveyed a message of pure *tawḥīd* and came with a religious faith based on tangible facts and laws rather than myths and mysteries.

The surah seems to point to the scrolls of Moses, while the reference to the sea appears to be a reference to the Red Sea where Pharaoh, with his false godhood, was drowned.

It is important to point out here that the Torah was a book of religion as well as a book of law and statecraft. The same applies to the Qur'an. The Gospel of Jesus, however, was supplementary to the Torah and an extension to it, introducing a limited number of concessionary rules. The Qur'an, however, represents the final and complete version of divine religion and law. It is the revealed divine message for all time to come, and remains today the sole authentic scripture ever received by a human being.

The surah emphasizes God's warnings to the unbelievers, threatening them with a bleak and wretched end, and reiterates His promise to the believers of everlasting happiness and prosperity for their self-sacrifice, purity, and integrity. They are quoted as saying:

"Among our people, we were fearful of God's wrath, but God was gracious to us and has protected us from the torment of the fire. We have prayed to Him from of old, for He is the Righteous, the Merciful." (26–28)

In this tense atmosphere of warning and promise, Muhammad is instructed to persevere with his mission and keep God in his sights. The surah says: "Therefore, admonish your people. God has been gracious to you, and with that you are neither a soothsayer nor a madman" (29). Muhammad was accused of being both, but how could he be either when the religion he taught is in harmony with human nature and based on intelligence and common sense?

Islam has the unique honor of being a refined and humane way of life that renounces ostentation, extremism, and perversion. As if to stress these facts, the surah confronts the skeptics and unbelievers with fifteen hard-hitting questions that are liable to bring them back to their senses and make them think. These questions are:

- "Do they say, 'He [Muhammad] is a poet and we wait for him to be struck by some misfortune'?" (30–31). Muhammad was not a poet and his Book is full of facts rather than fanciful ideas.

- "Do their minds allow them to think so?" (32). Rational people would not make such ludicrous allegations.

- "Or is it merely that they are wicked people?" (32). Only wickedness could explain their determination to perpetrate such falsehoods.

- "Do they say, 'He [Muhammad] has invented it [the Qur'an] himself'? Indeed, they have no faith. Let them produce a scripture like it, if they are truthful" (33–34). If the Qur'an were the work of a human being, what would prevent other humans from matching it?

- "Were they created out of nothing?" (35). How could anything be created out of nothing?

- "Or were they their own creators?" (35). Man is created and he cannot create a living soul.

- "Did they create the heavens and the earth? Surely they have no faith" (36). How could man have created the heavens or the earth when they were here before him?

- "Do they hold the treasures of your Lord?" (37). Do the skeptics believe that they could influence events and determine the destiny of the world?

- "...Or have control over them?" (37). If they do, then let them prove it! No. It is sheer arrogance driving them to make such claims.

- "Have they a ladder [reaching up to the heavens] and are able to eavesdrop [on God]? Let them bring a positive proof" (38). If the unbelievers could come up with divine revelation other than the Qur'an, then let them produce it!

- "Is it so that He would have daughters and you [the unbelievers] sons?" (39). Preferring male offspring, the Makkan Arabs were disdainful of having daughters, but nevertheless had the temerity to ascribe female offspring to God Almighty.

- "Are you [Muhammad] demanding of them [the unbelievers] any remuneration which they find hard to bear?" (40). Prophets seek the pleasure and grace of God and ask for no reward or recompense from anyone else.

- "Have they knowledge of the unknown and could they write it down?" (41). No, it is sheer bluster and they are completely ignorant.

- "Do they seek to conspire against you? Their conspiring shall backfire on them" (42). No matter how long the battle between truth and falsehood may last, justice shall be done and the truth shall prevail.

- "Have they a god other than God? Exalted be He above what they worship besides Him" (43). God is the only supreme Lord of all creation.

After these probing, hard-hitting questions, the surah indicates that the unbelievers are so stubborn and arrogant that they would not even recognize their punishment when it falls upon them. It says: "Even if they were to see part of the heavens falling upon them, they would still say, 'It is but a mass of clouds'" (44).

Thus, the surah counsels Prophet Muhammad to remain closer to God, to forge ahead with his mission and not to allow himself to be diverted from his main purpose, leaving his detractors to God to determine their fate. It closes with the soothing and reassuring words:

Therefore welcome your Lord's judgment with equanimity, for you are ever under Our watchful eyes. Give glory to your Lord whenever you rise, and praise Him in the nighttime and as the stars fade away. (48)

SURAH 53

Al-Najm
(The Star)

HUMAN KNOWLEDGE HAS THREE well-established sources: the human intellect, the five human senses, and divine revelation or inspiration which God bestows upon select individuals. This privileged knowledge is referred to elsewhere in the Qur'an when Jacob is reported to have told his sons: "'And I know from God that which you do not'" (*Yūsuf*: 86).

Knowledge received through revelation is real and absolute but it is only imparted to those with special personal gifts and traits that qualify them for such an honor and a privilege. Muhammad was a preeminent individual among this select group of human beings.

The present surah indicates how Muhammad had received revelation. It says:

By the star as it falls, your companion [Muhammad] has neither gone astray nor is he misled. And he is not speaking out of his own fancy. This is inspired revelation, taught to him by the Mighty and Wise one [the angel Gabriel]... (1–6)

Moses received his calling at Mount Sinai by the Red Sea where he was charged with carrying the banner of revelation for his generation, while Muhammad received his after several years of retirement and solitary meditation at a cave on Mount Ḥirā' near Makkah. His remit was to advance the word of God and establish His order on earth.

The surah asserts: "His heart and mind have never falsified what he had seen. How could you [the unbelievers] question what he had seen?" (11–12). The revelation Muhammad received was the truth which he truthfully and scrupulously relayed. The unbelievers question this fact because they: "succumb to their vain conjecture and prejudices, although their Lord's guidance has long since come to them" (23).

Throughout the ages, religion, revealed and unrevealed alike, has been the subject of much abuse, distortion, and corruption. Myths and superstitions about the Divine Being have crept into many religious beliefs, bringing religion into direct conflict with science. Religion and science are legitimate means for seeking the ultimate truth, but human caprice and tendentious manipulation have, in many cases, distorted the original and pristine divine message. The surah says:

They [the unbelievers] have no knowledge whatsoever of the claims they make; they merely succumb to conjecture, and conjecture is no substitute for truth. (28)

Religious knowledge is absolute knowledge, upheld and protected by divine revelation, based on rational argument and common sense. Any religious proposition or argument that does not stand up to rational and intellectual examination is not worthy of being approved or believed.

Distortion and tampering have crept into some Muslim doctrines, literature, and thought, and claims were made that Prophet Muhammad had praised the Makkan idols and approved of their veneration. Fortunately, such claims are not to be found in any of the trusty and authentic works of Islam, and have been completely disproved by rigorous and meticulous study.

The surah goes on to establish a fundamental principle regarding God's omnipotence and justice. It points to the route of man's success in his relationship to God and defines his limits and responsibilities within the overall message of Islam which guarantees man total freedom of choice. It says:

> To God belongs all that is in the heavens and on earth, and so He will recompense the evil-doers according to their deeds, and give those who do good a rich reward: those that avoid the most vile of sins and indecencies, although they may commit lesser ones. Your Lord's mercy is vast; He knows you best of all since He created you of earth and you were hidden in your mothers' wombs. Do not, therefore, be infatuated by your self-importance, for He knows best those who are God-fearing. (31–32)

The above passage confirms man's weakness and vulnerability to fall victim to his desires and prejudices. Sensible and mature believers should always be on their guard and look to God's guidance and grace to save them from falling by the wayside. They are ever ready to respond to God's call and seek His pleasure out of a desire to elevate and purify their souls and liberate themselves from greed and caprice.

The surah points out that the obstinate unbelievers shall face failure and disappointment. It says:

> Have you considered him who turns his back, who gives little then hardens [his heart]? Does he know, and can he see, the unknown? (33–35)

These characteristic features are typical of those who reject faith in God, past and present. They arrogantly refuse to acknowledge God, they look down upon others, and display a unique sense of selfishness and self-regard.

To reject Muhammad is to ignore the revelation given to him and all previous revelations. The surah says:

Has he [the unbeliever] heard of what is in the scriptures of Moses
[the Torah] and those of Abraham who had fulfilled his mission:
that no soul shall be made to bear another's burden; and that each
person shall be judged by his own labors alone; and that his labors
shall be assessed carefully and that he shall be accordingly rewarded
with generosity? (36–41)

The essence of religious belief is to know the Creator through His
creation and to recognize His power and authority over everything.
To suggest that life is self-generated, or that it is self-perpetuating
and that there is no place in this world for a Creator, is simply absurd.
The surah goes on:

And that to your Lord is the final return; and that it is He who created laughter and tears; and that it is He who grants death and life;
and that it is He who created the two sexes, the male and the female,
from a drop of ejaculated semen. (42–46)

Life is a gift from the Almighty who has power over all things. It
is an ongoing phenomenon—generations come and generations go.
The surah closes on a high note, vibrant with piercing assertions,
resounding in all directions, delivered in short hard-hitting strokes
of rhythm. It says:

And that He will bring all to life again; and that He grants wealth
and happiness; and that He is the Lord of Sirius [the mighty star];
and that He had destroyed the ancient people of ʿĀd and annihilated Thamūd leaving no trace of them. And before them the people of Noah who were more wicked and more seditious. And He
destroyed the overthrown cities [of Sodom and Gomorrah] so that
[ruins unknown] have covered them up. Which of God's blessings
does man then deny? (47–55)

Thus God removed the wicked and insolent communities of old, and destroyed their power and domination. Let this be a warning to others that He is capable of doing the same again at will and whenever necessary.

Muhammad was but one of many warners, preaching the same basic beliefs of *tawḥīd*. He denounced intercession with God and all superstition surrounding religious beliefs and practises, emphasizing that no man can control or decide another man's fate or destiny. The surah closes on an acerbic note to the cynics, asking: "Would you then question this revelation and laugh at it rather than weep?" (59–60).

SURAH 54

Al-Qamar
(The Moon)

THE SURAH OPENS WITH REFERENCE to a cataclysmic event as one of the major signs of the impending end of the world. It says: "The Hour is drawing near, and the moon is split asunder" (1). Other signs are cited elsewhere in the Qur'an, such as:

> When the eyes are bewildered and the moon eclipsed, and the sun and the moon are brought together, man will ask, "Whither shall I flee?" (al-Qiyāmah: 7–10)

A report by Ibn Masʿūd indicates that a splitting of the moon did occur at the time of Prophet Muhammad but the Makkans refused to believe it had happened and insisted that Muhammad was a mere sorcerer. The surah says: "They deny the truth and follow their own fantasies and prejudices. But all matters shall eventually be laid to rest" (3).

There will always be those who claim that Muhammad's efforts were in vain, since paganism and polytheism have survived and thrived through the ages, and the Muslims have failed to eradicate them. But the surah reiterates God's warnings to the unbelievers, saying: "Warnings have come to them with sufficient deterrence and profound wisdom, but would warnings be to any avail?" (4–5).

For man to respond to the call of God, his conscience must be alive and his heart must be pure. Throughout the Qur'an, God warns the unbelievers of the impending arrival of the Day of

Judgment and of the ill-fate of those who reject revelation. We read in the Qur'an that:

> As for the unbelievers, because of their misdeeds disaster shall never cease to afflict them or to fall close to their dwellings until God's will is fulfilled. (*al-Raʿd*: 31)

The present surah briefly cites the fate of earlier intransigent communities from the people of Noah onward, saying:

> Long before them, the people of Noah disbelieved and rejected Our servant and called him a madman and scolded him, but he called out to his Lord, "I am weak, Lord, and so You prevail over them!" (9–10)

Noah's experience of his people's rejection is typical and poignant and his plaintive cry for help can, even today, drive one to tears. God's response comes with speed:

> We opened the gates of heaven with pouring rain and caused the earth to burst with gushing springs, and so the waters met for a pre-destined purpose. (11–12)

Then it was the turn of ʿĀd, an arrogant and insolent people who were of strong physique and wealthy, who rejected the messenger sent to them. They also received their just deserts:

> We let loose on them a howling wind which snatched them away like trunks of uprooted palm-trees. How grievous was My scourge, and how clear My warning. (19–21)

Thus ordinary and familiar forces of nature, water, and air, become powerful tools in the hand of God to punish and destroy the wrong-doers.

Next comes an account of the fate of the people of Thamūd, and what the prophet Ṣāliḥ said to them because it was similar to what Muhammad said to his people. They questioned God's will to choose His messengers to convey His revelation, saying:

"Are we to follow a mortal from among ourselves? We would surely be mad and in grievous error. Was he [Ṣāliḥ] the only one of us chosen to receive the revelation? He is nothing but a presumptuous liar!" (24–25)

Ṣāliḥ had come to them with a sign in the form of a she-camel created from rock but they defied him and destroyed it, thereby incurring God's wrath and punishment which turned them into dry twigs of straw. The surah says: "We sent to them one cry and they became like dry wattle" (31).

The surah then turns on the people of Lot and their vile practices of sodomy and buggery which they institutionalized and practised publicly in their clubs and gatherings. It says:

They demanded his guests of him [for their pleasure] but We extinguished their eyesight and said, "Taste My punishment and My warning." And in the morning a heavy scourge overtook them. (37–38)

Lot condemned those indecencies and did his best to dissuade the people from perpetrating them but failed. The story says that Lot received a delegation of angels and that some of his people even tried to seduce them. Many of them were struck blind and their city was totally destroyed.

Homosexual practices have now become a feature of modern society and have brought with them the spread of HIV and AIDS, and instead of persuading people not to practise homosexual acts, religious and social leaders and educators are giving advice on safe sex and free condoms!

Finally, the surah cites the fate of the Pharaohs who were ruthless rulers and sought to dominate and enslave, saying:

To Pharaoh's people also came warnings. They rejected all Our revelations and signs, and so We smote them as only a Mighty and All-Powerful God could. (41–42)

The point here is that God's enemies will not prevail, no matter how powerful and mighty they may be. The surah goes on to address the disbelieving Makkans, saying:

Are your unbelievers [O Quraysh] better than them, or are you granted immunity in the scripture? Or do they say, "We are many and we shall be victorious"? They shall be routed and put to flight. (43–45)

That prophecy was fulfilled at Badr when the Makkan Arabs were dealt a humiliating defeat and lost a number of their most prominent leaders. A worse fate awaits them in the hereafter.

The surah closes with reference to the Day of Judgment when mankind—believers and unbelievers—will be set apart for accountability and reward. On the one hand there are the unbelievers:

The wrong-doers are doomed to bewilderment and a scorching fire. The day will come when they are dragged into the fire with their faces downwards and are told to taste the scourge of hell... (47–48)

On the other, there are the believers: "The righteous shall dwell in gardens with rivers running through them, honorably seated in the presence of the Mighty Lord" (54–55).

SURAH 55

Al-Raḥmān
(The Merciful)

THE WORD WITH WHICH THIS SURAH opens, "*Al-Raḥmān*
taught you the Qur'an" (1–2), and from which it derives its title, is
one of God's most exalted names and, besides the name Allah, is one
of the most frequently used in the Qur'an.

One of God's gracious blessings to mankind has been to provide
them with guidance for living. The Qur'an has encompassed all
previous revelation received by earlier prophets and messengers.
Its supreme teachings, principles, and ideas help mankind to lead a
normal and fulfilled life, for all time to come. The knowledge
and guidance the Qur'an brings are the first and foremost blessings
from God to Muhammad, the seal of the prophets. We read in the
Qur'an: "And He sent down to you [Muhammad] the Book
and wisdom, and He taught you that which you did not know"
(*al-Nisā'*: 113).

The Qur'an is a blessing also to all who study it and teach it to
others. Prophet Muhammad was reported to have said: "The best
among you is he who learns the Qur'an and teaches it." This noble
act of learning and teaching the Qur'an is a continuation of the
excellent tradition of God's prophets and messengers and a commendable contribution to the enlightenment and education of
individuals and communities.

Language is a feature unique to man, while eloquence of speech
is another divine blessing by which humans are able to articulate
ideas and concepts and communicate with one another in various
languages, accents, and dialects.

The surah goes on to assert that the whole cosmos exists and is sustained and controlled according to a predetermined and precise system; galaxies, stars, and planets are not simply drifting aimlessly in space. Every heavenly body has a set orbit and speed and is a part of a whole system which is closely balanced and tightly controlled. The same goes for plants that grow on earth; their life cycle is perpetuated according to a deliberate and well-integrated system.

The surah reflects a universe that is as well-regulated as a clockwork mechanism:

> The sun and the moon follow their precise course. Stars [or planets] and trees bow down [to God] in adoration. He raised the heaven high and set the balance of all things, so that you may not transgress the proper balance. (5–8)

This order in nature and the cosmic system may suffer disruption and disturbance as a result of human activity, folly, or abuse of the environment; natural resources may be plundered, the ozone layer could be ruptured, but the overall order and balance, being under the authority and control of the supreme Creator, shall be preserved and maintained until such time that God Almighty wills it to be otherwise.

In the meantime, men have the responsibility to establish justice in all their dealings with one another at all levels and in all spheres of life. The surah urges: "So give just weight and do not undercut the measure" (9).

God's blessings to mankind are varied and numerous. He has provided man with the fruits of crops, plants and trees on which man's nourishment and survival depend. These are also essential for the survival of animal life which, in turn, is vital and supplementary to human life. Moreover, the earth is richly adorned with the most exotic and beautiful flowers, blossoms, and vegetation for man's enjoyment and pleasure.

The surah has a distinctive refrain, repeated thirty-one times at regular intervals. It is a question addressed to the jinn and to human beings asking: "Which, then, of your Lord's blessings would you deny?" (13). Apart from that, the surah may be divided into four main sections, each dealing with a separate theme.

The first section deals with creation and the exquisite manner in which creation has been designed and integrated. The second one talks of death, resurrection, and punishment of the wrong-doers. The third section talks of faithful believers, while the fourth one speaks of those with a higher level of devotion to God.

Man's creation began with Adam who was created of earth and clay and black molded loam. From that beginning, the miracle of human creation continues to take place inside the mother's womb in stages, from a single fertilized egg that goes on to divide and grow into an embryo and then into a fetus; limbs and organs appear and the fetus gradually grows into a fully-developed human being.

The will of God is that mankind shall occupy and rule the earth for a prescribed period of time before all are overcome by death, only to be resurrected back to life to face accountability for their actions in this life. The surah asserts: "All that lives on earth must eventually die, but the face of your Lord, of majesty and glory, will abide for ever" (26–27). No one who has ever lived in this life shall be exempt from the final judgment in the hereafter. The righteous shall enjoy eternal peace and happiness while those who are condemned shall receive their just reward.

The surah says: "The wrong-doers shall be identified by their mark; they shall be seized by their forelocks and their feet" (41). This seems to indicate that the accountability and questioning process will be completed over a number of stages before a final judgment is passed.

The scolding of the neglectful continues to great effect through the repetition, again and again, of the refrain: "Which, then, of your Lord's blessings would you deny?" (36). It is used for a variety of ends: to highlight certain parts of the surah, to stress particular aspects, or to draw attention to specific scenes on the Day of Judgment. Here is an example:

> So when the sky is split asunder and turns red like a rose or stained leather, which of your Lord's blessings would you deny? On that day neither man nor jinn will be asked about his sins. (37–39)

The overall temper of the passage is one of anger and severe reprimand of those who are ungrateful and deny God's kindness and grace.

The surah concludes by giving a most beautiful and awe-inspiring description of the gardens in Paradise exclusively reserved for the most righteous of human beings, as well as those set aside for the rest of the believing men and women. These are depicted as opulent luxurious places, rich with green plants, lavish flowers, and flowing rivers. They are places of tranquillity, uninterrupted enjoyment, and everlasting peace.

Al-Wāqiᶜah
(The Inevitable Event)

LIKE *al-Ḥāqqah*, *al-Qāriᶜah* and *al-Sāᶜah*, the title of this surah, *al-Wāqiᶜah*, is one of the Arabic names given in the Qur'an to the Day of Resurrection. The surah's main features are quite distinct: it opens with a brief reference to the end of life on earth and the advent of the Day of Reckoning. It goes on to describe the three categories into which humankind will be divided in the hereafter: those who accepted the faith without question shall be the nearest to God, followed by the righteous who shall be to the right of God, and then the unbelievers who shall be to the left of God.

The surah then gives five arguments as evidence that resurrection is true and inevitable, and argues that to deny it is pure folly and futile. It concludes with a reference to the moment of death and to the fate of each of the three categories of humankind described above.

Being totally preoccupied with their day-to-day lives and worldly affairs, the majority of people cannot think beyond their material or physical existence. Many of them are, to say the least, skeptical about the resurrection and are quite adamant in their belief that death is the end of their existence.

Death is a most profound truth; today's dead are buried by those who too will die one day, and yet the latter continue to ignore death and live as if it would not happen to them. It seldom moves them to think or reflect on their convictions or conduct. As generations succeed generations, skeptics and disbelievers throughout the world seem to grow and increase, and become more vociferous.

By his very nature, man is argumentative, contentious, and stubborn. However, once this great cataclysmic event is suddenly set in motion, the curtain will fall and no human power will be able to stop it. The surah says: "When the inevitable event takes place, no one shall be able to deny it" (1–2).

Many a king or emperor shall be resurrected a feckless pauper, because they had not prepared for that momentous day, while others who were unknown and undistinguished shall be raised to the loftiest positions. "It shall abase some and lift others" (3). Many of those adorned in this world shall emerge bare on the Day of Judgment; the day when things shall be put aright and the truth shall prevail.

Some commentators give a literal interpretation indicating the physical fall and rise of parts of the earth such as mountains, buildings, and trees. The hadith often quoted to support this view says: "On the Day of Judgment, people shall be gathered on flat white sandy plains, without a single landmark."[36]

Elsewhere in the Qur'an, we read:

> They ask you [Muhammad] about the mountains. Say, "My Lord shall crush them to fine dust and reduce them to desolate waste, and you shall see neither peaks nor troughs." (*Ṭā Hā*: 105–107)

The two interpretations are complementary and there is no contradiction between them. The social upheaval that will destroy the false edifices of opulence, power, and status shall be accompanied by a geophysical calamity indicated by the words: "When the earth shakes and quivers, and the mountains crumble away and scatter into fine dust..." (4–6).

With the arrival of the Hour, then, a huge earthquake will strike, bringing everything toppling to the ground. Solid rocks shall

---

36 Narrated by al-Bukhārī.

crumble into fine dust. "The earth shall not be the same earth, nor shall the heavens, and all mankind shall stand before God, the One, the Conqueror" (*Ibrāhīm*: 48). Nobody knows when that event will occur—tens, perhaps hundreds, of centuries from now! The time span is irrelevant; what is more important is the outcome of this long history.

The surah indicates that, on that momentous day, mankind will be divided into three groups:

> You shall be divided into three multitudes: those on the right [blessed shall be those on the right], and those on the left [damned shall be those on the left], and those to the fore [they shall be foremost] who shall be brought nearer [to God] in the gardens of pure delight. (7–12)

The surah then goes on to give five different indications, derived from the physical world and from human experience, as evidence for the impending universal resurrection. The first indication is that whoever brought this world into being in the first instance can bring it to life a second time. The surah says: "We [God] have created you; would you not then believe [in the resurrection]?" (57).

Elsewhere in the Qur'an, God says: "It is He that initiated creation, and He renews it; that is easier for Him" (*al-Rūm*: 27). But, for God Almighty, there are no easy or hard tasks and so the verse goes on to say: "And to Him belongs the most exalted and unique attribute in heaven and earth, and He is the Mighty, the Wise One" (*al-Rūm*: 27). This incontrovertible argument is repeated on numerous occasions throughout the Qur'an, such as:

> "What!" they ask, "when we are turned to bones and dust, shall we be brought to life again?" Say, "Be you stones or iron, or any other entity you may think will never come to life." They will say, "Who will re-create us?" Say, "He that created you the first time round..." (*al-Isrā'*: 49–51)

The Qur'an urges man to examine very closely the world around him and to reflect deeply on the phenomenon of creation. There should be no doubt that we exist, and so the question is: how did we come to be here? The more one thinks about resurrection, the more foolish its denial seems to be. We read in the Qur'an:

> Do they not see how God initiates creation and repeats it; it is easy for God to do so. Say, "Roam the earth and see how God originated creation, and He will initiate the second creation. God has power over all things. He punishes whom He pleases and shows mercy to whom He pleases and to Him you shall be recalled."
> (al-ʿAnkabūt: 19–21)

The present surah captures this whole concept in the words: "We [God] have created you; would you not then believe [in the resurrection]?" (57).

The second argument says that God's ability to create is never exhausted; the phenomenon of creation takes place again and again, every day and every hour and every moment. As is the case with human beings, creation is an ongoing, renewable process. The surah expresses this concept thus:

> Look at the semen you discharge: do you create it yourselves or do We? It is We that ordained death among you, and We are equally capable of replacing you by others like you, and of recreating you in a form you cannot conceive. (58–61)

Indeed, semen is a fascinating substance! Every spurt of this bland fluid carries hundreds of millions of spermatozoa, minuscule creatures each of which carries all the human physiological and psychological characteristics. These are passed on from parent to child, a fact known to man for a long time.

610

How are spermatozoa manufactured in the testicles, the glands made of flesh and blood that feed on nutrients obtained from foods growing in the ground? The overall power that controls and regulates this process is God Almighty:

Who perfected everything He has created and created man out of clay. Then He made his offspring from a drop of plain fluid, and then molded him and breathed into him of His own spirit. He gave you hearing and sight and gave you hearts and minds, yet you seldom thank Him. (*al-Sajdah*: 7–9)

What is even more astonishing is that only one spermatozoon is needed to fertilize a female egg and produce a conceptuse. The rest are discarded, as if to point out that the making of a single human being requires next to nothing and that God can, if He so wishes, create billions more.

The third argument points to the multitude of marvels one can see every day: the countless plants with their various shapes, sizes and fruits, the flowers with their different colors, scents, and configurations.

Who has brought all this about? Farmers plough the land and plant the seeds, but leave the rest to God's will and power. All they have to do is look after the crop, reap the fruits and marvel at God's endowments. Such marvelous phenomena are bound to inspire fascination and curiosity as to what power lies behind them. They are liable to make one appreciate the realities of life and death.

The surah points to evidence for resurrection in the planting and gathering of crops, when it says: "Consider the seeds you sow! Do you make them grow, or do We? Had We willed, We would have rendered your crop a total wreck" (63–65). The life cycle is repeated continually throughout the universe. The resurrection of a dead human being cannot be less possible than making a plant grow out of a seed in the ground. God says: "God has brought you forth from the earth like a plant, and into the earth He will return you and then bring you back anew" (*Nūḥ*: 17–18).

Elsewhere He says:

And the earth We spread out and set upon it rigid mountains and brought forth from it all kinds of delectable plants. This We did as [a source of] enlightenment and an admonition to all penitent men. (*Qāf*: 7–8)

Such wonders and signs are liable to shake the oblivious and awaken the inattentive.

Human resurrection is just as real as the sowing and growing of seeds and plants out of heaps of peat, earth, and compost. How could any rational reasonable person deny such a fact that is demonstrated around us every single day?

Farmers may think that they are responsible for the growth of their plants and crops, and so the surah points out that God has the power to destroy the fruits of their labor. It says:

Had We willed, We would have rendered your crop a total wreck, and left you in total wonderment, exclaiming, "We have lost everything; nay, we have been robbed of our livelihood." (65–67)

The resurrection, like the growing of plants and crops, is a demonstration of the ability and power of the Creator that ought to inspire faith in the hereafter and the Day of Judgment. Let us dwell briefly on this concept.

Man is made up of body and soul. But is it true that man's excellence and elevation could only be attained by the denial of the body and the suppression of its needs and desires? There is nothing in the Qur'an or the Sunnah that supports this view.

Islam prescribes fasting and the experience of hunger and thirst. It demands the observance of prayer which could at times be strenuous.

Some people may have to struggle and work very hard to earn their living, while others might sacrifice their lives for the cause of God. But these are no more than manifestations of the challenges and ordeals of life in which the soul endures and suffers just as much as the body. If such pain were to be somehow mitigated or eliminated, life would lose its very essence and substance, and the reward for perseverance would be rendered meaningless.

Man is a unique creature, created by God in perfect order. It is absurd to believe that the human body should be degraded or abused in order to satisfy the soul or purify the spirit. How could this be the case since, when God Almighty created Adam, He invited him "to dwell, you and your wife, in Paradise and eat of its fruits to your hearts' delight wherever you will..." (*al-Baqarah*: 35). God's prophets and messengers were directed to: "Eat of that which is wholesome, and do good works..." (*al-Muʾminūn*: 51). There could be no question of intended deprivation in God's teachings.

God eased the lot of mankind by providing them with what they need by way of sustenance, asking them only to appreciate His grace and show gratitude in return. God says: "Believers, eat of the wholesome things We have provided for you and thank God, if indeed it is He you worship" (*al-Baqarah*: 172). Is this a negation of the flesh or an invitation to abandon material life?

God affirms in the Qurʾan that, after this human journey and experience on this earth, humankind will come back a second time to face God and account for their works. He says: "As We initiated the first creation, We shall repeat it. This is a promise We shall certainly fulfill" (*al-Anbiyāʾ*: 104).

In what form will this resurrection take place? Will it be in body only, or merely in spirit? Both are absurd concepts.

Humans shall always be human. They shall rise again with all the faculties, feelings, and emotions they possessed in this life. Their own bodies shall be a witness against them. The Qurʾan says:

Their ears and their eyes and their skins will testify to what they had been doing. They will say to their skins, "Why did you testify against us?" and their skins will say, "God, who makes everything speak, has made us speak. He created you the first time, and to Him you shall return." (*Fuṣṣilat*: 20–21)

Those who suffer and work hard in this life will be richly rewarded in the hereafter. Ibn Kathīr quotes a report by al-Ṭabarānī that, according to Prophet Muhammad, believing women in the hereafter will occupy a status higher even than that of the houris. When Umm Salamah asked: "In return for what?" the Prophet replied: "In return for their prayers and fasting and devotion to God!"

The hadith goes on to relate that, in the hereafter, believing women would say: "We shall have eternal life and will never die; we are the gentle ones who will never despair; we have settled down and shall never depart; we are contented and shall never be dissatisfied; blessed are we and blessed are our spouses..."

Those who strive and toil in this life will be restful in the hereafter. The notion that the destruction of the human body is permanent and irreversible, and that the hereafter is a world of souls and spirits alone, and that punishment and reward are abstract or spiritual only, is baseless and false. It is a concept that had filtered into Christianity from pagan man-made religions, based on myths and legends.

Advocates of asceticism and the suppression of the flesh represent a defeatist element in today's world, whereas modern civilization has gone farther than any other in satisfying the desires of the flesh, and has thrown up ways and forms in which it can be achieved that were never known even in the courts and palaces of the most affluent and corrupt kings and rulers of old. Inevitably, such erroneous beliefs have led to disastrous and sinful behavior.

The needs of the body are limited and easy to satisfy provided people can avoid extravagance and self-indulgence. Various talents and endeavors are rewarded in various forms and in different degrees. Some people appreciate what they receive more than they appreciate the giver. From our own experience, we know that the recognition and honor (such as the Nobel Prize, for instance), bestowed upon scientists and achievers mean very little to some unless complemented by substantial financial rewards. However, others direct their gratitude to the giver regardless of the value of what he gives them.

True believers adore God for His own sake and accept whatever He ordains for them, whether good or bad. However, as humans and believers, we need to experience the pleasure of reward, and ought not, therefore, to be so insincere as to claim that we are not seeking the material pleasures of Paradise but only to be with God and to enjoy the glory of His company!

Believers will indeed have the honor and the privilege of seeing God Almighty in person, but they will also enjoy the physical delights of being in Paradise, and there is no contradiction between the two. We read in the Qur'an that:

God has promised believing men and believing women gardens through which rivers flow, in which they shall abide forever, and wonderful mansions in the gardens of Eden, as well as greater pleasure and blessings from God. That is the most supreme triumph. (al-Tawbah: 72)

It is clear, then, that the divine pleasure is far more gratifying and enjoyable than any other reward.

Muslim ʿulamas are totally agreed that reward and punishment in the hereafter are material as well as spiritual, and this view is supported by a host of Qur'anic statements and hadiths.

We know, for instance, that Jesus and Yaḥyā (John, son of Zachariah) lived a celibate life, but they were not opposed to marriage and did not advocate celibacy or continence as a way of life for everyone else. Their mission was not to destroy or undermine human life, but their celibacy arose out of their own individual circumstances. Several prominent Muslim leaders and scholars also never married, but none of them promoted celibacy in their thought.

Similarly, vegetarians refrain from eating meat, and this might suit their bodies and personalities, and that is their choice because the consumption of meat is not a religious obligation. What is objectionable, however, is the attempt to impose such a tendency on everyone else and turn it into a way of life.

Some contemporary writers have claimed that Paradise is not a "market," meaning that its rewards are not material or physical! Such a view has been promoted as sublime and lofty, but in fact it is absurd.

In the history of Islam, one comes across legendary figures who sought and yearned for the pleasures and comforts of Paradise. Anas ibn Naḍr, in the heat of battle at Uḥud, was heard saying: "I can smell Paradise from beyond the mountain of Uḥud!" In a similar situation, Jaʿfar ibn Abū Ṭālib was fighting bravely and chanting: "How delightful is Paradise as it draws nearer. It is wonderful and its water is cool and refreshing!"

Was that yearning of such great and honorable believers for the delights of Paradise hallucinatory, as the detractors claim, and does it reflect a weakness on their part? Such people have been refered to in the Qur'an:

> Among the believers are men who have been true to their covenant with God: of them some have completed their pledge, and some [still] wait, but they have never changed [their determination] in the least. (*al-Aḥzāb*: 23)

Even Christian scholars have scoffed at the Muslim concept of hell and heaven as physical realities, but what spiritual contribution have these critics of Islam made to humanity? Has their condemna-tion of the material aspects of human life and their call for the sup-pression of the needs of the body done humanity any good at all? The reality is that their view of the human psyche is fundamentally flawed and that is one of the reasons that is driving people away from religion.

Man is an integrated combination of matter and soul and may only attain happiness and fulfillment under a system that equally rec-ognizes these two elements in him. Such was the essence of the teachings of all God's prophets, including Moses whom the Qurʾan quotes as pleading on behalf of his people:

"You, Lord, are our Guardian, so forgive us and have mercy on us, for You are the noblest of those who forgive. And ordain for us what is good both in this life and in the hereafter; to You alone we return." (al-Aʿrāf: 155–156)

Long before him, Abraham made this passionate prayer:

"My Lord, bestow wisdom upon me and admit me among the righ-teous, and bless me with a good reputation among posterity and count me among the heirs of the blissful Garden. Please also forgive my father, for he was of those who had gone astray, and do not hold me up to shame on the Day of Resurrection, when wealth and off-spring will avail no one except those who come before God with pure hearts; when Paradise is brought closer to the righteous and hell is revealed to the erring." (al-Shuʿarāʾ: 83–91)

The surah differentiates between two groups of the righteous: those who hearkened to the faith and those who fared well in their response to it. The rest are "those of the left." Some commentators confused this definition with that in *Fāṭir* which refers to those "of whom had brought wrong-doing upon themselves [the negligent] and some did not fare too badly and yet others strove to do their best" (*al-Fāṭir*. 32).

The present surah refers to all mankind, believers and unbelievers alike, while the reference in *Fāṭir* is to the Muslims only. This is clear from the preceding text which says:

> And then We bequeathed the Book to those of Our servants We have chosen, some of whom had brought wrong-doing upon themselves [the negligent] and some did not fare too badly and yet others strove to do their best. (*Fāṭir*. 32)

Al-Wāqiʿah goes on to point out that the most favored of the three groups, the third one, includes: "...many from the earlier generations and very few from the latter ones" (13–14).

Some commentators take the view that the earlier generations are followers of prophets and messengers prior to Muhammad and that the latter generations refer to followers of Islam. They argue that this is justified by the sheer number of prophets and followers.

My own view, however, is that the whole passage is a reference to the followers of Islam, with the early Muslims, who pioneered the establishment and spread of Islam throughout the world, representing the majority of the most favored group, and the rest coming from later generations who upheld the faith through hardship and adversity.

As for earlier prophets, their missions were short-lived and parochial. As Muslims, we have great respect for the followers of Moses and Jesus, but, adulterated and tampered with, their messages have long ceased to exist in their original form.

The surah affirms that the most important concession the first group gains in the hereafter is to be close to God Almighty, which is a sign of His pleasure. It says: "And those that were to the fore [in faith], shall have precedence [in the hereafter]; they shall be brought closer [to God], in gardens of delight" (10–12).

Those are the true believers whose faith had been completed and their aspirations fulfilled. They are full of praise and appreciation for their Lord; they glorify God with every breath. The Qur'an says: "Their prayer in Paradise is, 'Glory be to You, Lord!' And their greeting is, 'Peace!' And their closing prayer is, 'Praise be to God, Lord of all creation'" (*Yūnus*: 10). Like the angels, they glorify God constantly and tirelessly, with total serenity and contentment, by day and by night.

Those who, in this life, enjoyed reading and studying the Qur'an, shall derive even more enjoyment from doing so in the hereafter. Believers shall be fully and generously rewarded for their deeds and efforts in this life. They will be guests of their Lord in the auspicious company of angels and prophets. They will enjoy more than kings and emperors here on earth could ever dream of.

The wonders, blessings, and comforts of Paradise are beyond description or imagination. What we are told about it is very little indeed; no more than a taste of what it is really like. It is a place of total and complete devotion to God Almighty; devotion accompanied by an overwhelming feeling of happiness and contentment. It has reclining couches, studded with precious metal. "They recline on them face to face" (16). They socialize in an atmosphere of tranquillity, facing one another. "They are waited upon by immortal youths..." (17). who serve them with milk, honey, water and wine that are pure and healthy and which cause them to suffer "no giddiness or intoxication" (19).

Among the most famous features of Paradise are the virgin houris. These are said to be human beings, both men and women, of beguiling beauty, in the prime of eternal youth and freshness. In Paradise, humans undergo extensive biological and physiological changes for the better. Believers will be able to live together in bliss and happiness, as the Qur'an says:

They [the believers] are admitted into gardens of Eden, together with their righteous parents, spouses, and offspring. The angels come to them from every door and say, "Peace be upon you for your patience. Blessed is your final abode!" (*al-Raʿd*: 23–24)

The human body is a marvelous and awe-inspiring creation, but it has many shortcomings and embarrassing functions. This could be part of the test humans have to face in this life. To replace those functions with better ones is a step towards ultimate perfection.

The Qur'an, as a whole, gives glimpses of the rich rewards reserved for the believers in the hereafter. These are enough to inspire, reassure, and encourage people to long for those rewards and work hard to earn them.

This surah describes the rewards awaiting "those who are to the fore" and "those of the right," who are of greater number. There will be *sidr* (lotus) trees, which normally grow on water-rich land and have prickly thorns, that will be thorn-free. There will be clusters of banana trees, and expansive carpets of constant shade that never diminish with the heat of the sun, and continuously running water in the form of streams, springs, and fountains. Paradise has an abundance of fruit of all kinds available all the year round: "Neither governed by the seasons, nor forbidden" (33).

For those on the right, who are the mass of the Muslims after the first generation, there will be attractive and loving women, all of similar age.

The surah then turns to describe what awaits those "of the left," a reference to the mass of those who rejected God, opposed His messengers, denounced His message, and perpetrated corruption and injustice in the world. The surah talks of "scorching winds and seething water" (42), and of "shade of pitch-black smoke, neither cool nor refreshing" (43–44). Elsewhere in the Qur'an, God orders the unbelievers on the Day of Judgment to: "Go into the shadow that rises high in three columns, providing neither shade nor shelter from the flames" (*al-Mursalāt*: 30–31). The people "of the left" earned all this misery for their negligence and their lack of faith in God and their relentless hankering after their carnal and worldly desires.

Elsewhere, the Qur'an describes the unbeliever's life by saying:

He lived without a care among his people and thought he would never return to God. Yes; but his Lord was ever watching him. (*al-Inshiqāq*: 13–15)

The skeptics and the unbelievers completely discard any belief in the hereafter, and this is a prevalent feature of modern civilization and the root of all the evil and destruction witnessed in the world today. This is what the surah refers to when it says:

For they had been self-indulgent and persisted in committing the supreme evil, saying, "When we are dead and turned to dust and bones, shall we be raised to life again? And our forefathers, too?" Say, "Yes, those of old and those of the present age, shall be brought together for an appointed day." (45–50)

The surah goes on to elaborate on the punishment the unbelievers will face, saying: "'And then you, those who have gone astray and those who have rejected the truth, shall eat the fruit of *zaqqūm*'" (51–52). It is a bitter and foul fruit which dehydrates the body, causing the victim to crave for water. Alas! The only water the sinners shall have will be boiling water. The Qur'an asserts: "They are given scalding water to drink which will tear their bowels" (*Muḥammad*: 15). The surah says: "Such will be their state on the Day of Judgment" (56).

These scenes and descriptions of punishment and reward in the hereafter are given as incentives and as a means of enlightenment and education. They are very effective for a proper appreciation of the dire consequences of man's actions in this life. They prove as effective today in a world where science, arts, and the media all seem to enhance man's ignorance of God and accountability and encourage him to desert all religious and moral teachings. However, such an incentive alone might not be sufficient and would have to be augmented by a concerted effort to motivate the human mind to think and reflect more rationally about, and to believe in, God and His sovereignty and power over the whole world.

The fourth argument the surah advances in support of the resurrection can be found in the statement: "Consider the water which you drink. Is it you who pours it from the clouds, or We? If We will, We could turn it bitter; if only you would be thankful!" (68–70). Water is the essence and the fundamental element of life. God says: "And We made every living thing of water; would they not believe?" (*al-Anbiyā'*: 30).

Water covers four-fifths of the earth's surface and has the most fascinating cycle. Wind moves the clouds from, say, the Pacific basin to deposit their water in the Mediterranean region. The water falls to the ground and goes back into the oceans through a multitude of routes, only to evaporate again into the atmosphere and begin a fresh cycle. The Qur'an says: "And We sent down water from the sky in due measure, and lodged it into the earth, but We are perfectly capable of taking it all away" (*al-Mu'minūn*: 18). Indeed, He provides and He takes away! This surah confirms: "If We will, We could turn it bitter; if only you would be thankful!" (70).

The will of God is the only power capable of creation and destruction. Water, being the natural catalyst for life here and in the hereafter, is totally under the control of the absolute divine will. Water is the essence of life. God sends down the rain in a drizzle to nourish the earth and the human body. Rain water is purified in the atmosphere by certain chemical and electrical processes known to physicists, and these processes are also determined by the will of God Almighty.

The fifth argument is: "Consider the fire which you light. Is it you that create its wood, or We? We have made it a reminder and a useful tool for the traveler" (71–73). It has been proven scientifically that humans breathe in oxygen and breathe out carbon dioxide, a process which is reversed in the plant world. The green plants are a store of energy which is used by man to produce fire and heat. Life and death are so intricately intertwined together!

The properties of matter continue to be the focus of study and analysis. Chemical reactions produce substances with properties that are totally different from those of the original ingredients. Water, for instance, is used to quench thirst and put out fire, but its constituents of oxygen and hydrogen are essential for combustion and igniting fires.

Fields and forests are full of green trees, shrubs, and plants which, with time, wither, dry up, and decay in order to make way for fresh ones. The Qur'an expresses it thus:

You [God] merge the night into the day and merge the day into the night; and You bring forth the living from the dead and the dead from the living; and You give to whom You will unconditionally. (*Āl ᶜImrān*: 27)

Leaves and branches decompose and turn into humus, and that humus turns into fertilizer to enrich the soil and help trees and plants to grow and yield fruits and crops for consumption by animals and humans.

Every human being has two major appointments to keep, one sooner than the other. Following a limited span of life, man dies. The second appointment comes with the Resurrection. The Qur'an says: "He created you out of clay and decreed a fixed term in this world and another one known only to Him. Yet you are still in doubt" (*al-Anᶜām*: 2). It also says: "Our Lord, You will surely gather all mankind before You upon a Day that will undoubtedly come. God will not break His promise" (*Āl ᶜImrān*: 9).

The frequent references to the Day of Resurrection in the Qur'an are not meant, as understood by some ignorant people, as a threat to human civilization or to thwart human progress. Rather, they are aimed at breaking man's false pride and egotistic ambitions.

The need to remind humans of the Day of Judgment never ceases to exist. Such admonition helps control man's desires and moderate his arrogance. The normal human being, with enough common sense, and with a certain belief in the Resurrection, would never forfeit a life of eternal bliss or opt for short-term enjoyment in exchange for the rich rewards of the hereafter!

Modern science has succeeded in unveiling certain mysteries of natural matter and the physical world around us, but that does not disprove the purpose of existence or negate the role of man on earth, as expressed in the Qur'an: "He created death and life to test your actions" (*al-Mulk*: 2). In fact, the more man expands the frontiers of his knowledge and acquires more tools and ideas, the harder and the more demanding the test becomes.

The surah is brought to a close with a chilling challenge: Is man able to stem the force of God's will? Do humans have the power to prevent death? The surah says:

> When a man's soul reaches his throat and is about to leave him, and you are looking on, and We are closer to him than you, although you cannot see Us, why then, if you are not accountable, can you not bring the soul back, if you claim to be truthful? (83–87)

Death is inescapable and unpreventable; an inevitable event in every man's life that comes at a predestined moment, totally beyond human control. On the Day of Judgment, mankind will be sorted into groups according to their performance in this life.

"If he is of those favored by God, he will enjoy tranquillity and plenty and a garden of delight" (88–89). "If he is of the right, then he will be greeted with the words, 'Peace be upon you' from those of the right" (90–91). It is a greeting from the angels to those of the right for their triumph over life's temptations, and a precursor to their happy encounter with God Almighty.

"But if he is of the erring disbelievers, his welcome will be scalding water, and he will burn in hell" (92–94). This is a reference to those who are doomed and condemned to hell.

Thus the closing words of the surah reinforce its opening statements to give a complete, but concise, picture of what awaits mankind in the hereafter. Regardless of the outcome, the truth remains intact: "This is the indubitable truth. Praise, then, the name of your supreme Lord." (95–96).

SURAH 57

Al-Ḥadīd
(Iron)

THE WHOLE OF THIS SURAH was revealed in Madinah. It is addressed to the Muslims as a state and as a society. The Muslim society is distinguished by being a society devoted to God. From before dawn until well after sunset every day, Muslims frequent the mosque, the rulers as well as the ruled. The call to prayer is heard five times a day calling all Muslims to pray and fulfill their obligation to praise and glorify God Almighty.

Notwithstanding its upholding of the principle of "no compulsion in religion," a Muslim state is responsible for ensuring the establishment and practise of Muslim religious rites and obligations. It is expected to declare its allegiance to the One, Just and Merciful God and to His divine order. It is not surprising then that the surah opens with the words:

All that is in the heavens and earth gives glory to God; He is the Almighty, the Wise One. To Him belongs the sovereignty over the heavens and the earth. He gives life and He gives death, and He has power over all things. (1–2)

Today, we live in what is rightly called the age of science in which man has conquered space and, having landed on the moon, has gone on to reach farther planets in the solar system. Science has proved without much doubt that the sun and its satellites are mere specks in a vast universe teeming with stars and planets of every description. It is an expansive universe, larger than we can ever imagine, governed by precise and intricate laws and criteria that control our breathing, the movement of the tides in our oceans, the eclipse of heavenly bodies in space, and vast countless other universes that only God, in His infinite wisdom and knowledge, can fathom or comprehend. We stand in awe of such a boundless domain and the power that controls it, and all we can is to pray: 'Glory and praise be to God as much as His vast creation, as much as He could be satisfied, as much as the weight of His throne and the number of His words!'

Let us ask ourselves: Does a hen create the egg it lays? Does a cow manufacture the milk it produces? Is a mother the maker of the embryo growing in her womb? Is the farmer responsible for the creation of the seeds and the crops he cultivates? These beings are nothing more than instruments in the hand of the ultimate, predominant and creative power of God Almighty. The surah expresses it thus:

> He created the heavens and the earth in six days and then sat on the Throne. He knows all that goes into the earth and all that comes out of it, all that comes down from heaven and all that ascends to it. He is with you wherever you may be, and God is aware of all that you do. (4)

The mission of the Muslim community in the world is to recognize God's sovereignty and make the rest of mankind aware of it, to worship God, and to urge others to submit to Him. It is a community that stands for the right to worship God and opposes religious persecution in all its forms. Muslims believe in the right of all humans to live according to the beliefs of their choosing, and support all victims of oppression.

The surah goes on to chart the course the Muslim nation needs to pursue in order to fulfill its divine mission. God says: "Believe in God and His Messenger and give of that which He has put in your trust; for those of you who believe and give shall have a great reward." (7)

Faith and giving are two fundamental prerequisites for success. The surah then continues to elaborate on the same theme, pointing out that Muslims have no reason to shirk from their responsibility since a prophet had been sent to them to show them the way and to guide them in order that they might become the noblest nation ever raised up among mankind. How could they ever justify exchanging their faith for another ideology?

Muslims are today being strenuously tempted to abandon Islam and adopt a host of nationalist and socialist systems and ideologies. Some Muslim countries have succumbed to these pressures and millions of Muslims of all ethnic groups in various parts of the world are being railroaded into accepting un-Islamic and anti-Islamic ideologies. Such neo-paganism is severely condemned in the surah as it says:

> And what cause have you not to believe in God, while the Messenger earnestly calls on you to have faith in your Lord, and has taken a pledge from you to that effect, if you are true believers. He sends down to His servant [Muhammad] perspicuous revelations to lead you out of darkness and into the light. God is truly compassionate and merciful to you. (8–9)

The Arab nation, in whose language the Qur'an was revealed, is at the heart of the Muslim world community, straddling the world's richest region. But has this vast wealth been put to good use? Has it been invested in the service of Islam? Has it been wisely developed and looked after, or has it been foolishly squandered?

The wealth and resources of the Muslim world are being plundered and exploited in all directions, reaping more benefits for others than for the Muslims themselves, when they should have been employed in the service of the message of Islam. The surah asks, with evident irony:

And why should you not give to the cause of God, when [you know] God will inherit the heavens and the earth? Those of you who gave and fought before the conquest [of Makkah] and those who fought and gave thereafter, are not alike; the former shall receive greater honor. Yet God has promised all of you a good reward; God has knowledge of all that you do. Who will invest a benign loan with God, which He will pay back twofold, and receive a rich reward? (10–11)

The underlying principle here is that wise deployment of wealth in the service of the divine cause is a sign of true faith. Those who plunder their wealth shall end up as losers. On the Day of Judgment, they will be told:

"Today, no recompense shall be accepted from you, or from the unbelievers. The fire of hell shall be your home; it shall be your only resort, and a damned end it is!" (15)

For faith to be genuine and sincere, it must be based on recognition of God, on self-denial, and on kindness and compassion towards others. The Israelites could be a case in hand. In reference to them, we read in the Qur'an: "But because they broke their covenant We cursed them and hardened their hearts" (*al-Mā'idah*: 13). Harshness, cruelty, and haughtiness are not conducive to a sound and stable faith in God.

God and His Messenger have strongly advised against following in their footsteps, but many Muslims continue to have only a semblance of faith. We have seen people with scant knowledge and hardly any understanding of Islam looking down on other Muslims and passing judgment on issues of little significance as though they have been entrusted with the keys to Paradise.

The surah strongly condemns such an attitude, saying:

Is it not time that the hearts of true believers submitted fully to the will of God and the truth that has been revealed, and not be like those who were given the Book before them, but time took its toll upon them and their hearts grew hard...? (16)

Lack of sensitivity and compassion is a disease which demoralizes people and prevents the Muslim nation from fulfilling its obligations towards Islam. Humility and kindness, rather than arrogance and self-pride, are the qualities needed for harmony and agreement to prevail in the world.

The surah returns to its main theme of identifying the qualities of the community that would be trusted with God's message. It reiterates previous statements, saying:

The men and women who give for charity and invest benign loans with God, shall be repaid twofold and shall receive a generous recompense. Those who believe in God and His messengers are the truthful believers and valiant martyrs who shall be in their Lord's presence. They shall have their reward and their light... (18–19)

A martyr, in Islam, can be a person who gives up his life fighting for God's cause or one who follows in the steps of God's prophets and witnesses for the way of God and explains His revelation.

The key to true and genuine faith is one's actions in this world. Those who hanker after worldly pursuits and never seem to have enough of them are of no consequence in this context. The majority of people today are oblivious of the life to come and the dominant culture feeds their ignorance and delinquency while the proponents of revealed religion have lost the initiative and resigned themselves to failure. Such helplessness goes against the grain of a religion in which faith is built on study, reflection, and an understanding of the surrounding world.

The surah points out that Muslims are partaking in a crucial race which is won only by those who prepare for it. It says: "Strive for the forgiveness of your Lord and for a Paradise as vast as heaven and earth, prepared for those who believe in God and His messengers" (21).

It is the will of God that life on earth is a continuous struggle between those who believe in God and uphold His message and those who do not. God says: "Had God willed, He would have punished them, but He ordained to set you one against the other to test you..." (*Muḥammad*: 4). Today, the unbelievers have the upper hand; they control the land, the oceans, and the skies.

In this surah God says:

> We have sent Our messengers with veritable proof, and with them We have sent the Book and the criterion, so that men might establish justice, and We have sent down iron, with its mighty strength and many benefits for mankind, so that God may know those who will support Him and His messengers, without ever seeing Him or them. God is Powerful, Almighty. (25)

God created iron with special useful qualities in peacetime and in war. There is a hint here that these qualities should be studied and understood and harnessed for man's civilian and military advantage. In recent times, Muslims have neglected this aspect of scientific and technological study and so have lagged behind in these fields. The power of science and technology is essential for the protection of Islam and the progress and development of Muslim societies. Unless Muslims get to grips with modern scientific and technological advances and appreciate their value and power, they would not be able to assume the leadership of mankind again.

Muslims are going through a trying period. Other much weaker and smaller nations are draining their resources and controlling their wealth and their destiny. They need to be guided by this surah and appreciate its profound message.

The surah closes with a poignant piece of advice, urging the Muslims to revert to God and the message that Muhammad had brought to them. The earlier generations of Islam were elevated by the message of the Qur'an and catapulted to the highest positions of world leadership. They were few in number and had counted for nothing previously, but they worked hard and, within a very short period of time, registered the most phenomenal rise of any civilization in all human history. They went on to rule and lead the world for several centuries. That success can be repeated if Muslims return to the teachings of the Qur'an and revive the true spirit of Muhammad's message.

The surah ends on a note of promise and optimism, saying:

Believers, fear God and believe in His Messenger, and He will grant His mercy twice over and provide you with light to walk in and forgive you. God is Forgiving and Merciful. The People of the Book [Jews and Christians] should know that they have no control over the grace of God; that grace is entirely in His hands: He grants it to whom He wills, for God has grace in abundance. (28–29)

SURAH 58

Al-Mujādilah
(She Who Pleaded)

THIS SURAH WAS REVEALED in Madinah to a somewhat cosmopolitan community. It consisted of Muslims who were being prepared to carry a divine universal message to the rest of mankind, pagans steeped in ignorance and frivolity, the vestiges of self-possessed and ethnocentric Jews seeking to safeguard their interests and impose their wishes on their neighbors, and the hypocrites who were motivated by shameless self-interest and were ready to dance to every tune.

Its brevity notwithstanding, the surah deals with all these groups of the Madinan community. It deals with various aspects of family life, especially the question of divorce, setting out the proper manner in which it should be regulated, emphasizing that: "Such are the bounds set by God, and a woeful punishment awaits the unbelievers." (4)

It is worth noting that having outlined the rulings on divorce, the Qur'an tells us in *al-Baqarah*: 229: "Such are the bounds set by God, so do not transgress them." While in *al-Nisā'*: 13, having set out the rulings on inheritance, the Qur'an says: "Such are the bounds set by God. He that obeys God and His Messenger shall dwell forever in gardens through which rivers flow."

It is a unique feature of the Qur'anic style that it intersperses rulings with statements on faith and belief to indicate that they are part of the faith and a form of worship and veneration of God Almighty. In this surah we read:

Do you not see that God knows of all that is in the heavens and on earth? If three people talk privately together, He shall be their fourth; and if they are five, He shall be their sixth... (7)

As an expression of disdain for the Prophet and the Muslims, some Jews in Madīnah would play on the Arabic word *salām*, meaning peace, in the greeting: *assalāmu ʿalaykum*, peace be upon you, and utter instead *sām*, meaning death! The Prophet's wife ʿĀ'ishah was the first to bring this dubious behavior to his attention but he chose to rise above it until the revelation arrived saying:

When they come to you, they salute you in words other than those in which God salutes you, and they think to themselves, "Why does not God punish us for what we say?" Hell is scourge enough for them; they shall burn in it, a wretched fate! (8)

The surah directs the Muslims not to emulate the Jews and to avoid speaking evil among themselves. They should not be unduly concerned with the scheming and machination that went on between the Jews and the hypocrites who were colluding to isolate the Muslims. It says:

Intrigue is the work of Satan, who aims to cause distress to the believers, but it shall by no means harm the believers, except by the will of God. Let the believers place their trust in God alone. (10)

Islam grades people only by the sincerity of their faith and the depth of their knowledge. Prophet Muhammad used to ask for the wiser and more knowledgeable of his Companions to stand closest to him when performing prayer. This surah asserts: "God will raise to high ranks those among you who have faith and knowledge" (11).

Muslims have the greatest respect and adoration for Prophet Muhammad as the man who brought them God's revelation, led them out of ignorance and darkness, and introduced them to a life of guidance and righteousness. He, furthermore, deserved that love and devotion by virtue of his personal noble qualities. Nevertheless, love and admiration for Muhammad should be expressed with due dignity and honor, in order to allow him time to deal with the affairs of the community and preserve his privacy to attend to his personal and family needs. The surah directs:

> Believers, before you confer privately with the Messenger, give to charity, for that is best and purest for you. But if you do not have the means, be assured that God is Oft-Forgiving, Merciful. (12)

It teaches the Muslims to seek compensation for missing the privilege to speak directly and privately with the Prophet, by contributing constructively to the society at large. The surah goes on:

> Do you hesitate to give to charity before your private consultations [with the Prophet]? If you do not, and God has forgiven you, then observe regular prayer and give the obligatory alms... (13)

In a multi-religious society, where material and moral interests clash and intermingle, principles are bound to be tested to the limit. Some people are liable to give precedence to their own relatives or businesses over their beliefs and convictions.

Hypocrisy is a vile social disease that poses a great threat to society; a hypocrite would have no qualms about lying or perjuring himself. The surah says:

> Do you see those who have befriended a people who have incurred God's wrath? They belong neither to you nor to them. They knowingly swear to falsehood. God has prepared for them a grievous punishment. Evil indeed is that which they have

done. (14–15)

Bad habits die hard or, as the old Egyptian saying goes: 'The piper dies wiggling his fingers.' Those with a proclivity to lie and cheat in this life, will come to life in the hereafter with a similar tendency. The surah says: "On that day when God restores them to life, they will swear to Him as they now swear to you, thinking that they are covered. No, indeed! They are consummate liars" (18).

It would be futile and much too late for them to be saved, for: "Those who antagonize God and His Messenger shall be among the most disgraced" (20).

To gain salvation and purify their faith, God urges the believers to declare their allegiance, take pride in their beliefs, and support those with similar convictions.

The surah closes with a poignant assertion:

You shall not find those who believe in God and the Last Day offering friendship to those who antagonize God and His Messenger, even though they be their fathers or their sons or their brothers or their nearest kindred. God has inscribed faith in their hearts and strengthened them with a spirit of His own, and He will admit them to gardens in which rivers flow, where they shall dwell forever. God is well pleased with them, and they are well pleased with Him. They are the party of God; and God's party shall surely triumph. (22)

SURAH 59

Al-Ḥashr
(The Gathering)

SEVERAL DECADES BEFORE THE ARRIVAL in Madinah of
the Prophet and his followers, a large Jewish community had settled there. They professed to live by the laws of the Torah of
Moses, but they were hardly a flattering example for them. They
were not known for their fairness or enthusiasm for defending
divine revelation or for the advocacy of judgment and accountability in the hereafter. When Islam came, calling the Arab pagans
to abandon their idols and worship the One God, the Jews grew
rather indignant and uncomfortable. They resorted to undermining the integrity of Prophet Muhammad and to sowing seeds of
discontent in Madinah. From a very early stage, they undertook to
inoculate their community against Islam and built fortifications
around their settlements in preparation for confrontation with the
Muslims.

As an introduction to the expulsion of the Jews from Madinah,
the surah opens with glorification of God Almighty, saying: "All
that is in the heavens and on earth gives glory to God; He is
the Almighty, the Wise" (1). This echoes a similar celebration in
al-Anʿām: 45, which says: "Thus was the power of the wrong-doers
crushed. Praise be to God, Lord of all creation." The defeat and frustration of tyranny is a sweet achievement as it paves the way for
freedom and the exercise of one's rights and ensures peace and justice for all.

The Jews in Madinah felt and looked invincible. The surah says:

You did not think that they would get out, and they also thought that their strongholds would protect them from God. But God struck them whence they did not expect it, filling their hearts with such horror that they embarked on destroying their houses with their own hands, while being also destroyed at the hands of the believers. (2)

The Jews could have lived in Madinah in peace and security, but, without being provoked, they resorted to intrigue and plotting against the Prophet's life. As soon as it had become clear to Muhammad that the Jews were conspiring to kill him, he decided to expel them from Madinah. The surah explains: "Because they had antagonized God and His Messenger, and those who antagonize God should know that God is stern in retribution" (4).

The surah refers to this as the "first exile" (2), thereby implying a "second" one yet to come! The Jews have again, this century, established their own state. The question remains, however, as to whether it is a state that upholds and promotes the ideals of the Torah or contributes to human progress and to world peace and stability! Israel's unholy alliance with the United States of America and Europe is proving to be antagonistic towards the divine world order and seems to run contrary to the teachings of Moses, Jesus, and Muhammad. Not until the Muslims reform their situation and draw closer to God's way will justice be done in Palestine.

Having expelled the Jews, the Prophet distributed their land among the Makkan emigrants, the Muhājirūn, whose homes and possessions had been appropriated by the Makkans, thereby achieving a certain degree of social and economic balance among the people of Madinah. This step was necessary and befitting despite the generous hospitality afforded to the Makkans by their Madinan hosts, the Anṣār. The surah gives an even more compelling reason: "In order that it [the wealth] may not benefit only the rich among you" (7).

The surah describes the Muhājirūn thus:

> The poor Muhājirūn who have been driven from their homes and
> their possessions, who seek God's grace and blessings and support
> God and His Messenger. These are the true believers. (8)

Thus the Muslim community of Madinah was established on a fair
and equitable basis and it forged ahead to fulfill its great mission.

Today, there are many Arab, as well as Jewish, hypocrites who
use religion for their own self-promotion and self-aggrandizement.
They are allies of one another, reminiscent of those referred to in the
surah when it says:

> Have you seen the hypocrites who say to their fellow unbelievers
> among the People of the Book [Jews and Christians], "If you are
> expelled we will come with you; we will never obey anyone who
> seeks to harm you, and if you are attacked we will certainly support
> you." But God bears witness that they are lying. (11)

The Israelite belief in the hereafter is very fragile. The early books
of the Old Testament have very little to say about accountability,
reward, and punishment in the hereafter. They are, in the main, a
tedious narrative of episodes from the history of a dogged and rebellious people. Christianity, on the other hand, has become part and
parcel of today's materialist Western civilization in which people are
driven towards greed and concern for the here and now.

This surah comes with an earnest and urgent appeal to seek God
and pursue His grace and blessings at every turn. It says:

> Believers, fear God and let every soul look to what it has saved for
> tomorrow. Fear God, for God is cognizant of all that you do. Do
> not be like those who have forgotten God, so that He has caused
> them to forget themselves. They are the evil-doers. (18–19)

A wide and decisive conflict between the Arabs and the Jews seems inevitable. The Jews are certain to gain support from people in the West, from those who have abandoned the teachings of Christianity and who do not recognize Islam. The Muslims have to ask themselves: when are they going to submit to and abide by the rules of Islam? When are they going to adopt faithfully the directives of the Qur'an? Prophet Muhammad led his people from the mosque, and raised their cultural, social, educational, moral, and scientific standards to enviable heights which the Muslims have passed to the rest of mankind all over the world.

The surah describes the power of the Qur'an thus:

Had We revealed this Qur'an to a mountain, you would have seen it humble itself and break asunder for fear of God. Such are the parables We relate to people, so that they may reflect. (21)

Towards the end, the surah cites some twenty names of God Almighty, defining man's relationship to God and encompassing all aspects of life.

Under the leadership and influence of false and distorted religious systems, our world today is being controlled by evil and ill-gotten ideologies, in an endless struggle to achieve material progress. How well will this prepare man when he stands before God for judgment?

Al-Mumtaḥanah
(The Tested Woman)

A BELIEVER DOES NOT TOLERATE humiliation or infringement of his dignity, and does his best to resist those who wrong him. If overpowered, he would not give up but would await his chance to retaliate, in fulfillment of God's words: "And those who, when oppressed, seek to have the upper hand" (al-Shūrā: 39).

Muslims were subdued in Makkah and driven out of their homes, but they refused to surrender or relinquish their rights. A long drawn-out war with the non-Muslim Arabs of Makkah was inevitable and the confrontation was settled in favor of the Muslims. It would have been easier and less demanding to capitulate and take the soft option, but the surah responds to such an attitude by saying:

Believers, do not take My and your enemies as allies, appeasing them, when they have rejected the truth that has been revealed to you and have driven the Messenger and yourselves out [of Makkah] because you believe in God, your Lord... (1)

It is the essence of defeatism to seek to appease your enemy while he is doing his best to subjugate, crush, and humiliate you and undermine your beliefs and way of life. The surah says:

If they were to have the upper hand over you, they would be inimical towards you and would unleash their hands and tongues against you with evil, and they wish you would also disbelieve. (2)

641

Upholding a belief or ideology entails loyalty to and support for one's fellow-believers. This has been the case throughout human history, and the surah confirms:

> You have an admirable example in Abraham and his followers who said to their people, "We are clear of you and of all that you worship besides God. We renounce you: enmity and hatred shall reign between us for ever unless you believe in God and God alone…" (4)

This does not mean that Muslims are belligerent or are inclined towards being hostile, but it means that they stand up to aggression and defend their beliefs to the last. The surah defines the framework of the relationship between the Muslims and their enemies by saying:

> God does not forbid you to be kind and fair to those who have not waged war against you because of your religion or driven you out of your homes; for God loves the equitable. God does, however, forbid you to show friendship to those who waged war against you on account of your religion and drove you out of your homes and abetted others so to do. Those who make friends with them are wrong-doers. (8–9)

We have seen how international treaties and human rights conventions can be abused and ignored. We have seen tens of thousands of Muslims being attacked in various parts of the world, and being forced to give up their homes and live as refugees for years on end. Is this honorable? Is it fair? Would they be 'fundamentalist' fanatics if they retaliated and tried to regain their homes and possessions?

International peace and order must be maintained with fairness and respect for the human rights and dignity of all peoples and nations of the world. The more powerful and developed nations are only concerned with protecting their own people and interests; they show little concern for the welfare of others, which is totally unacceptable. Human and international relations of love and hate, of friendship and antagonism, must be established for the sake of God and nothing else. Appeasing or supporting a tyrant in order to gain favors, or opposing a just ruler for not giving you what you want are indications of a flawed faith; and so is all defective behavior.

The surah ends, as it begins, with emphasis on upholding the truth and renouncing alliances with those who reject God's revelations. It says:

> Believers, do not take as allies people who have incurred the wrath of God. These despair of the life to come as much as the disbelievers despair of the buried dead. (13)

Under the Ḥudaybiyyah treaty of 628 AC, the Makkans imposed the extraordinary clause, agreed to by the Muslims, that the Muslims of Madinah should not receive any emigrants fleeing Makkah while the Makkans were free to grant asylum to any defectors from Madinah. Prophet Muhammad accepted that patronizing provision, though it was soon to backfire on the Makkan Arabs, who later called for it to be rescinded.

During that period, however, a number of Makkan women accepted Islam and found themselves stranded in a hostile environment. Similarly, there were women who defected from the Muslim camp and made their way back to Makkah. It was at that time that word was received from God that the Muslim women from Makkah should be received and given refuge in Madinah. The surah says:

> Believers, when Muslim women emigrate and seek refuge with you, test them. God best knows how faithful they are. If you find them to be true believers do not send them back to the infidels... (10)

In the circumstances, the Muslims were instructed to compensate the Makkans whose wives had converted to Islam, and in this context the surah exhorts:

> Do not hold on to your marriages with unbelieving women; demand back the dowries you have given them and let the infidels ask for the dowries they had given. Such is the law which God lays down among you... (10)

These rulings proved fair and practical, but they did not remain in force for long since Makkah was soon to be reclaimed by the Muslims, bringing about an end to paganism and establishing the religion of *tawḥīd* in its place. In *al-Māʾidah*, we learn that Islam permits Muslim men to marry chaste Jewish and Christian women, but these are proving difficult to find in today's promiscuous Jewish and Christian societies.

The surah closes with an earnest instruction to Prophet Muhammad:

> Prophet, when believing women come to pledge their loyalty to you, that they shall associate nothing else with God, that they shall not steal or commit adultery or kill their infants or flagrantly spread slander or disobey you in any just matter, then do accept their loyalty and seek God's forgiveness for them... (12)

This is a reference to the Prophet's acceptance of women's oaths of loyalty at Makkah after the Muslims had recaptured it. This was done in the form of an oath by the women before the Prophet.

It is only decent and proper that relations between men and women are clearly defined and regulated in order to rein in the desires of the flesh and protect society against vice and corruption. False liberalism and free association between the sexes can lead to social chaos and the total collapse of morality and social cohesion.

Al-Ṣaff
(The Ranks)

GREAT MISSIONS REQUIRE STRONG SUPPORT and sincerity and cannot be upheld and defended with mere lip-service. Cowards and feeble-minded people have no leadership role to play. Falsehood is usually supported by audacious self-serving individuals, and can only be defeated by strong self-sacrificing believers who give all they have for the sake of upholding the truth and establishing the divine world order on this earth.

The Qur'an tells us: "Had He willed, God could have punished them, but He ordained that He might test you by means of one another" (*Muḥammad*: 4).

Empty threats and false claims achieve nothing. Hence the reproach: "Believers, why do you profess what you never do? It is most odious in God's sight that you should say what you do not do" (2–3). A believer devotes his whole life to the service of God. He blends with the world around him and acts in total harmony with his environment to sing the praises of God Almighty. Skeptics, on the other hand, are dissenters who represent an aberration, an anomaly, in God's vision of the world.

The surah opens with the assertion: "All that is in the heavens and on earth glorifies God. He is the Almighty, the Wise" (1). It then goes on to condemn those whose actions contradict their words, denouncing those communities that rejected God's guidance and showed hostility towards His messengers.

At the forefront of such communities were the early Israelites

645

who antagonized Moses and caused him no end of hardship. They lost their nerve when it came to facing their enemies and soon squandered the scriptures that were revealed to them. The surah elaborates:

> And remember Moses who said to his people, "My people, why do you seek to harm me when you know well that I am a messenger from God to you?" And when they went astray, God let their hearts go astray. (5)

They were castigated for their betrayal of Moses and their refusal to face his enemies.

The surah then goes on to state that Jesus had come with a message from God that was specific to a predetermined time and place. He was sent to lead the Israelites back to God's path, remind them of the Torah they had abandoned, treat their psychological and social ills, and pave the way for a universal message that would address the whole of humanity with the divine world order. It says:

> And remember Jesus the son of Mary, who said to the Israelites, "I am a messenger from God to you to confirm the Torah that was revealed before me and to bring you news of a messenger who will come after me whose name shall be Aḥmad..." (6)

The books of the New Testament, written several years after Jesus, make curious references to the same effect. Matthew 24 reads:

> And many false prophets will arise and lead many astray. And because wickedness is multiplied, most men's love will grow old. But he who endures to the end will be saved. And this gospel of the kingdom will be preached throughout the whole world, as a testimony to all nations; and then the end will come.

John 14 reports that Jesus had said: "If you love me, you will keep my commandments. And I will pray the Father, and he will give you another Counsellor to be with you forever…"

Who would preach the word of God throughout the world until the end? Who would this 'Counsellor' be whose message would endure for ever? Does this description fit any personality in history other than that of Muhammad?

I follow Muhammad because the Book he brought agrees with my instincts and with my conscience. I came to know God through my rational powers, having reflected on my own being and the world around me. The Qur'an is not in need of verification or authenticity from any other scriptures or prophecies. It contains the proof for its genuineness; it is totally self-evident.

The surah goes on:

And who is more wicked than a man who invents falsehood about God even as he is being invited to Islam? God does not guide the wrong-doers. They seek to extinguish the light of God [by blowing at it] with their mouths, but God will complete His light however much the unbelievers may dislike it. (7–8)

The human mind is the greatest gift God has given to man. Any belief or faith that is not founded on a rational and intelligent basis is worthless. Nevertheless, many people would rather close their minds and suspend their rational faculties altogether.

The surah closes with two important concepts that reinforce what it had already emphasized at the beginning. The first is that life is based on faith and hard work: "Believe in God and His Messenger and strive for the cause of God with your wealth and your souls" (11). The second is that believers must be ready at all times to uphold and defend the word of God. Just as Muslims respond immediately to the call for prayer, they must be prepared to serve the cause of God at all times using everything in their power.

The surah tells us that when he needed the support of his followers, Jesus evoked their faith in God. It says:

> Believers, be supporters of God's cause, just as Jesus the son of Mary said to the disciples, "Who will support me for the cause of God?" The disciples replied, "We will support the cause of God." (14)

Like Muhammad's Companions, the disciples of Jesus provided him with the strength and support he needed to propagate his message and fulfill his mission. Today, Islam is in greater need for Muslims to understand and appreciate the true meaning of the words: "Be supporters of God's cause" (14).

Al-Jumuᶜah
(Friday)

THE SURAH OPENS WITH AN EXHORTATION to the believers to glorify and revere God Almighty. It says: "All that is in the heavens and on the earth gives glory to God, the Sovereign, the Holy One, the Almighty, the Wise" (1). Whenever the call to prayer is heard, Muslims make their way to the mosque to join their fellow-Muslims in worshiping their Lord as an expression of praise to God and as a reflection of the unity of their community.

Friday is the highlight of the week for Muslims the world over. It is a day on which Muslims are urged to bathe and smell pleasant, and in which, according to Prophet Muhammad, there is a blessed hour during which a Muslim's prayers are certain to be answered.

The opening statement is also an indirect criticism of those Muslims who, on hearing of the arrival of trade caravans in Madinah, hastily left the mosque to engage in trading. The surah censures their action, saying:

> And when they see commerce or some other diversion, they rush to it and leave you [Muhammad] standing alone. Say, "That which God has in store is far better than any diversion or commerce, and God is the Best Provider." (11)

The surah asserts that Muhammad, the final messenger of God, was chosen from among the illiterate Arabs to convey God's final and universal message to mankind. That honor was withheld from the Israelites and the Christians because of the breaches they had committed and the distortions they had introduced into their respective religions. Their arrogance, stubbornness, and ignorance disqualified them. They proved unable to reform their own state, let alone be able to reform others or present a good example. The Arabs of the sixth century AC, on the other hand, were simple people with limited material ambition and were, therefore, more receptive and willing to devote all their energies to Islam. The surah says:

> It is He that sent forth among the unlettered people a messenger from among themselves to recite to them His revelations and purify them and teach them the Book and wisdom, though they had hitherto gone seriously astray. (2)

The Arabs did convey the message of Islam to other peoples all over the world and were assimilated into them, thereby forming a propitious link between humanity and God's revelation.

The Israelites had become too ethnocentric, parochial, and materialistic. The surah asserts:

> Those who were entrusted with the Torah and subsequently failed to fulfill their obligations are like a donkey laden with books. Wretched are those people who reject God's revelations. God does not guide the wrong-doers. (5)

Those qualities continue to be evident today. The Israelites do not appear to be capable of representing God's message or leading mankind towards His path. The surah adds:

> Say to the Jews, "If you claim that, of all men, you alone are the true friends of God, then you should wish for death, if you are truthful." But they will never wish for death because of what their hands have done. (6–7)

Sadly, many Muslims have today gone down that errant road, neglecting their responsibilities towards God's revelation and giving voice to materialistic, nationalist, and ethnocentric tendencies that have very little, if anything, to do with God or His message.

Those Muslims who are sincere should persevere and continue to work hard to revive the Muslim Ummah and enable it to play its proper role in the world and restore the sovereignty and prevalence of God's order over human life and world affairs.

SURAH 63

Al-Munāfiqūn
(The Hypocrites)

HYPOCRISY IS A MOST IGNOBLE human trait. It is a contradiction between a man's convictions and his behavior, when he falsely professes to believe in one thing but changes his expression or appearance, chameleon-fashion, to suit the moment or the situation in which he finds himself.

Hypocrisy takes several forms, dissimulation and perjury being the most obvious. Hypocrites are unprincipled individuals who lack decisiveness and stability; they go with the flow, guided only by their egotistic interests and selfish desires.

The surah addresses Prophet Muhammad:

> When the hypocrites come to you they say, "We bear witness that you are the Messenger of God;" and God knows that you are indeed His messenger and God bears witness that the hypocrites are dissembling. (1)

Hypocrisy cannot be hidden for long. It is usually reflected in a hypocrite's behavior and demeanor, or is easily exposed by unforeseen events.

This surah unveiled the hypocrites of Madinah who had for too long assumed a front of virtue and professed to be part of the Muslim community. The reality was quite different, since they were actively sowing seeds of discord and division among the Makkan Muhājirūn and the Madinan Anṣār. They would talk holiness while practising deceit and mischief. They would turn any trivial incident into a crisis and do their best to spread hostility and ill-will. The surah says:

It is they who say, "Do not give to those who follow the Messenger of God until they desert him." To God belong the treasures of the heavens and the earth, but the hypocrites do not understand. (7)

Both Makkan and Madinan Muslims had suffered great trials and tribulations; the former had left their homes and possessions behind in Makkah, while the latter had to receive the Muhājirūn and share everything they had with them. However, ʿAbd Allah ibn Ubayy, who was the chief hypocrite in Madinah, was heard making some very scathing remarks about the Makkan Muslims and inciting the Madinans against them. He would say: "Feed fat your dog and it will eat you!" The surah quotes him as saying:

"Once we return to Madinah [after the battle of Banū Muṣṭaliq] the honorable will drive the ignoble out of it." But honor belongs to God and His Messenger and the believers, but the hypocrites do not know it. (8)

These were the words of a troublemaker who wished to divide the Muslim community and undermine its strength.

ʿAbd Allah ibn Ubayy took that stance because he had been grooming himself to rule Madinah had the Prophet and his followers not emigrated to it from Makkah. With their arrival, his dream was shattered. However, instead of joining the Muslims in good faith and with sincerity, he chose the insidious cowardly approach. Had he come clean and apologized to the Prophet, he would have been pardoned and allowed to pursue his ambitions legitimately and within the principles and teachings of Islam.

The surah closes with valuable advice to all sincere men: "Believers, let neither your wealth nor your children divert you from the remembrance of God. Those who do so will indeed be the losers" (9).

SURAH 64

Al-Taghābun
(Loss and Gain)

THE SURAH OPENS WITH THE ASSERTION that the physical world and all that is in it sing the praises of the Creator because they recognize Him as such and submit to His commands. It says: "All that is in the heavens and the earth glorifies God. To Him belongs the sovereignty, and to Him all praise is due, and He has power over all things" (1).

As for humans, the situation is quite different. Many of them reject God and His teachings, deny His power and sovereignty, and denounce His messengers. We read elsewhere in the Qur'an: "He created man from a sperm, yet man immediately and openly dissented" (al-Naḥl: 4).

This surah highlights this perverse characteristic, saying: "It was He that created you: some of you disbelieve and some believe, and God is cognizant of all that you do" (2).

It is highly paradoxical when man shows disrespect towards God Almighty who has created him in the best form and endowed him with all his faculties and provided for him so generously. Some people refused to believe for the simple reason that God's revelation had come to them through other humans, arguing that it should have been brought by angels!

Sometimes it is difficult for some people to recognize the superior qualities of other individuals. This is more so in the case of those who are less intelligent, who tend to look with contempt at brighter and more discerning people. The surah says:

654

Have you not heard of those before you who disbelieved and so they tasted the deplorable outcome of their conduct, and a grievous punishment awaits them? That is because when their messengers came to them with clear revelations, they said, "What? Are ordinary mortals to guide us?" They disbelieved and turned away. But God was in no need of them; God is Self-Sufficient, Worthy of praise. (5–6)

It is in the nature of some people to seek to dominate others and suppress their talents. In fact, one can almost say that this is a characteristic of certain communities as well. God's messengers were humble and tolerant individuals, and to welcome them with disrespect and confrontation was most discourteous and ungracious. The surah then says:

The unbelievers claim they shall not be raised to life. Say, "By my Lord, you shall certainly be raised to life, and then you shall be told of all that you have done. That is easy for God to do." (7)

This denial is not new in the history of mankind but it has never been so widespread. Modern civilization is a materialistic civilization in which living the present life is revered above all else, and life after death is derided and dismissed as absurd nonsense.

This attitude is not confined to atheists or pagans but to followers of other divinely-revealed religions: Jews and Christians. They are not prepared to accept or tolerate the Qur'anic concept of the hereafter. Hence the need for a fresh approach for presenting Islam in a more effective and intelligent manner.

The surah says: "And so believe in God and His Messenger and in the light We have revealed" (8). That 'light' is the Qur'an, as referred to on numerous occasions in the Qur'an itself. The Qur'an is the only faithfully documented and fully authenticated word of God. It contains the best advice for an honorable and equitable life for all mankind. The Muslims are under an obligation to understand their Book and live up to the task defined for them in the Qur'an.

The surah goes on to talk about the Day of Judgment: "The Day He gathers you all, that shall be the day of recrimination" (9). On that day, many people will be full of regret and remorse for wasting their lives and squandering their abilities and energies. Prophet Muhammad is reported as saying: "Many people miss out on two counts: health and time."

Many will regret appeasing certain individuals because they were powerful or influential, and dismissing others because they were helpless. Many a wasted opportunity would be recalled! Many who disbelieved would wish they had not! Alas, then it will be too late; there will no chance for undoing what had already been done, and there will only be time for reckoning and accountability.

This surah was revealed in Madinah where the Makkan Muhā-jirūn and Madinan Anṣār were building the new Muslim state in the face of many odds and severe hostility. To reassure the Muslims during their hour of need, the surah says: "No misfortune falls except by God's will, and He will guide the hearts of those who believe in Him, for God has knowledge of all things" (11). The Makkan Muslims were driven out of their homes and their land because they chose to follow Muhammad and defend their convictions and beliefs. Not everyone can make such a sacrifice or gain such an honor.

Some Makkan Muslims hesitated, preferring to remain with wives and children in Makkah, and so lost out. Many people close their ears to the call of duty in order to stay in the comfort and company of their loved ones. To these God says: "Believers, among your wives and children there are enemies, so beware of them. But if you choose to overlook and pardon and forgive them, then God also is Oft-Forgiving, Merciful" (14). To cling too much to life's comforts could very well lead to betrayal and loss. The surah says: "Your wealth and your children are but a temptation, while God has great rewards for you" (15).

The resistance of corruption and aggression requires hard work and great sacrifices which faithful believers ought to undertake with courage and confidence. History tells us that some oppressors can only be defeated by faith and conviction. Criminals must not be allowed to have a free reign, otherwise there will be peace and security for no one. Hence the closing exhortation:

Therefore fear God to the best of your ability, and listen and obey, and give for the good of your own souls. Those saved from their own greed will be prosperous. (16)

Al-Ṭalāq
(Divorce)

THIS SURAH IS ALSO KNOWN as the shorter *al-Nisā'* chapter as it
contains a number of rulings relating to matrimony and family life. It
advocates strong and sound foundations for the family and deals with
some of the issues that threaten its stability and well-being. It forms
one compact unit that merits deep study and reflection. It is a very
good example of the power and effectiveness of Qur'anic presentation and debating style. The views expressed here are not my own
but those of many trustworthy scholars of the past. I have chosen
them only for their merit and because they happen to coincide with
my own views on the issues covered in the surah. Needless to say, my
views are open to criticism and discussion.

The surah opens with an earnest call to Prophet Muhammad as
the leader and benefactor of the Muslim Ummah, indicating the
gravity of the matter under discussion. Divorce is a very serious issue
with far-reaching consequences, not only for the person who initi-
ates it, his wife, their children and immediate family, but also for the
community as a whole. It therefore calls for regulation in order to
curb its abuse and minimize any injustice that may result from it.

For these reasons, God has specified certain times when divorce
could take place. It is not permissible during menstruation or confi-
nement, or during a post-menstrual period in which sexual intercourse has taken place. It has to be witnessed by two witnesses.
Once a wife receives the divorce notice from her husband, she must
remain in her home and must not leave it, since this pronouncement
is a warning signal in the process, rather than the end of the marital

relationship. It may still be possible to settle the dispute and save the marriage, once the circumstances leading to divorce have changed.

Fits of anger can dissipate and within two or three months the desire to reconcile and make up may prevail. This is what the surah alludes to when it says:

> Prophet, if you [the believers] divorce your wives, divorce them at the end of their prescribed period, and count the prescribed period accurately, and fear God, your Lord. Do not turn them out of their homes, nor should they leave, unless they have openly committed a flagrant act of indecency. These are limits set by God; he that transgresses God's bounds wrongs his own soul. You never know; God may, thereafter, bring about fresh circumstances. (1)

It is notable that the surah is full of admonitions and references to faith in the unseen and the resurrection, and to fear of God, as prerequisites for defusing tensions that could lead to the break-up of the family, and to bring about mutual tolerance and reconciliation. It says: "He that fears God, God will provide him with a way out" (2).

The surah outlines the rules for custody and nursing, and it seems clear that God Almighty does not wish a divorce to turn into wider social upheaval, or else the whole society would lose the essential bases of social and human cohesion.

Nevertheless, divorce as practised by Muslims has been associated with a great deal of unhappiness and injustice. Muslim jurists have tended to be lenient in dealing with divorce cases, and people have found it easy to divorce for the most trivial of reasons. Divorce under Islam has long been seen by non-Muslims as cruel and unfair to women, but this impression has been created by the behavior of the people and their interpretation of the rules, which are alien to the true spirit of Islam, rather than by the rules themselves. The rules given in this surah are hardly ever observed by Muslims today. Unfortunately, there is no shortage of jurists who are too ready to grant divorce for the most unsatisfactory of reasons and wreck homes and families at a stroke.

The reputation of Islam has been tarnished and its growth restricted by such irresponsible interpretations and practices. Islam's detractors were quick to exploit these negative aspects of Muslim life.

The second part of the surah can, therefore, be read as a warning to Muslims who ignore the proper rulings on divorce. The surah cautions: "Many nations have rebelled against their Lord's commandments and His messengers, and so We called them sternly to account and punished them severely, and they tasted the bitter fruits of their misdeeds..." (8–9).

This warning flows quite naturally and logically from the preceding arguments and statements relating to divorce. The surah seems to emphasize that a nation honored by God's revelation should not trivialize family life or take lightly the dangers that threaten its happiness and stability.

Furthermore, Muslim malpractices and misinterpretations of their religion should not become a hindrance to the spread of Islam or impede its progress and development.

The surah closes with emphasis on the fact that the world is a sign of God's power and existence and revelation is God's message to mankind. It says: "It is God who created seven heavens and as many earths. His command descends through them, so that you may know that God has power over all things, and that God's knowledge encompasses all things" (12).

This is a surah that Muslims should study carefully in order to understand its meaning and fully absorb its wisdom.

SURAH 66

Al-Taḥrīm
(The Prohibition)

THE PROPHET'S WIVES were the most chaste, virtuous and highly respected women ever to grace the earth. They accompanied the Prophet during his life and supported him in his mission. They, on the whole, lived up to the role and expectations defined for them in the Qur'an, but were, nevertheless, criticized on two occasions.

The first was over their unhappiness with the Prophet's austere life-style and their collusion to demand from him a higher spending allowance. However, once he explained to them that his aim in life was not to prosper or become wealthy but to serve God and seek His pleasure and blessings in the hereafter, they acquiesced and chose to live according to his terms.

The second instance was when some of his wives, mainly driven by jealousy, tried to take advantage of his amiability and good nature. One of them, reported to be Ḥafṣah, once told him that his breath smelt unpleasant and he explained that he had eaten some honey at the house of Zaynab, one of his other wives. Ḥafṣah commented rather sarcastically: "The bees must have been feeding on foul flowers!" The Prophet promised never to eat Zaynab's honey again and asked Ḥafṣah not to relate the episode to anyone else.

It soon transpired, however, that there was collusion, out of sheer jealousy, between more than one wife, aimed at causing the Prophet to lose interest in his wife Zaynab. The Prophet was upset at this behavior and decided to stay away from all his wives to the extent that some people thought he had divorced them all!

It was in order to ease the tension and censure the culprits that this surah was revealed, opening with the words:

> Prophet, why do you prohibit what God has made lawful to you, seeking to please your wives? God is Forgiving and Merciful. God has granted you exoneration from your oaths... (1–2)

The majority of Muslim scholars are of the opinion that no one has the right to prohibit what God has made lawful, and to do so is tantamount to an oath that can only be reversed by an act of atonement. The surah then turns to address the two colluding wives (reportedly, ʿĀʾishah and Ḥafṣah) saying:

> Your hearts have committed a grievous error, but if you repent you shall be pardoned. If, however, you conspire against him [Muhammad], know that he is protected by God, Gabriel and the righteous among the believers, and that the angels are, moreover, his supporters. (4)

ʿĀʾishah and Ḥafṣah were being severely reprimanded for their mistake, urged to desist and repent or face castigation and ostracism. The surah then addresses the Prophet's wives, advising them to be considerate, reasonable, and polite in their dealings with him, warning them that:

> It may well be, if he were to divorce you all, that his Lord would provide him with better wives than you, subservient to God, believing, devout, penitent, worshiping, and devoted; formerly married or virgins. (5)

The Prophet's laudable qualities should not be abused by his wives, nor should he be maligned for being the good and gentle man he was. The Prophet's household should not be a place for jealousy and ill will, but rather a haven for the adoration of God and preparation for the hereafter and devotion in the pursuit of God's pleasure and blessings.

By way of severe reprimand to those wives who had upset the Prophet, the closing part of the surah cites the wives of the prophets Noah and Lot who let their respective husbands down in fulfilling their mission, and in fact betrayed them to their enemies. It says:

> God sets an example to the believers in the wife of Noah and the wife of Lot. They were married to two of Our righteous servants and they betrayed them, but their husbands could in no way protect them from God. They were told, "Enter the fire along with those who are entering it." (10)

The betrayal was not sexual infidelity; rather, they failed to stand behind their husbands and give them the support they needed to fulfill their obligations as messengers of God commissioned for a crucial leadership role among their people. Their shameful attitude caused those wives to be condemned and to enter the fire of hell with other wrong-doers.

Personal accountability is a fundamental Islamic principle. On the Day of Judgment every man will be for himself: no father shall fend for a son, or husband for a wife. While the Pharaoh is destined for hell, the surah points out that his wife will reside in Paradise, not affected by the consequences of his transgressions.

A little earlier, the surah urges believers to ensure that their homes and their families are raised in accordance with God's teachings in order to protect them against doom and perdition. It exhorts: "Believers, guard yourselves and your families against a fire fuelled with men and stones..." (6).

It goes on to point out that God does not expect from human

beings total infallibility, but to learn from their mistakes and always seek the path of proper and decent behavior. He urges them to be vigilant and to acquire strong consciences that would always steer them towards the right path. It says:

> Believers, turn to God with sincere repentance, so that your Lord may forgive you your sins and admit you to gardens through which rivers flow... (8)

Some Orientalists have expressed disapproval that God Almighty should be concerned with a marital tiff within Muhammad's household! In his book *The Life of Muhammad*,[36] the late Egyptian scholar, Muḥammad Ḥusayn Haykal points out that the episode was certainly more worthy of mention in the Qur'an than the one recorded in the Old Testament of Lot being lured by his two daughters to become intoxicated in order to sleep with them!

It is certainly more worthy of mention than another Old Testament story about a prophet of God sleeping with his daughter-in-law! Some Orientalists, tend to exaggerate their perceived shortcomings of the Qur'an while totally overlooking those of their own scriptures.

---

36 See Muḥammad Ḥusein Haykal, *The Life of Muhammad*, translated from the Arabic by Ismaʿīl Rāgī al Farūqī (London, Shorouk International, 1983).

SURAH 67

Al-Mulk
(Dominion)

THIS LIFE DOES NOT END WITH DEATH, but is resumed in another life. False religious belief bemoans this fact and looks at it with pessimism, rather than urging its followers to work hard in preparation for the eternal life to come.

To be able to face up to modern ideologies, it is essential to state one's stance regarding the hereafter. This would, in turn, necessitate a proper understanding of life and the whole purpose of our existence.

Dismissal of the idea of the hereafter, or refusal to understand it, betrays a degree of intellectual impotence which does not become the believer. This is what the present surah emphasizes very strongly by saying: "He who created death and life, so that He may put you to the test and see whose deeds are the best..." (2); "He created seven heavens, one above the other. You shall find no discrepancies in the Merciful's creation..." (3); "We have adorned the lowest heavens with lanterns..." (5).

We see widespread preoccupation in Muslim societies with the material and trivial things in life, and an excessive tendency towards the pursuit of greed and pleasure. Herein lie the causes of the material and spiritual malaise sweeping the Muslim world today. It is no wonder that the surah highlights the fate of the unbelievers as a warning to the believers. It says:

And every time a multitude [of unbelievers] is thrown therein, its [hell's] keepers will ask them, "Did no one come to warn you?"

665

They will reply, "Yes, indeed! A warner did come to us but we rejected him and we said that God had revealed nothing and people were deluding themselves." They said, "If only we had listened or tried to understand, we should not have been among those in hell." (8–10)

A believer is more intelligent and more capable of understanding life and the world. According to Islam, belief in God is firmly based on a rational grasp of the purpose of life and the signs God has established all around us. It is sad that Muslims today are trailing behind, with no say or influence over world affairs.

Belief in God has its unique and mysterious way of influencing the human soul, motivating individuals to incredible levels of action and sacrifice. It makes some give up all material pleasures, or sacrifice their lives, for the sake of compliance with God's revelations. Thus the surah promises: "Those who fear their Lord although they cannot see Him shall be forgiven and richly rewarded" (12).

With belief in God and the hereafter comes the power to control, harness, and manage the material resources of the world for the good of humanity. The surah says: "It is He who has made the earth subservient to you, so go about its regions and eat of His provisions, for to Him all shall be resurrected" (15). Man's real future happiness and success are not in this world but in the life to come.

The opening verse in this surah asserts that God has complete sovereignty over the world, while verses in other surahs in the Qur'an affirm that God also controls man's sustenance and well-being, that the destiny of the earth and the heavens is under His power, and that in His supremacy He has no equal or rival.

Thus God asks the unbelievers:

Are you confident that He who is in heaven would not cause the earth to sink beneath you and shake violently? Or are you confident that He who is in heaven would not shower you with stones? You will soon know the truth of My warning... (16–17)

The Qur'anic expression: "He who is in heaven" is one of several such expressions referring to God's Throne and in no way restricts God's presence to the 'heavens'. His knowledge, hearing, sight, and control reaches every soul and every thing, anywhere in the universe. Nothing escapes His attention or is beyond His reach, as the Qur'an elsewhere asserts: "To God belongs the east and the west and whichever way you turn there shall be the face of God. God is Omnipresent and All-Knowing" (*al-Baqarah*: 115).

It also states: "No three persons talk together in secret without Him being their fourth; nor five without Him being their sixth; nor fewer or more, without Him being present with them wherever they may be" (*al-Mujādilah*: 7). And we read: "And He is with you wherever you are" (*al-Ḥadīd*: 4).

God's omnipresence should never be in doubt and it would be impertinent to ask in what form that omnipresence is manifest. This is one of the many facts in our existence that we shall never be able to encompass or comprehend. God is closer to us than our own souls, but we cannot see Him and we shall not be able to conceive the reality of the divine essence or form. All we need to appreciate is our total dependence on His grace, power, and generosity, and the complete insignificance of everything else besides Him. The surah emphasizes this by saying:

> Who can defend you like an army besides the Merciful? The unbelievers are under total delusion. And who can provide for you if He withholds His sustenance? Indeed, they persist in rebellion and rejection. (20–21)

As it comes to a close, the surah turns to address the unbelievers who wage war against the Prophet and his followers. It asks them about the purpose and wisdom of their aggression if they could not understand God's message and appreciate it. How could they justify their folly?

667

It asks:

Say [Muhammad], "What would you say if God were to destroy me and those with me or be merciful towards us? Who would protect the unbelievers from a grievous scourge?" Say, "He is the Merciful. We believe in Him and in Him we put our trust, and you shall soon know who is evidently in error." (28–29)

It ends by asking the materialists who deny the existence of God a pertinent question: "Say, 'What if the water you have became inaccessible, who else would provide you with running water?'" (30).

SURAH 68

Al-Qalam
(The Pen)

THE SURAH OPENS with a general reference to the pen: "By the pen and by the written word." (1) This could be a reference to the pen as an essential instrument of knowledge and education, or, more appropriately, a reference to the recording of the Qur'an itself and the wisdom it contains. For, the Qur'an is undoubtedly the most important book known to mankind; every single letter in it was directly revealed from God Almighty and remains pure and unadulterated. God had chosen for its dissemination and propagation the most honorable person ever to walk this earth, in spite of what his detractors may say. The surah affirms: "You are not, by the grace of your Lord, insane, and a boundless reward awaits you, and you are of the highest moral caliber" (2–4). The enemies of divine revelation are destined to lose and be exposed, as history has already proved.

The surah cites the parable of: "The owners of the orchard" (17), in order to indicate to the Makkan unbelievers that their initial animosity towards Islam would be turned to an acknowledgement of its truth. The story goes that the 'haves' refused to share with the 'have-nots,' and so God destroyed the crops and fruits of their garden, causing them to regret their actions and cry: "'Woe to us! We have transgressed. It may be that our Lord will give us a better one in its place, for we do turn to Him in humble petition'" (31–32).

God does indeed forgive those who repent and express remorse for their errors. This was the case with the Makkan Quraysh who had initially opposed Islam and later accepted and supported it.

Those who persist in their rejection and hostility will have no future with God. The surah asks with incredulity: "Are We to treat the Muslims the same as the wrong-doers? What has come over you? How do you make such a judgement?" (35–36). In defining their values, the unbelievers always seem to resort to illogical and nonsensical criteria, and so God Almighty scoffs at them saying: "Or do you have a Book in which it tells you that you can have whatever you choose?" (37–38). In fact, they have no basis for their fancies and wishful thinking. All they are promised is a stern punishment, and when it comes, they shall regret their actions and it would be too late. The surah says: "The day the dreaded event unfolds and they will not be able, when asked, to prostrate themselves" (42). They would have no excuse then because they had ample opportunities to make amends but they squandered them, and God would then say: "Therefore, leave to Me those that deny this revelation: We will lead them step by step to their punishment, without them even knowing it" (44).

Prophet Muhammad was commanded to convey the message to his people and persevere in that task, no matter how arduous or demanding it was. The surah exhorts: "And so await with patience the judgment of your Lord and do not be like him [Jonah] who was swallowed by the whale…" (48). Muhammad made great sacrifices and suffered untold hardship but persevered and fulfilled his mission, leaving for all mankind a universal legacy of values and principles.

From the very beginning, Muhammad was aware that his mission was universal. The universality of Islam is stressed on numerous occasions in the Qur'an, and the surah, being an early Makkan revelation, contains one of the clearest references to it. It says:

And the unbelievers would all but devour you with their eyes when they hear Our revelations, and they say, "He is surely possessed." Yet it [the Qur'an] is nothing less than a message to all mankind. (51–52)

SURAH 69

Al-Ḥāqqah
(The Reality)

MANY BELIEVE THAT THIS LIFE is the only reality, but are not sure if this belief will remain with them after they die and face another life which would be the eternal reality. We should ask what happened to the hundreds of generations that have come and gone. Have they not all died, most of them suddenly and without warning? There shall come a time when all the people who have ever lived shall be gathered together to face up to the consequences of their deeds in this life.

Many communities had renounced the messenger God had sent to them. Some of them were punished in this world but the punishment of others has been deferred. Its time will come:

> When the trumpet is sounded once, and when the earth and the mountains are raised and then in one mighty crash are shattered to pieces. That is the Day when the inevitable cataclysm shall take place... (13–15)

That will be the time for accountability and judgment. "He who is given his record in his right hand will say, 'Here it is, read my book! I knew that I shall face my judgment...'" (19–20). But: "He who is given his record in his left hand will say, 'I wish I had never been given my record or known my judgment...'" (25–26).

Materialism has permeated all aspects of modern civilization, and a feverish race for selfish material gain has engulfed the whole world.

People are dismissive of God, of religious practices and of altruistic acts of any kind. Those communities that have inherited divine revelation have failed to translate it into an effective, workable system; rather, some of them have become a liability to the mission with which they are charged. They have let their prophets down miserably. Some of them have amassed enormous wealth and enjoy extravagant luxuries, but are loath to help the poor and the needy or to support charitable causes. It is these, according to the surah, that God sends for punishment when He says:

> Take him and bind him, and then throw him in the fire of hell, and then fasten him with a chain seventy cubits long. For he did not believe in God, the Most High and did not care to feed the poor. (30–34)

Several societies today continue to accuse Muhammad of being an imposter prophet, and view Islam as no more than a sham religion. But did Muhammad gain, personally or materially, from proclaiming Islam and defending it? What did he gain for the sacrifices he had made and for insisting that he was no more than a humble servant of God Almighty and had no powers to determine the destiny of any human being?

Muhammad was supremely placed to lead humanity along the path to God Almighty, and he was an ideal paradigm for loyalty and trustworthiness. The surah affirms these truths thus:

> I [God] swear by all that you see and all that you cannot see, that it [the Qur'an] is uttered by a noble messenger. It is not the word of a poet: how little you believe! Nor is it the word of a soothsayer: how little indeed you reflect! It is a revelation from the Lord of all creation. (38–43)

The surah warns that were Muhammad to ascribe to God words He had not revealed to him, he would face stern punishment. It says:

If he [Muhammad] had invented some of these words, We would have seized him by the right hand and then cut off his arteries and none of you could have protected him. (44–47)

The Qur'an, the pure unadulterated word of God, shall remain the bedrock of faith for all mankind, for all time to come. It will always be a fountain of guidance and righteousness, and a clear proof for the honesty and integrity of its proponent.

SURAH 70

Al-Maʿārij
(The Ways of Ascent)

AT THE BEGINNING of this surah, God refers to Himself as 'Lord of the Ways of Ascent'. This calls to mind another Qur'anic reference to God as: "the Exalter of rank, Lord of the Throne" (*Ghāfir.* 15). This is an indication of the vastness of God's realm which may take humans fifty thousand years to traverse, while angels, especially the Archangel Gabriel, can travel it within a short time. We read in *al-Naml* (40) that the Queen of Sheba's throne was taken from Yemen to Syria in a flash.

The surah refers to the Makkan Arab who foolishly challenged God to inflict a speedy punishment upon himself and his people for their rejection of the revelation. Little did he know that his request was very easy to achieve, and the surah goes on to give signs of the impending apocalypse, saying: "When the heavens will be like molten brass, and the mountains like tufts of wool, and no friends shall ask after each other" (8–10).

God has instilled in man instincts and desires that tend to pull him towards immoral and self-indulgent acts, and He has urged him to resist their power of temptation. Those that tame and overcome such desires shall be successful. That is the essence of faith (Arabic: *īmān*); a force for purification and excellence, and a beacon that leads to God's pleasure. The surah expresses it thus:

Man was created with a restless disposition. When evil befalls him he is despondent, and when blessed with good fortune, he turns mean and niggardly. Not so those who observe prayer, who are

674

steadfast in their praying, and who recognize in their wealth a right for the needy and the deprived, and those who truly believe in the Day of Judgment... (19–26)

In these few words, God outlines a number of great virtues of Islam that lead those who practise them to success and Paradise. It is a pity to see many Muslims today neglecting these fundamental aspects of their great religion, thereby failing to benefit from the numerous advantages it offers them, as clearly outlined in the Qur'an. God makes it clear in the Qur'an that the road to Paradise is littered with hardship and hurdles that have to be overcome. It is only through trials and tribulations that the caliber and quality of individuals can be tested and determined.

The surah asks:

But what has befallen the unbelievers, that they scramble towards you [Muhammad], swamping from right and left? Do they all hope to enter a garden of delight? No! They know well of what We have created them. (36–39)

This is a reference to the Makkans who would gather around Prophet Muhammad in order to listen to what he was saying, not with the intention of understanding and accepting the faith, but rather to find out what new ideas he was trying to introduce into their beliefs and way of life. Such a negative attitude was self-defeating, and they would go away with little benefit.

The surah asserts that God is capable of choosing the right people to carry His message forward; the dithering and the indecisive shall be left behind and in the hereafter will occupy a lowly position.

Nūḥ
(Noah)

ONE OF THE MOST AMAZING ASPECTS of Noah's experience is that he spent nine and a half centuries in teaching and guiding his people and some of them continued to resist and reject his advice. Such a long time would have been sufficient to reform whole nations, but they chose to persist in their deviation and intransigence. The only thing left for Noah was to resort to God Almighty for help and direction.

> He said, "My Lord, I have pleaded with my people night and day, but my pleas have only added to their aversion. And every time I call on them to seek Your forgiveness, they thrust their fingers into their ears and draw their clothes over their heads and become obstinate and grow ever more arrogant." (5–7)

One wonders if those who deny God's power and reject the truth are not suffering from some intellectual defect. There are psychological, as well as intellectual, reasons for refusing to recognize God Almighty and for choosing instead to submit to worldly and human powers.

The proof for God's existence cannot be found in a complex mathematical formula. It is something that the human heart and mind perceive instinctively. The surah relates how Noah directed his people to such proof: "'Can you not see that God created seven heavens, one above the other, and in them He made the moon a light and the sun a lantern? God has brought you from the earth like a plant and He will return you to it and then raise you forth afresh'" (15–18).

Humans live on the produce of the land. Who devised the process by which crops and plants are converted into proteins and other nutrients to sustain life and growth, and who supervises it? Who controls the movement of the stars, planets, and other heavenly bodies? It is totally absurd, and outright arrogance, to suggest that either man himself or any other presumed deity could have been the power behind creation.

The surah indicates that, after those many long years, Noah lost patience with his stubborn people and so pleaded:

> "My Lord, do not leave a single unbeliever on the face of the earth.
> If You spare them, they will lead Your servants astray and they will
> breed none but wicked and ungrateful offspring." (26–27)

Denial of God Almighty, once entrenched in a society, becomes hard to remove and breeds generation after generation of people "whose wealth and offspring bring them nothing but perdition" (21). It begets people who believe that: "We have more wealth and more offspring, and will never be punished" (*Saba'*: 35). More grievous is when the disbelievers assume the right to deny believers the right to live and practise their faith. Elsewhere in the Qur'an we read: "And the unbelievers said to their messengers, 'We shall expel you from our land unless you embrace our creed again'" (*Ibrāhīm*: 13).

This ungodly stance assumes many forms in different societies, and believers in many parts of the world today are suffering at the hands of arrogant unbelievers.

SURAH 72

Al-Jinn
(The Jinn)

IN THIS SURAH ARE SPECIFIC REFERENCES to the Christian doctrine that considers Jesus as the son of God and a component of godhood. This belief had spread over many parts of the old world and was taken as true by many generations until the Qur'an was revealed and denounced it completely, asserting instead that God is One and without offspring. Some jinn also seem to have adopted this Christian doctrine but discovered its falsehood when they heard the Qur'an. The surah tells us:

> Say, "It is revealed to me that a group of jinn listened and said: 'We have heard a most wonderful Qur'an which gives guidance to the right path and we have believed in it and will never henceforth worship anything besides our Lord.'" (1–2)

They went on to elaborate the new principles they had learnt. "'Exalted be our Lord who has taken neither a wife nor a son'" (3). They condemned those who advocated the old belief: "'And that the foolish among us have uttered falsehood against God'" (4). They regretted their ignorance and naïveté: "'And we never thought that any men or jinn could ever tell anything untrue against God'" (5).

This erroneous belief had been accepted by many humans and spread far and wide among innocent people. The jinn continue: "'And that some men have sought the help of jinn and these have misled them into further error'" (6). These foolish humans and jinn

SURAH 72 • *Al-Jinn*

thought that no further revelation would be forthcoming, and no more messengers would come to put things right and establish the true doctrine of *tawḥīd* and reassert God's power over all creation.

In reality, whenever falsehood is bolstered by authority or force and is adopted by those who have power and influence, it would flourish and take root in society. The Christian doctrine of the trinity was adopted and reinforced by the might of the Roman empire which enabled it to spread widely until Muhammad emerged and refuted that belief and stemmed its propagation.

The jinn came to know of the new religion as it began to reach many lands. They listened to the Qur'an being recited by thousands of people and were able to learn that God is One and without ancestry or offspring.

The jinn knew that a sea change was taking place in the world and that the divine revelations descending upon mankind through Muhammad were being heavily guarded. They said:

> "And we sought to reach the high heaven but found it filled with mighty wardens and fiery comets. And we used to eavesdrop on it but whoever eavesdrops now will be met with flaming darts lying in wait for them." (8–9)

The divine protection afforded the Qur'an in heaven was extended to it on earth, and has ensured its absolute preservation for all time to come.

Having heard the Qur'an, it seems that some of them rejected it while others accepted its message and said: "'And when we heard the guidance we believed in it; and whoever believes in his Lord shall fear no diminishment or injustice'" (13).

This should not surprise us human beings because, like them: "'Some of us are Muslims and some are wrong-doers. Those who embrace Islam would have pursued the right path, but those who do wrong shall become the fuel of hell'" (14–15).

I was once asked if I had encountered a jinn and said that I had not. I was then asked how I could believe in something I have never seen and I replied that not all that exists is visible. Bacteria, for their small size, as well as some heavenly bodies, being so far away, are not visible to the naked eye. The Qur'an confirms the same about the jinn when it says that Satan: "…and his minions see you whence you cannot see them" (*al-Aʿrāf*: 27). It is not possible that human beings are the only inhabitants of this vast universe. What would be the point of building a skyscraper only to have the ground floor occupied and leave the rest of it vacant? As Muslims we firmly believe in the existence of mankind, the jinn and the angels.

The surah makes the most profound observation when it asserts that it is not sufficient for man simply to recognize God Almighty but he must also fulfill certain obligations towards Him. Some people do acknowledge God's existence, power, and authority but conduct their lives in a way that takes no account of Him whatsoever. The surah alludes to communities that received divine revelation but ignored its teachings and left it by the wayside, and says: "If they had pursued the right path, We would have bestowed on them abundant rain, to test them thereby. He that turns away from his Lord's remembrance, He will inflict upon him a severe punishment" (16–17). Ingratitude is the worst form of disrespect.

The closing verses are a testimony to Muhammad's faith and integrity as a messenger. The surah exhorts him to declare:

Say, "I worship none but my Lord and take no others besides Him." Say, "It is not in my power to cause you any harm or to bring you to right conduct." Say, "No one can protect me from God, nor shall I find refuge except in Him." (20–22)

There are even today people who claim the power to forgive the wrong-doers and to possess the key to salvation and eternal life. Such claims stem largely from ignorance and lack of understanding of God's power and status. Muhammad himself, God's own last messenger to mankind, could not claim such a unique prerogative. The surah says:

> Say, "I cannot tell whether the scourge you are threatened with is imminent, or whether my Lord has deferred it for a later day. He alone knows what is to come and He reveals that knowledge to no one." (25–26)

Muhammad was a faithful and diligent servant of God who has established the creed of *tawḥīd* and ensured its spread to all corners of the globe. Today, Muhammad's followers are to be found among every human community on earth, worshiping God Almighty, invoking His name, and promoting God's noble cause.

Al-Muzzammil
(The Mantled One)

SURAH AL-AN^CĀM GIVES A CONCISE and accurate description of the life and mission of Muhammad. It says: "Say, 'My prayers and my devotions, my life and my death, are all for God, Lord of all creation: He has no partners. Thus I am commanded, and I am the first of those who submit to His will'" (*al-An^Cām*: 162–163).

Muhammad's life, unlike any other, was wholly devoted to the service of God and His message. His task was not limited to the confines of Arabia, but to raising a community that would change the direction of humanity altogether, for all time to come. His nation was to carry the banner of truth in the face of all odds. His sixty years on this earth were not devoted to reform merely one generation but to establish the tenets of *tawḥīd* all over the globe, for ever, and to raise the men and women that would carry it forward for posterity.

In the early days of his mission, Muhammad was urged to: "Spend most of the night in prayer; half of it, a little less or a little more, and recite the Qur'an in slow, measured, rhythmic tones" (2–4). There was going to be no more time for comfort or relaxation because: "We are about to pass on to you words of enormous gravity" (5).

The Qur'anic revelations Muhammad was about to receive would charge him with great responsibility and demand of him diligence and hard work. He would spend most of the night in prayer and by day he had to proclaim the message and confront his detractors. He had only God Almighty to depend on, and so he had to devote time to His praise and glorification in order to draw of His power and strength and be able to face his enemies.

God reassures Muhammad, saying: "We have in store for them heavy fetters and a blazing fire, and food that chokes and a harrowing torment" (12–13). This would be their fate "on the Day that the earth and the mountains shake violently, and the mountains crumble into heaps of shifting sand" (14). The surah thus depicts a frightening and awesome scene that should incite people to think and reflect on their life and their future after death.

Muhammad is a paradigm for men who fear God and are conscious of their accountability to Him. His Companions emulated his example and learnt from him how to combat falsehood and confront evil. But God, in His infinite mercy, relieved the rest of the Muslims of the obligation to pray for most of the night and urged them to attend to their daily duties and responsibilities. The surah says:

And God knows precisely the length of night and day, and He knows that you cannot spend the night in prayer, and so He was merciful towards you. Now recite of the Qur'an as much as is easy for you to recite. (20)

This concession is not without conditions. It is, in fact, a reward for other duties required of the believers. The surah elaborates: "God knows that there are among you some who are sick and others who travel far and wide seeking God's bounty, and yet others fighting for the cause of God" (20).

The Muslim nation needs people who build as much as it needs those who protect and defend, because there are predators constantly looking to strike at the first sign of weakness or neglect. When the Muslim nation is attacked or subdued, the truth is in danger of being undermined or destroyed altogether.

Al-Muddaththir
(The Cloaked One)

THIS SURAH SEEMS to have been revealed before the preceding one, but it is not correct to say that it was the first surah to have been revealed. Its timing appears to coincide with the end of a hiatus in the receipt of revelation by Muhammad and a longing for it on his part. The opening verses give a glimpse of some personal aspects of Muhammad, the Messenger.

It says: "You who are wrapped up in your cloak, arise and give warning, and glorify your Lord" (1–3). Muhammad is being instructed to warn the polytheist Arabs to beware their folly, and exhorted to acknowledge God's glory and greatness. The Arabic phrase *Allāhu akbar*, God is the greatest, has become the motto of Islam and Muslims everywhere. It is part of the call to prayer, the *ādhān*, and is said at the beginning of every prayer. It is also used as a rallying cry on the battle field.

The instructions continue:

- "And purify your clothes" (4). Clean your body and the clothes you wear, for cleanliness is a sign of faith and an Islamic ethic.

- "And keep away from all wickedness" (5). Avoid all immoral and wicked behavior.

- "And give with modesty" (6). Give for the sake of God and do not overestimate the value of what you give to others.

- "And be patient in the service of your Lord" (7). Persevere and put up with all hardship for the sake of God.

Having warned the Makkans of the horrors of the Day of Judgment, the surah makes an oblique reference to one of the most vociferous opponents of Muhammad in Makkah who described the Qur'an as sorcery. He was a man of great wealth and influence, uniquely acknowledged for his literary prowess. It says: "Leave to Me the man I created lonely and helpless and then gave him vast riches and sons to be by his side" (11–13). The contempt afforded to this chieftain is, of course, extended to his followers and supporters. The surah continues: "I will cast him into hell. Would that you knew what hell is like! It spares nothing and nobody…and over it are nineteen" (26–30). The number nineteen refers to the angels guarding hell and those who are in charge of punishing the guilty.

The surah goes on to draw attention to natural and cosmological phenomena such as the moon, the day, and the night, stressing the gravity of man's responsibility and accountability. It says:

Nay! By the moon and by the night as it withdraws and the morning as it reveals itself, it [hell] is one of the mightiest events. It is a warning to all mankind; those who wish to go forward and those who wish to go backward. (32–37)

Man's tendency to advance or lag behind is not determined haphazardly, but is directly linked to his eagerness and sincerity. The surah goes on to say:

Every soul shall be bound to its own deeds, except for those on the right hand who revel in gardens enquiring of the wrong-doers, "What has brought you into hell?" They would reply, "We did not observe the prayer, nor did we ever care for the needy." (38–44)

They would be reaping what they had planted, and their crooked ways would never have led them to success. "No pleas from any ancestors shall ever avail them" (48).

What, other than sheer arrogance, caused people to resist the truth and turn away from the message of Islam? They would demand that God should send angels to them individually to address them with Islam, before they would accept and believe. They resented the fact that Muhammad had been chosen as a messenger of God. The surah says:

> What is the matter with them? Why do they turn away from this reminder like frightened asses fleeing from a lion? Indeed, each one of them demands scriptures of his own to be unrolled before him. (49–52)

This jealousy and aversion to the truth remains alive today. Messengers can only remind their people of God and His blessings, and it is up to each individual to believe or not. "Nay, this surely is an admonition. Let him who will, take heed" (54–55). God will help those who help themselves.

Al-Qiyāmah
(The Resurrection)

A TRUE BELIEVER IS EXTREMELY sensitive to error; as soon as he commits a misdemeanor his conscience begins to prick him and his heart fills with regret. Faith is a powerful deterrent and a strong incentive to righteousness. Self-reproach, whenever necessary, purifies the soul and reinforces one's moral character. God, in the surah, swears by the "self-reproaching soul" as the seat of faith and true belief. People and societies that have no regard for God Almighty and do not believe in their accountability to Him lose their moral standards because they dismiss as fantasy the judgment that is to come.

The opening verses in this surah revolve around these ideas. It says:

I swear by the Day of Resurrection, and the self-reproaching soul! Does man think that We shall never put his bones together again? Indeed, We have the power to restore to perfect order the very tips of his fingers. (1–4)

God takes away life and He gives it back; He is capable of reconstructing the most intricate fingerprints in their original distinct form.

Humans will be brought back to life after death in order to account for their deeds. The surah affirms: "Man shall on that day be told of all his deeds, from first to last" (13). One of man's most consistent failings is his lack of appreciation of the gravity and

687

importance of the Day of Judgment. Were people to grasp the true impact of this concept, human life would take an altogether different course.

The surah presents a detailed description of the Day of Judgment and the events that precede and follow it. It also gives advice to Muhammad not to seek to hasten the arrival of the revelation which he, understandably, was eager to receive. The Qur'an was given to Muhammad piecemeal in order for him to be able to memorize it and relay it to his people faithfully and efficiently.

God reassures Muhammad, saying: "We shall impart it to you and ensure its recital; so listen to it when it is read and follow its reading. We shall then make its meaning clear to you" (17–19). This is a cast-iron divine guarantee that the Qur'an shall remain intact and complete for all time to come.

Before the Day of Judgment there is a phase through which every human being must pass: death! But how conscious are we of this fact? The surah goes on:

> But when a man's soul is at the top of his chest and those around him cry, "Can anyone spare him?" When he knows it is the final parting and the pangs of death assail him—on that Day all shall be driven to your Lord. (26–30)

Alas! The hustle and bustle of life tends to blind man's vision of these ominous scenes! But, the surah asks: "Does man think he will be free of responsibility?" (36).

The world has not been created for sport. People will one day be accountable to God Almighty and be answerable for their actions and for what preparations they have made for the hereafter. It is curious that, despite the tremendous advances made in the scientific field, man continues to be ignorant of his Creator and oblivious to the realities of the Day of Judgment.

Al-Insān
(Man)

AS TWO MEN PASSED BY A GRAVEYARD, one of them asked: "Do you know what these graves are saying to us?" "What do they say?" asked the other. "They say: 'We were once like you, but one day you shall be like us!'" he replied.

Indeed, ask yourself where were you, and most people in your generation, a hundred years ago? The opening verse in this surah has the answer. It says: "Has there not been upon man a long period of time when it was nothing, not even a thing to be thought of?" (1).

We were all once nonexistent, but then God brought us to life and gave us hearing and sight. One day we shall be taken away from this world to face our Creator. But in what state shall we be when we return to life again? The surah says:

For the unbelievers We have prepared chains and manacles and a blazing fire. The righteous will drink from a cup a mixture of camphor, a fountain where the servants of God go to drink. (4–6)

The surah is almost totally devoted to describing the opulence and the splendor of Paradise that await the faithful. It says: "When you behold the scene you will see great opulence and a realm of vast riches" (20). It is a reward to the believers for their faith and devotion: "This is your reward, and your endeavor is hereby accepted and recognized" (22).

The second half of the surah is devoted to extolling the virtues of God's final message to mankind and its role in shaping individuals and societies. The social and moral influences of society on individuals cannot be underestimated. Changing society according to the teachings and principles of the Qur'an is liable to bring about a righteous and upright nation. The surah says:

> We have sent down the Qur'an to you [Muhammad] piecemeal; therefore be patient and await the judgment of your Lord, and do not yield to the wicked and the unbelieving. (23–24)

Remembrance of God must be a continuous vocation, by day and by night. The surah exhorts: "And remember the name of your Lord morning and evening, and at night pray to Him and glorify Him for most of the night" (25–26).

The surah cites a human trait which is true throughout the ages, that: "The unbelievers love this fleeting life too well, and leave behind them [all thought of] a grief-laden Day" (27). It is a fact that people tend to become occupied with their desires and worldly affairs and forget about death and the hereafter. In today's world, talking of the hereafter is almost a taboo while people no longer respond to the mention of death.

This is not a call to morbidity or pessimism but a condemnation of laxity and indifference, and an invitation to overcome our whims and desires. It is important that we know where we have come from and where we are going. The surah says: "This is indeed an admonition, so let him that will take the path that leads to his Lord" (29). God guides those who seek the right path and clears the way for the believers, and He leaves the neglectful to their own devices. The surah ends with: "He takes into His mercy whom He will, but for the wrong-doers He has prepared a grievous punishment" (31).

Al-Mursalāt
(Those Sent Forth)

IN A SIMILAR FASHION TO *al-Dhāriyāt*, this surah opens with a description of wind:

> By those sent forth [winds] as they blow in swift succession; by the raging tempests that scatter things far and wide and then separate them one from another; and by those that carry the revelation, to remove blame or to warn. (1–6)

Air, still or moving, is the elixir of life on earth. It is by the grace of God that we breathe the air that surrounds us. Nevertheless, some people would persist in denying God's favors and blessings.

Wind is a curious phenomenon. It is pleasant when it is calm or when it is blowing gently, but when it is stormy it turns into a destructive force, bringing ruin and devastation. The wind plays a crucial part in the movement of the clouds that carry rain to various parts of the world.

The surah makes a curious reference to: "Those that carry the revelation, to remove blame or to warn" (5–6). We know that air is the medium through which sound waves travel, and those who receive God's revelation would either accept or reject it. The wind carries God's words to people to warn the rejectionists and place the onus on the believers.

We note that most commentators are of the opinion that the two verses refer to the angels, but this misinterpretation has come about due to their ignorance of the now established fact of physics that sound travels through the air.

In the surah God calls the wind in its various forms as witness to the truth of the resurrection and judgment. It goes on to describe the Day of Judgment thus:

> When the stars are blotted and the sky is rent asunder and the mountains are obliterated and the messengers are gathered on the appointed day; for what day had they been deferred? For the Day of Judgment! Would that you knew what the Day of Judgment is like! (8–14)

There shall come a day when this intricate well-structured cosmology will collapse and be built afresh according to a new system. In the new life truth shall be established and justice will prevail.

The surah has a refrain, repeated ten times, warning the disbelievers thus: "Woe on that day to the disbelievers!" (15). It variously occurs following a warning or a reference to a cosmological marvel, a historic event, or a piece of advice. It first occurs following a threat to the disbelievers, reminding them of the punishment they had received in this life and of what happened to those who preceded them.

The surah turns to talk about creation and how God Almighty creates out of nothing. How does man's creation come about? It is an arduous process that starts from a plain fluid, expelled through the urethra. The surah says: "Did We not create you from a plain fluid, which We placed in a safe receptacle for a fixed period of time?" (20–22). It is in that receptacle, the mother's womb, that humans are formed and shaped, intelligent and asinine alike, and then emerge in such a marvelous, functioning, fully-developed state. Who directs this breathtaking process and supervises it? The surah says: "It is We who determine and We are the best to determine" (23).

God's grace and blessings are countless, and Muslims are exhorted to recall as many of them as possible in prayer and under all conditions.

The surah goes on to say: "Have We not made the earth a home for the living and for the dead?" (25–26). This is an allusion to the force of gravity which holds everything to the earth. Water covers four-fifths of the earth's surface; what keeps it there and prevents it from spilling over or shooting up into the atmosphere? It is out of His infinite mercy and grace that God Almighty has made the earth attract things towards it and hold the life system together on its surface. Furthermore: "We have set up on it huge mountains, firmly built, and provided you with fresh water to drink" (27).

The surah then describes scenes of punishment in the hereafter and what awaits believers and disbelievers among all mankind therein. It says: "This is the Day of Judgment on which We will assemble you all, together with those who had come before. If ever you had a cunning stratagem against Me, now is the time to use it! Woe on that day to the disbelievers!" (38–40). As the final hour descends, a grave and gloomy prospect awaits the unbelievers; they shall be left dazed and totally bewildered.

The surah closes by asking what revelation other than the Qur'an the unbelievers are prepared to accept, saying: "In what message, after this, will they believe?" (50). Is there a better example of God's words? Is there a more authentic and creditable revelation other than the one Muhammad has expounded? The Qur'an is the book of truth that exposes all falsehood. Indeed: "In what message, after this, will they believe?" (50).

SURAH 78

Al-Naba'
(The Great News)

EVERY COMMUNITY TO WHICH A MESSENGER has come and claimed a divine commission, has the right to question his credentials and examine his assertions, and judge him accordingly. Let us then ask: what did Muhammad proclaim? He said that God existed, and he advanced powerful and unprecedented arguments and evidence for that. He said that there is only one God, the Creator of all that is in the heavens and the earth, and that all creatures, regardless of their state or status, submit totally to His power and will. He further asserted the inevitability of the Day of Judgment and the accountability of every responsible adult, and declared that: "Who-ever does an atom's weight of good shall see it, and whoever does an atom's weight of evil shall see it also" (*al-Zalzalah*: 7–8).

Why should anyone reject these tenets or denounce Muhammad for proclaiming them? Has anyone come with anything better?

This surah says to the Makkan unbelievers: If you are not convinced of what Muhammad is saying, look at the physical world around you and reflect upon its creation. It asks: "Did We not spread the earth like a bed, and set the mountains firmly like pegs, and created you in pairs?" (6–8).

For the last fourteen centuries, human society has, besides Islam, seen many religions and ideologies, and should be able to judge their veracity and record fairly. The fact of the matter is that, under such scrutiny, Islam would stand out above all the rest. In other words, one would be hard put to deny that Muhammad's mission is a true representative of the old as well as the new authentic divine revelation, and that other creeds are man-made. To believe in Muhammad is to believe also in Moses, Jesus, Noah, and Abraham.

The surah consists of four parts. The first one is a description of the physical world and of man himself, ending with verse 16. The second is a brief description of the Day of Judgment: "The time of the Day of Judgment is fixed. It is when the trumpet is sounded, and you shall come forth in droves" (17–18). The numerous references in the Qur'an to the resurrection are intended to counteract man's love for life and worldly things.

The third section describes the punishment awaiting the wrong-doers: "Hell is ready and waiting, a home for the transgressors, where they shall abide for ages" (21–23).

The fourth, and final, part describes the rich rewards awaiting the good and the righteous: "The righteous shall surely triumph. Theirs shall be gardens and vineyards, and young virgin maidens" (31–33).

The believers shall also experience true happiness and their faces shall glow with contentment, in the company of the angels, praising and glorifying their Lord. Their happiness will be complete as they settle down in rosy gardens, surrounded by exquisite young female companions. The surah then asserts: "That Day is sure to come, and so let him who will, seek a way back to his Lord" (39).

On that momentous Day, those conscious of God will be successful, while the cynics will have nothing to show for their life here and will regret their actions when it would be too late. The surah warns: "We have forewarned you of an imminent scourge: when man faces his record and the unbeliever pleads, 'Would that I were dust!'" (40).

We leave Muhammad's detractors with the following questions: What did he gain for himself by proclaiming his message? Was his crime that he was ardent in promoting it and pursuing its goals? Was he wrong to confront the corrupt and the tyrants of his time?

Al-Nāziʿāt
(The Setting Stars)

MY PERSONAL INTERPRETATION of the opening verses of this surah is that they draw attention to heavenly bodies that float in space, in continuous motion, at various speeds, but without engines to propel them or navigators to direct them in their respective assigned orbits.

> By the stars that set, and those that move at a lively pace, and the stars that float at will, and those that race away in their orbits, and those that govern the affairs of the world... (1–5)

However, this whole complex system is destined to come to an abrupt end, and all these phenomena will disappear. When will that happen? "When the trumpet sounds its first thundering sound followed by a second one" (6–7).

This huge cataclysmic quake will bring everything tumbling down. The whole world will be turned upside down and people's hearts will be filled with horror and anticipation. The unbelievers will then ask in bewilderment: "'Are we really to be returned to life, after we have become hollow bones?'" (10–11).

Skeptics in this life doubt the warnings of God's prophets and messengers. They deny that the dead shall ever be brought back to life. They would say: "'In that case, our return will be a total loss'" (12).

They gradually begin to realize that their denial and lack of faith had been an unwise preparation for such a momentous event. The surah asserts: "But, it will be only a single blow and they shall all be alive again" (13–14).

Twentieth-century atheists are not really very much different from the sixth-century pagan Arabs who had a purely materialistic and existentialist view of life: people are born, they die and are buried. There is no more to life than that! What would they say or do when they are brought to life again?

The surah goes on to cite the Pharaoh as an example of intransigence and arrogance. The Pharaoh is a prototype of men who can be found in all walks of life. They are usually selfish, ruthless megalomaniacs who have no concept of justice and who would not flinch from violating the rights of others.

The surah then turns to address the whole of mankind, questioning their callousness and lack of faith in God. It asks: "Are you harder to create than the heaven which He has built? He raised it high and fashioned it..." (27–28). Compared to other creatures, man is small and weak; he should know better than to deny the truth or act like a tyrant. Man needs to be conscious of God and to seek to earn His mercy and forgiveness. The power man has been given over other creatures ought to be harnessed and employed in the service of God and to praise and thank Him.

Towards the end, the surah returns to its opening theme: the resurrection and punishment and reward, pointing out clearly that this life is but a precursor to the life to come.

It says: "Thus, when the supreme calamity strikes, the day when man will recall all his labors and hell is brought in full view for all to see..." (34–36). On that day, mankind will be divided into two groups: those who succumbed to their weaknesses and desires and those who submitted to God and served His cause. The surah explains:

He who transgressed and preferred the life of this world shall have his final abode in hell; but he who feared standing before his

697

Lord and curbed his soul's desires shall have his final abode in Paradise. (37–41)

Despite their denial, skeptics have the audacity to be curious about the time when the final Hour might arrive. The surah says: "They ask you [Muhammad] about the Hour, 'When will it come?' But how are you to know? Only your Lord knows its appointed time" (42–44).

What good is it to the unbeliever to know when the world will end when he is not prepared for the life to come? Existence is one complete and continuous cycle and death is but a short interval between this life and the next. It is only in the hereafter that we shall know the real value of our life in this world. The surah asserts: "The day they witness that Hour, they will think they stayed [in the grave] but one afternoon, or one morning" (46).

SURAH 80

ʿAbasa
(He Frowned)

THE PROPHET WAS BUSY ONE DAY addressing a group of prominent dignitaries from the Quraysh tribe, in the hope that their joining the small community of Muslims would influence a large number of Arabs to turn to Islam too. A blind man, called ʿAbd Allah ibn Umm Maktūm, interrupted him, demanding his attention and asking to talk to the Prophet. Muhammad was perturbed, and it showed on his face. He ignored the blind man and continued his appeal to the Makkan notables.

This is the background to this surah which says:

> He [Muhammad] frowned and turned away when the blind man came towards him. But how would you [Muhammad] know that he might not be reformed, or that he might not take heed and benefit from your admonition? (1–4)

The Prophet appreciated the reproach and thereafter became more deferential and accommodating towards Ibn Umm Maktūm. He would call him "the man my Lord censured me about!" It also became Muhammad's practise to leave Ibn Umm Maktūm in charge of Madinah whenever he had to leave it for any reason.

The surah then continues to expound the nature of God's message. It is a message to be passed on orally as well as in written form. Those who receive this message should reflect on it, appreciate its meaning, respond to God's call and prepare for the hereafter. Alas! Not all people react in a positive way to God's message.

699

Many people are oblivious, or have no interest in knowing how or why they have come to be alive. Man starts life as a drop of fluid, then develops and grows into a full human being. Few people stop and reflect sufficiently on how they have reached this stage and what power has brought them to it. They totally forget Almighty God, the source of their existence and sustenance. The surah enquires:

> From what did God create him [man]? He created him from a drop
> of fluid and then decided his destiny; He then paved the way before
> him, and then caused him to die and be interned. When He wills,
> He will certainly bring him back to life. (18–22)

In the course of life, man forgets all this and becomes occupied with fulfilling his worldly goals and aspirations. Inevitably, he neglects his obligations towards God Almighty. The surah says: "By no means, he must fulfill God's commands" (23).

Skeptics and unbelievers are always arguing against the resurrection and the Day of Judgment. They refuse to accept them and recognize only their present existence. The surah cites a simple argument as proof for resurrection by saying:

> Let man reflect on his food. We pour water from the sky, and We
> cause cracks to appear in the ground through which We cause to
> grow corn and grapes and fresh vegetation and olives and palm trees
> and rich fields... (24–30)

How did all this come about? How did the various plants, fruits and trees come to have their distinct flavors, colors, smells, and structures? Whoever caused them to grow out of dirt and peat must be capable of bringing humans back to life, and of making everyone face up to their record.

The surah goes on: "On the Day the deafening siren sounds, a man shall forsake his own brother, his own father and mother, his own wife and children. Each one of them, that Day, shall be preoccupied with his own plight" (33–37). But today, people are seldom concerned about heaven and hell or punishment and reward!

On that Day: "Some faces will be beaming, smiling and delighted, while others will be in total gloom, covered with dust and darkness" (38–41).

It is a real pity that modern science has not, as yet, been able to go beyond physical and material reality. It continues to refuse to look into questions of metaphysics in any serious way at all.

Al-Takwīr
(The Folding Up)

THE SURAH LISTS TWELVE CATACLYSMIC EVENTS that will accompany the resurrection and the advent of the Day of Judgment.

1. "When the sun is folded up," (1) and its light and energy disappear and darkness engulfs the whole world.

2. "When the stars fall," (2) and are scattered aimlessly in space.

3. "When the mountains are annihilated," (3) and broken into pieces and strewn as dust.

4. "When pregnant she-camels are abandoned," (4) with no one to care for them.

5. "When the wild beasts are gathered together," (5) from their remote habitat.

6. "When the oceans boil over and flare up," (6) overflowing the land and sweeping away everything in their path.

7. "When human souls are sorted out," (7) and returned to their respective bodies.

8. "When the daughter killed in infancy is asked for what crime she was killed," (8–9) the questioning begins.

9. "When the scrolls are laid open," (10) and every human being is presented with his or her life history.

10. "When the sky is removed," (11) and completely transformed.

11. "When hell is made to burn fiercely," (12) ready to engulf the evil-doers.

12. "When Paradise is brought near," (13) to the believers with all its luxury and opulence.

That will be the time when: "Every soul shall know what it had done" (13). The verses list briefly the precursors for universal resurrection and the fate awaiting every human being.

Despite the fact that the earth is one of the smallest planets in the solar system, and that the solar system itself represents but a tiny part of the universe, mankind is afforded the highest status and respect in God's estimation. Nevertheless, man's response to God's message and his relationship with the Almighty is often faltering and inconsistent.

In this surah, God calls the galaxies and stars as witnesses to the validity of the Qur'an and the integrity of Muhammad's mission as guidance to all mankind and a mercy from God. It says:

I swear by the shining stars that recede by day, and by the stars that rise and set, and by the night when it spreads its darkness, and the morning as it first breathes light, that this is the word of a most honorable messenger. (15–19)

The majesty of the physical world is evidence of the eminence of revelation, both of which are signs of God's existence and power. The recitation of the Qur'an moves the human heart and brings one into harmony with the rest of the world, and puts all creation in direct contact with God Almighty.

The surah mentions the Archangel Gabriel, sometimes referred to in the Qur'an as *Rūḥ al-Quds*, pointing out that he is greatly favored and most highly trusted by God: "He is endowed with power and high rank by the Lord of the Throne; he is obeyed there in heaven and faithful to his trust" (20–21).

It was Gabriel who conveyed God's revelation to Muhammad, who received it and relayed it to mankind faithfully. Muhammad thoroughly absorbed the teachings and spirit of the Qur'an, reflected them in his person and behavior, and strove hard against all odds to translate them into reality and establish them as a basis for a civilization that has spread to all corners of the globe and left its indelible mark on the history of mankind.

Despite it being among the earliest Qur'anic revelations, this surah very clearly establishes the universality of the message of Islam. It castigates Islam's detractors in Makkah, saying: "Whither then will you go? This is a message to all men: to those among you that have the will to be upright" (26–28).

Man's duty is to make the effort. Everyone will be rewarded according to what he or she has done.

SURAH 82

Al-Infiṭār
(The Cataclysm)

IN THIS LIFE, MAN IS CONSTANTLY required to watch the sky, marvel at the stars that adorn it and admire its symmetry and perfect design. The Qur'an asserts: "He created seven heavens, one above the other. You will not see any flaws in the Merciful's creation. Turn up your eyes: can you detect a single crack?" (*al-Mulk*: 3).

When the final Hour comes, everything is turned upside down. It is a time "when the sky is rent asunder; when the stars scatter and the oceans roll together; when graves are disinterred, and every soul shall know the good and the evil it had done" (1–5).

Let us visualize the scene: cracks all over the skies; stars shooting and falling in every direction; the oceans overflowing; and graves opening up and throwing out their contents, with the dead being prepared for resurrection in total bewilderment.

With this cataclysmic event in mind, a reprimand is given:

Man, what has possessed you to disobey your gracious Lord who created you in a perfect upright form? He shaped you in whatever shape He willed. (6–8)

Man will ask himself: What have I done during my life to prepare myself for this momentous day? In this life, man would sooner overlook divine advice and be led astray by his whims and desires. He tends easily to linger and fall behind when called upon to work hard and make sacrifices.

For most people, the advent of the hereafter will come as a shock, and they will be told: "You deny the Last Judgment, but there are guardians watching over you, noble recorders who know all that you do" (9–12). Throughout one's life, faithful angels accurately and meticulously record one's every action. On the Day of Judgment, every human being will be presented with a true and full account of their life before their final destination is decided. "The righteous will surely dwell in bliss, but the wicked shall burn in hell" (13–14).

Al-Muṭaffifīn
(The Stinters)

THIS SURAH CONTINUES in a similar vein to the preceding one, elaborating the strong and binding relationship between deeds and rewards. This link may have, at times, been misunderstood or distorted in Muslim societies. There have always been selfish individuals who only think of their own needs and interests, even if these are unfair or unjustified, and have no consideration for the needs of others, no matter how legitimate. Such greedy self-seeking people are a threat to society as a whole.

The surah describes them as: "Those who exact full measure when taking from others, but defraud when they measure or weigh for others" (2–3). Their dishonesty is not limited to buying and selling alone, but it influences their behavior in many other fields of life.

There are people who value their possessions dearly, but consider other people's property as fair game. Human life cannot proceed normally when such contradictory and destructive tendencies prevail, nor can progress be made when such self-centered views reign. The Qur'an warns:

We made the foul deeds of those who do not believe in the life to come seem fair to them, and they blunder about in their folly. Such are those who shall be sternly punished and in the hereafter shall be the biggest losers. (al-Naml: 4–5)

Belief in God and the Day of Judgment protects people against such foul deeds, and deters them from committing acts of aggression or violating the rights of others. The surah says menacingly: "Do these not know that they will be raised to life one momentous day, when mankind will stand before the Lord of all creation?" (4–6).

Nevertheless, a man's fate in the hereafter is not decided by a few casual misdemeanors, from which believers are usually absolved, but rather by deliberate and consistent patterns of misbehavior. Prophet Muhammad is reported to have said: "As one commits a sin, it leaves a black spot in one's heart. If one desists, seeks forgiveness, and repents, one's heart will be cleansed; but if one repeats the offense, the black spot enlarges until it covers the whole of one's heart." This is what the surah refers to when it says: "No! Their misdeeds have left a stain on their hearts. No! On that day they shall be obscured from their Lord, and they shall enter the fire of hell" (14–16). The renowned Muslim scholar, Ḥasan al-Baṣrī said: "The stain on the heart is the result of repetitive offending that renders the heart blind until it withers away."

Those for whom lowly behavior becomes a habit and who get used to living like animals shall be barred from entering the gates of heaven. They make no effort to raise their principles or morals and so they remain dishonorable and inferior. The surah asserts: "Truly, the record of the sinners is destined for *Sijjīn* (a squalid place in hell); and would that you knew what *Sijjīn* really is! Their record is a sealed book. Woe on that day to the disbelievers who deny the Day of Judgment" (7–11).

On the other hand, those who uphold the faith and are happy to persevere and face the hardships of persevering in their commitments to God, and support His cause, shall have a different fate altogether. The surah says:

The record of the righteous is destined for *ʿIlliyyūn* (a lofty place in Paradise); and would that you knew what *ʿIlliyyūn* really is! Their record is a sealed book, witnessed by the favored angels. The righteous will surely dwell in bliss. They will look around them from reclining seats, and on their faces you would recognize the glow of joy. (18–24)

The early pioneers of Islam displayed great faith and sincerity, but their small numbers and meager resources left them easy prey for others. Nevertheless, God Almighty has compensated them for what they had suffered and allocated for them rich and wonderful rewards.

The surah says:

The evil-doers would mock the believers, winking at one another as they pass by them. When they meet with their own folk they speak of the believers with jest... (29–31)

These scenes are repeated in our own time, as disbelievers sneer at the faithful and mock their beliefs. It is not a new phenomenon, nor should the believers complain about it.

The earlier generations of Islam showed great fortitude and innovative spirit in all fields of life. Their triumphs have produced one of the greatest human civilizations whose influence has reached all corners of the globe.

The latter generations, however, have not fulfilled their duty. They have inherited the glory and the wealth but not the talent or the drive of their predecessors. They would not be able to spread the word of Islam while they fail to adhere to its precepts in their personal as well as communal lives. Today, true and honest believers have to fight on two fronts: a domestic as well as an external front; the one is just as demanding as the other.

SURAH 84

Al-Inshiqāq
(The Rending)

TO US, THE SKY MAY SEEM to be a vast blue dome. We know very little of its structure or the life forms that may exist in it. However, God tells us in this surah that, when the Hour comes, the sky will be split asunder. The surah says: "When the sky is rent apart, and duly submits to its Lord's will..." (1–2). We are also told that the earth will be flattened and will throw up all that is buried underneath it.

The Qur'an tells us that at the beginning of creation, God ordered the sky and the earth "to come into existence, willingly or unwillingly." (*Fuṣṣilat*: 11) When the end of the world comes, they shall have no option but to obey God's will and command.

Then comes the moment of truth for mankind. The surah says: "Man, you are diligently toiling on towards your Lord, and you shall meet Him" (6). This life is a time of hard work, responsibility, and challenge. It is also a time for choice.

He that is given his record in his right hand shall have a lenient reckoning, and shall go back rejoicing to his people. But he that is given his record behind his back shall bewail his fate and be thrown into a blazing fire. (7–12)

Presenting the wrongdoer with his record from behind his back, forcing him to take it with the left hand, is a sign of derision and humiliation. God turns away from him as he had turned away from God in his previous life, denying His existence and rejecting His message. God was aware of his actions; "Indeed, His Lord was ever watching him" (15).

The surah goes on, in the inimitable Qur'anic style, to draw attention to certain physical phenomena, saying: "I call to witness the reddish glow of the sky preceding the sunset, and the night and all it brings together, and the moon in her fullness, that you [mankind] shall pass from stage to stage" (16–19).

My personal interpretation of this passage is that it is a reference to the trials and tribulations of the Muslim experience on this earth; its triumphs and setbacks. I was inspired to come to this conclusion while reading the report of al-Tirmidhī, on the authority of Abū Saʿīd al-Khudrī, who reported that one day, having performed the *ʿaṣr* prayer, Prophet Muhammad stood up to address the congregation. He spoke on a wide range of subjects relating to the coming of the Hour. At one point he said: "Life is green and sweet. God has put you in charge of it to see how you would fare. Once one knows the truth, one should not fear any human power in upholding it..." Abū Saʿīd added that people in the congregation started looking at the sun and wondering how long it would be before the day was over, when the Prophet said: "What is left of this life so far is equal to what is left of your day, so far."

Whatever time is left before the coming of the Hour represents the history of the Muslim nation which has emerged in the world towards the end of time. The crucial question now is: Have Muslims fulfilled their mission towards humanity? Have they made a difference to the quality of life on this earth? Have they learnt all the lessons of history?

On the Day of Judgment, Muslims will be asked how far they have adhered to the Qur'an, and how they have presented its teachings to the rest of the world. The surah asks: "Why then do they not have faith, or prostrate themselves when the Qur'an is read out to them?" (20–21).

Al-Burūj
(The Constellations)

THE SURAH OPENS with the declaration: "By the heaven with its constellations; and by the appointed Day [of Judgment]; and by the witness and what is being witnessed, cursed be the people of the trench" (1–4). This is a reference to huge trenches in the ground filled with burning substances into which believers have sometimes been thrown as punishment for their faith. This has been the fate of numerous believers throughout human history, meted out to them at the hands of tyrants whose cruelty and ruthlessness know no bounds.

I have personally known some martyrs and felt that they had only existed for such a great feat. They have nothing but disdain for their oppressors and the falsehoods they propagate, and have no qualms about giving up their lives for what they believe to be right. I once heard such a martyr say shortly before his death: "To die for the truth is life itself!" Over fifty years ago, a group of young Muslims came to bid me farewell as they were preparing to go to war in Palestine, and I never saw any of them again, but their bravery and heroism were the talk of their generation!

There is a story of a woman who, as she and her son were being led to the trench of fire, hesitated slightly, probably due to a mother's instinctive feelings for her son. But when the son urged his mother that she had nothing to fear because right was on her side, she stormed into the fire!

SURAH 86

Al-Ṭāriq
(The Night-Visitor)

By the sky, and by the night visitor. And what will explain to you what the night visitor is? It is the star of piercing brightness. (1–3)

IN THE UNIVERSE THERE ARE DARK PLANETS, such as the earth, which are dull and emit no light, and there are stars, like the sun, that glow and radiate light. The "night visitor" referred to in this surah is one such star, which the Arabs identify as al-Shāhid (meaning "the witness" or "the proof"), and is normally visible at sunset. It could also be a reference to a group of bright stars.

"Every soul but has a guardian," (4) and God provides watch over every human being, to record his or her deeds and actions.

The surah goes on to affirm: "Let man reflect on what he was created from. He was created from a gushing fluid that issues from between the loins and the ribs" (5–7). The Qur'an speaks with such authority and precision on matters of science, that there have been reports of modern embryologists being filled with amazement and admiration at such accurate statements on the various stages of human conception, which are unique to the Qur'an.

It is common knowledge that human conception begins with the ejaculation of the male sperm and is controlled by a number of glands connected to the nervous system. However, the human being is also the product of nutritive substances provided by the environment in which we live, and in which water, sun, energy, and soil, among others, all play a part. Yet some people deny the miraculous aspects of creation, forgetting that one day they will have to

713

account for their denial—the day "when men's consciences will be searched, and man shall be helpless and with none to support him" (9–10).

The surah goes on to elaborate on God's mighty creation: the earth is plowed and produces plants, the skies gush with rain and the seeds are planted and grow to ensure that the cycle of life is maintained; helpless weak babies develop into strong, full-grown men and women. What power, other than God's, lies behind these amazing phenomena of creation and regeneration?

The Qur'an comes to establish truth:

It is a decisive statement, free of any flippant trifle. They scheme, and I, too, scheme. So bear with the unbelievers, bear with them for a little while. (13–17)

Al-Aʿlā
(The Most High)

Praise the name of your Lord, the Most High, who has perfected the creation of all things; Who has ordained their destiny and guided them. (1–3)

THIS IS A REFERENCE TO THE LOFTINESS and magnificence of God Almighty. It does not signify geographical or physical height as Pharaoh in his foolishness understood it when he, as the Qur'an relates, said: "Hāmān, make me bricks of clay and build for me a tower that I may climb up and reach the god of Moses" (al-Qaṣaṣ: 38), or as a Russian astronaut seemed to believe when, on his return from space, he said that he could not see God anywhere out there!

Muslims praise God and glorify Him several times a day. We believe that God sits on His Throne which encompasses the whole of the cosmos, and that all this is beyond the restraints of matter and the constraints of time and space.

God is exalted and powerful and it is far beyond the capabilities of the human intellect to comprehend or encompass His power. Human mental ability has not exhausted the secrets of the atom, let alone fully perceived the glory and greatness of God.

God has created all things from nothing and in perfect order. He proportioned things to complement one another and to exist and function in harmony. Science tells us that the quantity of water on our planet remains constant. People, animals, plants, and all other creatures consume water in various ways and in huge quantities that are replenished through a process of vaporization, condensation and precipitation.

"He brings forth the green pasture, then turns it to withered grass" (4–5). Both of these states have their uses for life, vegetation, and the environment.

"We shall allow you [Muhammad] to recite [the Qur'an] so that you forget none of it…" (6). This is to reassure Muhammad that God would support him to deliver the message of Islam and would facilitate the task for him, because it is a timeless and tolerant message. "We shall guide you to the smoothest path, and so admonish, if admonition be of use" (8–9). Muhammad's duty was to exhort and remind people of God; the wise would heed the call and follow him, but the foolish would walk away. "He that fears God will heed it, but the wicked sinner will avoid it, and shall enter in the great fire" (10-12).

Man is capable of achieving excellence as well as of failing woefully, but these are not brought about by wealth or power. What good would it do one to own the whole world while earning the wrath of God? "Successful shall be the one who purifies himself, who invokes the name of his Lord and prays" (14–15). Most people, alas, are blinded by fleeting and immediate enjoyments and ignore the requirements of the life to come. Al-Ḥasan, the Prophet's grandson, is reported to have said: "I know of no misunderstood truth worse than death; it knocks at every door, but it is as though it has never snatched a youngster or an elderly person." The surah asserts: "Yet you [unbelievers] prefer this life, although the life to come is better and more lasting" (16–17).

Al-Ghāshiyah
(The Overwhelming Event)

THE SURAH OPENS WITH a reverberating question: "Have you
heard of the overwhelming event?" (1). The title of this surah, *al-
Ghāshiyah* (The Overwhelming Event), denotes the Day of Resurrection because it is a day when people's minds will be overwhelmed. The surah then continues to provoke fear and hope
through promises and threats, before it calls on the Arab mind to
look around its environment and observe the camels and the mountains and the stretching horizons. The Arabs were directed to
conclude that only the One God was deserving of worship and that
the idols they had inherited should be abandoned.

The surah closes by defining the mission of the Muslim community, namely to enlighten and remind. As people forget or overlook
the purpose of their existence, Muslims are expected to take up the
task of confronting ungodliness and evil in the world. They draw
their power and strength from the Qur'an, the book that had
brought them honor and respect, but which they have now all but
neglected.

The surah threatens the wrong-doers with misery, describing
their faces: "On that day there shall be downcast faces, worn out,
haggard" (2–3). They will drink seething water and eat food of no
benefit to them. As for the believers, they will be in a different world
altogether. "There shall be radiant faces, of men pleased with their
labors, residing in a lofty Paradise" (8–10). Paradise is a place that is
free of idle talk or vain chatter, because such behavior does not befit
wise and pious people.

Believers should use their minds to increase understanding of the world and that which lies beyond its physical presence. "Would they not reflect on how camels were created and how the heavens were raised on high?" (17–18). It is an open invitation to mankind to reflect on all aspects of the universe and all its phenomena and creatures. Very few of the early Muslim scholars can escape the criticism that they were too infatuated with the study of Hellenistic Greek philosophy rather than devoting their attention to the study of the Qur'anic philosophy of matter.

The surah then makes a most profound statement which encapsulates the essence of the mission of Islam. It says: "Therefore, admonish, for you are but a warner; you have no power over them" (21–22). This is a clear affirmation that Muslims are not directed to establish a tyrannical, colonialist community steeped in greed, but a community that liberates the human mind and directs mankind towards perfection. A Muslim state is not established for the benefit of one particular race or ethnic group; rather, it is the outcome of sincere and honest endeavor to please God Almighty.

Virtue in today's world has been stifled as evil, injustice, and vice find protection and promotion. There has never been a greater need for a believing authority to rise to protect the good, establish justice, and work for faith and reform. Whatever the outcome, the final return shall be to God Almighty: "To Us is their return, and We will bring them to account" (25–26).

SURAH 89

Al-Fajr
(The Dawn)

THE SURAH OPENS by drawing attention to the dawn, a symbol for the recession of darkness and the birth of daylight. It also draws attention to "the ten nights" (2) which, according to the majority of commentators, is a reference to the first ten nights of the sacred month of Dhū'l-Ḥijjah, the twelfth month of the Islamic calendar, which include the Day of ʿArafāt, and the Day of Sacrifice—the ninth and tenth days of the month, respectively. On these days every year, Muslims from all over the world converge on Makkah for the pilgrimage, praising God and venerating His sacred House, the Kaʿbah.

Next comes the reference to: "all that is dual and all that is single, and the night as it falls" (3–4). This is an allusion to time, which is one of the most mysterious and intriguing aspects of creation that can only be measured by its effects.

The surah draws attention to these phenomena to reassure Muhammad that God would support him and give him, and his religion, the upper hand, and that He would thwart his enemies and frustrate their efforts, no matter how powerful or ruthless they might be. It asks Muhammad to recall earlier history. The surah says:

Are you not aware how your Lord had dealt with [the tribe of] ʿĀd, the people of Iram, the city with many pillars, the like of whom had never existed anywhere in the land? And with Thamūd who had cut their dwellings among the rocks of the valley? And with Pharaoh, firm of might? (6–10)

719

Ancient communities may not have conquered space or excelled in material science, but, as their remains would testify, they were efficient masons and craftsmen. Elsewhere in the Qur'an, God directs the Arabs who rejected Muhammad's call, saying:

Would they [the Arabs] not tour the earth and see the fate of their predecessors? They were more powerful; they tilled the land and built upon it more than they have built... (*al-Rūm*: 9)

As a result of their arrogance, however, their power led them to ruin and destruction, and "Your Lord let loose upon them a scourge of punishment; for your Lord is ever on the watch" (13–14).

The surah then turns to that abominable human trait of living for the day and neglecting future accountability. It says:

As for man, when his Lord tests him by exalting him and bestowing favors upon him, he would say, "My Lord has been generous towards me." But when He tests by withholding His favors, he would say, "My Lord despises me." But that is not true. (15–17)

God apportions people's livelihoods and fortunes in this life according to principles and criteria known only to Him. God tests people with affluence and with poverty, with victory and with defeat. His generosity does not necessarily reflect pleasure nor is the lack of it an expression of wrath. God tries all people in a variety of ways in order to determine their final resting place in the hereafter.

God does not favor a person with wealth in order for that person to flaunt it and tell his peers: "I am richer than you and I have the stronger following" (*al-Kahf*: 34). The receiver of such favor is expected to share his wealth with others and help the needy and alleviate the hardship of the poor. Similarly, He does not withhold fortune from others in order to demoralize them or invoke in them envy and jealousy towards the well-off, but to strengthen their ability to endure and learn to rise above greed and lust for money.

Differences in wealth and material possessions among human beings have existed throughout human history. Having asserted that fact, the surah goes on to say:

No! But you show no generosity towards the orphan, nor do you vie with each other to feed the poor. You devour the inheritance of others with greed, and you love riches dearly. (17–20)

Bread wars have broken out in almost every generation. They are wars motivated by greed rather than altruism, and by niggardliness rather than beneficence. It is disheartening to note that religious teachings have been discarded and ignored, while licentiousness is running rife. In modern times, communists have branded God a tyrant and taken it upon themselves to redistribute wealth, resulting in far greater tyranny and injustice.

However, what have Muslims contributed to the modern world? Hardly anything. Through their behavior and life-style, and their misrepresentation of their faith, Muslims today have rendered a great disservice to Islam. We see Muslims despairing of obtaining justice, dignity, and respect in their own countries and seeking them instead in foreign lands. Could matters get any worse, or should we look for justice only in the hereafter?

When the earth is crushed to fine dust, and your Lord emerges with the angels in their ranks, and hell is brought closer—on that Day man will remember his deeds. But what shall remembering avail him? He will say, "Would that I had sent forth [good deeds] for my [future] life!" (21–24)

For the wrong-doers, that will be the time for bitter regret and remorse, but it will be too late. As for the conscientious believers, it will be a day of triumph and rejoicing. The closing verse of the surah confirms this by saying: "O serene soul! Return to your Lord, joyful, and pleasing in His sight. Join My servants and enter My Paradise" (27–30).

It has been reported that Abū Bakr expressed great admiration for these verses when a man recited them in the presence of Prophet Muhammad. The Prophet said: "The angel shall greet you with these words when you die." That was certainly a special privilege for Abū Bakr, such a distinguished and loyal Companion of Muhammad, and these gracious and heartening words shall also be a compliment that God will extend to every human being who submits to His will and behaves with decency and righteousness.[37]

---

37 Narrated in al-Ṭabarī.

SURAH 90

Al-Balad
(The City)

THE OPENING VERSE: "I swear by this city," (1) draws attention to the city of Makkah, where Prophet Muhammad was born and lived, to which the next verse refers: "And you are a resident of this city" (2). Makkah was also a city of paradox, because although it was a sanctuary and an inviolable city, Muhammad faced the rejection and persecution of its people.

Nevertheless, the identity and history of Makkah epitomizes God's promise to Abraham and his son Ishmael, who built its central shrine, the Ka'bah, and prayed to God: "Our Lord, send forth to them [the Arabs of Makkah] a messenger from among themselves to declare to them Your revelations, teach them the Book and wisdom, and purify them" (*al-Baqarah*: 129). This would fit well with the interpretation that "the parent and his offspring" in the third verse is a reference to Abraham, the founder of monotheism, and Muhammad, a descendant of Ishmael and the seal of the prophets, who established the religion of monotheism firmly on this earth.

Man was brought to this world with a heavy burden of responsibility: "We have created man in a state of turmoil" (4). God's teachings and the laws of the Shari'ah were revealed to help him rationalize and control his desires. The surah questions the wisdom of disbelief in God and His judgment: "Does man, then, think that no one has power over him?" (5). This echoes what is said elsewhere in the Qur'an: "Does man think that We shall not gather his bones back together again?" (*al-Qiyāmah*: 3).

723

Man even gloats in spending his wealth, saying: "'I have squandered vast riches'" (6). What good would wealth do if one is going to meet one's Lord stripped of faith and righteousness? The surah asks: "Does he [man] think that none can see him?" (7). Indeed, every human being shall be questioned by God on how he had earned his wealth and how he had spent it.

God then goes on to remind man of the bounties He has bestowed upon him, saying: "Have We not given him two eyes, and a tongue and two lips, and shown him the two routes [of right and wrong]?" (8–10). It was time man used those faculties God had given him to break away from blindly following the heedless traditions of the forefathers, to scale the heights, submit to God Almighty, and seek the path of faith and righteousness. It was a big step to take. It would entail a great deal of will-power and moral courage. It would mean: "The freeing of a bondsman, or the feeding, on a lean day, of an orphaned relative or a needy person in distress" (12–16).

To that the surah adds: "And to be one of those who believe and exhort one another to perseverance and to mercy; these shall be of the right side" (17–18). These are all features of the people of Paradise, who seek excellence in all they do. Believers are alert, active, and astute people who strive to do good until the day they die, after which they will be rewarded with life in Paradise, according to their deeds.

Those who are bent on evil and wrongdoing shall have a different end. "Whereas those who deny Our revelations shall be of the left side, overwhelmed by fire, closing in upon them" (19–20).

The surah alludes to the fact that earlier prophets and messengers were not successful in bringing all the people of the Arabian peninsula into the fold of God's revealed religion, a task which was only achieved by Muhammad, the seal of the prophets, who came from the heart of Arabia and founded a community that was to carry the torch of faith to all corners of the globe.

SURAH 91

Al-Shams
(The Sun)

THE SURAH OPENS BY drawing attention to: "The sun and its midday brightness and the moon as it rises after it" (1–2). From earth, the sun looks to the naked eye like a small disc, while astronomers tell us that, in fact, the sun's mass is 330 times the earth's mass and 150 million kilometers away from it. It has nine planets orbiting it, including our own planet earth, presently inhabited by around six billion people. We also learn that, in addition to our Milky Way, there are countless other suns and galaxies which, despite their vastness, occupy only a fraction of this boundless universe.

Surely, the vastness, intricacy, and order of the universe are signs for the omnipresence and omnipotence of its Creator, as stated in the Qur'an: "To God belongs the east and the west, wherever you may turn there shall be the face of God. God is Omnipresent and All-Knowing" (*al-Baqarah*: 115).

This small planet, earth, is the home of the human race who have been given the free will and the power to choose. Some believe in God while others do not. The Qur'an tells us that angels, all over this universe, pray for the salvation of the believers:

> Those [angels] that carry the Throne, and those surrounding it, sing the praises of their Lord in whom they believe and seek His forgiveness for the believers (*Ghāfir.* 7);

and:

The heavens above them are well-nigh shattered, while the angels sing the praises of their Lord and seek His forgiveness for those on earth. (*al-Shūrā*: 5)

This surah, together with other short ones, consists of concise, sharp, but powerful facts, concepts, and instructions. They are the most commonly read surahs during the Muslim prayers (salah) for their informative, inspiring, and stimulating value.

This surah is a powerful assertion that success lies in purifying the human soul, and that spiritual and moral corruption, neglect, and ignorance would only end in failure and ruin. The surah cites the example of the people of Thamūd who were arrogant and oppressive, and whose civilization consequently disintegrated.

SURAH 92

Al-Layl
(The Night)

THE CYCLE OF NIGHT AND DAY is a familiar daily occurrence.
During these alternate periods of light and darkness, people seek
various pursuits and shape their future in this life, and the life to
come. Some will end up in Paradise while others shall go to hell.
A man's destiny is determined by his deeds: good ones shall bring
happiness and success, and evil ones shall bring misery and doom.

Having drawn attention to the phenomenon of night and day,
the surah declares:

He that gives in charity and is conscious of God, and believes in
goodness, We shall lead along the smooth path; but he who is niggardly and arrogant, and disbelieves in goodness, We shall lead
along the arduous way. (5–10)

There have been times when Muslims were negative regarding
their own potential and preferred sloth and indolence, thereby forfeiting their prestige and their future. They behaved foolishly and
misunderstood God's guidance, squandering their faith through
complacency and superstition. Generosity, honesty, and fear of
God must be combined with total and undivided devotion to His
cause.

This is not an easy goal to achieve. Most people worship wealth,
fame, and power, and are only prepared to pursue their own selfish
objectives and glory. One cannot help but wonder whether, nowadays, the whole of human activity is centered around pomposity and

ostentation, and whether honesty is now the exception. The surah draws attention to him:

> …who spends in charity to purify his soul, expecting recompense from no one, save for the sake of his Lord, Most High; and he shall find satisfaction. (18–21)

Were people to cleanse their hearts of the love of money and worldly things, and seek success in the hereafter, mankind would be spared a great deal of evil and suffering, and many a devastating war might be averted.

SURAH 93

Al-Ḍuḥā
(Daylight)

THE QUR'AN IS OFTEN DESCRIBED as 'light' (*nūr*). We read: "So believe in God and His Messenger and the light We have sent down" (*al-Taghābun*: 8); and, "But We made it [the Qur'an] a light with which We guide whomever We wish of Our servants" (*al-Shūrā*: 52).

There is no doubt that for Prophet Muhammad, the Qur'an was a source of light which accompanied him for the rest of his life. During the early days of revelation, there were times when there were some extended pauses, which Muhammad's detractors interpreted as signs of God's displeasure. It was on one such occasion that this surah was revealed, reassuring Muhammad that: "By the light of day, and by the night when it is still, your Lord has not forsaken you [Muhammad], nor does He despise you" (1–3).

Commentators have pointed out that these are indications of the times when revelation began and paused, with a period of rest in between since receiving revelation used to be a trying experience. There was no question, though, of God abandoning His Messenger. In fact: "The life to come holds a richer prize for you than the present one" (4).

Muhammad started with a few followers, but he was soon in charge of a growing community which was to form the bedrock of a great Islamic civilization that will survive for as long as man remains on this earth. During that period of his life, Muhammad received a considerable amount of revelation and worked very hard to establish

729

the foundations of Islamic civilization and change the course of human history. The Book he had received remains intact and as accessible to us today, and is a testimony to the glory of Islam and the greatness of its Messenger and mentor.

The surah promises more: "And your Lord shall give you more and you shall be satisfied" (5). What, then, would Muhammad be granted? He passed away at the height of Islam's struggle for survival in the face of growing opposition, and was buried in a room adjacent to his humble mosque in Madinah. He left this life penniless. His successors carried the banner forward relentlessly and were shining examples of perseverance and fortitude.

God chose prophets of the highest caliber and from the most noble stock. He would then nurture and train them through experience and hard work, and take full charge of their upbringing to polish and refine their characters and performance. God said to Moses: "And you shall be reared under My watchful eye" (*Ṭā Hā*: 39), and He said to Muhammad:

Await the judgment of your Lord: We are watching over you. Praise the glory of your Lord when you rise, and at nighttime, and at the setting of the stars. (*al-Ṭūr.* 48–49)

In the present surah, God says:

Did He not find you an orphan and give you shelter? Did He not find you at a loss and guide you? Did He not find you poor and provided for you? (6–8)

There is no question here of Muhammad, or of any of the other prophets, being heedless or disbelieving prior to their commissions—as some ancient writings had suggested. Rather, they were in need of guidance to the universal truth and to the means that would qualify them to lead their communities. It is this guidance with which God favored them.

God provided enough for Muhammad to live decently and com-
fortably, but he was no rich emperor. Having reminded him of
God's grace, the surah tells Muhammad: "Therefore do not wrong
the orphan, nor turn away anyone seeking help, and proclaim the
blessings of your Lord" (9–11).

Muhammad is instructed elsewhere in the Qur'an to: "Give
warning. By the grace of your Lord you are neither a soothsayer nor
deranged" (*al-Ṭūr.* 29).

Muhammad was chosen to convey and promote God's message
and save nations of mankind. As the Qur'an puts it: "You are but a
warner; and God is the guardian of all things" (*Hūd:* 12).

SURAH 94

Al-Sharḥ
(The Consolation)

THIS SURAH IS A CONTINUATION from the one preceding it, in content as well as style, and, in a similar manner, begins by posing a number of questions. The Prophet's heart was lifted and his spirits were raised by the knowledge and the prestige conferred upon him by God, as affirmed elsewhere in the Qur'an:

> God has revealed to you the Book and given you wisdom and taught you what you did not know before. God's favor upon you has been tremendous indeed. (*al-Nisāʾ*: 113)

Muhammad was born into a society that was living in darkness and ignorance. At that time, the whole world was in the grip of corrupt and bogus systems and religions. He was charged with a heavy burden which, initially, he undertook with little support from those around him. But God was always there to guide him and look after his progress. The surah asserts: "Have We not comforted your heart and lightened your burden which has weighed heavily on your back?" (1–3).

The most fundamental principle of Muhammad's message is pure *tawḥīd*. It is a simple, clear, and rational belief, free of paradoxes and contrived doctrines. The confirmation of Muhammad's message is inextricably linked to this universal principle.

It is the same principle taught and advocated by all prophets and messengers of all time, and Muhammad's advocacy of it raises his prestige (verse 3) and is an endorsement of the unique and distinguished origin of *tawḥīd*.

Many people in the West—as did people in Arabia fourteen centuries ago—have accused Muhammad of being an imposter, which is a result of their denial of *tawḥīd* and the very existence of God Almighty. They believe that the world is self-sustaining and that life is self-perpetuating. If they can make such claims regarding God, they would not hesitate to direct vile accusations against humans. The Qur'an tells us:

> We know only too well that what they [the non-believers] say grieves you [Muhammad]; but it is not you that they are disbelieving; the evil-doers deny God's own revelations. (*al-Anʿām*: 33)

In the present surah, God Almighty advises His Messenger to persevere and persist in confronting the rejectionists, no matter how vicious their methods and attacks are. He reassures him that the future is his and his followers': "With every hardship comes ease; every hardship is followed by ease" (5–6). The original Arabic syntax conveys an impression of restricted hardship but an abundance of ease.

The surah closes with an exhortation to strive and struggle further in God's cause, with no flinching or letup, saying: "As you fulfill one duty turn to another, and seek your Lord in earnest." (7–8) Islam is a religion of honesty, truth, and justice—qualities that are most urgently needed in today's world, where frivolity and trivia are rampant, and where justice and truth are being deserted and suppressed. The lesson the surah conveys to Muhammad's followers is clear and poignant.

Al-Tīn
(The Fig)

THE SURAH OPENS WITH an affirmation that, as the fig and olive
trees are real, and as Mount Sinai is real, and as Makkah, the city of
peace and security, is real, man was created in the best physical and
spiritual form (verses 1–4). Plants and trees, such as figs and olives,
are natural phenomena that testify to God's greatness and glory. Out
of mud, peat, and earth grow such sweet, pure, and fragrant fruit.

Some commentators are of the opinion that figs, olives, Mount
Sinai, and Makkah are references to lands where some of God's most
senior and noble messengers had emerged. ʿAbd Allah ibn ʿAbbās is
reported to have said that the fig is a symbol of the shrine Noah built
on Mount Jūdī at the end of the Great Flood; olives are a reference
to the shrine in Jerusalem erected by Abraham, after he had built the
Kaʿbah in Makkah; Mount Sinai is where God spoke to Moses and
commissioned him to be a messenger; and the city of peace is
Makkah, the cradle of Islam.

These splendid phenomena and noble and blessed lands are a
testimony to a great universal truth: that man was created in the best
form, not only physically, but also mentally and spiritually. Man's
intellect, wisdom, and intelligence have been the most distinguishing factors of his being. However, Prophet Muhammad was reported to have said: "God does not give much weight to your looks or
outward appearance, but to what is in your hearts."

The spirit that God had blown into man has made him a uniquely
important creature. The surah indicates that man's initial state is one

of wholesomeness, but the environment into which a person is born is liable to corrupt and demean his character and personality. Elsewhere in the Qur'an, we read:

> Turn your face steadfastly towards the true faith, the natural form in which God has created mankind. God's creation shall not be corrupted. This is the universally true faith, though most people may not realize it. (*al-Rūm*: 30)

When people abandon faith in God Almighty and allow their basic original nature to be corrupted, they sink to degrading levels of evil behavior, committing monstrous acts, such as infanticide, burning wives with their dead husbands, gratuitous torture, oppression, greed, and apostasy.

Man's basic pristine and righteous nature can be preserved with devotion to and fear of God; otherwise man's faith withers away. The surah goes on to assert: "...and thereafter We reduce him to the lowest of the low, except the believers who do good works, their reward shall be everlasting" (5–6).

Then it addresses man with a sharp and most profound question: "What then, in view of this, could make you [man] deny the faith? Is God not the Most Just of all judges?" (7–8).

Why, the surah asks, having been shown the right path, should people turn, and divert others, away from it? Worse still, how could they replace God's true religion with other false or inadequate ones?

The Prophet taught that after reading the last verse of this surah, one should say: "Indeed! And I am a witness thereto."

SURAH 96

Al-ʿAlaq
(The Blood Clot)

BEFORE HIS CALL TO PROPHETHOOD, Muhammad used to spend time alone in the cave of Ḥirā', just outside Makkah, in meditation and reflection, away from the hustle and bustle of Makkah and the misbehavior of some of its inhabitants. He loathed the idols which the Arabs used to worship, and the many bogus religious traditions built around them. However, he did not know any better.

One day while in the cave he heard an unfamiliar voice calling him several times to: "Recite…" He inquired as to what he should recite, and was eventually told to:

> Recite in the name of your Lord who created. He created man from a clot of blood. Recite! Your Lord is the Most Bountiful, who by the pen taught man what he did not know. (1–5)

These were the first words of Qur'anic revelation Muhammad had received.

As God was able to create man from a clot of blood, so too could He choose an illiterate man for His most illustrious mission. Muhammad had no ambitions to become a prophet or receive revelation, and was genuinely overwhelmed by the experience, but as soon as he realized the nature of his task, he embarked on building the community of Islam, similar to what earlier prophets, such as Abraham and Moses, had done. A fair and objective assessment of Muhammad's life and his career would reveal that he fulfilled that

736

honorable task to the highest standard. He stands out as a foremost leader and benefactor of the whole human race.

Later Muhammad was to receive the verses: "Indeed, man over-reaches himself by thinking that he is Self-Sufficient. But to your Lord shall all things return" (6–8). Poverty can indeed lead to depri-vation and humiliation, but why should wealth cause a person to overreach himself and transgress? Moderation and temperance are far more befitting virtues. Nevertheless, many people, as they grow wealthier, tend to look down on others and become arrogant, obli-vious of their accountability in the hereafter for their deeds in this world.

The surah also admonishes the unbelievers who reject God's rev-elation and denounce those pious servants who wish to worship God. It says: "Have you ever considered him who tries to prevent a servant [of God] from praying? Have you considered whether he is on the right way, or enjoins true piety?" (9–12). Elsewhere in the Qur'an, the unbelievers are asked:

> "What has brought you into hell?" They will reply, "We never observed the prayers, nor did we ever feed the hungry. We simply joined in with those who argued and disputed and denied the Day of Resurrection." (*al-Muddaththir*. 42–46)

The affirmation of God's existence and sovereignty, the observance of the rites of prayer and the institution of zakah to ensure proper distribution of wealth were at the heart of the dispute between Muhammad and his Makkan opponents for about thirteen years. They shall remain central to the ongoing religious debate between Muslims and non-Muslims, with no possibility of any compromise on the part of the Muslims.

The surah continues with its strong admonition, saying: "You see how he [the unbeliever] denies the truth and turns away from it! Does he not realize that God is aware of everything?" (13–14). The debate between the Muslims, who understand life in terms of rights and responsibilities, and those who view man as his own master, with no accountability or subordination to a higher authority, will continue to focus on these important issues.

The surah warns the unbeliever that: "If he does not desist, We will drag him by his forelock, his lying, sinful forelock" (15–16). It is a formidable warning some Makkan chiefs chose to ignore.

SURAH 97

Al-Qadr
(Power)

REVELATION BEGAN ON a night known as *laylat al-qadr*—the night of glory and splendor. There is no agreement on the exact date of this night, but it is taken to fall in the last ten nights of Ramadan, the ninth month in the Muslim calendar. Since this is a lunar calendar, the birth of the new moon, marking the beginning of each month, varies throughout the year, making it difficult to determine exactly on which night *laylat al-qadr* actually falls. Muslims wishing to offer additional voluntary prayers on that night are urged to do so every night during the last half or third of the month of Ramadan.

The beginning of the revelation of the Qur'an to mankind was undoubtedly a most auspicious event that should be commemorated with prayer and devotion. The Qur'an is God's own word and final revelation to mankind. It is a gift and a blessing to the world, as attested by the words:

> Would that you knew what the Night of Power is! It is better than a thousand months. Hosts of angels and the Spirit [the Archangel Gabriel] are dispatched on that night by their Lord's leave with decrees for all manner of purpose. (2–4)

Elsewhere in the Qur'an, *laylat al-qadr* is described as the night on which "the fate and destiny of all creatures are carefully determined by Our commandments. We send messengers as a blessing from your Lord" (*al-Dukhān*: 4–6).

The Qur'an contains all the principles, rules, teachings, and guidelines necessary for the organization of human life and behavior in this world. It is the only source of inspiration and true guidance. A cursory comparison between the Qur'an and other allegedly divinely-revealed books available today would bear this out.

The night the Qur'an was sent down was also a night of peace, one of Islam's main objectives in this world. But peace can only be attained when justice is established on earth.

SURAH 98

Al-Bayyinah
(The Proof)

THIS SURAH SUMMARIZES the history of the world. During the sixth century AC, western Asia and north Africa were dominated by the Christian Roman empire, while the rest of the world as far as China and India was inhabited by pagans and followers of polytheist religions.

By the end of the seventh century and the advent of Islam, the world map was completely transformed, with the whole of Arabia, north Africa, the Nile valley, Anatolia, and Mesopotamia coming under the umbrella of Islam.

Genuine Christians welcomed Islam and many of them voluntarily and willingly embraced it and understood Muhammad's mission as a fulfillment of their own scriptures. Elsewhere in the Qur'an, we read:

> Those who were endowed with knowledge before its [the Qur'an's] revelation prostrate themselves when it is recited to them and say, "Glorious is our Lord. Our Lord's promise has been fulfilled." They fall down upon their faces, weeping, and it makes them ever so humble. (*al-Isrā'*: 107–109)

In another surah we read:

> Those to whom the scriptures were given rejoice in what is revealed to you, while some deny parts of it. Say, "I am commanded to serve God and associate none with Him. To Him I call people, and to Him I shall return." (*al-Raʿd*: 36)

In yet another surah we read:

> Thus We have revealed the Book to you [Muhammad]. Those to
> whom We have given the scriptures believe in it, and some of these
> [the Arabs] also believe it. (*al-ʿAnkabūt*: 47)

It is a historic fact that Islam spread especially widely among those
people who had been Christian, and that the arrest of its progress
was due to internal reasons which it is not appropriate to discuss
here. In addition to the Christians, many Magians, Buddhists and
pagans also embraced Islam.

How did this come about? The answer lies in the power and
charisma of the Qur'an. The surah says:

> The unbelievers among the People of the Book [Jews and
> Christians] and the pagans would not abandon unbelief until a clear
> proof was given them: a Messenger [Muhammad] from God recit-
> ing purified text wherein there are veritable principles. (1–3)

The timeless principles and codes expounded in the Qur'an continue to be relevant and applicable to all human situations, if they are
genuinely and seriously asserted and upheld. However, human
nature is such that some people do recognize the truth but would
rather act according to their whims and desires.

Among the earlier communities who had received revelation,
some people chose to ignore its teachings or tamper with them,
some had even dared to kill the messengers who delivered that revelation to them and persecute those who rose to teach and enlighten
them. The surah records these actions thus:

> The people of the Book had only come to disagree among them-
> selves when the veritable proof had come to them. They were enjoi-
> ned to serve God with devotion, and to worship none but Him, to
> observe the prayers and give alms. That is the true faith. (4–5)

Knowledge, it seems, is no guarantee of righteousness; intellectual error or ignorance of the truth may be forgiven and can be rectified, but the deliberate promotion of evil and corruption of the soul are unpardonable.

The surah makes it clear that the fate of such greedy, selfish, and corrupt people who abuse religion is doomed:

Those of the People of the Book and the pagans who disbelieve shall burn forever in the fire of hell. They are the vilest of all creatures. (6)

God's justice towards humans is assured, and were He to withhold His grace and benevolence from anyone, they would have no hope of redemption. But God is Forgiving and Magnanimous and His door is always open to those who choose not to forfeit their future and their salvation.

The surah closes with a poignant reassurance for the conscientious believers who are ever vigilant and take heed of God's teachings. It says:

Those who believe and do good works are the noblest of creatures. Their rewards awaiting them with their Lord shall be gardens through which rivers flow, where they shall dwell forever. God is well pleased with them, and they are well pleased with Him. Thus shall the conscientious be rewarded. (7–8)

Early Muslims who carried Islam to the world were impeccable models for the spirit of the Qur'an, and wherever they went, with them went justice, tolerance, and humanity. The weak, the deprived, and the oppressed of the world found a real savior in Islam, which has protected their dignity and self-respect.

743

SURAH 99

Al-Zalzalah
(The Earthquake)

THE HOUR OF UNIVERSAL RESURRECTION will be preceded by an enormous earthquake that will shake the whole of the planet. Earthquakes manifest themselves in many different ways, and with widely varying degrees of magnitude; some may last a few seconds, others a few minutes, but their effect is often devastating and always frightening.

The effect is even more calamitous if an earthquake is accompanied by explosions and volcanic eruptions, which appears to be the scene described in the surah, thus: "When the earth is rocked by a mighty earthquake and throws up her burdens, and man wonders what has happened to her…" (1–3).

An endless series of questions will be asked then in an endeavour to grasp what is going on and what the end will be, and so: "On that Day the earth shall reveal all her history, as your Lord would have instructed her" (4–5).

Human beings will, as a result of that tumultuous event, come to appreciate the significance of that momentous Day and realize that the moment of truth and accountability has arrived. "On that Day, people will be dispatched in various directions to be shown the fruits of their labor" (6).

Accountability, on that Day, shall be meticulous and to the very last atom, and people will wish that their evil deeds had never existed. This is borne out elsewhere in the Qur'an, where we read:

The Day shall come when every soul will be confronted with whatever good it has done, and will wish that it were a long way away from its evil deeds. (*Āl ʿImrān*: 30)

The surah ends with a most profound and succinct statement: "Whoever does an atom's weight of good shall see it, and whoever does an atom's weight of evil shall see it" (7–8).

When asked one day about the rate of zakah that should be paid out for donkeys, the Prophet is reported to have made reference to verse 7 of this surah, as the most comprehensive and concise reply.

745

Al-ʿĀdiyāt
(The War Steeds)

TO FLOURISH AND TAKE ROOT, religious faith has to be strongly defended and protected. Without this protection, falsehood would have a free rein. Human history is replete with corrupt and oppressive rulers who have dominated millions of people by brute force and trampled over values of justice, honor, and dignity. According to many, might is right, and it is also true to say that for right to be adequately safeguarded, might must also be present.

In this surah, God swears by certain means usually associated with power and jihad. He says:

> By the panting steeds as they charge forth, striking fire with their hooves and galloping to assault at dawn, with trails of sand, blazing into the heart of the battlefield; man is ungrateful to his Lord! (1–6)

The scene is of knights on horseback, fighting fiercely; horses panting and jostling against each other, with their hooves striking the ground, giving out sparks of fire; and fearless riders bravely thrusting forward. For the unbelievers, defending false and corrupt beliefs, such scenes represent the moment of truth when they shall realize their errors and pay for them with their blood.

Jihad is necessary to revive faith in God, to weed out corruption and evil, and to ensure the health and well-being of society. This is as true today as at any time in history, not least because of the prevalence and dominance of corruption and injustice everywhere, as the surah points out, saying: "Man is ungrateful to his Lord! To this he himself bears witness" (6–7).

The materialistic nature of contemporary civilization, its ungodliness and the extent of its denial of judgment and accountability in the life to come, must be unprecedented in human history. The surah affirms man's weakness in his devotion to wealth and warns:

Is man not aware that when the dead are raised from their graves, and men's hidden thoughts are laid open, their Lord shall on that day be fully aware of them? (9–11)

Al-Qāri'ah
(The Calamity)

PRIOR TO THE COMING of the Hour of universal resurrection, a thunderous sound will erupt that will shake the whole world and be heard by everyone. This is described elsewhere in the Qur'an: "Listen on the Day when the crier will call from near-by; the Day when they [mankind] will hear the fateful cry. That will be the Day they will rise up from their graves" (Qāf: 41–42).

All shall rise up in fear and anticipation, wondering what is happening. This surah tells us:

It is the calamity! What could the calamity be? Would that you knew what the calamity is! It is the Day when people become like scattered moths and the mountains are turned into tufts of carded wool. (1–5)

The mountains collapse upon themselves and are reduced to rubble. People are dispersed and scattered like moths in all directions, everyone for himself, not knowing their destiny or destination.

Their fate would by then have already been sealed and: "He whose weight [of good works] is heavy in the balance shall dwell in bliss; but [as for] he whose weight is light in the balance, shall plunge in the womb of the Pit" (6–9). The word 'mother' is used in the Arabic original metaphorically since, at times of anxiety, one seeks the comfort and security of one's mother's bosom. But those whose good works are meager or worthless shall be engulfed by "a scorching fire" (11).

Al-Takāthur
(Worldly Gain)

THE SURAH IS ADDRESSED to the idol-worshipers and, conceivably, everyone infatuated by worldly goods, who pays no attention to the life hereafter. These people are driven by greed, live for the moment, and devote all their energies and resources to material comfort and enjoyment. Their whole life is a struggle for the accumulation of wealth, until they are laid to rest in their graves.

However, they seem to overlook the fact that the grave is but a temporary abode, a mere bridge to another life of accountability, judgment, and punishment or reward. Elsewhere in the Qur'an we read:

> The trumpet will be blown and, behold, they will rise up from their graves and hasten to their Lord. "Woe to us," they will say. "Who has roused us from our resting-place? This is what the Merciful has promised, and the messengers have told us the truth." (Yā Sīn: 51–52)

They are in for a huge surprise: "You shall know. You shall before long come to know" (3–4). The unbelievers are told: "Indeed, if only you knew the truth with certainty! You will see the fire of hell" (5–6). Had they believed and heeded the call of God's messengers, they would have spared themselves the torment of hell, but they chose to turn away from them, and are therefore told: "You will see it [hell] with your very eyes" (7).

Furthermore, they would be questioned about their wealth:

"Then, on that day, you shall be questioned about the affluence you enjoyed" (8). They would be told: "You have squandered your wealth during your life and enjoyed it" (*al-Aḥqāf*: 20).

People shall be questioned about the wealth and affluence they accumulated and enjoyed in this life, and about the reason why they did not show any gratitude for it. The enjoyment they had in this world would not last, and they would have to face up to God's humiliating punishment. Elsewhere in the Qur'an, we read: "That is for the delight you took in falsehood on earth and the frivolity you enjoyed" (*Ghāfir*: 75).

SURAH 103

Al-ʿAṣr
(The Flight of Time)

THIS BRIEF SURAH SUMMARIZES the essence and outcome of all human activity for all time. God says: "By the flight of time, man is in total loss" (1–2).

Time goes on, and people live and die, generation after generation, and era after era. People of the same generation may live under similar circumstances and traditions, but their destinies may go in totally different directions, depending on their moral and religious beliefs. The moral quality of human life is far more important, and the truth is no less honorable or illustrious if it is recognized by a minority.

Those who deny the sovereignty and power of God shall end up as fuel of hell in the hereafter, whereas the believers who, despite the odds, persevere in upholding the truth shall be the real and final winners in the ordeal of life.

True believers are few and far between, and in some generations of human history may even seem odd, but they are promised great rewards. The surah singles them out: "Except for those who have faith and do good works; who exhort each other to uphold the truth and to perseverance" (3).

This surah became a motto, a pledge of loyalty and brotherhood, among the Companions of the Prophet. It was traditional, according to reports, for Muhammad's Companions to recite this surah together before they shook hands and departed. The renowned scholar, al-Shāfiʿī, was reported to have said: "If this was the only surah to have been revealed, it would have been sufficient."

751

To persevere for the sake of the truth could expose one to persecution and hardship, and therefore to uphold the true faith and triumph with it requires persistence, tenacity, and a strong will.

SURAH 104

Al-Humazah
(The Slanderer)

SLANDER IS, AND HAS BEEN, one of the most effective weapons of propaganda used against believers throughout history. The Qur'an alludes to this behavior when it says: "The evil-doers mock the faithful and wink at one another as they pass by them" (*al-Muṭaffifīn*: 29–30). In modern times, propaganda and psychological warfare of this kind have been much more systematic and effective.

As the Qur'anic revelation was being received by Muhammad, groups of Makkans who were wealthy and did not need to earn their livelihood would gather together to mock the Muslims and scoff at Muhammad and Islam. This surah was revealed as a warning and a threat to those slanderers. It says: "Woe to every back-biting slanderer who amasses wealth and sedulously hoards it, thinking his wealth will secure him immortality" (1–3).

Slanderous activity takes various forms including verbal jeering and abuse, or gestures and gesticulations. It can be expressed in writing or caricatures or depictions of all kinds. Slanderers are usually idle people, with money and time to spare, or people who are paid to pursue such wasteful and futile activity.

They should, however, beware God's wrath, for He says: "He [the slanderer] shall be thrown into the all-consuming fire. And what will explain to you what the all-consuming fire is like? It is God's own raging fire, which will scorch the hearts and engulf the slanderers from every side, in towering columns" (4–9). They shall be entrapped in a towering inferno, from which they shall have no means of escape.

Al-Fīl
(The Elephant)

AROUND 571 AC, the Abyssinians organized an army in Yemen to raid Makkah and destroy the Ka'bah, God's holy house. The army included a number of elephants, which were to be used in combat for the first time in Arabia.

The news left the Arabs of Makkah despondent, totally unprepared to resist such an attack. Many of them took flight to the mountains, leaving the Ka'bah as well as their own homes to their fate. For the Christian Abyssinians, the whole campaign was a misguided and pointless one. There was no justification for it, since they had a cathedral in Sana'a, where they used to worship, and could have left the Arabs to worship at the Ka'bah.

The expedition ended in tragedy. The Abyssinian army was attacked by a barrage of stones thrown by birds flying overhead, reminiscent of those thrown at the people of Lot whose town had disappeared under the ground.

Historians say that, on the way back to Sana'a, the Abyssinian army, including its chief Abrahah, was wiped out by a plague of smallpox. The surah records this historic event in the following words:

> Have you not considered how your Lord dealt with the people of the elephant? Did He not confound their stratagem and send against them flocks of birds which pelted them with clay-stones? (1–4)

Historians also say that Prophet Muhammad was born in that

year, known to the Arabs as 'the Year of the Elephant'. His birth was, therefore, a good portent for the future prosperity and security of the Quraysh, referred to in the following surah, as a prelude to the advent of Islam and its rise from Makkah, the mother of all towns, to all corners of the globe.

Quraysh

SOME COMMENTATORS VIEW this surah as complementary to, or a continuation of, Surah *al-Fīl* which precedes it.

Being strategically situated astride Europe and Asia, the Arabian peninsula has, since early times, been a vital trade route between these two continents. As renowned traders, sixth-century Arabs formed an important link between the Romans to their north and the Indians to their east and south. Regular trade caravans would cross the peninsula in both directions, carrying all manner of goods and merchandise.

The Quraysh people of Makkah, and its surrounding towns, were to benefit greatly from this most fortuitous situation.

For the good and protection of the Quraysh in their winter and summer journeys, they should worship the Lord of this House [the Kaʿbah] who has provided them with food to satisfy their hunger, and security from all danger. (1–4)

Peace and security are a prerequisite for prosperity and political and economic freedom. With their strong and tenacious character, the Arabs truly epitomized free spirit which, in turn, made them most suitable candidates for shouldering the message of Islam and passing it on to the rest of humanity.

SURAH 107

Al-Māʿūn
(Charity)

SINCERE AND PIOUS PEOPLE are always ready and eager to help others. True religion encourages its followers to provide support for the weak, sustenance for the poor, provisions for the orphan, and guidance for those who have lost their direction in life.

Neglect of these virtues has given credence to godless and materialistic ideologies such as communism which swept across nearly half of the world, wreaking havoc upon millions everywhere.

Had believers, not least the Muslims themselves, upheld their faith and observed their religious beliefs, humanity might well have been spared many catastrophes.

Religion, as the surah implies, means charity, tolerance and compassion. It says: "Have you considered him who rejects faith? It is he who turns away the orphan and has no urge to feed the poor" (1–3).

This brief surah is a denunciation of religious bigotry, stressing that helping the needy is as fundamental an aspect of faith as observing the prayers. It warns the negligent of frightful consequences.

Al-Kawthar
(Good in Abundance)

THIS VERY BRIEF SURAH is like a short sharp message of good news addressed directly and personally to Prophet Muhammad. It was to console him for the loss of all his male children at a very early age. According to Arabian custom before Islam, the loss of male offspring was considered a great misfortune because it signified the cutting off of a father's name and ancestry, and his fading into obscurity. A man not survived by his sons was thus given the pejorative Arabic name *al-abtar* (sonless).

The surah came to reassure the Prophet that God's grace and generosity towards him were great and unparalleled. He was favored by receiving the Qur'anic revelation; he was selected as a messenger of God to all mankind; and he is loved and revered by millions all over the world. In every moment that passes someone, somewhere, is praying for Muhammad or praising his name.

Muhammad should undoubtedly be the happiest of all God's creation; he is the mentor, the benefactor, the model, and the leader of mankind, for all time.

God says: "We have given you in abundance [of all good things], so pray to your Lord, and sacrifice" (1–2). This is a reference to prayers performed on the occasion of Eid, which is normally followed by the sacrifice of animals, usually sheep, cows, or camels, whose meat should be distributed among the poor and the needy.

Then God says: "He that hates you [Muhammad] shall fade into obscurity" (3). This is a reference to those who lampooned the Prophet and taunted him for the non-survival of his sons.

It also conveys the reassurance that, in God's sight, Muhammad was praiseworthy and deserving of God's grace and generous rewards.

SURAH 109

Al-Kāfirūn
(The Unbelievers)

THE SURAH OPENS WITH the following words: "Say, 'Disbelievers, I do not worship what you worship, nor do you worship
what I worship" (1–3). This statement brings to mind a similar one
we find in verse 145 of *al-Baqarah*, which says:

> If you [Muhammad] give the People of the Book every proof they
> would not accept your qiblah, nor would you accept theirs; nor
> would any of them accept the qiblah of the other.

These statements confirm that it is impossible for one religious faith
to be universally accepted. It is far more sensible and realistic to
acknowledge and recognize the existence of different ideologies and
beliefs and endeavor to coexist with them.

In Surah *Hūd*, we have seen how the Qur'an summed up the
whole history of mankind, and the endless conflict between those
who believe in God and those who do not. God says to Muhammad
in that surah:

> Had your Lord wished, He would have made the whole of
> mankind as one nation, but they shall continue to be at odds, except
> for those to whom your Lord has shown mercy. (*Hūd*: 118)

As Muslims, we do not seek to eradicate other religions. It has
been the overwhelming majority view among scholars and jurists
that Muslims should only take up arms in order to confront insur-
gency, sedition, or hostility. No use of force can ever be justified to

760

compel people to accept a particular religion or creed. It would only breed more conflict and hatred.

Hence the surah reemphasizes the point, saying: "I shall never worship what you worship, nor will you worship what I worship. You have your own religion, and I have mine" (4–6).

The surah lays down one of the most fundamental principles in international relations: the recognition of all religious faiths, and the promotion of good neighborliness and constructive dialogue.

However, it must also be recognized that some world powers today do nurture suspicion about Islam and do have designs against it. This negative attitude towards Islam and the Muslims must be addressed in order for the Muslims to have an equal chance of protecting their faith and practicing their way of life in peace and security.

Al-Naṣr
(Victory)

THIS SURAH WAS REVEALED towards the latter days of Prophet Muhammad's life and was understood, by the more adroit of his Companions, as a portent for his impending departure from this world. It says:

> When God's succor comes and victory is complete, and you [Muhammad] see people coming to God's faith in their multitudes, give glory to your Lord and seek His forgiveness. (1–3)

Muhammad was being urged to devote more time to praising God and pleading for His mercy and forgiveness.

The victory of Islam began with the fall of the idols of Makkah and the spread of the message of Islam from Arabia in all directions. Its central message is that God is One, and none else is worthy of veneration and worship.

Muhammad had done well to discharge his duty to eradicate the myths and superstitions associated with religious belief. It was time for him to return to His Lord to receive his well-earned reward. He had worked extremely hard and suffered a great deal. He worshiped God with greater devotion and sincerity than anyone could; he fought in battles until he was wounded; and he suffered the loneliness of his struggle, but his faith and trust had never been shaken.

Some may wonder why Muhammad had not been allowed to live longer to enjoy the triumph of Islam, but that would not have been in the character of a prophet. Muhammad was not seeking any personal glory or world domination. He was of humble means, and during the latter days of his life, when he was at the peak of authority, he had to borrow food with which to feed his family from a Jewish retailer who asked for collateral. At that time, Muhammad was in command of a formidable fighting force that was sweeping Arabia and was poised to challenge the Roman Empire.

It would not have dented his reputation if he had asked one of his wealthy Companions to provide the collateral on his behalf, but he did not, and he gave the Jew his shield as security for the loan. When Muhammad died, his shield was still mortgaged to that Jewish merchant.

Muhammad made no material or personal gain out of fulfilling his responsibilities, and once his task was completed, he was looking forward to meeting his Lord and Protector. He departed to join that most lofty company of angels and earlier prophets and messengers who are "honorably seated in the presence of a Mighty King" (*al-Qamar.* 55).

Al-Masad
(The Fiber)

THE SURAH OPENS with a vehement attack on one of Prophet Muhammad's most bitter adversaries, his uncle Abū Lahab.

> May the hands of Abū Lahab perish, and may he himself perish!
> His wealth and all that he has gained shall not avail him. (1–2)

Abū Lahab was a wealthy and influential figure among the Arabs of Makkah, but he soon came to grief. He was one of Muhammad's staunchest opponents, harboring intense resentment towards him, and sparing no effort to slander him and his message.

It is reported that one day the Prophet went to the hillock of al-Safa, near the Kaʿbah in Makkah, and called the names of the prominent clans of the Quraysh. A crowd, including his uncle Abū Lahab, gathered around him, and he addressed them saying: "If I were to tell you that enemy cavalry were in the valley preparing to attack you, would you believe me?" They replied: "Indeed, we would. We have never known you to lie." The Prophet continued to warn them of God's severe punishment and to explain his mission, when Abū Lahab interrupted angrily: "Damn you for the rest of the day! Is this what you wanted to tell us?" It was shortly afterwards, according to the reports, that this surah was revealed to Muhammad. The reports go on to say that Abū Lahab started to throw stones at the Prophet.

Of all Muhammad's uncles, Abū Lahab remained for the rest of his life a most vicious opponent. This deep-seated animosity passed on to his sons—those of whom who were married to daughters of Muhammad decided to divorce them,—and to his wife. She was a vicious, evil, and malicious woman who dedicated herself to slandering Muhammad and smearing his name. She was a sister of Abū Sufyān, Makkah's most prominent leader and the closest it had to a military general.

The surah was revealed during the early days of Islam, and there was ample opportunity for Abū Lahab to retract his allegations and join the Muslims, but he persisted and so the surah asserts that:

> He shall roast in a flaming fire, and so shall his wife, that carrier of firewood. She shall have a rope of entwined fiber round her neck. (3–5)

These powerfully graphic idiomatic expressions indicate that the woman was zealous in her pursuit to revile the Prophet, and fanatical in her hostility to Islam.

Abū Lahab, it seems, could never see Muhammad as anything other than the poor orphan boy brought up by his grandfather, ʿAbd al-Muṭṭalib, and his uncle Abū Ṭālib. He could not accept that Muhammad could be chosen to receive divine revelation or be commissioned for prophethood. He was blinded by his prejudice and jealousy all his life.

SURAH 112

Al-Ikhlās
(Purity of Faith)

GOD IS ONE; He is neither two nor three. He has no spouse nor offspring. He is Supreme and Omnipotent. The Qur'an tells us: "God says, 'Do not take two gods; He is the One God, so fear Me'" (*al-Naḥl*: 51). Elsewhere in the Qur'an, we read: "Do not say, 'Three gods.' Refrain from saying so for your own good. God is but One God; far too highly glorified is He to have a son" (*al-Nisā'*: 171).

The principle of *tawḥīd* is the very soul of Islam. In comparison to God, as we come to know Him through the Qur'an, everything and everyone else is utterly powerless and helpless. The Qur'an abounds with strong arguments supporting this principle:

Never has God begotten a son, nor has there ever been any other god besides Him. Were the opposite to be true, each god would govern his own creation, and some would have overwhelmed others. Exalted be God above their falsehood. He knows the unknown as well as the manifest. (*al-Mu'minūn*: 91–92)

Were there other gods in the heavens or earth besides God, both heavens and earth would have been ruined. None shall question Him regarding His works, but all else shall be questioned. (*al-Anbiyā'*: 22–23)

Advocates of the doctrine of the Trinity believe in three coequal partners in the godhead, who are in fact one: the Father, the Son and the Holy Spirit, existing in total harmony.

They also believe in the crucifixion of Jesus, which raises the question: who was actually crucified: one of the three or all three? If the three are one, and the 'one' was crucified, does that mean that God was out of existence for a time before He came back to the world? But, if the Son only was crucified, how could he be 'God'?

People are, of course, free to believe what they wish to believe, and this surah, which is said to be equivalent to 'one third' of the Qur'an, gives a most concise definition of the essence of Islamic belief. "Say, 'God is One, the Eternal God. He begot none, nor was He begotten. None is equal to Him'" (1–4). God is unique, and there is nothing that can be likened to Him. There is nothing that can be equal to Him. He could, therefore, have neither been a father nor a son. He is the Eternal to whom all creation refers and will return.

The very nature of the cosmic structure does not allow for multiple gods. It is nonsensical to believe that there is an independent god for the sun and another for the earth, or one for the animal kingdom and another for the plants, or one for the African continent and another for Europe. The cosmic order is an integrated whole, set up, designed, run, and controlled by a single self-sufficient power. This power regulates the operation of the human digestive system and the orbiting of planets and stars in the infinite universe. The plants grow out of the ground, the dawn breaks every day, and the sun and the moon move in their charted courses in accordance with His will.

Rational and sensible contemplation of these issues could only lead us to believe that there is only the one God, without a partner, the Sovereign, to Whom belongs all praise, the All-Powerful and Omnipotent.

Al-Falaq
(Daybreak)

GOD ANSWERS THOSE WHO PLEAD with Him and seek His protection. This surah and the one that follows it teach us how to seek God's protection against all kinds of ill-feelings and evil intentions, which we constantly encounter in life. God says: "We try you with evil and good to test you" (*al-Anbiyā'*: 35); and: "We have tried them [the Israelites] with adversity and prosperity, so that they might mend their ways" (*al-Aʿrāf*: 168).

Evil and harm may come from numerous sources: germs, insects, animals, and people. They may strike at daybreak or in the middle of the night, the latter being a popular time with thieves, criminals, and merchants of death and corruption.

One seeks refuge also from "the mischief of conjuring witches," a reference to sorcery and witchcraft, which some people believe to exist, ascribing them to devils and evil spirits, human as well as jinn. Ibn Ḥazm, the Andalusian scholar, and the Zahirite school of Islamic fiqh refuse to believe in sorcery, while the idea is mixed with a great deal of mythology and folklore and has to be taken with much skepticism.

One needs to seek God's protection against envy, which reflects a hatred of other fellow-humans and an evil desire to see them deprived of comfort and success.

A great deal is also said in folklore about the "evil eye," most of which is false and exaggerated, but there is no harm in seeking refuge with God from its possible damaging effects.

SURAH 114

Al-Nās
(Mankind)

THE SURAH OPENS WITH this passionate exhortation:

Say, "I seek refuge in the Lord of mankind, the King of mankind,
the God of mankind…" (1–3)

Refuge is being sought with God Almighty from the insinuations of
the devils of both the jinn and humankind. As humans, we have no
knowledge of how the jinn act and behave, but we are able to feel
their influence and presence in our life. In view of this frailty it is,
therefore, necessary for us to seek God's help and protection against
their potential scheming and ill-will.

We seek refuge: "From the evil of the stalking whisperer," (4)
who acts by stealth to release venomous insinuations in the hearts
and minds of men.

Elsewhere in the Qur'an, God says:

We assigned for every prophet enemies: devils of men and of jinn
who inspire one another with false and vain ideas. (*al-Anʿām*: 112)

It appears that the human devils relish influencing actions while the
jinn devils enjoy confusing people and leading them astray, thereby
complementing one another.

Nevertheless, devils are barred from having any power to force
anyone to do anything they do not want to do, but the greatest

769

danger lies in their persuasive and inciting skills. Having been warned, those who fall for the devils' intrigues would have only themselves to blame.

The surah warns against adverse or corrupting psychological and mental influences that can affect human behavior, urging believers to ward against them and seek protection and safety with God Almighty.

INDEX OF QUR'ANIC QUOTATIONS

The index below provides details of related verse references additional to those mentioned in the chapter on each Surah.

2. Al-Baqarah

verse(s)	page no.
35	613
83	302
109	574
115	667, 725
129	723
145	760
165	188
172	613
177	512
216	316–317
226–227	381
229	633
245	51
247	541
249	175
257	66
259	43

3. Āl ʿImrān

verse(s)	page no.
9	623
27	623
30	745
78	64
145	69
166–167	192
181	51
186	377

4. Al-Nisā'

verse(s)	page no.
13	633
41–42	286
46	64
69	3–4
90	183
103	5, 449
113	603, 732
131	8
157	94–95
171	433, 766
174	380

5. Al-Mā'idah

verse(s)	page no.
13	629
70	154
98	513
119	512

6. Al-Anʿām

verse(s)	page no.
1	308, 525
2	623
33	733
38	404
45	407–408, 637
52	400
86–89	128
112	361–62, 769

128	583
146–147	37
155	546
162–63	682

7. Al-Aʿrāf

verse(s)	page no.
27	562, 680
66	222
67–68	222
74	226
75–76	225
82	221
86	227
87	227
88	227
128	264
131	70
146	515
155–156	617
168	768
169	329
185	308

9. Al-Tawbah

verse(s)	page no.
6	92
9–10	19
13	19
14–15	564
72	615

10. Yūnus

verse(s)	page no.
10	512, 619
41	177
72	128
90	543

11. Hūd

verse(s)	page no.
12	731
27	480
48	490
118	760
118–19	48

12. Yūsuf

verse(s)	page no.
39	408
56	314
86	594

13. Al-Raᶜd

verse(s)	page no.
17	261, 340
23–24	620
31	600
36	741

14. Ibrāhīm

verse(s)	page no.
13	677
13–14	356
48	609

15. Al-Ḥijr

verse(s)	page no.
14–15	304, 345
97–98	340

16. Al-Naḥl

verse(s)	page no.
2	486
4	654
51	766
72	21
97	20–21
112	173
121	504

17. Al-Isrā'

verse(s)	page no.
3	504
6	314
40	539
49–51	609
58	320
60	489
107–109	741

18. Al-Kahf

verse(s)	page no.
32–46	331
34	720
58	205

19. Maryam

verse(s)	page no.
73–74	341
75	100, 155
93–95	288

20. Ṭā Hā

verse(s)	page no.
5–7	288
39	730
105–107	608

21. Al-Anbiyā'

verse(s)	page no.
10	494

22	198
22–23	766
27–28	203
30	622
35	466, 768
58	491
64	388
74	237
83	499
96–97	320
98–99	543
104	613
105	302
107	194

22. Al-Ḥajj

verse(s)	page no.
40	48–49

23. Al-Mu'minūn

verse(s)	page no.
18	622
51	613
91–92	766
96	521

24. Al-Nūr

verse(s)	page no.
62	161
63	577

25. Al-Furqān

verse(s)	page no.
20	48
42	361

26. Al-Shuᶜarā'

verse(s)	page no.
41–42	468
83–91	617
111–14	305

27. Al-Naml

verse(s)	page no.
4–5	707
31	497
40	674
91–92	252

28. Al-Qaṣaṣ

verse(s)	page no.
14	237
15–21	404
16	404
38	715
44	501

29. Al-ʿAnkabūt

verse(s)	page no.
19–21	610
45	252
47	742
53–54	204

30. Al-Rūm

verse(s)	page no.
9	720
21	21
27	609
30	735

31. Luqmān

verse(s)	page no.
32	504

32. Al-Sajdah

verse(s)	page no.
7–9	611

33. Al-Aḥzāb

verse(s)	page no.
23	616

34. Saba'

verse(s)	page no.
23	486
35	677

35. Fāṭir

verse(s)	page no.
18	445
32	617–18
41	127

36. Yā Sīn

verse(s)	page no.
51–52	749

38. Ṣād

verse(s)	page no.
8	206, 540
29	546

39. Al-Zumar

verse(s)	page no.
4	40
15	535
64–66	433
74	350

40. Ghāfir

verse(s)	page no.
7	725
15	674
40	21
75	750

41. Fuṣṣilat

verse(s)	page no.
11	710
20–21	614
26	562

42. Al-Shūrā

verse(s)	page no.
5	726
15	182
39	641
52	276, 729

44. Al-Dhukān

verse(s)	page no.
4–6	739

45. Al-Jāthiyah

verse(s)	page no.
36–37	2

46. Al-Aḥqāf

verse(s)	page no.
20	750

47. Muḥammad

verse(s)	page no.
4	48, 631, 645
15	621

49. Al-Ḥujurāt

verse(s)	page no.
15	161

50. Qāf

verse(s)	page no.
7–8	612
41–42	748

51. Al-Dhāriyāt

verse(s)	page no.
53–54	400

52. Al-Ṭūr

verse(s)	page no.
29	731
48–49	730

53. Al-Najm

verse(s)   page no.
42–43   257

54. Al-Qamar

verse(s)   page no.
20   224
40   494
55   763

55. Al-Rahmān

verse(s)   page no.
29   321

57. Al-Ḥadīd

verse(s)   page no.
4   667

58. Al-Mujādilah

verse(s)   page no.
7   667
8   204
21   160

63. Al-Munāfiqūn

verse(s)   page no.
5   67

64. Al-Taghābun

verse(s)   page no.
8   380, 729

67. Al-Mulk

verse(s)   page no.
2   624
3   705
19   125

69. Al-Ḥāqqah

verse(s)   page no.
44–47   533

71. Nūḥ

verse(s)   page no.
17–18   612

74. Al-Muddaththir

verse(s)   page no.
42–46   737

75. Al-Qiyāmah

verse(s)   page no.
3   723
7–10   599

77. Al-Mursalāt

verse(s)   page no.
30–31   620–21

78. Al-Naba'

verse(s)   page no.
9–11   449

83. Al-Muṭaffifīn

verse(s)   page no.
29–30   753

84. Al-Inshiqāq

verse(s)   page no.
13–15   621

86. Al-Ṭāriq

verse(s)   page no.
15–17   545

96. Al-ʿAlaq

verse(s)   page no.
9–12   450

99. Al-Zalzalah

verse(s)   page no.
7–8   694

112. Al-Ikhlāṣ

verse(s)   page no.
1–4   288

GENERAL INDEX

Aaron (brother of Moses), 336–37, 417

ʿAbd al-Muṭṭalib, 765

Abel, 96–97

Abrahah, 754

Abraham, 271, 368, 499

   and the idol and star-worshipers,
127–28, 327–28, 347, 388, 427,
490–91, 642

   as an advocate of *tawḥīd*, 12, 263,
358–59, 405, 642, 723

   as a prophet, 14, 290, 450

   confrontation of, with a king, 26

   construction of Kaʿbah by, 723, 734

   construction of shrine by, 734

   in the Old Testament, 10, 271, 587

   offering of Ishmael in sacrifice by,
491–92

   prayer of, 617

   progeny of, 65, 234, 264

   qualities of, 450, 489, 499, 504

   testimony of faith of, 398

   visit of angels to, 271, 587

abstinence, sexual, 57. *See also*
   asceticism, religious; celibacy

Abū Bakr, 163, 183, 184, 216, 516, 722

Abū Jahl, 260

Abū Lahab, 764–5

Abū Sufyān, 765

Abū Ṭālib, 420, 765

Abyssinia

   hijrah to 185, 275, 324, 433

   raid on Makkah by army of, 754

accountability, 233, 299, 310, 422, 479,
534, 685, 688

   according to one's limits or
capabilities, 125

   and free will, 155, 233, 373, 374

   and judgment, 134, 140, 226, 345,
411, 602, 605, 663, 671, 694, 744

   deferment of, 339

   for misleading others, 276–77

   in Jewish faith, 10, 637, 639

   of nations, 140, 286, 542, 554

   only for one's own actions, 89, 177,
182, 208, 445, 468, 532

   rejection of, after death: 141, 142,
315, 344, 556, 559, 687, 749;
by pagan Arabs, 343, 394;
in modern civilization, 198, 199,
266, 301, 344, 432, 483, 548, 621,
655, 747; *See also* free will

ʿĀd, 139, 151

   nature of the, 224, 400–1, 560–61,
563, 600

   punishment of the, 218, 224, 524,
560–61, 587, 597, 600, 719

   rejection of Hūd's message by the,
221–24, 600

Adam, 613

   creation of, 43, 605

   expulsion of, from Paradise, 144, 158,
337, 338–39

   in the Old Testament, 281

   offspring of, 96–97, 143, 145, 148,
157, 270, 303

   temptation of, 143, 151, 158, 338,
526

   weakness of, 303, 337, 526

adhān, 105, 533, 570, 626, 649, 684

adoption, 452–53

agnostics and agnosticism, 106, 108, 119,
122, 127, 129, 197, 354, 399, 436,
523, 554

   See also unbelievers and unbelief

General Index

Ahl al-kitāb. See People of the Book
AIDS, 39, 60, 601
ʿĀʾishah, 58, 377–78, 634, 662
alcohol. *See* intoxicants
ʿAlī ibn Abū Ṭālib, 92
alms-giving. *See* charity; zakah
al-ʿamal al-ṣāliḥ, 199–200. *See also* good
  deeds
angels
  arguments among, 501
  as 'daughters of God', 492, 539
  as guardians of hell, 685
  as guardians watching over humans,
    125, 459, 515, 527, 582
  as messengers to Abraham, 271, 587
  as messengers to Lot, 601
  as messengers to Mary, 42
  as messengers to Zachariah, 41
  as servants obedient to God, 86, 157,
    203, 233, 435, 539
  as supporters of Muhammad, 462, 662
  as supporters of Muslims in battle,
    163, 172
  as worshipers glorifying God, 346–47,
    512, 515, 530, 534, 695, 725–26
  belief in, as tenet of faith, 28, 680
  influence of, on man's behavior, 525–
    26
  instruction to, to prostrate before
    Adam, 142
  invisibility of, 120, 525–26
  nature and responsibilities of: 157,
    268, 276, 386, 471, 486, 515, 527,
    530, 585, 721, 725–26, 739;
    as recorders of man's deeds, 706,
    708;
    as takers of souls at death, 75, 125,
    131, 136, 149, 172, 277, 278, 387,
    527, 567;
    greeting those entering heaven,
    251, 620, 624–25, 722
  Pharaoh's demand for, to accompany
    Moses, 543
  speed of, 674

unbelievers' demand for angel to
  accompany Muhammad, or to
  bring revelation, 119–120, 217, 267,
  304, 386–87, 654, 686
unsuitability of, for role of
  prophethood, 345
See also Gabriel
animals, slaughter of, 38, 89, 359, 363,
  758
Anṣār, 161, 175, 638, 652–53, 656
apostasy, 289, 735
Arabic. *See* Qurʾān: Qurʾānic language
Arabism and Arabisation, 253, 523
Arabs
  Arab–Jewish relations, 6–7, 31, 35,
    36, 65, 184–85, 573, 640
  Arab nationalism, 136, 176, 477, 536
  Arabs of Makkah. *See under* Makkah
  as custodians of revelation, 36, 130,
    133, 140, 252, 476, 522, 530, 535,
    542, 649–50
  as illiterate pagans, 30, 36, 78, 115,
    117, 168, 182, 251, 281, 343, 408,
    425, 478, 717
  conversion to Islam of, 129, 213, 254,
    346, 383
  customs of pre-Islamic Arab society,
    59, 298, 452, 492, 758
  insincere converts to Islam among
    the, 580
  negative attitude and response of,
    towards Muhammad and Islam, 53,
    167, 206–7, 218, 251, 267, 287,
    369, 419–20, 473, 476–77, 493,
    522–23, 524, 546. *See also* Makkah,
    opposition of Arabs of, towards
    Muhammad and Muslims
  negative characteristics of, in modern
    society, 34, 136, 523, 528, 535–36,
    538, 548, 628, 639
  responsibility of the Arab nation, 140
  transition of, to a leading nation, 27–
    28, 139–40, 259, 276, 346, 447, 546
  See also Qurʾān, Arabs' rejection of

the
'Arafāt, 364
 Day of, 719
armed robbery, 97, 428
arrogance, 148, 225, 737
 as a human trait, 2, 370, 462, 624
 consequences of, 212, 469, 481, 514–
  15, 720, 727
 of 'Ād, 400, 524, 600
 of Jews, 15, 16, 32, 42, 84, 96, 476,
  650
 of nations, 28, 118, 401, 450, 517
 of Noah's people, 676
 of Pharaoh, 214, 397, 404, 543, 697
 of Thamūd, 226, 406, 726
 of unbelievers, 66–67, 86, 129, 131,
  165, 354, 369, 380, 410, 477, 511,
  593, 596, 686
arrows, divining, 89
asceticism, religious, 146–47, 319, 613–
 14, 617. *See also* abstinence, sexual;
 celibacy
Asmā' bint 'Umays, 275
asylum seekers, protection of, 92, 178,
 275. *See also* hijrah
awliyā' Allah, 200
āyāt. See God, evidence for the
 existence of; miracles

Babylonians, 293
Baghdad, 350
Banū Ḥanīfah, 572
al-Baṣrī, Ḥasan, 708
Battle of Badr, 45, 47, 160–67, 169–70,
 172, 260, 357, 369, 547, 589, 602
Battle of the Trench, 458–59, 571
Battle of Uḥud, 30, 44–47, 49–51, 63,
 160, 192, 616
beast, appearance of the, as portent of
 the end of the world, 411
'Big Bang' theory, 228–29, 344
Bilāl, 570
Bilqīs, 404–6, 497,
 throne of, 674

black holes, 256–57
boastfulness, 79, 312, 444. *See also*
 arrogance
bondsman, freeing of, 724
brotherhood in Islam, 175, 453, 579,
 751. *See also* Ummah
burial, 454
business matters
 dishonesty in, 707
 fairness in weights and measures, 135,
  227, 299, 401, 604
 honoring pledges and contracts, 299
 partnership with non-Muslims in, 105
Byzantines
 Christianity under the, 103
 defeat of the, by the Persians, 434
 Muslim attitudes towards, 111
 war waged against the, by the
  Muslims, 105, 178–79, 182–83, 185,
  186–91, 195, 245

Cain, 96–97
Caliph(s), 92, 169, 171, 185, 242, 253,
 317, 514, 516, 559
call to prayer. See *adhān*
celibacy, 615–16. *See also* abstinence,
 sexual; asceticism, religious
charity
 giving of, as a token of faith, 367,
  449, 627–28, 657, 727, 728, 757
 recipients of, 190
 reluctance to give, 67
 spending in, 61, 286, 630, 635, 720
 See also zakah
children
 adoption of, 452–53
 as an ornament of life, 314
 as a test, 167, 653, 657
 custody of, following divorce, 658–59
 death of male, 758
 enemies among, 656
 parental responsibilities towards, 24,
  58, 169, 453
 prayer for, 393, 559

777

rejection of faith by, 559
responsibilities of, towards parents,
298
showing kindness towards, 71
weaning, 24
See also infanticide; orphans
Christianity
and the Arius doctrine, 186
as a belligerent force, 103
Christian attitude to Muhammad, 82,
349–50, 434, 464, 532
Christian attitude to the Qur'an, 101,
253, 272, 587
Christian belief in God, 10, 31, 53
Christian-Muslim relations, 31, 72–
73, 89, 103–5, 108, 111, 185, 186,
429–30, 433, 644, 754
conversion to Islam of Christians,
111, 185, 253, 307, 420, 434, 532,
741–42
erroneous doctrines and practices
within, 43–44, 84–86, 94–95, 110,
113, 185–86, 281, 326, 346, 425,
466, 531, 614, 616, 649–50, 655,
678–79
God's covenant with the Christians,
92–93
hostility of Christians towards Islam,
429–30, 554, 574. *See also* Crusades
Islamic approaches to addressing
Christian ideology, 11, 12, 15, 43–
44, 54
lenience of Christians towards
criminality, immorality and
materialsim, 107, 186, 407, 639
religio-centricity of Christians, 11, 95
schism within: 93, 110–11;
St. Bartholomew's Day massacre,
181
See also Gospel; Jesus
civilization, contemporary
attitudes towards God within, 65, 85,
149, 226, 399, 426, 519, 553
disguised polygamy within, 457

family life in, 297–98, 428, 444
hostility towards Islam within, 430,
521
materialism within, 266, 313, 344,
401, 432, 437, 459, 521, 639, 655,
671, 747, 757
nature of, 28, 98, 149, 175, 199, 221,
225, 240, 377, 379, 399, 401, 448,
449, 457–58, 483, 520–21, 535, 553,
640, 718, 733
rejection of accountability after death
by, 198, 199, 301, 344, 548, 621,
655
scientific materialism within, 410
sexual immorality within, 60, 271,
377, 379, 401, 407, 428, 601, 614
clothing. *See* dress
coercion in religion, prohibition on 30,
74, 105, 133, 181, 183, 186, 208,
290, 356, 521, 552, 559, 626, 760–
61
communism, 721, 757
Companions of the Prophet, 383, 570,
634, 683, 751, 762, 763. *See also*
Anṣār; Muhājirūn; *and names of*
individuals
consultation, mutual (*shūrā*), 535
corruption, 258, 401
causes of, 176, 329, 439, 542, 553,
735
consequences of, 62, 329, 547, 726
death sentence for spreading, 97
divine punishment for, 296, 297, 378,
524, 620, 743
eradication of, 292–93, 408
political and economic, 226–27
protection of society against, 20, 376,
379, 644, 657, 746
symptoms of, 221, 296
See also oppression
crime, 107, 392
lenience towards, 60, 98, 107
punishment for, 98, 99–101, 106–7,
197, 298–99, 376, 392–93, 535

social consequences of, 67, 98–99,
299, 657
See also homosexuality; infanticide;
murder; sexual relations, illicit;
slander; theft
Crusades, 94, 112, 429
cycles of nature, 255, 270, 485, 581, 604,
611–12, 623
See also water: water cycle

David
accusations of adultery against, 496–
97
as a king, prophet and leader, 351,
466, 494
as recipient of the Psalms, 302
curse of, on Israelite unbelievers, 108
in arbitration over ewes, 495–6
qualities of, 348, 465
repentance of, 496
See also Psalms
da'wah
emigrating to participate in, 75
failure to propagate Islam effectively,
528
methodology of engaging in, 290–91,
516, 552, 579
al-Dawālībī, Dr. Muhammad Ma'rūf, 94
Day of Judgment, 2
accountability on the, 113, 125, 134,
140, 226, 284, 299, 310, 339, 344,
345, 349, 394, 411, 421–22, 445,
462, 464, 479, 532, 548, 554, 597,
602, 605, 656, 663, 671, 687, 688,
694, 707–8, 744, 748
criteria for judgment, 33
deferment of punishment until the,
204, 220
events of the, 315–16, 335–36, 350,
352, 487–88, 525, 582, 606, 608,
609, 614, 624, 671, 683, 688, 692,
696, 697, 700–1, 702, 705, 710,
744, 748
inevitability of the, 116, 288, 519,

536, 582, 608, 623, 624, 694
length of the, 448
no exemptions from the, 605
punishment of unbelievers on the:
327, 330, 338, 411, 432, 470, 507–
8, 511, 544, 670, 717, 748;
and their followers, 260–61, 461,
468–69, 487, 500, 602
receiving one's record on the, 305,
316, 671, 706, 710
response of unbelievers on the, 372,
449, 470, 487, 511, 670, 696, 717,
721
resurrection of both body and soul on
the, 613–14, 687, 723
signs of impending end of the world,
136, 320, 411, 544, 599, 674, 702,
744
timing of the last hour, 157, 204–5,
284, 431, 446, 483–84, 528, 609,
681, 695, 698
See also punishment, divine; hell;
Paradise
death, 607, 716
approach of, 89
as a divinely ordained event, 269,
448, 605, 610
as a transitional phase, 143, 312, 698,
749
of Jacob, 12
of Jesus, 43
of Muhammad, 183
man's inability to prevent, 624, 688
predetermination of moment and
place of, 69, 302, 446, 624
unbelievers' response at the moment
of, 131, 136, 372
See also angels: nature and
responsibilites of, as takers of souls
at death; life after death
debts, unpaid, 453–54
destiny
and acceptance of God's will, 316–17,
355, 466

and moment of death, 69, 624
God as controller of creation's, 70,
   125, 224, 257, 260, 443, 447, 464,
   666, 715, 739
God as controller of man's, 55, 125,
   127, 190, 316, 656, 700
inability of one man to control
   destiny of another, 598, 672
man's behavior, as determiner of his,
   296, 445, 727
of those whom God wishes to
   confound, 100, 155–56
of those whom God wishes to guide,
   155, 656
predestination and free will, 155–56,
   373
devils
   as companions assigned to
      unbelievers, 542, 583
   as enemies of prophets, 361, 769
   attempts to tamper with revelation
      by, 486
   luring believers away from Islam, 126,
      134, 425, 527, 583, 769–70
   punishment in hell of, 329
   Solomon's command over, 498
   See also jinn; Satan
Dhū'l-Ḥijjah, 363, 719
Dhū'l-Kifl (Ezekiel), 348, 499
Dhū'l-Qarnayn, 307, 309, 319–20
dissension
   among groups and nations, 140
   among the Christians, 93
   among the Jews, 10
   and discord:
      sown by man, 194, 320, 652;
      sown by Satan, 248, 302, 578
   and ijtihad, 348, 437–38
   and 'innovation', 320
   as a human trait, 437, 654
   dangers of, 438
   fitnah, 18
   See also sectarianism
divorce, 21–24, 80, 658–60

of unbelieving women, 644
payment of dowry following, 59
payment of *khulaʿa* following, 23
regulation of, 21–22, 633, 658–59
treatment of women following, 21–
   22, 24, 658–59
waiting period following, 381–82, 659
woman's right to divorce husband,
   23–24, 57
dowry, 23, 58, 59, 644
dreams, interpretation of, 234, 237, 241–
   44
dress
   asceticism in, 147
   cleanliness in, 684
   for prayer, 147
   'garb of piety', 144–45
   rulings on clothing, perfume,
      cosmetics and jewelry, 379
   symbolism of clothing, 144, 148
   women's, 457, 460–61
   See also ihrām
duress, renouncing faith under, 289
   See also coercion in religion

earthquakes, 519–20, 608, 696, 744
Eid, 758
elderly
   neglect of the, 297–98, 444
   respect for the, 71, 577
   See also parents
Elijah (*Ilyās*), 490
Elisha (*al-Yasaʿa*), 499
emigration. *See* hijrah
enemies of Islam and Muslims, 6–7, 15,
   73–74, 104–5, 165, 182–83, 194–95,
   429–30, 458–59, 642–43, 653–54
   grace period extended to, 179
   persecution of and hostility towards
      early Muslims by pagan Arabs, 53,
      120, 167, 168, 177–78, 180–81, 306,
      369–70, 394, 571–72, 764–65
   present-day hostility towards
      Muslims, 23, 111, 360, 450, 567,

642–43

See also Christianity: hostility of Christians towards Islam; Crusades; hypocrites; Jewish-Muslim relations; unbelievers

environment, abuse of the natural, 481, 547, 604

envy, 340, 574, 721, 768

equality, 363–64, 399, 541
  during salah, 400
  sexual, 20–21

Eve, 144, 338

evil
  accountability for evil actions, 694, 744–45
  actions of unbelievers, 19, 173, 180, 194
  as a test, 466, 768
  battle between good and, 48, 264, 339–40, 360, 431
  consequence of evil acts, 366, 445, 552, 727
  directive not to perpetrate, 422
  distinguishing between good and, 380, 462
  effects of, on society, 109, 220–21, 422
  evil-doers: 52, 104, 124, 152, 163, 188, 399, 449, 709, 733, 753; fate of, 411, 474, 487, 544, 563, 724
  good deeds make up for evil ones, 220, 403
  Muhammad's mission to eradicate, 201
  promotion of, as unpardonable sin, 743
  recent wars as works of, 20
  requirement of Muslims to combat, 364, 564, 683, 717, 746
  requital of evil with evil, 21, 79, 200, 423, 477, 535, 596
  requital of evil with good, 521
  responsibility for, 70, 293
  salah and revelation as protection against, 329, 522, 530
  seeking forgiveness for committing, 54, 78, 123, 290, 403
  seeking God's protection from, 768, 769
  speaking evil words, 107, 262, 634
  unbelief as root of, 621, 735
  See also devils; jinn: devils among the; Satan

evil eye, 768

faith. *See* God (man's relationship with), belief in; *īmān*; waverers (weak in faith)

false accusation
  defamation, 579
  directive not to bear false witness, 393
  in Tuʿmah case, 77
  of adultery, 377
  rumor-mongering, 190–91, 377, 578
  See also slander

falsehood and lies
  as opposed to *ḥaqq* or *īmān*, 356, 565
  concerning Muhammad, 123, 190
  eradicating or combatting, 163, 645, 683
  faith as a protection against, 645, 746
  influence of, on society, 261–62, 679
  inventing, about God, 36, 64, 131, 134, 149, 284, 310, 432, 508, 509, 511, 533, 647, 678
  listening to, 100
  punishment for, in hereafter, 131, 149, 289, 432, 508–9, 511, 635–36, 750
  stemming from Satan, 361–62
  See also slander

family affairs, 20–25, 56–61, 79–81
  families in Western society, 297–98, 428
  family disputes, 21
  fragmentation of the family, 81, 559
  preservation of the family unit, 17, 379, 393, 658–59

treatment of children and kinfolk, 71,
298, 438–39
values of the Muslim family, 341, 663
fasting, 8, 612, 614
Ramaḍān, 546, 739
Fāṭimah (daughter of the Prophet), 98
fighters
as an instrument of God, 160
disobedience of Muslim, in battle, 46
divine support given to Muslim, 164,
459
martyrs, 4, 48, 49–50, 69, 141, 164,
195, 566, 613, 616, 630, 666, 712
motives of, for bearing arms, 171–72,
357, 760–61
payment of, 169
reward of, 69, 192, 194–95
See also jihad (in war time)
fire, 623
fire worshipers, 295
trench of, as a human punishment,
712
use of plants as fuel for, 485, 489, 623
See also hell
fitnah (sedition), 18. *See also* dissension;
sectarianism
fiṭrah (natural disposition), 18, 425, 435,
437, 674, 734–35. *See also* human
nature
Flood, the Great, 151, 222–23, 490, 600,
734
in Jewish scriptures, 10
See also Noah
food, 581
as a divine blessing, 254, 278–79, 283,
353–54, 700, 756
intoxicants, 112
of hell, 489, 549, 683, 717
prohibitions on, 37–38
Qur'anic directive to eat wholesome,
89, 112, 368
free will, 155–57, 355, 474, 596
and accountability, 339, 374, 710–11
and destiny, 70

exercising, in choosing to listen to or
follow Satan, 79, 271
man's freedom to accept or reject
God and His message, 78, 127,
133–34, 157, 183, 232–33, 307, 312,
373, 525, 725
man's status above the animals by
virtue of his, 301, 462
See also accountability
future, knowledge of the, 124, 241, 269,
317, 360, 445–46

Gabriel, the Archangel
and Ḥassān ibn Thābit, 527
in Christian belief, 288, 346, 425
role of, 203, 332, 486, 594, 662, 704,
739
speed of, 674
gambling and games of chance, 89
al-Ghazālī, Abū Ḥamid, 380
ghusl, 649
God (as the Supreme Being) 26, 116,
124–27, 201–3, 278–80, 289, 325,
385, 475, 504, 666, 715, 767
as the Creator and life-giver, 2, 34,
55, 70, 150, 229, 255, 263, 278,
335, 427, 610–12, 627
omnipotence of, 114, 150, 255, 257,
279, 285, 288, 300, 321, 354, 443,
448, 474, 481–83, 509, 519–20, 584,
597, 604
omnipresence of, 125, 229, 667, 715,
725
omniscience of, 124–25, 217, 257,
269, 288, 446, 463, 513, 634, 667
oneness of. See *tawḥīd*
self-sufficiency of, 80, 156, 203, 341,
363, 406, 427, 444, 474, 568, 588,
655
God (man's relationship with)
belief in, 52, 91, 115–16, 199–200,
203, 260, 289, 304, 308, 312, 355,
356, 381–82, 435, 666, 680. *See also*
rational thought

duty of gratitude towards, 173, 212, 280, 283, 390, 438, 504–5, 519, 613

forgiveness of sins by: 55–56, 77–78, 123, 168, 220–21, 290, 370, 511, 513, 514, 534, 565, 572, 669, 708, 743;

as God's prerogative, 680–81

help and succor of, 3, 126, 156, 163–64, 210–12, 230, 322, 348–49, 409, 519, 769–70

man's ingratitude towards, 230, 303, 357, 438, 444, 504, 519, 588, 606, 680, 746, 750

mercy and grace of, 2, 36, 56, 230, 389, 445, 471–72, 504, 596, 603, 632

praise and worship of, 1–2, 340, 363, 459, 588, 593, 619, 626, 627, 645, 649, 654. *See also* prayer

God-consciousness (awareness and fear of God; *taqwā*), 7–8

as a characteristic of believers, 7–8, 56, 105, 200, 277, 360, 509, 512, 527, 579

as a means of achieving victory, guidance, and success, 171, 423, 727

as a protection against Satan and wrongdoing, 158, 238, 527

danger of lack of, 338, 381, 680

distractions from, 653

man's need of, 23, 697

Muhammad's mission to raise, 469

Qur'anic directives to remain God-conscious or to fear God, 8, 19, 22, 37, 51, 54, 55, 80, 90, 97, 105, 133, 159, 202, 352, 369, 371, 396, 400, 461, 577, 632, 639, 657, 659

remembrance of God throughout the day, 159, 449, 459, 519, 690

reward and deliverance for God-conscious, 51, 218, 330, 339, 423, 507, 566, 583, 695

salah as a means of achieving, 336

God, evidence (*āyāt*) for the existence of, 21, 26, 122, 131–32, 151, 202, 206, 212, 250, 254–57, 267, 279, 282–83, 285, 296, 380–81, 385, 390–91, 395, 435–36, 438, 445, 451, 467, 475, 481–82, 520, 528, 529, 534, 551–52, 586, 612, 660, 676, 703, 725. *See also under* cycles of nature; stars; sun; water: water cycle

Gog and Magog, 319–20, 350

good deeds, 13, 15, 53, 97, 140–41, 199–200, 220, 309, 314, 361, 368, 403, 445, 511.

Gospel (New Testament), 31, 90, 101, 108, 109, 130, 195, 281, 287–88, 326, 388, 562, 590, 646–47. *See also* revelation

gravity, force of, 256, 534, 586, 693

greetings, 72–73

on visiting someone's home, 379

offensive, 204, 634

hadith. *See* Muhammad, sayings of

Ḥadīth al-ifk, 377–78

Hadramawt, 560

Ḥafṣah, 275, 661–62

Hajj, 719

grace period granted to Muhammad's enemies during, 179

iḥrām, 89

in years 9 and 10 A.H., 184

main rituals of, 358–59, 363–64

promise of, after Ḥudaybiyyah, 569, 575

Qur'anic directive to complete, 8

shaving hair for, 575

ʿumrah, 8, 571–72

unbelievers prohibited from performing, 182

Hāmān, 418, 715

al-Ḥasan (grandson of the Prophet), 716

Hawāzin, 572

Haykal, Muḥammad Ḥusayn, 664

heaven. *See* Paradise

heavens. *See* sky
hell
  as a physical reality, 616
  description of, 620–21, 685, 753
  duration of punishment in, 33, 330
  fire of, 312, 344, 602, 703
  nature of punishment in, 344, 488–
    89, 625, 672, 683, 689
  nature of water in, 142, 489, 620,
    621, 625, 717
  occupants of, 141–42, 155, 199, 219,
    261, 302, 321, 330, 384, 500, 509,
    544, 555, 583, 620, 665, 685–86,
    753
  reasons for punishment in, 399, 432,
    511, 519, 737, 749
  Sijjīn, 708
  zaqqūm tree in, 488–89, 549, 621
  See also punishment, divine, in the
    hereafter
al-Ḥijr valley, 267
hijrah, 75, 161, 275–76
  from Makkah to Abyssinia, 185, 275,
    433
  from Makkah to Madinah, 6, 50, 53,
    75, 161, 175, 643
  of the Prophet, 163–64, 306
  status of Muslims who did not make
    the, 175, 275, 643, 656
  See also Muhājirūn
Himyar, 561
Ḥirā', 594, 736
HIV. *See* AIDS
Holy Spirit, 110, 185, 288, 326, 739,
  766–67
homosexuality
  lesbianism, 60
  Lot's campaign against, 221, 271, 407,
    428, 601
  permissibility of, in the West, 60, 99,
    186, 271, 401, 428, 601
  punishment for, 60, 271, 401, 407,
    601
  Qur'anic directive to punish those

    who engage in, 60
  See also Lot
houris, 614, 619
Hūd, 368
  deliverance of, 218, 224
  mission of, 221–22, 223–24, 400,
    560–61
  See also ʿĀd
Ḥudaybiyyah, Treaty of, 569–571, 573–
    575, 643
human nature, 11, 39, 78, 102, 115, 164,
    211, 221, 230, 232, 282, 291, 296,
    354, 435, 437, 440, 466, 591, 742.
    See also *fiṭrah*
humility, 166–67, 299
  as a quality of a believer, 106, 146,
    248, 630
  of prophets, 240, 319, 655, 672, 762–
    63
  towards children, 298
  towards God, 4, 31, 53, 95, 113, 118,
    150, 159, 366, 531
Ḥunayn, 572
hygiene, personal, 379
  bathing on Fridays, 649
  cleanliness in clothes and person, 684
  See also *wuḍūʾ*
hypocrites, 66–67, 85, 190–94, 633,
    652–53
  as a threat to the Muslim community,
    8, 66, 73, 81–82, 187, 188, 190–94,
    566–68, 571–72, 634, 639, 652–53
  neglect of religious duties by the, 25,
    67–68
  punishment of the, 81, 100, 457, 461,
    567, 635
  See also unbelievers and unbelief

Iblīs. *See* Satan
Ibn ʿAbbās, ʿAbd Allah, 58, 72, 513, 734
Ibn ʿAbd al-ʿAzīz, ʿUmar, 253
Ibn Abū Ṭālib, ʿAlī, 92
Ibn Abū Ṭālib, Jaʿfar, 616
Ibn Ashur, Fāḍil, 450

Ibn ʿAṭāʾ, Wāṣil, 92
Ibn ʿAṭiyyah, 559
Ibn Ḥanbal, Aḥmad, 57
Ibn Ḥaram, ʿAbd Allah, 50
Ibn al-Ḥārith, al-Naḍr, 442
Ibn Ḥārithah, Zayd, 452
Ibn Ḥazm, 43, 768
Ibn Jarīr, 72
Ibn Kathīr, 513, 514, 614
Ibn al-Khaṭṭāb, ʿUmar. *See* ʿUmar ibn
al-Khaṭṭāb
Ibn Kulthūm, ʿAmr, 225
Ibn Masʿūd, 599
Ibn al-Muʿaṭṭal, Ṣafwān, 377
Ibn al-Muṭʿim, Jubayr, 589–90
Ibn Naḍr, Anas, 616
Ibn Thābit, Ḥassān, 527
Ibn Ubayy, ʿAbd Allah, 45, 73, 377–78,
653
Ibn ʿUmayr, Muṣʿab, 50
Ibn Umm Maktūm, ʿAbd Allah, 699
Ibn al-Walīd, Khālid, 245, 560
Ibn Zayd, Usāmah, 74
idolaters, 78, 134, 148, 168, 749
Abraham's campaign against, 327–28,
347, 490–91
attitude of, towards God, 133, 399,
538
attitude of, towards Muhammad, 431
ban on, attending mosques, 182, 184
demand for a sign by, 122
granting asylum to, 92
Israelite idol-worshipers, 153
Qurʾanic approach in addressing, 115,
197, 371
rejection of life after death by, 281
relations between Muslims and, 178
sun, moon or star worship by, 127,
404–5, 497, 528
See also unbelievers and unbelief
idolatry, 6, 148, 169, 182, 184, 360, 435,
478. *See also* unbelievers and
unbelief
idols

as a Satanic abomination, 89
destiny in hell of, 399, 487
destruction of, by Abraham, 347, 491
destruction of Makkan, 182, 570
impotence of, 408, 421, 538–39, 556
Muhammad's attitude towards, 595,
736
worship of the golden calf, 153
Idrīs (Enoch), 348
ignorance
advice to Muhammad to shun the
ignorant, 158
as root or symptom of unbelief: 121,
129, 208, 230, 352–53, 354, 380,
502, 567;
of pagan/polytheist Arabs, 148, 478,
633
Christian doctrine stemming from,
39–40, 84, 433
committing evil out of, then
repenting, 56, 123, 290
Islam's attempt to rid people of, 115–
16, 259, 478
misleading others through, 134, 276–
77
pursuit of knowledge to overcome,
516–17
Satan's desire to keep people in, 362
speaking on religious matters of
which one is ignorant, 23, 71, 103,
199
iḥrām, 89
iḥsān, 200. *See also* good deeds
īmān, 199, 200, 304, 308, 356, 674. *See
also* God (man's relationship with),
belief in
immorality, 107, 109, 144, 240, 377,
401, 674, 684. *See also*
homosexuality; indecency;
promiscuity; sexual relations, illicit
indecency, 60, 146–47, 221, 240, 286,
298, 377, 379, 442, 535, 659. *See
also* homosexuality; immorality;
promiscuity; sexual relations, illicit

infanticide, 135, 298, 413, 492, 644, 702, 735

inheritance, 57–59, 86, 453, 721

intoxicants, 89, 112, 514

invisible world, 463, 526, 680, 701

Iram, 719

iron, 301, 320, 465, 609, 631

Isaac, 234, 264, 328, 348, 499

Ishmael, 264, 348, 491–92, 499, 723

Islam, 13
  as a balanced religion, 103
  as a holistic religion, 423
  as a source of peace, 93
  as a tolerant religion, 105, 106, 183, 290, 521
  as a universal religion, 30, 31, 102, 103, 130, 385, 447, 531, 670, 704
  as religion of truth, 575
  as religion preached by all the prophets, 12, 13, 31, 128, 385, 405
  as submission to God, 13, 148, 282, 355, 405, 443, 507, 630
  key principles of:
    belief in God, 13, 666;
    belief in God's books, 130, 181–82;
    belief in God's messengers, 130;
    belief in jinn and angels, 680;
    belief in the hereafter, 157, 663;
    pillars of Islam, 8, 210, 212–13, 261, 327, 363, 612–13, 766–67;
    teachings of Islam, 38, 55, 102, 106, 135, 146, 379, 435, 449, 733
  mission of, 11, 385, 410, 718
  Muslims as custodians of, 75, 364, 440, 648; rejection of, 30, 521

Islam, spread of
  among the People of the Book, 111, 253, 307, 420, 532, 741–42
  by peaceful means, 532
  geographical, 111, 129, 178–79, 195, 245, 253, 254, 307, 346, 383, 420, 426, 455, 531, 532, 533, 724, 741, 762
  obstacles to the, 183, 190, 455, 554, 660
  opposition to the, by Jews, 554, 573
  See also *daʿwah*

Iẓhār al-Ḥaqq (Sh. Raḥmat Allah), 64

Jacob (*Yaʿqūb*)
  and Joseph, 234–36, 246–48
  as a prophet, 12, 328, 499
  in Jewish scriptures, 10, 287
  prohibition on foods by, 38
  qualities of, 348, 499, 594

Jerusalem, 38, 40, 292, 293, 405, 406, 734

Jesus (*ʿĪsā*)
  as 'God' in Christian belief, 346, 767
  as 'son of God', 39–40, 43, 86, 94–95, 110, 288, 326, 544, 678, 767
  birthplace of, 368
  celibacy of, 615–16
  conception and birth of, 34, 39–40, 42, 324, 326
  curse of, on Israelites, 108
  death or crucifixion of, 43, 84, 94–95, 281, 767
  disciples request to, for a meal from heaven, 88
  mission and status of, 37, 42, 325, 326, 544, 646, 648
  refutation of divine status of, 113, 185–86, 346
  second coming of, 44, 544

Jewish–Muslim relations, 103–10, 184–85
  agreements between Muslims and Jews, 16, 100
  attitude of Jews towards Muhammad, 82, 349–50
  conflict between Jews and Muslims at Khaybar, 572–74
  feigned acceptance of and insincerity towards Islam by Jews, 35–36, 92
  hostility of Jews towards Islam, 6–7, 16, 30, 31–32, 34–36, 51–52, 62, 573–74, 637–38

offensive greetings given by Jews to
Muslims, 204, 634
rejection of Muhammad's
prophethood by the Jews, 558
See also Jewish scriptures; Jews;
Judaism; Madinah, Jewish
community of
Jewish scriptures 10,
adulterations in the, 64, 281, 457, 498
discrepancies between the, and the
Qur'an, 10, 271, 281, 287–88, 587,
664
failure to preserve, intact, 62, 130,
272, 646, 650
misinterpretation of the, 63–64
the Old Testament, 64, 101, 103,
281, 388, 639
the Talmud, 36–37
the Torah (the Book of Moses), 10,
31, 34, 36, 37, 38, 90, 99, 101, 103,
108, 109, 130, 195, 231, 281, 287–
88, 292, 320, 347, 398, 450, 489–
90, 529, 563, 590, 597, 646, 650
See also Psalms; revelation
Jews
as a 'chosen people', 36–37, 425, 531,
548, 553, 573, 650
as descendants of Isaac, 264
as recipients of revelation, 133, 152,
272, 476, 553, 650
attitude of, towards Jesus, 82, 349
betrayal of Moses by the, 646
decline in power of the, 184–85, 638
diaspora of the, 154, 293
'first exile' of the, 638
God's covenant with the, 9, 17, 52,
84, 90, 91, 629
in the Sinai wilderness, 96, 153, 337
negative traits and actions of the, 32–
34, 36, 51–52, 62, 107, 214–15,
553, 633, 650
political fortunes of the, 292–93, 295
relations of, with pagan Arabs, 99–
101

the Ṭuʿmah case, 77
See also Jewish-Muslim relations;
Jewish scriptures; Judaism
jihad (in peace time)
as sacrifice and hard work, 17
broader definition of, 263
campaigning against injustice, evil
and oppression, 109, 364, 535, 578,
641, 657
reward for those who sacrifice and
struggle in God's cause, 64, 275,
383, 590
role of wealth and power in, 314–15
striving, spending, and sacrificing in
God's cause, 51, 161, 187, 192, 194,
365, 427, 432, 508, 568, 580, 629,
647–48, 733
struggling to protect one's religion
and way of life, 360
supporting a good cause, 72
See also charity
jihad (in war time), 17–20
as a deterrent, 173–74
as a test of faith, 45–46, 47, 48, 69,
161, 164, 189–90, 458, 572
avoiding committing aggression, 19,
178–79, 181, 183
behaviour during battle, 164–65, 170,
171, 174, 565
defeat in battle through disunity and
weakness, 47–48
during the sacred month, 18
engaging in, in response to
aggression, 19, 178, 180, 357, 578,
641–42
grounds for engaging in, 18, 19–20,
73–74, 171–72, 174, 196, 641, 746
making adequate preparations for
battle, 47, 63, 164
misconceptions about, 17–19
prayer of Muhammad before battle,
163
praying during battle, 76
prescription of fighting, 18–19, 72,

169, 174, 178, 180–81, 195, 357,
564–65
prohibition on befriending aggressors,
642
refusal or reluctance to fight, 67, 68–
69, 162, 187, 189–90, 192, 507, 567
role of women in battle, 49
size of army not a key factor in, 164,
174–75
spending in support of the war effort,
51, 193
treatment of prisoners of war, 74,
173, 565
treatment of women captured in war,
456–57
See also Battle of Badr; Battle of the
Trench; Battle of Uḥud; fighters;
self-defense, right to; spoils of war
jinn
acceptance of Islam by, 563, 679
accountability of, 534, 606
adoption of Christian doctrines by,
678
belief in, as tenet of Islam, 680
devils among the, 361, 526, 768, 768–
70
duty of, to worship God, 435, 588
influence of, over man, 525–26, 583,
678
invisibility of, 525–26, 562, 680
paying heed to the Qur'an, 562, 678–
79
power of, 563
punishment in hell of, 155, 220, 232
rejection of Islam by, 679
righteous, 526
Solomon's army of, 498
jizyah, 183–84
Job (*Ayyūb*), 348, 498–99
John (*Yaḥyā*, son of Zachariah), 41,
325–26, 348, 615–16
Jonah (*Yūnus*), 213, 348–49, 490, 670
Joseph (*Yūsuf*, son of Jacob), 152, 234–
49, 314, 370, 408, 516

Joseph (suitor of Mary), 42
Judaism, 102–3, 107, 109–10
belief in the hereafter in, 639, 655
dietary laws under, 37–38
imposition of, and breaking of the
Sabbath, 153, 290
punishment for adultery under, 99–
101
See also Jewish-Muslim relations;
Jewish scriptures; Jews
justice (divine). *See* law, Islamic:
sharīʿah; punishment, divine;
reward, divine
justice (human)
absence of, as threat to family, 81
exercising, towards Muslims, 578
exercising, towards non-Muslims,
100, 181–82
importance of, to society, 80, 146,
297, 718, 733, 740
in retributive killing, 299
in the Ṭuʿmah case, 77–78
in weights and measures, 135, 299,
604
Qur'anic directive to be just, 135, 286
revelation as source of earthly, 522,
631
role of Muhammad in establishing,
195–96, 201, 532, 564
superiority of sharīʿah over human
legislation, 97–99, 423
towards Muslim women, 22–23, 58
See also law, man-made
Kaʿbah, 589–90, 719
as a place of worship and peace, 569,
574, 575, 754
as a symbol of *tawḥīd*, 359
as the *qiblah*, 38
attempted destruction of the, 754
construction of the, 358–59, 723, 734
custodians of the, 168
debarring from visiting the, 18, 168,
358
first call to prayer from the, 570

purging of the, 182, 184
ṭawāf (circumambulation), 359
Kant, Immanuel, 241
Khawārij, 92
Khaybar, 184, 572–74
al-Khiḍr, 316–18
al-Khuḍrī, Abū Saʿīd, 711
khulaʿah, 23
knowledge and learning, 71, 436, 465,
    516–17, 595, 634, 669
Korah (*Qārūn*), 422

law, Islamic (divine)
    application of, 78, 101, 102, 118, 252,
        529, 633, 644, 723
    distortion and neglect of, 98, 134, 451
    governing family life, 21–22, 377, 658
    ijtihad, 102, 103, 437
    importance of, to Muslim society, 27,
        90, 97, 112, 379
    in the hands of the ignorant, 71
    revelation as the source of, 63, 97–98,
        101–4, 295, 430, 489–90, 563, 590
    sharīʿah, 97, 103, 104, 381–82, 723
    See also penal code, Islamic
law, man-made
    Arabs as pioneers in field of law, 27
    as heresy, 186
    bias and failure in human legislation,
        67, 98, 423
    governing people of all religious
        persuasions, 100–1
    governing rights of women, 23
    replacement of Islamic laws with, 64,
        99, 382
laylat al-qadr, 546, 739
leadership qualities, 317, 541, 645
    of nations, 259–60, 384, 427, 460,
        631–32
    of prophets, 123–24, 234, 317, 385,
        450
lesbianism. *See* homosexuality
lies. *See* false accusation; falsehood;
    slander

life, 711
    as a gift, 283, 373, 597
    as a means to recognize God, 373
    as a test, 137, 321, 348–49, 355, 367,
        391, 425, 426, 435, 466, 492, 510,
        624, 631, 665, 675, 720, 768
    as a transient, fleeting state, 270, 280,
        297, 329, 432, 535, 690, 716
life after death, 198, 435, 485, 554, 556,
    581, 605, 607–14, 665, 671, 687–88,
    689
    belief in, 157, 312, 582
    rejection of belief in, 230, 280, 301,
        312, 313, 315, 329, 343, 344, 352–
        53, 354, 410, 448–49, 463–64, 548,
        559, 581–83, 621, 655
    See also Day of Judgment; death
The Life of Muhammad (Haykal), 664
light
    and shadow, 375, 390, 620
    God as *al-nūr*, 375–76, 380
    God as ordainer of darkness and, 115,
        131, 308, 375, 422, 482, 525
    revelation as, 130, 336, 411, 473, 628,
        655, 729
    synonymous with guidance, 66, 93,
        132, 156, 258–59, 265, 380, 507,
        537
lightning, as a sign of God, 436
logic. *See* Qurʾān: logic and rationality
    of the; rational thought
Lot (*Lūṭ*), 347–48
    as a messenger, 490
    campaign by, against sodomy, 221,
        271, 401, 406–7, 428, 601
    in the Old Testament, 664
    people of, 139, 151, 218–19, 267,
        271, 389, 401, 407, 428, 601, 754
    Sodom and Gomorrah, 389, 406–7,
        587, 597
    wife of, 663
    wisdom of, 237
Luqmān, 443–44

Madinah (*Yathrib*)
  attempted siege of, 458–59
  establishment of the first Islamic state
    in, 6, 25, 27, 28, 53, 75, 175, 181,
    192, 458–59, 571, 633, 638–39, 643,
    652–53, 656
  Jewish community of, 6, 9, 13, 16–
    17, 30, 31, 32, 34, 51, 65, 99–100,
    185, 634, 637–38
Madyan, Moses' sojourn in, 416
Madyan, people of, 139, 151, 361, 419
  call to, to believe in God, 226–28
  destruction of, 219
  rejection of Shuʿayb's message by,
    227–28
  See also Shuʿayb
Magians, 72, 355, 742
mahr. See dowry
maintenance, women's entitlement to,
  following divorce, 24
Māʿiz, 106–7
Makkah
  Abyssinian campaign against, 754
  as a sacred city, 411, 719, 723
  as the cradle of Islam, 734
  conquest of, 184, 414, 569–70, 574–
    75, 644, 762
  conversion of population of, 129, 254
  drought in, 547
  history of, 723
  opposition of Arabs of, towards
    Muhammad and Muslims, 181, 185,
    213, 272, 274–75, 281, 304, 306,
    330, 370, 386–88, 389, 394, 414,
    433, 458, 571, 641, 656, 685
  protection of Muslims resident in,
    574–75
  purging of, of idolatry, 182, 184
  Quraysh tribe of, 304, 364, 669, 675,
    756
al-Manār (Riḍa), 37, 63
mankind's role on earth, 1, 9, 256, 462,
  525, 624, 666
manslaughter, 74

marriage
  as a religious obligation, 379
  erosion of institution of, 428
  fairness in, 80
  forced, 57
  marital disputes, 80
  marital relations, 60–61
  prohibition on marrying adulteresses,
    377
  purpose of, 21, 436
  reconciliation, 80, 659
  right to chastise wives, 61
  sanctity of, 284
  with non-Muslims, 105, 644
  See also divorce; polygamy; women,
    Muslim
martyrs. *See under* fighters
Mary (mother of Jesus), 39–42, 86, 325
  as a prophet, 343
  Christian concept of, 110, 326
  conception and birth of, 40–41
  integrity and innocence of, 326
  Jews' slander of, 84
Mina, 364
miracles, 124, 310–11, 478
  demand for: 119–20, 255;
    from Muhammad, 121–22, 158,
    251–52, 253, 303–4, 342, 345, 395,
    419, 431
  of prophets, 42, 419, 439, 473. *See*
    also under individual prophet's names.
  Qurʾan as a, 342, 395, 431
mockery, 105, 117, 228, 272, 579, 709,
  753
modern life. *See* civilization,
  contemporary
Mongols, 99, 350
monotheism. See *tawḥīd*
month, sacred, 18, 88
moon, 685, 711, 725
  Abraham and moon worship, 127
  appearance of, in Joseph's dream, 234,
    241
  as a means of reckoning time, 131,

206, 739
as a portent of the end of the world,
    599
as a source of illumination, 391, 475,
    676–77
directive not to worship the, 528
subservience of the, to God, 150,
    257, 263, 279, 482, 528, 604, 767
Moses (*Mūsā*)
    and al-Khiḍr, 316–318
    as recipient of revelation, 450, 489–
        90, 590, 594
    birthplace of, 368
    call to prophethood, 417, 594, 734
    divine favours bestowed on, 237, 730
    early life of, 413–19
    flight from Egypt, 398, 419, 543
    God's forgiveness of, for killing
        Egyptian 403–4, 416
    in the Sinai wilderness, 96, 419
    mission and status of, 31, 318
    mission to and confrontation with
        Pharaoh, 70, 139, 152, 334–35,
        336–37, 396–97, 417, 468, 516,
        542, 547
    mission to the Jews of, 139, 153, 258–
        59
    mother of, as a prophet, 343
    prayer of, 617
    slandering of, 461
    staff of, 335, 398, 403
mosques
    as the focus of the community, 25
    ban on unbelievers from attending,
        182
    closure of, 360
    congregational prayer in, 392, 649
    right of self-defense to protect, 48–
        49, 357, 360
    rival mosque of the hypocrites, 193–
        94
    those who seek to destroy, 15, 20
mountains
    as dwelling places, 226, 267, 285

changes to, as sign of impending Day
    of Judgment, 315, 335–36, 608,
    671, 674, 683, 692, 702, 748
creation of, by God, 268, 283, 344,
    408, 475, 525, 612, 693, 694
mountain of Uḥud, 49, 616
parable of revelation being given to a
    mountain, 640
refusal of, to undertake man's task on
    earth, 462
Mount Ḥirā', 594
Mount Jūdī, 734
Mount Sinai, 589–90, 594, 734
Muhājirūn, 53, 161, 175, 638, 639, 643,
    652–53, 656
Muhammad
    accusations levelled against: 345, 386–
        88, 469, 494, 533, 557, 591, 595,
        672, 733;
    of being a sorcerer, 494, 500–1,
        591, 599;
    of being insane, 469, 487, 587, 591,
        669;
    of being possessed or bewitched,
        301, 369, 387, 670
    approaching death of, 182–83, 762
    as a devoted servant of God, 306,
        309, 455, 558
    as an illiterate man, 418, 736
    as an orphan, 730
    as a recipient of revelation, 594, 649,
        732, 758
    as a witness on the Day of Judgment,
        286
    as the 'seal of the prophets', 7, 9, 307,
        317, 385, 455
    birth of, 755
    call to prophethood of, 736
    demand for miracles from, 121–22,
        158, 251–52, 253, 303–4, 342, 345,
        395, 419, 431
    divine protection and support for,
        662, 719, 730
    etiquette to be observed when

addressing, 577–78, 635
graying hair of, 216
household of, 454, 460, 663
human status of, 157, 345
prayers of, 375, 459, 472, 683
prophecy of advent of, in earlier
  scriptures, 231, 307
qualities of: 333, 564, 669, 672, 682–
  83, 758;
  as a leader, 453, 634–35, 640
Qur'anic directives, advice and
  reassurance to, 123–24, 177, 219,
  266, 272–73, 274, 310, 334, 340,
  360, 371, 394, 423–24, 452–57,
  474, 501, 521, 557, 563, 590–91,
  593, 668, 680, 682, 684–85, 716,
  718, 730, 731, 733, 758, 760
role and mission of: 195–96, 201, 251,
  259, 282, 286, 305, 310, 333, 361,
  385, 410, 411, 426, 453, 455, 469,
  501, 558, 570, 584, 598, 670, 672,
  682–83, 703, 704, 729–30, 732,
  736–37, 762–63;
  as a mere warner, 217, 307, 361,
  385, 455, 501, 557, 716, 718, 731;
  in delivering the Qur'an, 206–9,
  307, 496, 501, 537, 595, 634, 649,
  650;
sayings (hadith) of, 3, 4, 58, 71, 73,
  74, 98, 99, 147, 154, 163, 216, 238,
  275–76, 277, 315, 328, 332, 363,
  366, 370, 375–76, 420, 425, 484,
  511, 519, 546, 575, 577, 603, 614,
  711, 722, 734
state of, when receiving revelation,
  366
See also wives of Muhammad
murder, 74, 97, 135, 298–99, 392
  killing of prophets, 16, 84, 110
  See also infanticide
Musaylimah, 572
Muslim nation. *See* Ummah
Muslims, conflict between, 578
Muslims, God's covenant with the, 1,

37, 90–91, 93, 113, 135, 250–51
Muslims, negative characteristics of, 136,
  155, 580, 582–83, 629, 721, 727.
  See also Ummah, state of the, today
Muslims, Qur'anic directives to the, 8,
  88–89, 135, 165–67
  about asceticism, 89, 112, 613
  about fighting, 164, 165, 169, 170,
  195, 365, 565
  about relations with peaceful non-
  Muslims, 183, 429
  about relations with the Prophet, 460,
  577, 635
  about treatment of prisoners of war,
  74, 565
  about worship, 8, 17, 262, 365, 459
  not to betray God or His Messenger,
  167
  not to dispute with one another, 170
  not to emulate those hostile to Islam,
  634
  not to inherit women, 59
  not to mock others, 579
  not to rely on hearsay, 578
  not to slander others, 461
  not to take Jews and Christians as
  protectors, 89, 103–4, 105
  not to take those hostile to Islam as
  friends or allies, 89, 636, 641, 643
  to avoid the polytheists, 132
  to bear true witness, 80–81, 88
  to believe in God, His Messenger,
  and divine revelation, 81, 160–61
  to be patient, 17, 54
  to be truthful, 135, 461
  to do good works, 365
  to fear, remember and obey God, 54,
  88, 97, 166, 170, 459, 461, 632,
  639, 653, 657
  to guard against hellfire, 663
  to repent, 664
  to spend or give, 8, 262, 657
  to strengthen each other, 54
  to support God's cause, 97, 187, 648

to take pride in faith, 636

to uphold justice, 80–81

Mu'tah, 186, 188

Mu'tazilah school of thought, 92

natural disposition. See *fiṭrah*; human
nature

Nebuchadnezzar, 293

needy

entitlements of the, 57, 169, 298, 359,
438–39, 758

neglect of the, 61, 306, 672, 721, 737,
757

religious obligation to support the,
51, 61, 524, 675, 720–21, 724, 731,
757

Negus, 185

New Testament. See Gospel

niggardliness, 193, 392, 568, 674, 721,
727. See also wealth and property

night

alternation of day and, 26, 150, 482,
551, 623, 727

as a divine favour to man, 263, 279,
371

as a sign of God, 296, 390, 528

as a time of man's punishment, 139,
205, 212

as a time of sleep and rest, 125, 131,
436, 519

laylat al-qadr, 546, 739–40

Muhammad's Night Journey, 292,
450

swearing by the, 685, 703, 711, 729

See also prayer, additional voluntary,
at night; sleep

Noah (*Nūḥ*)

class distinction during the time of,
399–400

construction of shrine by, 734

fate of son of, 222–23

mission of, 214, 305, 396, 427, 489–
90, 676–77

nature and role of, 83, 128, 318, 504

people of, 139, 151, 361, 396, 480,
514, 597, 600, 676

prayers of, 223, 600, 676–77

wife of, 24, 223, 663

See also Flood, the Great

oaths, 19, 21, 381, 570–71, 644, 662

old age. *See* elderly; senility

Old Testament. *See* Jewish scriptures

oppression

by the Israelites, 292

causes of, 296, 370, 472

consequences of, 118, 141, 168, 214,
564, 726, 735

emigrating to escape, 6, 75

imperialist, 85

Muhammad's mission to eradicate,
195–96, 564

obligation on Muslims to combat,
109, 364, 535, 564, 578, 641, 657,
712

of Muslims, 53, 168, 677

of women, 22–23, 25

punishment of those who engage in,
119, 257, 264–65

within the family home, 81

See also corruption

orchard owner, 309, 312–13, 314, 669

orphans

entitlement to a share in spoils of
war, 169

lack of generosity towards, 721, 757

marriage to orphan girls, 80

obligations towards, 61, 453, 454, 724

protection of property and rights of,
56, 80, 86, 135, 299, 731

ozone layer, 547, 604

Paradise

as a physical reality, 616

as a reward for believing women, 614

as a reward for righteous believers,
21, 39, 50, 140–41, 198, 339, 393,
500, 507, 512, 544, 549, 583, 631,

689, 695, 708, 717, 724, 743
description of, 566, 602, 606, 615,
619–20, 665, 689, 695
glorification of God in, 381, 619
ʿIlliyyūn, 708
Muhammad's night journey to, 450
occupants of, 140–41, 198, 219, 251,
278, 512, 583, 602, 606, 614, 619–
20. *See also* houris
proximity to God in, 618
yearning for, in battle, 616
parents
attesting against, 80
cursing of, by offspring, 559
duty to show kindness towards, 61,
135, 297–98, 444
rights of natural, 453
peace
as a prerequisite for prosperity and
freedom, 756
emigrating to safeguard, 75
exchanging greetings of, 72–73, 123,
391, 634
greetings of, in the hereafter, 198,
251, 278, 512, 619, 620, 624
in Paradise, 140, 583, 605, 606
Islam as a source of, 93
justice and fairness as a guarantee for,
146, 642, 740
Makkah and the Kaʿbah as places of,
574, 734
spouses as a source of, 21, 142, 436
war and: 18–19, 174, 195–96, 568,
578;
non-aggression towards neutral
unbelievers, 30, 73, 101, 179, 181,
183, 545
penal code, Islamic, 97–99, 101, 106–7,
135, 298–99, 376–77. *See also* law,
Islamic
People of the Book
accountability of the, 15, 79, 84, 109,
464, 742–43
Muhammad's mission to the, 14–15

Qur'anic directives to the, 11–12, 35,
39, 86, 89–90, 108, 110–11, 632
relations between Muslims and the,
31, 34, 36, 53, 72, 82, 103–13, 428–
30, 574, 639, 644
religious unity of the, 10, 15, 31, 53–
54, 85, 101, 130, 371, 429, 558, 760
response to the Qur'an by the, 35,
132, 253, 272, 420
See also Christianity; Jewish-Muslim
relations; Jewish scriptures; Jews;
Judaism
People of the Cave, 43
Persian empire
conflict between Byzantine Christians
and the, 111, 185, 187, 188, 434
conflict between Muslims and the,
171, 178–79, 383, 426
Pharaoh
and Joseph, 244, 314
and the sorcerers, 334, 335, 397, 417,
468
arrogance of, 543, 697
demand by, to see God, 418, 715
drowning of, 398, 543, 587, 590
final submission to God by, 543
Moses' encounter with, 70, 334–35,
396–98, 542–43
oppression of the Jews by, 10, 153,
398, 413, 547, 587
refusal of, to believe God's
revelations, 152, 397, 404, 542–43,
602
wife of, 24, 61, 663
pharaohs, 139, 214, 219, 389, 421, 602
Pharisees, 42–43
polygamy, 57, 59, 456–57
polygamous prophets, 264, 495, 498
See also wives of Muhammad
polytheism. *See* idolaters; idolatry;
unbelievers and unbelief: *shirk*
poor. *See* needy
prayer
additional voluntary: 739;

at night, 39, 220, 294, 306, 326, 340, 375, 392, 449, 505–6, 593, 682–83, 690, 730, 739

benefits and purpose of, 5, 329

call to. *See adhān*

collective worship, 25, 336, 392, 400

direction of, 38, 760

for forgiveness, 29, 39, 514, 518

for glorifying and expressing gratitude to God, 559, 593, 626, 693, 730

importance of *al-Fātiḥah* in, 4–5

in times of need, 126, 438, 504, 510

joint, with Christians, 44

non-observance of, 79, 329, 685, 737

observance of: 69, 106, 146, 159, 161, 262, 273, 366, 392, 449, 535, 612, 674–75, 716, 737;
   enjoined on Jesus, 326;
   enjoined on People of the Book, 742;
   Qur'anic directives to observe or perform, 5, 8, 17, 150, 220, 294, 306, 336, 340, 365, 384, 437, 449, 518, 635, 690, 758

of Abraham, 264, 617, 723

of Job, 348, 499

of Jonah, 349

of Joseph, 240

of Mary, 40–41

of Muhammad, 163, 306, 375–76, 459, 472, 589, 634, 682

of Solomon, 498

of Zachariah, 41, 325–26

on occasion of Eid, 758

preparations for, 88, 90, 147, 336

preventing others from praying, 18, 449–50, 737

reluctance of hypocrites to perform, 67–68

reward for, 85, 91, 392, 614

shortening, when travelling or under attack, 75–76

success and support promised to those who pray, 123, 357, 365, 716

timings of salah, 5, 159, 220, 294, 306, 392, 435, 449, 459, 505, 682, 730

predestiny. *See* destiny

prejudice, racial, and ethnic conflict, 93, 176, 225, 413

privacy, right of women to, 460–61

promiscuity, 57, 240, 271, 298, 376–77, 382, 428, 458, 644. *See also* homosexuality; immorality; indecency; sexual relations, illicit

property. *See* wealth and property

prophets and messengers, 343, 423
   as servants of God, 14, 203, 214, 396, 530, 592
   belief in the, 12, 82–83, 130, 630, 631
   hostility towards, 121, 139, 259, 266–67, 280, 356, 368, 386, 396, 467, 481, 587, 655, 677, 742
   Israelites' attitude towards and treatment of their, 10, 16, 84, 110
   mission and role of the, 52, 81, 129, 132, 168, 357–58, 361, 528, 541
   qualities of the, 107, 128, 129, 237, 328, 340, 345, 368, 395–96, 480, 497, 499, 536–37, 563, 730
   testing of, and hardships endured by the, 343, 345, 348–49, 357, 361–62, 450, 494–95, 515
   unity of religion taught by, 3, 12, 13, 83, 102, 111, 128, 231, 347, 349, 368–69, 397, 405, 603, 732
   See also under individual prophet's names

Psalms, 302, 350–51

punishment, divine
   deferment of, until the Day of Judgment, 204–5, 220, 230, 473, 532, 552
   inevitability of, 205–6, 589
   in the hereafter:
      for ascribing partners to God (*shirk*), 346;
      for falsehood, 131, 432, 511;
      for rejecting God and revelation,

82, 133–34, 199, 224, 260–61, 289,
302, 330, 338, 461, 468–69, 487,
500, 524–25, 620–21, 670, 672, 693,
743, 749;
for wrongdoing, 15, 265, 312, 507–
8, 535, 544, 602, 695, 707, 717
on earth, 117–19, 133, 139, 152, 200,
211–12, 226, 259, 266, 290, 297,
316, 421, 428, 466–67, 473, 508,
524, 583–84, 588, 597–98, 660. *See
also under names of individual tribes.*
See also corruption, divine
punishment for; Day of Judgment;
hell; wind, as a source of divine
punishment
purity, inner, 144–45, 148, 553, 590

qadr. See destiny
qiblah, 38, 760
qiyām al-layl. See prayer, additional
voluntary, at night
Queen of Sheba. *See* Bilqīs
Qur'ān, 216, 294–95
Arabs' rejection of the, 167, 206–8,
267, 272, 386–88, 529
as a confirmation and extension of
previous revelation, 9–10, 31, 83,
101–2, 128, 129, 133, 207, 236,
281, 349, 369, 385, 419, 528–29,
531, 542, 563, 603
as a divine revelation, 121, 131, 132,
138–39, 207, 249, 266, 280–81, 334,
430, 455, 478, 503, 522, 546, 556,
656, 669, 673, 739
as a means of salvation, 282, 286
as a miracle, 342, 395, 430–31
as a protection against Satan, 158
as a reminder, 336, 494
as a source of guidance, instruction
and law, 7, 26, 37–38, 97, 99, 138,
236, 254, 258–59, 265, 282, 286,
290, 299, 308, 342, 473, 507, 537,
552, 556, 590, 603, 656, 673, 729,
740

as a source of strength and unity,
208–9, 295, 717
as a warning, 116, 133, 138, 265, 309,
337, 347, 421, 447, 478, 522, 524,
530, 542, 546, 563, 666, 690
as God's definitive, conclusive
message, 317, 385, 402, 590, 739
as light (*nūr*), 380, 655, 729
as spirit, 276, 486
as the truth, 132, 209, 282, 307, 369,
447, 503, 693, 714
authenticity of the, 216, 479, 529,
590, 647, 703
authorship of the, 207, 218, 236, 287,
430, 503, 557, 672–73
benefits deriving from the, 208, 276,
703–4
benefits of studying the, 291, 308,
603, 619
challenge to the Arabs to compose a
similar scripture, 207, 231, 591
God's promise to preserve the, 268,
362, 513, 679, 688
lessons from history in the, 47, 214,
222, 236, 334, 337, 402, 418–19,
451, 479–81, 489, 517, 566, 597–98,
719, 720
logic and rationality of the, 126, 198,
431, 584, 713
merit of teaching the, 603
opening letters of surahs (*muqaṭṭaʿāt,
fawātiḥ*), 333, 478, 513, 530, 556
perfection of the, 7, 26, 308, 309,
507, 669, 673
prostrating on hearing the, 307, 323,
711, 741
Qur'anic language, 252, 254, 287,
288, 332, 337, 522–23, 530, 538,
550, 582
Qur'anic style, 25, 126, 142, 156,
198, 209, 287, 288, 513, 565, 633,
658
recitation of the: 252, 306, 505, 682–
83, 703;

giving full attention to, 139, 158,
393, 688;
talking during, 526, 562
revelation of the:
beginning of the, 546, 736, 739;
buzzing sound during, 366;
final verse in the, 8;
in stages, 307, 388, 688, 690, 729
swearing by the, 478, 494
universality of the message of the,
369, 455, 742
Verse of the Throne (*āyat al-kursī*), 26
See also under Muhammad; Muslims,
Qur'anic directives to the;
revelation
Quraysh. *See* Makkah, Quraysh tribe of

racism, 33, 65, 225
Raḥmat Allah, Shaykh, 64
Ramadan, 546, 739
Ramses II, 413
rational thought, 282, 374, 390, 469,
474–75, 532, 551, 595, 647, 666
See also God, belief in; Qur'an, logic
and rationality of the
reconciliation
between husband and wife, 24, 80,
659
between warring believers, 578
following warfare, 45
Red Sea, 398, 419, 543, 587, 590, 594
reform, social, 259, 292, 682
religious unity. *See* unity of religions
repentance
admission to Paradise for the
penitent, 329, 583
door for reform remains open, 393
for minor misdemeanors, 220
God's allowance for weakness and
correction, 339
God's forgiveness of those who
repent, 78, 123, 221–22, 225, 252,
290, 506, 511, 513, 514, 515, 534,
572, 662, 664, 669, 708

God's guidance of the repentant, 531
in the face of misfortune, 438, 510
moment of death being too late for,
136
of David, 495
of Solomon, 497–98
responsibility, personal and social, 58,
65, 102, 130, 155, 183, 277, 299,
355, 364, 438–39, 535, 604, 626,
757
revelation, 594–95
as 'the Spirit', 276
attempts at fabricating, 305, 533
custodianship of, 32, 36, 133, 140,
528
divine origin of, 83, 231, 334, 486,
522, 536, 551
exploitation of, 476
marginalization of, 437
modification, distortion or loss of, 14,
62, 130, 272, 281, 425, 595, 618,
742
not taking, lightly or in vain, 22, 53
purpose of, 149, 230, 282, 336, 376,
478, 650
rejection or denial of, 15, 31, 35–36,
67, 82, 84, 120, 122, 126, 131, 136,
138–39, 140, 149, 151–52, 154, 156,
172, 199, 210, 224, 259, 289, 302,
338, 450, 511, 514, 542, 670
unity of, 31, 83, 102, 128, 223, 302,
429, 528, 531, 590, 603
waḥī, as a means of communication
between God and man, 394, 536
See also Gospel; Jewish scriptures;
law, Islamic, revelation as the
source of; Psalms; Qur'ān; unity of
religions
reward, divine, 552
for good intentions, 505
for resisting seduction, 238
of believers: 11, 15, 20–21, 51, 69,
78, 83, 85, 200, 221, 230, 237, 275,
331, 339, 361, 509, 534, 535, 548,

565, 570–71, 578, 629–30, 666;
in Paradise, 21, 39, 50, 53, 140–41,
194, 198, 203, 250–51, 278, 312,
330, 335, 393, 442–43, 500, 507,
512, 544, 549, 558, 566, 570, 583,
602, 614, 615, 619–20, 636, 689,
695, 708–9, 717, 724, 743
of doers of good, 199–200, 230, 235,
277–78, 309, 312, 314, 361, 423,
455, 596
of non-Muslim believers, 15, 53, 420
preference for, in the hereafter rather
than in this life, 46, 315, 341, 421,
535, 624
See also Paradise
Riḍā, Shaykh Muḥammad Rashīd, 37,
63, 102–3
robbery, armed, 97, 428
Romans, 189, 383, 420, 426, 429, 434,
572, 679
rumor-mongering. *See* false accusation;
slander

Sabians, 355
Sacrifice, Day of, 719
al-Ṣafā, 303, 764
Ṣaḥābah. See Anṣār; Companions of the
Prophet; Muhājirūn; *and under
names of individuals*
salah. See prayer
Ṣāliḥ, 368
and al-Ḥijr, 267
deliverance of, 218
mission to Thamūd, 224–26, 601
plot against, 406
See also Thamūd
Sāmirī, 337
Sanaʿa, 754
Sarah (wife of Abraham), 264, 587
Sāriyah, 242
Satan
abominations devised by, 89
as a jinn, 562
as enemy of Islam, 526

as sower of doubt and despair in
minds of believers, 499, 511
as sower of falsehood, discord and
intrigue, 9, 302, 362, 578, 634
as tempter and enemy of mankind, 5,
9, 66, 79, 126, 143–44, 145, 158,
234, 270–71, 302, 329, 405, 472,
527
as tempter of Adam, 143–44, 151,
158, 338, 526
fate of those who follow, 79, 154,
282, 484
influence of, over unbelievers, 118,
526, 567
rebellion of, against God, 13–14, 323,
354, 424
seeking God's protection against, 41,
158
true belief and salah as a shield
against, 145, 158, 270, 329, 527,
634
See also devils
Saul (*Ṭālūt*), 540–41
sawm. See fasting
science
accuracy of the Qur'an on scientific
phenomena, 431, 713
advances in: 624, 626;
leading to a recognition of God,
242fn., 475, 549
and religion in conflict, 552–53, 595
God not bound by law of causality,
40
limitations to scientific understanding,
229, 257, 701, 715
Muslims' contribution to, past and
present, 27, 256, 320, 631
no grounds in, for rejection of God,
354
physical laws as evidence for God's
existence, 122, 549, 623
role of religious sciences, 552–53
scientific materialism, 410, 554
scientific understanding:

of mass and energy, 406;
of the human body, 269, 713;
of the universe, 256, 525, 586, 626–27
sectarianism,
among Arabs, 136–37
among early communities, 349–50
and the Khawārij, 92
attempts to sow division among
Muslims, 194, 272, 652
fitnah, 18
in Christianity, 93, 111, 327
Islam as a means of overcoming
schism, 93
rejection of Islam resulting in schism,
13
warning against, 136–37, 437
See also dissension
self-defense, right to, 18, 19, 20, 357.
See also war, fighting in response to
aggression
self-interest, 45–46, 68–69, 245, 313,
388–89, 468–69, 572–73, 707, 727–28. *See also under* wealth and
property
semen, 278, 352, 353, 367, 474, 485,
597, 610–11, 654, 692, 700, 713,
736
senility, 283
sexual relations, illicit, 298, 392
adultery, 99–100, 101, 106–7, 298,
377, 644
disguised polygamy, 57
impact of, on society, 39, 60, 240,
376–77, 379, 382, 428, 644
See also homosexuality; immorality;
indecency; promiscuity
al-Shaʿbī, 72–73
al-Shāfiʿī, 751
sharīʿah. *See* law, Islamic
Shayṭān. *See* Satan
Sheba
people of, 466–68, 561
Queen of. *See* Bilqīs

ships and sailing vessels
damage to fishermen's boats by al-
Khiḍr, 318
man's use of, as sign of God's favour
and existence, 26, 263, 436, 445,
482, 534, 552, 585
reaction of those in peril at sea, 211
shirk. *See* unbelievers and unbelief
shrines, 41, 465–66, 734
Shuʿayb
mission of, 227–28, 401–2
people of, 267, 368
See also Madyan
signs. *See* God, evidence (*āyāt*) for the
existence of
Sinai
desert of, 96, 368
Mount, 589–90, 594, 734
singing, 442
sinning, perpetual, 708. *See also*
unbelievers and unbelief:
transgressors
Sirius, 597
sky
as 'God's residence', 667
changes to the, as sign of impending
Day of Judgment, 606, 692, 703,
705, 710
God as creator of the sky and
heavens, 26, 115, 127, 150, 156,
202, 229–30, 257, 263, 268–69, 278,
302, 308, 344, 375, 390, 408, 436,
447, 471, 475, 482, 510, 519, 520,
525, 534, 538, 549, 556, 563, 584,
586, 589, 604, 627, 660, 665, 697,
705, 710
sovereignty of God over the sky and
heavens, 26, 80, 85, 86, 114, 116,
205, 256, 258, 282, 288, 300, 311,
324, 346, 363, 371, 381, 396, 448,
486, 531, 537, 554, 570, 572, 596,
626, 653, 654, 666
See also water: rainfall
slander 521, 579, 644, 753

against ʿĀ'ishah, 377–78
against Jesus, 84
against Mary, 42
against Moses, 461
against Muhammad, 123, 190, 287, 521, 764–65
against prophets, 280
gravity of slandering virtuous women, 377
punishment in hell of slanderers, 378, 461, 753
scandal-mongers, 457
See also falsehood; false accusation
slaughter of animals, 38, 89, 359, 363, 758
slave, freeing of, 724
slavery, 103, 237, 258, 417
sleep
  as a sign of God, 436
  foregoing, to pray. *See* prayer, additional voluntary, at night
  God having no need for, 26
  Muslims overcome by, at Badr, 164
  purpose of, 131, 390, 392, 449, 505–6, 519
Sleepers in the Cave, 310–11
social differences, 260, 283–84, 297, 314, 341, 399–400, 423, 439, 540–41, 721. *See also* wealth and property
social relations, 55, 72–73, 183, 356, 376, 378–79, 642–43, 644, 760–61. *See also* Ummah
society, modern. *See* civilization, contemporary
Socrates, 553
Sodom and Gomorrah. *See* Lot.
sodomy. *See* homosexuality
Solomon
  and the ants, 404
  as a king and prophet, 466, 494, 498
  divine gifts bestowed on, 348, 404, 498
  fondness for warhorses, 497
  mission to Bilqīs, 404–6, 497

shrines and statues of, 465–66
temple of, 293
testing of, by God, 497–98
wives of, in Old Testament, 457, 498
sorcery, 768
  during the time of Pharaoh, 335, 397, 417
  unbelievers' accusations of, 119, 230, 419, 465, 587, 685. *See also* Muhammad: accusations levelled against, of being a sorcerer
soul
  angels as takers of, at death, 125, 131, 136, 149, 172, 278
  appointment of guardian over, 713
  at moment of death, 624, 688
  corruption of the, 743
  death of, only by God's leave, 69
  forfeiting, on Day of Judgment, 140, 506, 535
  God as creator and ordainer of destiny of, 34, 55, 86, 127, 443, 667
  God does not overburden, 135, 369
  just requital of, on Day of Judgment, 8, 33, 345, 349, 547, 705, 745
  means of benefiting or purifying, 4–5, 146–47, 208, 282, 329, 507, 657, 687, 726, 728
  no soul bears another's burden, 445, 504, 597
  resurrection of, on Day of Judgment, 315–16, 582, 614, 685, 702–3
  sacrificing or striving with one's, for God's cause, 580, 647, 666
  suffering of the, in life, 613
  wronging one's own, 22, 78, 511, 659
sperm. *See* semen
spoils of war, 160, 162, 165, 169, 456–57, 571, 572–73, 574
stars, 594, 696, 703, 712, 713
  as tokens of God's power and existence, 268, 299–300, 390, 475, 482, 586
  black holes, 256–57

changes to appearance of, as portent
of Day of Judgment, 692, 702, 705
creation of, by God, 255, 334, 391
in Joseph's dream, 234, 241
Milky Way, 448, 725
al-Shāhid, 713
Sirius, 597
subservience of, to God's commands
and control, 2, 150, 279, 443, 448,
584, 586, 604, 677, 767
statues, 465–66, 502. *See also* idols
stoning to death, 99, 101, 311
sun, 725
and the Sleepers in the Cave, 310–11
as a means of reckoning time, 131,
206, 294, 306, 448, 482, 711
as a sign of God's existence and
creative power, 390, 391, 475, 528,
677
Bilqīs and the sun-worshipers, 404–5,
497
changes to, as a portent of the end of
the world, 136, 599, 702
directive not to worship, 528
in Joseph's dream, 234, 241
solar system, 391, 448, 520, 525, 626,
703
subservience of, to God's laws and
commands, 150, 257, 263, 279, 409,
482, 519, 604, 767
superstition, 63, 135, 146, 374, 595, 598,
727, 762, 768. *See also* sorcery

al-Ṭabarānī, 614
Tabuk, 186, 190, 193
Ṭā'if, 375
taqwā. See God-consciousness
Tatars, 350
tawḥīd, 86, 408–10
and the concept of the trinity: 110,
185–86, 209–10, 288, 326–27, 346,
433, 766–67;
the identity of Jesus, 15, 43, 86, 94–
95, 326, 544, 678, 767

as a key principle of Islam, 8, 109,
209, 210, 261, 297, 302, 355, 766
as a message conveyed by all
prophets, 128, 347, 399, 405, 732
as a purifying belief, 435
denial of God's fatherhood, 40, 309,
321, 372, 492, 503, 539, 678
evidence for, in the physical world,
308
Hajj as an expression of, 358–59, 360,
363
Qur'an as an advocate of, 11, 207,
216, 309, 333, 371–72, 433, 503,
529
See also God (as the Supreme Being)
taxation, 183–84, 253. See also zakah
testament, making a, 89, 483
Thamūd, 139, 151, 224–26, 400
and the she-camel, 304, 406, 601
nature of Thamūd society, 224, 226,
406
punishment of, 218, 226, 401, 524,
597, 601, 719, 726
rejection of Ṣāliḥ's message by, 225–
26, 406, 540, 601. *See also* Ṣāliḥ
Thaqīf, 572
Thātu al-Salāsil, 188
theft
concealment of, 77
penalities for, and highway robbery,
97, 98, 428
Ṭuʿmah case, 77
undertaking not to commit, 644
time, 719, 751
God's perception of, 361
man's perception of, 373
time management, 449
al-Tirmidhī, 711
Titus, 293
trade. *See* business matters
travelers
entitlement to financial support, 298,
438–39
entitlement to spoils of war, 169

trinity. See under *tawḥīd*

truth, 261, 509

and the Day of Judgment, 140, 327, 608

betraying the, for short term gain, 109

conflict between, and falsehood, 9, 228, 356, 592

creation and universal, 269, 278, 280, 549, 556

distortion of the, 141

by People of the Book, 11, 16, 35, 44, 86, 90, 130

God as the source of, 43, 201, 250, 253, 312, 354

God's guidance of those responsive to the, 133, 259

guiding others to the, 156

ignorance of the, 743

Islam as the religion of, 191, 575, 733

Muhammad as conveyor of the, 85, 123, 250, 369

prophets as advocates of the, 356, 361, 515, 563

Qur'an as embodiment of the, 31, 77, 102, 111, 132, 207, 209, 210, 231, 282, 295, 307, 312, 369, 420, 430, 447, 503, 565, 595, 625, 693, 714

refusal to defend the, 67, 162

rejection of the, 117, 118–19, 120, 121, 133, 167, 227, 250, 289, 293, 362, 388, 432, 470, 508, 514, 521, 524, 540, 621

requirement to defend and uphold the, 108, 160, 161, 232, 340, 578, 683, 712, 751–52

requirement to verify the truth of hearsay, 578

reward for upholding the, 509

Satan's desire to pervert the, 362

truthfulness: 113, 135, 393, 512; of Muhammad, 218, 478

Ṭuʿmah, 77–78

ʿUmar ibn ʿAbd al-ʿAzīz, 253

ʿUmar ibn al-Khaṭṭāb, 169, 171, 242, 275, 317, 341, 366, 514, 559–60

Ummah (Muslim nation)

and the Qur'an, 132, 259, 295–96, 402, 542

as a 'middle nation', 27–28

birth of the, 447, 682

characteristics of the, 201, 262, 424, 533–34, 535, 626, 632, 683, 718

contribution of the, to civilization, 27, 632

fraternal bond of the, 175

need of the, to reform, 63, 651

relationship of the, to God, 28–29, 156

responsibilities of the, 356, 364, 402, 459–60, 575–76, 578, 627–28, 630, 711, 717

state of the, today, 136, 155, 171, 176, 263, 286, 293–94, 320, 383, 440, 451, 455–56, 460, 465, 477, 576, 628, 631, 640, 651, 665, 709

Umm Salamah, 614

ʿumrah. See Hajj

unbelievers and unbelief

atheism, 129, 149, 167, 554, 697

kuffār (unbelievers), 82, 85, 117–18, 120, 122–23, 129, 157–58, 168, 180, 204–5, 210, 252, 289, 301–2, 312, 315, 321, 344, 354–55, 358, 472, 508–9, 510–11, 602, 621, 647, 655, 677, 685–86, 710, 749

shirk (ascribing partners to God; polytheism), 64–65, 78, 115, 126, 134, 142, 148, 153, 156, 167–68, 203, 206, 213, 216, 256, 280, 284, 300, 303, 331, 343, 360, 374, 399, 408, 421, 433, 444, 472, 502, 538–9, 556–57, 766–67

transgressors, 108, 131, 141, 153–54, 157, 168, 265, 316, 372, 469, 487, 488–89, 500, 507–8, 544, 583, 596, 708, 717

General Index

See also agnostics and agnosticism;
  enemies of Islam; hypocrites;
  idolaters; idolatry; punishment,
  divine; waverers
unity of religions, 11, 12, 13, 15, 31,
  102, 531
  need to recognize all religious faiths,
    760–61
  See also revelation, unity of

Vatican, 94
vegetarianism, 616
vicegerency, 525, 666. *See also*
  mankind's role on earth
volcanic eruptions, 352, 744

war
  fighting in response to aggression,
    18–19, 30, 71, 74, 174, 178–83,
    357, 358, 578, 641, 642. *See also*
    fighters; jihad (in war time); self-
    defense, right to; spoils of war
water
  as a symbol of racial purity, 225
  as the source of all life forms, 344,
    622
  dependence of man on God for, 622,
    668
  drought, 547, 560
  for drinking, 279, 391, 585, 693
  in hell, 142, 489, 620, 621, 625, 717
  in Paradise:
    quality of, 566, 616, 619, 620;
    rivers of Paradise, 39, 53, 91, 113,
    198, 387, 507, 566, 570, 602, 606,
    615, 633, 636, 664, 743
  rainfall: 118, 164, 534, 622;
    for irrigation and plant growth,
    145, 150, 212, 254–55, 263, 279,
    282, 314, 335, 353, 363, 390–91,
    408, 436, 475, 528, 539, 585, 700,
    714
  rivers: 390, 585;
    God as provider of, 118, 263, 408–

9, 474
seas and oceans, 409, 474, 482–83,
  552, 702. *See also* Red Sea
sweet and salt, 408–9, 474
water cycle, 390, 622, 715–16
See also Flood, the Great
waverers (weak in faith), 68–69, 76, 81,
  187, 189, 210–11, 263, 329, 355,
  382, 427, 438, 504, 510–11, 567,
  580
wealth and property, 312–15
  affluence, greed and materialism, 32,
    108, 190, 225, 296–97, 313, 315,
    330, 341, 392, 400–1, 439, 467,
    468, 506, 554, 560, 665, 707, 721,
    737, 749, 750
  as a divine gift, 297, 313, 314, 422,
    438
  as a test, 167, 284, 340, 422–23, 466–
    67, 629, 720, 724, 750
  belief that, can secure immortality,
    753
  fair distribution of, within society,
    298, 423, 638, 720, 737
  insignificance of, in the sight of God,
    341
  leaving behind, after death, 331, 506,
    547, 608
  not to judge people by their, 389,
    540–41, 543
  ostentatious spending or squandering
    of, 61, 298, 401, 628, 724, 750
  proper use of, 315, 422, 628, 675, 684
  pursuit of commerce, 649
  spending of, in moderation, 61, 298,
    392, 737
  unlawful appropriation of, 61
  See also inheritance; niggardliness
wind, 551, 585, 691–92
  as a source of divine punishment,
    360, 561, 587, 600, 620
  for man's benefit, 409, 436, 498
  role of, in the water cycle, 145, 150,
    314, 390–91, 474, 585, 622, 691

wine, 89, 243, 566, 619. *See also* intoxicants

wives of Muhammad, 454–57
  addressing, from behind a curtain, 460
  'Ā'ishah, 58, 377–78, 634, 662
  behavior of, 662
  dress code of, 457
  Ḥafṣah, 275, 661–62
  Muhammad's period of abstinence from, 662
  prohibition on remarriage of, 454
  Qur'anic criticism of, 661–62
  status of: 454–55;
    as 'Mothers of the Faithful', 456
  Umm Salamah, 614
  Zaynab, 661

women, Muslim, 21–25, 57–59
  dress code of, 460–61
  enemies among wives, 656
  on the battlefield, 49
  protection of emigrant, 643–44
  rights of: 22
    to be treated kindly, 58, 59;
    to consent to marriage, 57;
    to divorce husband, 23, 57;
    to education, 58;
    to financial support, 58;
    to inherit, 57–58;
    to keep their dowries, 59–60;
    to maintenance, 24;
    to refuse polygamous marriage 57;
    to remain in family home, 59, 659
  status of, in Paradise, 614
  See also divorce; polygamy; wives of Muhammad

worship. *See* prayer
wuḍū', 88, 90

al-Yarmuk, battle of, 245
Year of the Elephant, 754–55
Yemen
  as land of Bilqīs, 405, 497, 674
  Byzantine Christians' loss of, 434
  launch of Abyssinian campaign from, 754
  tribes of, 151, 368, 560

Zachariah, 41, 325–26, 348
Zahirites, 768
zakah
  introduction of, 117
  Jesus commanded to give, 326
  obligation on People of the Book to give, 91, 742
  payment of, as a sign of genuine faith, 85, 106, 182, 357, 366, 728
  Qur'anic directive to give, 8, 384, 635
  rate of, for donkeys, 745
  redistribution of wealth through, 262, 737
  reluctance to pay, 507
  warning about not giving, 524
  See also charity; needy
Zaynab, 661